37

8

43
42
41
40

46
45

44

47
48
49

50

64 65 66 67 68

69

39

53
52

51

63 71

70

54
55
56
57

73 72
75 74

32

38

36

79

78
76

77

58

80

34 35

33

81

82
83

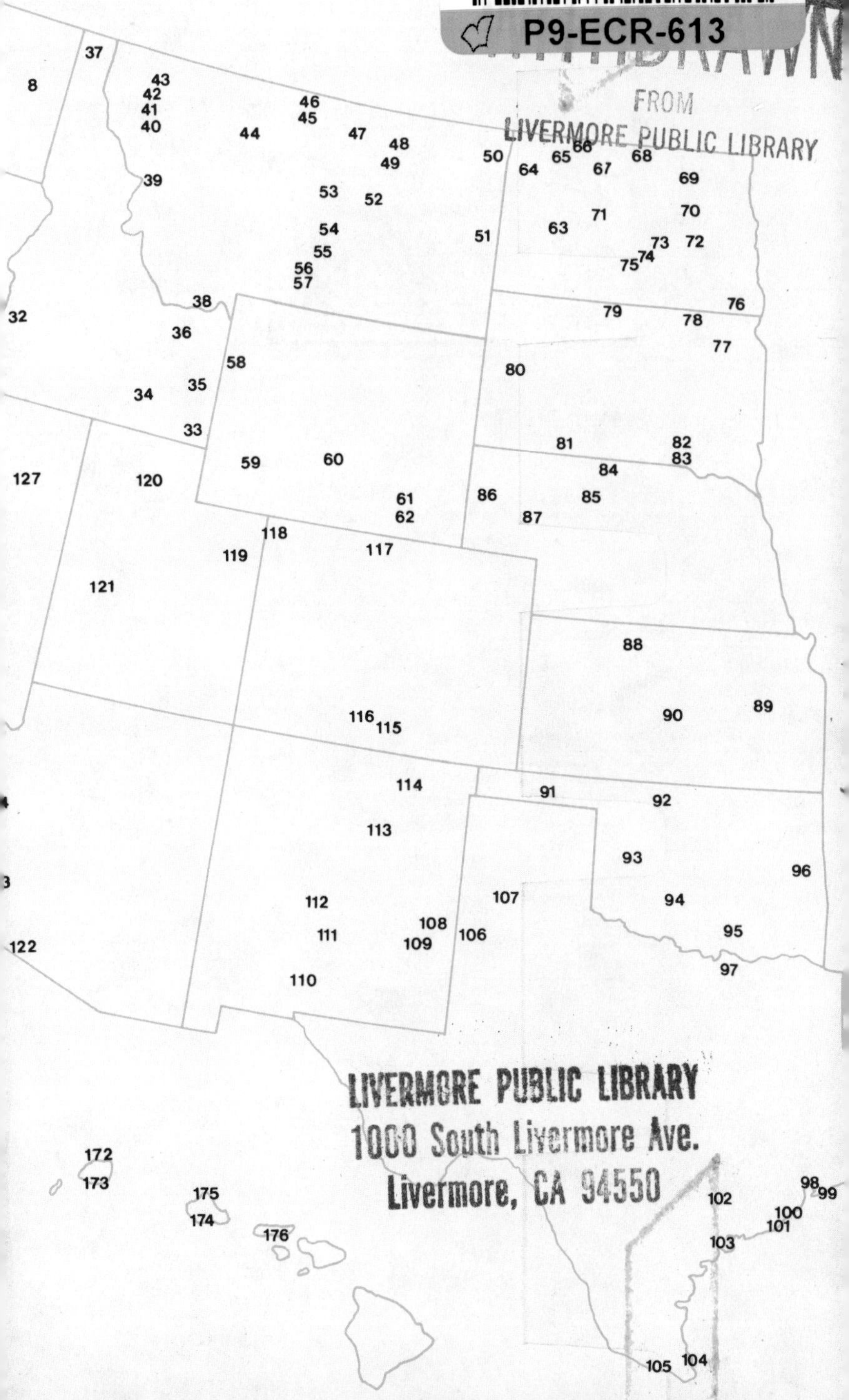

59 60

84

85

86

87

127

120

61
62

118

119

117

121

116 115

114

113

88

90

89

91

92

93

96

112
111

108
109

106

107

94

95

97

110

172
173

175
174

176

102

98 99
100
101

103

122

105 104

GUIDE TO
THE NATIONAL
WILDLIFE REFUGES

GUIDE TO
THE NATIONAL
WILDLIFE REFUGES

Laura and William Riley

ANCHOR PRESS/DOUBLEDAY
GARDEN CITY, NEW YORK
1979

Library of Congress Cataloging in Publication Data
Riley, Laura.
Guide to the national wildlife refuges.
Includes index.
1. Wildlife refuges—United States. I. Riley,
William, 1931–   joint author. II. Title.
QH76.R54   917.3′04′926
ISBN: 0-385-14014-2
Library of Congress Catalog Card Number 78–60300

". . . come, men, to see the wonders which may be discovered in Nature . . ."

Leonardo da Vinci, *Madrid Codex I*

CONTENTS

Contents　　　xiii

FOREWORD

For a great many years the prevailing philosophy in managing our wildlife refuges seems to have been a commitment to anonymity—the less people knew about the refuges, the better.

This is a secret that we can no longer keep.

People have discovered the natural treasures that these refuges hold, and wildlife managers who once worried only about flocks of birds and herds of animals now have to be concerned also with flocks of people and herds of curious tourists.

Now that the secret is out, the challenge for the Department of the Interior and U. S. Fish and Wildlife Service is to meet the public demand for more extensive outdoor experiences while protecting the wildlife for which the refuges were created.

A second challenge, which this guide helps meet, is to educate the public about what they can see and what they can do at the refuges to enrich their lives and increase their understanding of the interdependence of all living things. Implicit in this is the understanding that when people enter these special areas they must make every effort to meet nature on nature's terms—not on human terms. Those who visit the refuges must have a reverence for the wildlife residing there, and must take care to see that it is not damaged or unduly disturbed.

CECIL D. ANDRUS
Secretary of the Interior

ACKNOWLEDGMENTS

In producing this book we had the enthusiastic cooperation of Lynn Greenwalt, James Pulliam, and Marcus Nelson and their staffs at the Washington headquarters of the U. S. Fish and Wildlife Service. We also visited virtually every staffed refuge in the country and many of the unstaffed ones and interviewed hundreds of refuge managers and assistants, who filled out extensive questionnaires and helped in many other ways, including checking our write-ups for accuracy. We were assisted as well by naturalists from all over the country who provided background information. All these are listed by geographic region.

We also wish to thank Evelyn Richter, who assisted in making complex (and often-changed) travel plans as well as in many other ways; Laura Etz, who provided helpful botanical knowledge; the tireless typists of Business Services in Pittstown, New Jersey; the Hunterdon County Library; Cathy Dolan and Mary Madden; and finally Vincent Abraitys, Robert Arbib, Priscilla Barton, Dr. Robert Brodey, and John DeMarrais who read the manuscript and provided so many helpful suggestions and corrections that it would be impossible to overstate our debt to them. Any errors that may remain are our responsibility and we earnestly solicit corrections from readers for possible future editions.

Laura and William Riley
Pittstown, New Jersey
January 1979

I. THE NATIONAL WILDLIFE REFUGES

The national wildlife refuges of the United States are unmatched by those of any other country in the geographic span they cover, the diversity of habitat they provide, and the variety and numbers of wild creatures they harbor.

Brown bear, largest land carnivore in the world, roam the Alaskan refuges. Tiny painted buntings nest by the thousands in coastal Georgia and South Carolina islands. Bald eagles congregate in great numbers in sanctuaries along the Mississippi River. Ducks and geese by the millions darken the sky as in a bygone age when they visit Tule Lake in California's Klamath Basin. Primeval alligators, once endangered, bellow through the night, protected in Louisiana, Georgia, and Florida marshes. Mountain sheep look down over the Arizona Kofa desert.

There are more than 380 of these remarkable places throughout this country. They cover more than thirty million acres and harbor substantially every kind of wild animal native to the continent. It is an extraordinary list, including more than 220 species of mammals, more than 600 of birds, 250 of reptiles and amphibians, over 200 species of fish, and uncounted numbers of plants, from wild orchids to unique kinds of palm trees. The species include most of those on the endangered list, and the refuges are often a chief reason for their continued survival.

Proposed refuge additions in Alaska and elsewhere would more than double this acreage.

Most of these refuges are open to the public for wildlife-oriented activities, which vary with the refuge, ranging through nature observation, photography, to backpacking, fishing, and hunting (governed by special refuge rules determined yearly based on the wild populations). There is information available for most of these, and about half also have professional wildlife managers and assistants on the grounds.

This book tells where these refuges are, how to get there, what there is to see and do, where a visitor can stay or camp nearby, best times to visit, any special equipment needed, and how to get more information. It contains almost 200 maps to help in quickly locating the refuge. The information is based on hundreds of hours of interviews as well as personal observation by the authors at more than 170 of the staffed refuges and many that are unstaffed. Every fact has been double-checked, once by refuge personnel and once by the national office of the U. S. Fish and Wildlife Service in Washington.

Many of these refuges were established for special purposes, as was the first, little Pelican Island in Florida, created by Theodore Roosevelt in 1903 to protect nesting birds from human marauders. Later came Wichita Mountains in Oklahoma and National Bison in Montana for the bison or American buffalo. Kofa in Arizona and Desert in Nevada harbor desert bighorn sheep. Sheldon Antelope in Nevada and its companion refuge, Hart Mountain in Oregon, were set aside for the pronghorn antelope.

The trumpeter swan was brought back from near extinction in the forty-eight states at Red Rock Lakes in Montana—and even persons with but a glancing interest in wildlife know of the whooping crane and its stand against extinction at Aransas Refuge on the Texas Gulf Coast.

Other refuges provide habitat for creatures that while not technically endangered have felt the pressure of onrushing civilization, such as National Elk in Wyoming; Kodiak for the Alaskan brown bear; Kenai in Alaska and Agassiz in Minnesota for the moose.

Many are aimed at providing special refuge for birds while they are breeding, migrating, and wintering. These include great breeding bird sanctuaries in the north-central "prairie pothole" region, and others strategically located along the various flyways for migratory and wintering protection.

Most refuges, even those set aside for a particular species and purpose, have evolved quickly into general refuges for all the types of wildlife that can be sheltered within the appropriate environment—as the prairie potholes with shrubbed areas that serve not only waterfowl but passerines and small mammals. Grasslands where pronghorns graze also are nest habitat for longspurs and grouse.

Each of these refuges is unique, containing a different ecological composition with different combinations of plant and animal habitats from any other. Refuges as close together as Iroquois and Montezuma in upstate New York show quite different migration patterns. Dramatically different are Brigantine, the great coastal New Jersey refuge with large numbers of migrating waterfowl and raptors, and New Jersey's Great Swamp Refuge, inland and just a short distance from New York City, with its deer and wood ducks.

Many refuges, increasingly in recent years, are close to metropolitan areas, such as Tinicum in Philadelphia, Mason Neck near Washington, D.C., Nisqually on Puget Sound in the Seattle-Tacoma-Olympia metropolis, and San Francisco Bay Refuge. These offer refuge not only to wild creatures but also to their human neighbors, who can escape urban clamor and encounter wild creatures in their natural homes.

Many refuges were brought back from places that had been all but destroyed by deplorable practices—fire, drainage, erosion. Acquired when almost worthless, they are lessons in how land can be brought back to beauty and productivity. There are many of these, outstanding being Seney in Michigan's upper peninsula, Moosehorn in northeast Maine, and Piedmont in Georgia.

Mingo . . . Mattamuskeet . . . Iroquois . . . Montezuma . . . Loxahatchee—even the names are evocative. Sabine and Lacassine and Catahoula; Kootenai and Malheur and Shiawassee—names of wild places, of explorers and Indian tribes. Laguna Atascosa, Cabeza Prieta, Bosque del Apache—the list goes on and on (and how much more appropriate for these great natural places than the few that bear the names of human public benefactors, however worthy).

They offer chances to experience the country in many places as it was when the first explorers saw it, when the whole continent was a wilderness. The Great Dismal Swamp in Virginia is like this, and Okefenokee on the Georgia-Florida line, and the great river bottom refuge, White River in Arkansas, and there are many in the West, like Charles M. Russell in Montana, little changed since Lewis and Clark came through in their exploration of the Missouri River in the early 1800s.

Not all the species of birds and mammals are commonly present every place, of course, but most can be seen by the careful, quiet, persistent observer at one or another of the refuges. The larger mammals, generally most affected by human disturbance and diminishing habitat, are warier, but they include black bear, wolves, wolverine, lynx, bobcat, mountain lion or cougar, ocelot, jaguarundi, and coyote, and a wide range of herbivores including elk, caribou, mountain goat, musk-oxen, and mule, blacktail, and whitetail deer, plus the water-dwelling mammals, the sea and river otter, northern and California sea lion, manatee, walrus, and a half dozen kinds of seal. Of the smaller mammals, beaver and muskrat are present in large numbers, also opossum, raccoon, skunk, fox, weasel, marmot, ground and flying squirrel, badger, marten, fisher, rabbit, hare, and many others.

Of the more than six hundred bird species on the refuges, many are of special interest to birders. Those in this category which occur commonly or abundantly at any of the refuges are listed in detail following the introduction to each geographic region.

Waterfowl include great numbers of geese, several races of Canadas, snows in both color phases, white-fronted, Ross', barnacle, and emperor; the ducks, mallard, black and mottled, gadwall, pintail, canvasback, green- and blue-winged and cinnamon teal, wigeon, shovelers, common and Barrow's goldeneyes; buffleheads, old-squaws, ruddy and harlequin ducks, and the wood duck, called the most beautiful duck in the world.

But the refuges are far from being "duck farms." Among other waterbirds are whistling, trumpeter, and mute swans; white and brown pelicans; the lovely long-legged wading birds—six kinds of herons, four of egrets, four ibises, and the breath-taking roseate spoonbill; and shorebirds and pelagic sea birds by the many millions, plovers, sandpipers, gulls, terns, shearwaters, puffins. Raptors include both bald and golden eagles, four species of kite including the endangered Everglade kite, prairie and peregrine falcons, Cooper's, rough-legged, and ferruginous hawks, ospreys, and many others. There are commonly eleven kinds of owls, eleven kinds of hummingbirds, prairie chickens, pheasants, more than a dozen woodpeckers, and a tremendous number of small songbirds—warblers, buntings, too many to list here but described in detail throughout the book. Most refuges have lists showing relative abundance by seasons, and many are among the country's best birding spots, showing high counts in the nation in the annual Audubon Society Christmas Bird Count.

One way to understand the value and importance of these refuges is briefly to contemplate the unthinkable, and suppose they were all to cease to exist. The loss can hardly be imagined. Literally millions of wild creatures—most of those just described—would shortly cease to exist or be under desperate pressure, for except for some of our semidomesticated lawn and garden birds and mammals, most wild creatures require wild land, both to support the unpolluted food chains of which they are a part and to provide needed places where they can rest and reproduce. There is less and less of it every day.

There are several ways to use this book effectively. If you wish to learn quickly what is in a particular region, turn to the introduction to that region. It provides summaries of refuges there and a map showing their general location. If you want to know about a particular refuge, find it in the table of contents. To determine where a certain wild creature can be found, look it up in the index.

In visiting a refuge there are a number of *do's* and *don'ts* that will help make your time there productive and enjoyable.

•Visit early and late—not midday, when most birds and other wildlife are least active. Best is close to dawn and dusk; worst, between 11 A.M. and 3 P.M. Use the midday for a nap or picnic lunch. This is worth any inconvenience—at dawn in December Bosque del Apache becomes a magical place of thousands of sandhill cranes and snow geese coming awake, stretching and muttering and gathering to fly to feeding grounds. Dusk at Ding Darling on Sanibel in May can see long lines of sunset-lit roseate spoonbills coming in to roost.

•Spend some time on the walking trails. Many refuges have excellent auto tour routes where much wildlife can be seen (and often they are more readily observed from a car, which serves as a good blind). But try the trails, too, to feel and experience the wildness of the place. Walk quietly. Stop from time to time and just look around, without talking. It takes a while for wildlife to forget you're there and resume their activities. Visit and talk later. You'll see more.

•Don't expect manicured grounds. Refuges are not parks, nor are they intended for picnicking or other non-wildlife-related recreation. Most wild creatures require cover as well as food and water, and these necessities usually mean marsh and woods and lots of "edge" where different habitats come together.

•Try to acquire some understanding of what you are looking at. What is there in the habitat that attracts these particular creatures? If they are not residents, where did they come from and where are they going? At what stage of "succession" is the habitat? No natural place is static—brush becomes woodlands and then climax forest. Ponds become marshes and then dry land. What geological forces shaped the refuge? Use the refuge leaflets to help in understanding. It will make your trip far more interesting.

•If coming from any distance, write or call the refuge office ahead of time, and stop by. Usually the staff can tell you what's been seen lately and almost always suggest ways to best see the refuge. Always inquire in advance before coming to see a certain creature or natural event, to be certain it is appearing on schedule (nature changes, and they don't always). Remember words such as "common" and "abundant" involve certain assumptions: "common" eagles are not as numerous as "common" starlings; and, any wildlife observation requires a careful, quiet viewer ("Refuges are not zoos," staffers are fond of saying).

•Take insect repellent (not always needed but one can be miserable without it); binoculars and if possible a spotting scope; field guides such as Peterson's or the Golden Book on birds, and others for various interests; proper clothing—specifically, layered clothing if it's cool, several light garments rather than one thick one because these can be adjusted to changing conditions; hat, sunglasses, and so on. In sparsely populated and remote areas, be sure your gas tank is kept full; take a canteen and some food and at least a modest first-aid kit; be sure you have a jack and a good spare tire.

•STAY IN THE CAR where specified on tour routes. You will see more, and so will those behind you. In fact, obey all refuge signs. "Closed" means what it says. It may be a road that is unsafe, or one that passes near a nesting colony that will be disturbed. If you have any doubts, ask at headquarters. Permission will sometimes be granted to serious and responsible persons to enter such areas.

•If you see something of particular interest, tell the staff about it. Many refuges keep logs of interesting goings on, available to all visitors.

•Best to write or call ahead for motel reservations, just in case—especially at peak travel times.

•If in any doubt, clarify refuge hours. Most refuge offices are open Monday to Friday, but the refuges themselves more often than not are open all year from dawn to dusk, a few, twenty-four hours a day.

•One simple rule for good wildlife viewing is to stop and look back every so often. Both mammals and birds often freeze or duck back as visitors pass, then resume their activity soon thereafter. Remember, wild creatures that are easy to see seldom survive long.

•Human activity on refuges must be consistent with wildlife welfare. Stay out of nesting areas; don't pick or remove plants; leave artifacts—teepee rings, pony express stations—as you find them.

Every visit to a refuge is different. Every person sees something slightly altered from one who precedes or follows; and if a person comes again and again, he or she sees a different thing every time. This is the essence of a natural situation. It can cause disappointment—or, more frequently, elation. It is one of the sources of fascination to those who come to love and enjoy refuges and come again and again, never knowing what they will see—but observing and understanding more every time. It is part of the dynamic nature of the natural state and wildness itself not to be predictable.

Because of space limitations we have not dealt in this book with the history of the refuge movement, its current problems and issues, nor the interesting developments in refuge management practices. Some things, though, should be said. As Rachel Carson put it, "the preservation of wildlife and of wildlife habitat means also the preservation of the basic resources of the earth, which men as well as animals must have in order to live." George Laycock pointed out in his excellent book *The Sign of the Flying Goose*, "Seldom a day passes when a wildlife refuge somewhere in the country is not threatened by forces that would turn out the wildlife." Sometimes the idea is to use a refuge for a bombing range, sometimes for a highway, sometimes as a picnic ground or waterskiing lake. The threats are constant, and not always turned back. Each has required a mobilization of effort of those who love wild places to save the day.

To those seriously interested in current problems and potentials of the refuges, the comprehensive "Final Environmental Statement on Operation of the National Wildlife Refuge System" prepared by the Fish and Wildlife Service of the Department of the Interior and including statements by such key private organizations as the National Wildlife Federation, National Audubon Society, Defenders of Wildlife, Sierra Club, the National Wildlife Refuge Association, and many state wildlife agencies is an indispensable guide. This book also includes the Leopold Report, a study by an advisory committee appointed by Interior Secretary Udall during the Kennedy Administration whose distinguished members have provided in brief and readable form a wise and comprehensive "philosophy for the Refuge System." Other excellent reports have been made by Defenders of Wildlife and the National Wildlife Refuge Association.

If there is one single reason for refuges, it is to provide a different kind of place from that described over a century ago by an Indian chief named Sealth, and quoted recently by the League for Conservation Legislation: "There is no quiet place in the white man's cities," Sealth wrote, "no place to hear the leaves of spring or the rustle of insect's wings . . . The white man does not seem to notice the air he breathes. Like a man dying for many days, he is numb to the stench. What is man without the beasts? If all the beasts were gone, men would die from great loneliness of spirit, for whatever happens to the beasts also happens to man. All things are connected."

II. THE NORTHEAST AND MID-ATLANTIC STATES

There are twenty-two staffed national wildlife refuges open to the public in the eleven Northeast and Mid-Atlantic states and each of them is within a day's drive of one or more of the area's major metropolitan areas. Five of them—*Parker River* and *Great Meadows* near Boston, *Great Swamp* in northern New Jersey near New York City, *Tinicum* in Philadelphia, and *Mason Neck* just south of Washington, D.C.—are within an hour or so of the heart of those cities.

Despite their proximity to great numbers of people, the refuges of this area share with those of the South and West the presence of wild creatures in woods and marsh, river and sea, and the absence of most of the noises and sights of modern urban civilization. It is a combination that pleases the senses and lifts the spirits.

Beginning in the North along the Canadian border are *Moosehorn* in the northeastern corner of Maine and *Missisquoi* in northwestern Vermont. Moosehorn is famous for its large nesting population of woodcock, the bird with the spectacular courtship flights that occur each spring. From early April to mid-May some of the hundreds of nesting pairs are active each daybreak and dusk—the males soaring into the air, circling, then plummeting with whistling wings downward toward a clearing, leveling off only a few feet above the ground as the female watches from the edge of the woods near her future nest. Missisquoi offers superb canoeing through delta passages where the Missisquoi River meets Lake Champlain, with good views of beaver, muskrat, great blue herons, gallinules, and common goldeneye ducks, together with charming nature trails along the river and its backwaters.

In upstate New York are *Iroquois* and *Montezuma*. Iroquois, in the northwestern corner of the state, is noted for its massive waterfowl migrations in spring, with up to 25,000 ducks and 100,000 geese. Montezuma, in the north-central section, has a more spectacular migration in the fall. It also is noteworthy as the site of a program aimed at reintroducing bald eagles, absent for twenty-five years. *Erie,* located near its namesake city in northern Pennsylvania, is a little-known refuge which has an unusually good population of nesting warblers and raptors and excellent stands of wild flowers such as painted, purple, and white trilliums, hepaticas, bloodroots and dwarf ginsengs, trout lilies and phlox.

Along the Massachusetts coast are Parker River and *Monomoy* and just inland, Great Meadows in Concord. The Parker River area has been the locale of many rare bird sightings in recent years, including the Ross and ivory gulls and Hudsonian and bar-tailed godwits. It benefits both from its location—on Plum Island jutting out into the Atlantic Ocean—and from its proximity to Boston's colony of expert naturalists.

Monomoy is one of the loveliest of all the country's refuges—a 2,600-acre island located a short but treacherous distance over water just south of Cape Cod. It is a wilderness area, remote and unpeopled even in August, and the site of beautiful and varied plant life, ranging from dune grass, seaside spurge, and beach pea to fruiting viburnum, sweet pepperbush, highbush blueberry, and rose mallow.

Great Meadows serves as an oasis not only for the wild creatures that inhabit it but also for the human residents of the Boston area who can be seen on its trails along the Concord and Sudbury rivers not far from Walden Pond, some absorbed in viewing the birds and mammals, others occupied with their own thoughts. Nearly four million persons live within thirty miles of its boundaries, yet even at the busiest times it is a quiet and natural place.

Trustom Pond, together with a neighboring Audubon Society tract, encloses the only protected coastal pond of consequence in Rhode Island. Although its 350 acres make it small compared to most refuges, its charming and pleasant trails which wander across old fields and through overgrown orchards to the pond make it worth a visit. Also of interest here is a flock of about two hundred graceful mute swans, an introduced bird which lives year-round and nests here.

Great Swamp in New Jersey was almost New York City's fourth jetport, until some six thousand citizens and 462 organizations banded together in 1960 to purchase it and donate it to the refuge system. Now its more than six thousand acres of wooded swamps, fresh-water marshes, bogs, and uplands produce some four thousand young wood ducks each year and provide habitat for more than two hundred species of birds, mammals such as deer, muskrat, fox, mink, otter, and beaver, and a wide array of interesting botanical species.

Brigantine, on New Jersey's southern coast, is among the most famous of all the nation's refuges and draws visits from naturalists from all over the world. Something of natural interest is going on there all year-round. In early summer Canada goose parents herd their young around the dikes in great numbers. By late summer the shorebird migration has begun, followed by blue- and green-winged teals and pintails in September, black and northern shoveler ducks and brant in October, and climaxed by great flocks of snow geese in November. Winter is a good time for viewing predator species, including occasional bald eagles and peregrines, and in spring the shore and wading birds reappear to begin the natural year again.

Less than a mile from the end of one of the runways at Philadelphia International Airport and adjacent to downtown Philadelphia is Tinicum National Environmental Center, which, though not designated as a refuge, is managed as one. Wild rice grows and green herons nest there; short-eared owls hunt its open areas in fall and winter and there are even small populations of deer, racoon, opossum, and skunk. There is a good trail around the fresh-water marsh, well used by many of the local citizens whose efforts led to the establishment of Tinicum.

The Delmarva Peninsula, a narrow neck of land that is bordered on the west by Chesapeake Bay, on the north by Delaware Bay, and on the east by the Atlantic Ocean, can be traversed easily in a long weekend. Along its coasts are five varied and interesting refuges. *Bombay Hook* on Delaware Bay is most famous for its Canada geese; over fifty thousand rest in its marshes at the peak in late October. But the refuge also has an excellent shorebird migration in late summer as well as some unusual and colorful breeding birds as prothonotary warblers and blue grosbeaks. Diamondback terrapins, once close to extinction, now nest commonly there, as do incredible numbers of horseshoe crabs.

Prime Hook, farther down the bay, offers an outstanding canoe trail—a watercourse more than fifteen miles long that winds down Prime Hook Creek through woods and marsh along which otter, muskrat, bitterns, and herons can be seen. *Eastern Neck* across the peninsula on Chesapeake Bay also is easily accessible by water. But this island of about 2,300 acres also has about ten miles of hardtop and graveled roads, a nature trail and boardwalk into the marsh.

Blackwater, about fifty miles farther south in Maryland, provides habitat for three endangered species in one small, remote area of the refuge—a patch of mature pine woods where the southern bald eagle, the red-cockaded woodpecker, and the Delmarva fox squirrel all nest. While the red-cockaded is seldom seen, fall visitors have a good chance of seeing both the eagles and the squirrels and are sure to see huge concentrations of waterfowl—up to 85,000 Canada geese and 100,000 ducks in mid-November.

On the Atlantic Ocean just over the Virginia line is *Chincoteague*, famed for its oysters, for the beauty and diversity of its habitat, for its miles of wild beaches and dunes and for its wild ponies, said to have descended from a Spanish herd shipwrecked here in the 1500s. The refuge is highly accessible. During summer there is both a daily wildlife safari—a narrated 15-mile land tour of the refuge—and a boat cruise around the island. There are auto trails and several foot trails, and even special provision for handicapped persons—wheelchair ramps and a trail on which a blind visitor can follow a hand line while touching and listening.

Mainland Virginia contains four refuges. Mason Neck, about 1,100 acres of woods and marsh on a peninsula in the Potomac River estuary, was established in 1969 through efforts of local citizens aided by The Nature Conservancy determined to protect it as a nesting site for endangered southern bald eagles. *Back Bay* with its sister refuge *Mackay Island* occupies miles of Atlantic Ocean coastline south of Virginia Beach. Their oceanic outlook frequently provides unusual offshore bird sightings, especially after winter storms, and this area often leads the nation in the annual Audubon Society Christmas Bird Count for such as gannets, loons, and jaegers.

Presquile was named when it was "almost an Island" in Virginia's historic James River, but since 1934 it has been an island in fact, severed from the banks by a navigation channel cut across its narrow neck. Reachable by private boat or refuge-operated ferry, it is memorable for its remote feeling and the diversity of its habitat.

The *Great Dismal Swamp* is a 63,000-acre tract of brooding swampland in southeast Virginia whose beauty and prolific plant and animal life contradict its name. Its mammals include black bear, bobcat, mink, white-tailed deer, and otter. It is the only known habitat for the Dismal Swamp shrew and one of the few places to see rare dwarf trilliums and silky camellias, which are sometimes here by the thousands. There have been bird sightings here that can only be called fantastic—as ten thousand pine siskins and one million robins. George Washington, who owned part of this swamp and surveyed it in 1793, called it "a glorious paradise" and, remarkably, it still is.

The following is a list of some birds of special interest found in common or abundant status at the refuges of this region.

Birds Common or Abundant at Seasons Indicated:

S: Spring   s: Summer   F: Fall   W. Winter

Gannet: Back Bay, SFW; Monomoy, SF.
Great Cormorant: Moosehorn, W.
Louisiana Heron: Chincoteague, SsF.
Least Bittern: Bombay Hook, s; Great Swamp, s; Mason Neck, s;
    Prime Hook, s; Tinicum, SsF.
Mute Swan: Brigantine, SsF, Montezuma, SF; Trustom Pond SsFW.
Brant: Brigantine, SFW; Chincoteague, SFW.
Common Eider: Monomoy, SFW; Parker River, W.
Cooper's Hawk: Eastern Neck, SF; Erie, SsFW.
Rough-legged Hawk: Blackwater, W; Bombay Hook, W; Erie, SW;
    Montezuma, W; Prime Hook, W.
Bald Eagle: Blackwater, SsFW; Eastern Neck, SF; Erie, F.
Ruffed Grouse: Erie, SsFW; Montezuma, SsFW; Moosehorn, SsFW.
King Rail: Back Bay, SsFW; Blackwater, SsF; Bombay Hook, SsF;
    Prime Hook, SsF.
Turkey: Erie, SsFW; Presquile, SsFW.
American Oystercatcher: Chincoteague, SF.
Piping Plover: Chincoteague, Ss; Monomoy, SsF.
Whimbrel: Chincoteague, Ss; Monomoy, s.
Red Knot: Chincoteague, Ss; Erie, SF; Monomoy, Ss.
White-rumped Sandpiper: Missisquoi, s.
Stilt Sandpiper: Chincoteague, s.
Arctic Tern: Monomoy, Ss.
Royal Tern: Chincoteague, SsF.
Caspian Tern: Chincoteague, SF.
Black Skimmer: Brigantine, SsF; Chincoteague, SsF.
Chuck-will's-widow: Back Bay, s; Chincoteague, Ss.
Olive-sided Flycatcher: Missisquoi s; Moosehorn, SsF.
Common Raven: Moosehorn, SsFW.
Boreal Chickadee: Moosehorn, SsFW.
Cerulean Warbler: Montezuma, SF.
Pine Grosbeak: Moosehorn, W.
Grasshopper Sparrow: Great Dismal Swamp, F; Eastern Neck, SsF;
    Erie, Ss; Presquile, SsF.
Henslow's Sparrow: Erie, Ss.

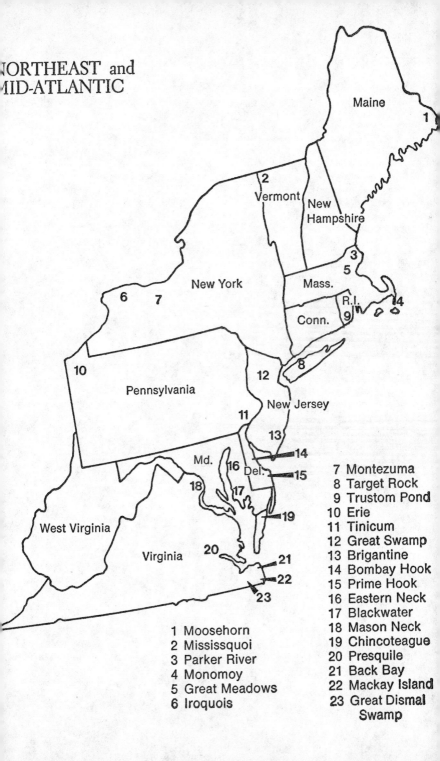

NORTHEAST and MID-ATLANTIC

Maine

1

Vermont

New Hampshire

2

New York

3

5

Mass.

R.I.

6   7

Conn.

9

4

10

8

12

Pennsylvania

New Jersey

11

13

Md.

14

16   Del.

18   17

19

West Virginia

Virginia

20

21

22

23

1 Moosehorn
2 Mississquoi
3 Parker River
4 Monomoy
5 Great Meadows
6 Iroquois

7 Montezuma
8 Target Rock
9 Trustom Pond
10 Erie
11 Tinicum
12 Great Swamp
13 Brigantine
14 Bombay Hook
15 Prime Hook
16 Eastern Neck
17 Blackwater
18 Mason Neck
19 Chincoteague
20 Presquile
21 Back Bay
22 Mackay Island
23 Great Dismal
   Swamp

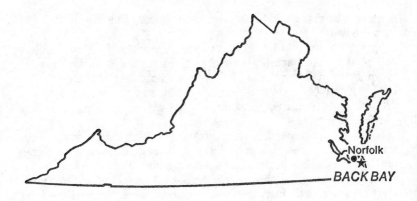

Norfolk

BACK BAY

BACK BAY (Virginia)

Back Bay is a beautiful and varied 4,589-acre refuge fronting on the Atlantic Ocean on one side and Virginia's Back Bay on the other, with ocean, bay, fragile dunes, and upland-woods habitat that at times support some of the largest bird concentrations anywhere.

In recent years, the highest numbers on the National Audubon Society's annual Christmas Bird Count were recorded here for gannets, red-throated loons, whistling swans, snow geese, gadwall, Forster's terns, parasitic and pomarine jaegers, and Swainson's thrushes. Gadwall recently numbered 12,000 an all-time count record for that species.

But good wildlife observation is possible most of the year. Many thousands of yellow-rumped warblers are here in all but summer (when they go north to breed)—sometimes hundreds in a single bayberry clump, and a "pishing" sound made by blowing air through the lips may summon fifty or more.

Snow geese in glistening white throngs arrive in November and stay until mid-February, peaking near twenty thousand. There are also large numbers of Canada geese and ducks—mallard, black, teal, wigeon, and a dozen others, including surf scoters and other sea varieties.

In the dunes, the visitor can spot the rare Ipswich (Savannah) sparrow—not by walking there, because this area is off limits even to refuge personnel; but through binoculars from the beach. One can also see gannets from the beach—a spotting scope is helpful but not necessary to make out these large white birds wheeling and diving into the water.

Spring observation of shore and marsh birds as well as warblers and smaller land birds begins in April and continues until they start south again in August. Especially common are great blue, green, little blue and black-crowned night herons, snowy and great egrets, yellowlegs, sanderlings, turnstones, black-bellied plovers, and king and Virginia rails.

Many of these overflow from *Fisherman Island*, a fantastic thousand-acre refuge administered by Back Bay and located near the north end of the Chesapeake Bay Bridge and Tunnel, where thousands of wading and shore birds nest—oystercatchers, willets, royal and caspian terns, glossy ibises, and many others. Because the land narrows sharply, great numbers of birds also pour through this natural neck in seasonal migration—arctic nesters such as pectoral and semipalmated sandpipers, and the rare peregrine falcon.

Public access to Fisherman Island is restricted, but most of the birds that nest there and most of those that funnel through fan out to appear at some point at Back Bay as well as at Mackay Island Refuge, also administered by Back Bay, six flight miles to the south (but a twenty-mile drive).

Among the smaller birds commonly nesting at Back Bay are indigo buntings, brown thrashers, meadowlarks, towhees, prothonotary, prairie and yellow warblers, bobwhite quail, flickers, cardinals, Carolina and long-billed marsh wrens, the latter furnishing one of the highlights of the refuge year with their twilight singing flights, many hundreds at a time, in the marsh in June and July.

Another extraordinary sight is the overflight of whistling swans in late November, sometimes twenty thousand in a two-day period, seeming to fill the sky with their graceful presence—most of them en route to winter at nearby Mattamuskeet Refuge, although several thousand usually stay at Back Bay.

Ospreys and barn owls frequently nest in a double-decker arrangement on duck blinds in the waters outside refuge boundaries—the ospreys on top, the barn owls inside.

Nutria—beaver-like South American imports—are frequently seen in the canals, sometimes with young resting atop the mother where they nurse on her back. Gray fox are sometimes on the dikes along with feral hogs, wild for generations now, deer, muskrat, and, less visible, mink, otter, and weasel. March hibiscus, creamy plume grass, and acres of goldenrods and black-eyed susans make a stunning display—but worth searching for also are the tiny lady's tresses orchids and insectivorous sundews.

To see these, drive a mile along the beach road to the visitor's contact point. Park, and walk along the beach and dikes for up to ten miles or so.

Mackay Island Refuge is smaller (842 acres), but with more upland and fresh water and well worth a visit. One can see there good seasonal concentrations of waterfowl—sometimes hundreds of canvasback, sixteen thousand American wigeon, and forty thousand coot. There are also some smaller birds not commonly present at Back Bay—fox sparrows, orchard orioles, goldfinches, Carolina chickadees, red-headed woodpeckers, yellow-billed cuckoos.

Plum Tree Island Refuge—a 3,275-acre habitat for waterfowl, marsh and shorebirds—is also administered by Back Bay. But it is a former bombing range with unexploded ordnance considered dangerous and therefore public entry is prohibited.

How to get there: From Norfolk take I-64 south to Road No. 44 (toll road), exit at Independence Boulevard and take Independence-Holland Road south; left on Princess Anne Road; left on Sandbridge Road; then right on Sandpiper Road to refuge entrance.

Open: Daylight hours all year.

Best times to visit: Winter and spring.

What to see: Snow geese, ducks, sea and shorebirds, and sometimes warblers in large numbers.

What to do: Wildlife observation from walks and roads; boating in Back Bay (boat rentals nearby); crabbing; excellent fishing in bay for bream, crappie, and bass up to 10 pounds, in surf for blues, trout, and channel bass (no hunting).

Where to stay: MOTELS—Many in Virginia Beach (Crowded in season). CAMPGROUNDS—One mile north of refuge; and on Knotts Island, 6 miles south.

Weather notes: Hot in summer but generally pleasant all year.

What to take and wear: Sturdy footgear for off-trail areas.

Points of interest nearby: Seashore State Park, 10 miles north, with resident eagle, northern limit of Spanish moss; Great Dismal Swamp Refuge, 40 miles west. Pocahontas and Trojan state waterfowl management areas, adjacent to refuge.

For more information: Back Bay National Wildlife Refuge, Pembroke Office Park, Pembroke Building №2, Suite 218 Virginia Beach, Virginia 23462. Phone: (804) 490-0505.

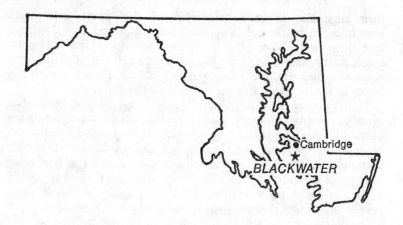

●Cambridge
★
BLACKWATER

BLACKWATER (Maryland)

Undoubtedly at some point three endangered species have occurred at the same time in a single tree in a remote part of this 11,800-acre refuge on the eastern shore of Maryland which is almost 60 per cent marsh and water, with a little mixed hardwood and pine woods.

The three species are the southern bald eagle, which usually has about seven successful nests every year on the refuge; the Delmarva fox squirrel, which exists in good numbers; and the red-cockaded woodpecker, rare here and throughout its range. But in one recent year a red-cockaded nesthole was seen just two feet under an active bald eagle nest, in a locale where the Delmarva squirrels commonly leap from branch to branch and make their own nests in forks of loblolly pines.

Not endangered but a chancy sight is the nutria, a marsh-dwelling rodent native to South America unrelated to the beaver but much like it in appearance. They were released in the southern United States in the 1930s, and spread widely. This is the northern edge of their range—they literally freeze their tails off when it gets too cold, and older animals can be recognized in this way. For this and other reasons they are cyclic, sometimes easy to see and sometimes difficult —but interesting. The female mammary glands are high on the sides and the young go with their mother shortly after birth, riding on her back and nursing while she swims.

The Delmarva squirrels differ from the resident gray squirrels in their large size—at least twice that of the others—their thick chinchilla-like coats, and their fuzzy, heavily furred ears. One can spot them easily. The refuge sometimes sets up a blind to photograph them, using a horizontal log as a lure to bring them in close range—for they will, it is said, go sixty yards out of their way to run across such a log, especially one with a little elevation.

This is a good place for eagles. The area that includes the refuge often has twenty productive nests—the most for its size of any place outside Florida (for some reason, they are less troubled here by the pollution that still makes the eagles' existence problematical farther up on the eastern shore). The visitor may see a half dozen at fairly close range while driving around the auto tour route.

The red-cockaded woodpecker is another matter, and while it is possible to see one, it is an extremely lucky visitor who does.

Ducks and geese are one of the prime sights, and also photographic subjects—especially in mid-November when peaks of 85,000 Canadas and 100,000 ducks may be here, including mallard, black ducks, gadwall, pintail, green- and blue-winged teal, wigeon, shoveler, and merganser. Many beautiful photographs have been taken of the waterfowl flying against a sunset—along the tour route but also in the fields next to refuge headquarters, where the geese (mostly Canadas but also snows) group by the hundreds, sometimes thousands. (But don't try during a full moon at hunting season—the wary, intelligent birds have learned to feed by night then, which makes them understandably inactive in daylight hours.)

Travelers can also spot deer—the white-tailed and also a small herd of sika deer, actually a small Asiatic elk which was released in the region several decades ago from an estate, and which has prospered. The best way to see deer is to go out early or toward dusk, drive slowly, and look carefully into the backs and corners of field edges. This is also true of the other mammals—raccoon, red fox, opossum, skunk, and a few otter.

The refuge has an observation tower, woodland walking trails, and a four-mile auto tour route from which most of the refuge wildlife can be seen at one time or another—pied-billed grebes, seven heron species, ospreys (which also nest), whistling swans, quail, marsh and red-tailed hawks, and a fine array of shorebirds. For this reason, visitors are asked to stay in their cars to lessen disturbance and maximize the viewing for all.

Still, some of the small birds are best seen closer—and for this, the walking trails may be best, as for the yellow-billed cuckoos, brown-headed nuthatches, red-bellied and pileated woodpeckers, Acadian flycatchers, wood pewees, hermit and wood thrushes, yellow-breasted chats, long-billed marsh wrens, orchard orioles, white- and red-eyed vireos, and dozens of others which occur here in good numbers.

There are two satellite refuges also administered from Blackwater: Glen L. Martin Refuge, a salt marsh island in Chesapeake Bay with habitat for ducks and wading birds; and Susquehanna, a one-acre island in the Susquehanna flats near Havre de Grace, formerly prime habitat for canvasbacks and redheads but altered by river damming upstream and other factors. Both of these are remote and extremely difficult of access and visitors are not encouraged.

How to get there: From Washington take the Chesapeake Bay Bridge, then south on Route 50 to Route 16 (1 mile beyond Cambridge), right on 16 to Church Creek, left on Route 335, and 4 miles to refuge sign; turn in left.

Open: Wildlife drive and visitor center September 1 to May 30 (closed Christmas Day).

Best times to visit: Mid-October through December.

What to see: Eagles; deer; Delmarva fox squirrel; waterfowl concentrations; nutria.

What to do: Auto and hiking trails; photography (blind for fox squirrel photography available on reservation basis); wildlife photo contest in March (mail in for entry); check at Visitor Center for other scheduled programs.

Where to stay: MOTELS—In Cambridge, 12 miles north, and Easton, 27 miles north. CAMPGROUNDS—At Madison and Taylor's Island, 8 and 20 miles northwest on Route 16

Weather notes: Few extremes.

What to take and wear: Comfortable clothing appropriate to season.

Points of interest nearby: Old Trinity Church, 3 miles west of Church Creek, active continuously since Revolutionary War and beautifully restored and maintained. Hooper Island, 25 miles southwest—interesting isolated fishing community with large numbers of migrating flickers, marsh and sharp-shinned hawks, and kestrels, in September–October. But take a picnic—there's no restaurant.

For more information: Blackwater National Wildlife Refuge, Rt. 1, Box 121, Cambridge, Maryland 21613. Phone: (301) 228-2677.

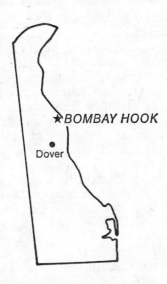

BOMBAY HOOK

Dover

BOMBAY HOOK (Delaware)

One of the wondrous and common sights at this 15,136-acre wetland refuge is the Canada geese coming into the marsh at dusk—wave after wave, looking in the distance like clouds on the horizon until their V-forms become visible, filling the air with their cries and finally "whiffling" their wings as they drop down over the waving grass.

Then they simply disappear from view. The tall *Spartina alterniflora*, which is one of the most desirable plants known for wild-life cover and food, appears exactly as before. It is like a fascinating optical trick. Their presence is clear from the ever-increasing calling as thousands more join them, drifting down like falling leaves into the bright rust-colored cover, which then looks entirely empty.

This goes on until dark, when not even the marsh can be seen—and sometimes long afterward, for the geese here, as in some other places, have learned under hunting pressure to feed at night by moonlight. (They have also learned, it is reliably said, how to tell the exact hour when a field is opened to hunting; when a blind is safe to approach; and what is prudent height when flying a hazardous area. No one who has watched Canada geese long underestimates their intelligence.)

Bombay Hook is a prime stopping place for the Canadas, whose population has increased enormously in recent years, due partly to changes in agriculture from truck farms to row crops such as corn and soybeans, and also to the mechanical corn picker which leaves more grain in the field. They peak here sometimes in late October at up to fifty thousand birds—and this is only a relatively small share of the population estimated at up to a million over the Delmarva peninsula. One cannot go far in this area without seeing Canada geese.

Snow geese also come in good numbers, and ducks—pintail, wigeon, ringneck, scaup, bufflehead, hooded and common merganser, and those that also nest here—mallard, blue-winged teal, gadwall, wood and black ducks. (The Canadas also have a small nesting group, and broods of these are an engaging sight in June.)

But impressive as the waterfowl are (and many of them stay the winter), they are only part of the story.

The shorebird migration in late summer is as good as anywhere in the East. Appearing commonly or abundantly are pectoral and least sandpipers, short-billed dowitchers, both yellowlegs, turnstones, black-bellied plovers, occasional golden plover, whimbrel, and godwit, to mention a few. Four species of rail nest regularly—king, clapper, Virginia, and sora—as do least bitterns and green herons. Six heron species stay here from midsummer through fall.

Red-shouldered and red-tailed hawks nest, as do barred and great-horned owls, and in the upland, bobwhite and ring-necked pheasant.

And, notable among the small birds, there are almost always breeding prothonotary warblers, blue grosbeaks, orchard orioles, grasshopper sparrows, and Louisiana waterthrushes, and commonly nesting scarlet tanagers, sharp-tailed and seaside sparrows, Kentucky warblers, Acadian flycatchers, indigo buntings, and a great many others.

Bald eagles and ospreys have nested here but with little recent success, and egg analysis showed some of the highest pesticide levels ever measured.

A fascinating sight is the diamondback terrapins, once close to extinction but now regular visitors to the shore and dikes in late July, digging holes to deposit their eggs. Another is the horseshoe crabs, renowned for their blue blood and ancient lineage, which gather at the water's edge in almost incredible numbers—perhaps millions—for their courtship and mating.

There are also deer, their fawns appearing in June, fox, muskrat, opossum, squirrel, woodchuck, and a few otter to be seen by the careful observer. In fact, the refuge calendar lists interesting natural events for every month in the year.

There are observation towers, hiking trails, and an excellent twelve-mile auto tour route for seeing all this—but a fine way also is to get a small boat and go out on the bay side to explore the shore and tidal guts. Out there, it can seem as if there is nothing in the world but you and the sky and marsh and birds.

How to get there: From Dover take Route 13 north to Route 42, then east to Leipsic and north on Route 9 to refuge sign (about 2 miles).

Open: Daylight hours all year.

Best times to visit: All year interesting—summer less comfortable with biting insects.

What to see: Geese; ducks; fine shorebird migrations; scarlet tanagers; occasional prothonotary warblers; diamondback terrapins.

What to do: Auto and hiking trails; observation towers; Allee House (handsome restored old farmhouse on refuge, open to weekend afternoon visitors). Fishing and crabbing permitted in boats in navigable streams (but not from refuge land). Limited hunting for waterfowl, deer, and upland game.

Where to stay: MOTELS—At Dover, 10 miles south. CAMPGROUNDS—One near Dover on Route 13; also at Blackbird State Forest, 20 miles north.

Weather notes: Most seasons pleasant but midwinter subject to brief snowy periods. Roads when wet may become impassable, especially if geese consume much of the gravel on them for grit to aid digestive processes. Check with headquarters on road conditions.

What to take and wear: Comfortable clothing appropriate to the season.

Points of interest nearby: Two state wildlife management areas border the refuge, Woodland Beach to the north and Little Creek to the south. Island Field archeological dig, a substantial Indian excavation, is open to visitors, about 20 miles south. John Dickinson mansion, historic home, 14 miles south.

For more information: Bombay Hook National Wildlife Refuge, R.D. 1, Box 147, Smyrna, Delaware 19977. Phone: (302) 653-9345.

BRIGANTINE

Atlantic City

BRIGANTINE (New Jersey)

It is hard to think how a nature-oriented person could visit Brigantine and not come away happy with the experience. There is always something to see—concentrations of waterfowl in the fall, shore and wading birds and warblers in the spring. The calendar of wildlife events furnished by this 20,197-acre south Jersey coastal refuge has something going on in every month.

Even in January and February there are diving ducks, rough-legged hawks, short-eared owls, an occasional whistling swan, bald eagle, or great black-backed gull, and large groups of sea ducks visible offshore.

And in May and June the dikes of the auto tour route can seem covered with Canada geese and their downy young broods (many quite willing to cooperate with photographers).

Most spectacular in the fall are the large numbers of ducks and geese, which begin with blue- and green-winged teal and pintail in September, then Canada geese, black and shoveler ducks and brant in October, and the snow geese in November for a peak of more than 150,000 waterfowl of a dozen or so species, which may linger into mid-December.

Of these, ornithologists particularly monitor the arrival of the brant, for Brigantine harbors at times 90 per cent of the Atlantic population of this small dark goose which leads a precarious existence, its numbers having varied from 238,000 to 41,000 on its return south from its egg-laying grounds in a small area north of the Arctic Circle. If the weather has been adverse during the few weeks when nesting is possible there, brant may absorb their eggs and not breed at all. Their diet is limited to a few plants—they nearly became extinct during an eelgrass blight in the 1930s. So it is good news when young birds appear with the adults in good numbers.

Visitors can see all this activity from three self-guided walking trails and an eight-mile auto tour route. Leaflets point out the fresh and brackish water impoundments. Fiddler crabs change their color with day and night. And one can sight seaside and sharp-tailed sparrow habitat, waterfowl nesting areas, and osprey poles and tree snags where eagles perch. (Travelers can see peregrine falcons too, especially near the platform where young peregrines, in a program with the Cornell Laboratory of Ornithology, are being introduced to the wild in an effort to restore a population hard hit by pesticide use.)

One can spot tall wading birds almost anywhere from the dikes—little blue and great blue herons, snowy and great egrets, Louisiana and black-crowned night herons, and glossy ibises. The latter are especially likely at the beginning of the tour route. American bitterns, while not common, usually appear somewhere along the way. Mute swans are around most of the time, and whistling swans usually spend their nights in the refuge in November and December, feeding in the nearby Wading River until freeze-up.

Warblers appear in refuge uplands in migration—more than a dozen species are common (black-and-white, blue-winged, northern parula, Canada, blackpoll, pine, prairie) and a dozen others less so. Kinglets are seen in spring and fall and the golden-crowned stay the winter.

Brigantine also has impressive shorebird populations—skimmers with their outsized lower bills that plow the water surface for food and nest near here in the largest numbers in New Jersey; colorful oystercatchers out on marshy islands; and literally thousands of willets, rails, and gulls, with lesser numbers of various terns and plovers. Many of these nest in large numbers but off by themselves, and the refuge is strict in curbing access to their breeding areas and patrolling them twenty-four hours a day to prevent disturbance.

Because of its largely wetland habitat, Brigantine does not have a large mammal population, but they are here—deer, fox, cottontail rabbit, raccoon, squirrel, skunk, weasel and especially muskrat and otter. One of the best ways to see these latter is to go early to the northwest corner of the tour route, and park and watch.

The rare Pine Barrens tree frog, sometimes called our most beautiful frog, with its bright green skin and plum body stripe, lives close to the refuge in good numbers and sometimes strays over.

The Holgate Unit of the refuge is excellent for shorebirds. It has no visitor facilities but can be reached by driving south to the end of Long Beach Island.

Other subrefuges administered from Brigantine are:

Barnegat Refuge—Two areas totaling 7,580 acres of coastal marsh with a varied population of wetland birds, especially rails. It is located between West Creek and Barnegat, and one of the best ways to view it is from the dikes in the adjacent Manahawkin State Management Area.

Supawna Meadows Refuge—A tidal marsh and waterfowl nesting area three miles northwest of Salem. Land acquisition is continuing; no public access now but future development is contemplated.

How to get there: From Atlantic City take Route 30 to Absecon, then Route 9 for about 4.5 miles to Great Creek Road in Oceanville. Turn right there to refuge headquarters. (The Intracoastal Waterway bisects the refuge and boat landings are nearby.)

Open: Sunrise to sunset all year.

Best times to visit: Spring and fall.

What to see: Concentrations of geese and ducks; shorebirds; warblers; birds of prey.

What to do: Photography (blinds available, also many opportunities on tour routes); observation tower; trails. Film and slide lectures by prearrangement. Limited hunting for waterfowl. Fantastic fishing offshore all year, and ice fishing nearby. Boating (rent or bring one for a memorable look at the coastal marsh). N. J. Audubon has interesting fall and spring activities in nearby Cape May and Pine Barrens.

Where to stay: MOTELS—On Route 9 and 30, around Absecon. CAMPGROUNDS—At Wharton State Forest and Bass River State Forest, adjacent to refuge on north.

Weather notes: Variable all year—come prepared for possibility of change. Coastal winds blow away much heavy snow, but accentuate cold and dampness.

What to take and wear: Waterproof footgear a good idea on the trails. Bring along a warm jacket November through March. Ice clamps for footgear on a glazed winter day.

Points of interest nearby: Wharton State Forest (see CAMPGROUNDS —Part of interesting Pine Barrens. Bass River State Forest also has swimming. Stone Harbor worth a visit, if near Cape May, for its fascinating heronry, located right in the center of town.

For more information: Brigantine National Wildlife Refuge, P.O. Box 72, Oceanville, New Jersey 08231. Phone: (609) 652-1665.

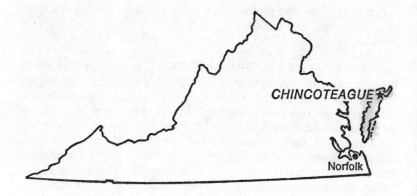

CHINCOTEAGUE (Virginia)

Chincoteague is one of the nation's outstanding refuges, both for the beauty and diversity of its wildlife and natural surroundings and the many opportunities available to the visitor to observe or become actively involved.

In season, visitors can see large numbers of snow and Canada geese and brant—one of the primary resting places for these interesting small geese from the Arctic; the famous wild ponies said to have descended from a Spanish herd shipwrecked here in the 1500s; sika and white-tailed deer; the rare Delmarva fox squirrel; otter families; fox; and some 260 species of birds large and small that are attracted to the diverse habitat on this barrier island which is bisected by the states of Maryland and Virginia and shared with the Assateague Island National Seashore.

More than a million persons a year visit this 9,460-acre tract of wild beach, loblolly pine forest, spartina marsh, and grassland for a great variety of nature-oriented activities such as is available in few other places.

Observation of the distinctive habitat and its creatures is, of course, primary and is possible in a number of ways, especially in summer when there is a daily wildlife safari—a narrated fifteen-mile land tour of the refuge—and a boat cruise around the island to see shorebirds feeding and large flights of herons and egrets leaving for their roosts, especially stunning at sunset. The land tour traverses quiet areas not otherwise open, and so sometimes affords sightings not otherwise possible.

But the person who prefers to do his or her own viewing can have an equally rich experience—on the wildlife drive, a 3.5-mile loop open to cyclists and hikers to 3 P.M., and cars after that; and on several foot trails. The Pony Trail goes through pine woods where sika and white-tailed deer, the endangered Delmarva squirrel (large and light gray), wild ponies, and woodland birds are seen. The Lighthouse Trail overlooks the Assateague channel. The 7.5-mile service road passes through several kinds of habitat. The Sensitivity Trail is for touching and listening—the visitor closes his eyes and follows a hand line. And there are ten miles of natural beach and dunes (special provision is made in many areas for handicapped persons, as, ramps for wheelchairs).

The abundance of birds can only be hinted at. The beautiful wading birds are here, many of them nesting on small offshore islands. There are common and red-throated loons; horned and pied-billed grebes; double-crested cormorants; mallard, shoveler, wigeon, blue- and green-winged teal, gadwall, pintail, bufflehead, black and wood duck; offshore eiders, scoters, oldsquaw; migrating hawks and peregrine falcons; nesting ospreys; bobwhite quail, rails, oystercatchers, and a great variety of shorebirds, including nesting terns, gulls, and skimmers.

Many small birds occur commonly and abundantly, including hermit, Swainson's, and gray-cheeked thrushes; seaside sparrows (and nearly always in winter some Ipswich sparrows, too); yellow-billed cuckoos; horned larks; brown-headed nuthatches; meadowlarks; kinglets; goldfinches; cardinals; gnatcatchers; white- and red-eyed vireos; and among warblers, the pine and prairie, magnolia, Cape May, black-throated blue, yellow-rumped, and yellowthroat.

The refuge has a program to transplant and release newly hatched loggerhead turtles, once native here, and visitors are asked to report any sightings. The results so far are inconclusive but some are believed returning to lay eggs. Visitors also can participate in the fall count of migrating hawks, a January nighttime census of the deer population, the Christmas Bird Count, and special bird-watching weekends held in late summer.

There is a Thanksgiving open house for waterfowl viewing, and at various times through the year art shows, decoy-carving contests, wildlife film showings, etc. When a storm casts a good supply of shells on the beach, an announcement is made for anyone who wishes to look them over for additions to his or her collection.

And, of course, a highlight of the year for many is the roundup and sale of the wild ponies that graze on the refuge most of the year. The herd, which is maintained now at 150, is sent swimming over to

Chincoteague Island the last week in July and the surplus over the prescribed number is auctioned off by the Chincoteague Volunteer Fire Company.

Chincoteague Refuge headquarters also administers *Wallops Island* Refuge, which consists of some 3,373 acres of marsh habitat on and near Wallops Island, Virginia. The refuge has a special permit from the National Aeronautics and Space Administration (NASA) for wildlife research and management, but otherwise there is no public access.

How to get there: From Dover, Delaware, take Route 13 south to Route 175 (about 5 miles beyond Pokomoke City, Maryland), east on 175 to Chincoteague Island, then east on Maddox Boulevard to Assateague Island and refuge signs.

Open: Entrance open 4 A.M. to 10 P.M., except Christmas and New Year's.

Best times to visit: Spring and fall—but any season can be rewarding.

What to see: Snow geese; brant; sika deer; otter; wild ponies; many others.

What to do: Auto, hiking and cycling trails; summer boat cruises; shelling; beachwalking; photography (blinds available); surf fishing (small fishing boats can be chartered through the refuge); limited deer hunting; a wide range of activities scheduled year-round.

Where to stay: MOTELS—A number on Chincoteague Island; also at Pokomoke City, 25 miles northwest. CAMPGROUNDS—Several on Chincoteague and on Assateague Island National Seashore (including canoeing campsites operated by National Park Service) and Assateague State Park.

Weather notes: Can be hot in summer but generally pleasant all year.

What to take and wear: Comfortable clothing appropriate to season.

Points of interest nearby: Virginia Coastal Reserve, interesting chain of barrier islands owned by The Nature Conservancy which can be visited by permission—contact Conservancy office in Wachapreague, 30 miles south.

For more information: Chincoteague National Wildlife Refuge, P.O. Box 62, Chincoteague, Virginia 23336. Phone: (804) 336-6122.

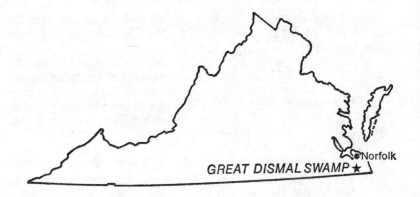

GREAT DISMAL SWAMP ★ ●Norfolk

GREAT DISMAL SWAMP (Virginia)

The Great Dismal Swamp is "a glorious paradise," said George Washington, who owned part of it and surveyed it in 1793. It still is. The 63,000-acre tract of brooding swampland, formed by forces active eight thousand to ten thousand years ago in this southeast corner of Virginia, is a unique ecosystem of natural inhabitants, some of them found nowhere else.

This is the only known habitat for the little Dismal Swamp short-tailed shrew, and one of the few places to see the rare dwarf trillium and silky camellia, which are sometimes here by the thousands.

Black bear are known residents, along with bobcat, mink, white-tailed deer, gray fox and otter.

The bird life is remarkable. Some eighty-eight species are known to nest, among the commonest the colorful pileated woodpecker, prothonotary warbler, and wood duck—but also the elsewhere uncommon Swainson's and a race of the black-throated green warbler known as Wayne's. There have been sightings which can only be called fantastic, for example, ten thousand pine siskins and one million robins.

As many as fifty male woodcocks have been observed in a single evening in one area, "peenting" and performing their stunning courtship flights.

More than a hundred bird species are designated as common or abundant (close to the total list in some refuges)—including orchard and northern orioles, scarlet and summer tanagers, blue and evening grosbeaks, ruby-throated hummingbirds, winter wrens, wood pewees, veeries, hermit thrushes, merlins, chimney swifts (nesting and roosting in hollow trees), and seventeen kinds of warblers. More hooded warblers can be seen here than at any other U.S. refuge.

Some of the cypress trees in the refuge are believed to be more than fifteen hundred years old, growing in peat soil firm enough for walking in most places but so malleable that a slim sapling can be thrust without great effort ten or fifteen feet straight down into it.

In watery places are found the Brimley's chorus frog, in the northern limit of its small range; and (with sharp eyes) the little grass frog, our tiniest frog—a half inch long.

The Dismal Swamp fish, blind or nearly so with only vestigial eyes, has evolved presumably because of the dark swamp waters, deeply stained by the peat vegetation. There is also the lovely little iridescent blue-spotted sunfish—and seventy-three species of butterflies.

This only starts to suggest the tremendous variety of sights and experiences available here along some 170 miles of roads and trails and around beautiful Lake Drummond in the center of the refuge, and from a canoe exploring its edges. (Excellent lists have been compiled, and a fine little booklet on the Great Dismal Swamp can be bought locally.)

It is steeped in history and lore as well. Patrick Henry once owned land here, and Robert E. Lee's father nearly did (he failed to come up with the purchase price). Robert Frost, stung by rejection of his poems by a lady he later married, came to the swamp contemplating suicide. Harriet Beecher Stowe set a novel here, and poems were written about it by Thomas Moore and Henry Wadsworth Longfellow. Legends of the Lady of the Lake arose from lights seen at night now believed to be foxfire—a luminescence given off by certain fungi on rotting wood.

In its more recent history large tracts of land given by the Union Camp Company through The Nature Conservancy and later the Weyerhaeuser Company led to its establishment as a refuge in 1973 and formation of a citizens' National Great Dismal Swamp Society to ensure protection forever of its fragile and irreplaceable habitat.

Also administered by Great Dismal Swamp is the Nansemond Refuge—208 acres of tidal marsh in the Nansemond River estuary for waterfowl and shore and wading birds. Access is difficult and by permit only.

How to get there: From Norfolk take Route I-64 east to its end, then 460 and 13 west for about 6 miles, taking the Suffolk exit. At the first traffic light turn left on Washington Street (Route 13) and left again at White Marsh Road (Route 642). The Washington Ditch entrance is about 7 miles from this point.

Open: Daylight hours all year.

Best times to visit: Fall and spring (birds are more vocal, and light better for viewing and photography).

What to see: Unique ecosystem including some plant and animal life existing nowhere else.

What to do: More than 100 miles of trails and roads (foot traffic only) for nature observation. Canoeing (boat rental nearby). Photography (photoblinds available). Limited deer hunting. Fishing (state license needed), but fishing is not outstanding; fishermen would have better results at the coast, two hours or less away.

Where to stay: MOTELS—At Suffolk, 5 miles northwest; others about 5 miles northeast. CAMPGROUNDS—In Feeder Ditch, boat access only; also Dismal Swamp State Park, just southeast of refuge. Private campground on U.S. 17 north of Feeder Ditch.

Weather notes: Summer can be warm and humid; winter roadways slippery and occasionally impassable.

What to take and wear: Sturdy walking shoes and a compass would be handy.

Points of interest nearby: Seashore State Park, 23 miles northeast; Back Bay National Wildlife Refuge.

For more information: Great Dismal Swamp National Wildlife Refuge, P.O. Box 349, Suffolk, Virginia 23434. Phone: (804) 539-7479.

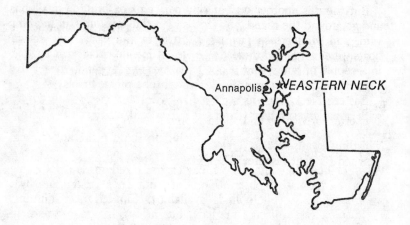

EASTERN NECK (Maryland)

One is quickly acquainted with the essence of this 2,286-acre island bordered by the Chester River and Chesapeake Bay by walking out a short distance on the boardwalk into the marsh at Tubby's Cove, shortly to the right after the refuge entrance.

Passing through a small patch of woods dominated by loblolly pine and American holly, small birds are everywhere: nuthatches, chickadees, thrushes, flycatchers, jays, yellowthroats, kinglets flying about, some resident and, in fall and spring, dozens of others stopping off on their way through.

Immediately beyond one emerges from the woods to a point of land with an observation tower surrounded on three sides by marsh and, past that, open water and an entirely different world. Muskrat houses are all around and, depending on the season, great numbers of Canada geese, mute and whistling swans, ducks of a dozen or so species, loons, grebes, and, farther out, black and white-winged scoters.

Marsh and red-tailed hawks glide by, and perhaps an occasional eagle. Ospreys nest regularly and successfully. Great blue herons prowl the edges. Sandpipers, yellowlegs, and an occasional shy rail probe the flats at low tide, and Forster's, common, and least terns dive for small fish during higher water.

It is an exciting place where one can spend hours.

But there is another way in summer: rent or bring a small boat and go around the island, and if it is high tide, explore Durdin, Shipyard, and Hail creeks (named because in the early days arriving boats were first hailed there). The entire six-mile circuit can be made in a couple of hours—but it can be interesting for much longer than that, especially tying up at Bogle's wharf for a picnic lunch.

Eastern Neck, with its secluded potholes and vast shoals covered with aquatic vegetation (damaged in a recent hurricane but coming back), has been a haven for waterfowl—especially black duck and whistling swans—for as long as anyone can recall in an area renowned for that resource. Kent County alone has an estimated half million ducks and geese on its ponds and farm fields during the height of the fall migration. More seem to come every year, reflecting a Canada goose population explosion partly caused by the introduction of the mechanical corn picker, which leaves grains the hand-pickers used to clean up, and on which the geese thrive (and farmers who lease their lands to hunting clubs don't complain).

Two structures on the refuge tell the story of its past and future. One, used now for youth groups and special projects, formerly was a spacious lodge known locally as the "millionaires' hunt club." The other is the converted refuge headquarters building, which was the first house in a planned development of part of the island, halted when the Fish and Wildlife Service at the last minute procured the land for a sanctuary.

One can enjoy white-tailed deer, along with good numbers of the endangered Delmarva fox squirrel—the only squirrel on the refuge, usually seen running in and out of the woods opposite the headquarters building. There are also woodchuck, raccoon, opossum, and skunk and cottontail rabbit which can be spotted by the quiet vigilant observer.

A great blue heron colony at the tip of the island supports about seventy-five nests. There are many pawpaws and consequently many zebra butterflies in August which lay their eggs exclusively on this shrub; also thousands of Monarch butterflies in migration, sometimes covering the vegetation at the south end. About ten miles of hardtop and graveled roads go through the varied habitat; there is a half-mile interpretive nature trail and a scenic vantage point near headquarters which offer a panorama extending on a clear day to the Chesapeake Bay Bridge and much of Eastern Neck itself, which surely must be one of the most attractive small refuges in the system.

How to get there: From Chestertown take Route 20 west and south to Rock Hall, then Route 445 south to the island and refuge signs.

Open: Sunrise to sunset all year.

Best times to visit: October through December.

What to see: Swans; geese; ducks; deer; Delmarva fox squirrel.

What to do: Observation platform; auto and hiking trails; photography (hunting blind can be used off season); limited deer hunting; fishing for blues, perch, and rockfish at entrance bridge and shoals around island; good crabbing (float a bushel basket on an inner tube and dip them up); boating (go around the island and explore creeks; boats can be rented nearby).

Where to stay: MOTELS—At Rock Hall, 7 miles north, and Chestertown, 21 miles north. CAMPGROUNDS—Three miles north of refuge on bayshore.

Weather notes: January–February can have bad ice storms, with alternate freeze-thaw. Refuge roads may be closed then, although one county road always stays open.

What to take and wear: Warm, waterproof gear in winter.

Points of interest nearby: Remington Farms, 12 miles north—an excellent wildlife and birding area with trails and self-guided tours open from March to mid-October.

For more information: Eastern Neck National Wildlife Refuge, Route 2, Box 225, Rock Hall, Maryland 21661. Phone: (301) 639-7415.

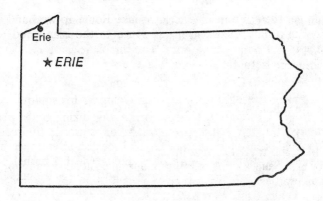

Erie

★ ERIE

ERIE (Pennsylvania)

The visitor to this 7,994-acre refuge in the northwestern corner of Pennsylvania—the only national wildlife refuge in this state—will be struck by the numbers of white-tailed deer and beaver. Both are visible almost everywhere in the fields and along the trails.

Working beaver lodges are located in ponds and impoundments throughout the refuge, and their busy occupants do not seem to mind being observed dawn and dusk; and the deer are seen in woods and fields winter and summer, and with their fawns from May through the summer.

The serious birder will be impressed by the numbers of nesting warblers—the magnolia, blue-winged, Blackburnian, black-throated green, and a half dozen others noted in the refuge's detailed and accurate bird list; and other frequently seen species as well—the Cooper's, red-shouldered, and sharp-shinned hawks; the ruby-throated hummingbird; and Henslow's sparrow.

Wild flowers, too, are beautiful at Erie, both on the main unit near Guys Mills, which accounts for about half the refuge acreage, and the Seneca unit, about eight miles north. The main unit, which has more upland and more roads and trails and impoundments (and supports the main waterfowl population), has a trail behind the refuge office where many of these can be seen—a succession from April through June of painted, purple, and white trilliums, hepaticas, bloodroots, dwarf ginsengs, trout lilies, and phlox.

The Seneca unit has more wetland and swamp forest where the

predominant species are hemlock, yellow birch, and beech, but also some stands of huge old sugar maple. It could be described as an ecological reservation for the various types of plants and animals that were indigenous to this area before the great forests were largely cleared—and since it has now been officially designated a natural area, it will remain that way.

Along a winding stream through this unit (there are no official trails, so you must find your own way) are five species of wild orchids, and numbers of ferns—the cinnamon, hay-scented, sensitive, Christmas, and royal, among others.

Also the Seneca unit nesting mourning, hooded, and yellow-throated warblers are found among clumps of blackberry canes grown up in old logged-over hemlock forest areas.

Ruby-throated hummingbirds nest in woods on both units, and their display can be seen by a delighted birder—the male flying up and then swinging down in an arc close to earth and up again, almost as if on a pendulum, while squeaking to draw the attention of a female to his performance and to his glittering crimson and green plumage (the display is easier to see than the tiny nests constructed of spider webs and bits of lichen).

Both sections have an excellent collection of owls—great horned and barred, which can occasionally be spotted in daytime on tree branches, and screech owls, which sometimes take up residence in wood duck houses and peer out in late afternoon.

Bobolinks, scarlet tanagers, and indigo buntings are common nesters, as are black-billed cuckoos, cedar waxwings, killdeer, grasshopper sparrows, ruffed grouse, pheasant, American bitterns, great blue herons—a rookery on the Seneca unit supports seventy or so nests—and waterfowl, including mallard, wood ducks, blue-winged teal, hooded merganser, black ducks, and Canada geese.

Waterfowl migration usually peaks in the spring about mid-April, and late October in the fall; and broods of ducklings and goslings are seen in refuge impoundments starting in late May.

An excellent self-guided hiking trail passes by beaver lodges, den trees, wood duck houses, carpets of club mosses and marsh marigolds, and bluebird houses put up by local Girl Scouts which are usually occupied each summer. There are numerous fox dens on the refuge which produce young almost every year. There are no formal auto trails but numbers of roads go through the refuge, especially the south unit.

Winter can be beautiful—especially on a day when a sparkling dry snow falls while the sun shines—and rewards the hardy hiker with such cold-season specialties as crossbills, pine grosbeaks, clouds of snow buntings, and sometimes a Lapland longspur or late hunting short-eared owl.

How to get there: From Franklin take Route 322 west about 12 miles to Route 173; north on 173 about 5 miles to refuge, 1 mile farther to refuge headquarters.

Open: Daylight hours, year-round.

Best times to visit: Spring and fall.

What to see: White-tailed deer and beaver; waterfowl; warblers in migration and through breeding cycle; hummingbirds; raptors, including red-shouldered and Cooper's hawks; Henslow's sparrows.

What to do: Photography; nature trails (auto and hiking); fishing for pike, crappie; hunting for deer, small game, and waterfowl, within state regulations.

Where to stay: MOTELS—A number in Meadville, 8 miles west. CAMPGROUNDS—Six miles west toward Meadville, with swimming and recreational facilities; also Allegheny National Forest.

Weather notes: Cold winters, sometimes with alternate freezing and thaw, drifting and blowing snow; also damp spells in April and August. These can make roads and trails hard to travel—check with refuge office.

What to take and wear: Wet-weather gear, especially footwear, in spring.

Points of interest nearby: Allegheny National Forest; Oil Creek State Park; also Titusville, 16 miles east, site of the first producing oil well in the United States, with a museum and nearby Pithole, old oil boom town.

For more information: Erie National Wildlife Refuge, R.D. #2, Box 191, Guys Mills, Pennsylvania 16327. Phone: (814) 789-3585.

GREAT MEADOWS (Massachusetts)

GREAT MEADOWS (Massachusetts)

Great Meadows may be unique among national wildlife refuges in its urban location, just fifteen miles from the center of Boston. It is surrounded by offices, stores, plants, an oasis for hundreds of wildlife species but also for the humans who come in numbers to visit from the busy surrounding area.

Nearly four million persons live within thirty miles of its boundaries, which enclose some four thousand acres of varied habitat along the Concord and Sudbury rivers, including marshes where water chestnuts, wild rice, and masses of golden lotuses bloom (the only place in Massachusetts where these plants grow in such profusion) and uplands where ring-necked pheasants are common throughout the year.

Some two hundred species of birds visit Great Meadows' 2,749 acres annually, and its mammals list covers twenty-six species, including opossum, raccoon, red fox, mink, striped skunk, otter, and, rarely, gray fox and flying squirrels. Appearing commonly and often nesting are solitary, warbling, and red-eyed vireos, and many warblers —among them the black-and-white, Nashville, parula, yellow, magnolia, yellow-rumped, black-throated green, chestnut-sided, blackpoll, yellowthroat, Canada, prairie, and palm.

Rails and wood ducks nest commonly—the refuge has produced as many as four hundred young wood ducks in a good year, encouraged by the many nest boxes provided—and a small black-crowned night heron colony has been active. Canada geese, mallard, black ducks, and blue-winged teal also nest here. An osprey comes to fish.

Migrant waterfowl and shorebirds make good bird-watching spring and fall, as do young broods in the water in midsummer. A glorious sight in the fall is the purple loosestrife, Queen Anne's lace, and goldenrod covering the fields as fall foliage starts to turn (loosestrife was first introduced in the United States in a backyard Concord garden).

Several trails are marked, including the Dike Trail, with a self-guiding leaflet, and the Black Duck Creek Trail, which runs alongside the creek where black ducks first appear in the spring. (Unfortunately, refuge ponds are sometimes heavily algae-coated in summer, a eutrophication problem caused by the daily emptying into refuge waters of some one million gallons of partially treated sewage.)

The refuge is in two units separated by several miles, both heavily used by persons who live and work nearby—business men and women taking a quiet hour at midday, families, and many school and other local groups. The red-winged blackbird colony, the decorative males highly visible in the spring as they expand their scarlet epaulettes and proclaim their territories from the tops of the cattails, has been studied as intensively as any in the world by local school science classes. (An interesting bit of information gained in one three-year study showed that the conspicuous male display was, contrary to previous belief, relatively ineffectual, for while the handsome ones were showing off, the females went off in the marsh grass and mated with less showy males that did no displaying at all!)

Great Meadows is equally popular in the winter for snowshoeing, cross-country skiing and ice-skating on the ponds, and winter birds such as chickadees, titmice, grosbeaks, and an occasional barred owl.

Access in peak times is limited to thirty-five cars, so best try for a morning visit. For several weeks in spring the two rivers flood—usually the last of March—and refuge trails may be muddy or off limits entirely.

Between the two refuge tracts lies Thoreau's Walden Pond, worth a sentimental pilgrimage even though it will disappoint many, its natural appearance marred by a public bathing beach on the east end. Still, the water is as crystalline as when Thoreau peered into it looking for shadowy pickerel, and a thirty-minute pondside walk to the original site of Thoreau's cabin passes through woods in which the main sound is still that of chickadees, nuthatches, and squirrels. Traffic noises are muffled by oak woods and undergrowth and one hears in the distance only the rattle of the Boston and Maine railroad train which Thoreau noted in his Journals years ago.

Around the cabin site, as in most woodland tracts roundabout, is an admirable collation of varied and multicolored mushrooms and other fungi for interested mycologists.

The area also is a treasure of historic places to see; and many communities with strong local conservation groups have set aside open areas available to horseback riding and hiking—the use varies with the town.

Oxbow Refuge is also administered by Great Meadows. It is named for the meanders taken by the Nashua River flowing through and creating ponds over its 662 acres, located in Fort Devens in Harvard, Massachusetts. Black and wood ducks stop over here and various others including pheasant, grouse, woodcock and ospreys. Trails have been made.

How to get there: From the center of Concord, Massachusetts, follow Route 62 northeast 2.5 miles to Monsen Road on the left, and refuge signs.

Open: Every day sunrise to sunset (except when closed by 35-car visitor limit).

Best times to visit: Spring and fall during migration and early nesting, though river flooding can prevent full use for several weeks in spring.

What to see: Spring warbler migrations; black-crowned night heron families in summer; fields covered with purple loosestrife, Queen Anne's lace, and goldenrod, and ponds with lotus bloom; wild rice and water chestnuts growing in marshes. Ducks and geese all seasons, but especially spring and fall.

What to do: Self-guided walking tour. Canoeing, boating, fishing and hunting in adjacent Concord and Sudbury rivers (though not in refuge boundaries). Skiing, showshoeing, iceskating on ponds in winter.

Where to stay: MOTELS—a number in nearby Concord. CAMPGROUNDS —Minuteman Campground, Littleton, Massachusetts, 10 miles west of refuge.

Weather notes: No unusual weather extremes, though sometimes quite cold in winter. Mostly pleasant the rest of the year.

What to take and wear: Comfortable clothing appropriate to the season. Waterproof footgear during spring floodtimes.

Points of interest nearby: Minuteman National Historical Park adjacent to the refuge, where the embattled farmers stood to start the Revolutionary War; Thoreau's Walden Pond (see text);

Massachusetts Audubon Society's Drumlin Farm, one of many sanctuaries operated by the Society, a listing available by writing Society Office, Dept. SM, in nearby Lincoln, Massachusetts 01773.

For more information: Great Meadows National Wildlife Refuge, 191 Sudbury Road, Concord, Massachusetts 01742. Phone: (617) 369-5518.

GREAT SWAMP (New Jersey)

The Great Swamp, bought from the Delaware Indians in 1708 for a collection of blankets, kettles, whiskey, and thirty pounds cash, was repurchased by citizens of this area for more than $1,000,000 in 1960. It could then become a national wildlife refuge instead of a metropolitan jetport.

More than 6,000 private citizens and 462 organizations raised the funds for the original 3,000 acres. Since then, additional acquisition has brought the area to more than 6,000 acres of wooded swamps, fresh-water marshes, bogs, and uplands. Now in north-central New Jersey a rich diversity of wildlife exists almost within view of New York's skyline.

Wood ducks, regarded by many as our most beautiful waterfowl, thrive here, producing some four thousand ducklings every year in nest boxes and natural cavities around the refuge. They are easily seen in the pothole ponds on the Pleasant Plains road approach to refuge headquarters, as well as on impoundments from observation and photography blinds located on the trails.

So are white-tailed deer, especially to the visitor who comes early in the morning or toward dusk. Muskrats build their winter lodges in the fall, and contend for mates in the spring. Fox, mink (their tracks alongside the waterways), occasional otter and beaver are also around. A few years ago, a black bear was sighted.

The bird list includes more than two hundred species. Common or abundant are the American and least bitterns, green and great blue herons, pheasant, woodcock (their spring courtship flights visible from refuge headquarters), kestrels, killdeer, Virginia and sora rails, barred and screech owls, and among the waterfowl, Canada geese, blue-winged and green-winged teal, mallard, and black ducks. Seasonally common or abundant small birds include the hermit, Swainson's, and wood thrushes, rose-breasted grosbeaks, scarlet tanagers, long-billed marsh wrens, flickers, kingfishers, and numbers of others. Common in warbler migrations, spring and fall, are black-and-white, blue-winged, northern parula, black-throated blue, blackpoll, chestnut-sided, Canada, black-throated green, and a half dozen others.

Visitors can see much of this rich variety from the auto drives and hiking trails, especially those into the wilderness area, which makes up more than half of the refuge and was the first tract so designated in the national wildlife refuge system.

Though surrounded by development, it is possible to get lost in this wild place full of bogs and great trees, oaks and beeches with trunks three and four feet in diameter. The rare blue-spotted salamander and bog turtle can be found here, along with a fascinating array of botanical species—ferns and mosses, wild lilies and orchids, and in the upland portions, gentians, primroses, marigolds, spring beauties. The refuge has excellent lists of all these, plus the various reptiles and amphibians which make this their home. (Access is limited to the sixty or seventy cars that can fit into the parking areas, however, so plan to go fairly early, especially in fine weather.)

The refuge is on the edge of a main raptor migration path along the Kittatinny Mountains, and gets interesting drop-ins during the fall of marsh and red-shouldered hawks, with occasional goshawks, ospreys, and eagles, and kettles of Cooper's and sharp-shinned hawks overhead. Redtails are around most of the year, as are red-shouldered.

Groups may arrange in advance for films, lectures, and slide talks at the refuge headquarters auditorium. The New Jersey Audubon Society, with headquarters in nearby Franklin Lakes, often schedules evening frog walks in the spring, under permit from the refuge.

How to get there: From New York City take the Lincoln Tunnel to the New Jersey Turnpike; Exit 14 to Route 22 to I-287 North. Exit at Basking Ridge onto Maple Avenue, left on Madisonville Road, right on Pleasant Plains Road to headquarters.

Open: Dawn to dusk through the year.

Best times to visit: Spring and fall.

What to see: Diversity of bird, animal, and plant life including deer, wood ducks, warblers.

What to do: Hiking and auto trails; observation platforms; photography (blinds available); limited 6-day deer hunt.

Where to stay: MOTELS—In Bernardsville, 3 miles northwest; Morris Plains, 10 miles north; Somerville, 20 miles west. CAMPGROUNDS —Mahlon Dickinson Reservation, 35 miles north.

Weather notes: Winters not usually severe but March–April and August can be wet.

What to take and wear: Waterproof footgear for off-boardwalk hiking, especially in wilderness area (compass handy there, too). Insect repellent in summer.

Points of interest nearby: New Jersey Audubon Scherman Wildlife Sanctuary, 4 miles west; Morristown National Historical Park (Revolutionary War encampment) 1 mile northwest; Somerset County Environmental Center, 1 mile west.

For more information: Great Swamp National Wildlife Refuge, R.D. 1, Box 148, Basking Ridge, New Jersey 07420. Phone: (201) 677-1222.

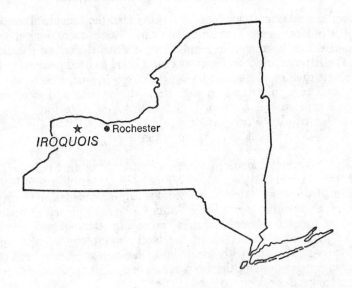

★ ● Rochester
IROQUOIS

IROQUOIS (New York)

A sign near the headquarters building of this 10,818-acre refuge warns against disturbing the Canada geese, so numerous here and accustomed to the idea of a refuge that they bring their broods of downy young to browse on the lawn in June and July.

Killdeer also—living up to their scientific name "vociferus"—join the group, flashing their wings and putting on their "broken-wing act" to lure visitors away from their nests on the ground nearby.

Spring and fall are in some ways the best times to visit Iroquois in the northwestern corner of New York State. Then the massive migrations of waterfowl come through—sometimes a hundred thousand geese alone in the area in the spring, and twenty-five thousand ducks. The first arrival of geese makes it seem to local residents like springtime at last after a hard winter and they themselves flock out to watch the heartening sight, creating bumper-to-bumper traffic on nearby roads in early April. But this tapers off and by later in the month the geese along with whistling swans and more than a dozen species of ducks can be viewed on the refuge ponds with relative ease —large concentrations of pintail in the spring and wigeon in the fall (the fall movements is nowhere near as impressive as the spring).

Of these, ten species stay to raise families, the most numerous being the stunning wood ducks—America's most beautiful duck—which produce more than three thousand young every year in four hundred nest boxes and in natural tree cavities. These are also used by the handsome hooded mergansers. The two species compete for the nest cavities, sometimes laying their eggs in such a disorganized way that mergansers end up with wood duck young and vice versa. One female may find herself attempting to incubate forty eggs of mixed parentage. When twenty or thirty of these hatch, she has as much as she can handle—sometimes more, judging from her harried behavior.

Spring warbler migration is famous locally along the Swallow Hollow trail in mid-May, with the Wilson's, cerulean, blackpoll, black-and-white, yellow, magnolia, chestnut-sided, bay-breasted, and many others, along with several vireos. Later on one can sight the nesting warbler species—the prothonotary, extending its range and finding holes in flooded timber along the creek; and both the blue- and golden-winged along with the hybrid that occurs where these two species' ranges overlap, the Brewster's warbler—and, far south of its usual range, the golden-crowned kinglet.

Well-laid-out trails are offered for cars, hikers, and canoeists. All are rewarding but the watercourse (one must get a permit for it) particularly so, as the paddler passes quietly through six miles of wetland inhabited by deer, green herons, fox, muskrat, raccoon, beaver (though one can see these elsewhere on the refuge too), and a variety of wild flowers that come out through the growing season. These include yellow and blue irises, lady's slippers, swamp loosestrife), white lizard's tails, and brilliant groupings of cardinal flowers in August.

A section of Oak Orchard Creek and adjoining natural areas have been officially designated a National Landmark; as such it has no formal trails but it is hikable and offers, besides birds and other wildlife, a climax forest of beech, birch, maple, and hemlock that, as far as is known, has never been cut. Some of the older hemlocks have trunks four feet in diameter; the beeches, five to six feet.

From the Cayuga Pool overlook it is possible to see floating nests of the pied-billed grebe in June, and in July young great blue herons from the colony that supports about two hundred nests of this stately bird in a remote refuge swamp area.

Other interesting nesting species include great horned and barred owls; least bitterns; many wood thrushes and rose-breasted grosbeaks; sora rails; red-tailed and red-shouldered hawks; woodcock, which put on their dramatic courtship flights at dawn and dusk through April, observable from the Casey Road; and screech owls and kestrels, which sometimes take up residence in surplus wood duck houses (when there is a surplus!).

Ospreys and occasional bald and golden eagles go through in the fall. By mid-December the ponds are frozen and the refuge covered with knee-deep snow that stays usually until ice breakup in March. But ice fishermen and cross-country skiers and snowshoers can see snow buntings, waxwings, redpolls, evening grosbeaks, and sometimes many horned larks—a recent Christmas Bird Count turned up more than a thousand; and the ice fishermen may pull out northern pike eighteen inches long from Ringneck Marsh.

How to get there: From Buffalo take New York Throughway to Pembroke exit, then north on Highway 77 to Alabama, New York, then 63 north to Casey Road and Headquarters sign.

Open: Daylight hours year-round.

Best times to visit: Spring and fall for migrants and spring flowers; summer for nesting birds, fawns, waterfowl broods.

What to see: Large numbers of waterfowl, especially Canada geese; also white-tailed deer, muskrat, spring wild flowers, wood warblers.

What to do: Photography (wooden blinds are available, overlooking waterfowl areas; can be reserved ahead); auto and hiking trails; overlooks; cross-country skiing, snowshoeing; canoeing; fishing all year (ice fishing in winter for northern pike); limited hunting for waterfowl, deer, and upland game.

Where to stay: MOTELS—In Batavia, 15 miles southeast; and Medina, 6 miles northwest. CAMPGROUNDS—In Akron, 15 miles west; Darien, 20 miles south; also Letchworth State Park, 45 miles southwest.

Weather notes: Winters cold, but not usually heavy snow cover.

What to take and wear: Heavy clothing in winter, waterproof footgear in spring and fall.

Points of interest nearby: Bergen Swamp, 28 miles east—a fascinating natural botanical area, 10,000 acres maintained by a private association, with dwarf trees; many orchids including the white lady's slipper, the bog turtle and Massasauga rattlesnake. Letchworth State Park (see CAMPGROUNDS) with spectacular scenic gorge and waterfalls and fine early October foliage colors. Also Tonawanda and Oak Orchard wildlife state management areas adjoining refuge.

For more information: Iroquois National Wildlife Refuge, R.D. # 1 Casey Road, Bason, New York 14013. Phone: (716) 958-5445.

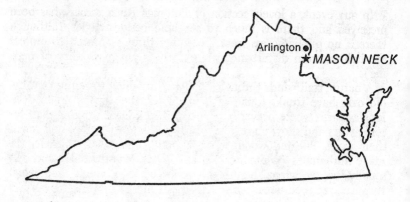

Arlington ● ★ *MASON NECK*

MASON NECK (Virginia)

This 1,661 acres of woods and marsh on the Mason Neck peninsula in the Potomac River, eighteen miles from Washington, D.C., became a national wildlife refuge in 1969, largely because private citizens, aided by The Nature Conservancy, were determined to protect it as a nesting site for endangered southern bald eagles. It was about to become a housing development instead.

They have had plenty to do since. Through "urgent notices" they have successfully resisted proposals to encroach on refuge land with an airport, a dredging project, a gas line, chemical aerosol spray experiments, application of chlorinated hydrocarbon insecticides to eliminate an insect which proved to be all but nonexistent, a sewage treatment plant, and an eight-lane highway.

It is probably not over; but, meanwhile, the eagles have a place they can call their own—altogether more than six thousand acres, for the whole peninsula is managed cooperatively to protect the eagles through regional and state parks, a state historic site, and other like-minded landowners.

The results even so have not been entirely heartening, for the eagles' numbers have continued to decline. The most recent did not hatch and, when examined, showed high pesticide levels. But a new plan offers some encouragement: a healthy egg transplanted from another area did hatch and the young successfully fledged. This practice will be continued in the hope that pesticides will be reduced and the transplanted birds will become a viable population once again.

In any event, a lovely section of Potomac River estuary has been preserved and there is much to see here besides eagles (although there is no public access from December through March to protect the habitat from disturbance while there is any possibility of nesting).

A nature trail winds through woodland in which towering century-old oaks have trunks four feet in diameter, then opens up to overlook a marsh where beaver have maintained a large working dam for some years and show up regularly early and late to inspect and repair their work. Pileated woodpeckers abound, along with flickers, titmice, nuthatches (white-breasted and some red-breasted), and seasonally, winter wrens, hermit, gray-cheeked, Swainson's, and wood thrushes, red-eyed vireos, scarlet tanagers, indigo buntings, and rusty blackbirds.

Deer are relatively unwary and easily seen. There are also fox, raccoon, and skunk, less commonly seen but all about at night.

Barred and great horned owls are common; woodcock, bobwhite, and a few turkey are around; in the marshy parts are numbers of green and great blue herons, great egrets, and mallard, black and wood ducks; and out in the river, scaup, bufflehead, and ruddy ducks sometimes are packed so tightly together they appear to be islands.

Several warblers are common much of the year—northern parula, prairie, Kentucky, yellowthroat, redstart, and yellow-breasted chat.

A good way to see all this is by canoe at high tide. Environmental education groups, with permission from the refuge office, can put in the water and explore the estuary and tidal guts. One feels, as the marsh birds seem to, that there is no one else around at all.

Also administered by Mason Neck is the Marumsco Refuge—sixty-three acres of fresh-water tidal marsh near Woodbridge, Virginia. There are no visitor facilities but travelers can see the refuge from adjacent Veterans Memorial Park.

How to get there: From Woodbridge go north on Route 1, take Route 242 east (Gunston Road), right on High Point Road for a half mile, then left into Woodmarsh parking lot. (Contact refuge office for current regulations, see below.)

Open: Office open weekdays all year. Refuge trail open dawn to dusk April 1–November 30, 7 days a week (closed December 1–March 31 to protect eagle nesting).

Best times to visit: April and October–November.

What to see: Eagles; deer; beaver, pileated woodpeckers in fall.

What to do: Trail birding; photography. Canoeing by permission for environmental education groups.

Where to stay: MOTELS—In Woodbridge, Virginia, 10 miles from refuge. CAMPGROUNDS—Pohick Bay Regional Park, 1 mile north; Prince William Forest, 10 miles south.

Weather notes: Summer can be unpleasantly hot and humid; otherwise generally temperate.

What to take and wear: Sturdy waterproof footgear may be handy on trails.

Points of interest nearby: Pohick Bay Regional Park and Prince William Forest (see CAMPGROUNDS)—attractive nature areas and trails. Gunston Hall Plantation, 1 mile north of refuge—beautifully restored home of George Mason, "Pen of the Revolution"—a state historic site.

For more information: Mason Neck National Wildlife Refuge, 9502 Richmond Highway, Lorton, Virginia 22079. Phone: (703) 339-5278.

★*MISSISQUOI*

●Burlington

MISSISQUOI (Vermont)

"Missisquoi" comes from an Abenaki Indian word meaning "Land of much grass and many waterfowl," a description as apt now as when the Indians alone were here. But that's not all. A morning walk along the nature trail in this refuge is likely to be punctuated by curious beaver slapping their tails on the stream surface to tell the other beaver you're coming—and then disappearing in the direction of their dome-shaped house, twenty feet across and ten feet high, built of whitened, barkless tree limbs.

In this northwestern corner of Vermont hummingbirds inspect and drink from the orange jewelweed. Yellowthroat and yellow warblers, which nest here, abound.

Alongside the trail flame-crested pileated woodpeckers, probably now our largest woodpecker and a year-round resident, have drilled more than a dozen of their square nest holes in a single giant dead elm.

In the first few minutes along the pine needle-cushioned walk one may start up woodcock a half dozen times, their wings whistling as they whir away. Ponds with golden-throated water lilies shimmer in the light. In season, songbirds delight the visitor, as do carpets of wild flowers in this 5,651-acre refuge established in 1942 primarily as a nesting place for water birds in summer and a resting place for them during migration.

Located on the northeast shore of Lake Champlain within a mile of the Canadian border, Missisquoi is the northernmost inland link in a chain of refuges at strategic points along the Atlantic Flyway in the eastern United States. Congregations of waterfowl are one of its outstanding sights. As many as ten thousand ducks—including the black duck, ring-necked, goldeneye, and wood ducks that nest here, and others such as nesting and migrant teal mallard, pintail shoveler, canvasback, and hooded merganser—gather in rafts at the peak of the spring and fall migration, normally April and mid-September.

The ideal time for walking the trails is probably from mid-August to October. The air is cool and fresh then, migrants are coming through, and the trees are beginning to blaze with color. (At other times foot travel may be restricted for various reasons, and it is well to check with refuge headquarters.) During breeding season dike areas heavily used as nest sites may be closed except by special permission. When hunting starts about October 1, other parts are closed to give protection and shelter to wild residents. And, being in large part on a diked river delta, some trails may be partly inundated during spring floods.

But even this has compensations, for Missisquoi is ideally seen by canoe, its quiet streams manageable by the novice. Virtually the entire refuge can be explored in this way, and wild creatures thus approached often seem less likely to startle and flee than when one is walking. Muskrat swim beside the boat, and migrating warblers, redstarts, water thrushes, and ovenbirds are in the low growth along the creeks.

By mid-June the trails are dry, and those who take them are rewarded by sightings of orioles, rose-breasted grosbeaks, and an unmatched atmosphere of woodland beauty and solitude, with no sounds other than birds, small frogs squeaking as they leap from the path, and leaves whispering in the breeze.

Broods of ducks are on the waterways—especially the goldeneyes, which sometimes "baby-sit" for one another and assume responsibility for as many as thirty chicks per parent.

There is a great blue heron colony; American bitterns, gallinules, and black terns nest, along with meadowlarks, marsh wrens, redtailed hawks, and barred owls (Missisquoi lists 185 birds as sighted here). Foragers will enjoy delicious fiddleheads of the ostrich fern, and wild blueberries.

Fishing is excellent—walleyed pike in the Missisquoi River in early

May are famous—and small- and largemouth bass, northern pike and occasional muskie; and ice fishing is popular in the winter.

In fact, for some the refuge is favored as winter closes in. Scoters and occasional eiders and old-squaws are here, and sometimes snowy owls. Saw-whet owls are resident in the pine stands, and the refuge's mammal population—deer, otter, red fox, and eastern coyote—may be more easily seen then, their tracks visible in the snow. Snowmobiles are not permitted, but snowshoeing and cross-country skiing are—for those who don't mind real winter weather. The refuge averages eighty-seven inches of snow a season, often more, with temperatures hovering around five to ten degrees and a cold snap around February that may hold at twenty or twenty-five below for a week or two.

How to get there: From Burlington, Vermont, take I-89 to Swanton exit then west on Highway 78 to the refuge, 2 miles west of Swanton.

Open: Daylight hours (walking trails may be closed at some seasons; see text and check refuge headquarters).

Best times to visit: Late summer and early fall.

What to see: Waterfowl, especially in migration; marsh hawks; yellow warblers; killdeer; sometimes coyote and fox.

What to do: Waterfowl hunting in the fall; fishing for walleyed pike, bass, bullheads. Group conducted tours can be arranged with the refuge manager. Canoeing—boats can be rented in Fairfax.

Where to stay: MOTELS—Several motels in Swanton and St. Albans (10 miles). CAMPGROUNDS—A state campground 16 miles away; 3 private campgrounds within 2 miles of the refuge.

Weather notes: Can be extremely cold in winter, 20 below or more.

What to take and wear: Waterproof footgear in spring; a windbreaker, at least, in spring and fall; warmest clothing in winter.

Points of interest nearby: Lake Champlain Islands offer excellent birding opportunities. Mud Creek State Management Area 5 miles west of refuge on Highway 78. Victory Bog in Burlington area 40 miles south. Green Mountain National Forest about 95 miles south of refuge (headquarters in Rutland). Excellent fall foliage in most of Vermont. Excellent skiing facilities within an hour of refuge.

For more information: Missisquoi National Wildlife Refuge, R.F.D. #2, Swanton, Vermont 05488. Phone: (802) 868-4781.

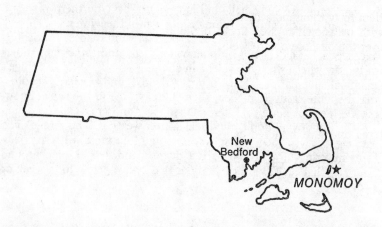

New
Bedford

★
MONOMOY

MONOMOY (Massachusetts)

Monomoy was the landing place in 1606 for the explorer Champlain when he broke a rudder. Before that, some say, it was a haven for the Vikings. Once a thriving fishing community, it has been separate from the mainland since a 1958 hurricane and since 1970 has been an official wilderness area. Few signs of mankind's past remain, and all except the lighthouse will be eliminated, as has been vehicular traffic, in accordance with the wilderness designation.

It is a spot that would have suited Thoreau in his quest "for a place where a man may stand and put all America behind him."

One can walk the eight miles of sandy beaches that edge this 2,700 acre island and see, at the height of the tourist season on populous nearby Cape Cod, perhaps a half dozen other persons all day long.

Birds concentrate in great numbers and variety, especially sea birds that are not seen at more inland refuges. If the Eskimo curlew, believed extinct, still exists, some birders feel that Monomoy is where it is most likely to be seen.

Fall migration begins early—as early as July for some northern nesters like the dowitchers—and builds to a peak in September, with abundant common shorebirds along with specialties such as the golden plover, Baird's and buff-breasted sandpipers and marbled godwits, and an infrequent jaeger, peregrine falcon, or wandering ruff from Europe. One can see up to 60 Hudsonian godwits, a species never glimpsed by the much-traveled Audubon. And in winter, more than forty thousand scoter and eider are commonly sighted offshore, with occasional massed flocks of up to a half million birds flying over the offshore ocean swells.

Spring migration, by contrast, is quickly over in late May and early June, as birds hurry to nest locations (warblers occur in greater numbers in fall, as their northward journey takes a more inland route).

In summer Monomoy has the largest colony of nesting least terns in Massachusetts, along with some two thousand pairs of common terns and five hundred pairs of roseate terns, and others—arctic terns, piping plovers, many Savannah sparrows, laughing and herring gulls, occasional willets and seaside sparrows and rarely skimmers and oystercatchers (Monomoy's total bird list includes 263 species).

Ducks and geese are still abundant in November—shoveler, pintail, wigeon, teal, ruddies, bufflehead, black along with pied-billed grebes and coot. In fact, the moderating ocean influence keeps Monomoy's fresh-water ponds open for more of the year than the mainland, and some of the highest populations of fresh-water waterfowl are seen here in November and December.

A number of small animals roam here also, including a small herd of deer, and some muskrat and opossum.

The plant life is beautiful, ranging from the dune grass, seaside spurge, and beach pea to primroses, orchids, and the inland fruiting viburnum, highbush blueberry, sweet pepperbush, shadbush, and black alder. In spring the hudsonia makes a carpet of silvery green and gold; pink rose mallows with 6-inch blooms burst forth in August; and in sheltered wet places along pond margins are occasional violets and sundews and the rare adder's tongue fern.

Surf fishing is erratic but can be very good, with bluefish averaging sometimes ten to fifteen pounds and striped bass up to twenty pounds or so (the die-hards' season starts in spring "when the whippoor-will calls"—but it's best after August).

All this does not come easily; Monomoy is surrounded by treacherous waters, shifting sandbars, and strong currents to confound and endanger even the expert boatman. At least one death every year is recorded among those who would visit and return from this island. It is best to try for a trip with someone who knows the waters intimately. Newcomers can find commercial fishermen by asking about in the center of Chatham, or at the Audubon Society in Wellfleet, or refuge headquarters.

It is worth it, if one can make the trip safely—for this bit of wilderness is a rare place, and with the protection of its wilderness status it will no doubt be even better in years to come.

Morris Island, the mainland section from which Monomoy was

detached by the hurricane, can be reached by crossing the causeway from Chatham, and contains a pleasant seaside walking area.

How to get there: From Boston, take Route 93 to U.S. 6, east to State Route 28, into Chatham. To get to Monomoy, inquire for boat (see text) or Massachusetts Audubon Society tour, Wellfleet (see below).

Open: Daylight hours.

Best times to visit: Spring, summer, fall—any good day with calm seas. Fall migrants peak in September.

What to see: Shore, marsh, and sea birds, sometimes by the many thousands. A wide variety of plant life, orchids, roses, heaths.

What to do: Surf casting for blues and striped bass.

Where to stay: MOTELS—Many in nearby Chatham. CAMPGROUNDS—Nickerson State Park in nearby Brewster (this may be crowded in summer and is first-come-first-served).

Weather notes: Often misty and cool—sometimes dense fog.

What to take and wear: A windbreaker is always a good idea here, and a sweater for ocean breezes, with warmer clothing in all but summer. Sun protection for bright days.

Points of interest nearby: Cape Cod National Seashore with some 10,927 acres (acquired or planned) of beach, heath, forest and ponds, picnic areas, horseback riding, nature trails and visitors' centers. Nauset Beach, setting for *The Outermost House* by Henry Beston. Tours of Nauset and trips to Monomoy are led in July-early September by Massachusetts Audubon Society from its Wellfleet Bay Wildlife Sanctuary, Box 236, South Wellfleet, Massachusetts. 02663.

For more information: Great Meadows National Wildlife Refuge, 191 Sudbury Road, Concord, Massachusetts 01742. Phone: (617) 369-5518.

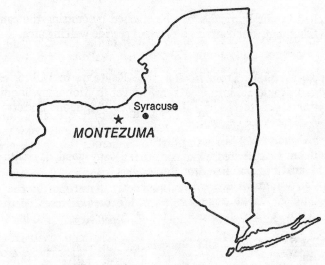

Syracuse

★
MONTEZUMA

MONTEZUMA (New York)

Bald eagles have thrived at Montezuma for the first time in a quarter century as the result of a joint program in which young birds have been taken from nests elsewhere and raised and released in the wild at this refuge.

The eaglets, taken from nonviable wild situations, were brought to this north-central New York State refuge starting in 1976. The project was started by the U. S. Fish and Wildlife Service, the State Department of Environmental Conservation, and Cornell University Laboratory of Ornithology. During the continuing program visitors have been able to view the young birds on their platform from an observation tower (not nearby, so a spotting scope would be helpful) and later overhead after they have begun to fly. (Long-range results of the "hacking" program were uncertain since eagles do not reach nesting maturity for five years. It is hoped that nesting eagles will reestablish in the area.)

For many visitors to this 6,432-acre refuge not far south of Lake Ontario and the Canadian border, the outstanding sight is the concentrations of waterfowl, and especially geese, in spring migration—100,000 Canadas at peak times in April, along with up to 10,000 blue and snow geese and 50,000 or so ducks (the numbers vary a little in fall, with perhaps 50,000 geese in late October and up to 81,000 ducks).

They can be viewed from many aspects of the five-mile self-guided auto tour route, the 1.4-mile Esker Brook Walking Trail, two observations towers, and about five miles of additional dikes open seasonally for hiking. Excluding small areas of upland woods and fields, most of Montezuma is marsh and swamp. It was not always so. The great wetland area which historically stretched another twelve miles northward from Cayuga Lake, about which early French explorers told of waterfowl so numerous they blackened the sky, all but disappeared after construction of the New York State Barge Canal in 1911. But droughts of the 1930s and their disastrous effects on waterfowl everywhere impelled interest in restoring such areas, and so Montezuma (so named because it reminded early explorers of tales told of the plains of Mexico) was established in 1937.

Mallard, wood duck, and blue-winged teal nest commonly, along with others that sometimes nest and sometimes move through to other areas—pintail, gadwall, wigeon, shoveler, redhead, merganser, and canvasback.

Other commonly nesting water birds include green herons, pied-billed grebes with their floating nests, coot, common gallinules, American bitterns, Virginia and sora rails, and black-crowned night herons, which have a colony out of sight in the cattails but which fan out to be easily seen around the dikes.

Red-tailed hawks also nest, as do ruffed grouse and pheasant on the limited upland areas, woodcock, killdeer, kestrels, great horned and screech owls, and some of the smaller birds—wood thrushes and veeries, indigo buntings, rose-breasted grosbeaks, vesper sparrows, goldfinches, red-eyed and warbling vireos, ruby-throated hummingbirds, and numbers of flycatchers, including both willow and alder, least, great crested, and eastern wood pewee.

Visitors can often see white-tailed deer, along with their fawns in summer which come out about the same time as the goose and duck broods. Woodchuck scurry about the fields and edges of the roads, and muskrat populate the refuge in the thousands, building their domelike houses and keeping the cattail areas open so they do not become so impenetrable they cannot be used for food and cover by the waterbirds.

Snapping turtles can be seen laying their eggs along the dikes in May and June, and a short time later the hollows where they have been dug up again by raccoon and skunk (a service to the duck broods which often fall prey to turtles). Carp, some several feet long, literally mob the dam structures by the thousands in spring while spawning, and later during lower water to seek oxygen, it is believed (interesting to see, but their presence in such large numbers is not welcome because their bottom-feeding habits increase water turbidity and temperature—thereby eliminating aquatic plants and invertebrates upon which young waterfowl feed).

Shorebird viewing is best in April and May and later in August, when short-billed dowitchers, greater yellowlegs, and a dozen or so species of plovers and sandpipers come through—in the latter time, seen against a background of brilliant purple loosestrife and pink blooms of the marsh mallow.

How to get there: From Syracuse take Interstate Route 90 west to Exit 41, then Route 414 south to 318 (at light); east on 318 to Route 5&20, east 1 mile on 5&20 to refuge entrance on left.

Open: Daily year-round.

Best times to visit: Spring and fall for migrants; summer for nesters and shorebirds.

What to see: Eagles June–September; geese in large numbers; shorebirds; white-tailed deer; muskrat; woodchuck.

What to do: Auto and hiking trails; photography (no blinds available but good opportunities along dikes); fishing in adjacent waters to refuge, mainly for bullheads; and hunting on limited basis for waterfowl, deer, and small game.

Where to stay: MOTELS—Several at Waterloo, Seneca Falls, and Auburn, within 10 miles. CAMPGROUNDS—Several on roads northeast of refuge; also at state parks in area, including Taughannock Falls, Watkins Glen, and Buttermilk Falls, 15–20 miles south. (Complete list of state parks available from state parks division in Albany.)

Weather notes: Influenced by proximity to Lake Ontario. Often cloudy and winters can be quite cold and windy but otherwise few temperature extremes. Snow usually not heavy but drifting, and trails are kept open to the observation tower.

What to take and wear: Comfortable clothing appropriate to the season.

Points of interest nearby: State parks (see campgrounds above) with impressive limestone formations; Howland's Island Game Management Area 12 miles northeast, beautiful with ponds, upland, diversity of birdlife; Cornell Laboratory of Ornithology, with raptor studies and bird-watching in Sapsucker Woods, 40 miles south.

For more information: Montezuma National Wildlife Refuge, R.D. 1, Box 1411, Seneca Falls, New York 13148. Phone: (315) 568-5987.

MOOSEHORN (Maine)

Moosehorn is rich in wildlife of many kinds—but its undeniable star is the woodcock, a small round bird with mottled brown markings so inconspicuous in its natural surroundings that it can sit a few feet from a viewer without being observed, yet it has one of the most spectacular mating displays in the world of nature.

The visitor can see these anytime between April 1 and about May 20, in clearings around the refuge at dawn or dusk. Refuge personnel will know where they are, and one can watch while the birds for which this 22,665-acre refuge was established in 1937 begin to stake out their territories and claim their females. It is a stunning sight as the male, triggered by a specific intensity of light at the beginning and end of day, soars hundreds of feet in the air, circles—outlining the area he has marked for his own, finally reaching a peak from which he plummets like a bullet, wings whistling as the air rips through his feathers, straight to earth, leveling out only a few feet off the ground. He may repeat the performance several times in the half light, while his intended presumably watches from the edge of the clearing, the site of a future nest, and listens to his twittering song.

Moosehorn, established for the study and protection of the American woodcock, has at least three hundred nesting pairs. More than two thousand birds may be present in the fall as they prepare to go south.

But many other natural inhabitants—over two hundred bird species and thirty-nine mammals—also have been seen and some are commonly resident at Moosehorn, located just six miles southwest of Calais (pronounced "callous"), Maine, in the easternmost tip of the United States. The refuge is made up of two tracts combining habitat ranging from upland and timbered areas to lakes, marshes, and streams.

On the Cobscook Bay side, where tides may reach twenty-eight feet—highest in the United States outside of Alaska—are harbor seals and porpoises; in the upland areas there are beaver in the ponds; in wooded areas black bear, deer, red fox, porcupine, snowshoe hare, and an occasional transient moose (the refuge was named for nearby Moosehorn stream, not because of a large moose population).

Common or abundant at all seasons except winter are double-crested cormorants, great blue herons, American bitterns, Canada geese, black, ring-necked, and wood ducks, blue- and green-winged teal, broad-winged and marsh hawks, sora and Virginia rails, whippoor-wills, nighthawks, kinfishers, meadowlarks, bobolinks, and a number of warblers, including the yellow, northern parula, Nashville, black-and-white, magnolia, yellow-rumped, chestnut-sided, and black-throated green. Many of these nest here. Bank swallows colonize several old abandoned gravel pits.

Present in good numbers at all seasons are loons, ruffed grouse, and owls—saw-whet, barred and great horned, though these are not always readily seen during the day; and, at the coast in spring and fall, scoter and shorebirds. Ospreys and sometimes bald eagles—both have nested here—may be observed swooping down for fish on both coastal and inland waters.

Spring is a good time for viewing migrant warblers and waterfowl, and if one arrives early enough—late March—one can spot such usually retiring creatures as mink and weasel as well, and otter playing where the ice still covers the streams, coming up through one hole and diving down another. The weather stays cool through May, with temperatures down to the twenties at night, though perhaps to the seventies by day; and the ground is moist, so waterproof and warm footgear and outerclothing are recommended.

About 1,800 waterfowl are present through the summer, but less visible because they are spread out over Moosehorn's fifty-nine man-made ponds and impoundments. These are lovely scenic spots, varying in size, surrounded by aspen, birch, spruce, and fir woods and fields marked with granite outcroppings left by glaciers—excellent places to stop for a picnic lunch (the refuge has no picnic sites as such, but permits lunching if visitors leave no litter). Visitors can see fall migrants in September and October, with foliage colors peaking about October 1.

Mammals, present all year-round (though bear and groundhogs are snoozing in winter), may be more visible when the leaves have fallen; and a photographer bent on taking a porcupine unawares is likely to be rewarded any time except winter and early spring if he walks quietly for an hour or so in the afternoon and listens for a quiet shuffling through the dry leaves, with a sharp eye out for a semi-shapeless object in a tree notch. ("Porcupines have their good points," locals are fond of saying, "but then again they have their bad points, too.")

The refuge has some sixty miles of trails, including several with self-guiding leaflets. Those interested in woodcock can accompany the crews which work in woodcock research from April to September, walking the woods to trap and band and note their activities. Contact the refuge office to arrange it a day or so in advance.

Moosehorn administers several other refuges. *Seal Island* is a 65-acre island located 25 miles offshore. Many pelagic birds visit here; eiders, Leach's petrels, and some puffins nest, but public access is denied because it is a former artillery range and live ordnance may still be present.

Petit Manan has 2,000 acres of peninsula and a nearby island with ducks, terns, gulls, and 190 acres of beaverflowages and fresh ponds. The peninsula is open to limited public use April 15–November 15; the island is restricted to research and wildlife studies by special permission.

Franklin Island is a twelve-acre island valued as a site for sea-bird nesting. Public use is confined to August 1–March 31, by permission.

Carlton Pond is a waterfowl production preserve for ducks and geese, covering 1,068 acres six miles south of Detroit, Maine, on Route 220 between Route I-95 and 202. Waterfowl is more concentrated than Moosehorn and highly visible.

Although *Matinicus Rock* is not a national wildlife refuge, it is administered cooperatively with the Coast Guard and Audubon Society. Puffins, arctic terns, and razor-billed auks nest here. Visitors can walk a trail laid out by Audubon and refuge personnel. Public use only by permission. For this as for other island refuges, visitors must arrange their own transportation, usually available through a lobster fisherman in a nearby coastal town such as Rockland, or the refuge manager can advise.

How to get there: From Bangor, Maine, take Route 9 to Baring, then Route 1 to Refuge Visitors' Center. Center is about 3 miles from refuge headquarters and about 100 miles from Bangor.

Open: Headquarters open 7:30 A.M. to 4 P.M. Monday through Friday; Visitors' Center 9–6 Monday through Friday and 10–6 weekends, June 15 through Labor Day.

Best times to visit: Spring and fall.

What to see: Nuptial flight of woodcock; a variety of ducks, also bitterns, rails, hawks, and warblers. Ruffed grouse abundant. Mammals—beaver, porcupine, snowshoe hare, fox, and sometimes deer and black bear. Bald eagles, especially in spring around marshes. Harbor seals along shore.

What to do: Cross-country skiing and snowshoeing in winter; snowmobiling on certain roads. Brook and lake fishing for trout, bass, and pickerel; ice fishing in winter; deer hunting as refuge conditions permit. Exhibits and wildlife films at visitors' center. Self-guided Nature Trails.

Where to stay: MOTELS—Several in Calais and Baring. CAMPGROUNDS —At Cobscook State Park, adjacent to Edmunds unit of refuge.

Weather notes: Temperatures on the cool side in spring and fall, often severe in winter.

What to take and wear: Footgear that will withstand damp ground; not always needed but a good idea. Sweaters and windbreakers in spring and fall. Warmest outerclothing November–March.

Points of interest nearby: Cobscook Bay State Park; Campobello International Park (Franklin Delano Roosevelt home). Machias Seal Island, nesting spot for puffins, administered jointly by Canadian and U.S. authorities.

For more information: Moosehorn National Wildlife Refuge, Box X, Calais, Maine 04619. Phone: (207) 454-3521.

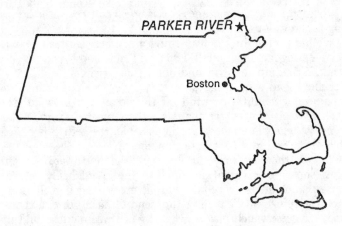

PARKER RIVER (Massachusetts)

The Parker River area is noted for some of the most unusual nature sightings in the country, indeed the world. The Ross' gull, one of the world's rarest birds, normally seen only in Siberia or Alaska and almost never south of the Arctic Circle, was spotted off adjacent Newburyport a few winters back and attracted worldwide attention and tens of thousands of persons to see it.

Other rarities have been an ivory gull, Hudsonian and bar-tailed godwits, gyrfalcons, and peregrine falcons, usually seen for several days in October.

Part of the reason for unusual appearances here may be the diversity of habitat, for the Parker River National Wildlife Refuge, occupying 4,650 acres on Plum Island and the mainland thirty-five miles north of Boston, offers on the one hand the coastal shore, dunes, and salt marsh, and on the other, fresh to brackish wetlands and upland growth with dense cover and lushly bearing fruited thickets. Because of these, delicate warblers may be seen feeding all winter long on its bayberries while sea ducks such as eider, scoter, and old-squaw swim in the icy waters offshore.

Lacy-plumaged snowy egrets journey here in summer and a prime view in early August is the gathering of five hundred to seven hundred of them to roost on a tiny island no bigger than one twentieth of an acre, feeding and preening as the sunset, brilliant here in the flat coastal terrain, turns their white feathers to rose crimson.

And, a little later, tree swallows by the tens of thousands flock to start their trip south, sometimes covering entire trees with their twittering congregations.

Something interesting is happening at Parker River all year long, though spring and early fall visits will suit most persons best—greenhead flies are about in midsummer and visitors need heavy use of repellent; and winters can be severe, for even a one-inch snow accompanied by a northeast wind off the ocean can blow to six-foot drifts and feel even colder than the thermometer's zero or below reading. When winter roads are impassable, the refuge is closed to all but visitors on foot (or skis or snowshoes).

But with the first thaw in February the northward movement begins—snow geese, brant in small numbers gradually joined by others—pintail ducks, wigeon, gadwall, green-winged teal—until by March the refuge may have five thousand Canada geese, a thousand or so snow geese which may stay as long as three months, and up to ten thousand ducks (these numbers may be even larger in the fall).

Ducks begin courtship activities with warm weather, and six males may be seen pursuing a single female, pulling tailfeathers from rivals, and engaging in aerial acrobatics. (Despite appearances, most probably have already paired by the time they arrive—and females return to their home areas to nest, while males usually take up a new residence if during the winter they have chosen a female they prefer from another area.)

Watching such a lively scene, it is worth remembering that with diminishing natural habitat, refuges such as this and others which form a chain of nesting and resting places in the coastal United States are not only pleasant stopovers but in some cases essential oases for the survival of many of these waterfowl species, at least in the numbers they now exist.

In early May the warblers start through, their numbers varying from year to year but in wide variety—almost every species common in the eastern United States has been seen at Parker River at some time or other. The shorebird migration in June is also notable, when they group, as in going south in August, in shallow marsh ponds (called "paanes") by the hundreds.

By late May and June, duck and goose broods are around, and purple martins are working at their colonies, nine of which return to houses on the refuge. There is a small ruddy duck nesting colony here, and also pintail ducks and gadwall—perhaps the farthest east these species nest in such numbers. Least terns often colonize a beach section, which is then closed to public access until the chicks are fledged. And in August, early shorebird migrants are on their way south again and sometimes two to three acres at a time seem almost covered by plovers, sandpipers, dowitchers, godwits, and an occasional avocet.

Even winter, with its severity, has its attractions, with snowy owls not uncommon and flocks of snow buntings, horned larks, and lapland longspurs.

Small populations of mammals are here—white-tailed deer, skunk, red fox, muskrat, and cottontail rabbit—the fox kits and young fawns sometimes seen on the roads in summer—and for the sharp-eyed, the well-named spadefoot toad, which can burrow eight to ten feet in the ground; this is its northernmost-known appearance.

Surf fishing is permitted on most of the refuge beach, and sizable striped bass are often here in large numbers; migratory waterfowl hunting is permitted on certain sections in fall. Blinds are available for photography, and visitors can go plum and cranberry picking during part of September and October. A two-mile self-guided walking trail through Hellcat Swamp passes both fresh- and salt-water marshes and dunes.

There is also a six-mile ocean beach for swimming, sunbathing, and picnicking—though the water is so cold that only a few visitors actually go in even on warmest days (swimming is at your own risk; there is a dangerous undertow offshore and there are no lifeguards).

Plum Island is one of the few natural barrier beach-dune complexes with its special life forms left in the northeastern United States; and its popularity and fragile habitat have led to rules limiting its use to 350 cars at one time. After that, the refuge is closed to autos until late afternoon. It is best therefore to arrive in the early morning, even in winter, on a pleasant weekend.

The subrefuges administered by Parker River include *Rachel Carson*—actually a chain of steppingstone refuges located near Wells, Maine, made up of salt marsh, upland growth, and hushed quiet stands of seventy-five foot white pines, more than four thousand acres acquired and named in honor of the late writer-environmentalist—quiet oases alongside busy commercial areas and well-traveled highways.

At *Wapack*, New Hampshire, the summit of this 738-acre mountain refuge is a vigorous mile hike from a quiet country road on the north side up a steep spur off the Appalachian Trail, but worth it for the occasional view of a red-tailed hawk hunting at eye level. White-throated sparrows nest abundantly. Blueberries grow thickly and can be picked. On a clear day (not every day!) you can see almost to the coast. Another approach is by driving to the summit of adjacent Pack Monadnock Mountain in Miller State Park, and hiking over by that trail.

Thacher Island, Massachusetts, is a rocky nest habitat off Rockport and a difficult boat landing; it is not open to the public.

John Hay, New Hampshire, is deeded as a refuge but the donor retains life estate. It was planned as an environmental education center.

Pond Island, Maine, has good striped bass fishing, nesting ground for eider ducks, but dangerous rip tides. The public is admitted, except during nesting season, but access is difficult. Expert boatmanship is required.

How to get there: From Boston, follow Route 1 north to I-95 and take Newburyport exit to Route 113 east. Follow refuge signs from Route 113.

Open: Dawn to dusk, except when closed for winter road conditions or by 350-car visitor limit.

Best times to visit: Spring and fall.

What to see: Large numbers of ducks, geese, migrating shorebirds and tree swallows; occasional rarities (such as Ross' gull), peregrine falcons, Ipswich sparrows, and ocean sunfish—weighing several hundred pounds, lolling offshore, their shark-like fins startling bathers. A half dozen or so snowy owls along with dovekies and guillemots sometimes on the winter beach.

What to do: Self-guided nature trails; fishing and hunting in season; clamming; swimming and picnicking; berry-picking. Observation towers and blinds available for wildlife study and photography.

Where to stay: MOTELS—Nearest and best motels are at Amesbury and Ipswich; if necessary try Salisbury, a resort area. Best to reserve ahead at busy times. CAMPGROUNDS—Salisbury Beach State Reservation at nearby Salisbury.

Weather notes: Cool spring and fall; bitterly cold in winter.

What to take and wear: A windbreaker might be helpful almost anytime. Otherwise, casual outdoor clothing. Insect repellent essential in summer. In winter, heavy insulated clothing and boots.

Points of interest nearby: Adjacent Newburyport, a historic clipper-ship port, has been restored and some of the country's finest Federalist architecture can be seen, with shops of many kinds. Also: Ipswich River Nature Center (off State Route 97); the Richard T. Crane Memorial Nature Reservation (tip of Argilla Road, Ipswich).

For more information: Parker River National Wildlife Refuge, Plum Island, Newburyport, Massachusetts 01950. Phone: (617) 465-5753.

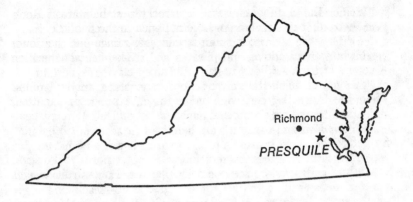

Richmond

PRESQUILE

PRESQUILE (Virginia)

Presquile was named when it was "almost an island"—merely an oxbow bend in Virginia's historic James River where birds and animals had lived for centuries in the swamp and marshland. Since 1934 it has been a separate entity, the result of a navigational channel cut across its narrow neck, and its changed situation has added to its attractions for wild and human creatures alike.

Access is by water only—by private boat or the refuge-operated cable ferry, both of which should be arranged ahead of time. Visitor facilities are extremely simple and the number permitted at one time is usually limited to around 60 at most, which refuge personnel feel helps make for an experience which borders on wilderness in places. Except during a limited deer hunt planned to keep the herd within healthy bounds, visitors are permitted to wander over its 1,329 acres of upland farmland and tidal woodland and marsh. (Waterproof footgear may be appropriate at some seasons, since except for the farmland, about 80 per cent of the island is subject to periodic flooding.)

Numbers of waterfowl winter here, first arriving in September and reaching peaks in mid-December of about eleven thousand Canada geese and seventeen thousand ducks—mallard, black, green-winged teal, pintail, wigeon, merganser, and the wood ducks which also nest here.

But more notable than concentrations of species is the diversity of fauna and flora.

Warblers coming in spring and present through the breeding season include the prothonotary, yellowthroat, black and white, prairie, pine, hooded, Kentucky and northern parula; as well as Louisiana water thrushes, three vireos, summer tanagers, grasshopper sparrows, bluebirds, orchard orioles, and pileated and red-bellied woodpeckers. A colony of bank swallows nests in the steep clay bank next to the navigational channel, the only one known within a hundred miles. There are Forster's terns, wild turkey, quail, killdeer, barred owls, and red-tailed and red-shouldered hawks.

Barn swallows and barn owls are here in their accustomed habitat, for before the island became a refuge in 1952 it was a farm, and several of the farm buildings still remain.

Muskrat and otter are seen occasionally; there are usually several red fox dens; and butterflies of varied species—black and tiger swallowtails, buckeyes, red admirals—flit about the black-eyed Susans and goldenrods in August.

A self-guided nature trail goes through examples of the varied habitat, including some stands of a curious silica-bearing plant called horsetail, which settlers used for scouring pots and which can serve as a nail file as well—and deer like to bed down in its thicker stands.

Canoes can be taken into the two creeks (after obtaining permission), and the adventurous can hike past a fine stand of thirty-foot bamboo into the swamp where the turkey and pileated woodpeckers like to spend their time. But swamp-walkers should wear boots (natives of the area can walk through it without getting their shoe soles wet, according to one legend, but those unused to its vagaries can sink down to the hips).

How to get there: From Richmond take I-95 to Exit 6E, east on Route 10 to Route 827 about 3 miles to the refuge ferry landing.

Open: All year; access by arrangement with refuge office, open 7:30 A.M. to 4 P.M. weekdays.

Best times to visit: Fall and spring but all year is pleasant.

What to see: Deer; waterfowl; bank swallows; bobwhite, quail, warblers.

What to do: Nature trail; wildlife observation; picnicking, limited deer hunting; seasonal boating and canoeing (bring own boat).

Where to stay: MOTELS—In Hopewell and near I-95 Exit 6E, north of refuge. CAMPGROUNDS—At Petersburg, 20 miles southwest; also Pocahontas State Park, 15 miles north.

Weather notes: Generally pleasant all year.

What to take and wear: Boots—hip boots if you wish to explore the swamp.

Points of interest nearby: Petersburg National Battlefield. Two of the nation's earliest plantations, Berkeley and Shirley, within a half hour's drive. A number of state and federal parks are in and around Richmond, 22 miles northwest. A monument near the ferry landing marks where Pocahontas saved Captain John Smith's life. Also near is Bermuda Hundred, oldest incorporated U.S. town.

For more information: Presquile National Wildlife Refuge, P.O. Box 620, Hopewell, Virginia 23860. Phone: (804) 458-7541 (office); (804) 458-4797 (Island).

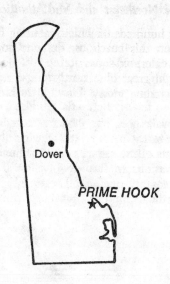

Dover

PRIME HOOK

PRIME HOOK (Delaware)

The best way to see this 8,926-acre marsh and upland refuge on the northern shore of Delaware is by canoe. A watercourse of more than fifteen miles winds down Prime Hook Creek through woods and marsh along which otter, muskrat, bitterns, great blue and green herons, and black ducks flourish, along with flowering mallows, water lilies, sweet pepperbushes, highbush blueberries, and the rare seaside alders. Pitcher plants are found in moist areas. It is a thoroughly delightful trip.

Other sightings around the refuge depend much on rainfall, since water control structures are minimal to nonexistent and in a dry year the wetland habitat can almost disappear. But it has fine potential and in a good year there may be concentrations spring and fall of 12,000 Canada and snow geese and up to 6,800 ducks—black, mallard, wood ducks, gadwall, and blue-winged teal, many of which also nest on the refuge when conditions permit; and in small numbers wigeon, pintail, bufflehead, and scaup.

Ospreys often nest successfully, and a good variety of shorebirds forage on the beach where the refuge has access. On a high tidal saltmarsh area in the south end several farm roads are open to walking. There are sandpipers, plovers, gulls, terns, seaside sparrows, and in the spring hundreds of willets scouting out nesting locations. (A winter walk on this beach can provide good offshore views of seaducks—scoter, eider, old-squaw).

Visitors can sight great blue herons and a number of other long-legged waders including glossy ibises, little blue herons, and great and snowy egrets.

A short boardwalk goes out into the marsh, and several public roads through the refuge permit good viewing of the area.

The upland parts of the refuge are not subject to water conditions and afford observations to the quiet visitor of deer, red and gray fox, raccoon, pheasant, quail, and various songbirds—goldfinches, meadowlarks, cardinals, indigo buntings, thrashers, mockingbirds, catbirds, Carolina wrens, and sometimes orchard and northern orioles and horned larks.

Warbler migrations can be active in April and September, with northern parulas, magnolias, yellow-rumped, blackpolls, yellowthroats, and others.

How to get there: From Rehoboth follow signs north on Route 14 about 12 miles, then east on Route 16 one mile to first blacktop to the left; follow this to the refuge office.

Open: From 7:30 A.M. to 4 P.M. weekdays through the year.

Best times to visit: Fall.

What to see: Waterfowl and shorebirds; occasional otter, deer, fox.

What to do: Trails; canoeing by permission on Prime Hook Creek (canoe rental available nearby); photography (hunting blinds available off-season by permission). Fishing good in Prime Hook Creek for largemouth bass and chain pickerel (some say the best in Delaware). Limited hunting for deer, upland game, and waterfowl.

Where to stay: MOTELS—Several on Route 14 south of refuge; a number in Rehoboth (more expensive and crowded during tourist season). CAMPGROUNDS—Several about 9 miles south and southwest of refuge; also at Cape Henlopen State Park, 9 miles south, April–November.

Weather notes: Fairly mild winters; summers hot and very humid.

What to take and wear: Waterproof footgear for hiking.

Points of interest nearby: Cape Henlopen State Park (see CAMP-GROUNDS)—good birding, especially for shorebirds after strong easterly winds. Lewes Beach, good for family outings. Delaware Seashore State Park from Rehoboth to Bethany, beautiful dune area.

For more information: Prime Hook National Wildlife Refuge, R.D. 1, Box 195, Milton, Delaware 19968. Phone: (302) 684-8419.

TARGET
ROCK
New York City ★

TARGET ROCK (New York)

Target Rock, named after a huge boulder said to have been used for target practice in the Revolutionary War, is as unlike a typical national wildlife refuge as can be imagined. One enters the eighty-acre former estate, the gift of financier, Ferdinand Eberstadt, past neat, pretty caretakers' houses and winds up at a thirty-two-room Georgian mansion where the refuge offices now are. Nearby is one of its chief attractions—impressive formal gardens where hundreds of rare species of azaleas and rhododendrons draw springtime viewers.

Still, it *is* a wildlife refuge and offers a variety of interesting natural sights and experiences for the visitor from the surrounding Long Island area or one traveling the forty-five-minute (more or less, depending on traffic) journey from New York City. School and nature groups particularly take advantage of this and the emphasis here on environmental interpretation and education.

A self-guided trail passes a variety of habitat, including dense thickets of greenbrier, grape, and bittersweet where small birds abound. Warbler migrations spring and fall are good, and flocks of white-crowned sparrows and magnolia warblers can sometimes be seen here, along with blackpoll and yellow warblers, mockingbirds, catbirds, towhees, cardinals, doves, kingbirds, and, in appropriate seasons, goldfinches and white-throated sparrows. Quail and pheasant are fairly common. A brackish pond often has great blue herons, snowy egrets, and kingfishers; the bluffs, which offer a fine view of Huntington Bay opening into Long Island Sound, are a traditional site for colonies of bank swallows (but stay away from the edge; there have been mishaps here).

The trail goes by a raccoon den tree, and there is at least one fox den on the refuge—fox are sometimes seen by persons getting out on the walks at dawn or dusk. Also owls—great horned, screech, and a few saw-whets and long-eareds. Sea ducks are seen in good numbers offshore in fall and winter, and the woodland surroundings are stunning—towering oaks and sycamores, with a great variety of interesting and unusual specimen shrubs and trees installed by the Eberstadt family; and dune plants and flowering cacti on the rocky beach.

Fishing from the shore can be excellent, for striped bass, flounder, weakfish, blackfish. An awesome sight here as at the Morton subrefuge sometimes is a school of perhaps 200 or 250 bluefish in an attack and killing frenzy, racing up and down offshore, feeding voraciously on smaller fish and driving them up onto the beach where they die by the thousands.

IMPORTANT: A visit to Target Rock, as to all of its subrefuges except Morton, is by permission only. Target Rock restricts access to fifty persons at one time. Permits may be obtained daily from the office, and in advance for weekend and holiday trips. The other units are, for the most part, presently open only to organized nature groups or for scientific research projects (though some public access areas are contemplated for the future).

At all the refuge units, sturdy waterproof footgear may be a good idea for serious hiking. Weather is pleasant to tolerable most of the year, though it can be hot and muggy in summer and zero or below in winter. Motels are available over most of Long Island, but they are expensive, and there are few campgrounds—one of them is East Wildwood State Park, ten miles from the Wertheim unit.

To reach Target Rock from New York City, take the Queens Midtown Tunnel to the Long Island Expressway, exit 49 and Route 110 into Huntington, and left on Main Street and Route 25A to West Neck Road. The refuge is at the end of this road.

For permits and other information contact: Target Rock National
    Wildlife Refuge, Lloyd Neck, Huntington, Long Island, New
    York 11743. Phone: (516) 271-2409.

The other units include *Morton* Refuge. Chickadees alighting on shoulders, head or hand may greet the visitor to this small but lovely 187-acre refuge on eastern Long Island, which also has deer, possum, raccoon, courting woodcock in the spring, nesting orchard orioles and redstarts, and a spectacular view along its bluffs and white sand beach (artists commonly come to paint and sketch). The former estate was the site of the introduction of Bartlett pears, apples, mulberry trees (for silkworm culture), shorthorn cattle and merino sheep to the area. Now it has nesting ospreys (with varying success), and, common seasonally, horned grebes, double-crested cormorants, green and black-crowned night herons, quail, ruddy turnstones, red-breasted mergansers, nesting gulls and terns, and a variety of other passerines, waterfowl, and shorebirds (sea ducks offshore in winter). There is a self-guided trail and good surf fishing (similar to Target Rock). The chickadees formed their friendly habits at the encouragement of a former resident and have continued to make friends ever since. It is located on Noyack Road off Route 27 between Little Peconic Bay and Noyack Bay, and is open nine to five all year.

Wertheim Refuge offers a fine natural waterfowl habitat, with 1,937 acres of brackish marsh, salt marsh, fresh meadows, and uplands, near Brookhaven. It has had successfully nesting ospreys, a widely viewed eight-point albino white-tailed buck, and many miles of roads and trails. Public access is considered for the future but no development yet.

Amagansett Refuge consists of a 36-acre tract of beach and dunes four miles east of East Hampton. It is the habitat for Ipswich sparrows (though they are not abundant) and has good fall hawk flights.

Conscience Point Refuge is a sixty-acre tract of fields, meadows, woodlands, and brackish marsh near North Sea, Long Island, planned for environmental studies. It has good varied habitat.

Seatuck Refuge is a ten-acre area with good resting and nesting areas for waterfowl as well as song and shorebirds; it is still subject to the life estate of its donors.

Oyster Bay Refuge consists of marsh and open bay covering 3,117 acres near the town of Oyster Bay, mostly closed to the public and of limited future use being largely covered with water. Adjacent areas are used for boating, fishing, swimming, and general recreation.

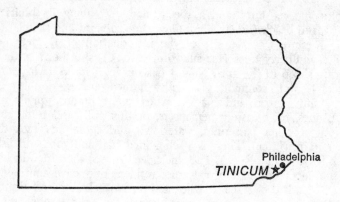

Philadelphia
TINICUM

TINICUM (Pennsylvania)

Wild rice grows and green herons nest in a refuge surrounded by highways, oil storage tanks, and dense housing development in this relatively new environmental center located within a mile of Philadelphia's International Airport.

It is almost a miracle that it became a refuge at all. Donated originally in the 1950s by the Gulf Oil Company to the City of Philadelphia and maintained as a public park, it was for a while the largest city-owned wildlife refuge in the United States (then 145 acres, expected eventually to be 1,250 acres). But urban financial problems and development changes threatened its continuation until citizens' groups came to its support and a transfer finally was arranged to the Fish and Wildlife Service. Its designation as a national wildlife environmental center reflects its function in educational work with schools and nature groups.

But it is managed as a wildlife refuge, and there is much to see here—especially in bird life.

Short-eared owls hunt in open areas in the late afternoon, especially in fall and winter—and several pairs stay to nest at the airport, in grassy places between the runways.

Common during all seasons are screech owls, pheasant, marsh hawks, downy woodpeckers, mallard and black ducks, Canada geese, pied-billed grebes, great blue herons, Carolina wrens, and mockingbirds, and most of the time except winter, snowy and great egrets, American and least bitterns, gallinules, black-crowned night herons, flickers, kingbirds, tree swallows, alder flycatchers, northern orioles, and indigo buntings.

Warbler migrations bring out birders around the area for northern parulas, Blackburnians, Cape Mays, bay-breasteds, and two dozen others that can be expected to be seen here, as well as solitary, warbling, red-eyed, and white-eyed vireos.

Visitors can view these birds commonly at times other than summer: white-crowned, vesper, swamp, and fox sparrows, pine siskins, purple finches, hermit and gray-cheeked thrushes, long-billed marsh wrens and nuthatches, both white-breasted and red-breasted.

Shorebird and hawk migrations are notable with good numbers of red-shouldered, redtails, and broadwings, concentrations sometimes in winter of five thousand pintail and six thousand ruddy ducks in the tidal marsh and Delaware River. And there is a small mammal population of deer, raccoon, opossum, and skunk.

A trail winds around the wetland, which is the last remnant of a once extensive fresh-water tidal marsh. There is an observation platform where taking good photographs are possible with a telephoto lens.

Citizens still take an intense interest in this refuge. The Philadelphia Conservationists are responsible for its visitors' center; the city garden club has planted hundreds of dogwoods and bayberry bushes; Youth Conservation Corps enrollees have put up bluebird boxes; the Concerned Area Residents for the Preservation of the Tinicum Marsh continues its support for the Center and recently sponsored legislation that added an additional seventy-eight acres of critical habitat to the original bill. Their contributions vividly underscore the role of this refuge as a sanctuary for humans and wildlife alike.

How to get there: From Philadelphia International Airport go northwest on Island Avenue, left on Lindbergh Boulevard, and continue on to the refuge entrance on 86th Street.

Open: Daylight hours all year.

Best times to visit: Spring and fall.

What to see: Excellent variety of birds; wild rice.

What to do: Hiking and cycling on trails; canoeing and fishing for bass and pickerel on Darby Creek; observation platform (also for photography).

Where to stay: MOTELS—Many near Philadelphia International Airport. CAMPGROUNDS—None nearby.

Weather notes: Winters can be windy and cold.

What to take and wear: Waterproof hiking boots needed in some places.

Points of interest nearby: Philadelphia historical sites (Independence Hall and Valley Forge National Historical Parks).

For more information: Tinicum National Environmental Center, Suite 104, Scott Plaza 2, Philadelphia, Pennsylvania 19113. Phone: (215) 521-0662 or 365-3118.

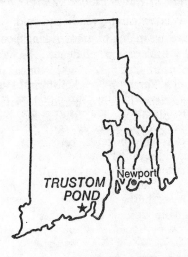

TRUSTOM POND (Rhode Island)

The most stunning sight for most visitors to this small refuge in our smallest state is probably the flock of introduced mute swans which sometimes numbers up to two hundred birds nesting and living year round at Trustom Pond.

Particularly appealing (though not always easily seen) are the downy young cygnets riding on the backs of their handsome parents in mid-June.

But the swans are far from the most significant natural attraction at this 365-acre sanctuary which, with an adjoining Audubon Society tract, encloses the only protected coastal pond of any size in Rhode Island.

Waterfowl in large numbers congregate during spring and fall migrations, and stay sometimes well into November. The upland area supports a healthy population of small mammals as well which in turn attracts interesting predators; and sea and shorebirds in impressive variety are counted on the small barrier beach.

Two nature trails wind several miles through basically upland scrub habitat, alfalfa hayfields crisscrossed with old stone walls and lined with wild cherry and apple trees, through clumps of blueberry, Tatarian honeysuckle, shadbushes, and oak and pine stands, both trails ending at the 160-acre brackish pond.

Most of the waterfowl on the Rhode Island checklist appear here at some time—brant, Canada, and snow geese, rarely in blue form; and among the ducks, mallard, black, gadwall, pintail, teal, wigeon, ring-necked, canvasback, scaup, goldeneye, bufflehead, eider, scoter, merganser.

Marsh and red-tailed hawks and kestrels are permanent residents, as are grouse, bobwhite, and ring-necked pheasant.

Cormorants, herons, egrets, and ospreys are common in the summer, and travelers can frequently spot yellow- and black-billed cuckoos, and occasionally bitterns, turnstones, killdeer, sanderlings, terns, and other sandpipers. Tree and barn swallows nest, as do yellow and prairie warblers (in the parking lot!).

Mid-April brings a showy blooming of the wild cherry and apple trees, shad and berry bushes, and lady's slippers growing alongside the trails; and equally glorious in a different way is their fruiting in the fall, when the winy fragrance of wild grapes fills the air on a crisp clear day.

But winter is the favorite season of many. Horned larks are common, and occasionally crossbills and grosbeaks. Coastal storms sometimes blow in such infrequently seen sea-birds as murres, dovekies, guillemots, and shearwaters. Fewer visitors come, but those who do —skiing or snowshoeing along the trails—can more easily spot the refuge's mammal residents—even, on a rare day, the heart-stopping sight of a red fox against the snow.

Trustom Pond and the adjacent 115 acres owned by the Rhode Island Audubon Society are jointly managed, with two naturalists available to assist and lead nature groups during summer months.

This and other refuges administered from Ninigret, Rhode Island, headquarters include the following:

Nantucket comprises forty acres of coastal beachland on Great Point, the northernmost tip of Nantucket Island, Massachusetts, about twenty-five miles south of Cape Cod and reachable by ferry from Hyannis or Woods Hole (the refuge is some distance from the ferry landing; and auto spaces must be reserved well ahead during crowded months). It shelters a wide variety of waterfowl and offers nest sites for terns; also surf fishing, excellent for blues.

Block Island, Rhode Island, is made up of twenty-nine acres on the island's northern tip, providing nesting grounds for gulls, terns, spotted sandpipers, and piping plovers, and spectacular sightings of spring and fall migrants.

Ninigret, Rhode Island, is a small section of barrier beach located off East Beach Road south of U.S. 1 near Charlestown. Foot travel only. Fishing off the beach.

Sachuest Point, Rhode Island, is a 228-acre peninsula near Middletown, part of which used to be a town dump, which shows what reclamation can do. Now it's a thickly fruited refuge for a large variety of birds—swallows, shorebirds, herons, hawks, and upland types such as pheasant and quail which flush along the 3-mile trail.

Salt Meadow, Connecticut, a 187-acre tract, recently a private gift, affords all kinds of habitat from tidal salt marsh to woodlands, and miles of trails, plus a beautiful old stone house dating to 1640, and a cabin built for and used by Mrs. Eleanor Roosevelt from trees felled in a hurricane. Admission is by permit from Ninigret headquarters.

How to get there: From Providence take U.S. Route 1, south to exit sign that says Moonstone Beach Road. Go south about ¼ mile to Schoolhouse Road, turn right and proceed to refuge.

Open: Daylight to dark.

Best times to visit: Fall and spring.

What to see: Large flock of nesting mute swans. Great variety of waterfowl and shorebirds.

What to do: Interpretive walks daily in July and August; schedule available from Ninigret headquarters. Walking trails. Surf fishing on beach; also sunbathing and swimming (however, a strong undertow should discourage all but strong swimmers). A beach parking fee is required by lessee of nearby beach mid-June to September.

Where to stay: MOTELS—5 miles north of refuge in Wakefield, or 7 miles south in Westerly. CAMPGROUNDS—Just off Route 1 in Burlingame State Park in Charlestown, 5 miles from refuge.

Weather notes: Normal for northeastern United States—no extremes.

What to take and wear: Comfortable casual clothing.

Points of interest nearby: Great Swamp State Refuge, 10 miles north of Trustom, has the only concentration of breeding ospreys in Rhode Island—4 active nests in recent years—and much other wildlife. Norman Bird Sanctuary, just north of Sachuest Point, is operated by the Audubon Society of Rhode Island, which has a number of other refuges, a list of which is available by writing to the Society offices, 40 Bowen Street, Providence, Rhode Island 02903.

For more information: Ninigret National Wildlife Refuge, Box 307, Charlestown, Rhode Island, 02813. Phone: (401) 364-3106.

III. THE SOUTHEAST

The refuges of the southeastern states harbor an extraordinary variety and number of birds, mammals, reptiles, and plants. *Mattamuskeet*, a large lake of mysterious origin in far eastern North Carolina, is wintering ground for twenty thousand whistling swans, an estimated one fifth of the North American population. This magnificent white bird with a seven-foot wingspread nests in Alaska and the northwest Canadian arctic, then migrates four thousand miles or so to Mattamuskeet where it may be seen in winter in numbers that whiten the lake. Nearby *Pungo* surrounds a similar though smaller lake, and commonly has up to twenty thousand Canada geese concentrated there in winter. *Pea Island*, on the Outer Banks of North Carolina, is southern terminus for the wintering snow goose, another long-distance migrant whose Latin name "hyperborea" means "beyond the north wind." Up to thirty thousand of these handsome birds, which breed in the arctic, winter here. This refuge, made up of beach, dunes, and bay, also has fifty or so sightings of peregrine falcons each year, harbors the rare Ipswich sparrow in winter, and, because of its seaward location, is one of the best east coast birding spots for pelagic species blown shoreward in winter storms. *Pee Dee*, an inland North Carolina refuge until recently still in development, has limited public access.

SOUTH CAROLINA

Carolina Sandhills, one of three South Carolina refuges, is home for over a hundred colonies of the endangered red-cockaded woodpecker, including some easily photographed, and also for the rare Pine Barrens tree frog. *Cape Romain* is a coastal refuge which includes Bull's Island, a barrier island of surpassing natural beauty which can be reached by day ferry. Its miles of deserted Atlantic beaches, interior trails, and fresh-water lakes are among the most beautiful natural areas in the East. On even less traveled smaller islands in the refuge most of the Atlantic population of American oystercatchers spend the winter.

GEORGIA

Piedmont, in central Georgia, is an upland refuge that has become world-renowned for techniques developed in reclaiming a depleted area and managing resources for both timber and wildlife. An outstanding example of this is management of mature pines for endangered red-cockaded woodpeckers, which are common here year-round. *Savannah* is a complex of refuges along the coast of Georgia and South Carolina. The home refuge has up to twenty thousand wood ducks visible at one time, and is a rich area for reptiles. The complex includes famed *Wassaw* and *Blackbeard* sea islands (accessible by boat) and *Harris Neck,* a peninsular refuge about forty-three miles south of Savannah. *Okefenokee* is one of the great primitive areas of the world—12,000 to 15,000 alligators live here as well as a tremendous range of natural inhabitants including 42 species of mammals, 233 of migrating and resident birds, 58 of reptiles, 32 of amphibians, 34 of fishes, and countless botanical species. Despite its wilderness aspect, parts of this refuge is easily accessible to visitors driving or on foot; the interior may be penetrated by boat.

FLORIDA

St. Vincent is an uninhabited tropical island lying off the Florida panhandle in the Gulf of Mexico. It is accessible only by small boat available from nearby ports, and for those willing to make the effort it offers 12,500 acres of beaches, high dunes, fresh-water ponds, and tidal marsh together with wooded interiors filled with magnolias and live oaks. Its location makes it a prime spring landfall for northbound migrants crossing the gulf. *St. Marks,* lying to the east along the panhandle, is an extremely diverse refuge. From open bay through shoreline, tidal flats, and creeks to fresh-water ponds and marshes, hardwood swamp, and upland pine woods, its varied habitat accommodates a wide variety of creatures, some in great seasonal numbers. *Lake Woodruff* in north-central Florida is a beautiful natural area appearing untouched by human activity. It is one of the few areas in the state where the rare Florida panther and black bear may be found. More commonly it is home to ospreys, eagles, and alligators. Manatees are here in summer months.

Chassahowitzka along Florida's central west coast is the site of fresh-water springs flowing millions of gallons of seventy-degree water every day of the year. This fresh water creates short but beautiful rivers that flow into marshy deltas and thence into the gulf. The refuge is noted for its wintering ducks—wigeon, black, mallard, and pintail, and for its large populations of graceful, long-legged waders. *Merritt Island*, across the state on the Atlantic Coast, is an overlay on the U. S. Space Center, and harbors more endangered species than any other refuge. Bald eagles are readily seen and up to 15 sightings of rare peregrine falcons in a single day have been reported. Brown pelicans nest here in good numbers (and the refuge administers *Pelican Island*, the nation's first refuge, established by President Theodore Roosevelt in 1903, as well as *St. Johns*, which is habitat for the endangered dusky seaside sparrow).

South Florida contains three of the nation's outstanding refuges. *Loxahatchee* includes one of the few pristine sections of Everglades remaining and is home to the rare Everglade kite as well as the limpkin. Bobcat and otter are common here; less common but present are the Florida panther and black bear. *J. N. "Ding" Darling*, on world-famous Sanibel Island off Fort Myers, has large concentrations of the showy and elegant roseate spoonbills, ospreys, wading birds, migrant and wintering shorebirds. Otter are readily seen in the refuge canals, as are alligators. The star of *Florida Keys* is the miniature Key deer—a fully antlered buck stands but twenty-eight inches at the shoulders. These creatures, nearly extinct less than a generation ago, have been restored to a stable population of 350–400 individuals. Their survival was due in part to their ability to swim from key to key and to subsist on the wild vegetation growing here. These refuges are also home to the American crocodile, the narrow-nosed relative of the alligator; other specialties include white-crowned pigeons, mangrove cuckoos, and nesting roseate spoonbills.

The following is a list of some birds of special interest found in common or abundant status at the refuges of this region.

Birds Common or Abundant at Seasons Indicated:

S: Spring   s: Summer   F: Fall   W: Winter

Brown Pelican: Cape Romain, SsF; Chassahowitzka, SsFW; Ding Darling, SsFW; Florida Keys, SsFW; Merritt Island, SsFW.
White Pelican: Chassahowitzka, SFW; Ding Darling, SFW; Loxahatchee, W; Merritt Island, SFW.
Wilson's Storm Petrel: Pea Island, sF.

Gannet: Cape Romain, W; Pea Island, SF.

Anhinga: Chassahowitzka, SsFW; Ding Darling, SsFW;
 Lake Woodruff, SsFW; Loxahatchee, SsFW;
 Merritt Island, SsFW; Okefenokee, SsFW; St. Marks, SsFW;
 Santee, s; Savannah, SsFW.

Magnificent Frigatebird: Chassahowitzka, SsF; Ding Darling, SsF;
 Florida Keys, SsFW.

Wood Stork: Chassahowitzka, SsFW; Ding Darling, sFW;
 Loxahatchee, SF; Merritt Island, SsFW; Okefenokee, sF;
 St. Marks, sF.

Glossy Ibis: Cape Romain, Ss; Loxahatchee, SsFW;
 Merritt Island, SsFW; Okefenokee, SsFW; St. Marks, SsFW;
 Savannah, SsF.

White Ibis: Cape Romain, SsF; Chassahowitzka, SsFW;
 Ding Darling, SsFW; Loxahatchee, SsFW;
 Merritt Island, SsFW; Okefenokee, SsFW; St. Marks, SsFW,
 Santee, SsF; Savannah, SsF.

Roseate Spoonbill: Ding Darling, SsF; Florida Keys, FW;
 Loxahatchee, W; Merritt Island, SF.

Whistling Swan: Mattamuskeet, FW; Pea Island, SFW; Pungo, FW.

Fulvous Whistling Duck: Loxahatchee, SsFW.

Mottled Duck: Ding Darling, SsFW; Loxahatchee, SsFW;
 Merritt Island, SsFW.

Surf Scoter: Cape Romain, FW; Pea Island, SW.

Black Scoter: Cape Romain, FW; Pea Island, SW.

Everglade Kite: Loxahatchee, FW.

Cooper's Hawk: Chassahowitzka, SsFW; Merritt Island, FW;
 Pungo, FW; Savannah, SFW.

Bald Eagle: Chassahowitzka, FW; Ding Darling, SsFW;
 Merritt Island, SsFW.

Osprey: Cape Romain, SsF; Chassahowitzka, SsFW;
 Ding Darling, SsFW; Florida Keys, SsFW;
 Lake Woodruff, SsFW; Mattamuskeet, Ss;
 Merritt Island, SsFW; Okefenokee, Ss; St. Marks, Ss;
 St. Vincent, Ss; Santee, SsF; Savannah, SsF.

Turkey: Chassahowitzka, SsFW; Piedmont, SsFW;
 St. Vincent, SsFW.

Sandhill Crane: Loxahatchee, SFW; Okefenokee, SsFW.

Limpkin: Chassahowitzka, SsFW; Loxahatchee, SsFW.

Purple Gallinule: Loxahatchee, SsFW; St. Marks, SsF; Santee, S;
 Savannah, SsF.

American Oystercatcher: Cape Romain, SsFW; St. Vincent, SsFW.

Wilson's Plover: Cape Romain, Ss; Chassahowitzka, SsFW;

Ding Darling, SsFW; Florida Keys, SsFW; St. Marks, S;
St. Vincent, SsFW.

Piping Plover: Ding Darling, SsFW; Florida Keys, SFW.

Whimbrel: Cape Romain, Ss.

White-rumped Sandpiper: Ding Darling, S; Pea Island, F.

Marbled Godwit: Cape Romain, S; Pea Island, F.

Gull-billed Tern: Cape Romain, Ss; Ding Darling, S;
Merritt Island, S; Pea Island, Ss.

Sandwich Tern: Cape Romain, Ss; Chassahowitzka, S;
Ding Darling, SsFW; St. Vincent, SsF.

Caspian Tern: Chassahowitzka, SFW; Florida Keys, FW;
Merritt Island, FW; Pea Island, F.

Black Skimmer: Cape Romain, Ss; Chassahowitzka, FW;
Ding Darling, SsFW; Florida Keys, SsFW; Loxahatchee SsFW;
Pea Island, SsF; St. Vincent, SsFW.

White-crowned Pigeon: Florida Keys, SsF.

Ground Dove: Cape Romain, sFW; Chassahowitzka, SsFW;
Ding Darling, SsFW; Florida Keys, SsFW; Loxahatchee, SsFW;
Merritt Island, SsFW; Okefenokee, SsFW; St. Vincent, SsFW;
Savannah, SsFW.

Mangrove Cuckoo: Ding Darling, Ss; Florida Keys, Ss.

Smooth-billed Ani: Ding Darling, SsFW; Loxahatchee, SsFW.

Red-cockaded Woodpecker: Piedmont, SsFW.

Gray Kingbird: Chassahowitzka, SsF; Ding Darling, SsF;
Florida Keys, SsF; St. Marks, Ss.

Scrub Jay: Merritt Island, SsFW.

Brown-headed Nuthatch: Cape Romain, S;
Carolina Sandhills, SsFW; Chassahowitzka, SsFW;
Mattamuskeet, SsFW; Okefenokee, SsFW; Pee Dee, SsFW;
Piedmont, SsFW; Pungo, SsFW; St. Vincent, SsFW.

Eastern Bluebird: Carolina Sandhills, SsFW;
Chassahowitzka, SsFW; Okefenokee, SsFW; Pee Dee, S;
Piedmont, SsFW.

Black-whiskered Vireo: Ding Darling, SsF; Florida Keys, SsF;
Merritt Island, s.

Painted Bunting: Cape Romain, Ss; Ding Darling, SFW;
Florida Keys, SFW; Loxahatchee, SFW; Merritt Island, W;
Savannah, SsF.

Bachman's Sparrow: Carolina Sandhills, SsF; Okefenokee, SsFW;
Savannah, SF.

SOUTHEAST

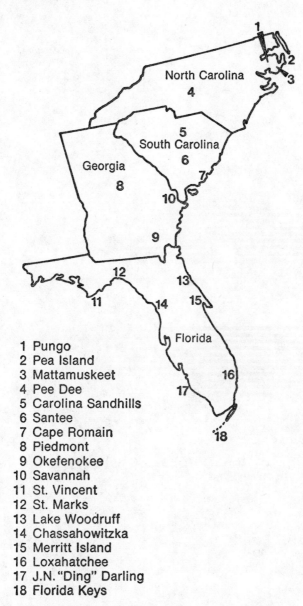

1 Pungo
2 Pea Island
3 Mattamuskeet
4 Pee Dee
5 Carolina Sandhills
6 Santee
7 Cape Romain
8 Piedmont
9 Okefenokee
10 Savannah
11 St. Vincent
12 St. Marks
13 Lake Woodruff
14 Chassahowitzka
15 Merritt Island
16 Loxahatchee
17 J.N. "Ding" Darling
18 Florida Keys

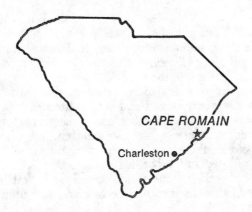

CAPE ROMAIN (South Carolina)

Cape Romain Refuge is 34,229 acres of widely varying habitat from open water sanctuary, sandy beaches and salt marsh to upland that encompasses dense forests of spreading live oaks, magnolias, pines, and palmettos, as well as fresh-water ponds and marshes. It includes barrier islands that probably were the first land spotted by settlers coming to the South Carolina coast. Now it is one of the outstanding wildlife refuges in the East, a mecca for nature watchers of many interests.

Most of the Atlantic Coast population of showy black-and-white oystercatchers winter here and feast on abundant supplies of their favorite food in these unpolluted waters, waiting until the wary crustaceans open their shells and then ripping in with crimson bills shaped like no other bird's to cut and paralyze the oyster's interior muscle.

Brown pelicans, endangered through much of their former range, nest commonly as do at least nine species of graceful wading birds, including glossy and white ibises, snowy and great egrets, great blue, yellow-crowned, and black-crowned night herons. Rare wood storks come in July in flocks of five hundred or more. Waterfowl of all kinds winter in large numbers—nineteen species, including abundant surf and black scoters, colorful wood ducks which also nest, and horned and pied-billed grebes.

Clapper rails are abundant all year, and whimbrels, dowitchers, and marbled godwits are common.

Ospreys nest, and terns—least, royal, and sandwich—raise families in colonies of thousands (which are patrolled and protected) on some of the more remote refuge strands. Black skimmers ply the waters, red and black bills agape to skim up small organisms, or rest on beaches, all facing into the wind.

Small birds are common to abundant in the woods and brushy areas—seasonally ruby-crowned and golden-crowned kinglets, hermit thrushes, brown-headed nuthatches, and cedar waxwings; nesting indigo and painted buntings, summer tanagers, ruby-throated hummingbirds, and northern parula warblers. Common all year are yellowthroats, pileated and red-bellied woodpeckers (and a few of the endangered red-cockaded ones), and screech and great horned owls. Small bird migrations, sometimes spectacular, occur from mid-March to early May.

Alligators up to 14 feet long bask on the banks on all but cooler days, grunting and bellowing and thinking about nesting in May; and otter, giving them a wide berth, swim and hunt wherever there is water. White-tailed deer are everywhere.

A rarer sight but always a possibility are the loggerhead sea turtles which crawl up and lay eggs on refuge beaches in greater numbers here than anyplace else on the Atlantic Coast—so much so that about thirty thousand eggs have been transplanted in recent years to other quiet Atlantic beaches in the hope of restoring these great sea creatures, whose shells sometimes measure four feet across, to their former range, once as far north as New Jersey. Visitors are not likely to see the adults which come up at night (though sometimes their heads can be spotted in the bay)—but occasionally a batch of young ones will explode from the sand and scamper to the water in the early morning.

The handsome red wolf is an even rarer sight. An experimental pair were brought to Bull's Island from Louisiana, where only a few still remain in the wild, in the hope they might survive here as a pure strain. The possibility is remote but tantalizing.

Access to the refuge varies; the best way is to go first to refuge headquarters at Moore's Landing, the only area of the refuge that can be reached except by boat. From there a boat leaves once a day taking visitors out and bringing them back from Bull's Island, a beautiful wild place that supports much of this varied wildlife.

Access to other refuge areas varies with the place and season; all are possible only by boat, and it is best to consult with the refuge before planning a trip. The waters can be treacherous.

How to get there: From Georgetown take Route 17 south about 40 miles to SeeWee Road and refuge sign; follow signs 5 miles to refuge headquarters located at Moore's Landing.

Open: Daylight hours all year.

Best times to visit: Spring and fall; winter too.

What to see: Great variety of birds of every kind; alligators; black fox squirrel; otter; possibility (very remote) of red wolves, loggerhead sea turtles. Old fort used as lookout for pirate ships.

What to do: More than 10 miles of trails; photography (photo blind available); limited archery deer hunting; fishing (devotees say the best anywhere for salt-water species like spot-tailed bass in surf, also largemouth bass in fresh-water lakes); also oystering and clamming.

Where to stay: MOTELS—In Mount Pleasant, 18 miles south; Charleston, 20 miles south. CAMPGROUNDS—Private, north of refuge 5 miles on Doar Road; and public in Francis Marion National Forest, 10 miles north on Highway 17.

Weather notes: Summers can be exceedingly hot and humid; sudden showers occur anytime but quickly pass.

What to take and wear: Raingear for sudden showers; insect repellent; lunch and comfortable shoes to Bull's Island.

Points of interest nearby: Francis Marion National Forest (see CAMPGROUNDS)—nature trails, one of the largest concentrations anywhere of endangered red-cockaded woodpeckers (information available in McClellanville). Historic Charleston, South Carolina; Fort Sumter National Monument.

For more information: Cape Romain National Wildlife Refuge, Route 1, Box 191, Awendaw, South Carolina 29429. Phone: (803) 928-3368.

CAROLINA SANDHILLS ★

Columbia

CAROLINA SANDHILLS (South Carolina)

The endangered red-cockaded woodpecker is a common resident here—probably more here than at any other national wildlife refuge. At least a hundred colonies of this small black and white bird with very particular breeding habits—so much so that they imperil his existence—are found in old longleaf pine woods in this 45,591-acre tract of rolling sandhills, remnants of dunes from an age when the Atlantic Ocean covered this area 55 million years ago.

Abuse of its resources by early settlers left it a wasteland forty years ago. It was established as a refuge in 1939, and its reclamation has been remarkable, supporting now a rich and varied flora and fauna that include a number of rare and endangered species, notably the eastern cougar (sometimes called a puma, panther, or mountain lion).

In addition, there are healthy populations of the Pine Barrens tree frog, sometimes called our most beautiful tree frog with its bright green plum-striped body, found only in small pockets here and in North Carolina, Georgia, and New Jersey. Sharing its wet hillside "seeps" are clumps of rare hooded pitcher plants, whose discarded trumpets with skeletal remains of small insects illustrate their carnivorous ways.

The tiny pyxie moss, a variety which is endangered, is also comfortably situated here, along with the eastern fox squirrel, whose status is undetermined—a large handsome squirrel, more than twice the size of the common gray variety, often coal black but sometimes with white ears and tail tip.

Visitors can easily view the red-cockaded woodpecker in the stands of fifty-year-old pines which it requires as a nest site—the nest holes always marked by outpourings of sap from small holes kept open by the birds (the function of this is unknown, although it does repel some predators, especially snakes). Each nest is tended not only by the parents but by two or more "nurse" birds, so that each nest is an active colony averaging six birds. Some of these are located immediately alongside the hundred miles of refuge roads and trails, where they make good photographic subjects (one group of nest trees located right behind refuge headquarters, in some years has featured not only the red-cockaded but also red-headed woodpeckers and flying squirrels).

Visitors also can observe beaver whose workings are conspicuous at most of the thirty man-made lakes and impoundments; white-tailed deer, especially when they browse, a dozen or so together, along the roads in late winter and spring; and less so, fox, bobcat, raccoon, opossum.

Mourning doves are extremely abundant—an estimated forty thousand, one of the highest recorded densities, and a research biologist has been studying their habits using telemetry for one part of the study.

Wintering here are some two thousand Canada geese and up to fifteen thousand ducks—mainly mallard, wigeon, black and wood ducks—plus good numbers of sharp-shinned hawks, hermit thrushes, and ruby-crowned kinglets. Common all year are bluebirds, meadowlarks, phoebes, Carolina wrens, quail, loggerhead shrikes, killdeer, and screech and great horned owls; and seasonally, summer tanagers, orchard orioles, yellow-breasted chats, white-eyed vireos, nighthawks, ruby-throated hummingbirds and northern parula, yellow-throated, hooded, pine, and prairie warblers.

Birdfoot violets, sundews, golden clubs, dwarf irises, passion flowers, beauty berries, trumpet creepers, and trailing arbutus are among the many flowering plants; and good lists are available of all the interesting natural flora and fauna.

How to get there: From Florence, take Route 52 northwest to Darlington; Route 151 west to McBee; then Route 1 north 4.5 miles to refuge headquarters.

Open: Daylight hours all year.

Best times to visit: December through early summer.

What to see: Endangered red-cockaded woodpeckers; rare Pine Barrens tree frogs and carnivorous pitcher plants; deer; waterfowl; beaver; extremely small chance of cougar.

What to do: Auto and walking tours; photography (blind available); observation tower; limited deer hunt; fishing, especially on Martin's Lake, for bass, bluegill, catfish (luck varies but the state's third largest bass was caught here).

Where to stay: MOTELS—At Hartsville, 14 miles southeast. CAMPGROUNDS—At Cheraw State Park, 25 miles north.

Weather notes: Fairly pleasant all year (lowest in winter usually 20).

What to take and wear: Boots will protect against sharp sandspurs.

Points of interest nearby: Cheraw State Park (see CAMPGROUNDS); Sandhill State Forest (with Sugar Loaf Mountain, unusual sandstone outcropping).

For more information: Carolina Sandhills National Wildlife Refuge, Route 2, Box 130, McBee, South Carolina 29101. Phone: (803) 335-8401.

CHASSAHOWITZKA (Florida)

Most of Chassahowitzka Refuge can be seen only by boat, and it is an unforgettable experience—estuarine salt marsh as far as the eye can see, interspersed with tidal streams and bars where graceful wading birds fish when low tide bares the mudflats.

At the river inlets are springs that churn up millions of gallons of water a day (or sometimes in just an hour)—crystal clear, as is the water everywhere, becoming bluish-green in the depths. For reasons not understood, the springs attract thousands of fish of dozens of species from both fresh and salt water—not feeding but seeming just to enjoy themselves, as if visiting a spa.

Flocks of white ibises are common, and there are thousands of coot, sometimes packed so densely together they seem like fair-sized islands rather than animate creatures; they scurry off a short distance over the water with their peculiar running gait at human approach, then settle into huge rafts a short distance away.

"Sometimes there are so many green sea turtles out there," said one local boatman, "it's hard to think they're an endangered species." They are mainly in the river mouths of the Homosassa or Chassahowitzka, both of which flow through the refuge to the sea. Visitors can watch them feeding in the channels to a considerable depth, almost as clearly in the crystalline water as in the air and basking on the surface, heads out, backs awash. Loggerhead turtles are common, too; in fact, the only easy way to distinguish them is by size, the loggerheads being larger, up to four feet across.

Endangered manatees or sea cows frequent the rivers in winter, leaving when the open waters warm up. Otter are common. The refuge has about 750 alligators as well. Bald eagles usually have several active nests each winter and fish commonly over the marsh channels —or sometimes follow one of the more numerous and only slightly smaller ospreys which may have already caught something they can steal (ospreys have as many as forty active nests on the refuge each year).

This 30,000-acre central-west-coast Florida refuge was established for wintering waterfowl, and up to twenty thousand of them are sometimes here—wigeon, black ducks, mallard, pintail—along with such other water-inclined inhabitants as loons, pied-billed grebes, gallinules, clapper and Virginia rails, least and royal terns, and both brown and white pelicans. Magnificent frigatebirds sail overhead, and anhingas pose with wings out to dry after a fishing trip.

And everywhere are the lovely long-legged waders—great blue and little blue herons, snowy and great egrets, black-crowned and yellow-crowned night herons, and ibises, which nest by the thousands on offshore refuge islands, along with orange-billed double-crested cormorants.

Fishermen in tidal river mouths have the treat of angling for both fresh- and salt-water fish at the same time—and sometimes, with the extreme visibility, of selecting which to go for ahead of time.

Land birds, including a number of passerines, thrive in the wooded upland fringe around refuge headquarters—prairie, pine, yellow-throated, and northern parula warblers, brown-headed nuthatches, and all the woodpeckers including pileated, red-headed, downy, and hairy (a few endangered red-cockaded nest just off the refuge).

Visitors should consult with refuge staff before planning a trip by boat, both to avoid hazards and to get around and see everything possible.

Cedar Keys, administered by Chassahowitzka, consists of four small subtropical barrier islands about four miles offshore supporting one of the largest nesting colonies of herons, egrets, brown pelicans, and other water birds in the South—sometimes two hundred thousand birds, including sixty thousand white ibises alone—along with perhaps the largest population of poisonous cottonmouth moccasins of any place its size in the world. A doctoral candidate doing a study on the cottonmouth tagged over seven hundred on the island. The two seem to exist in harmony: the snakes subsisting on fish leavings and eliminating rats as potential predators; the birds, which normally prey on small snakes, leaving them mostly alone.

Access to the islands is difficult and in any case restricted during nesting, usually from February through July. But the town of Cedar Keys is worth a visit, with its marine and nature museum—and most of the birds that nest on the keys are seen around the town in large numbers.

How to get there: From Tampa take Route 41 north to Route 98, left on 98 to Route 19, and north on 19 for 2 miles to refuge office.

Open: Refuge open year-round; office 7:30 A.M. to 4 P.M. weekdays.

Best times to visit: Wildlife here all year but weather pleasantest spring and fall.

What to see: Herons, egrets, pelicans, alligators, ospreys, sometimes manatees, otter, sea turtles; crystal-clear springs where thousands of fish congregate.

What to do: Photography (mostly scenics and wading birds); boating and canoeing (rentals nearby); limited waterfowl hunting; fishing, in salt and fresh water and combination of the two, for mackerel, speckled trout, bass, redfish, others. Refuge staff will conduct tours for organized nature and school groups if contacted two weeks in advance.

Where to stay: MOTELS—Homosassa Springs. CAMPGROUNDS—Homosassa Springs; also Withlacoochee State Forest, 4 miles east, and Ocala National Forest, 40 miles northeast.

Weather notes: Midwinter can be damp and chilly, midsummer hot and humid.

Points of interest nearby: Homosassa Springs, which produces 6,000,000 gallons of crystalline 74-degree water each hour to form the Homosassa River, where thousands of fish gather. Crystal River archeological site, 15 miles north. Cedar Keys, 40 miles north (see text). Ocala and Withlacoochee forests (see CAMPGROUNDS).

For more information: Chassahowitzka National Wildlife Refuge, Route 2, Box 44, Homosassa, Florida 32646. Phone: (904) 628-2201.

J. N. "DING" DARLING ★
Fort Myers

J. N. "DING" DARLING (Florida)

No serious naturalist visiting South Florida can afford to miss the 4,833-acre J. N. "Ding" Darling Refuge on Sanibel Island off the state's west coast for its matchless and wide variety of accessible natural life of both subtropical and temperate climatic zones.

Wading birds are particularly outstanding—herons, egrets, storks, and sometimes one third of the U.S. population of roseate spoonbills are here along the wildlife drive, which is bordered on one side by fresh and the other by salt water, periodically drained by tides and interspersed by grassy, brush, and mangrove habitat to accommodate almost every kind of bird possible to these zones. Also living here are alligators and other interesting reptiles; horseshoe crabs (that primordial species which has come down almost unchanged for 180 million years, mating sometimes by the thousands in a spectacular shoreline display); and mammals as well—otter sporting in the early morning along the canals, and, though extremely rare, an endangered Florida panther roaming along the dike.

The early visitor may see hundreds of snowy and great egrets in a feeding frenzy when a school of small chubs appears in the shallow waters. White ibises, great blue herons, yellow and black-crowned night herons are common as well. Shorebirds of various species are here in great numbers, passing through by the thousands sometimes in spring and fall and many staying to nest—black skimmers plying the waters with bills agape, snowy and Wilson's plovers, and many others.

Bald eagles soar overhead—they nest occasionally on the island and come over to fish from Pine Island, where a dozen or so nesting pairs are sometimes reported. Anhingas spread their moisture-absorbing wing plumage to dry. Ospreys are everywhere—nesting in the refuge as well as on power poles on the main road and nest structures erected by interested Sanibel citizens throughout the island.

In fact, the whole island which makes up the City of Sanibel is in effect a sanctuary and it would be difficult to visit here without seeing, for example, numbers of red-shouldered hawks, pileated and red-bellied woodpeckers and rare (though common here) brown pelicans; and birders who search can also find mangrove cuckoos and other more reticent species.

Warblers sometimes appear by the thousands in April migration, along with such others as indigo and painted buntings, blue grosbeaks, bobolinks, orioles, and others. A good place to see them is around the lighthouse and in the Bailey tract.

Rent a boat and explore the bay (though carefully as its waters are shallow and oyster and sandbars are common and hazardous)—ospreys nest by the dozens on channel markers; wintering white pelicans may be there by the hundreds, frigatebirds soaring overhead, an occasional swallow-tailed kite, and brown pelicans and wading birds on protected mangrove islands, along with a tremendous variety of water-oriented birds of all kinds, and porpoises, loggerhead turtles, and sometimes manatees in season.

Botanists will enjoy the varied and interesting vegetation which ranges from night-blooming cereus through gumbo limbo trees, strangler figs, mangroves, orchids, and air plants in profusion.

Sanibel is famous for its shell-strewn beaches, which are not as well supplied as before the island became so popular but still interesting (live shells should be returned to the water so the basic supply will not be diminished).

Loggerhead turtles nest and an active research program into this endangered species has its headquarters here. The gopher tortoise is commonly present in burrow homes up to forty feet long. Wild flowers are everywhere from March on through fall.

Excellent guides are available to point out the island's wildlife (best seen weekdays and non-holidays as crowds sometimes overwhelm the natural inhabitants in this increasingly and sometimes too popular island nature showplace).

Ding Darling also administers four mangrove island refuges, *Matlacha Pass, Pine Island, Pinellas,* and *Island Bay.* These support sizable populations of pelicans, herons, and egrets, and public access is prohibited when it may disturb nesting birds. Other subrefuges are *Passage Key* and *Egmont Key,* two islands in the Tampa Bay area to which public access by boat is permitted (Passage Key may be closed to public use during nesting); and *Caloosahatchee,* a river island, which has limited wildlife use and no public facilities.

How to get there: From Fort Myers take Route 41 south to Route 865, southwest to Route 867, west to Sanibel Causeway (toll); turn right on Periwinkle Way to Palm Ridge Road and refuge signs.

Open: Dawn to dusk.

Best times to visit: Things to see year-round.

What to see: Great variety of wading and shorebirds, passerines, alligators, otter, sometimes sea turtles, manatees, and uncommon gopher tortoises.

What to do: Eight miles of roads and trails for driving, hiking, photography (good from car windows); boating and canoeing (rentals nearby); fishing; shelling.

Where to stay: MOTELS—In Sanibel. CAMPGROUNDS—Sanibel and Fort Myers (reserve ahead); also Koreshah State Park, 17 miles south, and Collier Seminole State Park, 65 miles south (en route to Everglades).

Weather notes: Midwinter can be cool, rainy; midsummer hot, humid, hurricanes possible June–November.

Points of interest nearby: Sanibel-Captiva Conservation Foundation, nature center and trails; Corkscrew Audubon Sanctuary, nesting storks, 50 miles southeast; Everglades National Park, 90 miles south; Lee County Junior Museum and Nature Center and Thomas Edison's home and Gardens, Fort Myers; James Scenic Drive, outstanding birding, 90 miles south near Copeland.

For more information: J. N. "Ding" Darling National Wildlife Refuge, P.O. Drawer B, Sanibel, Florida 33957. Phone (813) 472-1100.

Key West ● FLORIDA KEYS

FLORIDA KEYS (Florida)

The diminutive Florida Key deer, miraculously surviving today, must be one of nature's most captivating creations. A fully antlered buck stands but twenty-eight inches high at the shoulders; a tiny spotted fawn less than a foot. The sight of one of these from April to August, teetering beside its mother, may incline the onlooker to shake his head in disbelief. As recently as 1950 the total number of these creatures was between twenty-five and fifty, brought close to extinction by habitat destruction and poachers who used fire, packs of hounds, hatchets, bludgeons, and guns to kill and drive them from the Florida keys that had been their homes since prehistoric times. Excellent swimmers, they have been found by boatmen a mile or more at sea plowing the emerald waters between islands, a capability that may have contributed to their bare survival, as does the surprising fact that many of the wild foods available to the deer on these keys are equivalent in energy content to commercial animal feeds.

None would live today except for the efforts of a handful of people who recognized the animals' plight in time and publicized it, arousing nationwide concern and leading to the establishment of a national wildlife refuge in 1954 to safeguard a sufficient area to ensure their survival. Now visitors to this south Florida refuge can be almost certain to see one of the most charming creatures of the animal world, numbering between 350 to 400 individuals in a stable and slowly growing population. They may be seen almost anywhere in the area but especially on Big Pine and No Name keys, where earth depressions over oolite limestone hold the fresh-water supplies they require.

Key deer are but one of a stunning array of natural phenomena in this rich area, including many rare and endangered species found nowhere else in the United States—such as the American crocodile, sharper-nosed kin to the alligator and found only here and in southwest Florida. Others include white-crowned pigeons, mangrove cuckoos, black-whiskered vireos, nesting roseate spoonbills, reddish egrets, and great white herons—now termed a color phase of the great blue and readily seen only here, distinguishable from the similar great egret by their large size and yellow, not black, legs.

Magnificent frigatebirds (also called man-o'-war birds) nest in the Marquesas Keys, where several hundreds circle at any time of the year, like great black cutouts against the deep blue sky, the males displaying their colorful breeding pouches, inflated like great scarlet balloons at their throats.

The dense and varied vegetation from both temperate and tropical zones includes species swept in by hurricane winds and tides over centuries, ranging through the various mangroves to the tall, sparse Caribbean pines. Tree trunks and branches support heavy beards of Spanish moss along with numerous epiphytes, ferns, drab and brightly colored orchids and crimson spikes of bromeliads. More than 450 species have been catalogued, many rare and endangered; a few, like the tree cactus, are unique in the world.

Key Deer Refuge (4,384 acres) and the two others it administers, *Great White Heron* Refuge (7,141 acres) and *Key West* Refuge (2,019 acres and one of the oldest in the system, established in 1908), all have their own boundaries, but for all practical purposes the visitor can regard them as one, extending sixty miles from Bahia Honda Key to the Marquesas, the farthest south of this chain of islands.

Great numbers of birds, especially the graceful long-legged waders, can be found almost anywhere—along U.S. 1, as well as the side roads from it. Egrets and shorebirds fish in the shallows and mudflats beside the bridges, where one can also sight an occasional raccoon, the local tribe often looking like bleached blondes, with honey-colored pelts and indistinct or no rings on their bushy tails. There are numerous osprey nests, some on crossarms of utility power poles. Boundaries for refuge and private lands are not too distinct, but for the most part well-behaved visitors can go anywhere. Visitors can obtain boats and there is no better way to see this stunningly beautiful refuge than out on the clear emerald waters, observing sea turtles and many varieties of fish to considerable depth, and watching pelicans, roseate spoonbills, and man-o'-war birds soar overhead.

How to get there: From Marathon take Route 1 south to Big Pine Key, right onto Route 940 (Key Deer Boulevard) to Watson Boulevard and left at sign to refuge headquarters. To go to visitors' contact nature trail continue on boulevard and turn off at refuge sign for Blue Hole and the trail.

Open: Headquarters weekdays only; refuge areas daylight hours all year.

Best times to visit: Fall, winter, spring.

What to see: Key deer; alligators; crocodiles; magnificent frigatebirds; great white herons; white-crowned pigeons; mangrove cuckoos; porpoises; sea turtles; other flora and fauna occurring rarely or nowhere else in the United States.

What to do: Walking trail and nearby Blue Hole, where alligators and perhaps crocodiles gather; nature observation by walking, driving, or boat (rentals, with guides if desired, available throughout area); photography (good from car or boat with telephoto for wildlife); wonderful fishing, from bridges, boats, in channels, flats, deep holes, for dolphin, mackerel, bonefish, many others. Snorkeling in shallow, clear water or over reefs from boat.

Where to stay: MOTELS—In Marathon, Key West, or through area. CAMPGROUNDS—Bahia Honda State Park; various others (marinas available for those coming by boat).

Weather notes: Summers seem burningly hot and humid to the uninitiated; otherwise beautiful through the year.

What to take and wear: Plenty of protective lotion and covering—the clear bright air and great reflection from water makes exposure to sun an extra hazard. Take nautical charts when boating and consult an experienced boatsman if going alone—it can be hazardous.

Points of interest nearby: Key West—Interesting historic place with tram tours. Bahia Honda State Park excellent for shorebird viewing.

For more information: Florida Keys National Wildlife Refuges, P.O. Box 510, Big Pine Key, Florida 33043. Phone: (305) 872-2239.

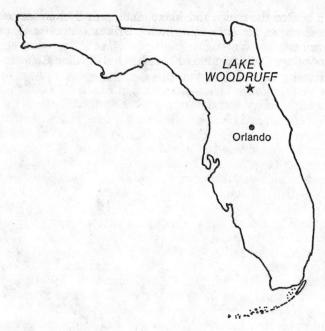

LAKE WOODRUFF (Florida)

Lake Woodruff is a beautiful natural area of over eighteen thousand acres of fresh-water marsh bordered by hardwood swamp and scattered pinelands, much of which appears untouched by human activity. Most of the birds and animals native to Florida can be found in the area at one time or another, including rare sightings of panther and black bear and, more commonly, ospreys, eagles, alligators, and a number of nesting warblers, especially the northern parula, pine, and yellowthroat.

Scrub jays are present, both on and just off the refuge. Red-shouldered hawks are common all year, screaming from the tops of longleaf pines and nesting. Armadillos, gentle armor-plated mammals from the Southwest, are common, lumbering along and foraging for insects in soft areas of low vegetation. The handsome little golden mouse builds its nests in trees, sometimes in thick "beards" of Spanish moss.

The refuge maintains several miles of trails and dike roads (mostly for walking only) through refuge lands, and along the railroad track which borders the refuge and where small birds flock in season. But the best way to see Lake Woodruff is by boat, either small power-boat or better, by canoe. One can put a canoe in the water at Alexander Springs Creek in the neighboring Ocala National Forest—also an extensive natural area with much to see—paddle down the St. Johns River, through Cross Creek and into Lake Woodruff (in the center of the refuge, but state-owned), taking three days.

Wild orchids and air plants grow on the trees which overhang the waterways like a canopy. The waters are so clear the vegetation and fish can be seen almost to the bottom. Manatees, rare over most of their former range but not uncommon here in summer, occasionally forage alongside such a canoeist. Herons and egrets fish along the banks, and alligators up to 14 feet or so climb out on mudflats, protected and seeming to know it.

In the lake, visitors can spot many of the osprey nests which are numerous over the refuge. There were 36 active families in a recent count of this large fish hawk, occasionally mistaken for a bald eagle (eagles also nest on the refuge). In winter, travelers can see some of the waterfowl which come here—blue-winged teal, ring-necked, sometimes a thousand or so of these, along with the wood ducks which are here all year and nest in boxes and natural cavities.

The refuge has begun a program to stock impoundments with apple snails, a great wildlife delicacy beloved by limpkins, which are here in small numbers, and sole food of the extremely rare Everglade kite. Perhaps in future years these will be seen here as well.

How to get there: From Deland take Route 17 north to De Leon Springs and refuge sign, then left one block to 40A and left on 40A to refuge headquarters. Trails and wildlife area are a mile west of headquarters.

Open: Daylight hours.

Best times to visit: November through April.

What to see: Ospreys, eagles, alligators, scrub jays, red-shouldered hawks, herons, sometimes otter and manatees.

What to do: Several trails, mostly walking; boating and canoeing (rentals available); limited deer hunt; fishing for bass, bream, catfish. Guided tours will be given for organized groups if contact is made in advance.

Where to stay: MOTELS—In Deland, 10 miles south. CAMPGROUNDS—At De Leon Springs, also Blue Spring State Park, 10 miles south, and Ocala National Forest, adjacent to refuge.

Weather notes: Midwinter can be cool, midsummers hot and humid.

Points of interest nearby: Blue Spring State Park (see CAMP-GROUNDS) often has wintering manatees; Ocala National Forest, walking and canoe trails and a fine natural area with occasional bear and panther sightings. De Leon Springs was discovered in 1513 by Ponce de Leon in his search for the fountain of youth.

For more information: Lake Woodruff National Wildlife Refuge, P.O. Box 488, De Leon Springs, Florida 32028. Phone: (904) 985-4673.

LOXAHATCHEE, FL (with star) and Fort Lauderdale marked on map

LOXAHATCHEE (Florida)

More than 140,000 acres of the vast legendary "River of Grass" that once covered the whole southern part of Florida as the Everglades, supporting immense populations of wildlife and plants found nowhere else, is in Loxahatchee Refuge. Loxahatchee is the northernmost remnant of that great natural area and encompasses some of the most pristine remaining parts.

Everglade kites, dark endangered birds of prey, fourteen inches long but with wingspreads up to forty-four inches that enable them to fly effortlessly over the marsh and settle so lightly that a blade of cattail will support them, are here in greater numbers than any other refuge. So are limpkins, handsome "crying birds" of the marsh (though with their mottled feathers, not easily seen), sharing the lush population of apple snails here that attracts and feeds them both.

Plant life is fascinating, with numerous native orchids and ferns, many of them visible along the boardwalk in the cypress swamp near headquarters. A single cypress may support several hundred pink-blossoming bromeliads and air plants along with "baton rouge," a strawberry-colored lichen on its trunk.

A walk along the marsh trail, especially at early morning or dusk, will turn up dozens of species of water birds—anhingas, ibises, gallinules, sometimes storks, bitterns, rails, herons of ten species, fulvous whistling ducks, and representatives of more than a dozen waterfowl that are common or abundant seasonally; pintail, wigeon, shoveler, teal, ring-necked, and mottled ducks which are here all year and nest.

Red-shouldered and marsh hawks, kestrels, and sharp-shinneds are common. So are Florida sandhill cranes, though they frequent more remote refuge areas—but they often can be seen winging their way to feeding areas or nightly roosts.

Alligators sun themselves on the levees (the refuge is bounded entirely by levees, all sixty miles of them available for hiking). Bobwhites cross from brushy and wooded areas where red-bellied woodpeckers live, along with indigo and painted buntings, white-eyed vireos, and hermit, gray-cheeked, and Swainson's thrushes. Smooth-billed anis are common. So are loggerhead shrikes, and in migration such warblers as the Cape May, magnolia, black-throated blue, and orange-crowned. Robins and swallows sometimes appear in wintering flocks of thousands.

Armadillos are common, as are bobcat and otter. Panther and bear are here, but rare and secretive and unlikely to be seen. Except for these two, most of the interesting natural inhabitants of Loxahatchee are where visitors can spot them at one time or another. Such is the dense cover, however, that one must be prepared to spend some time and look carefully. A bobcat, for example, whelped and raised a litter in a den on the marsh trail seen by almost no one, so wary and quiet were they.

The refuge has been increasingly the habitat of the apple snail, a delectable morsel to many creatures but the sole food of the endangered kite (one of the rarest of all birds in the United States, though more common farther south). Plans have called for twenty-eight miles of new dikes, in the hope of providing a place where this graceful flier, once common through the region before development and drainage, can always find food and habitat.

Hobe Sound Refuge, administered by Loxahatchee, is 965 acres along the Intracoastal Waterway and Jupiter Island, whose residents donated it to the Fish and Wildlife Service through The Nature

Conservancy to preserve one of the last undeveloped stretches of barrier beach and dunes in this highly developed area. Its three and a half miles of shore supports the densest sea turtle nesting habitat on the Atlantic Coast. Three species of endangered turtles use it for their crawls from May to August. The females emerging from the sea at night to lay their eggs in holes scoured out in the sand (weeping, for reasons not known, as they do so). They then re-cover the eggs with sand so that they are incubated by the sun's warmth. The turtles lay more than a hundred eggs in each nest. In recent years more than a thousand nests have been recorded, most of them for the loggerhead sea turtle but also for the green sea turtle and the leatherback. The last of these is the largest turtle in the world, its shell sometimes six feet across. It weighs up to 1,500 pounds. Its huge nest is large enough to drive a small car into.

Visitors to Hobe Sound have little opportunity to witness this awesome nocturnal spectacle, but they can sometimes watch manatees grazing on the shoal grassflats, and a variety of wading and shorebirds. Least terns also nest some years; when they do, their colony is roped off to protect them from disturbance (they also nest on the graveled roof of a nearby supermarket where they find even less disturbance except when washed out by torrential rains).

Refuge headquarters is located about six miles north of Tequesta on Route 1. It has a short nature trail. Jonathan Dickinson State Park, adjacent, has nature trails, pontoon boat tours up the Loxahatchee River, in some years an active eagles' nest, and camping. For further information contact Hobe Sound National Wildlife Refuge, P.O. Box 645, Hobe Sound, Florida 33455. Phone: (305) 546-6141.

How to get there: From West Palm Beach take Route 95 south to Boynton Road (northwest Second Avenue), then west until Boynton ends on Route 441 and south on 441 to refuge sign.

Open: Daylight hours year-round.

Best times to visit: Late fall, winter, spring.

What to see: Endangered Everglade kite; limpkins; Florida sandhill cranes; alligators; ferns and orchid air plants unique to the area.

What to do: Boardwalk, wildlife trail, interpretive displays, plus 60 miles of dike trails; boating (rentals available); photo blind; limited waterfowl hunting; fishing for bass, bream in good numbers, best March—May. Tours can be arranged at south end concession.

Where to stay: MOTELS—In Royal Palm, 20 miles north; Delray, Boynton, 15 miles east. CAMPGROUND—John Prince County Park in Lake Worth.

Weather notes: Summer can be oppressive; January subject to cold snaps.

Points of interest nearby: Everglades National Park, 60 miles south; Hobe Sound Refuge, 40 miles north; Key Deer Refuge, 125 miles south; Merritt Island Refuge, 120 miles north.

For more information: Loxahatchee National Wildlife Refuge, Route 1, Box 278, Boynton Beach, Florida 33437. Phone: (305) 732-3684.

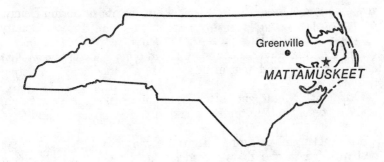

Greenville

MATTAMUSKEET

MATTAMUSKEET (North Carolina)

Mattamuskeet is a refuge essentially under water—covered with North Carolina's largest natural lake, which seems itself almost covered at times with waterfowl, the most spectacular being the large numbers of whistling swans that winter here—one fifth of the North American population.

It is the end of a journey of almost four thousand miles for these majestic once-rare white birds which nest diagonally across the continent in the northwest Canadian arctic. En route they passed over refuges such as Shiawassee in Michigan, Ottawa in Ohio, and several others, everywhere causing a stir as one of the memorable bird sightings of the year, for no creature is more admired for its grace and beauty.

Here they stay from November on and can easily be seen in large numbers either from the miles of auto and hiking trails in the marsh and upland that rim the lake or from Route 94, the seven-mile causeway that crosses over it. (To many, their call sounds more like a reverberating whoop than a whistle.)

The origin of Lake Mattamuskeet is something of a mystery. Some say it is a filled depression caused by fires long ago which burned out the upper layer of peat; others attribute its bowl shape to a meteorite landing from outer space. Whatever the cause, it is ideal feeding habitat now for all kinds of waterfowl—eighteen miles long and six miles wide and not much deeper than a swan's neck at any point, and even better since a recent invasion of acres of nutritious and succulent wild celery. Numerous Canada geese come here in addition to the upward of twenty thousand swans and a hundred thousand ducks of more than a dozen species, a far cry from its sorry state after repeated and luckily unsuccessful attempts to drain and farm it before it became a refuge in 1934.

Despite its small land area—the lake itself covers 40,000 of the 50,177 refuge acres and 4,000 more are in other impoundments—the remaining forest and marshland support a varied and interesting wildlife.

Occasional bobcat and black bear appear along with raccoon, mink, opossum, otter, muskrat, and nutria. One can readily see deer.

Bald eagles and peregrine falcons are winter visitors, and ospreys nest with fair success, despite pesticide problems, in ancient cypress snags on the western end of the lake—thirty-eight nests in one recent year with fifty-five young.

Barred, screech, and great horned owls are common all year, as are red-bellied and pileated woodpeckers, bobwhite quail, brown-headed nuthatches, kingfishers, meadowlarks, and northern yellowthroats. Great blue herons and great egrets occur at any time along the water's edge, and woodcock, killdeer, and snipe are common in winter.

Small numbers of endangered red-cockaded woodpeckers are in the older stands of loblolly pine, and another endangered species, the small tidewater silversides minnow, clings to existence in the lake shallows.

Also administered from Mattamuskeet are several small protected islands, as well as the following:

Swanquarter Refuge contains 15,500 acres of beautiful pine and hardwood swamp and marsh bordering Pamlico Sound. It is an important sanctuary for waterfowl with more diving ducks than Mattamuskeet—redhead, scaup, canvasback, bufflehead, and ruddy ducks —number of rails, and, in the woodlands, some of the rare red-cockaded woodpeckers. Bear appear from time to time, as do alligators, the northernmost location for that endangered species. There is a popular fishing pier. Eagles and peregrine falcons are winter visitors. Swanquarter is about ten miles southwest of Mattamuskeet. This is a good refuge to see by boat, and small boats can be rented nearby.

Cedar Island is an island refuge bordered by Core and Pamlico sounds. Its twelve thousand acres of mostly salt marsh provide excellent rest and feeding areas for many kinds of water birds. It is particularly noted as nesting habitat for black ducks, but also has a small representative population of mammals and songbirds. To get there, take Route 70 from Morehead City to Atlantic, then Route 12 to the refuge. It is a good place to view by boat as well.

How to get there: From Raleigh, take Route 264 east through Wilson, Greenville, Washington about 200 miles; at New Holland, turn left to Mattamuskeet Lake and refuge.

Open: Daylight hours all year.

Best times to visit: November through January.

What to see: Swans and waterfowl, good assortment of small birds.

What to do: Trails; photography; fishing in designated areas; no hunting in recent years—lead shot remaining in the shallow bottom continues to cause poisoning in feeding waterfowl, especially swans.

Where to stay: MOTELS—At Belhaven, 40 miles west; Fairfield, 10 miles north. CAMPGROUNDS—In Engelhard, 15 miles west; near Belhaven, Riverside Campground; and Pettigrew State Park, 50 miles northwest.

Weather notes: Summers are hot and humid; rest of the year generally pleasant.

What to take and wear: Windbreaker for cooler winter days.

Points of interest nearby: Cape Hatteras National Seashore, 100 miles east. Pea Island Refuge, 100 miles east. Swanquarter Refuge, 15 miles west. Cedar Island Refuge, 50 miles south.

For more information: Mattamuskeet National Wildlife Refuge, Route 1, Box N-2, Swanquarter, North Carolina 27885. Phone: (919) 926-4021.

Orlando● ★
MERRITT
ISLAND

MERRITT ISLAND (Florida)

Merritt Island, which came about as a happy afterthought in the creation of the vast U.S. space center here, is one of the great national wildlife refuges, 139,305 acres, with more endangered and threatened species of animals than any other continental refuge—plus large concentrations of many non-endangered species.

Housing and commercial construction had already begun (and no doubt would now cover this whole area, as it does much of this central Florida east coast) when NASA began buying the land from which the first man was rocketed off to the moon. It occurred to environmentalists and space people alike that there might be room for both here—and so it has proved. The refuge actually is an overlay on space center land, next to Canaveral National Seashore.

Among those species which would be under extreme pressure in this area except for the refuge are the southern bald eagle, which in some years has five active nests; the peregrine falcon, sometimes fifteen visible in a single day; the homely manatees, or sea cows; brown pelicans, which nest in even greater numbers than at nearby

Pelican Island—up to four hundred nests in one colony; the dusky seaside sparrow; American alligator; several species of sea turtles, which nest on the beaches, including the green, loggerhead, and, probably, the leatherback, largest of all living turtles, weighing up to 1,500 pounds (and with the unexplained ability to keep its cold-blooded body at warmer temperatures than the surrounding water). Other reptiles in this category are the eastern indigo and Atlantic salt marsh snakes; and among plants the hand fern, pond apple, and sea lavender, to mention just a few.

Equally interesting to most visitors are the throngs of beautiful birds, plants, and other animals which appear everywhere. While not necessarily endangered, they are here in such numbers as to be a rarity in most persons' experience.

Robins and tree swallows winter here in flocks of thousands and tens of thousands.

Visitors can see several dozen species and thousands of individual birds in the several miles' drive to the refuge headquarters, in the marsh and brushy areas immediately alongside the road. Especially apparent are the lovely long-legged waders, but also double-crested cormorants, grebes, black skimmers, rails, bitterns, and many kinds of shorebirds.

Almost every year in the annual Audubon Christmas Bird Count Merritt Island tallies among the highest in the nation in numbers of species—170 or so—and highest as well in the count of various individual species, such as merlins, palm warblers, kingfishers, yellowthroats, and dozens of others.

One of the few colonies of the rare wood stork is here, with every year three hundred or more nests of this majestic white bird (whose water requirements for breeding, luckily fulfilled here, are so exact that failure to meet standards causes them to abandon nests and young and even, if it occurs early enough, to fail to develop breeding plumage. They are not being finicky. The water levels are required for sufficient food supply).

Another of the several colonies here, some with thousands of nests, contains the largest number of species of any east coast heronry—eleven, including great blue, little blue, green, Louisiana, and black-crowned night herons, glossy and white ibises, and snowy, cattle, and great egrets.

King, clapper, and sora rails are common. Black rails are seen rarely due to their secretive habits.

Migrations in spring and fall can be spectacular, lasting for some species or other from September through April, with large numbers of kestrels, sharp-shinned hawks, and smaller birds—in the brushy areas Swainson's and worm-eating warblers, blackpolls, redstarts, and many others. Winter peak concentrations of waterfowl often reach seventy thousand or more of twenty-three species.

This only suggests the wealth of wildlife here, much of which is visible to anyone taking a little time to look quietly and carefully.

Pelican Island, administered by Merritt Island, was the beginning, in 1903, of the National Wildlife Refuge System. Even then for as long as anyone could remember it had been a roosting and nesting place for these large birds with huge feeding pouches in ponderous bills, so ungainly at rest but so graceful in the air, flying marvelously on wings spread seven feet or so across. Like many birds in the 1800s there seemed such an inexhaustible number of them that it mattered little if passing yachtsmen shot them for sport and market hunters slaughtered them. But eventually the killing, particularly of birds at the nest, aroused nature groups and, through them, President Theodore Roosevelt. Despite criticism he took the unprecedented step of creating, by executive order, a national wildlife refuge to be a sanctuary and protected breeding ground for native birds.

Since then buffer zones have been added to the 3.5-acre island until the refuge now encloses some four thousand acres of protected islands and water, where the pelicans—about three hundred to five hundred nesting pairs, along with numbers of herons, egrets, cormorants, ibises, frigatebirds, and others gather all year to feed, roost, and raise young. It is an impressive sight—birds seeming sometimes entirely to cover the tiny bit of land, hundreds soaring overhead almost anytime during the daylight hours.

It can be seen from the mainland at the town of Sebastian (a spotting scope would be helpful). Boats can be rented nearby to view the island and also used to explore the other refuge holdings in this beautiful Indian River area and up the Sebastian River, where almost any bird familiar to Florida waters is likely to be seen at one time or another.

St. Johns Refuge, administered by Merritt Island, consists of 4,241 acres of cordgrass salt marsh on the east side of the St. Johns River near Titusville, Florida. Its main reason for existence as a refuge is a small dark-streaked bird so inconspicuous in appearance and habits that, except in spring, when the male perches atop the cordgrass and sings a song that has been likened to that of a distant red-winged blackbird, it is impossible to estimate how many may be present. One recent spring, the census here showed twenty-eight singing males, almost all of the male dusky seaside sparrows in the world. It is one of the most endangered species of all.

For reasons not fully understood, this little bird is so habitat-specific it cannot survive without open horizons of savanna-like cord-grass prairies. Once this posed no problem, for vast areas here were just that. Now, with drainage, wildfires, highway construction and other development, this refuge, along with possibly some areas being set aside on Merritt Island for the few remaining birds, is its only remaining habitat.

Public access is restricted until more is learned about this small bird and particularly whether this land, much of it set aside only recently, will suffice, and whether it was set aside soon enough—for some creatures, once their population reaches a certain low, cannot recover even though breeding pairs remain. Meanwhile the census will be taken each spring when males fly to their perches and open their small throats to proclaim territories for quietly watching females, clearly unaware of their precarious condition and that they may not be singing for endless generations of dusky seaside sparrows to come. Sometimes questions arise about the wisdom of spending the sums required to set aside land for the chancy survival of such an inconspicuous small bird, which few persons have ever seen. The answer often cited comes from scientist William Beebe: "When the last individual of a race of living beings breathes no more, another heaven and another earth must pass before such a one can be again."

How to get there: From Orlando take the Beeline Expressway east to Route 95, north to Route 406, and follow 406 through Titusville to the refuge.

Open: Daylight hours all year (except when activities at space center close area).

Best times to visit: All year has fine wildlife but June–August least advantageous, with many seeking shelter from extreme heat (along with human visitors).

What to see: More rare and endangered species of plants and animals than any other continental U.S. refuge, including eagles, manatees, alligators, peregrine falcons, dusky seaside sparrows, brown pelicans, others—plus large concentrations of non-endangered.

What to do: Self-guided walking and driving trails, plus 100 miles of roads for on-your-own observation; photography (no blinds but photographers are encouraged to use their own, and refuge staff is happy to advise where and how); boating (rentals nearby); limited waterfowl hunting; fishing excellent year-round for (depending on season) trout, redfish, pompano, whiting, blues. Refuge films will be shown to groups by prior arrangement.

Where to stay: MOTELS—At Titusville. CAMPGROUNDS—At Titusville; also at Long Point County Park and Sebastian Inlet State Park, about 50 miles south (near Pelican Island Refuge).

Weather notes: Summers hot and humid; mosquitoes ferocious, and can last till Thanksgiving in a wet year. Some cool rainy days in January.

Points of interest nearby: Kennedy Space Center, with a variety of interesting tours; Canaveral National Seashore; Air Force Space Museum; Pelican Island Refuge. The Indian River Audubon Society has leaflet describing good birding places nearby in Brevard County, sometimes available at refuge.

For more information: Merritt Island National Wildlife Refuge, P.O. Box 6504, Titusville, Florida 32780. Phone: (305) 867-4820.

Savannah ●

OKEFENOKEE ★

OKEFENOKEE (Georgia)

Okefenokee is one of the great primitive areas of the world. Its dark, brooding cypress swamps hold one of the largest alligator populations anywhere, some twelve thousand to fifteen thousand of these primeval reptiles. Scarlet-crested pileated woodpeckers over a foot long hammer on its ancient moss-hung trees. Black bear and bobcat make their way silently along its forest paths.

Orchids bloom in almost infinite variety in remote areas, and carnivorous sundews, butterworts, and pitcher plants set their sticky traps for insects.

The swamp is not all dark and moody. Crimson-crowned Florida sandhill cranes prefer to perform their courtship dances on the wet grassland prairies. Otter ply the open waterways, snipe and killdeer visit their edges, and white ibises fly up by the hundreds from marshes which stretch golden in the sun as far as the eye can see.

Okefenokee is a mixture of fresh-water marsh, pine uplands and islands, dozens of small lakes and dense forest swamps extending over some 376,000 acres—about 650 square miles in the southeast corner of Georgia and north Florida with a tremendous range of natural inhabitants of all kinds. As examples, its lists of those identified on the refuge show 233 birds, 42 mammals, 58 reptiles, 32 amphibians, 34 fish, and hundreds of plants of every description.

Great colonies of graceful long-legged herons and egrets, white ibises and other wading birds cover almost two hundred acres and harbor an estimated seventy-five thousand nests. Red-cockaded woodpeckers make their homes in half-century-old pines, their trunks marked with white bands so refuge biologists—and visitors—can keep a watch on this endangered small bird. Prothonotary warblers, brown-headed nuthatches, yellow-billed cuckoos, chuck-will's-widows, wood pewees, Carolina wrens are seen commonly in low shrubs.

Everywhere are vistas that enchant the observant visitor and stimulate the photographer—dew-hung spiderwebs, red-billed gallinules stepping lightly across water lily pads, spectacular sunsets with striking compositions of moss-hung cypress trees silhouetted against red skies in the Chesser Prairie while waves of birds cross over to their nightly roosts.

The wonder is not in any one of these; it is in their total effect, which is stunning—that and two other factors. The first is its continued existence at all, through a long history of attempts to denude timber areas and drain its wetlands (the abandoned canal symbolizing this effort was finally called Jackson's Folly, and twenty-foot-deep peat beds continue to explode new islands to the water surface which eventually grow plants and trees that quake at a human footfall, a phenomenon that gave the swamp its Seminole Indian name "Land of Trembling Earth").

The second factor is that all this is able to exist as a wilderness showing little or no evidence of human activity, while at the same time, through careful resource management, much of it is accessible in some way to the visitor.

Three main entrances offer facilities for viewing the swamp on almost any knowledge level, with films, exhibits, tours, guides, auto, hiking and tram trails, observation towers, and picture windows through which deer and egrets may be seen at the swamp fringes. Night boat riders listen to alligators bellowing, frogs' choruses, and pick out with flashlights the red eyes of the alligators and green and gold ones of the frogs, owls, spiders, and others. Overnight canoe-camping trips deep into the swamp are available by limited reservation (filled well in advance) so each person can see and experience it individually.

"One thing certain," said a man who has been everywhere in the swamp many thousands of times, "it's different from anything else you'll ever see. And if you go every day for the rest of your life, it will be a little bit different every time. If you look around, there's always a little surprise. And always at bottom, the beauty and serenity of it that you can hardly convey. You have to see it for yourself, like a beautiful painting."

How to get there: Refuge office, open weekdays, is in Federal Building in Waycross, Georgia. Three main refuge entrances, open posted hours, are: *Okefenokee Swamp Park,* 13 miles south of Waycross on Routes 1 and 177. *Suwanee Canal Recreation Area,* 11 miles south of Folkston on Route 121/23. *Stephen Foster State Park,* 64 miles east of Valdosta on Route 94 and 177.

Open: 24 hours year-round.

Best times to visit: March through June (always interesting).

What to see: Tremendous diversity—233 species of birds, 42 mammals, 90 reptiles and amphibians, hundreds of plant species, flowering all year—but mainly, the swamp itself.

What to do: Walking and riding trails, boardwalks, observation towers, excellent interpretive exhibits, restored swamper's homestead, tram and boat tours, photography, canoeing, overnight canoe camping (by prior arrangement). Available for rental: boats, bicycles, guides for individual trips. Night tours for wildlife sounds, reflections of eyes. Fishing outstanding for warmouth, bass, pickerel, catfish, many others.

Where to stay: MOTELS—At Waycross, also Folkston and Fargo. CAMPGROUNDS—At Folkston, also Stephen Foster State Park, Laura S. Walker State Park, 10 miles southeast of Waycross; Crooked River State Park, 30 miles east of Folkston; along refuge canoe trails by special prior arrangement.

Weather notes: Wide-ranging temperatures—summer can be oppressive at 105 degrees, winter occasionally down to 13. Be prepared. Summer may have sudden heavy showers, quickly clearing—also violent electrical storms, during which it's important to keep a low profile.

What to take and wear: Raingear and a compass! Insect repellent for overnight campers in spring and summer.

Points of interest nearby: State parks (see CAMPGROUNDS); Cumberland Island National Seashore, 30 miles east of Folkston; Georgia's sea islands, about 50 miles east of Waycross.

For more information: Okefenokee National Wildlife Refuge, P.O. Box 117, Waycross, Georgia 31501. Phone: (912) 283-2580.

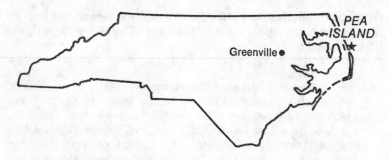

Greenville

PEA ISLAND

PEA ISLAND (North Carolina)

This 5,915-acre island is the end of the long journey south of the greater snow goose from its breeding grounds in the arctic, and the large once-rare birds can be seen here in winter in flocks that sometimes cover the refuge ponds with white.

Because they tend to stay in massed groups, their flights to and from feeding and resting places are spectacular, especially at dawn and sunset; and during the day they sometimes line the road through the sanctuary by the thousands, their heads tinged with orange from iron oxide compounds in the tundra where they feed and nest in the summer.

But they are only one of the fine natural aspects of Pea Island Refuge, a long finger of land located within Cape Hatteras National Seashore—on the outermost of the outer banks of North Carolina. Only a little over a mile at its widest, it narrows down in places to where, as the locals say, you can spit in the ocean on one side and Pamlico Sound on the other. In those places, it is little more than beach and dune held in place by sea oats; at its widest, it supports marsh and ponds which furnish food, shelter, and breeding areas to a wide variety of animal and plant life.

One can see the rare brown pelican here in the extreme north edge of its range. Peregrine falcons come through, usually from mid-September to mid-October—fifty sightings in one recent year. Swallowtailed kites are usually spotted at least once a year, as are purple gallinules, European wigeon and many sea birds, including shearwaters, may be seen occasionally on the beach, especially after a storm.

A chain of islands north of the refuge provides breeding habitat for a tremendous variety and number of water birds—gulls, skimmers, terns of various species—which are also seen during this time at the refuge; and refuge beaches also serve as nest areas from time to time.

Avocets and stilts have scattered nests in the marsh; and Atlantic loggerhead sea turtles crawl up on the beaches at night to lay their eggs, with an ongoing egg-transplant program from Cape Romain designed to increase their numbers. Sightings of the leatherback and green sea turtles are reported fairly frequently.

The Savannah sparrow is seasonally abundant in the dunes with some "Ipswich" sparrows among them, and seaside sparrows are common in the marshes.

Visitors can see otters fishing and sometimes frolicking in groups in the three main ponds which are bordered with footpaths and from two observation platforms. Muskrat and nutria are also present, and various small turtles and snakes, though none of a poisonous variety.

A colony of several hundred wading birds is visible from the north pond area—little blue, Louisiana, and black-crowned night herons, glossy ibises, and snowy, cattle, and great egrets. Fall shorebird migration is impressive; sometimes six thousand sanderlings stop along the beaches and mudflats along with comparable numbers of red knots, dowitchers, dunlins, and others. Later when the raptors start through, visitors can sight five hundred sharp-shinned hawks in a single day. And, along with the wintering snow geese are up to nine thousand Canadas and twenty or more kinds of ducks.

The marsh is full of flowers in the summer—marsh pinks, several rose mallows, purple, pink, and white morning glories, seas of blue-eyed grass, and scarlet and gold gaillardias, a garden escape which now makes itself at home everywhere here through November.

Altogether more than three hundred bird species have been identified on the refuge. Those listed as common or abundant at various seasons include magnolia, Cape May, northern parula and black-throated blue warblers, bobolinks, red-breasted nuthatches, pied-billed grebes, Wilson's storm petrels offshore, ring-necked pheasant, and king and clapper rails. Pea Island almost always heads the nationwide Christmas Bird Count list for at least one species—in recent years for sanderlings, short-billed marsh wrens, red-breasted mergansers, and yellow-rumped and Connecticut warblers.

How to get there: From Raleigh, take Route 64 east through Rocky Mount to outer banks and Nags Head; then south on Route 12 to Hatteras Island and refuge.

Open: Daylight hours all year.

Best times to visit: Something interesting here all year.

What to see: Warblers; wading and shorebirds; waterfowl; river otter and muskrat.

What to do: Wildlife observation from trails and platforms. Surf fishing on the beach for bluefish, trout (October–December best). No hunting on refuge or in 25,700 adjacent acres of Pamlico Sound by Presidential Proclamation.

Where to stay: MOTELS—In Nags Head, Kill Devil Hills, and Manteo to the north, Rodanthe, Avon, Buxton, and Hatteras to the south—all in 30-mile radius. Reservations advisable in tourist season. CAMPGROUNDS—Same as for MOTELS.

Weather notes: Winter chill factor with constant wind, and summer humidity uncomfortable when the breeze dies.

What to take and wear: A light waterproof windbreaker at any time. Warm clothing in winter.

Points of interest nearby: The refuge is within the boundary of Cape Hatteras National Seashore Recreation Area. Historic Fort Raleigh, Sir Walter Raleigh's famed lost colony, is near Manteo, and a monument to the Wright brothers' first successful flight is at Kill Devil Hills.

For more information: Pea Island National Wildlife Refuge, P.O. Box 1026, Manteo, North Carolina 27954. Phone: (919) 987-2394.

Charlotte

★ PEE DEE

PEE DEE (North Carolina)

Pee Dee Refuge was established in 1965 to serve as a wintering area for ducks and Canada geese, a nesting habitat for wood ducks and a sanctuary for the rare red-cockaded woodpecker, which exists here in small numbers.

It is now about 8,348 acres, but land acquisition still is not complete, and visitor facilities are limited. However, good sightings can be had in season of mallard ducks, pintail, gadwall, wigeon, blue-winged teal, ring-necked, and occasional bufflehead, as well as the Canadas—sometimes ten thousand ducks and up to five thousand geese.

The refuge interior is closed from October to April in order to serve as a quiet sanctuary for waterfowl during the surrounding area's hunting seasons; the rest of the time certain sections can be used for nature observation and fishing for bass and bream in refuge ponds.

Public roads encircle much of the refuge boundary, however, and also cut through in several places, and these are always open to travel and observation, though the visitor should beware of rattlesnakes.

Bobcat, fox, and beaver frequent the refuge, as do red-tailed and marsh hawks, and among the smaller birds flickers, kingfishers, nuthatches, chickadees, thrashers, and several warbler species. Wild turkey are here but in small numbers.

To reach Pee Dee take Route 74 from Charlotte east to Wadesboro, then Route 52 north six miles to the refuge. It is open seasonally. For further information contact refuge headquarters (open weekdays): Pee Dee National Wildlife Refuge, P.O. Box 780, Wadesboro, North Carolina 28170. Phone: (704) 694-4424.

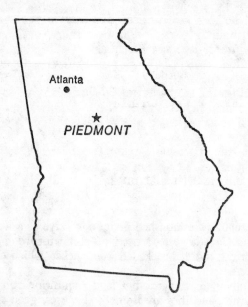

Atlanta

★ PIEDMONT

PIEDMONT (Georgia)

This refuge of 34,738 acres of mixed pine-hardwood forest in the Piedmont plateau of central Georgia is known the world over for techniques it has developed in reclaiming a depleted area and managing its resources concurrently for timber and wildlife. Piedmont and its personnel have won many awards for these achievements and visitors comes from as far away as Russia to see and learn—as well as to enjoy the results in the wildlife to be seen here now.

The endangered red-cockaded woodpecker is here in about sixty colonies and part of the forest management program is designed to support its needed habitat: pine trees which are at least fifty years old, having trunks with soft "red heart" centers which this small bird requires for its nest cavities. Brush is kept cleared in these areas, for this is another requirement; then the trees are watched carefully for the sap-encircled holes which means the red-cockaded has selected a spot for its breeding. This is the largest red-cockaded nest area in Georgia, and refuge forest management is on an eighty-year rotation cycle—longer than normally necessary—to ensure there will always be suitable habitat here for this small bird which has been excluded from most of its range by short-range lumbering practices.

Deer can be seen here in good numbers, as can the eastern fox squirrel, uncommon to rare now over much of its range, recognizable because of its size—more than twice that of the common gray—and often coal black or lightly marked with white. Turkey are here, and sometimes on a cloudy day they seem common—and they are; but for the most part they are wary and hard to see.

Beaver are almost certain to be seen, especially in early morning or toward dusk, and their workings are always visible. Also around, but taking a little more care to see, are fox, mink, raccoon, opossum, and bobcat—the latter more observable by tracks left in soft soil than by sightings of the beast itself.

Several thousand ducks winter on Lake Allison, mostly mallard, black, ring-necked, and wood ducks (the latter year-round residents).

Common all year are bluebirds, bobwhite, pileated and red-bellied woodpeckers, screech owls, brown-headed nuthatches, towhees, cardinals, mourning doves, yellowthroats, and pine warblers. Common seasonally are summer tanagers, indigo buntings, orchard orioles, prairie and hooded warblers, yellow-breasted chats, chuck-will's-widows, and four kinds of vireo—the white-eyed, red-eyed, yellow-throated, and solitary. Best time for songbird and other migrants is mid-April and late October.

At least thirty miles of roads are open for auto and foot travel, and one of the best walks is along beautiful Falling Creek—ask specific directions from the refuge office—where elevation slopes off sharply and there are rock slides and a series of small natural dams, and interesting mosses and wild flowers.

There are pitcher plants in March and April, and a little later the woods burst into bloom with dogwood, redbud, and wisteria—sometimes simultaneously.

The area is full of history—Sherman's troops marched through here on their way from burning Atlanta to the sea—and there are remnants from that time on the refuge, in rings still attached to trees where travelers tied their horses at old stagecoach stops.

How to get there: From Macon, take Route 129 north to Gray, then north on Route 11 to Round Oak. Refuge sign is just past Round Oak. Turn left and go 3.5 miles on blacktop to refuge headquarters.

Open: Daylight hours all year.

Best times to visit: Spring and fall.

What to see: Deer; beaver; red-cockaded woodpeckers.

What to do: Nature trails; photography (photo blind available); limited hunting for deer and small game; fishing for bass, bream, panfish.

Where to stay: MOTELS—At Forsyth, 18 miles west. CAMPGROUNDS—At Forsyth; also at High Falls State Park, 30 miles northwest.

Weather notes: Summers can be hot and humid; winter has periods of rain but no severe weather.

What to take and wear: Light raincoat might be useful; hiking boots for off-trail exploring.

Points of interest nearby: Ocmulgee Indian Mounds near Macon (National Park Service); Jarrell Plantation—a typical Georgia cotton plantation preserved from the 1800s, 8 miles from the refuge.

For more information: Piedmont National Wildlife Refuge, Round Oak, Georgia 31080. Phone: (912) 986-3651.

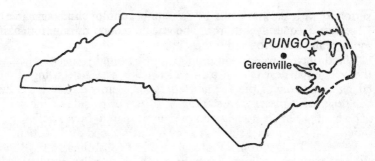

PUNGO (North Carolina)

Pungo Refuge was once part of the Great Dismal Swamp, with peat soil a dozen feet deep and covered with great cypress and white cedar trees. Now most of the surrounding area has been drained for farmland, and Pungo's wetlands and the swamp forest which is being restored serve as an oasis for wildlife.

Some thirty thousand wintering Canada geese are here from November to March, along with several thousand snow geese and swans and a dozen duck species, primarily mallard, wigeon, blue- and green-winged teal, pintail, black, and the wood ducks which also nest here. They are readily seen because while the refuge covers some twelve thousand acres, Pungo Lake is only a fourth that size and the concentrations, usually greatest in January, are almost always visible from the observation tower and from the several footpaths which lead from the eleven miles of graveled road to the lake.

At early morning this can be a dramatic sight when thousands of these birds stream out for an hour or so to feed in surrounding areas.

The tower is particularly good viewing because the walkway to it goes through marsh where numbers of other birds appear, including red-winged blackbirds, green herons, and occasional bitterns and rails.

The road passes through brushy upland where quail are abundant and various small birds are common seasonally—kingbirds, indigo buntings, cardinals, meadowlarks, mockingbirds, and in the woodland tracts flickers, Acadian flycatchers, and occasional prothonotary warblers.

Gallberry is an abundant shrub, with small but fragrant blooms and pollen which has made the refuge famous locally for gallberry honey, the product of beekeepers allowed to set up hives which they surround with electric wires to prevent bear from inspecting them. Observers frequently see bear, bobcat, raccoon, opossum, rabbit, squirrel, and a few fox and otter.

Wood duck houses produce up to four hundred young yearly, and the refuge has developed a plan which helps prevent starlings from taking over many of the 165 nest boxes for their own use: a smaller box designed especially for starlings is fitted to the side of the wood duck house. This is usually occupied immediately by a starling pair which then keeps other starlings away from the wood duck section.

To reach Pungo from Washington, North Carolina, take Route 264 east to Pantego, then Route 99 north eight miles and turn left for two miles at a church. The refuge is open every day. There is a limited deer hunt in the fall. Motels and campgrounds are located around Belhaven, eleven miles south. Weather and other conditions are similar to those at Mattamuskeet.

For further information contact Pungo National Wildlife Refuge, P.O. Box 267, Plymouth, North Carolina 27962. Phone: (919) 793-2143.

Tallahassee

ST. MARKS

ST. MARKS (Florida)

St. Marks Refuge in the Big Bend of the northwest Florida panhandle supports nearly every species of wildlife native to this section of the state—ospreys, eagles, alligators, otters, Canada geese, ducks, turkeys, herons, egrets, and small passerines, including a number of warblers. None is in huge concentrations, but all are here in comfortable numbers, including more than a dozen which are on the state and federal threatened and endangered lists.

The reason for this is the great diversity of habitat in these 64,000 acres of fresh-water ponds and marshes, brackish bays, tidal flats, hardwood swamps, and pine woods, with miles of shoreline and tidal creeks plus 31,500 acres of open water in Apalachee Bay that are closed to hunting.

As an example, the annual Christmas Bird Count taken by the National Audubon Society usually shows the count at St. Marks among the top 50 in the nation in number of species—often over 150—but seldom highest for any particular one. In a recent year these included 1,100 wigeon, 32 loons, 120 horned grebes, 60 snowy egrets, 17 marsh hawks, 11 bald eagles, 40 clapper rails, 57 killdeer, 85 short-billed dowitchers, 36 Forster's terns, 32 pileated woodpeckers, 36 hermit thrushes, 2,350 robins, 250 ruby-crowned kinglets, and a number of warblers, ranging through 935 yellow-rumped, 61 pine, 13 black-and-white, and 9 each of the white-eyed and solitary vireos.

This is a beautiful area where a visitor can wander on foot or bicycle over sixty miles of roads, some with self-guiding leaflets, some open to cars—or, one can put a boat or canoe into any of the refuge waters and explore the marshes and inlets and, weather and craft permitting, go on out in the bay. More than seventeen thousand acres of St. Marks is a designated wilderness—but except at peak times, much of it can seem to the visitor to be a de facto wilderness in any case.

Ospreys start building nests in February, males bringing huge branches which the females integrate into their bulky structures (or sometimes reject as unsuitable)—more than a hundred pairs within the three refuge units. There are five family groups of endangered red-cockaded woodpeckers, and their numbers are likely to increase with management of timber areas for this small bird whose nest-hole requirements include pines at least fifty years old with soft "red heart" centers. Wood ducks raise families in nest boxes and abundant natural cavities. Small birds abound in woods and brushy areas —yellow-billed cuckoos, Acadian flycatchers, blue-gray gnatcatchers, tufted titmice, summer tanagers.

Bear are here, though not in large numbers, the sight of one a tantalizing possibility nevertheless. Quiet visitors who get out on the trails early or stay out till dusk can see deer, armadillo, raccoon, opossum, otter, bobcat, feral hogs, and a few mink. Alligators bask on the banks on warm days.

Waterfowl concentrations occur mainly in the fall when a hundred thousand might be present in the bay or refuge ponds—redhead ducks, wigeon, pintail, blue-winged teal, mallard, gadwall. One can see herons and egrets all year any place there is water—and wood storks visit in summer and fall.

In June and sometimes continuing well into autumn the ponds are covered with white-blossoming water lilies, fifteen hundred acres of them, a stupendous sight. Overhead, an occasional swallow-tailed kite soars, along with Mississippi kites which nest on the refuge, but in such deep, remote places in the wooded swamp they are seldom seen there even by staff naturalists.

How to get there: From Tallahassee take Route 363 south about 20 miles to Route 98, then east .3 mile to refuge headquarters. To get to refuge entrance continue east on 98 to Newport then south on Route 59 to refuge sign.

Open: Daylight hours all year (office 8 A.M. to 4:30 P.M. weekdays).

Best times to visit: Fall through spring (though interesting all year).

What to see: Ospreys, eagles, alligators, waterfowl, red-shouldered and marsh hawks, good assortment of small birds including warblers. Historic lighthouse on tour route.

What to do: Some 60 miles of roads for walking and observing, including several interpretive; observation tower; boating and canoeing (rentals nearby); picnicking; fishing good, both fresh- and salt-water, for largemouth bass, speckled trout, redfish. Refuge staff with guide organized groups by prior arrangement.

Where to stay: MOTELS—At Wakulla Springs, 10 miles northeast; also Panacea and Shell Point, to the west. CAMPGROUNDS—In nearby Newport, also Ochlochnee State Park and Apalachicola National Forest, west of refuge.

Weather notes: January is cool, summer hot and humid with variety of biting insects.

Points of interest nearby: Wakulla Springs Lodge—a nature sanctuary with cruises to view wildlife (ospreys, limpkins, others) where the Wakulla River originates in a powerful spring flowing 83,000,000 gallons a day, and mastodon bones have been found. Also Fort San Marcos State Park in St. Marks, and the Wacissa River nearby, a major canoe trail.

For more information: St. Marks National Wildlife Refuge, P.O. Box 68, St. Marks, Florida 32355. Phone: (904) 925-6280.

ST. VINCENT (Florida)

For anyone who has ever wanted to be on a wild, beautiful, un-inhabited tropical island—here it is.

St. Vincent was named by Franciscan friars who came to establish missions in Florida's Big Bend in 1633. It is 12,489 acres of beaches, fifteen-foot-high golden dunes, fresh-water ponds and tidal marsh. In the wooded areas in the interior grow tall magnolias—flowering in spring and covered with scarlet in fall—great spreading live oaks, and a tremendous variety of other vegetation (one ogeechee tupelo tree is the largest of its kind anywhere, measuring 7 feet 11.6 inches around and sixty feet high).

Gulls and pelicans and sometimes swallow-tailed kites wheel over-head; ospreys and occasionally bald eagles fish in the ponds and offshore waters. Skimmers ply the shallows, scarlet bills agape to glean small surface organisms. Shorebirds congregate on tidal flats.

Access is by boat only, and the visitor must bring his own or rent one; but after that there are about eighty miles of shell-strewn beaches and sand roads that can be walked and explored.

Visitors can see peregrine falcons on the beaches in migration, along with various passerines (spring migrations, usually in April, can be spectacular) when small birds, including many species of warblers, make their first landfall for many hundreds of miles and come down to rest in beach vegetation.

Because it has more woods and shrubby upland than most barrier islands, birds nest here that are not usually seen on others—red-eyed vireos, brown-headed nuthatches, bobwhite quail, red-bellied and downy woodpeckers and a variety of warblers—northern parula, yellow-throated, yellow-rumped, and pine. Towhees and cardinals are common, as are marsh wrens, kestrels, and numbers of the large wading birds—great and little blue herons, white ibises, snowy and great egrets.

St. Vincent has been through a number of incarnations. Indians lived here centuries ago and left shell middens and artifacts that are still washing out on the beaches. More recently the island was stocked with exotic animals—elands, zebras, and others. Most of these have been removed, but sambur deer, of Asian origin and a cousin to our American elk—sturdy beasts weighing five hundred pounds or more, with large decorative antlers—remain and seem to thrive. Visitors can see them anywhere, along with white-tailed deer, feral hogs, raccoon, otter, alligator, and a few wild turkey.

Loggerhead sea turtles and a few rare leatherbacks—the largest turtles in the world—nest on the beaches.

Flowers abound, especially in spring—beach morning glories, marsh marigolds, purple swamp irises, fresh-water rose mallows and salt-marsh hibiscus, the small orchid-like bloom of blue sage, and rosemaries, fragrant shrubs which permeate the air with a lovely scent over the whole island.

How to get there: From Panama City take Route 98 southeast; just past Port St. Joe turn right on Route 30 about 15 miles to refuge sign and headquarters on right.

Open: Daylight hours by permission—check with refuge office, open weekdays (but telephone first since staff is in the field much of the time).

Best times to visit: Spring, fall, winter.

What to see: Ospreys, pelicans, shorebirds, white-tailed deer, and a few exotic sambur deer, vegetation ranging from dune grass and sea oats to tall magnolia trees—but mainly, a beautiful wild tropical island.

What to do: About 80 miles of beaches and roads for walking and nature observation. Photography—refuge staff are glad to help suggest where and how, with permission, to put up temporary blinds. Limited hunt for white-tailed deer, feral hogs. Fishing, in fresh-water ponds for largemouth bass and hand-painted bream (a colorful local subspecies) and surf for speckled trout, redfish. Boating—This is the only way to get to the island, and rentals and guides are available in the area. A slide show will be shown to groups by prior arrangement.

Where to stay: MOTELS—In Apalachicola. CAMPGROUNDS—At Indian Pass, also St. Joe Peninsula State Park, 12 miles northwest on Highway 98, and Torreya State Park, 80 miles northeast.

Weather notes: January can have cool, damp days, and many persons think midsummer's heat, humidity, and insects unbearable.

Points of interest nearby: St. Joe Peninsula State Park—trails, beach; Torreya State Park, with many botanical specimens found only in this area, including the Torreya tree, almost extinct in the wild (see CAMPGROUNDS). From here a beautiful canoe trip can be taken up a wild and undeveloped section of the Apalachicola River.

For more information: St. Vincent National Wildlife Refuge, Apalachicola, Florida 32320. Phone: (904) 653-8808.

Columbia ●

★
SANTEE

SANTEE (South Carolina)

Santee is the southernmost refuge where Canada geese which nest as far north as Manitoba and Saskatchewan come in large numbers to spend the winter, some twenty thousand of them, making this their cold-weather home after stopping off at refuges all up and down the east coast in a journey of some two thousand miles or so.

They are only one of the notable sights at this 74,000-acre refuge in the upper South Carolina coastal plain. The refuge was established in 1941 following construction of a reservoir on the Santee River by the South Carolina Public Service Authority which destroyed much of the area's natural waterfowl habitat.

Made up of approximately 4,340 acres of forest, marsh, and upland located around the large hydroelectric reservoir that resulted from the dam, it now harbors a tremendously varied spectrum of wildlife. These include such uncommon-to-endangered species as red-cockaded woodpeckers, found in old pine stands; alligators, near the northernmost point of their range; eastern fox squirrels—with grizzled gray and black markings; and occasional ospreys, eagles, and peregrine falcons.

Visitors can see bobcat, gray fox, and red fox, the best possibility being at first light from the observation tower where young kits are sometimes brought to learn the finer points of stalking waterfowl (and sometimes finding out it's a mistake to take on a healthy Canada goose). There are also mink, raccoon, muskrat, opossum, deer, and 150,000 or more wintering ducks of more than a dozen species—mallard, black, pintail, gadwall, teal, wigeon, redhead, canvasback, shoveler, ring-necked, scaup, bufflehead, three kinds of merganser. One can see all these from the foot trails which wind through varied habitat, including towering stands of eighty-foot pine.

One of the stunningly memorable sights is from a boat near the cypress stands on the lake where some four thousand herons, egrets, and ibises roost. At sunset they stream back in long undulating lines over the treetops from the direction of Santee Swamp—sometimes thousands overhead in a single moment, settling down in the ancient trees for the night.

Something interesting is happening all year. Short-eared owls flutter over the fields in the summer twilight. Purple gallinules are common then too, as are, for most of the year, such varied types among the 234 listed bird species as pileated woodpeckers, quail, yellow-throated and parula warblers, loggerhead shrikes, and red-shouldered hawks.

The refuge also contains one of the rare and interesting Carolina bays, the name given to a series of mysterious egg-shaped depressions scattered throughout Georgia and the Carolinas, many of which are being destroyed by draining and planting. Their origin is unknown, the best theory being that meteors struck the earth to form them. They range from two hundred feet to four miles in diameter, all oriented in the same direction, and having plant and soil types entirely different from the surrounding areas.

There is also a large mound where a Santee Indian chief reportedly was buried standing upright—accounting for its height—and on which the British built Fort Watson during the Revolutionary War, a position believed impregnable until Francis Marion and Lighthorse Harry Lee in a single night built a tower overlooking it and overcame the fort in a surprise dawn attack.

How to get there: From Sumter take Route 15 south to Summerton, then Route 301 eight miles south to refuge.

Open: Daylight hours all year.

Best times to visit: Fall through spring.

What to see: Large numbers of herons and egrets, Canada geese, endangered red-cockaded woodpeckers, alligators, eastern fox squirrels; Carolina bay—a unique natural area.

What to do: Trails; boardwalks; observation towers; boating (rentals nearby); limited deer hunt; superb fishing—Lake Marion has been rated one of the nation's top fishing spots, with rockfish weighing 55 pounds, largemouth bass 16 pounds, the world's record black crappie and others, including world-renowned landlocked striped bass.

Where to stay: MOTELS—Several in nearby Santee and North Santee, also Summerton. CAMPGROUNDS—Several in Santee and North Santee; also Santee State Park 8 miles south.

Weather notes: Summers hot and humid at times.

Points of interest nearby: Great Santee Swamp—huge, beautiful, wild area, north of refuge—you need a guide, but it's well worth it. Also: Four-Hole Swamp (Beidler Forest) 50 miles southwest; Congaree Swamp, 55 miles east; Francis Marion National Forest, 40 miles southwest; Edisto Gardens, 25 miles southwest.

For more information: Santee National Wildlife Refuge, P.O. Box 158, Summerton, South Carolina 29148. Phone: (803) 478-2217.

SAVANNAH (Georgia and South Carolina)

Tremendous numbers of wood ducks—often called our most beautiful waterfowl—along with hawks, wading birds, and alligators, in varieties and numbers occurring in few other places, are at home in Savannah. They live in 13,168 acres of fresh-water marsh and tidal rivers and creeks where the Savannah River borders both Georgia and South Carolina.

Savannah Refuge is one of the nation's oldest, started on lands occupied by a century-old rice plantation. The forty miles of dikes around its numerous impoundments were built by slave labor. So were the water control structures made entirely of cypress and heart pine wood which the refuge staff insists still work better than the modern metal ones. They regulate the flow of the twice-daily, seven-foot tides which come in here and provide a wide variety of habitats for a rich and diverse wildlife.

It is an ecosystem interesting to observe—for Savannah has a huge population of all kinds of rodents, rabbits, reptiles, and amphibians on its dikes, and these in turn attract creatures which prey on them, including some bobcat but especially raptors. Cooper's hawks along with red-tailed and red-shouldered are common and nest. Marsh hawks, sharp-shinneds, and kestrels are common seasonally, and occasional visitors throughout the year are merlins and peregrine falcons.

Among these prey animals are the numerous amphiumas and giant siren salamanders which look like catfish with legs and can be up to thirty inches long, and furnish the sole food for several snake species, including the beautiful rainbow snake and the mud snake, which is shiny black with red diamond-shaped markings on the sides. Savannah, in fact, is a herpetologist's paradise, the richest area in the eastern United States for a great variety of interesting reptiles, including the American alligator, whose population here is as dense as the area will presently support. They can be seen enjoying the sun on levees on most warm days.

Snipe are here in such numbers that they can be seen by the hundreds in midwinter, dotting the small floating mats of alligator weed along the wildlife drive—a staggering sight to the birder who has struggled for a fleeting glimpse of just one of these shy creatures.

Graceful, long-legged wading birds occur in large numbers—great and little blue herons, black-crowned and yellow-crowned night herons, glossy and white ibises. Great and snowy egrets nest in several colonies and fly in large V-formations to and from roosts and feeding areas morning and evening. Least and American bitterns are common, and wintering waterfowl include more than a dozen species.

Interesting plants are here as well—an unusual climbing fern, a Chinese parasol shrub, and tallow trees which descend from some Benjamin Franklin sent back from Europe. Altogether more than nine hundred species have been catalogued.

Mammals include white-tailed deer, raccoon, otter, and feral hogs, some of whose local ancestors date back four hundred years (watch out—they can be aggressive and when aroused have been known to dent cars).

Bald eagles and ospreys soar. Pileated woodpeckers are common in wooded patches. Orchard orioles are here, along with hermit thrushes, indigo and painted buntings, a variety of warblers in seasonal migration, and an impressive array of sparrows, including Bachman's, vesper, and sometimes Henslow's and LeConte's.

But no sight is more memorable than the multihued wood ducks, probably here in greater numbers than at any other refuge, staying all year and nesting, sometimes twenty thousand coming in at one time to roost in the late afternoon in patches of maiden cane and water lily in the east marsh.

Savannah Refuge also administers a complex of island refuges extending down the Georgia coast for some fifty miles, and twenty-eight miles into South Carolina. Most of these are barrier islands, although some are connected to the mainland by roads. Those which are offshore have access by boat only, and in some cases this is not easy access—as much as eighteen miles across open water where tides and water currents and depths can be variable and treacherous. Only experienced boatmen should attempt such a trip. Sometimes boats are available for rental, and guides also. A fisherman might be persuaded to take along a visitor. Some access is on a permit-only basis; always in daylight hours only (no camping permitted). Refuge staff are willing to help plan and arrange trips if contacted in advance. Public facilities in all cases are limited and likely to remain so—for these are wild places, acquired and maintained for their wild inhabitants and for visitors who will take these on their own terms, willing to walk wild trails, to seek out and observe the wary and inconspicuous as well as the obvious. The visitor who approaches these beautiful islands from this view is likely to reap a rich experience.

To the south, as they occur down the coast, are *Pinckney Island, Oysterbed Island (Tybee Refuge), Wassaw Island, Harris Neck, Blackbeard Island,* and *Wolf Island,* all administered by Savannah.

Pinckney Island. (Under Savannah) This refuge consists of 4,052 acres of marsh, woods, and some upland on Pinckney and four other small islands next to Hilton Head off the South Carolina coast. Cooper's hawks, brown pelicans, alligators, quail, deer, wild turkey, and a variety of waterfowl, herons, and shorebirds are common seasonally and year-round. Pinckney's entrance is on Route 278 five miles east of Bluffton, South Carolina; the other islands are reachable by boat only. The refuge was acquired fairly recently by donation. Access has been on a limited permit-only basis.

Tybee Refuge. Here are one hundred acres of largely spoil bank, once a lighthouse station in the mouth of the Savannah River, and used mainly now as a resting and feeding place for shore and migratory birds—skimmers, turnstones, clapper rails, brown pelicans—also, periodically as a nesting area for least terns. Diamondback rattlesnakes are abundant. It is twenty-four miles down river from Savannah through treacherous currents, and access is difficult.

Wassaw Island. This is believed by many to be the most beautiful of Georgia's famed "Golden Isles." It was established as a refuge by private purchase and donation through The Nature Conservancy—10,085 acres of wide beaches, spectacular dunes thirty feet high, with stands of sea oats, trails that wind through virgin stands of pine and live oak, their trunks covered with resurrection fern, and thousands of acres of fertile and unspoiled fresh- and salt-water marsh. Endangered red-cockaded woodpeckers nest, as do alligators and ospreys. Clapper rails and painted buntings are abundant, along with most of the graceful wading and shorebirds common to the region. Loons are common fall and winter visitors.

Loggerhead turtles crawl ashore on summer nights to scour out several hundred nests and lay hundreds of eggs, their activities monitored by youth groups for the Savannah Science Museum.

Access is by boat only. A marina is located at Isle of Hope, and transportation may be arranged from local Savannah marinas.

Harris Neck. The impressive numbers of birds of all kinds that are attracted to these 2,687 acres of varied grass and timberland, freshwater and salt marsh, mudflats and brush make it a mecca for birders. The local Audubon Society holds its annual Christmas Bird Count here because Harris Neck is certain to have the greatest variety of species in the area.

Nesting colonies are fantastic—tens of thousands of ibises, herons, egrets, storks, night herons, some roosting but most nesting in concentrations that cover the vegetation, sometimes producing two and three broods a year in a season that starts in early spring and may go into September. The sight of these great birds flying from the marsh to feed and coming back at night, sometimes hundreds of ibises alone, will never be forgotten.

Canada geese nest in a resident flock of about three hundred that often acts as a decoy to attract others unusual for this area such as brant and snow and white-fronted geese.

Cooper's hawks are uncommon. White-tailed deer are abundant; so are alligators. Painted buntings and northern parulas delight the eye everywhere but especially around former airstrips dating from when the tract was a military airbase. Many kinds of sparrows also like this place, as do yellow-throated vireos, orchard orioles, summer tanagers, and prairie and hooded warblers. Clapper rails, willets, and marsh wrens are predominant in the wet grasses, and thousands of ducks spend fall and winter on the ponds.

Access to some areas is closed during the nesting season, and closed to driving on some weekends. To check schedules, call the Savannah Complex office. Otherwise, Harris Neck can be reached by following Route 17, forty-three miles south from Savannah then east on Route 131 to the refuge entrance.

Blackbeard Island. This wild, beautiful 8,618-acre barrier island was named after the notorious pirate who was said to have buried treasure here (never unearthed). It was bought by President John Adams in 1800 as a source of oak timbers for navy sailing ships, making it longer in government ownership than any other refuge. After that it was a yellow fever quarantine station and finally in 1924 a wildlife sanctuary. Now loggerhead turtles crawl up on Blackbeard's nine miles of white beaches and lay eggs through the summer months; willets, sanderlings, oystercatchers, and black skimmers patrol the sands and brown pelicans wheel and dive offshore.

One of the densest populations of alligators anywhere is at home on the fresh-water ponds, apparently not interfering with large wintering flocks of waterfowl—ring-necked, canvasback, wigeon, teal, and sometimes sixty thousand lesser scaup—or with what many think is the best fresh-water fishing anywhere for bluegill, bass, and shellcracker.

Clapper rails nest in the marshes, and flickers, pileated and redbellied woodpeckers, and wild turkeys take advantage of the wooded areas. Painted buntings are common, as are cardinals, yellowthroated warblers, Carolina chickadees, and ground doves—along with a few chachalacas, a Mexican species which was introduced on a neighboring island and made its way here. A heronry supports more than a thousand nesting pairs of herons, egrets, ibises, and anhingas. Small white-tailed deer (smaller than the mainland animals) wander about commonly.

But it is the beautiful island itself and its remote, primitive atmosphere that provides a memorable experience for most visitors.

Access is by boat only, and this can be arranged at Shellman's Bluff, located on the eastern end of Shellman's Bluff Road, which is about fifty-one miles south of Savannah on Route 17.

Wolf Island. Along with neighboring Egg and Little Egg islands, 5,126-acre Wolf Island Refuge consists largely of a narrow strip of ocean beach backed by sea oats, sandbars, scattered myrtle bushes and cedars, and dense salt marsh. These are heavily used by clapper rails, herons and egrets, brown pelicans, some passerines, and a variety of shorebirds. A few oystercatchers and willets nest. Loggerhead turtles come ashore and lay eggs on the beaches. Surf fishing can be good, especially on Egg Island, where large channel bass are sometimes caught. But for the casual visitor, the dense vegetation restricts movement to all but a narrow stretch of beach, so it is of limited enjoyment compared with other areas available. For those who wish to try, boat transportation may be arranged from Shellman's Bluff (see Blackbeard).

How to get there: From Savannah take Route 17 north 13 miles to refuge sign. (Complex Headquarters is in Federal Building, Savannah.)

Open: Daylight hours all year.

Best times to visit: All year is interesting; weather least pleasant in midsummer.

What to see: Great numbers of wood ducks; snipe; Cooper's hawks; purple gallinules; wading birds and waterfowl; 11 species of sparrows; numerous and unusual reptiles, also plants. Remnants of old rice plantations and wooden dikes, here before refuge was established.

What to do: Five-mile nature drive, also 40 miles of dikes and roads for hiking, nature observation, photography. Limited hunting for waterfowl, sometimes feral hogs. Fishing for bass, bluegill, also landlocked flounder and striped bass that come up river and are caught in impoundments. Guided tours for organized groups by prior arrangement.

Where to stay: MOTELS—In Hardeeville, South Carolina, and Savannah. CAMPGROUNDS—Near Hardeeville, also Skidaway Island State Park, 15 miles south.

Weather notes: Midsummer hot, humid, buggy; midwinter, occasional frost.

Points of interest nearby: Hilton Head Island, 31 miles east—historic sites, nature walks (contact local Audubon Society); Savannah has interesting old restored sections, tours; Georgia Ornithological Society, 755 Ellsworth Drive NW, Atlanta, has Georgia guide, checklists, and advice for areas throughout state.

For more information: Savannah National Wildlife Refuge Complex, P.O. Box 8487, Savannah, Georgia 31402.

IV. THE GREAT LAKES STATES

There are sixteen staffed national wildlife refuges open to the public in the six Great Lakes states. Five are located in Minnesota, three in Wisconsin, two in Michigan, and one each in Illinois, Indiana, and Ohio. Two of the major refuges—*Upper Mississippi* and *Mark Twain*—are not confined to a single state but stretch out for hundreds of miles of bottomlands and river, starting at Wabasha, Minnesota, and touching Minnesota, Wisconsin, Iowa, Illinois, and Missouri before reaching the southernmost unit, just above St. Louis, Missouri.

MINNESOTA

The refuges offer a diversity of habitat and wildlife. In Minnesota there is *Agassiz* (pronounced Ag'-uh-see), a 61,000-acre watery remnant of Lake Agassiz (which once covered an area larger than all of the present Great Lakes) which harbors a herd of about four hundred moose. *Big Stone*, another Minnesota refuge, has two-billion-year-old red granite outcroppings, virgin prairie, and a spot where western grebes can be observed throughout their entire courtship, mating, and nesting cycle. *Rice Lake* is in a region of flat bogs laced with glacial moraine. It has much the same wild feeling as Boundary Waters Wilderness Area.

Sherburne, only an hour's drive from the Twin Cities metropolitan area, is a new refuge which came into being largely due to citizen action and is particularly interesting to see as a wildlife refuge in the development stage. *Tamarac* is in northern Minnesota, the locale of historic Indian hunting and camp grounds. It is rich in artifacts, wild rice (which is still harvested in the traditional way from canoes by Chippewa Indians), and wildlife—coyote, deer, beaver, and bear. Its fall foliage, including golden birches and aspens, crimson maples, sumacs, and maroon oaks, is among the most brilliant anywhere.

WISCONSIN

In Wisconsin, *Horicon* is famed for its numbers of wild geese—in excess of 100,000 each fall. *Necedah* harbors flocks of sandhill cranes and their courtship dances can be seen there in spring. *Trempealeau* contains remnant stands of virgin prairie and work is now underway there to re-create a much larger prairie habitat.

MICHIGAN

Seney, in the upper peninsula of Michigan, is a wildlife paradise, remade from timbered-over, burned-over, diked, and drained land which had failed for every other purpose when it was taken over by the Service in the 1930s. In its 153 square miles of pine woods, bogs, and lakes dwell bear, otter, bald eagles, and loons, among hundreds of other species of birds, mammals, reptiles, and amphibians. *Shiawassee* is within the Saginaw-Midland-Bay City industrial complex. Yet it is famous for its spring migration of thousands of whistling swans heading north from their wintering area along the mid-Atlantic Coast (predominantly at *Mattamuskeet* Refuge in North Carolina) to their breeding grounds in far northwest Canada and Alaska.

ILLINOIS AND INDIANA

Crab Orchard in Illinois is a historic goose wintering area and an interesting example of how wildlife and industry can coexist. *Muscatatuck* in southern Indiana is prime wood duck habitat—over one thousand of these most colorful ducks may be there at one time. It also is one of the most notable warbler nesting areas in the region.

OHIO

Ohio's *Ottawa*, on the shore of Lake Erie and east of Toledo, is a significant remnant of a 300,000-acre marsh that once stretched seventy-five miles from Port Clinton, Ohio, to Detroit, Michigan. Among its notable sights are up to four thousand black-crowned night herons which nest on a nearby island, also a part of the refuge system, and come to Ottawa to feed.

In terms of migration of waterfowl, the Mississippi River is the main Midwest Flyway, and the hundreds of miles of Mississippi and

Illinois rivers contained in *Upper Mississippi* and *Mark Twain* comprise necessary habitat for migrating ducks and geese and the bald eagles which follow them south. During fall migration Upper Mississippi harbors a good part of the world's population of canvasback ducks and over half a million waterfowl regularly visit Mark Twain during the fall and winter. Upward of three hundred eagles, including a few golden, were counted there in a recent winter census.

The following is a list of some birds of special interest found in common or abundant status at the refuges of this region:

Birds Common or Abundant at Seasons Indicated:

S: Spring   s: Summer   F: Fall   W: Winter

Red-necked Grebe: Agassiz, SsF; Big Stone, s; Rice Lake, SF; Tamarac, SF.
Eared Grebe: Big Stone, S; Tamarac, S.
White Pelican: Agassiz, SsF; Big Stone, SsF.
Yellow-crowned Night Heron: Big Stone, S; Crab Orchard, Ss.
White-fronted Goose: Big Stone, SF.
Goshawk: Big Stone, SF; Tamarac, W.
Cooper's Hawk: Big Stone, SsFW; Mark Twain, W; Necedah, SF; Sherburne, S; Shiawassee, SsF.
Swainson's Hawk: Big Stone, SsF.
Golden Eagle: Necedah, F; Shiawassee, SF; Tamarac, F.
Bald Eagle: Agassiz, F; Big Stone, SsFW;
Chautauqua, W; Crab Orchard, W; Mark Twain, W;
Necedah, F; Rice Lake, SsF; Shiawassee, SsF; Tamarac, SsF;
Upper Mississippi, sFW.
Osprey: Big Stone, SsF; Tamarac, SsF.
Prairie Falcon: Big Stone, SF.
Peregrine Falcon: Big Stone, SF.
Merlin: Big Stone, W.
Sharp-tailed Grouse: Rice Lake, SsFW.
Gray Partridge: Big Stone, SsFW.
Sandhill Crane: Agassiz, SF; Necedah, SsF; Seney, SsF; Shiawassee, SF.
American Avocet: Big Stone, Ss.
American Golden Plover: Big Stone, SF; Ottawa, SF.
Hudsonian Godwit. Big Stone, SsF.
Marbled Godwit: Big Stone, SsF.

Upland Sandpiper: Big Stone, Ss; Crab Orchard, Ss; Rice Lake, SF.
Stilt Sandpiper: Chautauqua, F; Rice Lake, SF; Shiawassee, SF.
Northern Phalarope: Agassiz, F.
Glaucous Gull: Big Stone, SF.
Snowy Owl: Big Stone, W; Rice Lake, W; Shiawassee, W.
Saw-whet Owl: Big Stone, F; Tamarac, SsFW.
Chuck-will's-widow: Crab Orchard, s.
Gray Jay: Tamarac, SFW.
Common Raven: Agassiz, W; Rice Lake, W; Seney, SsFW;
    Tamarac, SFW.
Eastern Bluebird: Big Stone, SsF; Crab Orchard, SsFW;
    Necedah, F; Rice Lake, SsF; Seney, F; Sherburne, SsF;
    Shiawassee, SsF; Tamarac, SsF; Upper Mississippi, SsF.
Bohemian Waxwing: Tamarac, W.
Northern Shrike: Agassiz, W; Big Stone, SFW; Rice Lake, W;
    Tamarac, SFW.
Philadelphia Vireo: Big Stone, S.
Mourning Warbler: Big Stone, S; Necedah, SF; Shiawassee, SF.
European Tree Sparrow: Mark Twain, SsFW.
Pine Grosbeak: Big Stone, W; Rice Lake, W; Seney, W;
    Shiawassee, W; Tamarac, SFW.
Hoary Redpoll: Big Stone, W.
Red Crossbill: Big Stone, SFW; Seney, W; Tamarac, SFW.
White-winged Crossbill: Big Stone, FW.
Henslow's Sparrow: Big Stone, Ss; Muscatatuck, SsF.
LeConte's Sparrow: Big Stone, F.
Harris' Sparrow: Big Stone, SFW; Crab Orchard, W;
    Rice Lake, SsF; Seney, SF; Tamarac, SF.
Lapland Longspur: Big Stone, SW; Rice Lake, SF; Shiawassee, SF;
    Tamarac, SFW.

GREAT LAKES

1 Agassiz
2 Tamarac
3 Rice Lake
4 Big Stone
5 Sherburne
6 Upper Mississippi (Headquarters)
7 Trempealeau
8 Necedah
9 Horicon
10 Seney
11 Shiawassee
12 Mark Twain (Headquarters)
13 Crab Orchard
14 Muscatatuck
15 Ottawa

AGASSIZ (Minnesota)

Agassiz harbors as great a variety of waterfowl and other wildlife as any national wildlife refuge—but its most imposing resident, without doubt, is the moose. It weighs in at up to nine hundred pounds and stands seven feet high at the shoulders, with a rack of antlers that may spread five feet across in breeding season. "When you find one on the road," said a refuge employee, "you almost feel you could drive your truck under it." It looks even bigger when you are on foot.

Agassiz' 61,487 acres of marsh and woodland in the northwest corner of Minnesota occupy part of the huge prehistoric glacial Lake Agassiz, which once covered an area larger than the Great Lakes. Historically settlers were attracted to it because of its wild game. Over the centuries it was so ill-used by timbering, burning, overtrapping, hunting, and drainage attempts that it was tax-delinquent and almost sterile when it was made a national wildlife refuge in 1937. Its comeback has been spectacular.

The refuge now contains more than two dozen lakes and ponds of various sizes where sixteen species of ducks are common throughout the warm season, producing in a good year more than eighteen thousand ducklings—blue-winged teal, mallard, pintail, gadwall, wigeon, shoveler, and, among the diving ducks, redhead, ruddy, canvasback, scaup. A population of Canada geese usually has several hundred young. In migration in spring (April–May) and fall (peaking mid-

October) the refuge may see several hundred thousand ducks and tens of thousands of geese, including blue and snow geese as well as the Canadas.

The mammal list is equally impressive. The moose herd on the refuge area is estimated to number up to four hundred; white-tailed deer two thousand; and the visitor going along the trails is almost certain, with any care, to see beaver, muskrat, skunk, perhaps mink, opossum, raccoon, and there are also bobcat, fox, otter, porcupine, coyote, badger, bear, squirrel, and a few fisher and gray wolves.

A fascinating area—though not easy to reach or navigate when there (and, being fragile, requiring permission from the refuge)—is a quaking bog in the north end—a floating mat of sphagnum moss and other vegetation supporting tamarack and black spruce trees thirty or forty feet tall which literally quake, or bounce visibly, at a visitor's footfall. Growing there amid the ground story of leatherleaf ferns are bog laurels, callas, pitcher plants, and orchids.

There are also, in migration, 150 or so rough-legged hawks; around 200 whistling swans; hundreds of white pelicans; usually several peregrine falcons; and a shorebird movement in fall (none in spring due to flooding) that usually includes dowitchers, yellowlegs, several species of sandpipers, stilts, avocets, golden plovers, and Wilson's phalaropes.

Five species of grebes are seen here—the western, pied-billed, eared, red-necked, and horned, and all are nesters. A great blue heron colony in the northwest section supports seventy-five pairs. LeConte's sparrow is not too difficult to find; and others which nest in fair to good numbers include killdeer, black-crowned night herons, American bitterns, marsh and red-tailed hawks, sharp-tailed and ruffed grouse, snipe, black terns, Franklin's gulls (a colony of some 25,000), great horned owls, flickers, long-billed and short-billed marsh wrens, veeries, cedar waxwings, warbling vireos, among warblers the Tennessee, Nashville, yellow, yellowthroat, and the clay-colored and sharp-tailed sparrows.

Visitors can spot the first moose calf around May 1, and white-tailed fawns about three weeks later, along with the first waterfowl broods on the various ponds. This is where moose are often seen, too, chewing on aquatic plants and other vegetation and seeking respite from insects.

A herd of twenty or thirty elk is in the area, though usually seen on a state and private area about five miles northeast of the refuge.

The auto and hiking trails offer good opportunities to see most of these, and refuge personnel can be helpful in advising where they have been recently—particularly the active beaver lodges, where large beaver can be observed almost every dawn or dusk, chewing on aspens and building their lodges.

Winter is the least hospitable season; nearby Thief River Falls is often the coldest spot in the nation, and winds sweeping over the flat terrain (only one foot of slope per mile) accentuate this. But for those who don't mind, there are (when roads are passable) black-billed magpies, ravens, northern shrikes, redpolls and some hoary redpolls, snow buntings, snowy owls, and the resident mammals, including winter weasels or ermines. Of the refuge's 270 birds on its list, only thirteen are left through this bitter season, and most humans who can, emulate the migrants.

How to get there: From Thief River Falls take Highway 32 north to Holt; then east on County Road 7 about 11 miles to refuge headquarters.

Open: Daylight hours every day except when winter driving conditions do not permit. Refuge headquarters open 8–4 weekdays; weekend visits can be prearranged.

Best times to visit: Spring and fall, for migrants, spring breeding plumage and fully antlered moose and deer in fall.

What to see: Moose, large concentrations of waterfowl; grebes; deer; beaver; skunk; wild flowers; a quaking bog.

What to do: Self-guided trail, auto and hiking; observation tower; photography; limited hunting for moose and deer; fishing in nearby lakes (a wide variety of water recreation available at Lake of the Woods resort area, 75 miles northeast).

Where to stay: MOTELS—A number in Thief River Falls, 23 miles southwest. CAMPGROUNDS—In Thief River Falls and Old Mill State Park, 20 miles west; and other state parks (see *Points of Interest,* below).

Weather notes: Extremely cold and occasionally bitter in winter; sometimes rainy in spring and can be cool anytime. Check with office on trail and road conditions in wet or snowy weather.

What to take and wear: Warmest clothing in winter; a windbreaker or sweater anytime; waterproof footgear in spring and summer.

Points of interest nearby: Three state wildlife management areas adjoin the refuge; also Old Mill State Park, 20 miles west; Lake Bronson State Park, 30 miles northwest; Hayes Lake State Park, 40 miles southeast; Itasca State Park—headwaters of the Mississippi—75 miles southeast. Lake of the Woods, 75 miles north-east, has wide-ranging recreational facilities.

For more information: Agassiz National Wildlife Refuge, Middle River, Minnesota 56737. Phone: (218) 449-4115.

BIG STONE (Minnesota)

Much of this 10,795-acre southwest Minnesota refuge has been in the making for almost two billion years, when pressures deep within the earth began to push up molten rock which eventually cooled in such lovely colors that the resulting granite blocks are known worldwide for their ruby-red hues.

The outcrops were first exposed about ten thousand years ago when the last glacier receded from ancient Lake Agassiz, which once covered a region larger than the Great Lakes, and the runoff cut a canyon through here leaving the great stones visible everywhere— 125 acres of them on the refuge alone. They are some of the oldest rocks on earth. Now, they form parts of beautiful hiking trails; a background, in earth-filled fissures and shallow depressions (where Indians once ground corn), for multicolored and unusual plant species; and a gentle slope from which some of the interesting wildlife here can be seen.

Establishment of Big Stone Refuge is credited to the push given by one man—Lem Kaercher, editor and publisher of the Ortonville, Minnesota, *Independent*. It was his idea that a mistake was made when the Whetstone River was channelized, causing severe siltation in Big Stone Lake as well as flooding problems downstream, and that it could be rectified with better-planned water control and utilization of the results to benefit wildlife. He won public and official support, and the refuge is part of the result.

It is a refuge of considerable beauty; besides the stunning granite outcroppings, the well-planned trails for auto, hiker, skier, and canoer pass through scenes of marsh, swamp, and woodland, and patches of virgin prairie grassland that can only be called idyllic, and where much of the wildlife here can be seen. Mink and raccoon frequent the streams, and there are white-tailed deer, beaver, thirteen-lined ground squirrel, muskrat, fox, badger—the mammals list gives thirty-five species.

The birds are equally enjoyable and impressive—the first verified sightings in Minnesota of yellow-crowned night herons, little blue herons and snowy egrets, and the first nesting pair of snowies. These were in a colony which accommodates somewhere around three thousand birds—great blue herons, black-crowned night herons, great egrets, cattle egrets, and five hundred nests of double-crested cormorants.

There is also a colony of twenty-five or so pairs of western grebes which can be observed (from an overlook by the water control spillway near state highway 75) through their entire nest cycle, starting with their courtship dances on the water to the fledglings riding about on their parents' backs.

Swainson's hawks also nest here as do red-tailed hawks, kestrels, twelve species of ducks, pheasant, woodcock, black-billed cuckoos, American bitterns, marsh wrens, screech and great horned owls, Forster's and common terns, five kinds of swallows, dickcissels, northern and orchard orioles, and vesper and grasshopper sparrows.

Notable among the plants are ball cacti and prickly pears, unique for this area with purple and yellow blooms in early June; fameflowers and polypodium and adiantum ferns. There is a continual succession of flowers from spring snow-melt to winter freeze-up, especially on the prairie grasslands (lead plants and purple and prairie clovers, coneflowers, black sampsons, gayfeathers and pasqueflowers).

Among the granite outcroppings the blue-tailed skink survives in its only known habitat in this part of Minnesota.

Spring and fall are the best times to come—in April and May for the spring migrants, and September to November for the fall. Flights of several hundred white pelicans appear (and a good number nest in Marsh Lake, twenty miles southeast, where they can be seen from a bluff near Louisburg)—along with whistling swans; some ten thousand Canada, blue, and snow geese; and twenty species of ducks, which peak at about thirty thousand birds about the first of April and mid-September. Bald eagles come through and can be seen almost any day in the latter half of October.

Broods of wood ducks, pintail, shoveler, redhead, blue-winged teal, and ruddy ducks appear in June, and flickers call from their nests in the wooded areas.

The Big Stone headquarters also administers wetland areas in Traverse, Lac qui Parle, Yellow Medicine, and Big Stone counties. These are natural prairie potholes open to the public for hiking and nature watching, though with few visitor facilities. Together with potholes throughout the other north-central states, these constitute the primary duck-producing habitat in the United States. Maps and directions are available from the refuge office.

How to get there: From Ortonville take Route 75 about 2 miles south to railroad crossing, red barn, "Granite View Farm," and small sign, "U.S. Fish and Wildlife Tour Route." Turn right onto refuge. (Ortonville is about 150 miles west of Minneapolis on Route 12.)

Open: Daylight hours year-round; office, weekdays. Some areas may have restricted use during nesting or hunting seasons and inclement weather—check with office.

Best times to visit: Spring (April–May) and fall (September–November).

What to see: Waterfowl, including numbers of ducks and geese both nesting and migrant, a variety of herons, egrets, and grebes; white-tailed deer; unusual rose granite outcroppings and wild flowers and plants unique for this area.

What to do: Photography; auto touring, hiking, canoeing, and ski trails; fishing (best in the spring for walleyed pike) and hunting for upland game and deer.

Where to stay: MOTELS—Several on Highway 12 near Ortonville, and in Milbank, South Dakota, 9 miles west; also Morris, 40 miles northeast. CAMPGROUNDS—At foot of Big Stone Lake, Ponderosa, and on Route 12 near Ortonville; also at Meadowbrook State Park 9 miles northwest on Route 7.

Weather notes: Winters can be windy and quite cold, with weeks below zero. Summers are often hot and humid with temperatures over 100° F.

What to take and wear: Spotting scope if possible, for colony viewing. Footgear with nonslip soles for walking on granite rocks; heavy pants or tall boots to protect from prickly pear cacti (and pliers to pull out spines if necessary).

Points of interest nearby: Big Stone State Park on Route 7, 9 miles northwest. Lac qui Parle State Refuge and State Park 35 miles south on Route 7. Nesting white pelicans on Marsh Lake, 20 miles southeast. Big Stone Lake has resorts and yearlong recreational facilities of all kinds.

For more information: Big Stone National Wildlife Refuge, 25 NW Second Street, Ortonville, Minnesota 56278. Phone: (612) 839-3700.

CRAB ORCHARD ★ Marion

CRAB ORCHARD (Illinois)

Crab Orchard in southern Illinois is unique among U.S. refuges for its combination of high public use—as many as two million visitors a year—and its wildlife living adjacent to the nation's main federal maximum security prison. The refuge shares its 43,022 acres with industries that employ fifteen hundred persons in the manufacture of missile parts, explosives, sporting goods, and display cases. There are facilities for swimming, boating, camping, and waterskiing—and a herd of more than two thousand white-tailed deer and flocks of waterfowl that number seasonally as high as a hundred thousand Canada geese and thirty thousand ducks. (Until recently the refuge also ran its own railroad!)

It works as well as it does largely because the main resident wildlife populations, which also include fox, coyote, raccoon, woodchuck, and a variety of songbirds and upland game, keep mainly to quieter portions of the refuge which for parts of the year are closed to high public use; and the main areas of overlap—the three sizable lakes and land around them—are used by the wild and human visitors mostly at different seasons.

The geese begin arriving in September after most warm-weather recreation is over, and though some of them move on through, most of them stay until March, when they go elsewhere to breed as do the ducks—mainly mallards, but including more than a dozen other species as well. There are also good numbers of migrating shorebirds—among them upland sandpipers (which also nest here) and spotted and pectoral sandpipers.

Hawks nest commonly—red-tailed, red-shouldered, broadwings, kestrels, and occasionally a Cooper's or marsh hawk.

Wild turkey, absent from the area for many years, have been seen more often in recent years and now apparently reproduce on the refuge. Turkey vultures nest commonly and have been seen bringing up families in hollow trees in the woods.

Even such retiring birds as black- and yellow-crowned night herons, green herons, and an occasional American bittern find a way to breed, mostly on the fifty or so small ponds which are in approximately half of the refuge that is closed to most public use. It is here that the industrial residents are found, in structures scattered physically (because they were built in World War II to make and store explosives and some still serve this purpose). They could not now be easily separated from refuge lands (and after its establishment in 1947, local towns successfully resisted the loss of jobs that would have resulted from their closure).

Much of the wildlife seems almost as much at home there as it does in the 4,050 acres that have been designated a wilderness area never to be disturbed by human activity. And though this area is closed for most purposes, visitors can see much of its wildlife from the twenty-plus miles of roads which one can walk or drive twenty-four hours a day, every day in the year. (The wilderness area is open to foot travel only, for hiking, hunting, fishing, and trapping.)

In both areas, great horned and barred owls are common, as are chuck-will's-widows, whip-poor-wills, and nighthawks—not readily seen except at dusk, but their voices fill the summer night air. And there are good populations of songbirds—seasonally Acadian flycatchers, wood pewees, yellow-billed cuckoos, ruby-throated hummingbirds, parula and prothonotary warblers, orchard and northern orioles, and for most or all of the year, Carolina wrens, cedar waxwings, goldfinches, cardinals, meadowlarks, brown thrashers, mockingbirds, and bluebirds.

Because of the proximity of Southern Illinois University the refuge has been closely studied by students who have investigated its trees, vines, flowers, fish, reptiles, mammals, and almost anything one might want to know about them. (Deer are sometimes seen wearing scarlet collars and streamers, part of a research project.) As a result, numbers of interesting reports are available as well as excellent lists of everything from the prehistoric paddlefish that inhabit Crab Orchard Lake to the cucumber tree—a type of magnolia, one of the 114 tree and shrub species—and 108 herbs and vines, which include the lovely trout lily, purple trilliums, bluebells, star-of-Bethlehem, silky asters, and various kinds of ferns that grow in the woods areas.

Refuge managers feel it is encouraging that all this can coexist with such heavy and varied public use. But occasionally they draw the line. One visitor asked if he could parachute into the lake from a helicopter. They turned him down.

How to get there: From Marion take Highway 13 west to Route 148, south on 148 about 1.5 miles to refuge sign and headquarters on right.

Open: Parts of the refuge, including information office at fire station on Route 148, are open 24 hours, all year.

Best times to visit: March through mid-May and October through December.

What to see: Canada geese; white-tailed deer; good assortment of songbirds.

What to do: Auto and hiking trails; observation tower; photography (deer and geese can be approached within range of a telescopic lens); wide variety of recreation in public use areas—swimming, boating, waterskiing, picnicking; limited hunting for waterfowl, quail, and deer; and fishing, best spring and fall, for bass, crappie, channel catfish, and bluegill, within state regulations.

Where to stay: MOTELS—Available at Marion, Carbondale, and most towns in area. CAMPGROUNDS—Three on refuge, with tents, trailers, and campers permitted; also at Giant City State Park, 3 miles southwest.

Weather notes: July and August hot and humid, fall and early winter can be wet and cool.

What to take and wear: Raingear suggested, with boots if hiking in wet clay soil.

Points of interest nearby: Ferne Clyffe State Park, 10 miles south, and Giant City State Park, 3 miles southwest, with unusual sandstone-limestone outcroppings, hiking trails. Horseshoe Lake

State Wildlife Area, 40 miles southwest, good fishing and birding. Shawnee National Forest, which covers much of southern Illinois, borders the refuge on the south.

For more information: Crab Orchard National Wildlife Refuge, P.O. Box J, Carterville, Illinois 62918. Phone: (618) 997-3344.

HORICON (Wisconsin)

Horicon in east-central Wisconsin is famous for its Canada geese, which congregate here in larger numbers than anywhere else in the world—upward of two hundred thousand at times in the past, causing ten-mile traffic jams for hours on adjacent roads when visitors come to see them during peak spring and fall migration times.

It is a case of a refuge succeeding too well. When Horicon was established a small captive "call" flock was brought in to attract others. All the habitat requirements were here, and by 1948 there were 2,000; in 1958, 51,000; 1968, 130,000; and by 1975 the population was estimated at times at 208,000—a large percentage of the entire Mississippi Flyway flock. It caused problems both real and potential (goose depredation on neighboring farms, threat of disease outbreak which could decimate most of the Flyway geese, and crowding out of other species, especially ducks, which have an equal need of the refuge lands).

A control program to move the geese on sooner to winter quarters farther south, and of adjusting the habitat to provide cover and food designed more specifically for other wildlife users, has brought their numbers closer to an optimum of a hundred thousand during peak times.

The difference would hardly be noted by the visitor during March and April and again in early October and November, when the sound Aldo Leopold called "goose music" enlivens the air and the sky is filled, perhaps against a brilliant sunrise or sunset, by the honkers (a scene listed by the Fish and Wildlife Service as one of the outstanding photographic opportunities on national wildlife refuges).

But now, there is much else besides—some 239 species on the list of birds seen here, as well as raccoon, deer, opossum, muskrat occurring commonly, with occasional badger, fox, and skunk.

Tennessee, palm, and black-throated green warblers are common migrants, and redstarts, red-eyed and warbling vireos, yellowthroats, black-and-white and yellow warblers nest commonly. So do both eastern and western meadowlarks, yellow-headed and red-winged blackbirds, bobolinks, marsh wrens, wood thrushes, kingbirds, indigo buntings, swallows, and a number of sparrows—swamp, song, chipping, and Savannah.

Summer brings numbers of waterfowl broods since the refuge produces about six thousand young ducklings every year—blue-winged teal, redhead, ruddy, and mallard most commonly. It is also the time for wading birds, for one of the largest heronries in the country is located on Four-Mile Island in the neighboring state-managed wildlife area, which occupies the southern third of this 21,000-acre marsh.

Great blue herons, great egrets, and black-crowned night herons make up the island's nesting population which can number 6,400. The refuge restricts public access during the breeding season, but these birds, as well as least and American bitterns, are visible in marshlands throughout the area when they go out to hunt their food.

Winter is less hospitable—thirty-below-zero temperatures are not unusual—but skiing and snowshoeing are permitted on the refuge. The mammal population is more easily seen against the sparse landscape, and there are usually rough-legged hawks hovering over the fields, as well as such common permanent residents as ring-necked pheasant, re-tailed hawks and chickadees, nuthatches and horned larks.

The refuge provides auto and hiking trails. It also permits hunting. But regulations are adjusted yearly according to refuge conditions, so check with the refuge office. Visitors can fish, but no great claims are made for it—the shallow marsh waters cannot easily support a good fish population year-round in this climate. Waters on the adjoining state area are opening to canoes; also worth a visit are nearby Kettle Moraine State Park, with interesting land forms left by glaciers, and

Horicon Ledge County Park, with limestone ledges which offer dramatic views.

But perhaps the most interesting feature of Horicon is the marsh itself—one of the largest cattail marshes anywhere, supporting a tremendous ecosystem of wildlife of all kinds. Scoured out by the Wisconsin glacier some ten thousand years ago, it was first used by Indians whose mounds remain. With settlers and lumbering, a dam was built in 1846 and the marsh became the world's largest manmade lake—fifty-one square miles. But farmers whose land was flooded organized opposition to it, and the dam was removed in 1869 and drainage started. Had modern techniques been available then, the plan probably would have succeeded—but they were not, luckily for Horicon. It failed, and after a twenty-year fight by conservationists, the refuge was established in 1941.

For some, the best experience of the refuge is the highly visible waterfowl—but for others, it is to go to the edge of the marsh at dawn or dusk and just sit quietly and watch and listen to the chorus of birds calling and singing, with an occasional frog chiming in. It is, said one, "like a wonderful concert."

Horicon also administers two small refuges, *Green Bay* and *Gravel Island*, in Lake Michigan. Designated wilderness areas, they support herons, gulls, and waterfowl. Access is rocky and difficult and only authorized by a permit issued by the refuge manager for scientific and research purposes.

How to get there: From Madison take Highway 151 north to Route 49, just east of Waupun; Route 49 east for about 4 miles to Country Road "Z". Right on "Z" and south 3 miles to entrance road for refuge office. Watch for refuge headquarters sign.

Open: Dawn to dusk year-round, weather permitting (some areas may be closed for specific purposes during year, as in hunting and nesting seasons. On these, check with refuge office, open 7:30 A.M. to 4 P.M. Monday through Friday).

Best times to visit: Spring and fall for migrants; summer for waterfowl broods.

What to see: Large concentrations of Canada geese and many other waterfowl and songbirds; showy trilliums, Dutchman's breeches, other wild flowers; deer, raccoon, muskrat.

What to do: Auto tours and walking trails; photography; some fishing (northerns and bullheads) and hunting, varying from year to year; cross-country skiing, snowshoeing in winter.

Where to stay: MOTELS—A number in and near Waupun, Mayville, and Horicon and farther away in Beaver Dam. CAMPGROUNDS— A private campground in Horicon; Fond du Lac County Park Campground north on County Road MM from Waupun; Dodge County Ledge Park located 2 miles east of Horicon north on Highway 28 to Raasch Road.

Weather notes: Winters may be severe at times with 30-below temperatures; summers pleasant, no other temperature or weather extremes.

What to take and wear: Comfortable clothing appropriate to season.

Points of interest nearby: Horicon Marsh Wildlife Area—the southern third of Horicon marsh, adjoining the refuge, managed by the Wisconsin Department of Natural Resources. Fishing, hiking, canoeing, and large heronry. Kettle Moraine State Park, east of refuge—unique geological features formed by glaciers. Horicon Ledge County Park, south of refuge—limestone outcroppings form ledges providing fine views of marsh and area.

For more information: Horicon National Wildlife Refuge, Route 2, Mayville, Wisconsin 53050. Phone: (414) 387-2658.

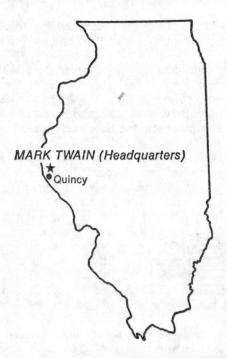

MARK TWAIN (Headquarters)
★
●Quincy

MARK TWAIN (Illinois, Missouri, Iowa)

Named after the man who gave *Life on the Mississippi* reality in the imaginations of many generations of readers, the Mark Twain National Wildlife Refuge is a chain of twelve separate divisions, ranging in size from 600 to 4,800 acres each, spread along 250 miles of the Mississippi River and 180 miles of the Illinois River.

The refuge totals thirty thousand acres of river bottomlands, backwater channels and sloughs, some islands and timbered uplands. Its divisions stretch along the Mississippi River from Muscatine, Iowa, south almost to St. Louis, Missouri, and upstream on the Illinois River from the Mississippi River to thirty-five miles north of Peoria, Illinois.

In addition to the refuge lands themselves, the Mark Twain Refuge is engaged in cooperative management of another 86,000 acres of General Plan Lands owned by the U. S. Army Corps of Engineers but under shared management with the states of Illinois, Iowa, and

Missouri. Also located along the Mississippi and Illinois rivers, these lands are managed for public recreation and wildlife habitat protection.

In total, and individually, the divisions of the Mark Twain Refuge provide habitat for a wide variety of wildlife. As a sampling, Chautauqua Refuge near Havana, Illinois, one of the older sections, has tremendous concentrations of shorebirds, especially in August. As many as two hundred thousand have been present at one time on the exposed mudflats and shorelines of Chautauqua Lake: lesser yellowlegs and golden plovers, pectoral, stilt, and least sandpipers.

The Chautauqua Refuge in December may have a hundred thousand ducks, mostly mallard. The various divisions of the Mark Twain Refuge as a whole may have as many as a half million or more ducks during the fall season, ranging through more than a dozen species: mallard, wood ducks, wigeon, pintail, black, goldeneye, redhead, canvasback, scaup, and ring-necked.

A major function of most of the divisions is to protect and enhance wood duck nesting in tree cavities and nest boxes in timbered areas. The Big Timber, Chautauqua, Meredosia, and Gardner divisions all contain many timber-edged sloughs and lakes preferred by "woodies."

Eagles winter in large numbers. An Illinois Natural History Survey in a recent January survey showed 718 eagles, including several golden eagles, on the river areas, with 300 of these within the refuge boundaries.

There are nine great blue heron/great egret colonies in or near refuge lands, and hundreds are sometimes seen at Chautauqua and on Fox Pond at the Louisa Division. Louisa also has a scenic overlook which offers a breath-taking view of the entire Mississippi River flood plain and the bluffs which follow it, especially when fall foliage colors peak in mid to late October.

Located north of the Gardner Division near Fort Madison and Keokuk, Iowa, is a section of the Mississippi River which is extremely important to migrating canvasback ducks. Each fall up to seventy-five thousand of them rest and feed on this pool with large numbers of scaup and ring-necked ducks. Peak numbers occur in late November and early December; Illinois Highway 96 provides many good viewing points.

Visitors can often make spectacular sightings in fall and spring of geese, particularly the Canadas and snow geese but also smaller numbers of blues and white-fronteds. The Gilbert Lake Division has an auto pull-off from Illinois Highway 100 from which the geese may be viewed as they feed in the fields.

Quail and pheasant are common in upland areas. Barred, great horned, and screech owls are around all year (not all of these in all divisions, of course) and common all year among the smaller birds are red-bellied, red-headed, and pileated woodpeckers, Carolina wrens, cardinals, goldfinches, blue jays, and nuthatches. Common in all except winter are flycatchers (Acadian, great crested), swallows (tree, bank, rough-winged, barn, and cliff), vireos (red-eyed, white-eyed, and warbling), prothonotary warblers, mockingbirds, redstarts, indigo buntings, and many others. (Large numbers of hummingbirds are sometimes attracted to fields of thistles and primroses at the Cannon Division.)

Mammals present on the refuge include fox, coyote, raccoon, mink, opossum, beaver, and large numbers of muskrat, squirrel, rabbit, and white-tailed deer.

Motel accommodations and campgrounds are available near most of the refuge divisions, and boat liveries are near many.

Fishing and wildlife observation account for most of the public refuge use, although limited hunting is permitted in some places within state and federal regulations.

Some of the divisions have boat ramps and nature trails; others are wild and undeveloped. Of these, some will have trails and public facilities constructed and others such as Gardner and Big Timber may remain forever wilderness, open to those willing to take a boat out through somewhat hazardous waters and hike in. This can be challenging but rewarding, for one can see the river and its islands almost exactly as the first explorers and settlers did—as Mark Twain saw them, in *Life on the Mississippi* as ". . . utter solitudes. The dense, untouched forest overhung both banks of the crooked little crack, and one could believe that human creatures had never intruded there before."

One cannot plan to see all the Mark Twain Refuge in a day, or even a few days. It might be best to plan to see only one or a few divisions at a time. In any case, because of the changing state of development of the various refuges, one should make contact ahead of time to learn the current status of open areas and permitted activities in the various areas. Their contact points are:

Mark Twain National Wildlife Refuge (Quincy Headquarters and Gardner Division), P.O. Box 225, Quincy, Illinois 62301. Phone: (217) 224-8580.

Mark Twain National Wildlife Refuge (Calhoun, Batchtown, and Gilbert Lake Divisions), Box 142, Brussels, Illinois 62013. Phone: (618) 883-2524.

Mark Twain National Wildlife Refuge (Louisa, Keithsburg, and Big Timber Divisions), R.R. No. 1, Wapello, Iowa 52653. Phone: (319) 523-6982.

Mark Twain National Wildlife Refuge (Clarence Cannon National Wildlife Refuge and Delair Division), P.O. Box 88, Annada, Missouri 63330. Phone: (314) 847-2333.

Mark Twain National Wildlife Refuge (Chautauqua and Meredosia National Wildlife Refuges and Cameron Division), R.R. No. 2, Havana, Illinois 62644. Phone: (309) 595-2290.

MINNESOTA WATERFOWL PRODUCTION AREAS

Minnesota has almost seven hundred small wildlife areas, ranging in size from a few dozen to hundreds of acres, maintained for the purpose of furnishing breeding habitat for a wide variety of waterfowl. Most have few if any special visitor facilities but are open for hiking, photography, and general nature-watching as long as they offer no disturbance to wildlife. In nonbreeding seasons cross-country skiing, snowshoeing, fishing, and hunting may also be permitted.

Typically they contain one or more prairie wetlands surrounded by grassland and brush, which attract many species of wildlife as well as birds. Ducks, geese, and swans are frequent visitors to these areas during spring and fall migrations, as well as deer, pheasant, gray partridge, a few ruffed and sharp-tailed grouse, some prairie chickens, and various shore and wading birds. Heavy duck and goose nesting occurs all spring and early summer. Young broods of several species are visible by mid-late summer.

For the nature-oriented person a visit to any of these can be highly rewarding (since the terrain is largely unimproved, hiking boots and sometimes waterproof clothing and footwear may be a good idea). Motels and campgrounds are available near most of these wetland areas, which are located in nineteen counties in west and south-central Minnesota. Visitors can obtain a listing and maps from: Manager, Minnesota Wetlands Complex, Route 1, Box 26A, Fergus Falls, Minnesota. Phone: (218) 739-2291.

Indianapolis

MUSCATATUCK★

MUSCATATUCK (Indiana)

The duck that Audubon called "this most beautiful bird" with its silken crest and plumage of scarlet, purple, blue-black, green, and gold receives much attention here, as well it might—for, as he said, "the great beauty and neatness of their apparel and the grace of their motions always afford pleasure to the observer."

This pleasure is multiplied many times at Muscatatuck, named by the Algonquin Indians "land of winding waters" because of the meandering of the heavily wooded Muscatatuck River, a historic nesting place for the wood duck. Once brought low by overhunting and habitat destruction to the point that it was threatened with extinction in the 1930s, it is plentiful here (and its status no longer worrisome due to a long period of protection). One can sit quietly by Mutton Creek marsh and see hundreds of these exquisite birds resting on the water, or calling and flying back and forth to the woods and river beyond.

Behind the headquarters of this 7,700-acre southern Indiana refuge, which was located here in large part because of its traditional attraction for wood ducks, there are sometimes a thousand of them at one time, resting, feeding, and taking off all at once with a rush of dazzling wings that is a stunning experience.

But this is a diverse refuge with upland fields and woods of tulip, beech, maple, and oak trees as well as bottomland stands of sweet gum, sycamore, river birch, ash, and pin oak. A wide variety of wildlife also like it here, in addition to large numbers of waterfowl—Canada geese and more than a dozen species of ducks.

Visitors can easily see white-tailed deer, especially in early morning and toward dusk, in the fields and wood edges. There are also many fox (you have to be a little more careful and lucky to see them), plus woodchuck, rabbit, squirrel, raccoon, muskrat, beaver, and mink.

Muscatatuck is also known over the State of Indiana for its songbirds, which are abundant and encouraged. It is hard to see how an alert observer could come here during summer without seeing numbers of brilliant indigo buntings. Cardinals abound all seasons of the year, and common sights year-round are goldfinches, towhees, meadowlarks, bluebirds, robins, brown thrashers, mockingbirds, kingfishers, and pileated, red-bellied, and red-headed woodpeckers.

Many warblers nest commonly in their preferred woods, shrubbery, or prairie habitat—cerulean, Kentucky, yellow-throated, prairie, blue-winged, yellow, prothonotary, and some parulas. Henslow's sparrow is here, and flycatchers enjoy the insects around the moist soil—the Acadian, least, alder, willow, great crested, wood pewee, and kingbird.

Great blue herons are here commonly all the time, and so are great horned and barred owls, red-tailed hawks and killdeer, which nest in every suitable habitat, including the refuge headquarters gravel parking area, putting on their "broken-wing act" to lure cars (sometimes insensitive to their displays) away from their nests.

Because of its fairly recent origin—the refuge was established in 1966 but the land not all acquired from private ownership until almost a decade later—much of the land supports not only wild flowers but colorful remnants of cultivated gardens—iris and sweet peas among the cardinal flowers and black-eyed Susans. There are also a number of old orchards with fruit that is relished not only by the wildlife but humans who come out for the mushroom, fruit, and nut gathering (permitted in quantities appropriate to personal use). They gravitate especially to a stand of forty persimmon trees of a delicious seedless type.

Muscatatuck is on the Flyway for the greater sandhill cranes which gather in concentrations of ten to twenty thousand at Jasper-Pulaski State Fish and Wildlife Area in northern Indiana before going south for the winter, and sometimes as many as three thousand can be seen going over in November. Sometimes small groups stop at Muscatatuck, and it may be that after it has been an established refuge a little longer, the great birds will begin to stop down with them in larger numbers.

If the hospitality at this refuge's attractive new visitors' center means anything, they will.

How to get there: From Indianapolis take I-65 south to Seymour. Approaching Seymour take the North Vernon exit to Route 50 east, and continue on 50 for 3 miles to the refuge entrance.

Open: Sunrise to sunset every day through the year. (Office hours 8 A.M. to 4:30 P.M. weekdays.)

Best times to visit: Spring and fall.

What to see: Wood ducks; white-tailed deer; varied songbirds and waterfowl.

What to do: Nature trails. Photography (blinds available). Film and slide shows and guided tours available by prearrangement. Gathering of mushrooms, fruit, and nuts. Fishing for bass, catfish, and bluegill, and hunting, mainly for rabbit and quail, within state regulations.

Where to stay: MOTELS—In Seymour, 4 miles west of refuge. CAMP-GROUNDS—Thirteen miles west on Route 258. Also Hardy Lake State Recreational Area, 25 miles south; and Starved Hollow Lake State Area, 25 miles west.

Weather notes: Wet in March–June and hot, humid periods in summer, but relatively pleasant most of the year.

What to take and wear: Might need raingear, also waterproof hiking boots if venturing far off trails.

Points of interest nearby: State recreational areas (see CAMP-GROUNDS); Brown County State Park 35 miles northwest, artists' mecca famed for natural beauty, especially fall foliage in mid-October (but reserve accommodations well ahead).

For more information: Muscatatuck National Wildlife Refuge, P.O. Box 631, Seymour, Indiana 47274. Phone: (812) 522-4352.

NECEDAH
★
La Crosse

NECEDAH (Wisconsin)

The greater sandhill crane, a majestic slate-colored crimson-crowned bird standing four feet tall with wingspread up to eighty inches, was so reduced in numbers a few years ago that it was placed on the endangered species list. Its comeback since protection is such that it can be seen in flocks of 450 or so when it stops at Necedah in spring and fall, in one of the larger concentrations of this still-rare bird on any national wildlife refuge.

Several pairs nest here, and their courtship dances in spring (and occasionally in fall) are one of the fine sights at Necedah as the great birds gather, in something like a square dance, and crouch and spring into the air, waving their wings and calling, a yodeling cry that can be heard for miles.

Visitors can easily spot their gatherings in fields along the eleven-mile self-guided auto trail and from a high observation tower. The tower scans much of this forty-thousand-acre central Wisconsin refuge, reclaimed in 1939 by Presidential Executive Order from land ill-used in successive timbering and abortive drainage and agricultural attempts.

The area now is a combination of marsh, woodland, and restored prairie that furnishes food and habitat for a wide variety of wildlife. The prairie is maintained by controlled burning.

Ducks and geese stop by in large flocks in spring and fall (depending on weather conditions up to fifteen thousand geese and twenty thousand ducks, including mallard, merganser, black, teal, wigeon, and wood ducks). Many of them nest on the refuge (wood ducks have even colonized the nearby town of Necedah, nesting in natural cavities in the many silver maples there, and townspeople take the same pride in them that other communities do in robins and purple martins).

Warblers also come through in good numbers in spring and also whistling swans, usually several hundred at least. Ruffed grouse can be heard, and sometimes observed in their courtship drumming, and woodcock on their high flights at dawn and dusk to proclaim their territories and claim a mate. Observers occasionally see wild turkey, too, the toms demonstrating before a group of hens—though this is the northern fringe of their historic range in Wisconsin, and they are not common.

Two of the common and colorful summer nesters are the scarlet tanager and the red-headed woodpecker, its scarlet head and flashing white wing patches highly visible throughout the year; and bitterns, pied-billed grebes, and red-tailed and marsh hawks raise broods. Deer are seen in good numbers and beaver and badger less often (watch for a badger along the auto trail, taking off like a small tank).

One can hear whip-poor-wills through most of every summer night. Fall foliage color peaks the last half of September, and is beautiful, and there is a good fall hawk migration, with sharp-shinneds and Cooper's commonly seen.

Winter is more tolerable than at many more northern refuges, and the auto trail is on township roads which are usually kept open in all but the most severe weather. Horned larks and snow buntings rise in clouds against the landscape, along with tree sparrows, redpolls, goldfinches, evening grosbeaks, and good numbers of rough-legged hawks, which hover over the windswept winter fields. Sometimes one can sight two dozen in a single day's outing, when snow cover is not too deep.

One of the stunning sights here is the fall gathering of migrating bald eagles. They gather often in a group of as many as a dozen or so in certain trees, resting and feeding on their way south. The refuge has built sturdy wooden photo blinds into the ground in two places to observe the eagles and the waterfowl and sandhill cranes. The former is best seen in November, the latter in April and October. Visitors can reserve blinds.

Parts of the refuge remain closed during nesting and hunting seasons—check with the refuge office on this. But the entire refuge is open to all in July, especially for blueberry picking, which is popular; and in the winter, when snowshoeing and cross-country skiing are permitted on the refuge.

Necedah also manages several waterfowl production areas jointly with the state. These are small habitats from forty to three hundred acres mostly with no special visitor facilities. They are seasonally available for wildlife-oriented activities including hunting, hiking, and nature watching. A list of locations is available from the refuge office.

How to get there: From I-90-94 at Tomah take Highway 21 east to the refuge, or from I-90-94 at Mauston take County Road Q north to Highway 80. Continue north into the Village of Necedah, turning left on Highway 21 and on to the refuge. Signs will direct you onto the refuge.

Open: Seasonally open from sunrise to sunset for permitted activities —for further information inquire at headquarters' office, which is open 7:30 A.M. to 4 P.M. Monday through Friday.

Best times to visit: April and October for migration.

What to see: Greater sandhill cranes in some of the largest concentrations anywhere in Wisconsin. Migrating eagles, grouse, waterfowl. Rough-legged hawks in winter. White-tailed deer, beaver, muskrat, occasional badger. Variety of wild flowers—blazing stars, lady's slipper, orchids. Occasional massive monarch butterfly migration in early August, covering refuge buckwheat fields.

What to do: Photography; auto tour and interpretive trails; deer hunting; snowshoeing and cross-country skiing; blueberry picking. Guided tours can be arranged in advance for groups.

Where to stay: MOTELS—Several in Tomah, Necedah, and New Lisbon. CAMPGROUNDS—Private campground east of Necedah on Highway 21, watch for signs. State Meadow Valley Campground on boundary of refuge, limited facilities, open September–December 31.

Weather notes: Pleasant weather most of spring, summer, and fall; winters can be quite cold with snow cover most of January–March.

What to take and wear: Appropriate to season.

Points of interest nearby: Sandhill State Experimental Game Farm near Babcock, west of refuge; International Crane Foundation in Baraboo, which studies cranes worldwide and has many live examples on premises; scenic resort area of Wisconsin Dells, 50 miles to the south.

For more information: Necedah National Wildlife Refuge, Star Route West, Necedah, Wisconsin 54646. Phone: (608) 565-2551.

OTTAWA (Ohio)

During nesting season up to four thousand black-crowned night herons regularly visit this northern Ohio refuge which is the remainder of a marsh of some 300,000 acres that a century ago stretched seventy-five miles along Lake Erie from Port Clinton, Ohio, to Detroit.

Less than 10 per cent of that vast acreage remains, mostly in small parcels in the hands of hunting clubs; but Ottawa Refuge is an exception to the general drainage and development of the area. It still retains virgin patches of Black Swamp Woods and upland habitat as well as marshlands that help feed and support pheasant all year-round, as well as large numbers of geese, ducks, and swans, some nesting, some stopping over on their migration routes.

One is quickly introduced to the wildlife inhabitants of this 5,794-acre refuge. Along the entrance drive is a pond which may be lined with killdeer and yellowlegs. Geese and ducks are visible in the field nearby, the geese with their young broods in summer.

Ottawa has had its habitat problems. The huge surrounding marshes once acted as a giant sponge for the whole area, soaking up the brunt of storms and floods from shallow windy Lake Erie where stormy waves may crest up to twenty-eight feet. Development and drainage left the few remaining marshy areas increasingly vulnerable to these forces and in 1972 a giant storm wiped out the dikes now necessary for maintenance of the shore wetlands, and their reconstruction and maintenance is an ongoing project, along with restoration of the vegetation needed for wildlife support.

Even so, one can see many thousands of ducks and geese in October and November from both the Mississippi and Atlantic flyways—Canadas along with snows and a few white-fronted geese; and mallard and black ducks, along with a good assortment of pintail, gadwall, teal, wigeon, ring-necked, canvasback, scaup, goldeneye, and many others, with only slightly lesser numbers in the northward flight in spring.

Ottawa is a pivotal waterfowl migration point, where part of the Mississippi and Atlantic Flyway populations separate on their southward fall journeys and rejoin when they return north in the spring. Perhaps a thousand whistling swans are present on the refuge in April, en route from their wintering area on the South Atlantic Coast to their nesting grounds in the Far North. The sight of the large graceful white birds is so popular locally that a Swan Day is declared by the state, and school classes and family groups come out to witness their spring visit.

Warbler migration also brings many viewers in the spring, with common sightings of black-and-whites, Tennessees, Nashvilles, magnolias, Cape Mays, black-throated blues, and Blackburnians and many others as well as the chestnut-sideds and yellows which nest here. There is a seven-mile self-guided walking trail, in four loops so that one may go the whole distance or take only part of it. Altogether they cover the four main habitat types, and the Blue Heron loop, the closest to refuge headquarters, goes through two patches of the original virgin Black Swamp Woods.

Along the trail visitors can see some of the mammal residents—deer, muskrat, raccoon, woodchuck, cottontail, and red fox (but it is necessary to walk quietly to do so).

Five photo blinds are available, sturdily built on the edge of the ponds, well disguised with cattails—and many of the ducks and geese, as well as great blue and black-crowned night herons, may be seen from them.

Both these herons nest in numbers at *West Sister Island*, nine miles out in Lake Erie—nine hundred pairs of great blues and up to two thousand pairs of black-crowns at a recent yearly estimate. But the water is deep around the island so most of these birds return daily to Ottawa to feed, and they are a common sight. West Sister Island is a satellite refuge administered by Ottawa and designated a wilderness area in 1975; public access is by special permit only to protect the heronry. (Several hundred great blue herons can be seen at Ottawa year-round.)

Many ducks nest at Ottawa as well—among them redhead, shoveler, and wood ducks, for which two hundred nest boxes are tended on the refuge; also kingfishers, red-headed woodpeckers, ovenbirds, meadowlarks, indigo buntings, red-tailed hawks and spotted sandpipers, screech and great horned owls, and a pair of bald eagles have been active in recent years.

The 2,500-acre Crane Creek State Wildlife Experiment Station is adjacent, and the two work cooperatively in many ways, including goose production work, bird banding, and a controlled goose hunt in the fall.

Ottawa National Wildlife Refuge (5,794 acres) includes three separate divisions: Ottawa Division (4,683 acres) where the refuge headquarters is located, Darby Marsh Division (520 acres, thirteen miles east of Ottawa Headquarters), and Navarre Marsh Division (591 acres, six miles east of Ottawa Headquarters) not owned but leased and managed by the refuge system.

Other refuges administered by Ottawa:

Cedar Point (2,245 acres, ten miles west of Ottawa Headquarters) has been managed largely as a waterfowl nesting and stopping place with public access limited to those with special permission.

West Sister Island (77 acres, nine miles north of Ottawa Headquarters) is an important heronry for great blue and black-crowned night herons. West Sister Island has been designated as a wilderness area. No access is permitted except by special permission.

How to get there: From Toledo take Route 2 about 15 miles east to refuge entrance sign.

Open: Sunup to sundown, every day. Headquarters office open 7:30 A.M. to 4 P.M. weekdays.

Best times to visit: October and November, also spring.

What to see: Ducks and geese, migrating in spring and fall and with broods in summer; also migrant whistling swans, more numerous in spring. Black-crowned night herons; Great blue herons; shorebirds.

What to do: A 7-mile self-guided walking trail, with more trails and tours planned for completion soon. Photography blinds. A limited controlled goose hunt in fall. Limited fishing in Lake Erie for walleyed pike, perch, white bass. Boats for rental in Port Clinton.

Where to stay: MOTELS—A number in Toledo or nearby Oregon, also Port Clinton, a lakeside resort area (these are generally more expensive). CAMPGROUNDS—7 miles east of the refuge off Route 2; also several at Port Clinton.

Weather notes: No extremes, but winds off Lake Erie can be raw and uncomfortable in early spring and fall, and strong northeasterly storms can arise suddenly off Lake Erie, with hazard to boaters.

What to take and wear: Comfortable seasonal clothing.

Points of interest nearby: Crane Creek State Park, adjacent to the refuge, excellent for warblers and others. Oak Openings Park, a 3,000-acre tract owned by the Toledo Park Board, 18 miles west of the city—a little distant but worth it for the amazingly varied habitat and wildlife attracted to it.

For more information: Ottawa National Wildlife Refuge, 14000 West State Route 2, Oak Harbor, Ohio 43449. Phone: (419) 897-0211.

RICE LAKE (Minnesota)

This entire refuge of 20,287 acres in east-central Minnesota, typical of the region's great, flat bog country laced with glacial moraines, approximates a wilderness experience. The power line extends to the refuge headquarters; beyond that there is little sign of civilization, and the possibility, and often the reality, to the patient naturalist of seeing deer, moose, black bear, coyote, beaver, mink, eagles, gray wolves, even a rare lynx, and some of the largest concentrations of ring-necked ducks anywhere in this country.

Both ruffed and sharp-tailed grouse perform their courtship, drumming and dancing in the grassland areas and aspen clearings; eagles can be spotted almost any day in the fall (a pair usually nest here, though an ambitious beaver came close to cutting down their nest tree, a giant aspen, a few years ago); and occasional interesting western species, at the easternmost edge of their range—black-billed magpies, western bluebirds, yellow-headed blackbirds.

October is the favorite time for many, with fresh cool days, fall foliage colors peaking in mid-October, and waterfowl in considerable numbers—up to sixty thousand ring-necked, along with mallard, black ducks, wood ducks, and blue-winged teal, many of which also nest here, and Canada, snow, and some blue geese.

There is a good fall raptor migration, usually with an occasional peregrine as well as merlins, Swainson's, roughlegs, bald eagles, and a few golden eagles. A number of hawks summer and nest here—red-tailed, marsh, broadwinged, and a few Cooper's, sharp-shinned, and ospreys.

But spring is beautiful also with its northbound migrants—swans, geese, ducks, and some sandhill cranes; upland sandpipers; numbers of warblers; and the return of such commonly nesting songbirds as the swallows—five species common here; cedar waxwings; eastern kingbirds; yellow-billed cuckoos; scarlet tanagers; rose-breasted gros-beaks; ovenbirds; bobolinks; northern orioles; and ruby-throated hum-mingbirds.

The spring wild flowers are out in lovely progression from ice breakup in March with bloodroots, trilliums, gentians, yellow and showy lady's slippers, Dutchman's breeches, pitcher plants, hepat-icas, columbines, tiger and Turk's-cap lilies, and many others (but until June, the visitor should be prepared for changeable weather and keep raingear handy).

Summer is a pleasant season, with few hot spells—seldom does the thermometer rise above ninety degrees—and nights are cool. Visitors can enjoy broods of ducks and geese, also nesting loons and great blue herons. Most of the refuge's sights are visible (though not the actual nests) from some two miles of foot trails and seven miles of refuge roads which can be traveled by car.

A major food plant for the waterfowl is wild rice, and the crop is also shared by local Chippewa Indians, starting in mid-September. Many of those who participate in the harvest are descendants of tribal villages once located on the shores of Rice Lake and old sugar maples on the refuge still bear scars where they were slashed by Chippewas using their sap to make maple sugar.

The refuge receives few human visitors in winter, but snow bun-tings are common then, along with pine and evening grosbeaks, red-polls, a few crossbills and Lapland longspurs, rough-legged hawks, and snowy owls. Great horned, screech, and saw-whet owls are com-mon all year. Look for the latter at any time, sitting quietly in the daytime in the low branches of a spruce tree.

The most exciting aspect of Rice Lake is probably not what jumps out at you at every turn—for, like any wildlife refuge, the wild crea-tures that abide there are more interested in keeping their own com-pany than that of humans. Seeing them takes quiet patience. But there is always the possibility of seeing a great range of birds and ani-mals, at any time and almost any place. Many of the black bear sightings were by anglers at the fishing bridge.

And the best sightings of badger were made when a family took up residence in a burrow under the refuge entrance road, and were observed there for many weeks by early summer visitors.

Rice Lake also administers two small boulder islands in Mille Lacs Lake, nest sites for gulls and terns, and the Sandstone Unit, 2,240 acres about forty miles southwest of the main refuge, with nesting habitat for ruffed and sharp-tailed grouse and waterfowl. Public access is not permitted onto these areas.

How to get there: From Duluth take U. S. Highway 210 west 65 miles to McGregor; then U. S. Highway 65 south 5 miles to East Lake; then west 2 miles on gravel road to refuge headquarters.

Open: Dawn to dusk daily year-round (certain areas may be closed to public use at times as in breeding or hunting season—check with office).

Best times to visit: Fall is the general favorite—especially October, with fall migrants; foliage colors; fresh, cool weather.

What to see: Great variety of birds and mammals, including large concentrations of ring-necked ducks and other waterfowl; eagles; deer; beaver; muskrat; occasionally bear and coyote; some western bird species such as magpies; spring wild flowers; Indian burial mounds.

What to do: Photography; fishing from entrance road bridge and in nearby areas and Mississippi River for northern and walleyed pike and bullheads mostly; some small game hunting; facilities in nearby Mille Lacs resort area (Mille Lacs is a famous walleye lake). Ski resorts near Hill City and Duluth.

Where to stay: MOTELS—In McGregor, 7 miles north; Aitkin, 20 miles west; farther away in Cloquet (35 miles east) and Brainerd (40 miles west). CAMPGROUNDS—North of McGregor and near Aitkin; also permitted in Chippewa National Forest 65 miles north of refuge; and Savannah State Park, 30 miles north.

Weather notes: Pleasant and cool most of year, though changeable and unpredictable April–June; can be extremely cold in winter (40 below not uncommon!).

What to take and wear: Keep raingear handy in spring, even if the day looks pleasant; warmest clothing in winter.

Points of interest nearby: Savannah State Park, trails and historical points of interest; Kimberly Wildlife Area, on western refuge boundary; Northwoods Audubon Center, 40 miles southwest; Boundary Waters Wilderness Area, 160 miles north.

For more information: Rice Lake National Wildlife Refuge, R.R. ⌗2, McGregor, Minnesota 55760. Phone: (218) 768-2402.

SENEY (Michigan)

Visitors can enjoy an extraordinary variety of wildlife—from nesting bald eagles to otter sliding down snowbanks and black bear with their cubs—at this 153-square-mile refuge, which was built on reclaimed land which had failed for almost every other purpose.

Ruffed grouse appear and perform their courtship act with whirring wings on a "drumming log." Loons carry their chicks about on their backs and utter their wild cries at dawn and dusk during the two-hour visitors' evening tour. Stately sandhill cranes, standing three feet tall with wingspreads of almost seven feet, gather with their young in flocks of three hundred or more.

Even the little yellow rail, rare and extremely shy, has been found here in numbers. Visitors can summon it by tapping stones together, making a sound that is similar to the rail's own call.

The 95,455-acre tract located in the Great Manistique Swamp in Michigan's far northland next to the Canadian border is ideal for wildlife, with twenty-one ponds—over seven thousand acres of open water—dotted with nesting islands, interspersed with open fields and sandy ridges supporting woodlands of mixed deciduous and ever-green growth.

Once it was quite different. During timber cutting in 1870–90, Michigan's Upper Peninsula was nearly stripped of its pine forests. Afterward fires, often deliberately set, all but destroyed the humus soil. Then unscrupulous developers drained and sold it for agriculture, and when this failed the land reverted to the state for taxes. At last in 1934 the State of Michigan recommended it be developed as a national wildlife refuge, and its present status began the following year.

Now over two hundred species of birds live here, as well as mink, muskrat, coyote, porcupine, fox, bobcat, skunk, weasel, raccoon, white-tailed deer, and a few timber wolves, an endangered species.

Commonly nesting are American bitterns, marsh hawks, killdeer, woodcock, black-billed cuckoos, great horned owls, nighthawks, ravens, hermit and Swainson's thrushes, cedar waxwings, red-eyed vireos, and a number of warblers—the black-and-white, Nashville, yellow, magnolia, black-throated green, chestnut-sided, Canada, pine, palm, and yellowthroat.

Common nesters among the waterfowl include goldeneye, common and hooded merganser, wigeon, blue-winged teal, mallard, ring-necked, black, and wood ducks.

A popular attraction for visitors, especially those with cameras, are the broods of Canada geese which are everywhere, even on the lawn of the visitor center, from mid-June to mid-July.

But wildlife of all kinds is omnipresent. An active beaver lodge has been built behind the nearby refuge manager's house, and trunks of birch trees on the visitor center's lawn have been protected with chicken wire since a prize specimen fell to the gnawings of one of these furry neighbors. Kingfishers and bank swallows have built nest tunnels in sand banks along the self-guided auto tour route.

A naturalist leads a two-hour auto tour every evening from June 15 through Labor Day, and a seven-mile self-guided auto tour is open from late June through September 30. There is also a 1.4-mile self-guided walking trail with a hundred-foot observation tower.

The refuge has set up a telescope at one point and left it focused on one of the eagles' huge seven-foot nests, so they can be observed through the nest cycle from incubation until the young birds are up flapping their wings in exercise routines and finally taking off on their first flights.

Almost a third of Seney is a wilderness area, including a significant strangmoor bog, a Registered National Landmark. The public is denied access from March 1 through July 31, but after August 1 permits may be obtained for hiking in. Camping is not allowed.

Two refuge pools are open to summer fishing, and all are open for ice fishing in winter (these ponds contain large northern pike—not often caught; but the head of one captured by an otter measured twelve inches long). There is a hunting season in fall for upland game and deer.

Fall foliage colors peak starting in mid-September, and are a brilliant sight on a clear day with gold aspens and birches and scarlet maples mixed with evergreens all reflected in the quiet water against a blue sky. Dozens of varicolored mushrooms and other fungi appear around the woods and trails (along with delicious morels, available for the picking earlier in the season).

Winters are relatively mild due to the refuge location between the moderating influences of Lake Michigan and Lake Superior—the average low is around fifteen to twenty degrees—and ideal for snowshoeing and cross-country skiing. Snow buntings are abundant then, and pine grosbeaks, redpolls, siskins, and red crossbills are a common sight. The landscape, due to the surrounding Great Lakes, is every night dusted lightly with fresh snow, so that each winter morning is a pristine sparkling vista.

Seney also administers *Huron Islands,* a group of eight small islands located three miles offshore in Lake Superior about forty miles east of Houghton, Michigan. Pink and gray granite cliffs rise nearly two hundred feet from the water, supporting nesting colonies of herring gulls and some common terns and double-crested cormorants. Designated a wilderness area, public access is by permit only and only West Huron Island is open to the public except by special permission.

How to get there: From Sault Ste. Marie take state route M-28 west about 80 miles to M-77 at Seney, then follow M-77 south 5 miles to refuge entrance.

Open: From 8 A.M. to 6:30 P.M. daily June 15–Labor Day; 8 A.M. to 4:30 P.M. weekdays rest of year. Visitor center open daily April 1 through October 31.

Best times to visit: Between Memorial Day and Labor Day—visitor center, exhibits, and all public use facilities are open daily (snow cover, perhaps several feet deep, may limit access except on skis or snowshoes November 1–April 15).

What to see: Canada geese; sandhill cranes, bald eagles; deer, otter, bear, and a variety of other waterfowl and land animals.

What to do: Photography—especially for geese. Fishing and hunting in season (the Fox River east of the refuge is reputed one of the finest brook trout streams in the country, with specimens taken up to 5 pounds). Skiing and snowshoeing in winter. Self-guided trails, both walking and auto, and guided tour each summer evening. Films, slide shows, and exhibits at visitor center.

Where to stay: MOTELS—Limited accommodations at nearby Seney and Germfask; standard motel accommodations at Newberry (30 miles east) and Manistique (35 miles southwest). CAMPGROUNDS—Several state forest campgrounds within 10-mile radius of refuge. Excellent private campground in nearby Germfask and in Newberry (30 miles east).

Weather notes: Moderate for latitude due to location between two Great Lakes—subzero weather is unusual in winter—but snow accumulations may reach several feet.

What to take and wear: Not always needed but best to have along—good boots and raingear.

Points of interest nearby: Pictured Rocks National Seashore, Munising; Hiawatha National Forest; Indian Lake; Big Spring and Tahquamenon Falls State Parks.

For more information: Seney National Wildlife Refuge, Star Route, Seney, Michigan 49883. Phone: (906) 586-9851.

SHERBURNE
★

● ⟩Minneapolis

SHERBURNE (Minnesota)

Sherburne, 30,479 acres of wetland, woodland, and upland situated
on a large glacial outwash plain in central Minnesota, became a refuge largely as a result of citizen action—conservationists and sportsmen's organizations who knew of its history as a lush wildlife area,
and petitioned the government to set it aside and restore it to its
original condition.

This was done in 1965, and the land finally was accumulated and
purchased ten years later. Work remains to be done, in planting and
establishing marshes and impoundments and making them hospitable to a balanced wildlife population. But much can be seen here.

Deer are abundant, along with such other mammals as ground
squirrels, both the Richardson's and the attractive little thirteen-
lined; pocket gophers, their mounds seen everywhere (though the
gophers are not, except at night); and occasionally fox, coyote,
badger, and porcupine.

Hawks appear in good numbers during fall migration (September–November)—especially marsh and Cooper's hawks, which
also have nested here; and red-tailed and kestrels are common to
abundant through the seasons. Common waterfowl, which also nest
here, are mallard, blue- and green-winged teal, shoveler, wood ducks,
loons, pied-billed grebes, and Canada geese, with a captive goose
flock planned as the nucleus of a future wild population. Bitterns are

common through the warmer months, as are great blue and green herons, some of which fan out from a sizable heronry located near St. Cloud. Swans and sandhill cranes migrate through, and a few of the cranes stay to nest.

Woodpeckers, especially the red-headed, are colorful and commonly seen. So are bluebirds, for which several hundred homes have been put up on the refuge, and rose-breasted grosbeaks and indigo buntings.

There are roads open to auto touring and hiking trails, and the Mahnomen Trail winds through the site of a prehistoric Indian village, partly excavated, believed to date back 6,500 to 10,000 years.

There is also a ski trail in winter, which is a beautiful but cold season (see *Weather Notes*). Horned larks are common, along with goldfinches, nuthatches, hairy and downy woodpeckers, and occasional visits by rough-legged hawks, goshawks, and snowy owls. Specialties reported on the Christmas Bird Count include a Lewis' woodpecker, Townsend's solitaire, black-backed three-toed woodpecker, and Bohemian waxwing. Screech and short-eared owls stay all year.

Wild flowers are beautiful—whole fields of snowy pasqueflowers in spring, followed by blue spiderworts, showy butterfly weeds and the purple and pink milkweeds, coneflowers in the prairie areas, and purple asters in fall.

Occasionally the refuge has a bumper crop of wild rice, when it grows so thickly the waterfowl cannot easily get in and use it. Then it is opened up to public harvesting, in the Indian manner, with one person propelling the boat, the other bending the stalks and shaking loose the kernels. Part of the rice must be given to the refuge, which uses it to reseed. This occurs in late August, and is so popular the refuge plans to repeat the practice in years of plenteous crops.

Sherburne also administers the Round Lake Waterfowl Production Area, a two-hundred-acre wild tract with wetlands, but with no public facilities, located near Arden Hills, southeast of the refuge.

How to get there: From Minneapolis-St. Paul (about 50 miles southeast) take Highway 169 north to refuge sign, 4.5 miles north of Zimmerman; then west 5 miles to refuge.

Open: Daylight hours every day year-round.

Best times to visit: Mid-April to mid-May, and October, for wild flowers and migrants. Fall colors peak usually first half of October.

What to see: Waterfowl; abundant red-headed woodpeckers, kestrels, black-billed cuckoos, bluebirds, loons, ruffed grouse, deer, ground squirrels, both Richardson's and thirteen-lined. Occasional foxes. Pocket gophers, their mounds omnipresent. Prehistoric Indian mounds.

What to do: Auto and hiking trails; fishing and hunting; showshoeing and ski trails in winter. Canoeing when water conditions permit. Photography blinds available. Harvesting wild rice when there's a bumper crop; and gathering of berries, cherries, mushrooms, and nuts in designated areas. Hunting for small and big game and waterfowl; fishing for walleye and northern pike (up to 27 inches) according to state regulations.

Where to stay: MOTELS—At Princeton, 10 miles northeast; Monticello, 15 miles south; Elk River, 20 miles southeast; St. Cloud, 25 miles west. CAMPGROUNDS—Sand Dunes State Forest, immediately south of refuge; several others within 4 miles on roads east, west, and south of refuge.

Weather notes: Spring is a short season, last half of April—after that weather can be hot and sticky. Can be quite cold in winter (propane gas sometimes solidifies in tanks) but beautiful—dress warmly.

What to take and wear: Well-insulated clothing in winter (see *Weather Notes*); prepare for heat and humidity in summer.

Points of interest nearby: Sand Dunes States Forest, just south of refuge.

For more information: Sherburne National Wildlife Refuge, Route 2, Zimmerman, Minnesota 55398. Phone: (612) 389-3323.

SHIAWASSEE ★

Flint

SHIAWASSEE (Michigan)

Some seven thousand whistling swans stop over every spring at Shiawassee, a sight that one refuge manager found "like thinking of heaven, you get a peaceful state of mind just seeing them feeding and flying by."

It is awesome to see such a congregation of these graceful birds with seven-foot wingspreads, filling the air with their muffled, musical whistling calls, whitening the fields and skies with their family groups as they pause for a month between mid-March and mid-April to rest and feed between their wintering grounds along the Atlantic Coast and their nesting areas thousands of miles away to the Northwest, some of them north of the Arctic Circle.

Shiawassee, largely an 8,900-acre diked flood plain at the point where six rivers come together to flow into Saginaw Bay, attracts many other forms of wildlife, however. Ducks and geese peak in their fall migrations at about eighteen thousand geese (mostly Canadas but also good numbers of snow and blue geese) and fifty thousand ducks. The ducks are mostly black and mallard, but also wigeon and teal, pintail, wood duck, merganser, and a few others.

The geese begin coming in spring as early as February, the ducks shortly afterward, and their passage through continues until about mid-April. Fall migration starts in mid-September and continues until December, birds constantly coming and leaving so that the number present at any one time is only a small indicator of the tens of thousands streaming through. (Swans are a spring phenomenon, taking a different route on the fall journey.)

Shiawassee has a well-marked, five-mile self-guided walking wildlife trail, in three loops for those who wish to take it a little at a time. Visitors can view many of these sights from the trail, and some others as well. In the spring, fawns, young woodchuck and fox families play about the trail area. (It is, of course, necessary to walk quietly in order not to startle them.) In all seasons there are white-tailed deer from the refuge herd of several hundred feeding in the early morning and at dusk.

Young broods of ducks and geese (most of the geese are the maxima, or giant race of Canadas) are around most of the refuge waters by early summer, as are American bitterns and great blue and green herons, the latter such common nesters they often set up housekeeping in local backyards. A great blue heron colony supports 150–200 nests every year plus a few great egrets. Other common summer residents include red-tailed, marsh, and broad-winged hawks, killdeer, sora, coot, swallows (tree, bank, barn, and rough-winged), rose-breasted grosbeaks, redstarts, brown thrashers, kingfishers, common and black terns. Among the shorebirds are dowitchers and spotted sandpipers.

Most years one can see a bald eagle family, operating from a nest in the area, from February through November, carrying off a fish or occasionally an unlucky muskrat. And in winter, visitors can readily sight horned larks and ring-necked pheasant (both commonly present all year) along with tree sparrows and snow buntings, and a few snowy owls.

There is fishing in the area for pike in the rivers, for perch all year in Saginaw Bay (through the ice in winter), and for chinook and coho salmon which spawn in the fall and winter in the Cass, Shiawassee, and Flint rivers. Water quality has been poor but is improving. A limited-permit goose hunt is managed jointly with the adjacent Shiawassee State Game Area, with steel shot shells required. Winter skiing is available at resorts within fifty or a hundred miles of the refuge in all directions.

Subrefuges also administered by Shiawassee include the following:

Wyandotte, actually two islands in the Detroit River near Wyandotte. It was formerly an important resting feeding place for waterfowl. Poor water quality has cut its use in recent years.

Lake St. Clair includes some four thousand acres of shallow water and marsh on Lake St. Clair near Detroit, a resting area for ducks. Fishing is permitted but not hunting.

Michigan Islands consists of five small islands totaling 364 acres, established for herons, gulls, and terns. Three—Scarecrow, Pismire, and Shoe—are designated wilderness areas. The public is permitted but no disturbance whatever is tolerated. Trips can be arranged from Beaver Island.

How to get there: Take State Route 13 from Saginaw, 7 miles to refuge.

Open: From 8 A.M. to 4:30 P.M. weekdays.

Best times to visit: Spring (March–May) and fall (October–November).

What to see: Large numbers of migrating swans in spring, and congregations of geese and ducks in spring and fall; fox families, deer and fawns along dikes.

What to do: Self-guided nature trail with good photographic opportunities in season. Fishing in rivers for pike, and in Cass, Shiawassee, and Flint rivers for fall-winter spawning chinook and coho salmon, in Saginaw Bay for perch year-round, through ice in winter. A limited-permit goose hunt on refuge each fall. Ski resorts within 50–100 miles of refuge in all directions.

Where to stay: MOTELS—A number in Saginaw and nearby. CAMPGROUNDS—Several in Saginaw but often crowded. Otherwise find one between Vassar and Mayville, 40 miles from refuge.

Weather notes: Usually no temperature extremes, but road conditions can close the nature trail for periods in the spring.

What to take and wear: Waterproof boots and hiking boots are recommended.

Points of interest nearby: Shiawassee State Game Area, adjoining to the west.

For more information: Shiawassee National Wildlife Refuge, 6975 Mower Road, Saginaw, Michigan 48601. Phone: (517) 777-5930.

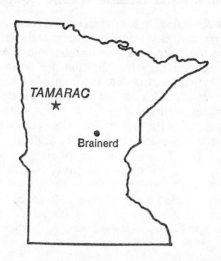

TAMARAC (Minnesota)

Most of the 42,725 acres in this northeast Minnesota refuge has never seen a plow, and there is a feeling of wildness about it best expressed by the yelping howl of the coyote, commonly heard at dawn and dusk throughout the year, and the cry of the nesting loon through most of spring and summer.

The person standing at one of the many historical spots where Indians have buried their dead and battled over this lush territory where rice grew thickly and wild game flourished can have the feeling of going centuries back in time, as if almost nothing has changed since the Sioux and Chippewa contended there.

And indeed, though the mightiest stands of timber have been cut over, much remains that is the same.

Chippewas still harvest wild rice in the ancient way—one man guiding the canoe, the other pulling the stalks over with flails and tapping them to let the ripe kernels fall in the boat, filling a canoe with as much as three hundred pounds of grain.

A quiet visitor can see deer and beaver. Beaver lodges are usually located in Jim's Marsh and various other places visible from the road as well as porcupine, muskrat, mink, otter, black bear, and a few bobcat and moose, and, rarely, timber wolves.

In recent years there have been at least two producing nests of bald eagles, eight nesting pairs of ospreys, and three great blue heron colonies, the largest with seventy-five nests.

Flat Lake, in back of refuge headquarters, one of two dozen lakes and impoundments on the refuge, has so many northern pike spawning each year that up to a hundred thousand are taken out each winter to stock other lakes (since Flat is so shallow that winter often kills most of its population).

Fall foliage colors, with the golden birches and aspens, crimson maples and sumac and maroon oaks, are so brilliant (usually peaking about October 1) that even refuge personnel who have seen them many times say the sight in the fall sunlight "makes you want to squint your eyes."

Bohemian waxwings sometimes come in flocks of thirty or forty to devour the scarlet fruits of the mountain ash trees.

Many of the wild flowers along the roads and in back areas may be descendants of those that grew a century or more ago in this undisturbed land—prairie lilies, showy lady's slippers, Indian paintbrushes, marsh marigolds, asters—one twenty-acre bog swamp is often almost covered with lady's slippers in the spring. And there are flowering shrubs—serviceberry, chokecherry, highbush cranberry, wild plum—something blooming during the whole growing season, with morel mushrooms popping up almost anytime under the quaking aspens (though more in spring).

Part of the reason for the great variety of flora and fauna is the wide-ranging habitat, from shallow lakes, scrub swamp and bog, woodland potholes in all stages of succession, up through second-growth aspen and hazel brush, forests of upland and lowland northern hardwoods, and red, white, and jack pine.

Ducks and geese come in good numbers. One of the great sights is the scaup, which often migrate from west to east, and show up sometimes in flights of forty thousand, especially in late October. But there are also canvasback, ring-necked, redhead, and wigeon—up to fifty thousand of these; and the returning nesters, the wood ducks, mallard, goldeneye, and blue-winged teal. Wood ducks, often called our most beautiful duck, are a breath-taking sight in nuptial plumage and some years are the most common breeding waterfowl on the refuge, making homes in natural tree cavities (often old pileated woodpecker holes) and producing as many as two thousand young. (Spring migrants start through after snow melt in late March and peak about May 10; fall migration begins in September and peaks about October 20.)

Summer brings waterfowl broods on the lakes, and a prime sighting is that of a parent loon in stunning black and white breeding plumage, with two or three downy youngsters riding on its back or nestled under a wing, only the tiny head peeking out. Ruffed grouse, after their courtship drumming rituals, lead their fluffy young along woodland trails.

And while winter can be extremely cold—the record is minus 46° F., and frost is possible in every month of the year—it is, as the saying goes, a dry cold, with little wind, so that subzero weather here seems not so bitter as elsewhere. It is a beautiful season—not only the glittering ice and snow-laden landscape, but the colorful magpies, purple finches, redpolls, blue and gray jays, grosbeaks—sometimes a feeder will be visited by four hundred at one time. Sometimes there are goshawks, snowy owls and crossbills along with gray partridge and northern and three-toed woodpeckers.

There are two hiking trails, each a little more than a mile long, a five-mile ski trail, and fifteen miles of roads.

Tamarac also administers two small island subrefuges in Hungry Lake, ten miles to the south—wild areas with public access but no visitor facilities.

How to get there: From Fargo, North Dakota, take Highway 10 for 45 miles east to Detroit Lakes, Minnesota, then Highway 34 for 8 miles east to Becker County ✕29, then 10 miles north to the refuge.

Open: Daylight hours every day all year; weather permitting.

Best times to visit: Spring and fall.

What to see: Great variety of wildlife, both mammals and birds, including bald and golden eagles, wood and goldeneye ducks, loons, deer, beaver, bear. Spectacular fall foliage. Wild flowers in profusion from early spring on, including lady's slippers. Fall harvest of wild rice by Chippewa Indians, mid-August to early September.

What to do: Photography is for the patient—thick foliage in summer interferes with light and viewing—but the subjects are here. Limited hunting and fishing, for deer, upland game, and waterfowl; walleye up to 10 pounds and northern pike up to 18 pounds (ice fishing in winter). Cross-country skiing. No snowmobiles. Hiking and auto trails.

Where to stay: MOTELS—A number in Detroit Lakes, 18 miles southwest. CAMPGROUNDS—On Shell Lake and Island Lake, east of refuge (both tents and vehicles). Also Buffalo Lake just west of refuge, and many in Detroit Lakes area.

Weather notes: Extremely cold in winter. Short heavy thunderstorms can occur in June and July.

What to take and wear: Warmest clothing in winter, and at least a windbreaker most of the year (frost has been recorded in every month of the year here).

Points of interest nearby: Hubbel Pond State Wildlife Area, bordering refuge. Smokey Hills State Forest just east; Itasca State Park (headwaters of the Mississippi) 20 miles to the northeast. Several other state forests and numerous federal Waterfowl Production Areas are located within 30 miles.

For more information: Tamarac National Wildlife Refuge, Rural Route Box 66, Rochert, Minnesota 56578. Phone: (218) 847-4355.

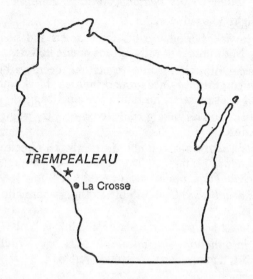

TREMPEALEAU

TREMPEALEAU (Wisconsin)

Much of this part of west south-central Wisconsin used to be known as the Trempealeau Prairie, a grassland with vegetation six feet tall supporting buffalo, elk, and prairie chickens, as well as Indian villages. Remnant stands of those original grasslands remain and major portions of the rest of this 707-acre refuge are being restored to that condition, affording opportunities to observe this unique type of habitat.

The best time to see prairie wild flowers, such as the tall gayfeather and others, is late summer. Birds such as the thrushes, flycatchers, woodpeckers, and swallows can be sighted earlier; ruffed grouse and quail and the refuge's mammal population—deer, fox, thirteen-lined ground squirrel, and a few badger—can be seen by the patient observer all year long.

The refuge has both auto and hiking trails with explanatory leaflets, and ski trails in winter. Guided tours and slide shows can be arranged for groups by contacting the refuge manager in advance.

How to get there: From Winona, Minnesota, cross river on Minnesota Highway 43 to Wisconsin Highway 35, then southwest 8 miles, then south 1 mile to entrance.

Open: Daylight hours all year.

Best times to visit: Spring and fall for warblers and small birds migrating. Midsummer to early fall for prairie flowers.

What to see: Distinctive prairie vegetation; deer; warblers; grouse; Bell's vireos; thirteen-lined ground squirrels; black squirrels (color phase of fox squirrels), fox, and occasional badger.

What to do: Auto and hiking trails; cross-country skiing, snowshoeing in winter.

Where to stay: MOTELS—A number in nearby La Crosse, Wisconsin, and Winona, Minnesota. CAMPGROUNDS—Facilities available in Perrot State Park, 3 miles east of refuge.

What to take and wear: Comfortable clothing—normally no weather extremes.

Points of interest nearby: Perrot State Park, hiking trails.

For more information: Trempealeau National Wildlife Refuge, Route ⅟1, Trempealeau, Wisconsin 54661.

Minneapolis

UPPER MISSISSIPPI
(Headquarters)

UPPER MISSISSIPPI RIVER WILDLIFE AND FISH REFUGE (Minnesota Headquarters)

A tragic boating accident led to the establishment in 1924 of this 284-mile-long refuge which includes the Mississippi River and lands alongside it from the mouth of the Chippewa River at Wabasha, Minnesota, to Rock Island, Illinois.

While Will Dilg, a Chicago advertising executive who founded the Izaak Walton League and whose son drowned in the river while the two were fishing, does not deserve sole credit—there were many who helped—he was a prime mover. There is a statue in his honor in Winona, but his major monument is the refuge itself—enjoyed by millions of persons annually in activities ranging from bird-watching and photography to cross-country skiing on its borders, fishing, boating, and camping on its island sandbars.

It is a stunning and unique example of what a national wildlife refuge can be, sheltering some 270 species of birds, 50 mammals, 45 amphibians and reptiles, and 113 kinds of fish, as well as uncounted interesting plant varieties in its 194,000 acres.

A large percentage of the world's population of canvasback ducks can be seen during fall migration in some of the pools near La Crosse, Wisconsin, and a hundred bald eagles in late fall around the waters near Lansing, Iowa. Colonies of herons and egrets, some of them sheltering several hundred nests, occur every twenty miles or so along its length, which crosses the boundaries of four states—Iowa, Minnesota, Wisconsin, and Illinois. Occasional endangered peregrine falcons are seen—and because of its central position between the Atlantic and Central flyways, and north and south, it has wildlife overlapping from wide areas—eastern and western meadowlarks, redwinged and yellow-headed blackbirds, great blue and yellow-crowned night herons.

The best way to see the refuge is by boat—almost any kind of boat. A houseboat can tie up to sandbars at night, and be let through locks in the dams which have been built at intervals along its length. There are boat ramps along the shore at frequent intervals, and detailed maps of the river and refuge land areas and visitor facilities available from refuge headquarters and the various district offices. A nine-foot navigation channel is kept open by dredging by the U. S. Corps of Engineers, which cooperates with the U. S. Fish and Wildlife Service and consulting environmental interests in managing refuge lands and waters. Dredge spoil has built up some of the islands used by wildlife and by campers.

But it can be seen very well also from the continuous system of highways known as the Great River Road which closely follows its boundaries, with many pull-offs for observing wildlife (a spotting scope as well as binoculars would be helpful here) as well as superb views of the bluffs which in places rise sheer for five hundred feet or so from the river bed. Especially notable outlooks are from bluffs at Winona and LaCrescent, Minnesota; Alma, La Crosse, and Cassville, Wisconsin; Lansing, McGregor, and Dubuque, Iowa; and Savanna, Illinois. Fall colors peak around mid-October to early November.

With a canoe, put in the river at almost any point, you can explore wilderness-like sloughs and backwaters containing beaver, muskrat, otter, and visited by fishing herons and egrets, rails, and in spring and fall, warbler migrations along the upland edges. It is a wondrous experience to meander in a boat through blossoming water lilies and lotuses in June—fields as large as forty acres covered by the white and golden blossoms. Later in the fall, muskrats build their domelike winter homes of dying sagittaria stalks. Getting back in the bottomland backwater sloughs "you could almost get lost," said one who had been there (the charts are well marked, however)— "you're all by yourself and you almost feel like a wilderness explorer. It's another world. You feel as if you've gone back a little bit in time."

White-tailed deer are numerous and sometimes swim out to the islands. One can camp on these islands for as long as fourteen days, without a permit.

Colorful wood ducks nest in great numbers along the bluffs—the river is a major breeding area for them (some two thousand young are produced each spring) and for a number of other waterfowl species. Thousands of whistling swans come through in migration, gathering on the Weaver Marsh north of Winona.

The diversity is due partly to the varied habitat around the dams —deep water in pools just behind the dams; wide marshes of sagittaria, wild celery, and bulrushes; and timbered areas in the drier parts just below the dam.

As a result, both diving and dabbling ducks are attracted—teal, wigeon, shoveler—scaup, goldeneye, bufflehead—and shorebirds such as spotted sandpipers nest in numbers.

Whip-poor-wills occur commonly; also barred and great horned owls, yellow-billed and black-billed cuckoos, five kinds of woodpeckers, five kinds of swallows, rose-breasted grosbeaks, bluebirds, waxwings, vireos, red-tailed hawks, and numbers of others.

Fishing is good all year for bluegill, crappie, catfish, and others— bass up to eight pounds, walleyes to fifteen.

There are nature trails all along the way, and good photographic opportunities (though it is a good idea to have a portable blind for serious work). One of the best of these for observing is Lansing, where sometimes fifty or sixty bald eagles, and occasionally a golden eagle, will gather in fall or spring migration, and a dozen or so will stay the winter. Patience will allow fairly close-range observation and the refuge managers can advise where the eagles have been seen recently.

The district offices also have excellent checklists of birds, mammals, reptiles, and amphibians found in the areas.

How to get there: Refuge lands and waters extend on both sides of the Mississippi River from Wabasha, Minnesota, to Rock Island, Illinois. Boat landings are located all along the river; district offices at six locations (see below).

Open: Daily all year.

Best times to visit: Spring and fall for migrants; early summer for nesting and resident birds and flowering water plants; late fall for migrating eagles.

What to see: Great range of wildlife—some of the standouts being great concentrations of canvasback ducks as well as other waterfowl; swans, herons, and egrets; migrating and wintering eagles; deer, otter, beaver, muskrat, mink.

What to do: Photography, boating, camping, swimming, picnicking, waterskiing, fishing year-round and hunting in season on specific areas. Boats available for rental at marinas in most areas.

Where to stay: MOTELS—Many; in communities along river. CAMP-GROUNDS—A number, both public and private, along river; also camping permitted on river islands. Contact refuge offices.

Weather notes: Spring and summer best; summers can be sticky in lower portion, and winters below zero even in south, with humidity and winds making it seem even colder.

What to take and wear: Waterproof gear and protective coverings for binoculars and camera equipment in boats.

Points of interest nearby: Many scenic outlooks along the way with spectacular views of bluffs and river course, especially when fall foliage colors peak in October. Also a number of state parks—as, Effigy Mounds National Monument at McGregor, Iowa, and Mississippi Palisades State Park near Savanna, Illinois, both with extraordinary scenic views.

For more information:

Upper Mississippi River Wild Life and Fish Refuge, 122 West Second Street, Winona, Minnesota 55987. Phone: (507) 452-4232.

Upper Mississippi River Wild Life and Fish Refuge, Savanna District P.O. Box 250, Savanna, Illinois 61074. Phone: (815) 273-2732.

Upper Mississippi River Wild Life and Fish Refuge, Cassville District, P.O. Box 51, Cassville, Wisconsin 53806. Phone: (608) 725-5198.

Upper Mississippi River Wild Life and Fish Refuge, LaCrosse District, Room 208, Post Office Building, Box 415, LaCrosse, Wisconsin 54601. Phone: (608) 782-6039.

Upper Mississippi River Wild Life and Fish Refuge, Lansing District, P.O. Box 128, Lansing, Iowa 52151. Phone: (319) 533-4850.

Upper Mississippi River Wild Life and Fish Refuge, Winona District, Route One, Trempealeau, Wisconsin 54661. Phone: (608) 539-3620.

V. THE MID-SOUTH

The predominant habitat of the mid-South refuges is hardwood bottomland. It occurs mostly along rivers that feed into the Mississippi and into which, quite frequently, the Mississippi backs up and overflows. The characteristic trees of this habitat, such as bitter pecan and overcup oak, provide rich forage for a variety of nut- and seed-eating creatures which in turn are food for predators like raccoons, bobcat, and occasional black bear and cougar. Intermittent flooding has kept these bottomlands mostly unpeopled and wild—in some cases the visitor can see what the Indians saw but only by the same means the Indians saw it, by traveling on foot or by canoe.

The mid-South also has a number of interesting refuges surrounding or overlaying man-made reservoirs—created rather than preserved wildlife oases—and three extraordinary Gulf Coast refuges. Among them they provide habitat for a wide variety of wildlife.

TENNESSEE

Tennessee, the northernmost state in this region, has four national wildlife refuges, all lying in the western half of the state. *Reelfoot,* along the Kentucky border, was formed by a great earthquake in 1811 and 1812 which caused the forty-five-square-mile basin to fall thirty-five to forty feet and the waters of the Mississippi to rush in like a tidal wave to fill it. It is one of the best places in the United States for endangered bald eagles, wintering between one hundred and two hundred each year. It also has an extraordinary warbler migration. *Hatchie* is 11,555 acres of bottomland locally best known for its large population of wintering waterfowl. It also boasts excellent warbler migrations, particularly for such as the blue-winged, magnolia, chestnut-sided, bay-breasted and rare Swainson's. *Tennessee* Refuge is an overlay on TVA's Kentucky Lake. Wild turkey are seen year-round here along with both bald and golden eagles in winter.

Cross Creeks is rolling hills, rock bluffs, and rich bottomland. Noted primarily for wintering waterfowl, it also has good spring and fall shorebird and songbird migrations.

ARKANSAS

Arkansas is one of the nation's richest states in terms of wildlife. *Big Lake* and *Wapanocca* are both located in the northeastern corner of the state near the Mississippi River. Both have beautiful stands of virgin cypress and are particularly advantageous to see by boat. *Holla Bend* in the northwest is noted for its summer population of scissor-tailed flycatchers. *White River* in the east-central part of the state is in what is often called the duck capital of the world. Its hardwood bottomlands provide habitat for black bear, white tailed deer, and turkey, and good nesting populations of such small birds as cerulean, prothonotary, parula, and yellow-throated warblers. Mississippi kites are common in spring and summer and in a good year up to two thousand wood storks may visit the refuge. *Felsenthal*, just above the Louisiana border, is a true wilderness with limited visitor facilities but excellent wildlife, including alligators, bobcat, river otter, gray and red fox, and probably the endangered eastern cougar.

MISSISSIPPI

Mississippi has three primary national wildlife refuges, each quite distinct. *Yazoo* near the western border has a spectacular wood duck population, producing around twelve thousand of this most beautiful bird each year, and they are everywhere on the refuge. It also is one of the few places where the cougar is regularly reported—every two weeks or so. *Hillside*, at the eastern edge of the delta, is still being developed. It has good populations of wintering waterfowl along with year-round deer, coyote, and bobcat. *Noxubee*, in eastern Mississippi, has one of the nation's largest populations of red-cockaded woodpeckers and excellent numbers of wild turkey and deer in a beautiful and rich habitat reclaimed from a near biological desert.

ALABAMA

Wheeler in Alabama was the first national wildlife refuge to be created on a power reservoir—part of TVA's Wheeler Reservoir in 1938. It is excellent not only for waterfowl but also for muskrat, beaver, bobcat, and fox, and has an unusually interesting population of bats, including two endangered species. *Eufaula* on the Alabama-Georgia border has been called by the Georgia Ornithological Society one of the ten best birding areas in the state.

Choctaw in the southwestern part of the state is still relatively un-developed. It is notable for its extensive (several thousand nests) cattle egret heronry in a cypress lagoon across from the field office.

LOUISIANA

Louisiana was Audubon's favorite state and even today one can see why. Its refuges are rich and extensive. *D'Arbonne*, almost on the Arkansas border, is still in development with very limited trails. An excellent canoe or boat trip can be made through D'Arbonne Bayou —fifteen miles of stream through high banks of mosses and ferns timbered with cypress and bitter pecan, overcup oak and tupelo. *Catahoula*, just north of Alexandria, is a restored bottomland hard-wood area noted both for waterfowl and good populations of some of the more spectacular small birds such as prothonotary warblers, painted and indigo buntings, and orchard and northern orioles. *Sabine* and *Lacassine* are coastal refuges along the western Gulf. Sabine is the larger and has besides waterfowl a population of some nine thousand alligators; roseate spoonbills are there year-round. Lacassine consists of about thirty-two thousand acres of which six-teen thousand are in a marsh known as Lacassine Pool. Its wintering populations of waterfowl reach 750,000 and its long-legged waders in summer are in the tens of thousands, including more than five thou-sand white-faced ibises.

Delta, at the very end of the Mississippi River and therefore of both the river and the Gulf, is forty-nine thousand acres of shallow ponds, bayous, and marsh with a bit of upland. It's remoteness and wild aspect, together with staggeringly prolific bird life, make it one of the nation's great refuges, but also one of the most difficult of ac-cess. While of interest all year, Delta is best in spring when thou-sands of migrating small birds drop in, often to their first landfall in hundreds of miles after their northward flight across the Gulf of Mexico.

The following is a list of some birds of special interest found in common or abundant status at the refuges of this region.

Birds Common or Abundant at Seasons Indicated:

S: Spring   s: Summer   F: Fall   W: Winter

White Pelican: Delta, SFW; Sabine, SFW.
Olivaceous Cormorant: Lacassine, SsFW; Sabine, SsFW.

Anhinga: Catahoula, SsFW; Delta, S; Lacassine, Ss.
Least Bittern: Catahoula, S; Delta, SsF; Eufaula, s; Lacassine, SsF;
    Reelfoot, SsF; Sabine, Ss; Wheeler, Ss.
Wood Stork: Catahoula, sF; Noxubee, s.
Glossy Ibis: Delta, SsFW.
White-faced Ibis: Delta, SsFW; Lacassine, Ss; Sabine, SsFW.
White Ibis: Catahoula, s; Delta, SsFW; Lacassine, Ss; Sabine, SsFW.
White-fronted Goose: Lacassine, SFW.
Fulvous Whistling Duck: Lacassine, SF.
Mottled Duck: Catahoula, FW; Delta, SsFW; Lacassine, SsFW;
    Sabine, SsFW.
Mississippi Kite: Reelfoot, sF; White River, Ss; Yazoo, Ss.
Cooper's Hawk: Tennessee, SsFW.
Golden Eagle: Tennessee, FW.
Peregrine Falcon: Delta, SFW; Holla Bend, SW.
Turkey: Hatchie, SsFW; Reelfoot, SsFW; Tennessee, SsFW;
    Waponocca, SsFW; White River, SsFW.
King Rail: Delta, SsFW; Lacassine, SsFW; Sabine, SsFW;
    Wheeler, SsF.
American Oystercatcher: Delta, Ss.
Wilson's Plover: Delta, SsF.
Piping Plover: Catahoula, SsFW.
American Golden Plover: Lacassine, S; Reelfoot, S.
Whimbrel: Delta, S.
Upland Sandpiper: Holla Bend, S; White River, S.
White-rumped Sandpiper: Delta, S; Sabine S.
Black-necked Stilt: Delta, SFW; Holla Bend, SF; Sabine, W;
    Wheeler, F.
Wilson's Phalarope: Holla Bend, SF.
Royal Tern: Delta, SsFW.
Caspian Tern: Delta, SsFW.
Black Skimmer: Delta, SsFW; Sabine, SsFW.
Ground Dove: Eufaula, SsFW.
Scissor-tailed Flycatcher: Holla Bend, SsF.
Western Kingbird: Delta, S.
Yellow-bellied Flycatcher: Delta, S.
Philadelphia Vireo: Delta, S.
Swainson's Warbler: Delta, S; White River, Ss.
Worm-eating Warbler: Delta, S; Hatchie, S.
Golden-winged Warbler: Delta, F.
Painted Bunting: Catahoula, SsF; Delta, SF; Yazoo, SsF.
Lincoln's Sparrow: Delta, S; Hatchie, S.

THE MID-SOUTH

1 Holla Bend
2 Big Lake
3 Wapanocca
4 White River
5 Felsenthal
6 Reelfoot
7 Cross Creeks
8 Tennessee
9 Hatchie
10 D'Arbonne

11 Catahoula
12 Sabine
13 Lacassine
14 Delta
15 Yazoo
16 Hillside
17 Noxubee
18 Wheeler
19 Choctaw
20 Eufaula

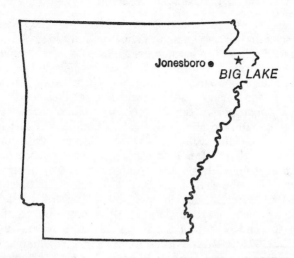

Jonesboro ● ★
BIG LAKE

BIG LAKE (Arkansas)

Big Lake Refuge, established in 1915, is one of the nation's oldest—
almost seven thousand acres made up of an intricate maze of creeks
and open water areas, virgin cypress-tupelo swamp and flooded timberland with a little upland twenty miles west of the Mississippi
River. It roughly surrounds the body of water for which it was
named. Almost every species of duck common to the Mississippi
Flyway can be here during migration, and some spend the winter—
mallard, pintail, wigeon, blue-winged teal, ring-necked, scaup, and
hooded merganser, sometimes twenty-five thousand at peak times,
along with as many as three thousand Canada geese.

There are good numbers of songbirds as well, especially during
spring migration when naturalists in recent years have made many
forays looking for a bird widely believed to spend at least some time
here: the exceedingly rare Bachman's warbler.

Until recently at least its presence had not been authenticated,
but their lists showed various other interesting residents and pass-
ersby: Lincoln's sparrows, Philadelphia and warbling vireos, Swainson's and gray-cheeked thrushes, rose-breasted and blue grosbeaks as
well as the more familiar dickcissels, gnatcatchers, crested flycatchers,
wood thrushes, towhees, ruby- and golden-crowned kinglets, brown
thrashers, loggerhead shrikes, prothonotary, Nashville, and black-
throated green warblers, and red-eyed and white-eyed vireos. Red-

shouldered and red-tailed hawks appear along with Cooper's; also barred and screech owls and numerous chuck-will's-widows.

In the past, Big Lake has been accessible only by boat—a fine trip in which the visitor can thread his or her way for miles (take a compass) through cypress swamps and bayous where beaver, muskrat, wood ducks, hooded mergansers, kingfishers, great blue herons, and six species of woodpeckers can be seen, as well as many of the warblers. But a dike road along the western boundary is due to be completed soon, and the visitor then will be able to view from this vantage as well with a better look at deer, opossum, raccoon, and other mammals commonly present (canoes are not appropriate as any wind roughens the shallow waters). Wintering waterfowl have always been visible from Route 18.

Big Lake, in many ways similar to Wapanocca Refuge to the south, is at the end of one of the largest drainage systems in the world—the St. Francis River Basin Project, 215 miles long and 53 miles wide. Until recently five canals drained into it, bringing silt and pesticide-laden water. Fishing, once outstanding, deteriorated. A restructuring now has created a bypass whereby in all but floodtimes, these do not enter the refuge, and the situation, including the fishing, has improved (though occasional high floodwaters still are a hazard).

How to get there: From Memphis take I-55 north to Exit 21; then Route 140 west to 181, north on 181 and west on Route 18 to refuge headquarters, just past floodway bridge.

Open: Daylight hours all year (however, waterways are closed in winter as sanctuary to wintering waterfowl).

Best times to visit: Spring and fall.

What to see: Wintering waterfowl; virgin cypress stands; songbirds; and someday, it is hoped, the Bachman's warbler.

What to do: Boating (rentals available at adjacent Mallard Lake); walking and driving road, due to open soon; limited hunting for squirrel, raccoon; fishing good for bass, bream, crappie.

Where to stay: MOTELS—Blytheville, 15 miles west; and West Memphis. CAMPGROUNDS—Big Lake Wildlife Management Area, adjacent to refuge.

Points of interest nearby: Big Lake Wildlife Management Area (see CAMPGROUNDS)—includes Mallard Lake, which holds state record for largemouth bass. Also Wapanocca National Wildlife

Refuge, 50 miles south; White River National Wildlife Refuge, 125 miles south.

For more information: Big Lake National Wildlife Refuge, P.O. Box 67, Big Lake, Arkansas 72442. Phone: (501) 564-2429.

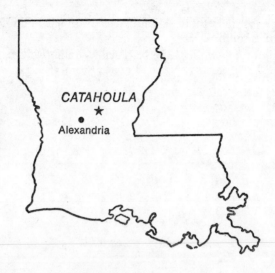

CATAHOULA
★
● Alexandria

CATAHOULA (Louisiana)

Prothonotary warblers, those small birds of wet woodlands whose orange-gold plumage matches the robes of the papal notaries or scribes of the Roman Catholic Church (from which their name derives), sometimes nest in boxes vacated by bluebirds outside the headquarters of this refuge. The area covers 5,308-acres of river delta bottomland hardwoods in south-central Louisiana. The warblers are only one of numbers of creatures which appreciate this habitat.

Beaver are busily at work on dams in Cowpen Bayou, stopping only occasionally to bask atop their lodges—their workings always visible. Visitors often see deer. Waterfowl concentrations through the winter months fill the air with birds—moving between the refuge and adjacent Catahoula Lake—beginning with pintail, mallard, blue- and green-winged teal, gadwalls, wigeon, and later the divers such as ring-necked, canvasback, scaup, along with snow and a few white-fronted geese.

This is an historic waterfowl area, as piles of bones in old Indian heaps indicate, and Catahoula Lake was a resting (and consequently hunting) ground long before the refuge was established. With the addition of twelve-hundred-acre Duck Lake on the refuge, it is expected to attract even more birds in future years.

Catahoula is an example of how a misused area can be restored and made a haven for natural inhabitants of all kinds. When acquired, it had been mostly cleared, the forest understory gone, a bare remnant of bottomland hardwoods that once covered the area for miles around. Now wildlife, finding good cover and food plants here, abound.

Small birds rest during migration and many stay to nest in the now-dense forest understory growth and upland areas—colorful painted and indigo buntings, cardinals, summer tanagers, orchard and northern orioles, meadowlarks, wood thrushes, Acadian flycatchers, yellow- and black-billed cuckoos, woodcocks, Carolina chickadees—all these in good numbers—along with hairy, downy, red-bellied, pileated, and some red-headed woodpeckers. Barred owls are common all year, and so are both red-shouldered and red-tailed hawks.

Anhingas, unusual for this area, are common seasonally feeding on crayfish along the bayou. Also common are great blue, little blue, green and yellow-crowned night herons, snowy and cattle egrets and wood storks, sometimes several hundred visiting the refuge at one time. Wood ducks are abundant, nesting both in natural tree cavities and nest boxes. There are also some bobcat, raccoon, opossum, skunk, nutria, otter, armadillo, delta fox squirrel, coyote, and a few fox.

In the past the refuge has had problems with water, the Mississippi River backing up and spreading over the area—once the refuge office was partly submerged by floodwater—and refuge roads were generally impassable to vehicles from November to April. But dikes, new buildings, and rerouting of roads are expected to change this and make the refuge open to travel most if not all the time. And the roads and trails are beautiful, winding along the bayous through old trees hung with Spanish moss. In any case, they are always open to foot travel—just bring boots, which are handy anyway for getting off and hiking the firebreaks to see small birds which seek more densely covered areas.

How to get there: From Alexandria, take Route 28 east to Route 84, then left 1 mile to refuge sign.

Open: Daylight hours.

Best times to visit: October through May—but check with refuge about winter road conditions during wet periods.

What to see: Beaver, deer, waterfowl, good small bird population (prothonotary warblers sometimes nest at refuge headquarters).

What to do: Walking and driving trails; observation towers and blinds; canoeing; limited hunting for squirrels, deer; fishing, especially in spring when timberlands flood, bass move in to spawn and minnow populations explode.

Where to stay: MOTELS—Alexandria, 40 miles southwest. CAMP-GROUNDS—North of refuge 2 miles; also in Saline Wildlife Management Area on adjoining Catahoula Lake.

Weather notes: Summers hot and humid, otherwise generally pleasant—but any heavy rainfall upstream creates possibility of river backup and flooding here.

What to take and wear: Waterproof footgear for walking, especially off-trails.

Points of interest nearby: Adjoining Catahoula Lake, historic waterfowl area; Saline Wildlife Management Area, on the lake; Kisatchie National Forest, near Alexandria.

For more information: Catahoula National Wildlife Refuge, P.O. Drawer LL, Jena, Louisiana 71342. Phone (318) 992-5261.

CHOCTAW (Alabama)

Choctaw Refuge is 4,218 acres of bottomland hardwoods and agricultural fields interspersed with lakes and sloughs on the Tombigbee River in southwestern Alabama where waterfowl and alligators find ideal habitat, for it is flooded much of the time. Sometimes even the refuge field headquarters is an island, the only high ground in the area and reachable only by boat. Then even the numerous beaver, their homes inundated by water levels which can rise thirteen feet overnight when the Mississippi backs into the Tombigbee (it can happen any time between October and April, even without a local rain), seek driftwood islands, to return later with the deer and wild turkey to live off the food plants in the fertile woodlands when they are dry.

Choctaw is a relatively undeveloped refuge; its bird list is preliminary and the wildlife population still is being explored. Woodpeckers including sapsuckers, brown thrashers and cardinals are commonly observed; warblers find the refuge hospitable in spring. Cattle egrets have an impressive rookery of several thousand nests in a cypress lagoon across from the field office, the white birds and their young families almost covering the trees and audible at some distance with their noisy squabbles from mid-May to June (a silent alligator often waiting underneath for one of the unsteady young to make a mis-step).

Red-tailed and red-shouldered hawks are common. So are fire ants, which show their indomitable survival instincts (which no one doubted) during floodtimes, when large clusters of them are seen clinging together in floating clumps on the water, the bottom ones drowning but the top ones making it through to form a new colony when the waters recede.

A trip to this refuge should follow a check with the refuge office to learn which areas are open, and whether a car or boat or on foot is the appropriate mode of travel.

How to get there: From Jackson (refuge office) go northwest on Route 69 to Coffeeville; west on 84, turning right or north to Barrytown; at "T" turn right through Womack Hill to Lenoir Landing turnoff, and right 2 miles to refuge.

Open: Daylight hours (but parts of refuge closed most of the year for waterfowl sanctuary or poor driving conditions—best check with refuge office which is open weekdays).

Best times to visit: Late fall, early spring.

What to see: Wood ducks, turkeys, woodpeckers, beaver.

What to do: Nature observation from refuge roads—or waterways, as the case may be, since the entire refuge is flooded at times (usually dry May to September). Boating (obviously) and fishing—some say the best in three states—for white and black bass, crappie, bream, and catfish.

Where to stay: MOTELS—In Jackson. CAMPGROUNDS—Bladon Springs State Park, 26 miles south.

What to take and wear: Sturdy waterproof footgear.

Points of interest nearby: Salt Springs Game Sanctuary, 13 miles south of Jackson (noted for wild turkey; permission required from state conservation department for entry).

For more information: Choctaw National Wildlife Refuge, 2704 Westside College Avenue, Jackson, Alabama 36545. Phone: (205) 246-3583.

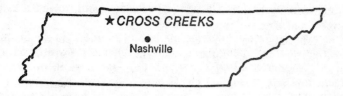

Nashville

★CROSS CREEKS

CROSS CREEKS (Tennessee)

Cross Creeks Refuge is a beautiful area of rolling hills and high rocky bluffs around 8,862 acres of rich bottomland in north-central Tennessee where thousands of waterfowl stop and spend the winter. They begin to arrive in October when the hills are suffused with colors ranging from golds through deep reds of chestnut and red oak, maple, sweet-gum, and hickory, and continue building to a peak in December and January when there may be fifteen thousand Canada geese and seventy-five thousand ducks on the refuge ponds, creeks, and impoundments. This is one of the best times to be here.

One of the most exciting sights comes when the waterfowl seem to sense the coming of a cold front bringing cold rain or even sleet and snow. Refuge staff believe barometric pressure may give them the message; at any rate, they pile into some of the water areas, particularly those with sheltering woodlands and abundant food supplies—a favorite is Elk Reservoir—and thousands can be seen in flight at once, calling and settling and flying up again to seek a more advantageous spot to stay and rest and feed until the bad weather has passed.

Bald and golden eagles are usually present in small numbers in winter, and a few rough-legged hawks. Marsh hawks are common, along with red-tailed and red-shouldered, all year, preying on field rodents and rabbits. Barred owls are common, as are red-bellied, red-headed, downy, and a few pileated woodpeckers, and Carolina chickadees and tufted titmice in the wooded, brushy areas.

Local birding groups from Clarkesville and Nashville come out to Cross Creeks at least three times a year; first in December and January for the waterfowl—mostly Canada geese with a few snows and blues, and the ducks, primarily mallard but also black, gadwall, wigeon, teal, pintail, ring-necked, and scaup; then in March and April and again in mid-September and October for the migrants, which include shorebirds—yellowlegs, semipalmated plovers and pectoral, least, and solitary sandpipers—and songbirds such as Swainson's thrushes, tree swallows, and Tennessee, blackpoll, yellow-rumped, and black-throated green warblers.

Loggerhead shrikes are here all year, as are bluebirds, cardinals, meadowlarks, and goldfinches, and in all except winter, yellow-throated warblers, redstarts, red-eyed vireos, wood thrushes, and brown thrashers. There are lovely flowers in the spring, dotting the fields and hillsides with red, yellow, and purple in May and June.

Cross Creeks was established in 1962 to compensate for the loss of Kentucky Woodlands Refuge which was partly covered over when Barkley Dam was built for flood control. Fishing is good but not as good as formerly, due to still-frequent periodic flooding from the Cumberland River. It is a refuge where the visitor should not seek rare exotic species but a good population of small birds common to the area, and large numbers of waterfowl in season against a beautiful natural setting.

How to get there: From Clarkesville take Route 79 south to Dover, then left on Route 49 for 2.2 miles to County Road leading to refuge headquarters.

Open: Daylight all year (but some roads may be closed at various times for banding work or weather conditions; visitors are asked to check at office or adjacent manager's house).

Best times to visit: October through January.

What to see: Large waterfowl concentrations.

What to do: Twelve miles of auto and hiking trails. Fishing for bass, crappie, bream. Slide shows will be given for groups on prior arrangement.

Where to stay: MOTELS—in Dover; also Paris Landing State Park, 16 miles west (also has boats and marina). CAMPGROUNDS—Paris Landing State Park; also Land Between the Lakes, 10 miles west.

Weather notes: July through September can be very hot.

Points of interest nearby: Tennessee Refuge, 35 miles southwest; Fort Donelson National Battlefield Park, 4 miles south; Land Between the Lakes (see CAMPGROUNDS), numerous recreational facilities, (boating, swimming, horseback riding, trails).

For more information: Cross Creeks National Wildlife Refuge, Route 1, Box 229, Dover, Tennessee 37058. Phone: (615) 232-7477.

D'ARBONNE (Louisiana)

D'Arbonne Refuge, 17,421 acres of pinelands, hardwood bottomlands, and small lakes and ponds through which winds the scenic Bayou D'Arbonne, is sanctuary for the endangered red-cockaded woodpecker as well as for long-legged herons and egrets and various smaller birds. Numbers of beaver live in its wet areas, which are considerable since 90 per cent of the refuge can be flooded at times (the water level can fluctuate as much as thirty feet)—mostly in the spring but it can be any time between November and July with backup from the D'Arbonne River. (For this reason the refuge should be contacted about access during such times.)

White-tailed deer live here, as well as raccoon, opossum, bobcat and fox, coyote, some alligators, red-shouldered and red-tailed hawks, occasional ospreys and various songbirds; several species of woodpecker are in the forested sections.

D'Arbonne is of recent acquisition as a refuge, and facilities for visitors are mostly in the process of development. The trails are in a largely primitive state. More trails are planned, along with an observation tower overlooking concentrations of wintering ducks on watered bottomlands, boat launch ramps, and a headquarters with visitor center.

One of the best ways to see the area is by boating or canoeing down the D'Arbonne Bayou, which winds down about fifteen miles of twists and turns through the entire refuge from north to south, through high banks of mosses and ferns and areas timbered with tall cypress and bitter pecan, overcup oak and tupelo gum, with an occasional glimpse of some of the wildlife residents in a beautiful semi-wilderness setting.

How to get there: From Monroe take I-20 west. Exit at Mill Street (Route 143). Continue north on 143 about 13 miles to refuge entrance.

Open: Daylight hours.

Best times to visit: Spring and fall.

What to do: Nature observation; fishing; limited hunting; boating.

Where to stay: MOTELS—In Monroe. CAMPGROUNDS—In Kisatchie National Forest, west of refuge, and Cheniere State Park, south of refuge.

Points of interest nearby: Felsenthal Refuge, 40 miles north.

For more information: D'Arbonne National Wildlife Refuge, P.O. Box 3065, Monroe, Louisiana 71201. Phone: (318) 325-1735.

New Orleans

DELTA

DELTA (Louisiana)

Louisiana was the "favorite portion of the Union" for the great bird artist, John James Audubon, and some of the wondrous sights at Delta and Breton refuges offer ample reason why. Indeed, they may not be very different today from what he saw—hundreds of thousands of water birds finding rest, food, and nesting sanctuary on barrier islands in and around the delta where one of the longest rivers in the world empties into the sea. Sometimes they almost cover the brilliant sands and gold-green vegetation with their nests, and when they fly up they seem literally to fill the air—long-legged white egrets, red-billed skimmers, a great variety of shore and wading birds and immense concentrations of waterfowl. It is an experience that can leave the onlooker breathless.

Delta Refuge is forty-nine thousand acres of shallow ponds, bayous, marsh, and a bit of upland located in the mouth of the Mississippi; Breton Refuge, farther out in the Gulf, established as a refuge in 1904, is nine thousand acres of sandy beaches made up of the Breton Islands and the chain of Chandeleurs. Both are administered from headquarters located on Delta, and both can be reached only by boat. The forty-three-foot radar-equipped twin diesel *Skimmer II*, owned by the refuge, takes small groups of ten, twenty, or so out to see and explore Delta, and trips can be arranged any day in the week by contacting the refuge manager in advance (and sometimes smaller numbers can be combined with others to make up such a group).

Otherwise, visitors to Breton are on their own (though occasionally the refuge staff may permit company on a trip they are making anyway)—which means they need an extremely seaworthy craft, preferably with sleep-aboard capacity since no camping is allowed and it takes at least three and a half hours to the Chandeleurs (until recently, at least, there were no convenient boat rentals nearby). Visitors to Delta may take a canoe over on the *Skimmer II* and use it in the bayous, but this is not recommended on Breton and the Chandeleurs, and visitors to the latter are urged to consult the refuge on their plans.

Whatever the effort expended, the results are certain to make it seem worthwhile. The scene itself, a world of blue sky and sea, white sand and hundreds and sometimes thousands of birds visible at all times, is stunningly wild and beautiful. The list of birds to see which spend most if not all the year at one or both of these refuges is not only long but impressive in the great numbers seen.

For example: common and abundant species include frigatebirds, purple gallinules, white pelicans, peregrine falcons (not in large numbers but always here in season), red-tailed and red-shouldered hawks, ospreys, least and American bitterns, and eleven species of graceful ibises, herons, and egrets. Wintering waterfowl sometimes exceed a half million, including blue and snow geese and thirteen duck species. Nesting and commonly present shorebirds include oystercatchers, whimbrels, Wilson's plovers, pectoral and white-rumped sandpipers, least and Caspian terns, and many others (nesting areas are patrolled and protected from public disturbance).

Sea turtles nest on the Chandeleurs. Deer are present on Delta.

Some of the most impressive sights are in spring migration, when great numbers of small birds come in from across the Gulf, sometimes to their first landfall in hundreds of miles, weary and highly visible—rose-breasted and blue grosbeaks, indigo and painted buntings, scarlet and summer tanagers. There are as many as twenty-five warbler species, along with tremendous flights of tree swallows—sometimes sixty thousand, skimming over the inland ponds or just stopping to rest a little while before moving on north.

How to get there: From New Orleans, take Route 10 east to Gretna, then Route 23 south through Venice. Just beyond Venice turn left at stop sign to Delta-Breton Refuge boat dock.

Open: Daylight hours except during waterfowl season when refuge is closed.

Best times to visit: Fine sights all year but heavy fog can close in December through February.

What to see: Shore and wading birds and waterfowl, plus small birds in migrations (usually best in late March); also deer and nutria.

What to do: Boating (own boat or by arrangement on refuge boat, see text); photography; observation tower; sport shrimping and fishing, fresh and salt water depending on season and location, best in fall starting in September but good most of time for redfish up to 10 pounds, speckled and white trout, largemouth bass, others.

Where to stay: MOTELS—Limited and at least until recently somewhat spartan accommodations in Empire, 20 miles north of Venice. CAMPGROUNDS—None in immediate area.

Weather notes: Normally pleasant except for possible periods of fog and cool rain December–February and hurricane threats July–September (in this case, refuge is evacuated).

What to take and wear: Protective sun lotion; waterproof boots.

Points of interest nearby: Louisiana State Waterfowl Management Area—marsh, similar to refuge. Fort Jackson, interesting old river fortification about 4 miles north.

For more information: Delta-Breton National Wildlife Refuges, Venice, Louisiana 70091. Phone: (504) Pilottown 3-3232 (ask New Orleans toll operator for this mobile radio Pilottown number).

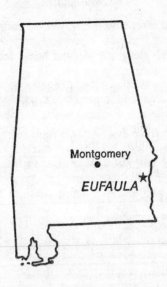

EUFAULA (Alabama-Georgia)

Eufaula Refuge, 11,160 acres of upland, woods, and marsh superimposed on Lake Walter F. George, a Corps of Engineers reservoir project in the Chattahoochee River at the southern boundary between Alabama and Georgia, has been called by the Georgia Ornithological Society one of the ten best bird walks in that state.

Its varied habitat, plus its agricultural fields planted largely in wildlife foods, give it an appeal to a broad spectrum of bird life, and others as well. Threatened alligators reproduce here. A sizable herd of white-tailed deer, often several dozen, wander around the roads in the early morning, with their spotted fawns starting in April. Raccoon, squirrel, chipmunk, and beaver (whose dams sometimes cause havoc at refuge water control structures) and lesser numbers of red and gray fox, otter, mink, and bobcat thrive in Eufaula.

Birders like it in spring and summer for bitterns, gallinules, wood ducks, and many kinds of shore and wading birds—commonly great and little blue herons, great and cattle egrets and black-crowned night herons, snipe, coot, killdeer, and both greater and lesser yellowlegs. In fall and winter, they suggest watching for high hawk populations, both bald and golden eagles, and varied duck and goose species—Canadas, here all year, along with some wintering snows, and duck concentrations that usually peak around forty thousand—

mallard predominant, but also black ducks, gadwall, pintail, blue-and green-winged teal, wigeon, shoveler, ring-necked, canvasback, bufflehead, ruddy, and merganser. Wood ducks are here all year and nest.

The annual Christmas Bird Count usually goes well over a hundred species; those noted in one recent year included, some in sizable numbers, brown-headed nuthatches, winter, Bewick's, and short-billed marsh wrens, hermit thrushes, cedar waxwings, ruby- and golden-crowned kinglets, bobwhite quail, woodcock, snipe, mourning and ground doves, Bonaparte's gulls, grasshopper, vesper, and Le Conte's sparrows, seven woodpecker species, seven hawks, and five kinds of owls.

The refuge is eye-pleasing as well, especially when golden lotus blooms cover large water areas, and wood ducks bring their downy broods to seek rest and shelter among their large bright green leaves.

How to get there: From Eufaula take Route 431 north about 10 miles to state park information office, then right 2.5 miles to refuge headquarters.

Open: Dawn to dusk.

Best times to visit: Fall, winter, spring all good.

What to see: Waterfowl; deer; some alligators; good variety of bird species.

What to do: Thirteen miles of roads for driving or hiking; photography (mainly for waterfowl, near water and food plants); limited dove and waterfowl hunting; fishing excellent—sometimes fantastic—especially in spring for bass, crappie. Guided tours for groups by arrangement.

Where to stay: MOTELS—in Eufaula. CAMPGROUNDS—Lake Point State Park, adjoining refuge.

Weather notes: July–August extremely hot and humid.

Points of interest nearby: Lake Point State Park (see CAMPGROUNDS) —various recreational facilities, especially water-oriented; beautiful historic homes in Eufaula (just drive down the main street, if time go through the Shorter Mansion).

For more information: Eufaula National Wildlife Refuge, Route 2, Box 97-B, Eufaula, Alabama 36027. Phone: (205) 687-4065.

El Dorado ● **FELSENTHAL**
★

FELSENTHAL (Arkansas)

This sixty thousand acres of bottomland hardwoods and peripheral pine forest in southeast Arkansas interspersed with lakes and sloughs around the confluence of the Saline and Ouachita rivers must have seemed a paradise in the eyes of the Indians who once inhabited it. Its fertile basin supports a superb wildlife ecosystem with many kinds of oaks and other fruited vegetation on which deer, wild turkey, waterfowl, and a wide variety of other birds and mammals feed. In the surrounding upland pine stands, endangered red-cockaded woodpeckers find homes in large numbers.

Much of this relatively new refuge has been, at least until recently, largely unexplored and unvisited—a wilderness harboring alligators, bobcat, river otter, gray and red fox, squirrel, and raccoon. Here, too, the extremely rare and endangered eastern cougar (or panther) is still believed to roam. Wood ducks nest in its cypress-studded backwater ponds; beaver are active in large numbers in its creeks and bayous; and large populations of a half-dozen woodpecker species are seen commonly, including the spectacular flame-crested pileated—plus nuthatches, chickadees, titmice, and various other smaller birds common to brush and woodland, as well as raptors and barred and screech owls.

Good numbers of waterfowl have always been attracted to this area, and with future development, including a 21,000-acre shallow wooded pond, populations can be expected in fall and winter to peak most years in the many tens of thousands of mallard, pintail, gadwall, and others.

Access has never been easy—at least by land. The old logging roads have been in a largely primitive state, but mostly walkable. However, the whole refuge is subject to periodic flooding, with water levels that can rise quickly at times up to twenty feet. For this reason it is best to contact the refuge office about conditions. Until future development is complete, boating in the Saline River and its Eagle Creek tributary, together with the other lakes and sloughs, is the best way to see Felsenthal.

How to get there: From El Dorado take Route 82 about 40 miles west to the refuge.

Open: Daylight hours year-round. (Office weekdays only.)

Best times to visit: Winter and spring.

What to see: Waterfowl; deer; other swamp woodland species.

What to do: Nature observation; boating; hunting; fishing excellent (and with planned development expected to become even better) for bass, crappie. About 40 miles of rough, unimproved logging roads mostly unfit for autos but open to foot travel in dry weather. Refuge facilities extremely limited.

Where to stay: MOTELS—In Crossett, Arkansas, about 6 miles west of refuge. CAMPGROUNDS—in Moro Bay State Park adjacent to west side of refuge, but 30 miles by road.

Weather notes: Frequent flooding—visitors should inquire as to current conditions from headquarters.

What to take and wear: Waterproof footgear and insect repellent.

Points of interest nearby: Seventeen-hundred-acre Lake Georgia Pacific, adjacent to refuge—trails, fishing, excellent birding; Levi Wilcoxon Demonstration Forest, 20 miles east; Moro Bay State Park (see CAMPGROUNDS).

For more information: Felsenthal National Wildlife Refuge, P.O. Box 279, Crossett, Arkansas 71635. Phone: (501) 364-8700.

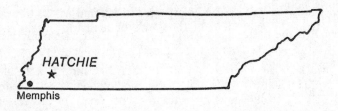

HATCHIE

★

Memphis

HATCHIE (Tennessee)

Hatchie Refuge is 11,556 acres of beautiful bottomland hardwood forest filled with meandering streams and oxbow lakes and some vegetated upland, a type of tremendously fertile wildlife habitat that has become an extreme rarity in southwestern Tennessee. As such it supports deer, wild turkey, beaver, waterfowl, and a good variety of small birds in greater numbers than anywhere else in this area.

Wood ducks and hooded mergansers are common all year and nest. Migratory and wintering varieties of waterfowl reach peaks of up to sixty thousand—about 75 per cent mallards but a good assortment also of gadwall, black, pintail, teal, wigeon, with some canvasback and redhead. Geese, mostly Canadas but with a few snows and blues, peak around five thousand (but a severe northern winter can bring up to thirty thousand to the refuge).

Raccoon are also common, some trapped by the state and removed to other areas where their populations have dropped; along with squirrel, opossum, and some bobcat, their wariness making them harder to see; and in lesser numbers, river otter and coyote.

Members of the Memphis Ornithological Society come regularly, but especially in spring and fall migrations, when large numbers of bobolinks, Acadian flycatchers, redstarts, and Tennessee and Swainson's warblers are usually here, along with hermit, gray-cheeked, and Swainson's thrushes, golden-crowned kinglets, vesper and Lincoln's sparrows, rose-breasted grosbeaks, northern orioles, and good numbers of perhaps two dozen other warblers—including the worm-eating, blue-winged, magnolia, chestnut-sided, bay-breasted, Wilson's and Canada.

A breeding bird census in June shows some of these stay and nest, along with northern parula and prothonotary warblers, dickcissels, indigo buntings, yellow-breasted chats, yellow-billed cuckoos, Acadian and great crested flycatchers, mourning doves, killdeer, chuck-will's-widows, bobwhite quail, three kinds of owls and five kinds of wood-peckers, including the large showy pileated.

But it is the bottomland hardwood forest itself that many visitors enjoy most—quiet, remote-seeming even a few miles from busy high-ways, shaded and cool on the hottest day (usually five to fifteen de-grees cooler than sunlit areas)—it is sanctuary for wildlife and human alike.

Visitors' facilities have been in the process of development; but walking primitive trails (keep an eye out for cottonmouth water moccasins) will not bother the visitor with an appreciation for such things.

How to get there: From Memphis take I-40 east to Exit 52, then east on Route 76 about 1.5 miles to refuge sign. Take this turnoff or Powell or Windrow Road—all lead into the refuge. Head-quarters is in nearby Brownsville.

Open: Daylight hours (but bad weather, floods, and hunting can close roads. Check with refuge office weekdays, where permis-sion is usually given anytime for foot travel and nature observa-tion).

Best times to visit: Spring through fall.

What to see: Waterfowl; deer; wild turkey; woodpeckers, good as-sortment of small birds spring and summer.

What to do: About 15 miles of roads for driving and hiking (some-times mucky in wet weather). Limited hunting for deer, rac-coon, squirrel. Fishing for catfish, crappie, bream. Boating, es-pecially float trips down the Hatchie, a designated state scenic river which forms refuge boundary. Guided tours for groups by prior arrangement.

Where to stay: MOTELS—In Brownsville area. CAMPGROUNDS—Near I-40 Providence Exit; also Chickasaw State Park, 40 miles south-east.

Weather notes: Winter damp, cold; summer hot, humid.

Points of interest nearby: Chickasaw State Park (see CAMPGROUNDS); Reelfoot National Wildlife Refuge, about 70 miles north; Ten-nessee National Wildlife Refuge, about 70 miles northeast.

For more information: Hatchie National Wildlife Refuge, Browns-ville, Tennessee 38012 (901) 772-0501.

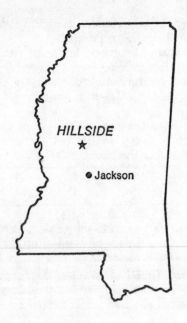

HILLSIDE (Mississippi)

Up to sixty-four thousand waterfowl, both ducks and geese, spend the fall and winter and sometimes almost blacken the fields at this fifteen-thousand-acre refuge, named for the rolling sandhills which separate this section of the state from the flat Mississippi River delta land and are said to have been made by prehistoric sandstorms.

Raptors, especially marsh hawks in good numbers, are common along the miles of diked roadbeds which bound Hillside and form an all-weather vantage point from which most of the refuge wildlife can be viewed.

Beaver are busy along these levees, cutting down saplings to keep open pathways and natural areas among the densely forested timber and brush, and their dams are regarded as helpful in slowing water flow in floodtimes (which occur often, sometimes flooding the entire refuge. This land was acquired by the Corps of Engineers in 1968, to serve as a silt collection system for the Yazoo basin, and only became a refuge in 1975).

Deer are fairly plentiful, coyote and bobcat less so, but they make appearances early and late around open areas and in the

White pelicans with great nine-foot wingspreads are seen off "Ding" Darling Refuge in Florida in late winter and later fly diagonally across the country to nest in northern breeding grounds, including such refuges as La Creek in South Dakota, and Medicine Lake in Montana. *Laura Riley*

Snow and Canada geese and many kinds of ducks concentrate in tremendous flocks in fall migration, at Montezuma, Horicon, Bombay Hook, and in other areas—but nowhere in greater numbers than in the Klamath Basin, where there may be several million. *U. S. Fish and Wildlife*

The bald eagle, our national symbol, on the endangered list because of pesticide pollution and habitat destruction, finds sanctuary in Alaska and in refuges such as Lake Andes in South Dakota and along the Upper Mississippi, where hundreds often winter. *U. S. Fish and Wildlife*

Musk-oxen are massive arctic beasts known for their stolid herd defense against an enemy, forming a circle which predators like wolves find it difficult to penetrate. But repeating rifles proved their downfall. They have made a comeback at Nunivak Refuge off the Alaskan coast. *U. S. Fish and Wildlife*

Great herds of caribou roam the Arctic Wildlife Range, northernmost U.S. refuge. When thousands gather in early fall the range is a sea of antlers, the air filled with the sound of their soft grunts and oddly clicking leg bones. *U. S. Fish and Wildlife*

The great egret is common at refuges across the southern United States and is often seen farther north along with such others of the lovely wading birds as great blue herons, snowy and cattle egrets, white and glossy ibises, and occasional storks. *Laura Riley*

The majestic whooping crane, five feet tall with 7.5-foot wingspread, once reported to be extinct, survives, gradually increasing its numbers, wintering at Aransas on the Texas coast. Sandhill-crane foster parents at Grays Lake Refuge are raising whooper young in a novel survival project. *U. S. Fish and Wildlife*

The ordinarily mild-mannered prairie chicken performs striking courtship dances in spring, strutting and inflating colorful throat sacs which deflate with a booming sound that can be heard long distances. Attwater Prairie Chicken Refuge in Texas was established to protect an endangered subspecies. *U. S. Fish and Wildlife*

The osprey or "fish hawk" is often mistaken for the bald eagle because of its similar size and markings. It ranges across the United States. Similarly hurt by pesticides, it still nests successfully at Wassaw, Blackwater, Chincoteague, Moosehorn, Metcalf, and others. *Laura Riley*

No more beautiful small bird exists than this green, purple, and scarlet sprite. Mostly a southern resident, it nests commonly on Bull's Island and at Catahoula and Savannah refuges. *William Riley*

Songbirds are abundant at many refuges, particularly warblers during spring migration in which waves may come in late April or early May. Wilson's, prothonotary, prairie, pine, palm, and many others flock at coastal landfalls where they may touch down after long oceanic passages—Delta, St. Vincent, and others. *William Riley*

The cougar or mountain lion, also locally called panther or puma, is rare through most of its range now. Wary because of human persecution, it still can be seen occasionally at such refuges as Yazoo and Ruby Lake. *U. S. Fish and Wildlife*

The American bison or buffalo once roamed the United States in numbers estimated at sixty million. By the late 1800s all but a few were gone. A nucleus herd was taken to the new Wichita Mountains Refuge in 1907. They thrived and now are at such refuges as National Bison Range, Fort Niobrara, and Sullys Hill. *U. S. Fish and Wildlife*

fields which are planted in soybean, millet, and other wildlife foods.

Small birding, at least until recently, had not been fully explored, but cardinals, blue jays, chickadees, titmice, and numbers of woodpeckers are common in the brush and hardwood bottomland.

The ducks—primarily mallard, pintail, shoveler, and teal—often find rest and sanctuary in borrow pits alongside the dikes as do numbers of pied-billed grebes and great blue herons. Geese, mostly Canadas but with a few snows, usually number somewhere around two thousand about the first of the year. Bald eagles can sometimes be seen at that time.

Also administered from Hillside are *Panther Swamp*, a fifteen-thousand-acre bottomland hardwood swamp with good deer and waterfowl populations, acquired in 1978 with Nature Conservancy assistance; and *Morgan Brake*, a small (299-acre) bottomland swamp located about five miles north of Hillside and acquired in 1977. Until recently at least, neither of these refuges has had facilities for public access.

How to get there: From Yazoo City, Mississippi, take highway 49E for 10 miles north to refuge entrance sign.

Open: Sunrise to sunset, year-round.

Best times to visit: Winter and spring.

What to see: Waterfowl; raptors; beaver; deer.

What to do: Wildlife observation—miles of dike roads; limited deer hunting; excellent fishing in borrow pools.

Where to stay: MOTELS—In Yazoo City. CAMPGROUNDS—In Thornton, 4 miles west; also Holmes County State Park, 26 miles east.

Weather notes: Summers are extremely hot and humid.

What to take and wear: Waterproof footgear a necessity in refuge interior.

Points of interest nearby: Panther Swamp National Wildlife Refuge, located 18 miles southwest; Morgan Brake National Wildlife Refuge, located 5 miles north. Holmes County State Park; Delta National Forest, 35 miles southwest.

For more information: Hillside National Wildlife Refuge, P.O. Box 107, Yazoo City, Mississippi 39194. Phone: (601) 235-4355.

HOLLA BEND (Arkansas)

Holla Bend, an old oxbow in the Arkansas River nestled between the Ozarks on the north and the Ouachita Mountains and National Forest to the south, became a refuge largely through efforts of local sportsmen and conservationists. Established in 1957 on 4,083 acres of Corps of Engineers land acquired for a flood control project, it now supports large populations of wintering waterfowl and eagles, as well as other interesting natural inhabitants, including many scissor-tailed flycatchers in the warm months and deer all year round.

When the waterfowl are in, from late fall through January—peaking at up to fifty thousand ducks and five thousand geese—they can be seen in great numbers flying back and forth early and late between the river nearby to the agricultural fields on the refuge where they feed, largely on vegetation planted on shares with local farmers and left there for wildlife benefit. Closely observing them most of the time from the tops of lone cottonwood trees are the eagles, sometimes a dozen or more at a time, which prey on the weak and injured waterfowl. They are mostly bald eagles (the dark brown-headed ones are immature birds) but a few golden eagles also are here.

The ducks are predominantly mallard with some gadwall, pintail, wigeon, and blue- and green-winged teal; the geese are both snows and Canadas, along with a resident flock of Canadas which were established as a decoy flock to bring in others when the refuge was started and now, their purpose accomplished, continue to produce downy broods on a pond behind the refuge field headquarters (eery "wounded blackbird' calls from loudspeakers are designed to frighten predators away from the nests).

The visitor who gets out early or stays till dusk can see white-tailed deer on the roads; also apparent are coyote, raccoon, armadillo, attractive red and gray fox squirrels, beaver, and, less readily seen, bobcat. Black bear occur rarely. Presumably they are moving between the mountain ranges.

One of the beauties of the refuge is the population of scissor-tailed flycatchers that arrive in early April and are visible nearly every daylight hour until they leave in October, perching on fence posts and power lines, their long deeply forked tails streaming behind, and nesting in brushy areas along the river.

Holla Bend is also good for dickcissels and sparrows—larks and field sparrows are common all year and in fall and winter whitethroats, white-crowns, fox, Lincoln's and sometimes Le Conte's and vespers are here. Bell's vireos are common in the spring—listen for them singing down the slopes on the main road in—as are the whiteeyed and red-eyed; common through the breeding season are wood thrushes, brown thrashers, summer tanagers, orchard and northern orioles, and all year meadowlarks, shrikes, bobwhite, killdeer (nesting on the roads sometimes), red-bellied woodpeckers, mourning doves (sometimes in huge flocks of five thousand or so), screech and barred owls, great blue herons and red-tailed and red-shouldered hawks.

Shorebird migrations can be interesting in a wet spring, with upland, pectoral, and spotted sandpipers, Wilson's phalaropes, snipe, and an occasional golden plover.

How to get there: From Russellville, take Route 7 south; about 2 miles beyond Dardanelle turn left on gravel road, Route 155, and proceed 6 miles to refuge entrance.

Open: Daylight hours all year.

Best times to visit: Fall through early spring.

What to see: Wintering bald and golden eagles; concentrations of ducks; Canada geese; white-tailed deer; scissor-tailed flycatchers in warm months.

What to do: Sixteen miles of roads and trails for riding, hiking; photography (blind for waterfowl, eagles); quail dog training; limited dove and deer hunts; fishing, sometimes very good spring and fall for largemouth bass, crappie.

Where to stay: MOTELS—In Russellville, Dardanelle. CAMPGROUNDS —Corps of Engineers campground, 6 miles south; also Mount Nebo State Park, 10 miles west, and Petit Jean State Park, 15 miles east.

Weather notes: Dry hot summers and wet cool winters can create poor road conditions.

Points of interest nearby: Ozark National Forest starts 5 miles north, Ouachita National Forest 10 miles south; Hot Springs National Park, 75 miles south, can have outstanding birding; also Petit Jean and Mount Nebo State Parks (see CAMPGROUNDS).

For more information: Holla Bend National Wildlife Refuge, P.O. Box 1043, Russellville, Arkansas 72801. Phone: (501) 968-2800.

Lake Charles

★ *LACASSINE*

LACASSINE (Louisiana)

The first reaction of a visitor seeing sixteen-thousand-acre Lacassine Pool for the first time is often "how peaceful it is"—for it seems almost like another world, with its great expanse of water and islands of marsh vegetation as far as the eye can see, shining gold and dark green against the clear water and blue sky. Contrasted to sounds of traffic and civilization, it seems dead quiet. Then one becomes aware of an undercurrent murmur that may build until it is almost a dull roar, and closer scrutiny shows that the masses of what seemed islands of vegetation are in fact alive; they are great rafts of waterfowl, and the dull roar is their voices in continuous "conversation" among themselves.

It is a stunning sight and as they take off en masse, filling the air, sometimes moving only a short distance to settle again like a huge blanket, it is nothing short of awesome. Return another time, especially at dawn or dusk, and it may be quite a different scene, not so much for what is observed as heard—alligators bellowing, gallinules shrieking, and in the half light it seems a veritable jungle of hidden creatures.

Wintering populations of ducks and geese at this 31,776-acre refuge in southwest coastal Louisiana are among the largest in the nation, with concentrations sometimes of 750,000 birds in the fresh-water maiden-cane and bull's-tongue marsh and on the prairie—more than a dozen species of ducks and four of geese, settling in at the southern end of both the Mississippi and Central flyways. The snow geese are ending a heart-stirring three-thousand-mile journey from their far north nesting grounds, reflected in their scientific name, hyperborea—"beyond the north wind." Their companions, the white-fronteds are here in the greatest concentrations in the Mississippi Flyway—in spring, alongside fulvous whistling ducks, those curious waterfowl from Mexico whose long legs make them as good walkers as swimmers, which nest in rice fields around the refuge and concentrate here in spring and fall in the largest numbers of any U.S. refuge.

The list of common and abundant wading and other water birds at Lacassine is spectacular—snowy, cattle, and great egrets; great blue, little blue, tricolor (Louisiana), green, black-crowned and yellow-crowned night herons; white-faced and white ibises; least and American bitterns; purple gallinules, olivaceous cormorants, golden plovers, and many others.

During the summer months there may be in excess of five thousand white-faced ibises alone and tens of thousands of other long-legged waders present. Most of the species present also nest on the refuge, great blue herons and cormorants preferring the tall cypress trees in two small groves, while the others, including roseate spoonbills, take to the low-growing buttonbush and willow stands. Colonies here often contain as many as ten thousand birds in an area as small as five acres.

Eagles are winter visitors; so are peregrine falcons. Kestrels are common in the uplands. Mockingbirds, brown thrashers, orchard orioles, marsh wrens, water pipits, and yellowthroats are among the common small birds, and nutria and raccoon are a familiar sight.

Until recently, access to Lacassine's dikes and walkways has been limited due to lack of roads, although boats have been permitted in the channels and bayous. But plans for new right-of-ways and a visitor contact center make it likely access will be freer in the future. Refuge staff can sometimes arrange routings for good viewing and conduct tours for small groups if contacted in advance.

Also administered by Lacassine is *Shell Keys* Refuge, established in 1907, an eight-acre nesting colony offshore. Access is limited and difficult, by special permit only.

How to get there: Take Route 10 east to Welsh, turn right on Route 99, left on Route 14 to Lowry Road, then right 5 miles to headquarters (best phone ahead to see if staff has moved to new headquarters building).

Open: Daylight hours.

Best times to visit: Determined largely by weather and personal preference—something to see all year here.

What to see: Huge concentrations of waterfowl and wading birds, including large numbers of roseate spoonbills. Alligators. Various mammals, including nutria, deer, raccoon, armadillo.

What to do: Nature viewing from drive and walkways (some by permission only); boating; photography; limited waterfowl hunting; fishing considered good if you know where and how—6-pound black bass not unusual. (Refuge has about 100 miles of channels, but best take something larger than a canoe and consult refuge staff on plans.)

Where to stay: MOTELS—In Jennings or Lake Charles. CAMPGROUNDS —Adjacent to headquarters tract, or at Sam Houston State Park, 50 miles northwest—or anywhere along the beach in Cameron Parish.

Weather notes: Summers are humid; winter occasionally dips below freezing but doesn't hold there (find out if great blue herons are nesting; they don't start till cold weather is over for the year).

What to take and wear: Water-repellent gear—you never know.

Points of interest nearby: Sabine Refuge, 80 miles west; Rockefeller Wildlife Refuge, 60 miles west; Avery Island, 75 miles east; Kisatchie National Forest, 75 miles north; Atchafalaya Floodway, 80 miles east on Route 10.

For more information: Lacassine National Wildlife Refuge, Route 1, Box 186, Lake Arthur, Louisiana 70549. Phone: (318) 774-2750.

MISSISSIPPI SANDHILL CRANE (Mississippi)

The sandhill crane stands four feet tall with pearl-gray plumage and a red crown, wings that spread almost seven feet, a trumpeting call that can be heard for miles, and a spectacular mating dance in which the partners face each other and leap high in the air, feet forward and wings extended, then bow sedately and repeat this remarkable performance, sometimes again and again.

A refuge has been established for the endangered Mississippi subspecies of this striking bird on a tract of savanna, swamp, and pine forest purchased through The Nature Conservancy in the extreme southeastern corner of Mississippi, about ten miles east of Biloxi. There it is hoped that restoration of some of its habitat, reduced drastically through housing and commercial development, may allow repopulation here of this bird. The area will, of course, continue to have attractions for others which also prefer such wild places as these, including some notable plants—snakemouth orchids, grass pinks, meadow beauties, pitcher plants, sundews, and others.

Since it is one of the newest of the national wildlife refuges, there are—at least until recently—no visitor facilities and none in immediate prospect until plans can be completed for acquisition of breeding and resting sites and their protection and use. A visitor contact station, nature trail, and observation tower are part of a long-range plan.

For further information contact Mississippi Sandhill Crane National Wildlife Refuge, Gautier, Mississippi 39553. Phone: (601) 497-2380.

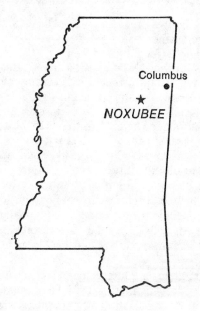

Columbus

★
NOXUBEE

NOXUBEE (Mississippi)

Noxubee Refuge, forty-six thousand acres of timber and uplands,
lakes and streams in east-central Mississippi, has one of the largest
populations of endangered red-cockaded woodpeckers anywhere,
along with giant Canada geese and good populations of deer and
wild turkey on land once abandoned as a near biological desert due
to deplorable land-use practices.

It is an excellent example of how land can be reclaimed after erosion and depleted topsoil have taken a severe toll. Good management practices since its acquisition in the 1930s by the Rural
Resettlement Administration have made it a garden for wildlife.

Wintering waterfowl number some sixty thousand—mallard, gadwall, pintail, teal, wigeon, shoveler, ring-necked, merganser, and
ruddy ducks all common, and wood ducks staying all year and nesting. A flock of about two hundred and fifty giant Canada geese,
started with a captive flock but now free fliers, are almost always visible from the observation platform through the winter and later in
the spring nesting season, incubating their eggs and leading their
downy chicks to forage around the edge of Bluff Lake.

Woodpeckers—handsome flickers, red-bellied, red-headed, and especially the large, flame-crested pileated—are common throughout the woodlands. These woodlands make up 90 per cent of the refuge, some in relatively level hardwood bottomlands, others in rolling pine uplands. It is in the latter, in trees a half century old or more which have developed the soft "red-heart" centers suitable for nest cavities, where the endangered red-cockaded woodpecker finds its home; the refuge manages its wooded acres with this little bird in mind, cutting no trees that might serve as breeding habitat.

About seventy nests of red-cockaded woodpeckers have been found. One can readily identify the active cavity trees because each day the birds peck open holes around the cavity which cause sap to run and leave the tree covered with shiny resin. There are various theories for this, including protection against predators, but none is conclusive; the birds can be seen at their chores most mornings in old trees near refuge headquarters and readily added to the birder's list.

Giant trees are here—a Durand oak, largest of its kind in the United States, 139 feet high, 16 feet 6 inches around the trunk with a 69-foot spread at the crown; and a Shumard oak, ranked second for its species, with a 107-foot spread.

Red-tailed and red-shouldered hawks are common; a few bald eagles and an occasional golden eagle are present in winter. White tailed deer and wild turkey are often around refuge roads and trails, especially in early morning. Beaver are here in good numbers, their workings always visible, as are squirrel, raccoon, and smaller numbers of red and gray fox and wary bobcat. Alligators are on the fringe of their range, but a small population persists. Quail and kill-deer are usually about the roadside and graveled area. Great blue herons and a few yellow-crowned night herons nest in old cypress stands.

Noxubee's Christmas Bird Count is usually around ninety species, with good numbers of cedar waxwings, brown-headed nuthatches, ruby-crowned kinglets, and wintering robins. Bluebirds are common all year, sometimes abundant in spring. Yellow-breasted chats and hooded warblers are nesters.

Several tracts on the refuge are regarded as so unusual by naturalists they are set aside as undisturbed natural areas—a loblolly pine-red cedar community, a pond with an array of unusual salamanders, and a creekbank bluff with ferns of a type not found normally so far south as this.

How to get there: From Starkville take Spring Street (or Oktoc Road) south off Route 12, bearing right at the fork, about 17 miles to the end of the blacktop. Turn right at that point and follow refuge signs.

Open: Daylight hours all year.

Best times to visit: Late fall though spring.

What to see: Wintering waterfowl, red-cockaded woodpeckers, bald eagles, resident flock of giant Canada geese, champion-size trees.

What to do: About 50 miles of driving and walking trails (some may be impassable in wet periods); observation platform; picnicking; limited hunting for deer, turkey, ducks, and small game; fishing for catfish, bass, crappie, bream.

Where to stay: MOTELS—In Starkville. CAMPGROUNDS—Seasonal on refuge; commercial at Starkville, also Oktibbeha County Lake nearby and Tombigbee National Forest, adjoining refuge.

Weather notes: Fairly pleasant all year but January–February can be cold; possibility of flooding January through April. July and August are hot and humid.

Points of interest nearby: Tombigbee National Forest, trails (see CAMPGROUNDS); Columbus area has beautiful ante-bellum homes, tours, especially Waverly Plantation.

For more information: Noxubee National Wildlife Refuge, Route 1, Box 84, Brooksville, Mississippi 39739. Phone: (601) 323-5548.

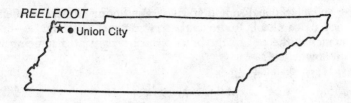

REELFOOT
★ ● Union City

REELFOOT (Tennessee-Kentucky)

Reelfoot Lake in the northwest corner of Tennessee, seasonal home for spectacular numbers of bald eagles, waterfowl, and migrating songbirds, was formed by devastating earthquakes in 1811 and 1812 which caused a two-thousand-mile area to rumble for months and the lake basin, then part of the Mississippi flood plain, to fall thirty-five to forty feet.

"The waters gathered up like a mountain fifteen to twenty feet perpendicularly," according to an eyewitness. "Groves of trees disappeared and fissures in the earth vomited forth sand and water . . . the atmosphere was so saturated with sulphurous vapors as to cause total darkness; trees cracked and fell into the roaring Mississippi."

Some said the Mississippi flowed backward three days to fill the forty-five-square-mile basin, the upper part of which is now 10,142-acre Reelfoot National Wildlife Refuge and, along with its notable natural inhabitants, one of the beauty spots of this part of the United States.

Majestic stands of virgin bald cypress tower over shallow-watered inlets, their bulbous trunks ringed with thickly blooming wild roses in spring and later with golden lotuses and water lily pads where purple gallinules forage.

Waterfowl occur in peak concentrations of 40,000 geese and 250,000 ducks in winter. Wood ducks are common all year. More than fifty-six species of fish inhabit its waters, including the curious and ancient paddlefish and bowfin. Mammals, though wary, are fairly readily seen early and late, including good numbers of white-tailed deer, beaver, raccoon, opossum, muskrat, fox, occasional bobcat, and young mink families hunting along the waterways, and swamp rabbits, look-alikes for the familiar cottontail but larger and not averse to swimming. An outstanding array of snakes and lizards are resident (protected from collectors), including the yard-long amphiuma salamander.

The endangered bald eagle at times appears in greater numbers than any place else of comparable size in the United States—between one hundred and two hundred almost every winter, roosting in swampy woodlands and going out to feed over the lake. They can be seen perched on snags and soaring overhead—or almost anywhere else in the area. It is not unusual to see twenty-five or thirty while driving Route 22 between Tiptonville and Samburg.

Reelfoot is a superb birding area. Naturalists come from all over the United States for its spring warbler migrations, when sixteen species may be seen commonly—and a dozen others less commonly—in waves starting in March and continuing until June. The peak is usually about mid-April, depending on weather. There also are orioles, Swainson's thrushes, tanagers, and many others, along wooded Grassy Island road.

Often Reelfoot is highest in the nation in the annual Audubon Christmas Bird Count for ring-necked and wood ducks and others, and highest in Tennessee in number of species due to its varied habitat of wooded bluffs, upland and swamp forest.

Red-tailed hawks are common; so are marsh hawks, especially in migration when sometimes hundreds can be seen on a single late fall day. Red-shouldered and rough-legged hawks appear in fair numbers, as do Cooper's, which nest near the bluffs. Ospreys nest, in recent years their only breeding place in Tennessee; Mississippi kites are summertime familiars, believed to nest but in areas so dense and remote even refuge staff seldom visit. Golden plovers are common in fall migration.

Huge flights of blackbirds, sometimes three million or so, mostly red-winged but six others as well, roost and scatter at dawn, returning in broad ribbons ten to three hundred feet wide across the sky for a half hour at dusk.

Ruby-throated hummingbirds are common nesters and flock around bird feeders. Six species of woodpeckers, including the large, striking pileated, are common in woods.

The lovely long-legged wading birds, including great and snowy egrets and great blue herons, nest but not as formerly, when tens of thousands occupied a large section of the lake. They left when the movie *Raintree County* was made here and the film company set off dynamite charges in the heronry to make them fly up for dramatic effect, and the birds have never since returned in such large numbers.

Lake Isom nearby is a subrefuge administered by Reelfoot, similar in natural inhabitants with a short drive open most but not all year. From Samburg take Route 22 west to the spillway, then left at the first paved blacktop road about two and a half miles to a refuge sign.

How to get there: Refuge proper has two units. Directions from Tiptonville are: to Grassy Island, Route 22 east about 15 miles to Route 157, north 2 miles to Walnut Log, then left 1.5 miles to refuge sign. To Long Point, north on Route 78 continuing after it becomes Kentucky Route 94, about 2.5 miles to first right on paved road, thence to sign. Refuge headquarters in Samburg may soon change.

Open: Daylight hours, but some roads close periodically to offer wintering waterfowl sanctuary. Check with office on viewing possibilities during this time.

Best times to visit: Nature observations superb most of the year.

What to see: Eagles, waterfowl concentrations, sometimes Mississippi kites and spectacular migrating warblers, beautiful vistas.

What to do: More than a dozen miles of roads and trails (see *Open*); photography; limited hunting for raccoon and squirrel; fishing excellent for crappie, bluegill, bass, catfish; boating (rentals nearby). Guided tours will be given for groups by prior arrangement.

Where to stay: In the 10 miles along Route 22 between Samburg and nearby Tiptonville are more than a dozen motels, several tent and trailer parks, and excellent restaurants and accommodations of all kinds at Reelfoot Lake State Park (but make reservations ahead during peak fishing times mid-March to June).

Weather notes: Midwinter can be blustery, midsummer hot and humid.

What to take and wear: Snake protection advised (not absolutely necessary if you're careful); insect repellent.

Points of interest nearby: Reelfoot Lake State Park (see *Where to Stay*) has a museum of Indian and nature lore, excellent guided tours of Lake and natural areas, trails, various other recreational facilities.

For more information: Reelfoot National Wildlife Refuge, Box 98, Samburg, Tennessee 38254. Phone: (901) 538-2481.

● Lake Charles

SABINE

SABINE (Louisiana)

For about an hour almost every afternoon of the year the visitor to Sabine Refuge can watch while roseate spoonbills fly overhead from their feeding grounds to their nightly roosts, their brilliant plumage matching if not overpowering the sunset.

To some this is probably the most memorable sight here. But to others, the prize would go to the alligators, which certainly are no longer an endangered species on this 142,846-acre expanse of fresh, brackish, and salt-water marsh in the southwest corner of coastal Louisiana. It is the largest waterfowl refuge on the Gulf Coast. Sabine has an estimated nine thousand alligators, and has transplanted thousands to other areas where their numbers are depleted. They are gradually increasing since the enactment of laws effectively protecting them in the United States. Before that, Sabine was a mecca for poachers; refuge personnel patrolled the marshes in teams every night, and it is due to their considerable courage in repeatedly facing threats on their lives that this healthy alligator population survived.

Because the alligators reproduce so commonly and visibly here, numbers of studies have been done on them, learning that the young are assisted by their mothers in hatching from eggs in nests of composting mounded-up vegetation: she hears their hatching grunts as they emerge from the shell, uncovers them, and sometimes will take a young one gently in her jaws and transport it thirty feet or more to the water (usually they will follow her, sliding down her muddy trail on the bank).

Visitors can sometimes see the young in late August—brightly colored, unlike their elders, in a mosaic yellow and black (but don't approach them; mother may be nearby and alligators, while normally peaceful, have tremendous damage potential when provoked. *Never* get between one and its family or its home waterway). The adults are best seen between April and October, though they may come out on a sunny winter day.

The refuge has a site where snow geese come daily in midwinter to gather grit, necessary for their digestive processes, and visitors can view them a little distance from headquarters on most mornings, sometimes in huge numbers. Usually a merlin or two can also be seen here, and often a wintering peregrine falcon.

Route 27 goes through the refuge and along it many of the impressive natural residents here can be seen—herons, egrets, ibises, spoonbills, some of which nest by the thousands on nearby islands; a dozen species of ducks, along with white pelicans and both oliva- ceous and double-crested cormorants. About four miles past head- quarters is an excellent walking trail where these and many marsh and shorebirds can be seen as well—purple gallinules, black-necked stilts—the great variety can only be suggested here. Sabine Refuge every year registers one of the nation's highest tallies in the Audu- bon Christmas Bird Count. Mammals are here also—a few deer, raccoon, opossum, armadillos (red wolves are listed as endangered and are seldom seen).

There is little habitat for small birds, except immediately around refuge headquarters; however, refuge staff are extremely helpful in directing visitors to spots where unusual bird sightings are available, especially in spring migration.

How to get there: From Lake Charles, take Route 10 west to Sulphur, then south on Route 27 to refuge signs.

Open: Daylight hours.

Best times to visit: Interesting things to see all year.

What to see: Alligators; spring migrants; snow geese; roseate spoon- bill flights.

What to do: Auto and walking routes; observation tower; snow goose grit site; photography; boating on 125 miles of canals and bayous from October 1 to March 1; limited waterfowl hunting; fishing, both salt- and fresh-water, for drum, redfish, catfish, many others, also crabbing.

Where to stay: MOTELS—In Sulphur and Lake Charles. CAMPGROUNDS —In Ward Four Parish Park, 14 miles north; Sam Houston State Park, 27 miles north; or anywhere along the beach in Cameron Parish.

Weather Notes: August hot and humid with deer flies; January to March can be rainy and blustery.

Points of interest nearby: Lacassine Refuge, 80 miles east; Creole Nature Trail, a driving tour mapped out by local parish, follows many local points of interest, including Rockefeller Wildlife Refuge. Refuge staff will advise on many other good birding spots open by permit—oil company roads, Hackberry and Peveto Woods, and numbers of others.

For more information: Sabine National Wildlife Refuge, M.R.H. Box 107, Hackberry, Louisiana 70645. Phone: (318) 762-5135.

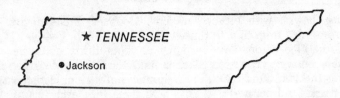

★ TENNESSEE

● Jackson

TENNESSEE (Tennessee)

Where the bandit Jesse James once farmed and Confederate General Nathan Bedford Forrest led his troops, wintering ducks and geese now feed and bald and golden eagles prey on their stragglers at Tennessee National Wildlife Refuge, an overlay on land bought and operated by the Tennessee Valley Authority for power and flood control in the 1940s.

When acquired the area was depleted by poor land use practices. The Tennessee Valley Authority created Kentucky Lake on the Tennessee River and the 51,358-acre refuge was superimposed on the project. Work began immediately to encourage wildlife by managing wooded areas and planting agricultural fields, often on shares with local farmers, in crops that would supply food and cover. It has succeeded to the point where Tennessee Refuge now has some of the most abundant and varied wildlife to be seen anywhere.

White-tailed deer and quail are common, wild turkey gobblers hold courting rituals in the spring (refuge staff can advise where), and the hens and poults appear in the fields in May and June.

Waterfowl are abundant, wintering concentrations sometimes reaching sixty thousand geese (the largest flock of Canada geese in the South) and three hundred thousand ducks, with so many mallards sometimes in the fields (where all these are closely visible from the roads) they appear almost a solid shimmering green from their shining head plumage.

And with the wintering waterfowl—in fact, studies show, fluctuating with the mallard—come the eagles, as many as sixty-five in some years of which about half may be golden. The latter is the largest wintering population of golden eagles anywhere this far east in the United States and the birds are usually readily seen on lookout posts near the roads.

Other raptors are common too—red-tailed, red-shouldered, and marsh hawks, with ospreys, merlins, Cooper's, broadwinged, and sharpshinned from time to time.

Great blue herons have a colony of about thirty nests, the only sizable one in Tennessee. Greater and lesser yellowlegs are here along the two hundred miles of shoreline in all but winter, as are least terns and pectoral and least sandpipers with a few Baird's and buff-breasteds sometimes in late summer and fall.

The swallows come in great flocks. More than a dozen warblers are common or abundant in migration with a dozen others only a little less so. Prothonotaries, yellowthroats, redstarts, chats along with some Kentucky and hooded warblers and red-eyed, white-eyed, and warbling vireos, stay and nest. Bluebirds are common all year as are killdeer, mourning doves, barred owls, Carolina wrens, loggerhead shrikes, and five kinds of woodpeckers.

Coyote are frequently on the roads in late afternoon; so are raccoon and opossum, more rarely bobcat, beaver, muskrat, mink, and fox along the water's edge where local lore says they switch their tails in the water to attract prey (don't count on it, though).

Ginseng grows in back areas, and in spring the hillsides are aglow with mountain laurels, wild azaleas, and flowering trees—dogwood, redbud, serviceberry (dogwood used to be commercially lumbered here for furniture spindles).

The refuge includes three separate units with varying habitat but the wildlife is about the same on all. Jesse James' old homestead was on the Duck River unit. No one knew he was anything but a farmer in those days, and neighbors only speculated as to why he always kept a mare saddled up and ready to go.

How to get there: Refuge headquarters is on Blythe Street in Paris. To get to the Big Sandy unit from Paris, take Route 69A to Big Sandy, then northeast on Lick Creek Road to entrance. For Busseltown, Route 641 to Parsons, 100 east to Mousetail Road, left to entrance. For Duck River, consult refuge office.

Open: Headquarters open weekdays; refuge, dawn to dusk.

Best times to visit: Fall and spring but winter is interesting too.

What to see: Wintering bald and golden eagles, waterfowl, wild turkey, deer, songbirds.

What to do: About 150 miles of roads and trails; boating; photography (blind available); limited deer hunting; fishing good for crappie in spring, bass in fall, sauger in winter (Paris has the "world's biggest fish fry" every spring with a queen, parades, bands, the works).

Where to stay: MOTELS—Many in Paris area. CAMPGROUNDS—At Paris Landing State Park, also Natchez Trace State Park, 30 miles southeast, and on the Duck River and Big Sandy units (this for youth groups only).

Weather notes: July–August usually hot and humid; January–February cold and damp.

What to take and wear: Take warm waterproof clothing and footgear any winter day.

Points of interest nearby: Tennessee Valley Authority Land Between the Lakes, 40 miles northeast—many recreational facilities; and the area is rich in state park natural areas and historic sites, such as Fort Donelson, 30 miles northeast, and Mount Zion National Historic Site on the refuge.

For more information: Tennessee National Wildlife Refuge, P.O. Box 849, Paris, Tennessee 38242. Phone: (901) 642-2091.

WAPANOCCA (Arkansas)

Wapanocca was a famous hunt club started shortly after the Civil War because of the apparently limitless wildlife, especially waterfowl, in this rich north Arkansas bottomland hardwood area just four miles west of the Mississippi River. Memberships sold for ten thousand dollars during the 1920s and were held by the wealthy and notable (including cabinet members) from around the United States. Agricultural drainage and stream channelization reduced the region's fertile habitat and its wildlife inhabitants to scattered remnants. This 5,484-acre refuge was started in 1961 with the support of descendants of some of the original club members to preserve a part of that rich area and bring back some of the concentrations once present. A good beginning has been made. Ducks winter here, sometimes in numbers to one hundred thousand—mallard, gadwall, wigeon, pintail, black duck—and geese have started up too, up to twenty thousand in recent years. Eagles sometime winter here.

There are abundant woodpeckers in the cypress-willow swamps and bottomland hardwoods—pileated, red-bellied, and red-headed, along with yellow-bellied sapsuckers—and a variety of songbirds both here and in the brushier upland areas—ruby- and golden-crowned kinglets, blue jays, Carolina chickadees, tufted titmice, yellowthroats and yellow-rumped warblers, cardinals, orchard and northern orioles, yellow-breasted chats and indigo buntings and sometimes large flocks of bobolinks.

Wild turkey and bobwhite quail are here in numbers all year, as are beaver, but these nocturnal creatures are most active from dusk to dawn. White-tailed deer are here along with raccoon, opossum, squirrel, and a few coyote.

One of the best ways to see Wapanocca is by taking a shallow johnboat out into Wapanocca Lake or a canoe in through the cypress swamp on both the north and south ends, but especially along the marked trail in the north. The trail threads through the flooded stands of tall cypress trees in dark waters where buttonbushes present feathery white blooms in the spring and drop round balls of seeds for the ducks later on. Beaver may note human approach by slapping their tails resoundingly on the water's surface. Woodpeckers hammer, great blue herons prowl, and a wood duck pair, sometimes with a brood in late spring, may appear around any curve. It is a lovely trip.

Future plans call for improved all-weather roads and boat launches and higher levees, since present levees have not prevented entry of silt and pesticide-laden waters which have resulted in the loss of more than a hundred acres of timber land. The hope is that higher dike walls will remedy this.

How to get there: From Memphis take I-55 north about 15 miles to Turrell-Route 42 exit; refuge office is about 2 miles east on 42 just past railroad underpass.

Open: Daylight hours all year (but roads and lake close seasonally to autos and boats to offer sanctuary to wintering waterfowl).

Best times to visit: Fall and spring (spring weekends can be crowded).

What to see: Wintering waterfowl; woodpeckers; beautiful cypress swamp.

What to do: About 5 miles of roads for riding or hiking (see *Open*); observation platform, boating (rentals available), limited hunting for raccoon, squirrel, rabbit. Fishing popular, especially in spring, for bass, bream, catfish.

Where to stay: West Memphis and Marion. CAMPGROUNDS—On I-55 at 10 miles south; also Shelby Forest, Lake Poinsett, and Village Creek State Parks, west of refuge.

Points of interest nearby: Crowley's Ridge, 40 miles west—interesting geological formations (also a state park with camping); St. Francis National Forest, 60 miles south; Big Lake National Wildlife Refuge, 50 miles north; White River National Wildlife Refuge, 75 miles south.

For more information: Wapanocca National Wildlife Refuge, P.O. Box 279, Turrell, Arkansas 72384. Phone: (501) 343-2595.

WHEELER (Alabama)

Wheeler was the first national wildlife refuge to be overlaid on a power dam project—part of the Tennessee Valley Authority's Wheeler Reservoir—in an experiment begun in 1938 to see if waterfowl could be attracted to such reservoirs. It has worked so well, attracting not only large concentrations of waterfowl but also a wide variety of other wildlife, that its example has been followed widely, not only over the United States but around the world.

Up to thirty thousand geese, mostly Canadas but also snows and blues, and seventy thousand ducks of two dozen species are here in winter, resting on the refuge's fifteen thousand acres of open water and feeding over its thousands of acres of cultivated upland, in some of the largest concentrations of the Southeast. It is a prime example of what can be done in creating habitat, for none of these areas existed as wildlife attractions before the 34,114-acre refuge was established. Since then, white-tailed deer have come to adapt to having Saturn rockets as neighbors—for two other government agencies, the Army's Redstone Arsenal and the Marshall Space Flight Center, occupy parts of this same government reservation (wood duck nesting poles and predator guards have been constructed of materials from Redstone scrap piles).

Muskrat and beaver are common, their workings visible on many waterways, bobcat and fox less so but frequently seen by quiet visitors on the roads early and late. Raccoon and opossum are numerous, and so are bats of a dozen species, sometimes flying out around dusk and roosting by day in limestone caves on the refuge. Two of these are endangered species—the Indiana and the gray, which has a protected nurse colony of some fifty thousand in one of the caves. It is so sensitive to disturbance during reproduction that even refuge personnel stay away.

Red-tailed hawks are common and, with the less common Cooper's, nest on the refuge. Bobwhite quail are common, and pheasant, turkey, and woodcock frequently are in the fields and woodlands. Barn owls nest in hollow trees, and screech owls also (when they don't prefer a wood duck house).

The refuge is popular with birders all year, and a center for the area's annual Audubon Christmas Bird Count, when more than a hundred species are often seen. Common all or part of the year are summer tanagers, indigo buntings, meadowlarks, ruby-throated hummingbirds (around the abundant orange trumpet creeper), Acadian flycatchers, Carolina wrens, mockingbirds, brown thrashers, yellow-throated and white-eyed vireos, yellow-breasted chats, ruby- and golden-crowned kinglets, horned larks, chimney swifts, yellow-billed cuckoos, six kinds of woodpeckers and grasshopper, vesper, and fox sparrows. Spring warblers come through in impressive waves, usually reaching a height in mid-April, and when stopped by a south wind switching to the north they appear to be everywhere—magnolia, yellow, black-throated green Kentucky, and a dozen others; and many of the hooded, black and white, prothonotary, and yellowthroats stay the summer and nest.

The countryside is lush with blooming dogwoods, redbuds, wild plums, azaleas, and fringe trees in April and with fall colors in early October.

The refuge office has excellent lists of its wildlife inhabitants, its birds, plants, mammals, and interesting fish and reptiles as well.

How to get there: From Decatur take Route 67 east 2 miles to refuge entrance.

Open: Daylight hours all year.

Best times to visit: Fall, winter, and spring.

What to see: Waterfowl concentrations; spring blooming; fall foliage; songbirds; good general spectrum of wildlife.

What to do: More than 100 miles of roads and trails; wildlife obser-

vation building (heated with one-way glass, microphone, open
in winter for seeing, hearing waterfowl); observation platform;
photography; boating (rentals nearby); fishing for crappie,
bream, bass, including fresh-water stripers; hunting (permits
required) for deer, small game; fruit and nut picking for personal use; guided tours for groups by prior arrangement.

Where to stay: MOTELS—In Decatur. CAMPGROUNDS—Point Mallard
Park, adjacent to refuge; also supervised youth groups on refuge
by special permit.

Weather notes: Winter can drop down around zero; midsummer so
hot and humid that all life, human and wild (except mosquitoes), slows to a near halt.

Points of interest nearby: Bankhead National Forest, 30 miles southwest; Wheeler State Park, 40 miles west; Monte Sano State
Park, 25 miles northeast; Point Mallard Park, adjacent to refuge,
various recreational facilities; Mooresville, also adjacent—one of
the oldest incorporated villages in Alabama (older than the
state)—it has existed almost unchanged for more than a century. Two Presidents worshiped at its church. Refuge geese graze
in the backyards of its beautiful old homes. A treasure.

For more information: Wheeler National Wildlife Refuge, P.O. Box
1643, Decatur, Alabama 35602. Phone: (205) 353-7243.

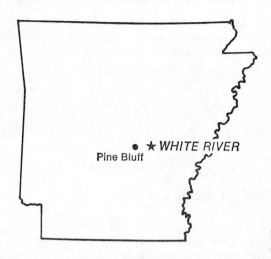

Pine Bluff ★ WHITE RIVER

WHITE RIVER (Arkansas)

This area calls itself the duck capital of the world, and when the sky over White River Refuge is full of up to 400,000 wintering ducks and 6,000 geese this seems no exaggeration—but there is much else as well on this 112,000 acres of mixed bottomland hardwood forest with 169 natural lakes and 125 miles of streams and bayous just 20 miles west of the Mississippi River in Arkansas.

White-tailed deer and wild turkey occur in large numbers—so many of the latter that hundreds have been trapped and transplanted to other areas. Now many places in Arkansas that will support wild turkeys have them, offshoots from this flock.

One of the healthiest populations of black bear in the eastern United States is here—an estimated 125, more than tripled since the refuge was established in 1935 and efforts started to make it the lush wildlife sanctuary it has become. The endangered eastern cougar also lives here, though it is rarely seen.

White River also is one of the best bird-finding places anywhere around, its songbird migrations notable, with good numbers of shorebirds as well, including upland sandpipers and golden plover in the spring. Many others nest, including, commonly, cerulean, prothonotary, parula, and yellow-throated warblers, yellow-breasted chats, indigo buntings, summer tanagers, dickcissels, northern and orchard orioles, wood thrushes, and ruby-throated hummingbirds. And, believed by many to be present but with no authenticated recent sightings, is the exceedingly rare Bachman's warbler. Swainson's, though rare, is seen regularly.

Mississippi kites are common in spring and summer, and in a good year up to two thousand wood storks will visit. A half dozen or so golden and bald eagles usually stop over in winter, and sometimes huge flocks of robins—one year an estimated eight million.

Showy pileated and five other woodpeckers are common to abundant all year, as are bluebirds, cardinals, brown thrashers, loggerhead shrikes, screech and barred owls, mourning doves, red-shouldered and red-tailed hawks, and sometimes tremendous numbers of blackbirds, regarded kindly by soybean and oats farmers when they go after troublesome army worms.

One of the best ways to see the refuge is by boat, going down the White River which bisects it, exploring side chutes and ponds and camping overnight, as is permitted March to November in designated sites. One would see one of the most impressive tracts of hardwood bottomlands anywhere, huge trees with five-foot trunks, a fertile ecosystem with lushly producing trees and shrubs, offering food and shelter for a great diversity of wildlife. Beaver abound. Some have learned to build their lodges on floating logs which become in effect beaver houseboats viable through all floods. Present though less readily seen are bobcat, coyote (some of them crossed with wolves and looking like half of each), otter, mink, as well as the endangered fat pocketbook pearly mussel in the river.

Various parts of the refuge may be closed in fall and winter to offer waterfowl sanctuary and because the refuge is subject to flooding—75 per cent of it is under water at least part of every year, and all of it some years. So best check with the office if in doubt.

Arkansas is a state with abundant wild flowers, and they bloom through all the long growing season. Fall foliage turns red just as the waterfowl start to return in numbers to gratify those who started White River to counter indiscriminate shooting practices when tens of thousands were slaughtered simply to prove marksmanship. Old photographs show trucks piled high with mallard duck heads alone to show the numbers shot, the bodies cast aside. Now this refuge attracts one of the largest concentrations of wintering waterfowl in the lower Mississippi Flyway, and if they do not totally blacken the sky, as perhaps when Hernando de Soto crossed the river here in 1521, sometimes they almost seem to.

How to get there: The office has been in DeWitt; the new head-quarters will be on Route 1 going south from DeWitt. The refuge itself is accessible also from Route 44 on the southwest end near Tichnor, and on the east from Route 85 and from Route 1 onto 316 and 318.

Open: Daylight hours March through October—other months best check with refuge office, as sections may be closed for waterfowl sanctuary or wet roads.

Best times to visit: Fall and spring.

What to see: White-tailed deer; Mississippi kites; turkey; waterfowl concentrations; possibly black bear; good variety of songbirds, possibly even Bachman's warblers.

What to do: About 75 miles of roads and trails; boating (rentals sometimes available); fishing for bass, crappie, bream, catfish; limited hunting for deer, turkey, squirrel, raccoon, sometimes waterfowl; camping seasonally; guided tours for groups with prior arrangement; waterfowl banding—visitors are invited to observe and participate, if they wish.

Where to stay: MOTELS—In DeWitt, Stuttgart, Helena. CAMP-GROUNDS—On the refuge March–October; also Lake Merrisach Corps of Engineers Park, south of refuge.

Weather notes: Winter sometimes touches zero; June and July hot and humid.

Points of interest nearby: Arkansas Post National Memorial, first white settlement west of Mississippi, with interesting nearby historical museum 20 miles south; and historical museum in DeWitt; beautiful old river bluff homes in Helena, 40 miles northeast.

For more information: White River National Wildlife Refuge, P.O. Box 308, DeWitt, Arkansas 72042. Phone: (501) 946-1468.

Greenville

★

YAZOO

YAZOO (Mississippi)

The wood duck has been called the most beautiful duck in the world —even its scientific name, *Aix sponsa*, refers to its spectacular breeding plumage, a breath-taking combination of reds, blues, green, bronze in striking patterns—and nowhere is it more intimately and abundantly visible than at Yazoo National Wildlife Refuge. Wood ducks sometimes seem to line the entranceway. They are common throughout the waterways, nesting in hundreds of houses as well as natural cavities. Refuge staff members had to put up hardware cloth over building chimneys to keep them from nesting there (after retrieving some of them unharmed from furnaces below). Once a staff member left his shed for a few minutes while building a wood duck house. When he returned a female wood duck was inside staking out a prior claim while her mate stood guard outside.

It would be hard to visit Yazoo without seeing a wood duck, and more likely a good many of them—about twelve thousand young ones are produced annually—and it is one of the world's eye-filling nature experiences.

But wood ducks are not all there is to see at this 12,470-acre refuge of diverse habitat ranging from agricultural cropland, planted largely in wildlife foodplants, to bottomland hardwood, in the heart of the Mississippi delta country.

White-tailed deer are equally visible, some resting and foraging near refuge headquarters; Canada geese, a resident flock of the giant species, are always around along with alligators—up to five hundred of this threatened species. In season, there are concentrations of wintering waterfowl—up to 6,500 snow and white-fronted geese in addition to the Canadas—and sometimes 150,000 ducks, predominantly mallard but numbers of nine other species as well.

Seldom seen by visitors but here in perhaps the largest numbers of any refuge is the rare and endangered eastern cougar. A reported sighting of this beautiful, wary animal occurs every two weeks or so. Family groups have been seen in recent years and the population is estimated at about a half dozen. Their screams can be heard at night.

A colony of herons and egrets, mostly cattle egrets but a half dozen others represented as well, some years accommodates twenty thousand nesting birds in summer in buttonbush and low-lying trees in the Deer Lake area—visible from the nature trail.

The wild turkey flock was recently estimated at three hundred birds. Mississippi kites are here in large numbers in spring and summer—sometimes sixty observed in a single day, usually flying over wooded portions (where they nest in dense and remote areas).

A few eagles, including goldens, stop each winter to rest and roost in a stand of tall cypress at the northeast corner of the lake.

Seasonally common are winter wrens, grasshopper sparrows, purple gallinules, Tennessee warblers, and hermit thrushes; and common nesters include painted and indigo buntings, northern and orchard orioles, dickcissels, gnatcatchers, ruby-throated hummingbirds, mourning doves, screech and barred owls, and five kinds of woodpeckers.

Coyote are occasionally spotted, some of them showing a heritage of red wolf strain. Beaver are common, their lodges visible in Gator Pond and Gin Slough.

And there are other mammals and birds as well, a variety that can be suggested by looking at the tracks left in soft ground on the trails after a rain—sometimes dozens of different kinds at one crossing, including bobcat, fox, raccoon, opossum, deer, mink, alligators, ducks, geese, and killdeer, and some of the small birds as well.

How to get there: From Greenville take Route 1 south 29 miles to refuge sign, then left 2 miles to headquarters.

Open: Dawn to dusk.

Best times to visit: Spring and fall.

What to see: Wood ducks; deer; wild turkey; alligators; waterfowl; Indian mounds dating from A.D. 400.

What to do: Twenty-six miles of walking and driving trails (some may close during wet weather); photography (blind available); limited hunts for deer, small game (no fishing in recent years due to heavy water pollution from agricultural chemicals).

Where to stay: MOTELS—In Greenville. CAMPGROUND—LeRoy Percy State Park, 8 miles north.

Weather notes: Midwinter can be cold, blustery.

What to take and wear: Waterproof footgear during rainy periods.

Points of interest nearby: Delta National Forest, 30 miles south; Lake Washington, 6 miles west (good birding, also boat launches); Vicksburg National Park, 60 miles south; Greenwood living farm project, 60 miles east; Winterville Mounds Historic State Park, 35 miles north; beautiful ante-bellum homes throughout area.

For more information: Yazoo National Wildlife Refuge, Route 1, Box 286, Hollandale, Mississippi 38748. Phone: (601) 839-2638.

VI. THE NORTH-CENTRAL STATES

The north-central refuges lie within the Great Plains, once a region of seemingly endless prairies and lakes, now mostly given over to intense agricultural activity, predominantly in corn, wheat, and cattle. They include some notable migratory waterfowl refuges along the Missouri River and on natural and man-made lakes, but the glory of this region lies in its nesting refuges for water birds and waterfowl. Nowhere else in the country are there so many places so well suited to this activity. Throughout the Dakotas and Nebraska (and also in Minnesota and Montana in neighboring regions) there are thousands of ponds and wetlands ranging in size from less than a hundred acres to many square miles, each providing nesting habitat for ducks and often for wading and shorebirds and geese as well.

These are called by the homely name of "prairie potholes." For the most part they are left over from the last glacier, scoured out by the retreating ice which left a hardpan or clay depression that holds water even in dry periods. Some of them are on named refuges; others are administered by wetland management districts under the U. S. Fish and Wildlife Service. Still others are privately owned, but subject to nondrainage easements sold to the government. Most are open to the public, but except for parking most have few if any visitor facilities. "Potholes" hardly describes them adequately—for they are jewels of marsh and water, small areas of remnant beauty that the first settlers saw in such profusion. They represent one of the great assets of these north-central states and it is to the credit of their citizens that many have been saved, for those not under such protection are steadily lost to drainage, this extraordinary wildlife habitat gone forever.

NORTH DAKOTA

The staffed refuges of North Dakota include some of the best of these superb natural areas. *Arrowwood* is a diversified refuge of prairie upland interspersed with wooded coulees and lakes in the east-central part of the state. Among its interesting wildlife inhabitants are sharp-tailed grouse, which have a dozen or more dancing grounds on the refuge. *Audubon,* named for the great naturalist-artist who visited this region in 1843 is outstanding habitat for water birds, the land here dotted with potholes and the eleven thousand acres of lakes holding more than a hundred and fifty islands. In spring and early summer thousands of breeding pairs of geese, cormorants, avocets, phalaropes, and eleven species of ducks can be seen from the four-mile auto tour route.

Des Lacs, one of four refuges along the Souris River near the Canadian border—the others are *Lostwood, J. Clark Salyer,* and *Upper Souris*—is at its best in spring when the visitor can see eared grebes in their gold-accented breeding plumage, ruddy ducks bobbing their bright blue bills in courtship display, and handsome western grebes in the water ballets with which they woo their breeding partners. Lostwood, administered from Des Lacs, is a unique area of beautiful, wild, and remote prairie grassland spotted with sparkling glacial lakes and potholes, woody thickets of aspen and snowberry and colorful wild flowers, the whole area almost untouched by human activity. J. Clark Salyer, named for one of the leading figures in this country's wildlife preservation efforts, has one of the nation's richest and most exciting bird populations with a list of over 250 species of which more than 125 nest. It is as well a great migratory refuge for shorebirds, geese, and ducks. Upper Souris may be the prettiest of the "Souris Loop" refuges—all of which you can see in a few days. It stretches for more than thirty miles along the river, which got its name—French for mouse—from the great numbers of those creatures which early French trappers found here. Within its boundaries is a diversity of habitat including river, lakes, marshes, prairie, and woodlands.

Sully's Hill in the eastern end of the state is one of the nation's first refuges, having been set aside by Theodore Roosevelt for big game preservation in 1904. Here in a relatively small space (just under seventeen hundred acres) are buffalo, elk, and deer, together with some of the region's most impressive migrations of small birds, especially warblers. *Tewaukon* in southeastern North Dakota is a productive water bird nesting refuge with ten duck species, including shoveler, mallard, pintail, redhead, canvasback, and blue-winged teal, along with bitterns, grebes, and herons.

SOUTH DAKOTA

Like its northern neighbor, South Dakota is extraordinarily rich in bird life, particularly water birds. *Lacreek,* along the state's southern border, has rare trumpeter swans, perhaps seen more easily here than anywhere, a large colony of nesting white pelicans, abundant American bitterns, and produces about ten thousand young ducks every year. Prairie dogs have two large colonies here and the near-extinct black-footed ferret may survive among them. The tiny swift fox is known to exist here in small numbers.

Lake Andes is best known for its wintering concentration of bald eagles, which appear around the refuge and its satellite *Karl Mundt* Refuge. In most years there are 100–150 of these majestic birds which fish and feed on waterfowl in and near the refuge, and particularly at the spillway of the Fort Randall dam. *Sand Lake* in the northeastern corner of the state has seven species of nesting raptors —Swainson's, sharp-shinned, Cooper's, red-tailed, marsh, and ferruginous hawks, as well as numerous kestrels, along with such interesting upland shorebirds as marbled godwits and upland sandpipers. *Waubay* is a lovely small refuge in the same region with equally impressive nesting populations which include red-necked grebes and common goldeneye ducks. Prairie wild flowers are outstanding.

NEBRASKA

Nebraska's ecologically unique sandhills region is the largest contiguous dune area in the western hemisphere. While its name seems to imply arid desolation, the reality is strikingly different. The hills are softly rounded and grass-covered, dotted with pure lakes formed when ground water, filtered by the sand, "perches" on impervious clay bottom between the hills. *Crescent Lake* in the western panhandle is a remote and beautiful refuge of almost fifty thousand acres in these hills. Upland sandpipers are abundant, as are the interesting Wilson's phalaropes, in which breeding plumage and nest-keeping roles of the sexes are reversed. Long-billed curlews are seen everywhere in spring and early summer as are pairs of avocets. *Valentine,* located in northern Nebraska, is similar to Crescent Lake, but even larger (though less remote), with 74,516 acres of sandhills, lake, and marsh. It is administered from nearby *Fort Niobrara,* a spacious big game reserve harboring large herds of buffalo, pronghorn antelope, mule and white-tailed deer.

KANSAS

Flint Hills, one of three Kansas refuges, rests in the vicinity of the country's largest remaining population of greater prairie chickens. It also is a key refuge for waterfowl migration in spring and fall. *Kirwin* has the largest flocks of migrating Canada geese in Kansas' portion of the Central Flyway, up to forty thousand in the fall with comparable numbers of white-fronted geese. *Quivira* is named for the vanished tribe of handsome, seven-foot-tall Indians discovered by Coronado in 1541. It attracts up to ten thousand sandhill cranes in fall migration and is notable for its breeding pairs of Mississippi kites, common throughout warm months here.

IOWA

Iowa has two refuges, *Union Slough* near the state's northern border and *De Soto* in the west along the border with Nebraska. About one third of De Soto lies in that state. Union Slough has a notable population of gray partridge. De Soto has one of the most spectacular fall migrations of waterfowl in the world with 150,000 or so snow geese regularly together with a dozen species of ducks. In peak years the refuge has as many as four hundred thousand geese and a million ducks in October and November, with up to seventy bald eagles following the waterfowl and wintering here.

MISSOURI

Mingo in southeastern Missouri has been a haven for wildlife since the Mississippi River changed course some eighteen thousand years ago and left an area of wetland and upland providing habitat for such creatures as swamp rabbit and wild turkey. It is rich in flora such as wake-robin, trillium, rue anemone, and in some isolated areas the spider lily and purple fringeless orchid. Several national champion trees also are found here. *Squaw Creek* in northwestern Missouri winters as many as two hundred bald eagles (and a few golden eagles) which regularly follow the migrating waterfowl to this refuge in the fall and stay on from mid-November to February. Sometimes as many as twenty-five or thirty may be seen roosting in a single tree.

Because of *Swan Lake* the nearby town of Sumner calls itself the Wild Goose Capital of the World and the name may be deserved. By late October there may be two hundred thousand of the honkers on this 10,670-acre refuge and their calling and chattering can be heard for more than a mile. To a visitor coming anywhere near the refuge at peak times they seem to be everywhere, in the fields, along the roads, as well as on the lake.

The following is a list of some birds of special interest found in common or abundant status at the refuges of this region.

Birds Common or Abundant at Seasons Indicated:

S: Spring   s: Summer   F: Fall   W: Winter

Mississippi Kite: Quivira, SsF.
Cooper's Hawk: Quivira, SsF; Swan Lake, SF.
Golden Eagle: Flint Hills, W; Kirwin, W; Quivira, SFW; Swan Lake, W.
Bald Eagle: Flint Hills, SFW; Kirwin, W; Lake Andes, W; Quivira, SFW; Swan Lake, FW; Squaw Creek, FW.
Prairie Falcon: Quivira, W.
Sharp-tailed Grouse: Arrowwood, SsFW; Crescent Lake, SsFW; Souris Loop, SsFW; Valentine, SsFW.
Greater Prairie Chicken: Flint Hills, SsFW; Valentine, S.
Gray Partridge: Arrowwood, SsFW; Audubon, SsFW; Souris Loop, SsFW; Union Slough, SsFW.
Snowy Plover: Quivira, SsF.
Long-billed Curlew: Crescent Lake, Ss; Quivira, SF; Valentine, Ss.
Upland Sandpiper: Audubon, SsF; Crescent Lake, Ss; Flint Hills, SsF; Lacreek, Ss; Souris Loop, s; Valentine, SsF; Waubay, Ss.
Baird's Sandpiper: Crescent Lake, SsF; Kirwin, SF; Quivira, SF; Sand Lake, Ss; Valentine, S.
Marbled Godwit: Audubon, Ss; Sand Lake, Ss; Souris Loop, F; Waubay, Ss.
Hudsonian Godwit: Squaw Creek, S.
Northern Phalarope: Souris Loop, SF; Waubay, SF.
Snowy Owl: Audubon, W.
Burrowing Owl: Lacreek, SsF.
Scissor-tailed Flycatcher: Flint Hills, Ss; Quivira, SsF.
Eastern Bluebird: Flint Hills, SsF; Union Slough, SsF.
Sprague's Pipit: Souris Loop, s.
Bohemian Waxwing: Souris Loop, SF.
Bell's Vireo: Flint Hills, SsF; Quivira, sF; Squaw Creek, Ss.
Bobolink: Arrowwood, Ss; Audubon, s; Crescent Lake, Ss;

Lacreek, Ss; Lake Andes, Ss; Swan Lake, S; Souris Loop, SsF;
Union Slough, SsF; Valentine, s; Waubay, SsF.

Blue Grosbeak: Quivira, SsF.

Lark Bunting: Audubon, s; Crescent Lake, SsF; Lacreek, Ss;
Souris Loop, Ss; Valentine, s.

Lark Sparrow: Crescent Lake, SsF; Quivira, SsF; Valentine, SsF.

Baird's Sparrow: Arrowwood, Ss; Audubon, Ss; Souris Loop, s.

Le Conte's Sparrow: Souris Loop, s.

Harris' Sparrow: Flint Hills, SFW; Quivira, SFW; Sand Lake, SF;
Squaw Creek, F; Souris Loop, SF; Tewaukon, SF; Waubay, SF.

Lapland Longspur: Arrowwood, SF; Audubon, SW; Flint Hills, W;
Lacreek, SW; Lake Andes, W; Sand Lake, W;
Souris Loop, SFW; Tewaukon, SFW.

Chestnut-collared Longspur: Audubon, Ss; Lake Andes, S;
Sand Lake, S; Souris Loop, Ss; Tewaukon, S;
Valentine, SF.

NORTH-CENTRAL

1 Des Lacs
2 Upper Souris
3 Audubon
4 J. Clark Salyer
5 Sully's Hill
6 Arrowwood
7 Tewaukon
8 Sand Lake
9 Waubay
10 Lake Andes
11 Lacreek
12 Fort Niobrara
13 Valentine
14 Crescent Lake
15 Kirwin
16 Quivira
17 Flint Hills
18 De Soto
19 Union Slough
20 Squaw Creek
21 Swan Lake
22 Mingo

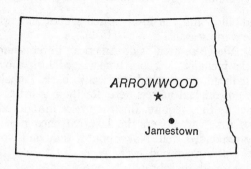

ARROWWOOD (North Dakota)

Arrowwood Refuge is a diversified 15,934-acre area of prairie upland interspersed with wooded coulees and a chain of four lakes in east-central North Dakota. Here western grebes perform their graceful courtship ballets, white-tailed deer along with some fox and badger thrive, and wood ducks, often called the most beautiful North American waterfowl, nest and flock in the largest population in this part of the United States.

Many of these, along with large groups of migratory waterfowl and shorebirds in spring and fall, can be seen on the approach to refuge headquarters along Lake Arrowhead, where there can be excellent small birding as well. The rest usually appear at one time or another (especially early and late) along the enjoyable 5.5-mile auto tour route which winds over softly green slopes, beside watered potholes, and alongside prairie dog burrows where litters of young "dogs" appear in May, leaping over each other in play and sometimes stopping to wash their mother's and each other's faces.

Sharp-tailed grouse have dancing grounds on a dozen or so small rises of ground where the males gather at dawn in the springtime to stomp down the grass, spread their wings and tails, inflate their gular sacs, and seek to impress females.

Baird's sparrows, sought-after by birders, are common here, and though not easily seen can usually be located with help and advice from the refuge staff (as can most of the interesting wildlife inhabitants). Common also are clay-colored sparrows and (at various seasons) Lapland longspurs, bobolinks, Tennessee and yellow warblers, bank and cliff swallows (these colonize in large numbers), gray partridge (most noticeable in coveys in the fall), red-tailed and marsh hawks, pied-billed and the lovely eared grebes, and white pelicans through the warm seasons.

Giant Canada geese nest, as do American bitterns and fifteen species of ducks including wigeon, blue-winged teal, shoveler, pintail, and some redhead, ring-necked, and canvasback. Probably the wood ducks were not original nesters here, for there is little woodland for the nest cavities they require. But they were introduced a few years ago. Houses were put up on the lakes to encourage breeding, to which they responded well. Now about a thousand wood ducklings are produced at Arrowwood every year, and they with the others begin to appear with their broods in June.

The hills and valleys, which were caused not by upthrust but by erosion from snowmelt runoff over the centuries, display wild-flower bloom from spring to frost—prairie roses, phlox, black sampsons, gaillardias—with yellow bladderworts in the marsh.

Arrowwood also administers a number of subrefuges and Waterfowl Production Areas, mostly of a water orientation though with varying wildlife, and most with few visitor facilities. Notable are *Chase Lake*, with a large white pelican nesting colony (visits are restricted during the nesting season) and *Long Lake*, which can have large flocks of migratory sandhill cranes. To arrange a visit to these, talk with the refuge office.

How to get there: From Jamestown take Route 281 north about 30 miles to refuge sign, just north of Edmunds; turn right 6 miles on gravel road to headquarters, which is a mile north of this road.

Open: Daylight hours April–September; after that may be closed for waterfowl sanctuary during hunting, check with office.

Best times to visit: May through September.

What to see: Waterfowl; white-tailed deer; sharp-tailed grouse; wood ducks; prairie dogs.

What to do: Auto tour route; hiking; picnicking; limited hunting for deer, fox, upland game; fishing; cross-country skiing and snowshoeing in certain areas.

Where to stay: MOTELS—Jamestown, 30 miles southwest. CAMP-GROUNDS—Jamestown and Carrington, also Jamestown Dam Recreation Area.

Weather notes: Winters harsh, most refuge roads impassable.

Points of interest nearby: Northern Prairie Research Center, Jamestown; Valley City National Fish Hatchery, 40 miles southeast.

For more information: Arrowwood National Wildlife Refuge, Pingree, North Dakota 58476. Phone: (701) 285-3341.

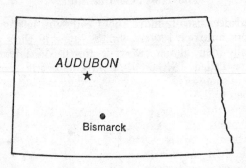

AUDUBON
★

● Bismarck

AUDUBON (North Dakota)

In 1843, Audubon journeyed up the Missouri River to explore the region and the native creatures of central North Dakota and make sketches for his paintings. His trip followed by a generation that of Lewis and Clark to this "beautiful level fertile plain" interspersed with glacial moraine knolls they saw around "Miry Creek." This 14,776 acres named for him is still superb habitat for water birds of all kinds, the land dotted with pothole ponds dating from the last glacier. The 11,000 acres of water hold more than 150 islands, which are a beautiful sight against the sparkling blue water, especially in spring when they are covered with golden wild flowers.

Nesting species include Canada geese, double-crested cormorants, avocets, eared, western, and pied-billed grebes, black-crowned night herons, rails, coots, black and common terns, Wilson's phalaropes, and eleven kinds of ducks. There are thousands of these, many of which can be viewed from the four-mile auto tour route (best with a spotting scope for picking out individual birds)—the nest sites in April and May, and by late May some of the goose and duck families among the marsh vegetation.

The grasslands are a fascinating sight as well. Wild flowers bloom from early spring through all the warm months—pasqueflowers, torch flowers, blazing stars, prairie violets, gaillardias, purple cone-flowers, needle and thread grasses, and pincushion cacti suggest the range and variety. Ring-necked pheasant and gray partridge both are common, and nest, as do red-tailed hawks, vociferous marbled godwits, upland sandpipers in large numbers, some sharp-tailed grouse, and among the small birds chestnut-collared longspurs, lark buntings, vesper and clay-colored sparrows, yellow warblers and long-billed marsh wrens. Baird's sparrows can often be seen.

White-tailed deer usually move about early and late, and in some years pronghorn antelope (severe winters can thin their ranks); red fox occasionally den along the tour road; Richardson's ground squirrels, aptly called "flickertails," are abundant around headquarters (where some of the best small birding is also) as well as on almost any open trail.

Waterfowl go through in good numbers in fall and spring, and shorebird migration can be interesting when water levels leave fertile mudflats, bearing out local belief that North Dakota can harbor more of these than most coastal areas, with dozens of species of sandpipers, plovers, yellowlegs, terns, gulls, and others. Sandhill cranes can be spectacular in fall; it is not unusual for thousands to stop by on their way south.

By late fall most of these have moved out; winter is harsh here with thirty-five-below readings and high winds common, and North Dakotans often point out there is nothing between here and the North Pole but a barbed-wire fence. But for those willing to brave the staggering chill factor, there are often snowy owls and good numbers of redpolls, Bohemian waxwings, snow buntings, and golden eagles.

Audubon Refuge also administers about seventy-five Waterfowl Production Areas in three counties, as well as wetland easement refuges. These are held largely for their habitat, with few if any visitor facilities. They are mostly open to the public, however, and the refuge office will supply information on how to see them.

How to get there: From Coleharbor take Route 83 north 4 miles to refuge sign, then right on gravel road .7 mile to headquarters.

Open: Daylight hours.

Best times to visit: Spring and fall.

What to see: Waterfowl and shorebirds, migrating and nesting. Deer, sometimes pronghorn antelope. Pelicans, cormorants. Indian "tipi" rings.

What to do: Eight miles of roads for driving, hiking. Photography (portable blind can be reserved ahead). Limited deer hunt; winter ice fishing for walleye, northern pike. Cross-country skiing and snowshoeing, check with office.

Where to stay: MOTELS—Garrison, 12 miles northwest; Underwood, 12 miles south. CAMPGROUNDS—Fort Stevenson State Park, 15 miles northwest; Lake Sakakawea State Park, 19 miles southwest; various others in Garrison Reservoir area.

Weather notes: Winters harsh, roads often impassable.

Points of interest nearby: Fort Mandan, restoration of Lewis and Clark campsite, 20 miles south; Stanton Indian Village, 35 miles southwest; Garrison Dam National Fish Hatchery, 14 miles southwest.

For more information: Audubon National Wildlife Refuge, Coleharbor, North Dakota 58531. Phone: (701) 442-5474.

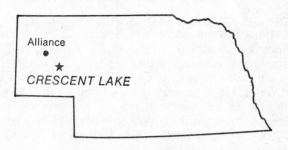

Alliance

★

CRESCENT LAKE

CRESCENT LAKE (Nebraska)

This wild, remote, and little-known refuge is one of the most interesting and beautiful in the system. Located on 45,818 acres in the rolling grass-covered sandhills of the Nebraska panhandle, it is in the largest continuous dune area in the western hemisphere. It is the remnant of a day when the sea washed over this region and huge crocodiles and later camels and rhinoceros roamed the land; its moisture-retaining soil structure supports nutritious vegetation in meadows and marsh and about 18 jewel-like ponds and lakes, most surrounded by dense nesting cover, some edged with trees, others open to the sky, attracting and supporting a widely varied wildlife population.

Sharp-tailed grouse have at least thirty known dancing grounds on or near the refuge where males gather in spring to stomp about, inflate their violet gular sacs and throatily entreat their mates.

The usually uncommon upland sandpipers are abundant on many areas here. So are Wilson's phalaropes—but look for the brightly plumaged *female* bird, because these reverse their sex roles. The males are dun-colored and incubate the eggs (sometimes forty-five thousand of these birds are on refuge waters in early May).

Long-billed curlews, showing their reddish wing linings and fantastic extended bills when they fly, breed commonly, as do avocets, striking black and white shorebirds with russet heads and necks in spring.

Northern phalaropes are common in spring. So are Swainson's thrushes, white-crowned sparrows, and in most warm months black-crowned night herons, marsh hawks, ring-necked pheasants, horned larks, Forster's and black terns, double-crested cormorants, eared grebes, pectoral sandpipers, Canada geese, a dozen kinds of ducks, along with lark buntings, bobolinks, lark and grasshopper sparrows, long-billed marsh wrens, and others. Several hundred white pelicans come through seasonally.

Both mule and white-tailed deer are here, the former in smaller numbers but more apparent as their curiosity leads them to investigate the visitor; the latter evident most often by their snowy "flags" as they beat a retreat. Pronghorn antelope are around as well, as are porcupine, raccoon, muskrat, pocket gophers, kangaroo rats, and coyotes (fewer of those lately due to high fur prices and intensive, including aerial, hunting off the refuge).

Wild flowers abound through the growing season, from the tiny star lilies in spring to the prairie coneflowers and blazing stars in August; and among the interesting reptiles and amphibians are the ornate box turtles, prairie race runners, and barred tiger salamanders.

One can marvel at vast areas seemingly untouched by human hands, and the best way to do it is simply to start out, driving slowly along trails, getting out and walking around ponds and brushy areas and looking closely with binoculars and field guide (low vegetation makes much of the wildlife here relatively easy to spot). Secondary roads may require four-wheel drive; consult the refuge office and map on this, and ask where interesting things have been seen lately.

Also administered by Crescent Lake is *North Platte* Refuge, 5,047 acres of lakes and grassland northeast of Scottsbluff, which offers resting habitat to large waterfowl concentrations—up to two hundred thousand ducks, mainly mallard—in migration. It is open to recreational use in summer but closed to provide sanctuary from October 1 through mid-January.

How to get there: From Oshkosh go north on West Second Street for 28 miles from intersection of Routes 27 and 26, following refuge signs all the way.

Open: Daylight hours.

Best times to visit: Spring and fall.

What to see: Upland sandpipers, long-billed curlews, sharp-tailed grouse and great spectrum of water and upland birds; deer; interesting sandhills formations.

What to do: Some 100 miles of roads for driving, hiking; photography (vehicle is a good blind); limited hunting for deer, antelope, upland game; ice fishing for northern pike, other times for bass, perch, bluegill.

Where to stay: MOTELS—Oshkosh and Alliance. CAMPGROUNDS—

Oshkosh and Alliance, also Smith Lake State Recreation Area, 50 miles north.

Weather notes: Winds can pile heavy drifts from an inch of snow; spring and summer rains hamper travel—check if coming from a distance.

What to take and wear: Four-wheel drive if planning to explore back roads; canteen if hiking cross-country.

Points of interest nearby: Scottsbluff National Monument, 105 miles west—ruts left by Oregon Trail still visible; Chimney Rock Historical Park, 85 miles west; Ash Hollow Historical Park, 50 miles southeast; Wildcat Hills Big Game Refuge (also fine birding) near Scottsbluff.

For more information: Crescent Lake National Wildlife Refuge, Star Route, Ellsworth, Nebraska 69340. Phone: (308) 762-4893.

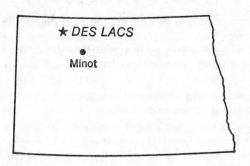

★ *DES LACS*

● Minot

DES LACS (North Dakota)

The approach to Des Lacs Refuge from the tiny nearby town of Kenmare gives a hint of what may be seen there—especially in spring: eared grebes in gold-accented breeding plumage building their floating nests in the river vegetation; ruddy ducks bobbing their bright blue bills in courtship display; mallard, scaup, and red-head ducks, with mates incubating eggs nearby; handsome western grebes, nicknamed "swan grebes" for their grace, preparing for the water ballets with which they woo their breeding partners.

Fifteen miles of roads go through this 18,881 acres of lake and marsh, mixed grass prairie and woodland following along the Des Lacs River north to the Canadian border, and a wealth of wildlife but particularly birdlife can be seen here from ice breakup in April until winter closes in again in November.

Sharp-tailed grouse are common and have numbers of dancing grounds where dozens of males may gather for their springtime displays, fanning out their tails and revealing lavender gular sacs for any females that may be shopping around (and judging from the females' nonchalant attitude they're often only browsing).

Birding is outstanding; birders who wish to add the Sprague's pipit or Le Conte's or Baird's sparrow to their list can almost certainly do so. For they are common, along with lark buntings, chestnut-collared longspurs, veeries, willow and least flycatchers, and in migration Lapland longspurs (with a few Smith's), Bohemian waxwings, Swainson's and gray-cheeked thrushes, and raucous, colorful black-billed magpies all year. (A pair of notable birders in Kenmare, Dr. and Mrs. Robert Gammel, have helped thousands of visitors to see some of these.)

Of the more than 250 species on the bird list, at least 140 have nested, some in great numbers. They include three other grebe species, sixteen kinds of ducks, giant Canada geese, black-crowned night herons, upland sandpipers, Wilson's phalaropes, avocets, Franklin's gulls, black terns, gray partridges, red-tailed and Swainson's hawks—these latter sometimes in large numbers.

Common and sometimes abundant are white pelicans, sandhill cranes, whistling swans, and a variety of shorebirds and warblers in spring and fall.

Ducks and snow geese may build up to migratory concentrations of 150,000 or more.

Visitors can usually see eagles in winter (though at other times too) along with snow buntings, redpolls, and occasionally snowy owls.

The mammal population tends to stay out of sight; but white-tailed deer are here, also red fox, beaver, muskrat, and mink, and occasional coyote, bobcat, and snowshoe hare. All are most readily spotted early or late on the trails.

The refuge has several suggested routes for seeing its wildlife, along with helpful maps; but ask as well where various species have been seen most recently.

Lostwood, administered from Des Lacs but with its own manager, is a gem. It is a unique area of almost 25,000 acres of beautiful, wild, remote prairie grasslands spotted with sparkling glacial lakes and potholes, woody thickets of aspen and snowberry and colorful wild flowers. Large populations of sharp-tailed grouse live here, along with breeding waterfowl, shorebirds and raptors, and such sought-after small birds as the McCown's and chestnut-collared longspurs, Sprague's pipits, Baird's and Le Conte's sparrows. To see all these in such an untamed atmosphere, the various inhabitants conducting their daily lives almost as if no human being had ever trod these places (and not too many have), is an unforgettable experience.

Ruby-eyed eared grebes with golden mating headgear are here in great numbers. So are lark buntings, avocets, willets, Wilson's phalaropes, red-head ducks, shovelers, canvasbacks, and a dozen other duck species (when water conditions are right this is some of the best duck breeding ground in the United States). Raptors include marsh, Swainson's, and red-tailed hawks.

White pelicans visit in the warm months; whistling swans and sandhill cranes come through in migration, along with thousands of ducks and geese; small birds such as veeries, thrushes, bobolinks, and horned larks abound. White-tailed deer are plentiful also, along with beaver, jackrabbit, thirteen-lined ground squirrels, coyote, badger, red fox, mink, and a few snowshoe hare.

A visit here may not be easily come by. The refuge, located just twenty miles west of Des Lacs on County Road 2 and then south on State Highway 8, is open during daylight hours all year, and has miles of roads that can be driven or hiked for nature observation. They are mostly unimproved roads, winding through needlegrass, bluegrass, and western wheatgrass prairies best traveled in good weather, and in the average North Dakota year there is quite a lot of the other kind—cold rains in spring and fall, and long, harsh winters. But any trouble taken for such a visit is well worth it, for there can be no more rewarding time for a naturalist than a fine day spent at Lostwood from May through September.

Des Lacs also administers a number of Waterfowl Production Areas as well as subrefuges—*Lake Ilo, Shell Lake, Pretty Rock, Stewart Lake, White Lake, Lake Zahl,* and the Crosby and Lostwood Wetland Management Districts. These contain varied wildlife, mostly of the wetland type, and limited visitor access. For information on how to arrange a visit, consult refuge headquarters.

How to get there: From Minot go north on Route 52 to Kenmare, then west on County Road 1-A, 1.5 miles to headquarters.

Open: Daylight hours (may be closed briefly for sanctuary during hunting).

Best times to visit: Spring, summer, fall.

What to see: Waterfowl and shorebirds, seasonally in large numbers; sharp-tailed grouse; deer; raptors; Sprague's pipits, Baird's and Le Conte's sparrows.

What to do: Fifteen miles of roads for driving, hiking; photoblind; boating; limited deer hunt; cross-country skiing, snowshoeing.

Where to stay: MOTELS—In Kenmare, or Minot for wider selection. CAMPGROUNDS—In Kenmare and Bowbells, 16 miles west.

Weather notes: Winters extremely severe (yearly temperatures can range from 40 below to 105 above).

Points of interest nearby: Tasker's Coulee Recreation Area, jointly managed with Kenmare City Parks; Salyer, Upper Souris National Wildlife Refuge (which see).

For more information: Des Lacs National Wildlife Refuge, Box 578, Kenmare, North Dakota 58746. Phone: (701) 385-4046.

DE SOTO (Iowa)

The sights and sounds of migrating waterfowl at this 7,820-acre southeast Iowa refuge (which lies about one third in Nebraska) can be a stunning, almost incredible experience. Watching from the observation tower or along the dike, one is overwhelmed by hundreds of thousands of snow geese, calling and flying en masse from their roosting spot to feeding areas and back again, and ducks going over in equal multitudes—the sky filled with birds.

They usually peak at 150,000 snow and blue geese (a snow color phase), along with some Canadas and white-fronted, and as many ducks, mostly mallard (but a dozen other species too). Their numbers have been at times even higher, as many as 400,000 geese and a million ducks at the height of seasonal migration in October and November, with lesser numbers seen in March and April. It is an unforgettable scene.

But so are the bald eagles, as many as seventy or more, which follow the waterfowl south from their breeding grounds in northern Minnesota and Wisconsin and spend the winter feeding on them and on fish in this 750-acre oxbow lake which was cut off when the Missouri River was channelized by the U. S. Army Corps of Engineers twenty years ago. They can be seen from November to March, soaring overhead, grouped in historic roosting trees, sometimes gliding by at eye level of the visitor in the observation tower at refuge headquarters.

All of this is widely witnessed, for De Soto has much public use—not only for wildlife but for other recreational activities. The refuge is open from mid-April to mid-September for swimming, boating, picnicking, fishing, mushroom picking, even waterskiing, and later in

October for a special auto tour route. There is also a limited fall hunting season, and ice fishing in January and February. A museum which holds relics from the cargo of the paddle-wheel steamship *Bertrand*, which sank in 1865 on what was then the Missouri River channel (now on refuge land)—clothing, equipment, even food supplies en route to the Montana minefields and preserved almost perfectly in the river silt—attracts many persons.

But the purpose of the refuge is wildlife, which it attracts in large numbers to its varied habitat of timber bottomlands (the only such large area in this section of the country) plus open fields and croplands, farmed on shares to provide wildlife sustenance.

The visitor driving quietly through the refuge in early morning or toward dusk often sees white-tailed deer—fifty or a hundred of them, if they are caught unawares; with their fawns in June and July. Other mammals, though normally wary, may be sighted at these times— coyote, fox, mink, raccoon, and, along the lake, muskrat, mink, and beaver.

Pheasant and quail are in upland areas and along roads, and red-headed woodpeckers sometimes seem to perch on every refuge sign. Red-tailed hawks are a common sight, overhead and perched on lookout points. Piping plovers and least terns have often nested on a sandspit in an isolated area. One can occasionally see them about the banks, as well as great blue herons and double-crested cormorants. Great horned and barred owls are common (though not commonly seen in daylight).

Common to abundant nesters among the smaller birds include bank swallows (they have a lakeside colony, best seen from a boat), rose-breasted grosbeaks, northern and orchard orioles, blue jays, dickcissels, redstarts, yellowthroats and yellow warblers, eastern wood pewees, least flycatchers, warbling and Bell's vireos, and mourning doves.

A curious resident is the paddlefish, which can grow up to six feet long and weigh up to 180 pounds. A primordial creature with a large paddle-shaped snout about which little is known, it was isolated from its ancient river home by the channelizing. It is caught only by snagging. The records for Nebraska and Iowa, over eighty pounds, have been caught at De Soto. If you're in a boat and see a large swirl as of something huge in the water, that's a paddlefish.

A curious plant is the horsetail or scouring rush, which covers acres of the refuge lowlands. This ancient plant contains so much silica, you can file your nails on it.

Wildlife has always been attracted to this place, and so have humans. Indians probably hunted the area extensively, and the explorers Lewis and Clark came this way on their route west, and camped near what is now the refuge.

How to get there: From Council Bluffs, go north on I-29 to Route 30 and refuge sign; then west about 6 miles on 30 to refuge entrance and headquarters area.

Open: Dawn to dusk mid-April to mid-September; otherwise variable depending on use. Check with headquarters, open weekdays all year (U. S. Route 30 observation tower always open). The auto tour is open for a 3-week period in mid-October.

Best times to visit: Spring and fall.

What to see: Great masses of snow geese and ducks in migration. Wintering eagles. Relics of unearthed Mississippi River steamboat, sunk in 1865 en route to gold fields. Deer, coyotes.

What to do: Nature trails. Photography (blind available by permit). Observation towers. In summer, wide variety of recreation permitted—swimming, boating, picnicking, waterskiing. Limited hunting for deer and waterfowl according to Iowa and Nebraska regulations. Fishing for crappie, bass, channel cat, and prehistoric paddlefish in summer; through ice in January–February.

Where to stay: MOTELS—At Blair, Nebraska, 5 miles west; near I-29, 5 miles east; at Council Bluffs, 25 miles south. CAMPGROUNDS— At Wilson Island State Recreation Area, adjacent to refuge on south.

Weather notes: Winter can be cold with subzero periods and penetrating dampness; spring often showery through mid-May.

What to take and wear: Raingear and windbreaker spring and fall; insulated clothing late fall and winter.

Points of interest nearby: Wilson Island (see CAMPGROUNDS); Fontenelle Forest, privately endowed natural area 25 miles south near Omaha; Fort Atchison at Fort Calhoun, historic site south of refuge in Nebraska.

For more information: De Soto National Wildlife Refuge, Route 1, Box 114, Missouri Valley, Iowa 51555. Phone: (712) 642-4121.

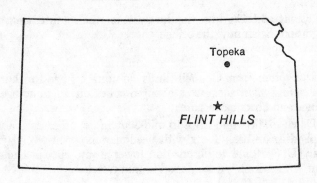

Topeka

★
FLINT HILLS

FLINT HILLS (Kansas)

Flint Hills Refuge in southeast Kansas is named for the rolling fossil-filled limestone range just to the west which formed when seas washed across this grassland area in ancient Permian times. This range runs the length of the state and often holds the largest concentrations of greater prairie chickens in the United States. Many of these wander over to the refuge when there is sufficient dry upland, although, as the refuge lies in the flood pool of the John Redmond Dam and reservoir, up to 90 per cent of its 18,500 acres can be inundated at times.

When this happens the refuge can accommodate up to a hundred thousand waterfowl in spring and fall migration, including Canada, white-fronted, and snow geese, and ducks of more than a dozen species. These include good numbers of redhead and canvasback, and also the blue-winged teal and mallard which stay and nest. Some of these also are here in winter along with the common and well-named goldeneye which is in good numbers *only* then. They furnish part of the attraction for the eagles (mostly bald but some golden) which frequent the dam area and prey on the fish there.

White pelicans come through in March and October, sometimes six hundred or so, en route to and from their southern wintering grounds. Snowy egrets and great blue and green herons appear in warm months and the greens nest, though there is no colony on the refuge. Marsh and red-tailed hawks are around most of the time.

Small birding can be rewarding; among those common in warm seasons are indigo buntings and dickcissels, northern and orchard orioles, Bell's vireos, grasshopper sparrows, red-headed woodpeckers, blue-gray gnatcatchers, and the lovely scissor-tailed flycatchers; and in migration Swainson's and gray-cheeked thrushes, usually some Le Conte's sparrows and sometimes many warblers, including the prothonotary, parula, Nashville, and orange-crowned.

Killdeer often nest at headquarters, and in winter Lapland longspurs and Harris' sparrows are common in the area, as are snowy owls in their periodic southerly invasions. Smith's longspurs have appeared in recent years in March.

The usually uncommon upland sandpiper is common to abundant. It is visible on fence posts in the spring and can always be found somewhere in warm months even when it tries to retire from view during its nesting.

White-tailed deer and coyote are here, most readily seen at dawn and dusk.

The refuge is not always easy birding. When roads are dry the visitor can travel through many inviting clumps of vegetation and open grasslands; in wet or flood times, however, these can be impassable, and a visitor from any distance should first check with the office—a good idea in any case to learn what is around. The staff almost always know where prairie chickens have been seen and in spring, where a view may be arranged, on or off the refuge, of their courtship-booming grounds.

How to get there: From Emporia take I-35 north to Route 130, then south to Hartford High School where turn right 3.5 blocks to refuge sign.

Open: Twenty-four hours (some areas closed in fall).

Best times to visit: Spring and fall.

What to see: Waterfowl concentrations; upland sandpipers; greater prairie chickens; occasional rarities.

What to do: Forty miles of roads for driving, hiking; interpretive trail; observation tower; hunting for deer, upland game, waterfowl; fishing, good in spring for white bass, crappie, channel catfish.

Where to stay: MOTELS—In Emporia, 20 miles northwest. CAMPGROUNDS—Primitive on refuge; also John Redmond Reservoir land.

Weather notes: Tornadoes possible through spring and summer.

Points of interest nearby: John Redmond Reservoir, various recreational facilities (3 others within 60-mile radius); home and newspaper office of famed Pulitzer Prize-winning editor William Allen White in Emporia.

For more information: Flint Hills National Wildlife Refuge, P.O. Box 128, Hartford, Kansas 66854. Phone: (316) 392-5553.

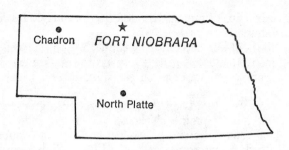

Chadron ★ FORT NIOBRARA

North Platte

FORT NIOBRARA (Nebraska)

Elk, bison, and antelope roam in herds as they did four hundred years ago on the prairie grasslands of north-central Nebraska—not in the numbers there were before the white men came, but it will almost seem so to the visitor looking out among the free-roaming herds at 19,124-acre Fort Niobrara Refuge.

White-tailed and mule deer are here as well—the former showing their fluffy white flags of tails as they lope up the rolling sandhills, the latter, more curious, edging closer to see what is going on.

A prairie dog "town" covers twenty acres or more, the small residents, which once numbered in the millions but were exterminated by land use practices over much of the West, fearless here as they scamper among their burrows.

Texas longhorn cattle, evolved from descendants of the fighting bulls of Spain and brought over by Spanish explorers and settlers—a bull can weigh a ton and full horn length extend nine feet—amble for the most part peacefully about the countryside (but don't get out of your car in the presence of any of these!).

Coyotes can be seen early and late. Porcupines lumber along almost anywhere, anytime.

Once, in prehistory, camels, elephants, and rhinoceros lived here —their fossil remains can still be seen on the refuge—and before that, vast seas covered this lush grazing vegetation, on which cattle raised in the sandhills can gain three pounds a day. Now, the bison (or buffalo), whose western populations were once estimated at sixty million but reduced to near extinction by the turn of the century, renew their hold on the land with young calves born in May. So do the massive-antlered elk, whose ancestors came over from Siberia; the pronghorn antelope, swiftest North American mammal, clocked up to seventy miles an hour; and the deer, their young appearing by June at the latest.

By July, clouds of dust are raised by contesting bison males pawing the ground in courtship and mating displays to start the whole process all over again; pronghorn and elk breeding displays begin in September.

Birding is excellent too. Large flocks of sharp-tailed grouse are present and a few greater prairie chickens, bald and golden eagles in winter. Upland sandpipers and long-billed curlews are common and nest. Wild turkey, pheasant, red-tailed hawks, and great blue herons are common. So are smaller birds such as black-headed grosbeaks, yellow-breasted chats, rock wrens, Say's phoebes, horned larks, grasshopper and lark sparrows, and occasionally a Townsend's solitaire.

Prairie wild flowers peak in June, with blazing stars and perhaps twenty other species blooming at once. Canoeing is enjoyable on the Niobrara River; so is the nature trail beside the waterfall. In the fall surplus animals, beyond the healthy number for the range, are rounded up and auctioned off, a popular event in early October. It is no easy trick for a man on horseback to herd a one-ton bull buffalo— "Generally we herd them just about anywhere they want to go," said one herdsman.

At Valentine Refuge sharp-tailed grouse dance and inflate lavender gular sacs on ancestral courting grounds. Shorebirds appear in huge flocks numbering in the tens of thousands in this beautiful and fascinating area of wild and remote-seeming grass-covered sandhills south of Valentine, Nebraska. It is administered from Fort Niobrara Refuge.

Sometimes the birds in these migratory concentrations have seemed impossible to estimate, when whole acres of shoreline and mudflats are shimmering with thousands of Wilson's phalaropes and dowitchers.

One can see why. Valentine is covered with appropriate habitat. There are 71,516 acres, 10,000 of which are water distributed among dozens of lakes and marsh areas, with the rest grassland, wet meadows, and rolling sandhills, all scenically beautiful—quiet and vast, seeming to stretch on forever. And the sight of ten thousand or more birds on one of these watery areas in spring and fall is more usual than otherwise.

The upland sandpiper is a common nester here; so are avocets, American bitterns, black-crowned night herons, eared, western, and pied-billed grebes, black and Forster's terns, and six species of ducks, along with small numbers of trumpeter swans. White pelicans are common in summer, ring-necked pheasant all year long, as are short-eared and great horned owls. Lark buntings, red-eyed and warbling vireos, and chestnut-collared longspurs are seasonally common and nest; mountain bluebirds do so occasionally.

Mule and white-tailed deer are present all the time, as are coyote (though less readily seen) and occasionally antelope.

More than forty miles of roads are open to driving and hiking, and blinds are available for observing and photographing the grouse and sometimes prairie chickens. Fishing can be excellent for bass, bluegill, and for northern pike through the ice in winter.

To get to refuge field headquarters take Route 83 south from the town of Valentine fourteen miles to Spur Route 16B, then right sixteen miles. Weather and other information is similar to that at Fort Niobrara.

How to get there: From Valentine take Route 12 east 5 miles.

Open: Daylight hours.

Best times to visit: April through October.

What to see: Bison, elk, longhorn cattle, antelope, mule and white-tailed deer, prairie dogs, turkey, sharp-tailed grouse, upland sandpipers; historic Fort Niobrara; relics of prehistoric wildlife inhabitants.

What to do: Fifteen miles of roads for driving, hiking (also 4,630-acre Wilderness Area in summer); horseback riding; self-guided trail; canoeing (rental available nearby); picnicking; photography.

Where to stay: MOTELS—In Valentine. CAMPGROUNDS—In Valentine; also Ballards Marsh State Park, 20 miles south.

Weather notes: Winters can be harsh; snow and rain can make roads impassable.

Points of interest nearby: Interesting area tours available in Valentine; also Valentine State Fish Hatchery; Merritt Reservoir, 26 miles southwest; Halsey National Forest, 50 miles southwest; Valentine National Wildlife Refuge, 90 miles northwest.

For more information: Fort Niobrara National Wildlife Refuge, Hidden Timber Star Route, Valentine, Nebraska 69201. Phone: (402) 376-3789.

HASTINGS WETLAND MANAGEMENT DISTRICT (Nebraska)

These are 15,200 acres of habitat acquired as Waterfowl Production Areas in seven Nebraska counties. They support a varying bird and other wildlife population in addition to waterfowl; generally surround shallow pond and marsh areas; are open for hiking and nature observation as well as seasonal hunting and fishing; and, except for parking areas, are mostly without visitor facilities. For location and further information contact the district office, Box 847, Hastings, Nebraska 68901. Phone: (402) 463-4888.

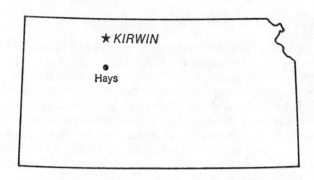

★ KIRWIN

• Hays

KIRWIN (Kansas)

The largest flocks of Canada geese in Kansas' well-traveled section of the Central Flyway, including at least six subspecies of this handsome bird, can be seen at Kirwin Refuge. This is a 10,778-acre overlay of a Bureau of Reclamation lake project in central Kansas just twenty miles west of the geographical center of the contiguous United States.

Visitors can sometimes see forty thousand Canadas during fall migration (and many more come through) with comparable numbers of white-fronted geese. In a good year—when ideal weather combines with sufficient water—there have been peak populations of more than two hundred thousand ducks, mostly mallard, gadwall, pintail, blue-winged teal, and shoveler, all of which nest in fair numbers.

Hundreds of sandhill cranes may be here in spring and fall; white pelicans; sometimes a few endangered whooping cranes en route from their northern Canada breeding grounds to south Texas; Franklin's gulls in large numbers; along with flocks of transient avocets, Wilson's phalaropes, Baird's sandpipers, Harris' sparrows, and a fair assortment of warblers.

A large "town" of black-tailed prairie dogs is a delight to visitors all year (when cold or wet weather does not preclude travel on some refuge roads) and white-tailed and a few mule deer browse early and late in the day. Badger are common, though nocturnal, and if they cannot always be readily seen, their burrows can, identified by their characteristic shape—somewhat like a half moon with the flat side on the bottom. Beaver live here; so do coyote and red fox, but high fur prices and intensive off-refuge trapping have reduced their numbers.

Birding can be enjoyable along brushy areas and in shelter belts— for there are probably more trees in Kansas now, as a result of planting programs, than a century ago. Raucous, colorful black-billed magpies are common all year. So are horned larks, red-shafted flickers, red-tailed hawks, bobwhite quail, and pheasant, and numerous seasonally are great blue herons, double-crested cormorants, vesper and lark sparrows, red-headed woodpeckers, and Swainson's hawks, which nest. Typifying the east-west crossover are the horned and eared grebes, eastern and Say's phoebes, eastern cottontails and black-tailed jackrabbits of the western plains.

The refuge has had water problems in some years, the result of drought plus changing farm practices, with more terraces and small ponds decreasing water going into the lake and more irrigation taking water out. This can mean less waterfowl habitat. Yet prairie chickens and turkeys have appeared more often recently, so such a change, if permanent, could mean a broadening of general wildlife habitat.

How to get there: From Phillipsburg take Route 183 south to Glade, east on Route 9 for 6 miles to refuge sign. Office is a mile south of sign.

Open: Twenty-four hours.

Best times to visit: Spring and fall.

What to see: Waterfowl; prairie dogs; pheasant; quail; deer.

What to do: Twenty-nine miles of roads for driving, hiking; interpretive trails; picnic areas; boating (rentals nearby); fishing—some say the best in Kansas for walleye; limited hunting for waterfowl, deer, upland game.

Where to stay: MOTELS—In Phillipsburg and Smith Center. CAMPGROUNDS—In Phillipsburg and Smith Center; also on refuge.

Weather notes: Changeable and windy—can be windiest place in interior United States; winters can be severe.

Points of interest nearby: Hansen Museum at Logan; old Fort Bissell, Phillipsburg; Cedar Bluff National Fish Hatchery at Ellis.

For more information: Kirwin National Wildlife Refuge, Kirwin, Kansas 67644. Phone: (913) 646-2373.

KULM WETLAND MANAGEMENT
DISTRICT (North Dakota)

This office manages Waterfowl Production Areas in four North Dakota counties, as well as several small refuges maintained largely for their waterfowl habitat, with varying wildlife and few visitor facilities, though open to the public. To arrange a visit, contact the district office, Box E, Kulm, North Dakota 58456. Phone: (701) 724-3598.

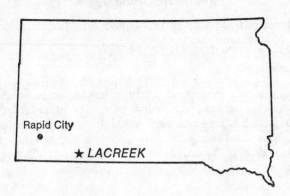

Rapid City

★ *LACREEK*

LACREEK (South Dakota)

Lacreek Refuge, 16,147 acres of marsh and grassland on the edge of the rolling sandhills in the southwest corner of South Dakota, is one of the richest areas in bird life in the country.

Trumpeter swans, once close to extinction, nest here and demonstrate their majestic strength and beauty in territorial and courtship displays from November to May. Lacreek is sometimes highest in the nation in the annual Audubon Christmas Bird Count for this stunning creature.

White pelicans, whose nine-foot wingspreads exceed the trumpeters' by only a little, pack together on two small islands, their nests just a few inches apart. This is one of the few places in the United States where they breed. They produce about two thousand young every summer. Their nests are intermingled with those of double-crested cormorants, and are preceded in the early spring by Canada geese which, in an unusual adaptation, sometimes nest colonially in the previous year's pelican nests before the pelicans return from the south. These geese of the giant *maxima* race, once thought extinct, have also used muskrat lodges as breeding structures and even constructed floating nests in bogs here.

American bitterns, shy denizens of the high marsh grass, are so abundant here that visitors can easily spot them.

The nesting of water birds of almost all kinds is phenomenal. About ten thousand young ducks are produced every year—mostly blue-winged teal but also green-winged, mallard, pintail, redhead, gadwall, wigeon, and canvasback. There are also nesting king, Virginia, and sora rails, Forster's and black terns, avocets, coots, western grebes, and black-crowned night herons.

The grasslands are equally productive with breeding long-billed curlews, upland sandpipers, ring-necked pheasant, and sharp-tailed grouse. Ask at the office where their dancing grounds have been located recently.

Marsh, Swainson's, and a few ferruginous hawks nest, as do great horned owls (often in a big cottonwood behind headquarters), burrowing owls (many in prairie dog holes), and short-eared owls, of which on a good day a dozen may be seen hunting in their mothlike flight over fields in the afternoon.

Lark buntings are abundant, as are yellowthroats and cliff swallows, which build solid masses of mud houses on headquarters buildings and bridges. You can see three kinds of longspurs seasonally. Eagles spend the winter here.

Mule and white-tailed deer browse on a marsh peninsula readily visible from the tour road, and bring their fawns out in June. One can hear and often see coyote in early evening. Muskrat build abundant houses in the marsh areas and beaver build lodges. Prairie dogs of the black-tailed variety have two large colonies, and the black-footed ferret, close to extinction, may survive in their company here. The tiny swift fox, also once believed to be gone, is now known to exist here in small numbers.

All except the rarest and most secretive of these can be seen from the refuge roads and, with a spotting scope, from the ninety-foot observation tower. This is the way refuge staff locate most of the more secluded swans' nests.

How to get there: From Martin take Route 18 east about 13 miles to (marked) gravel road, then south 5 miles to Tuthill and 1 mile west to refuge entrance. Headquarters is 6.5 miles southwest of entrance.

Open: Daylight hours.

Best times to visit: All year interesting (though blizzards, drifting snow, and rain can make roads seasonally impassable).

What to see: Trumpeter swans; white pelicans; sharp-tailed grouse; waterfowl; short-eared owls; deer; prairie dogs; sandhill plant associations; many others.

What to do: Twelve miles of roads for driving, hiking; self-guided tours; observation tower; photography (permits may be granted for temporary blinds); limited pheasant hunting; fishing on adjacent recreation area for trout and through winter ice for northern pike.

Where to stay: MOTELS—In Martin. CAMPGROUNDS—In Martin; also by permit at adjacent Little White River Recreation Area.

Weather notes: Blizzards in winter, muddy roads in spring (see *Best times* above).

What to take and wear: Spotting scope.

Points of interest nearby: McKelvie National Forest, 50 miles southeast; Wounded Knee National Historic Site, 25 miles west; Badlands National Monument, 60 miles northwest.

For more information: Lacreek National Wildlife Refuge, South Route, Martin, South Dakota 57551. Phone: (605) 685-6508.

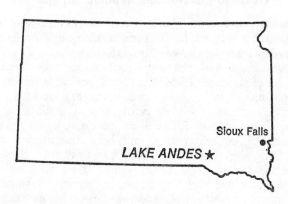

Sioux Falls

LAKE ANDES ★

LAKE ANDES (South Dakota)

The largest concentrations of endangered bald eagles in the contiguous United States can occur in fall and winter in and around Lake Andes Refuge and its adjacent Karl Mundt Refuge—100 or 150 in most years, though there have been as many as 280. They feed around Lake Francis Case and the spillway of the Fort Randall dam, on fish and on waterfowl which sometimes gather in the Lake Andes area in peak numbers of 200,000. These are mostly mallard but also green-winged teal, wigeon, pintail, and sometimes fifteen thousand Canada geese. All are in fine view from several points about the water areas, the eagles hunting from the rock cliffs or tall cottonwood trees, swooping down, scooping up a fish and returning to the cliffs to feed on it.

They roost at night on the Mundt Refuge, which was established specifically as an eagle sanctuary and is closed to public use, for the eagles are extremely sensitive to disturbance. There is, however, a public road which bisects it and from which the traveler can occasionally see the eagles, as well as the other wildlife that inhabit it—mule and white-tailed deer, rabbit, wild turkey, sharp-tailed grouse, and occasional bobwhite quail. The adjacent Corps of Engineers park and nature trail also may afford sights of these.

Waterfowl viewing can be impressive at any season—ten species of ducks nest here, although what is present depends to a great extent on water. In wet years when Lake Andes is full, there is much to see —not only ducks and geese and occasional whistling swans in migration, but white pelicans, bitterns, western grebes, cormorants, black-crowned night herons, long-billed dowitchers, sometimes golden plovers, upland sandpipers, Forster's and black terns and others, some of them also nesting. In dry periods these can dwindle almost to nothing, depending on the severity of the drought.

In any event, Lake Andes has a delightful nature trail which winds through most of the kinds of habitat of this part of southeast South Dakota—marsh, woods, brush, upland prairie, and pothole ponds—and in which a variety of wildlife can be seen. Bobolinks can arrive in large numbers in spring. Pheasant are common, as are red-headed woodpeckers, killdeer, dickcissels, and both eastern and western kingbirds. Long- and short-billed marsh wrens call from the cattails. Redhead ducks and teal nest. Great horned and screech owls roost. White-tailed deer rest and browse, an assortment of small birds, including warblers, pass through, and wild flowers bloom from spring through late summer.

Lake Andes also administers a wetland management district made up of small parcels of natural prairie marsh and upland spread over twenty counties—almost a hundred thousand acres in all, acquired as Waterfowl Production Areas and owned or held in perpetual easement. These are open for nature viewing and exploration, as well as hunting and fishing in season. They support a variety of wildlife as well as the waterfowl that nest. Some have prairie chickens; others a good supply of small mammals. They mostly are natural areas with no facilities other than parking areas. Persons wishing to visit them may contact refuge headquarters for information on what may be seen at the various tracts and maps telling how to find them.

How to get there: From Lake Andes (where headquarters is) go north past Lake Andes grain elevators 1 mile to unmarked paved road; turn east, go 6 miles straight to refuge sign.

Open: Daylight hours (nature trail closed in winter).

Best times to visit: Spring and fall through January.

What to see: Eagles; waterfowl; deer.

What to do: Nature trail; photography; observation tower; fishing; limited waterfowl hunting. Boating when water conditions permit.

Where to stay: MOTELS—Lake Andes. CAMPGROUNDS—At Lake Francis Case, 8 miles south.

Weather notes: Winters can be harsh with poor driving conditions; summers extremely hot.

Points of interest nearby: Lake Francis Case Recreation Area—

various recreational facilities, nature trail; Gavins Point National Fish Hatchery at Yankton.

For more information: Lake Andes National Wildlife Refuge, P.O. Box 279, Lake Andes, South Dakota 57356. Phone: (605) 487-7603.

MADISON WETLAND MANAGEMENT DISTRICT (South Dakota)

This district manages more than ~~twenty-one~~ thousand small wetland areas in southwest South Dakota, mostly small parcels acquired or held in easement because they hold glacial potholes and marsh which are valued for waterfowl production. In spring these produce hundreds of small ducks and offer habitat for other wildlife as well; while they are open to the public, most have few if any visitor facilities other than parking. To locate and get further information contact the District Office, Box 48, Madison, South Dakota 57042. Phone: (605) 256-2974.

Cape Girardeau ●
★
MINGO

MINGO (Missouri)

Mingo cannot fail to fascinate anyone with a serious interest in nature. Its many manifestations here range from the denizens of an ancient swamp where once the mighty Mississippi flowed, to wild turkeys, deer, and large concentrations of waterfowl, and some of the largest specimen trees in existence.

This 21,670-acre refuge in the southeast "boot heel" of Missouri has been a swamp and a haven for wildlife since the river changed course some eighteen thousand years ago. As such it attracted Shawnee and Osage Indians who made camp here, but it also inspired in them the fear that the mysterious atmosphere of a swamp often does, for they gave it its present name, which means treacherous and unreliable. A Confederate colonel during the Civil War, Jeff Thompson, earned the Civil War nickname "Swamp Fox" because he used it as a hiding place. Limestone bluffs with shallow caves still attest the river's long course through here; and the quiet of the wooded wetlands with their tall cypresses and tupelos surrounded by green duckweed and trailing vines with no sounds other than a bird calling or a turtle sliding into the water, quicken in the onlooker some of the same awe today.

About a fourth of the refuge is upland with oak-hickory succession and farmland, so the habitat is varied and more than two hundred bird species appear here, along with several dozen mammals and some sixty species of reptiles and amphibians. The whole history and ecology of Mingo has been carefully recorded and catalogued and is available to the visitor for reference.

Visitors can see waterfowl in good numbers in October–November and March. The birds peak sometimes at two hundred thousand ducks—mainly mallard but also pintail, green-winged teal, wigeon, gadwall, and shoveler—and twenty-five thousand geese, mainly Canadas with a few blues and snows. Many of these also winter here, and there is a smaller population which is resident and nests, mainly wood ducks and Canadas.

Wild turkeys, once rare in the state, are commonly seen here. So are great blue and little blue herons; red-bellied, red-headed, and pileated woodpeckers; orchard orioles; prothonotary, parula, cerulean, and yellow-throated warblers; red-tailed and red-shouldered hawks (with the Cooper's hawk occasional); Acadian flycatchers; blue-gray gnatcatchers; and quail. Bald eagles spend the winter—usually twenty-five or so.

A quiet walk, ride, or canoe trip at early morning or dusk will usually provide the visitor with sights of white-tailed deer and perhaps also raccoon, muskrat, opossum, and rarely a fox, mink, or bobcat.

Spring flowers are beautiful and a special tour is held in April to view them—bluebells, redbuds, wake-robin trilliums, rue anemones, Dutchman's breeches, dogwood, yellow rockets, and swamp buttercups—and in some isolated areas, spider lilies and purple fringeless orchids. Later there are large tracts of golden-blooming lotuses; in summer, trumpet creepers with their orange blooms attracting hummingbirds are everywhere; and scarlet cardinal flowers follow the roadsides in fall.

The trees are magnificent. Sixteen specimens found here are either national or state champions in size. One red maple is more than 10 feet around the trunk, one black gum almost 12, and a shagbark hickory is 118 feet tall with a spread of 50 feet. All these trees' measurements and locations have been recorded so the visitor can see and identify them.

Lists are available as well for the reptiles and amphibians. The hognose snake, which rolls over and plays dead if disturbed, is here, along with three poisonous ones—the cottonmouth, copperhead, and canebrake rattlesnake—which might not, so be careful. And there are lists of ferns, fungi, herbs, moles, and almost anything else imaginable, available for reference if not in leaflet form.

Like many similar places, Mingo was acquired as a refuge only after the land had been so abused by fires, overtimbering, and unsuccessful drainage attempts that it had been rendered almost useless for any other purpose. Naturalist Aldo Leopold once observed that the "central thesis of game management is this: game can be restored by the creative use of the same tools which have heretofore destroyed it—axe, plow, cow, fire, and gun." That has certainly been done here.

The refuge has three hiking trails, and special auto tours are held in April, October, and November. Visitors are welcome also to explore shallow caves along the Bluff Trail. A beautiful new visitors' center is snugged tastefully into the woods with interesting and imaginative displays as well as explanatory slide shows which can be seen during the day. Guided tours for groups can be arranged in advance.

How to get there: From Cape Girardeau take Route 74 west to Dutchtown, left on Route 25 to Advance, there turn right at 91 to get on Route C, take C to Arab, then south on 51 to Mingo.

Open: Dawn to dusk all year but certain areas restricted seasonally—check with office. Visitor center open 9 A.M. to 4 P.M.

Best times to visit: Spring and fall, though other seasons good too (summer can be uncomfortable for one unused to high humidity).

What to see: Waterfowl; eagles; interesting swamp habitat and remnants of old river bluffs; Indian campsites; huge trees (state and national champions); deer; wild turkey; great variety of plant and other natural life.

What to do: Nature trails; observation towers; horseback riding; bicycling; canoeing; photography (blind available); mushroom, berry, and nut picking; fishing March 15–September 30 for bass, bluegill, catfish, limited squirrel hunting and archery deer season within state regulations.

Where to stay: MOTELS—At Poplar Bluff, 25 miles southwest, and Dexter, 25 miles southeast. CAMPGROUNDS—Wappappello Lake, 10 miles west, and Duck Creek State Game Management Area, adjacent on north.

Weather notes: Summers hot and humid with little if any breeze. Rainfall averages around 46 inches yearly.

What to take and wear: Waterproof footgear, especially if venturing off boardwalk trails.

Points of interest nearby: Duck Creek and Wappappello Lake (see

CAMPGROUNDS)—both attractive natural areas with visitor facilities; Big Oak Tree State Park, 40 miles west near Charleston, good birding; Gaylord Laboratory, works nearby in waterfowl research, worth visit by serious naturalist.

For more information: Mingo National Wildlife Refuge, Box V, Puxico, Missouri 63960. Phone: (314) 222-3589.

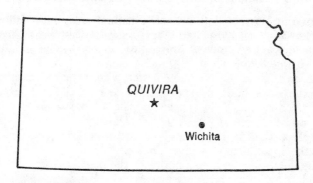

QUIVIRA

★

Wichita

QUIVIRA (Kansas)

When Coronado was searching for the seven cities of gold in 1541 he found instead a tribe of handsome seven-foot natives and called them, adapting the Indian word, Quivira, which symbolized for him the rich and plenteous natural life of all kinds that he saw here. When the next explorers came these giants had vanished. Yet some of the heritage of their times remains in this 21,820-acre refuge of marshes, low sandhills, and timbered shelter belts in central Kansas where Mississippi kites nest, eagles gather to follow the migrating waterfowl, and pheasant and bobwhite quail are everywhere.

White pelicans come through in flocks of sometimes six thousand in spring and fall and stay six weeks or so resting and feeding and soaring to great heights on nine-foot wingspreads. Sandhill cranes also appear in large numbers, up to 10,000 in fall, along with 100,000 Franklin's gulls, and in some years the majestic endangered whooping crane on its 2,600-mile flight from northern Canada to Texas.

Thousands of Canada and white-fronted geese and more than a dozen species of ducks may come through as well. Perhaps seventy-five thousand—depending on the weather—may stay the winter (Quivira has been highest in the nation for white-fronteds in the annual Audubon Christmas Bird Count). Lapland and chestnut-collared longspurs sometimes put in an appearance then too, as well as the spotted western version of the rufous-sided towhee, short-eared and long-eared owls, and bald and golden eagles.

The kites, which are common in all the warm months, usually have eight to ten nesting pairs on the refuge, some in cottonwoods around headquarters where they can readily be seen and instantly recognized by their swift swallowlike flight, taking large insects well into the evening, sometimes around lights. They are so numerous in the area they are a common "town bird" in nearby Stafford, where they raise broods in tall elms.

Swainson's hawks are common nesters also, as are Cooper's, and among the small birds, the beautiful scissor-tailed flycatchers, red-headed woodpeckers, Bell's vireos, dickcissels, lark sparrows, colonies, of cliff swallows, and of the shorebirds, least and black terns, snowy plovers, avocets, large numbers of American bitterns, and fair numbers of the uncommon upland sandpipers.

Prairie dogs sit up and take notice of the passing visitor along refuge roads, as do the burrowing owls which take over some of their holes for nests. White-tailed deer and coyote are here, best seen early and late in the day.

Wild flowers display from spring through summer—little blue lilies, milkweeds, blazing stars.

The refuge is almost exactly even with the geographical center of the contiguous United States and has considerable overlap of species —both eastern and western meadowlarks, cottontail, and black-tailed jackrabbit. Its bird list has more than 240 species.

A fine way to take it all in is to get a map and an excellent refuge leaflet telling when and how to see everything, and just follow the roads (staying away from soft ones in wet weather). It can be a treat for the naturalist in all seasons.

How to get there: From Hutchinson take Route 50 west to Zenith, then to Zenith Road right 8 miles (continuing as it becomes dirt) to headquarters.

Open: Daylight hours.

Best times to visit: Spring and fall.

What to see: Mississippi kites; pheasant; eagles; white pelicans; sandhill cranes and occasional whoopers; waterfowl; deer; prairie dogs.

What to do: Twenty miles of roads for driving, hiking; hunting for waterfowl and upland game; fishing. Guided tours for groups by arrangement.

Where to stay: MOTELS—In Hutchinson, 35 miles east; Great Bend, 35 miles northwest. CAMPGROUNDS—At Great Bend, Hutchinson.

Weather notes: Tornadoes and severe thunderstorms likely

May–June (western Kansas is one of the windiest locales in the interior United States).

Points of interest nearby: Cheyenne Bottoms Waterfowl Management Area at Great Bend—one of the greatest waterfowl concentrations of the Central Flyway spring and fall; the Hutchinson Planetarium, Fort Larned National Historic Site, 50 miles northwest.

For more information: Quivira National Wildlife Refuge, Box G, Stafford, Kansas 67578. Phone: (316) 486-2393.

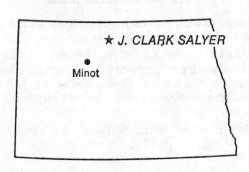

Minot

★ J. CLARK SALYER

J. CLARK SALYER (North Dakota)

This refuge has one of the nation's richest and most exciting bird populations. More than 250 species have been noted, ranging across the spectrum from sharp-tailed grouse on their dancing grounds in spring; Swainson's hawks in great numbers in fall—sometimes 150 in a single field in late September; water birds of all kinds, including five species of nesting grebes; and such small birds, rare elsewhere, as Sprague's pipits and Baird's and Le Conte's sparrows.

More than 125 species nest, some in great numbers—up to 17,000 Franklin's gulls and colonies of hundreds of double-crested cormorants and great blue and black-crowned night herons. An average year produces more than 17,000 ducklings—pintail, mallard, gadwall, and others.

White pelicans are here all summer, and thousands of sandhill cranes and whistling swans go through in migration.

The reason for all this is clear from a look at this 58,693-acre north-central North Dakota refuge with its tremendous diversity of habitat—36,000 acres of native and introduced grasslands, dense nesting cover and thick woodlands together with one of the outstanding waterfowl marshes in the Central Flyway winding along fifty-five miles of river bends and oxbows north to the Canadian border.

Fall can be a spectacular time to visit as well, with migrating shorebirds—northern phalaropes abundant, along with least, pectoral, and semipalmated sandpipers, yellowlegs, and others. There are also up to 150,000 geese, snows, white-fronts, and Canadas, and nearly a quarter of a million ducks of more than a dozen species. Aerial photographs of the refuge at such times, as well as the view from the observation towers, can have a fantasy look about them with seemingly countless birds in the air, on land and water, every place the eye can see.

Lapland longspurs are common in all but summer. Chestnut-collared longspurs are common nesters, as are upland sandpipers, avocets, marbled godwits, Wilson's phalaropes, marsh hawks, and, among the small birds, lark buntings, least flycatchers, northern orioles, and an unusually fine array of sparrows. Common all year are the sharp-tailed grouse (with two dozen dancing grounds on the refuge), gray partridges, horned larks, black-billed magpies, and in winter redpolls, snow buntings, and Bohemian waxwings. Bald and golden eagles may be around at any time.

This refuge is a prime example of land restoration after drainage, drought, poor farm practices, and market hunting had left it close to a wildlife desert when it was acquired in 1935. Nesting islands were built, the marsh restored, and vegetation offering food and cover was reintroduced.

The visitor can see all this, along with some of the white-tailed deer, coyote, beaver, mink, fox, and others of the mammal population—including some fluffy white albino muskrats which are usually here—from three excellent trails through the marsh, woods, and prairie (get out and peer down through the grasses for a botanist's trove of interesting plants) and a five- to thirteen-mile canoe route.

The refuge was named after J. Clark Salyer, an early leader in establishing the refuge system. Both are honored thereby.

Salyer also administers Waterfowl Production Areas in five counties, and seven wetland easement refuges, maintained largely for their habitat, with varied wildlife but few visitor facilities. To arrange visits to these, consult refuge headquarters.

How to get there: From Minot take Route 83 north 25 miles to Upham turnoff, then gravel road east 27 miles to Upham, then Route 14 north 2 miles to headquarters.

Open: Daylight hours.

Best times to visit: Spring through fall.

What to see: Migrating and breeding waterfowl; sharp-tailed grouse; white pelicans; Sprague's pipits; Baird's and Le Conte's sparrows; deer; occasional albino muskrats; others.

What to do: Twenty-seven miles of auto tour routes; 5- or 13-mile canoe trail (rentals in Minot); whole sandhill area open to hiking. Photography (blind available). Fishing can be good for walleye and northern pike. Limited hunting for deer, waterfowl. Two observation towers, one 150 feet high. Cross-country skiing, snowshoeing permitted on trails. Many public roads also cross refuge.

Where to stay: MOTELS—Minot, 50 miles southwest; Bottineau, 29 miles northeast. CAMPGROUNDS—In Towner; also Upham City Park, and Lake Metigoshe State Park, 43 miles northeast.

Weather notes: Winters harsh, heavy rains in fall and spring can make travel hazardous.

Points of interest nearby: Lake Metigoshe (see CAMPGROUNDS); International Peace Garden, 35 miles northeast; Upper Souris National Wildlife Refuge, 50 miles west.

For more information: J. Clark Salyer National Wildlife Refuge, Box 66, Upham, North Dakota 58789. Phone: (701) 768-3223.

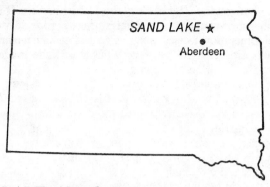

SAND LAKE (South Dakota)

No refuge has more impressive sights than Sand Lake, where the air and water at times are so filled with flying and resting waterfowl that it seems any more could not be accommodated and would have to go elsewhere.

Handsome black and white western grebes with ruby eyes—largest of the grebes and sometimes called the "swan grebe" for their grace —rise to webbed feet on the water's surface and perform their stunning courtship dances. Later they carry their downy young about on their backs (the offspring manage to cling even when the parents dive for food). As with many of the creatures at this 21,451-acre refuge of marsh, lakes, prairie, and woodland in the northeastern corner of South Dakota, the grebes are not especially shy and are readily seen from the dikes and spillways.

More than a hundred of the almost 250 species of birds seen here nest on the refuge. White pelicans crowd together on a small island with black double-crested cormorants fitting themselves onto the edge. Other nesters include seven species of hawks, the Swainson's, sharp-shinned, Cooper's red-tailed, marsh, ferruginous, and kestrel; four owls, the screech, great horned, burrowing, and long-eared; and a dozen kinds of ducks.

The upland sandpiper breeds commonly; so do marbled godwits, great blue and black-crowned night herons, ring-necked pheasant (seen everywhere), and among the small birds, long- and short-billed marsh wrens, dickcissels, horned larks, several kinds of swallows, and a few chestnut-collared longspurs.

By August the refuge may have, with breeding birds plus migrants,

6,000 pelicans, 500,000 Franklin's gulls, and in one small area alone, 100,000 shorebirds; and a little later up to 300,000 geese—both white and blue snow geese, along with the giant *maxima* Canada geese that nest here; and 300,000 ducks, with approximately the same population numbers in spring.

Warbler migrations in May can be fine indeed—twenty species sometimes can be found in the small shrubby wooded areas (each of which seems to have either a great horned owl or hawk nest in spring, and sometimes both).

White-tailed deer are plentiful around the open areas and show off their fawns in early summer. Almost every small watering area has a den of red fox and even badger don't seem as wary as usual.

Eagles come in fall and winter, when an occasional snowy owl also may show up, along with a few peregrine and prairie falcons, goshawks, and numerous redpolls, horned larks, and snow buntings.

The refuge has had a continuing reproduction program for the giant *maxima* race of Canada geese once thought extinct; this has been so successful that these magnificent birds now inhabit most of South Dakota and surrounding areas as well. Visitors can view these as well as other birds around the demonstration pond near headquarters.

The refuge has an excellent leaflet explaining what is here and how best to see it, and the knowledgeable staff is glad to tell what has been spotted lately and where.

Also administered by Sand Lake are the following:

Pocasse Refuge, consisting of 2,540 acres, mostly marsh and open water just north of Pollock, South Dakota. Up to ten thousand sandhill cranes may come through here in spring and fall along with ducks and geese, pelicans, and possibly a few whooping cranes. Beaver and deer also are present. Route 10 bisects the refuge, which is open dawn to dusk.

The Waterfowl Production Areas comprise more than a hundred units of small wetland habitat in nine counties totaling more than 150,000 acres owned or under easement, where waterfowl nest and various kinds of wildlife occur. These are wonderful natural areas maintained for their waterfowl production, and open to the public, though with few if any visitor facilities besides parking areas. For further information inquire at refuge office.

How to get there: From Aberdeen take Route 12 east 7 miles to Bath corner, then left 20 miles on County Road 16.

Open: Daylight hours.

Best times to visit: April–May and September.

What to see: Great variety and sometimes huge concentrations of various water-oriented birds; deer and red fox.

Where to stay: MOTELS—Aberdeen. CAMPGROUNDS—Richmond Lake State Recreation Area, 10 miles northwest.

Weather notes: Winters harsh, even April can be cold, windy, with poor road conditions.

Points of interest nearby: Sand Lake Recreation Area, adjacent; Ordway Prairie, owned by Nature Conservancy, 35 miles west—fascinating wildlife and habitat area; Dacotah Prairie Museum, Aberdeen; Waubay National Wildlife Refuge, 55 miles southeast.

For more information: Sand Lake National Wildlife Refuge, R.R. 1, Columbia, South Dakota 57433. Phone: (605) 885-6320.

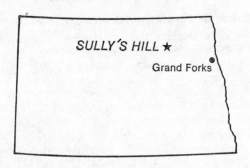

SULLY'S HILL ★
Grand Forks

SULLY'S HILL (North Dakota)

Sully's Hill is one of the oldest refuges in the United States. It was set aside by President Theodore Roosevelt for preservation of big game in 1904 when the buffalo, once one of the most numerous hooved animals in the world, had been driven to the edge of extinction. It became an official wildlife refuge by act of Congress in 1917, and small nucleus groups of six buffalo, fifteen elk, and four white-tailed deer, all of which had disappeared from the area, were brought here. All of these flourished and can be seen at all seasons (except when winter weather makes roads impassable).

The refuge also has one of the region's most impressive migrations of small birds, especially warblers, through the woods, grasslands, and brushy areas of this 1,674 acres of rolling glacial moraine hills in northeast North Dakota. In May an observant birder can sit quietly in one spot with binoculars and count forty species without moving —magnolia, prothonotary, black-throated, blue and black-and-white warblers, fox sparrows, vireos, and many others. Some of these nest as well.

There are colonies of bank swallows in the gravel pits; and a great variety of water birds of all kinds along the shores of little Sweetwater Lake on the refuge—Canada and snow geese, white pelicans in all the warm months, double-crested cormorants sharing the rocky nesting islands with the Canadas and some of the various ducks that nest on the refuge, including canvasback, shoveler, mallard, gadwall, wigeon, redhead, blue-winged teal, pintail and ruddy ducks. American bitterns, grebes, great blue and black-crowned night herons are here as well through the summer.

The auto tour route also winds by a sizable "town" of black-tailed prairie dogs, scampering about close at hand in all but the most inclement weather, so photographers need no blind to take fine pictures of them.

But it is the bison, elk, and deer that attract most visitors, and they are almost always in good view except when the elk and deer retire to care for their calves in relative seclusion in late May and June. The buffalo with their bright reddish-brown young do not seem to mind onlookers even when the calves are but a few days old.

Bison start contending for mates in late summer, pawing the ground and assuming threatening stances, while elks bugle in loud calls that can be heard for miles. A half dozen eagles, both bald and golden, begin to appear when the waterfowl do in fall, and stay until the refuge is fairly well frozen. By midwinter few birds are left in this frigid climate except redpolls, snow buntings, Bohemian waxwings (sometimes these are in large flocks), along with snowy owls from the north. This may be one of the best times to see the elk and other mammals, though—and while the refuge may be officially closed, one can get permission to enter and explore by checking first with refuge headquarters.

Birdwatchers are often allowed in before the 8 A.M. opening during prime warbler days, too.

Sully's Hill is administered from the *Devil's Lake* Wetland Management District, which also manages several satellite easement refuges and 34,832 acres of Waterfowl Production Areas in eight counties—small wetlands maintained largely for their habitat, open to the public but with few if any visitor facilities. Further information may be obtained from the district office, P.O. Box 908, Devil's Lake, North Dakota 58301. Phone: (701) 662-2924.

Lake Alice Refuge is also administered from this office. It is a relatively new refuge, in a state of development with, at least until recently, few if any visitor facilities. Large numbers of snow geese and ducks are present in migration, and, when water conditions are right, it is one of the state's best nesting marshes for redhead and canvasback ducks. Check with headquarters before planning a visit, however.

How to get there: From Devil's Lake take Route 20 then 57 south to Fort Totten Indian Reservation and refuge sign, then east to headquarters.

Open: From 8 A.M. to sunset May to November (headquarters area open all year, other roads also when passable under winter conditions).

Best times to visit: Spring through fall.

What to see: Bison; elk; white-tailed deer; prairie dogs; waterfowl; small birds.

What to do: Four-mile auto tour route; interpretive walking trail; picnicking; two scenic overlooks; photography (blind available); snowshoeing and cross-country skiing in winter.

Where to stay: MOTELS—Devil's Lake, 13 miles northeast. CAMPGROUNDS—Just north of Devil's Lake; also Ziebach Pass County Recreation Area, 4 miles west, several others nearby.

Weather notes: Winters bitterly cold.

Points of interest nearby: Cavalry Square, Fort Totten Historic Site; fishing can be good in Devil's Lake just off refuge for walleyes, northerns, white bass.

For more information: Sully's Hill National Game Preserve, Fort Totten, North Dakota 58335. Phone: (701) 766-4272.

SWAN LAKE (Missouri)

The name is Swan Lake but no one knows why anymore; swans are almost never seen here and this refuge of 10,670 acres in northwest Missouri is held in thrall by the Canada goose. The nearby town of Sumner, population 200, proudly calls itself the Wild Goose Capital of the World. Each fall it holds a Wild Goose Festival with a queen, parades, dances, and feasting, and its Bicentennial project was erection of the world's largest statue of a Canada goose—forty feet high, with a sixty-one-foot wingspread and an audiovisual presentation in the base.

The objects of all this attention start arriving in mid-September from their nesting grounds in the remote tundra of Hudson's Bay, and by late October they may number more than 200,000, resting and feeding on the refuge ponds and fanning out over fields in the area (farmers are recompensed in part for any depredation by hunter fees). Their calling can be heard for more than a mile, and to the visitor coming anywhere near the refuge boundary at peak times they seem to be everywhere, both on the ground and in the air.

It is an awesome and impressive sight, and though it is shared with some other species—sometimes up to 150,000 ducks, 2,000 white pelicans, and 30,000 snow geese—the Canadas clearly dominate the scene. It has been somewhat unexpected. Swan Lake was established as a refuge to offer rest and feeding grounds for ducks. Geese had not been here except as scattered sightings for years when the land was first set aside in 1937. Only twenty-five came in 1940. But by 1945 it had increased to ten thousand, and more and more came until it became clear they like it here, to put it mildly.

Interest in the species is not altruistic. It is rooted in the Canadas being a prime trophy for waterfowl hunters. After the birds' numbers increased, hunt clubs bought or leased most of the surrounding area until individual hunters complained, and state and federal authorities carved out the "Swan Lake Zone"—a move that has aroused some controversy—whereby the refuge is ringed by a belt of land in which sixty-three pit blinds have been constructed for use by hunters during a controlled, reservation-only season which starts in late October and continues until a given quota (in recent years twenty-five thousand birds) has been taken.

But their quarry have lived up to their reputation as intelligent birds. After the gunfire starts, they begin flying high, many out of gun range, when passing over the hunt zone, and only dropping down, rocking their wings like falling leaves, when safely over refuge land. One year of zone hunting, the quota was reached in fourteen days. Several times in recent years it has not been reached at all. (Still, reports show that 40 per cent of the adult geese banded here carry some shot in their bodies; and of those killed, the U. S. Fish and Wildlife Service statistics add 20 per cent to the mortality figures for those that die later of their wounds.) These carcasses are the primary food source for as many as a hundred bald eagles that winter on the refuge.

Despite the focus on the geese, other activities are offered and can be extremely rewarding. These are auto and hiking trails, and though these are closed in fall and winter to offer quiet sanctuary to the wildlife, the masses of waterfowl can be seen almost equally well from the observation tower by the refuge headquarters and the dike road by the lake.

Bobwhite are present commonly all year as are horned larks, mourning doves, cardinals, flickers, goldfinches, white-crowned sparrows, meadowlarks, red-headed and red-bellied woodpeckers, and screech, barred, and great horned owls (unhappily, prairie chickens, formerly residents, have not been seen in recent years). And seasonally common to abundant are great blue and green herons, great egrets, coots (as many as ten thousand), sora and king rails, killdeer, common snipes, hermit and wood thrushes, indigo buntings, and five species of swallow—cliff, barn, tree, and rough-winged, plus the purple martin.

The hawk migration in spring and fall is impressive, with common to abundant sightings of Cooper's, red-tailed, red-shouldered, rough-legged, broad-winged, and marsh, with a few merlin.

Of the mammals, the refuge supports a herd of about five hundred deer, and there are also about sixty coyote, some fox, raccoon, and opossum, our only pouched animal, these sometimes seen carrying young about on their backs after they have outgrown the pouch. The walking trail winds beside a sandbank where fox and coyote have had dens in some years—more recently coyote, whose numbers are up. It is an unexplained phenomenon that as coyote increase, fox go down in number, and vice versa.

How to get there: From Kansas City (about 100 miles) go north on I-35 to Route 36; east on 36 to State Route 139; south on 139 to Sumner; then south on Swan Lake Drive about 3 miles to refuge.

Open: Daily, dawn to dusk, March through September; otherwise closed except for special purposes or by permission (check with headquarters). Observation tower open all year.

Best times to visit: Spring and fall.

What to see: Massive concentrations of Canada geese; also ducks, snow geese, white pelicans, bald eagles, white-tailed deer.

What to do: Nature trails; photography (blind available and hunters' blinds can be used by permission); observation tower; conducted tours for groups by arrangement; fishing (for channel cat and carp); hunting.

Where to stay: MOTELS—At Chillicothe, 30 miles northwest of refuge, and Brookfield, 25 miles northeast. CAMPGROUNDS—Pershing State Park, 5 miles northeast.

Weather notes: Summer can be hot and humid, spring fairly wet, winters occasionally subzero. September and October are the prettiest, most pleasant months.

What to take and wear: Raingear, just in case, almost anytime.

Points of interest nearby: The world's largest statue of a Canada goose at Sumner, 3 miles away; Fountain Grove State Wildlife Area, 5 miles northwest, and Pershing State Park, 5 miles north —both attractive natural areas with trails (the latter features the boyhood home of World War I General John J. Pershing at Laclede).

For more information: Swan Lake National Wildlife Refuge, P.O. Box 68, Sumner, Missouri 64681. Phone: (816) 856-3323.

SQUAW CREEK (Missouri)

Anyone who wishes to see America's national bird can fairly well count on doing so by coming to Squaw Creek National Wildlife Refuge in late fall and winter.

Sometimes as many as two hundred bald eagles (and a few golden eagles) come to this 6,886-acre tract of varied marsh, timber, farmland, and upland prairie in the northwest corner of Missouri. They arrive in mid-November and stay on usually into February. They follow the waterfowl which are a sight in themselves. Up to 250,000 snow geese and 300,000 ducks flock here, a common count in spring from mid-February to April, and in fall, from the first of October to December (with enough staying over normally to provide a food source for the raptors).

The refuge supports one of the largest wintering concentrations of bald eagles in the United States. Immature birds come first (they are entirely dark and have not yet developed the white head and tail) and adults later, and while they are present they may be seen roosting in trees about the refuge—sometimes twenty-five or thirty in a single tree—or soaring in circles high in the air. Or, if the main pool is frozen over, it is not unusual to see a hundred eagles resting on the ice, or feeding there (perhaps on a fish or duck), or sunning themselves if it is a pleasant day. They are often visible from refuge headquarters as well as the roads. (A would-be photographer once rigged up a chickenwire blind on a canoe, concealing him so well an eagle carrying a duck landed on top of him, collapsing the blind and causing near-heart failure. His picture was out of focus.)

The snow geese are a spectacular sight in themselves, taking off in a single group, their calls heard for miles, an island of shimmering white against the blue sky or the water (accompanied by some blue and white-fronted and Canada geese, but in lesser numbers). The ducks—mostly mallard but also large numbers of pintail, shoveler, wigeon, blue- and green-winged teal, and gadwall—go among the standing marsh grass, where they are nearly invisible, the quiet marsh appearing entirely uninhabited until a hundred thousand or so take off with a rush of wings.

Some of the ducks stay to nest—teal, mallard, and pintail—but production is not high because of the abundance of predators—raccoon, red-tailed hawks, and turtles are among those that might take a young duckling.

White pelicans are another impressive sight: huge birds with nine-foot wingspreads coming through in numbers up to two thousand in September and April. Among the early fall shorebird migrants are long-billed dowitchers, Wilson's phalaropes, Hudsonian godwits, and lesser yellowlegs.

Great-horned and barred owls are common all year as are pheasant and quail; and in the breeding season, orchard and northern orioles, yellow-breasted chats, indigo buntings, red-bellied woodpeckers, blue jays, thrashers, eastern kingbirds, and red-eyed, warbling, and Bell's vireos.

Squaw Creek also has fine floral displays—Dutchman's breeches, phlox, and hundreds of redbud trees over the hillsides in spring; and in July, about a thousand acres of arrowheads and lotuses blooming gold and white on the refuge waters.

Of interest to reptile fanciers is the massasauga rattlesnake, not often seen but common in the refuge, though not in the surrounding area.

To geologists as well as the ordinary observer, the loess bluffs seen from many vantage points in the refuge are of particular interest— strange unstratified rockless hills of yellow windblown soil formed in glacial times, which later took a hard almost crystalline-like structure. It is a formation found along the river basin from Squaw Creek to Sioux City, but at few other places in the world.

Squaw Creek has fine trails for driving as well as walking—Pintail Point, which extends out into the water for a close view of the migrant waterfowl; and the Bluff Trail behind the refuge headquarters which climbs in easy steps to a spectacular view of the countryside and water areas. If you are driving, you may see as well some of the mammals which reside here—raccoon, beaver, muskrat, fox, and white-tailed deer. But proceed quietly and try early in the morning or toward dusk; these do not regard it their duty to be seen by visitors.

How to get there: From St. Joseph, Missouri, take Route I-29 about 30 miles north to the Rulo, Nebraska, Exit (#79); then Route 159 west for 2 miles to refuge headquarters.

Open: Daily, dawn to dusk (office weekdays 8 A.M. to 4:30 P.M.).

Best times to visit: All seasons have something to recommend them here, but August and late January–February probably least desirable.

What to see: Wintering eagles in large numbers. Masses of ducks and geese in migration. Unusual loess bluffs. Acres of lotuses and arrowheads in bloom.

What to do: Nature trails. Observation towers. Photography (photoblind available). Fishing for crappie, carp, and channel cat April–December (sometimes winterkills in shallow refuge waters, but new ones come with spring). No hunting on refuge.

Where to stay: MOTELS—Squaw Creek Truck Plaza, 2 miles east of refuge on Route 159; at Mound City, 5 miles north; Big Lake State Park, 8 miles east on Route 159. CAMPGROUNDS—Big Lake State Park (see MOTELS above).

Weather notes: Winters often 0 to 20 degrees F.; summers over 100. Spring and early fall can have sudden heavy rains making driving difficult on refuge roads.

What to take and wear: Raingear spring and early fall; warm clothing in winter.

Points of interest nearby: Bluff Woods State Recreation Area, 35 miles south of refuge, and Honey Creek State Area 15 miles south of refuge—both good birding and natural spots. St. Joseph Museum has extensive natural history collection including 500 mounts and 1,700 eggs from all over the world, and advice on natural places to see.

For more information: Squaw Creek National Wildlife Refuge, P.O. Box 101, Mound City, Missouri 64470. Phone: (816) 442-3570.

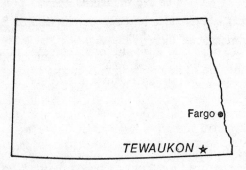

Fargo

TEWAUKON ★

TEWAUKON (North Dakota)

Tewaukon is spread over 8,444 acres of native grass, marsh, and wetland in the rolling prairie pothole region of southeast North Dakota. This is one of the most productive waterfowl areas in the nation, and this attractive refuge does its share with ten duck species that nest commonly.

It is a perfect habitat for water birds. Innumerable clay-bottomed glacial depressions and larger managed ponds are all filled with water in the spring. Pairs of shoveler, mallard, pintail, redhead, canvasback, and blue-winged teal flock here (and are seen everywhere)— in addition to others, such as pied-billed and western grebes (which perform their courtship dances), American bitterns, great blue, green, and black-crowned night herons, coots, black terns, Wilson's phalaropes, and Virginia and sora rails.

Double-crested cormorants nest colonially. By late August and September there may be buildups of nesting and migrant birds together. Sometimes fifteen hundred white pelicans appear along with two hundred thousand Franklin's and ring-billed gulls. Starting in October there are concentrations of up to eighty thousand ducks and a hundred thousand snow and Canada geese (with similar numbers of these coming through in the spring—birds from both the Mississippi and Central Flyways, for Tewaukon attracts some from each of these).

Visitors can observe pheasant and gray partridge all year, as well as white-tailed deer, along with their spotted fawns in May. Beaver have domed lodges on which their residents can be seen sunning on pleasant days. Thirteen-lined ground squirrels are everywhere, as are the little Franklin's and Richardson's ground squirrels. The latter are

North Dakota's state animal and have shorter tails, held erect, giving them their nickname "flickertail."

Birding can be good, especially in spring migration when Swainson's thrushes are common along with such warblers as the Tennessee, blackpoll, and yellow. Yellowthroats nest commonly, as do bobolinks, dickcissels, horned larks, chestnut-collared longspurs, and a good assortment of sparrows, including the grasshopper, clay-colored, Savannah and a few lark and Le Conte's.

Winters are so harsh that almost everything that can hibernate or fly away, does so. But hardy souls can usually find Lapland longspurs, snow buntings, redpolls, and Bohemian waxwings and perhaps a snowy owl.

Also administered from Tewaukon are Waterfowl Production Areas in three counties and three small easement refuges, *Lake Elsie* Refuge, *Storm Lake*, and *Wild Rice Lake*. These are maintained largely as natural areas for their excellent nest habitat, and have few if any visitor facilities other than parking. For information on how to see these, ask at the refuge office.

How to get there: From Lidgerwood take Route 11 west 13 miles to Cayuga, then south 5.5 miles on County Road 12.

Open: Daylight hours.

Best times to visit: Fall and spring.

What to see: Waterfowl; deer; beaver; Indian burial mounds.

What to do: Eleven miles of roads and trails for driving, hiking (can be closed during high water or snow or during hunting season); fishing for northern and walleyed pike; limited hunting for deer, pheasants.

Where to stay: MOTELS—Lidgerwood. CAMPGROUNDS—Silver Lake County Park, 9.5 miles west.

Weather notes: Winters can be extremely harsh—sometimes stays below freezing for three months straight.

Points of interest nearby: Tewaukon State Game Management Area, adjoining on north; Sheyenne National Grassland, 25 miles north; Northern Prairie Wildlife Research Center, 125 miles north in Jamestown; Sand Lake National Wildlife Refuge, 70 miles southwest.

For more information: Tewaukon National Wildlife Refuge, R.R. ✗ 1, Cayuga, North Dakota 58013. Phone: (701) 724-3598.

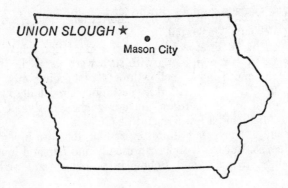

UNION SLOUGH (Iowa)

Union Slough is a 2,156-acre remnant of a preglacial riverbed, a narrow finger-shaped refuge six miles long and just a half mile wide, in land so flat that the wind, which not infrequently gusts up to sixty miles an hour, determines the direction of the slough's flow.

Sometimes it drains into the Blue Earth River to the north; sometimes south into Buffalo Creek, which becomes the East Fork of the Des Moines River. Indians called it Mini Okaoan Kaduza, "water which runs both ways." Its present name reflects its function as the juncture between two watersheds of rolling hills on both sides.

Its varied habitat, ranging through marsh, woods, and prairie upland even in this small 2,155-acre belt gives it an interesting wildlife population, one of the best in this section of north-central Iowa.

Ducks and geese coming through in spring and fall migration may peak at twenty-five thousand to fifty thousand birds, including as many as four thousand geese—predominantly Canadas but also some snow, blue, and white-fronted. Seventeen duck species are common migrants, including pintails, ruddy, gadwall, wigeon, shoveler, redhead, hooded and common merganser, ring-necked, canvasback, and scaup, and good numbers of mallard, blue-winged teal, and wood ducks stay to nest. (Peaks are usually reached in October and April.)

Ring-necked pheasant are abundant and gray or Hungarian partridge common all year. One can see their downy broods about the refuge roads and trails and in a stand of native prairie grassland on the north end in early summer. About the same time downy ducklings and a few Canada goslings can be seen on the ponds (particularly on Gabrielson Pool, where sometimes ten to fifteen wood duck broods can be seen from the bridge by the quiet visitor. Pied-billed grebes construct their floating nests there, too).

A few whistling swans usually touch down in spring and fall as well, and good groups of white pelicans—sometimes several hundred, most often in September.

The refuge has a good population of white-tailed deer, best seen at dawn and late afternoon along the trails and roads and around the deer-watching areas marked on the refuge map, in the south end near Route B-14, near the Indian Bluff Nature Trail. This is especially true in the winter, when they "yard up" in an interior area nearby.

The very quiet visitor can see other mammals—fox, raccoon, squirrel, rabbit, muskrat, mink, and a few beaver, their workings visible along the nature trail.

Common nesters among the small birds are cuckoos, meadowlarks, long- and short-billed marsh wrens, dickcissels, grasshopper and vesper sparrows, horned larks and yellow-headed and red-winged blackbirds. Sparrow hawks are here summer and fall. Screech and great horned owls are common all year, the screech owls sometimes taking up residence in unused wood duck houses.

Wild flowers bloom throughout the growing season—lavender and pink prairie clovers and milkweeds, masses of blue blazing stars, wild roses, marsh marigolds, Turk's-cap lilies, and Dutchman's breeches.

Blanding's turtles live here, along with snapping turtles weighing up to fifty pounds. The latter are prolific—seventy-nine eggs were once found in a single nest.

The refuge has seven miles of auto and hiking trails with explanatory leaflets and displays. Special auto tours are held on Sundays in April, July, and September, and guided tours and programs for groups can be arranged in advance. Parts of the refuge may be closed seasonally because of bad weather and to provide undisturbed sanctuary for waterfowl during hunting seasons (check with headquarters about this), but public roads cross through refuge lands every mile or so, and much can be seen from them.

How to get there: From Algona take Route 169 north about 15 miles toward Bancroft; turn right on state road A-42 at the south edge of Bancroft (a cemetery is on the northeast corner) and continue to the refuge sign.

Open: Headquarters open daily year-round; parts of refuge may be closed seasonally—check with office.

Best times to visit: Spring and fall.

What to see: Deer; migrating waterfowl; upland game birds.

What to do: Auto and hiking trails; photography (there is a photoblind); fishing in Buffalo Creek and gravel pits for bullhead and in March–April for northern pike. No hunting on the refuge.

Where to stay: MOTELS—Several in Algona. CAMPGROUNDS—Several near Algona, including Call State Park.

Weather notes: Spring can be rainy until mid-May; summers humid and winters down to 20 below. High winds (not uncommonly to 60 miles an hour) make cool weather penetrating.

What to take and wear: Waterproof footgear and windbreaker may be prudent at any season.

Points of interest nearby: Ingham State Wildlife Area, 40 miles west. Pilot Knob Park at Forest City, about 25 miles east. Grotto of Redemption at West Bend, southwest of Algona, about 30 miles.

For more information: Union Slough National Wildlife Refuge, R¾1, Box 32-B, Titonka, Iowa 50480. Phone: (515) 928-2523.

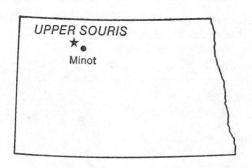

UPPER SOURIS
Minot

UPPER SOURIS (North Dakota)

Upper Souris may be the prettiest of the "Souris Loop" national wildlife refuges, with more than 32,000 acres extending over thirty miles of lakes, marsh, prairie, and woodlands along the Souris or Mouse River which loops down into North Dakota from Canada and got its name from the great numbers of mice which the early French fur trappers saw here. All these refuges are located on or near this river (the others are the Des Lacs, Salyer, and Lostwood refuges) and harbor outstanding wildlife populations as well. The small rodents include the engaging "flickertail" or Richardson's ground squirrel, North Dakota state mammal.

Upper Souris' lovely wildlife trail traverses most of this welcoming habitat, over softly contoured rolling hills, green and sprinkled with wild flowers in the spring, with long vistas of sparkling blue waters on the seven refuge ponds and lakes, interspersed with golden marsh vegetation where sizable populations of all kinds of water birds nest in May and June, and others come through in large numbers in spring and especially fall migration. Yet another lovely sight is the brilliant fall foliage in the wooded coulees.

Western grebes perform their graceful courtship ballets, rising to their webbed feet and tripping rapidly together on the water's surface, later appearing with downy young on their backs. They keep their seats even through the parents' feeding dives.

Double-crested cormorants and great blue and black-crowned night herons have nesting colonies of several hundred birds on Lake Darling, largest of the water areas.

Broods of Canada geese and fifteen species of ducks, including the spectacular wood ducks as well as mallard, teal, shoveler (the refuge produces several thousand ducklings yearly), can be seen by June, sometimes from the trails, or from the several Darling Lake crossings.

Hundreds of white pelicans are here all summer. Whistling swans go through in spring and fall, and sometimes thousands of sandhill cranes, though the latter are more often seen flying overhead than on the ground. Waterfowl may concentrate in flocks of up to sixty thousand geese, mostly snows but also Canadas and white-fronted, and fifty thousand ducks, along with large numbers of dowitchers, phalaropes, and other shorebirds.

White-tailed deer browse at dawn and dusk, and mink are a frequent sight along the watercourses. An occasional porcupine may be seen lumbering along almost anywhere.

Raptors, perhaps because of the rodents, like this place too. Swainson's hawks are common, as are marsh and red-tailed, rough-legged in fall and winter, occasional prairie and gyrfalcons, along with a half dozen or more bald and golden eagles on and off through the year. Short-eared owls fly out to hunt in late afternoons.

Sprague's pipits and Baird's and Le Conte's sparrows, outstanding "finds" for most birders, can usually be spotted.

Common all year are sharp-tailed grouse, which have two dozen or so active dancing grounds here, along with gray partridge, least and willow flycatchers, and lark buntings, and in winter waxwings, redpolls, sometimes grosbeaks, and usually a snowy owl.

How to get there: From Minot take Route 83 north about 15 miles, then west on County Road 6 (marked Lake Darling) for 13 miles to headquarters.

Open: From 5 A.M. to 10 P.M. daily.

Best times to visit: Spring and fall.

What to see: Waterfowl concentrations; western grebes; sharp-tailed grouse; whistling swans; white pelicans; Baird's and Le Conte's sparrows; and Sprague's pipit; white-tailed deer; beaver; sometimes mink.

What to do: Six miles of roads for driving, hiking; photography; observation tower; boating; picnicking; limited deer hunt; fishing good to excellent for northern and walleyed pike, both summer and through the ice. Cross-country skiing and snowshoeing permitted.

Where to stay: MOTELS—Minot, 28 miles south. CAMPGROUNDS— City Park in Carpio, 6 miles west.

Weather notes: Winters harsh, roads can be impassable.

Points of interest nearby: Theodore Roosevelt National Park, 100 miles west; Salyer National Wildlife Refuge, 55 miles east; Des Lacs National Wildlife Refuge, 35 miles northwest; Turtle Mountains State Park, 90 miles northeast.

For more information: Upper Souris National Wildlife Refuge, Rural Route #1, Foxholm, North Dakota 58738. Phone: (701) 468-5634.

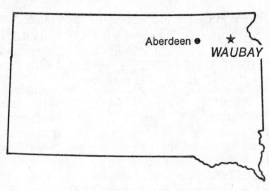

Aberdeen ● ★
WAUBAY

WAUBAY (South Dakota)

Waubay in Sioux Indian language means "nesting place for birds," an apt designation for this lovely small refuge in the prairie pothole region of northeastern South Dakota since, of the almost 250 bird species that have been seen here, more than a hundred are recorded as nesters.

These include two which are often uncommon, though here sometimes present in fairly good numbers: the red-necked grebe and the common goldeneye duck. It is one of the southernmost breeding records for both of these handsome birds.

Four other grebes nest as well. They are the horned, eared, pied-billed, and western (their impressive courtship water dances often visible from refuge headquarters) along with many bitterns, double-crested cormorants, great blue and black-crowned night herons, giant Canada geese, fifteen species of ducks and five kinds of hawks (the sharp-shinned, red-tailed, Cooper's, Swainson's, and marsh).

The reason for all this is the great variety of habitat in these 4,650 acres, which includes almost two dozen ponds and lakes, along with marsh, upland, and woods. Here can be found not only the tall cottonwoods and bur oaks usual to the region but other trees seldom seen in this area, such as prickly ashes, ironwoods, and basswoods, some of which are more than a century old.

Marbled godwits and upland sandpipers are common nesters; so are black terns, ring-necked pheasants, great horned owls, bobolinks, white-breasted nuthatches, four kinds of woodpeckers, grasshopper and vesper sparrows, and fair numbers of lark buntings and piping plovers. Black-billed cuckoos are common much of the summer.

White-tailed deer bring out their fawns in June, and young

beavers and muskrats can sometimes be seen atop their domed houses. Thirteen-lined ground squirrels make homes almost every place. Franklin's and Richardson's ground squirrels prefer overgrazed grasslands and roadsides, where they scamper about like miniature prairie dogs (Richardson's have short tails, Franklin's long).

Prairie bloom occurs all summer with a glorious peak in August— Maximilian sunflowers, orange wood lilies, bottle gentians, and masses of goldenrods. Migrations of waterfowl, shorebirds, and passerines can be interesting both spring and fall (though more for variety than great concentrations). By winter the hundreds of bird species have dwindled to a mere dozen or so—and refuge roads can have snowdrifts twenty-five feet deep. But for the hardy there can still be good birding with many redpolls and snow buntings around, Lapland longspurs, Bohemian and cedar waxwings, and sometimes gray partridge and a snowy owl.

Waubay also administers some twenty thousand acres of Waterfowl Production Areas in nine counties, small tracts averaging a hundred acres maintained for their outstanding nesting habitat and largely as natural areas.They shelter a variety of wildlife, open to the public but with little or no visitor facilities other than parking. For information on how to visit these, consult the refuge office.

How to get there: From Waubay take Route 12 east a mile to County Road 1 and small refuge sign, then north 8 miles to refuge sign and west 1.5 miles to office.

Open: Daylight hours (some areas close Labor Day).

Best times to visit: May and August–September.

What to see: Giant Canada geese, deer, western and red-necked grebes, goldeneyes, variety of others.

What to do: Ten miles of public roads through refuge; interpretive trail; tower; photography; limited deer hunt.

Where to stay: MOTELS—Webster, 20 miles southwest. CAMPGROUNDS —Pickerel Lake State Park, 5 miles north (see also points of interest).

Weather notes: Winters can be brutal, cold, snowy, roads blocked.

Points of interest nearby: Fort Sisseton State Park, 35 miles north; Sieche Hollow State Park, 25 miles northeast (camping at these also); Sand Lake National Wildlife Refuge, 55 miles northwest; 4 good birding areas—Rush Lake, 8 miles south, Bitter Lake, 15 miles south, Hedke's Pass, 5 miles southwest, Cormorant Island in South Waubay Lake.

For more information: Waubay National Wildlife Refuge, R.R. #1, P.O. Box 79, Waubay, South Dakota 57273. Phone: (605) 947-4695.

VII. THE SOUTHWEST

The refuges of the Southwest reach from the lower Colorado River Valley along the border between Arizona and California to eastern Oklahoma and down to the Texas Gulf Coast. Because of the size of this region and its widely diverse habitat, it harbors an extraordinary variety of wildlife.

ARIZONA

Beginning in the west are *Cibola, Imperial,* and *Havasu* refuges. All three are flanked by California and Arizona desert and their watery riverine lushness acts as a magnet for wild creatures. Havasu is the northernmost of the three and has particularly beautiful scenery. Its variety of habitat includes marsh, mountains, desert, and river bottom delta and even dense stands of Frémont cottonwood trees. Like the other two it is best seen by boat (rentals readily available), particularly through the Topock Marsh and Gorge. Cibola is the breadbasket of these three refuges with large areas farmed for wildlife food. One can make an excellent trip through Cibola and Imperial to the south by putting in at Blythe and floating down and through the two refuges to Martinez Lake. It is a sixty-mile trip with campgrounds available along the way (though not on the refuges). Some birds of special interest in these refuges include Gambel's quails, verdins, gila and ladder-backed woodpeckers, black-tailed gnatcatchers, Crissal thrashers, and Abert's towhees.

Southwest Arizona contains two of the nation's outstanding big game refuges—*Kofa* and *Cabeza Prieta.* Kofa is home to the bighorn sheep, descendants of the wild sheep of Asia and residents of this continent only since they crossed the land bridge from Siberia a half million years ago. Golden eagles nest here and among interesting birds are the elf owl and the phainopepla. Cabeza is more than a thousand square miles of mountains and desert, rough and remote land along the Mexican border. In addition to bighorns it harbors Sonoran pronghorn antelopes, collared peccaries, and such Mexican specialties as tropical kingbirds, white-winged doves, and coatimundis.

NEW MEXICO

Bosque del Apache, one of four primary New Mexico refuges, is also one of the outstanding in the nation. It is the wintering ground for thousands of sandhill cranes, among them the foster parents of several endangered whooping cranes. Its well-watered woods, fields, and marshes attract a wide range of easily visible wildlife from mule deer to coyote to huge flocks of waterfowl as well as an occasional mountain lion. *Maxwell* is an important nesting and feeding spot for waterfowl on the Central Flyway. Both it and *Las Vegas* have impressive raptor populations—nesting prairie falcons at Las Vegas; ferruginous hawks and bald eagles common in fall and winter at Maxwell with golden eagles common there all year. *Bitter Lake* winters a large percentage of the world's population of lesser sandhill cranes (up to seventy thousand birds) along with almost that many snow geese and up to a hundred thousand ducks of twenty species.

OKLAHOMA

Wichita Mountains in Oklahoma is one of the showplaces of the refuge system, with stunning scenery, large herds of buffalo, elk, and Texas longhorns and a prairie dog town quite accessible to visitors. *Optima* in the western section of the state is a relatively new and undeveloped refuge but has impressive populations of raptors including ferruginous, Harlan's, Cooper's, and rough-legged hawks and prairie falcons. *Salt Plains* contains the largest salt flat in mid-America including selenite crystals with a unique red-brown hourglass figure sought after by rock collectors. At *Tishomingo* visitors may see up to five thousand white pelicans in October. Migrating waterfowl may number up to four thousand geese, including Canadas, white-fronted and snows and as many as eighty thousand ducks of twenty or so species. *Washita* is another important link in the Central Flyway which for its small size accommodates an extraordinary number of waterfowl. *Sequoyah* in the eastern part of the state lies at the confluence of the Arkansas and Canadian rivers and is an important waterfowl refuge. Along with the ducks in the winter come the eagles, sometimes as many as sixty roosting in the tall cottonwood trees.

TEXAS

The refuges of Texas, like the state itself, cover a lot of ground. In the high plains of west Texas are *Buffalo Lake* and *Muleshoe*. When Buffalo Lake has water, which is not always, it is a prime stopping spot both for waterfowl and shore birds—up to eighty thousand geese and a million ducks in winter and thousands of shorebirds in spring and fall migrations. Besides its attractive down-home name, Muleshoe has one of the most spectacular wildlife sights of the North American continent—up to a hundred thousand sandhill cranes flying overhead and calling to one another on their way from their feeding grounds to their nightly roosts. This sight (and the sounds which accompany it) will stir the soul of anyone who cares at all about the wild; most years it can be seen almost every day at Muleshoe from fall to early spring. *Hagerman,* just north of Dallas, is something of a curiosity. Here white pelicans, migratory waterfowl, wading and shorebirds, deer, coyote, and bobcat intermingle and coexist with some two hundred operating oil wells.

Attwater Prairie Chicken was primarily established to harbor its namesake, a race of the greater prairie chicken in imminent danger of extinction. Once so numerous in the coastal tall grass prairie of east Texas that old-timers said their booming caused pain to sensitive eardrums, the total Texas population now is not more than about two thousand, of which about a hundred and fifty are on this refuge. This is one of a number of refuges to which The Nature Conservancy made an important contribution—by purchasing the original thirty-five hundred acres.

There are four Texas Gulf Coast refuges and one not far in from the Gulf along the Rio Grande. *Anahuac,* the easternmost of the group, is one of the few places in the world where the red wolf can still be heard howling at night, though for how long this will be true is in doubt, so reduced are the numbers of this creature. The refuge is also famous among birders for its rails—five or six species can be seen in spring migration on scheduled marsh buggy trips. *Aransas* is probably the most famous of all the refuges, primarily for its population of wintering whooping cranes, for many years at the brink of extinction and even now numbering only about seventy here. In addition it has the longest bird list of any refuge—three hundred and fifty species—and good populations of deer, collared peccary, alligator, and coyote. Although rarely seen, bobcat, wild boar, and mountain lion inhabit the refuge.

Laguna Atascosa near Corpus Christi maintains a great variety of temperate and subtropical wildlife. This includes not only coyote and bobcat, but also javelina and rare jaguarundi and spotted ocelot. Interesting border species of birdlife include chachalacas, pauraques, white-winged doves, white-tailed and Harris's hawks, kiskadee flycatchers, and groove-billed anis. Black-bellied (tree) ducks are abundant seasonally. *San Bernard-Brazoria* lies between Aransas and Laguna Atascosa and shares much of the wildlife of these refuges. Public access has been somewhat limited but the refuge does afford some outstanding sights, including up to a thousand wood storks and four hundred roseate spoonbills, with good populations of mottled ducks, king, clapper, black, and yellow rails.

Santa Ana is often called the jewel of the refuge system. One of the nation's smallest and most interesting refuges, it offers colorful inhabitants in an exquisite natural setting along the Rio Grande. Visitors can readily see the brilliant orange and black Lichtenstein's oriole, green jays, buff-bellied hummingbirds, white-fronted doves, groove-billed anis, and long-billed thrashers. The rare and secretive ocelot and jaguarundi are here also, and huge flights of white-winged doves roost in the refuge in September. A late winter or early spring trip to these east Texas refuges, perhaps including a side trip to the Big Bend area on the Rio Grande, is among the most interesting and exciting available to the naturalist.

The following is a list of some birds of special interest found in common or abundant status at the refuges of this region.

Birds Common or Abundant at Seasons Indicated:

S: Spring   s: Summer   F: Fall   W: Winter

Least Grebe: Laguna Atascosa, Ss; Santa Ana, SsFW.
Olivaceous Cormorant: Santa Ana, W.
Anhinga: Santa Ana, SW.
Reddish Egret: Laguna Atascosa, SFW.
Yellow-crowned Night Heron: Laguna Atascosa, FW; Washita, s.
Wood Stork: Anahuac, sF; Aransas, s; Attwater, F; San Bernard, s.
White-faced Ibis: Anahuac, SsF; Aransas, SFW; Attwater, Ss;
    Imperial, F; Laguna Atascosa, SsF; San Bernard, F.
White Ibis: Anahuac, SsF; Aransas, S; Laguna Atascosa, SsF;
    San Bernard, F.
Roseate Spoonbill: Anahuac SsF; Aransas, sF; Attwater Ss;
    Laguna Atascosa, F; San Bernard, sFW.

Black-bellied Whistling Duck: Laguna, Ss; Santa Ana, Ss.
Fulvous Whistling Duck: Laguna Atascosa, SF.
Mottled Duck: Anahuac, SsFW; Aransas, SsFW; Attwater, SsFW;
　　Laguna Atascosa, SsFW; San Bernard, SsFW.
White-tailed Kite: Laguna Atascosa, SsFW; Santa Ana, s.
Mississippi Kite: Salt Plains, s; Santa Ana, S; Washita, SsF.
Cooper's Hawk: Bosque del Apache, SW; Cabeza Prieta, SFW;
　　Cibola, W; Havasu, SFW; Kofa, SF; Laguna Atascosa, W.
Ferruginous Hawk: Muleshoe, SFW.
Harris' Hawk: Laguna Atascosa, SsFW; Santa Ana, SsFW.
Golden Eagle: Bosque del Apache, FW; Buffalo Lake, W;
　　Cabeza Prieta, SFW; Cibola, W; Kofa, FW; Las Vegas, W;
　　Muleshoe, FW; Salt Plains, W.
Bald Eagle: Bosque del Apache, FW; Cibola, W; Havasu, W;
　　Las Vegas, W; Salt Plains, W; Sequoyah, FW.
Osprey: Cibola, SF; Laguna Atascosa, FW.
Prairie Falcon: Cabeza Prieta, SsFW; Cibola, F; Las Vegas, SF.
Peregrine Falcon: Laguna Atascosa, F.
Chachalaca: Laguna Atascosa, SsFW; Santa Ana, SsFW.
Greater Prairie Chicken: Attwater, SW.
Scaled Quail: Bitter Lake, SsFW; Bosque del Apache, SsFW;
　　Las Vegas, SsFW; Muleshoe, SsFW.
Gambel's Quail: Bosque del Apache, SsFW; Cabeza Prieta, SsFW;
　　Cibola, SsFW; Havasu, SsFW; Imperial, SsFW; Kofa, SsFW.
Turkey: Aransas, SsFW; Laguna Atascosa, SsFW; Salt Plains, SsFW;
　　Wichita Mountains, SsFW.
Whooping Crane: Aransas, SFW.
Purple Gallinule: Anahuac, Ss; Laguna Atascosa, Ss.
American Oystercatcher: Laguna Atascosa, sF.
Wilson's Plover: Aransas, S; Laguna Atascosa, SsF; San Bernard, s.
Piping Plover: Laguna Atascosa, SW.
Snowy Plover: Aransas, SF; Bitter Lake, SsF; Buffalo Lake, s;
　　Havasu, sF; Laguna Atascosa, Ss; Muleshoe, SsF;
　　Salt Plains, SsF.
American Golden Plover: Anahuac, S; Attwater, S; San Bernard, S;
　　Sequoyah, S.
Whimbrel: Laguna Atascosa, SF.
Long-billed Curlew: Anahuac, SFW; Aransas, SFW;
　　Laguna Atascosa, SsFW; Muleshoe, F; San Bernard, SFW.
Upland Sandpiper: Anahuac, SF; Attwater, S; Hagerman, Ss;
　　Laguna Atascosa, SF; Tishomingo, S.
White-rumped Sandpiper: Hagerman, S; Laguna Atascosa, SF;
　　Salt Plains, SF; Sequoyah, SF; Tishomingo, S.

Baird's Sandpiper: Buffalo Lake, Ss; Hagerman, SF;
    Laguna Atascosa, SF; Las Vegas, SF; Muleshoe, SsF;
    Salt Plains, SF; Tishomingo, S; Washita, SsF.
California Gull: Havasu, S.
Gull-billed Tern: Anahuac, SsF; Aransas, S; Laguna Atascosa, SsF.
Royal Tern: Laguna Atascosa, SsF.
Black Skimmer: Aransas, SsFW; Laguna Atascosa, SsF;
    San Bernard, sF.
White-winged Dove: Cabeza Prieta, SsF; Cibola, Ss; Havasu, Ss;
    Imperial, Ss; Kofa, Ss; Laguna Atascosa, Ss;
    Santa Ana, SsF.
Ground Dove: Cibola, SF; Laguna Atascosa, SsFW;
    Santa Ana, SsFW.
Inca Dove: Aransas, SsFW; Havasu, Ss.
White-fronted Dove: Laguna Atascosa, SsFW; Santa Ana, SsFW.
Roadrunner: Bitter Lake, SsFW; Bosque del Apache, SsFW;
    Cabeza Prietta, SsFW; Cibola, SsFW; Havasu, SsFW;
    Kofa, SsFW; Laguna Atascosa, SsFW; Santa Ana, SsFW.
Groove-billed Ani: Laguna Atascosa, sF; Santa Ana, SsF.
Elf Owl: Cabeza Prieta, SsFW; Kofa, Ss.
Burrowing Owl: Buffalo Lake, Ss; Cibola, SsFW; Muleshoe, SsFW.
Short-eared Owl: Laguna Atascosa, W.
Pauraque: Aransas, SsF; Laguna Atascosa, SsFW; Santa Ana, SsFW.
Lesser Nighthawk: Bosque del Apache, SsF; Cabeza Prieta, SsF;
    Cibola, SsF; Havasu, SsF; Imperial, Ss; Laguna Atascosa, sF;
    Santa Ana, s.
White-throated Swift: Cabeza Prieta, Ss; Havasu, W; Las Vegas, s.
Costa's Hummingbird: Cabeza Prieta, SsFW; Cibola, Ss;
    Havasu, S; Kofa, S.
Black-chinned Hummingbird: Havasu, Ss; Las Vegas, s.
Broad-tailed Hummingbird: Las Vegas, s.
Rufous Hummingbird: Cabeza Prieta, S; Las Vegas, s.
Golden-fronted Woodpecker: Laguna Atascosa, SsFW;
    Santa Ana, SsFW.
Gila Woodpecker: Cabeza Prieta, SsFW; Cibola, SsFW;
    Havasu, SsFW; Kofa, SsFW.
Lewis's Woodpecker: Las Vegas, SsF.
Ladder-backed Woodpecker: Bosque del Apache, SsF;
    Cibola, SsFW; Havasu, SsFW; Kofa, SsFW; Laguna
    Atascosa, SsFW; Muleshoe, SsFW; Santa Ana, SsFW.
Tropical Kingbird: Santa Ana, Ss.
Scissor-tailed Flycatcher: Anahuac, SsF; Aransas, SsF;
    Attwater, SsF; Bosque del Apache, sF; Hagerman, SsF;

Laguna Atascosa, SF; Muleshoe, SsF; Salt Plains, SsF;
San Bernard, SsF; Santa Ana, SF; Sequoyah, SsF;
Tishomingo, SsF; Washita, SsF; Wichita Mountains, SsF.
Kiskadee Flycatcher: Laguna Atascosa, S; Santa Ana, SsFW.
Wied's Crested Flycatcher: Cabeza Prieta, Ss; Havasu, s;
Laguna Atascosa, Ss; Santa Ana, SsF.
Ash-throated Flycatcher: Bosque del Apache, Ss; Cabeza Prieta, Ss;
Cibola, SsF; Havasu, Ss; Imperial, Ss; Kofa, Ss.
Black Phoebe: Bosque del Apache, s; Cibola, SFW; Havasu, SsFW.
Hammond's Flycatcher: Havasu, S.
Vermilion Flycatcher: Laguna Atascosa, SFW.
Steller's Jay: Las Vegas, SsF.
Scrub Jay: Bosque del Apache, W.
Green Jay: Laguna Atascosa, SsFW; Santa Ana, SsFW.
Mountain Chickadee: Bosque del Apache, W.
Verdin: Cabeza Prieta, SsFW; Cibola, SsFW; Havasu, SsFW;
Imperial, SsFW; Kofa, SsFW; Laguna Atascosa, Ss;
Santa Ana, SW.
Bewick's Wren: Bitter Lake, W; Havasu, sW;
Laguna Atascosa, SsFW; Salt Plains, SsF; Tishomingo, Ss;
Washita, SsFW; Wichita Mountains, SsFW.
Cactus Wren: Bosque del Apache, sF; Cabeza Prieta, SsFW;
Kofa, SsFW; Laguna Atascosa, SsFW; Muleshoe, SsFW;
Santa Ana, SsFW.
Cañon Wren: Bosque del Apache, SsFW; Cabeza Prieta, Ss;
Kofa, Ss; Laguna Atascosa, SsF; Las Vegas, SsF.
Rock Wren: Bitter Lake, SsFW; Bosque del Apache, SsFW;
Buffalo Lake, SsFW; Cabeza Prieta, Ss; Havasu, FW;
Imperial, FW; Kofa, SsF; Las Vegas, SsF.
Long-billed Thrasher: Laguna Atascosa, Ss; Santa Ana, SsFW.
Curve-billed Thrasher: Cabeza Prieta, SsFW; Kofa, Ss;
Laguna Atascosa, SsFW; Muleshoe, SFW; Santa Ana, SsFW.
Crissal Thrasher: Cibola, SsFW; Imperial, SsFW.
Sage Thrasher: Bitter Lake, SF; Kofa, FW.
Western Bluebird: Bosque del Apache, F.
Black-tailed Gnatcatcher: Cabeza Prieta, SsFW; Cibola, SsFW;
Havasu, SsFW; Kofa, SsFW.
Sprague's Pipit: Attwater, W.
Phainopepla: Cabeza Prieta, SFW; Cibola, SFW; Havasu, SW;
Imperial, SW; Kofa, SFW.
Bell's Vireo: Hagerman, s; Havasu, s; Salt Plains, s; Tishomingo, Ss.
Lucy's Warbler: Bosque del Apache, s; Havasu, SsF.
Townsend's Warbler: Cabeza Prieta, S; Kofa, S.

Hooded Oriole: Cabeza Prieta, s; Havasu, s; Kofa, s.

Lichtenstein's Oriole: Santa Ana, SsFW.

Scott's Oriole: Cabeza Prieta, S; Kofa, s.

Bronzed Cowbird: Laguna Atascosa, Ss; Santa Ana, Ss.

Western Tanager: Bosque del Apache, S; Cabeza Prieta, SF;
    Cibola, SF; Havasu, SF; Imperial, S; Kofa, SF.

Pyrrhuloxia: Aransas, SsFW; Cabeza Prieta, Ss; Laguna Atascosa,
    FW; Santa Ana, FW.

Black-headed Grosbeak: Bosque del Apache, SF; Cabeza Prieta, SF;
    Cibola, SF; Havasu, SF.

Blue Grosbeak: Anahuac, SF; Aransas, SF; Bosque del Apache, Ss;
    Cibola, Ss; Hagerman, SsF; Havasu, s; Imperial, Ss;
    Laguna Atascosa, SF; Las Vegas, s; Muleshoe, s; Salt Plains, SsF;
    Tishomingo, S.

Painted Bunting: Aransas, SsF; Attwater, S; Hagerman, SsF;
    Laguna Atascosa, Ss; Salt Plains, SsF; Santa Ana, S;
    Tishomingo, SsF; Wichita Mountains, Ss.

Lesser Goldfinch: Bosque del Apache, SW.

Olive Sparrow: Laguna Atascosa, SsFW; Santa Ana, SsFW.

Green-tailed Towhee: Bitter Lake, S; Las Vegas, SF.

Brown Towhee: Kofa, SsFW; Las Vegas, SsF.

Abert's Towhee: Cibola, SsFW; Havasu, SsFW; Imperial, SsFW.

Le Conte's Sparrow: Anahuac, SFW; Attwater, SW.

Seaside Sparrow: Anahuac, SsFW; Aransas, SsFW;
    San Bernard, SsFW.

Botteri's Sparrow: Laguna Atascosa, SsF.

Cassin's Sparrow: Bitter Lake, SsF; Buffalo Lake, s;
    Laguna Atascosa, SsF; Santa Ana, s.

Black-throated Sparrow: Bosque del Apache, SsF;
    Cabeza Prieta, SsFW; Havasu, Ss; Kofa, SsFW.

Sage Sparrow: Bitter Lake, SFW; Bosque del Apache, SFW;
    Cabeza Prieta, FW; Havasu, W.

Harris' Sparrow: Hagerman, SFW; Salt Plains, SFW; Sequoyah, W;
    Tishomingo, SFW; Washita, SFW.

McCown's Longspur: Muleshoe, SFW.

Chestnut-collared Longspur: Muleshoe, W;
    Wichita Mountains, FW.

SOUTHWEST

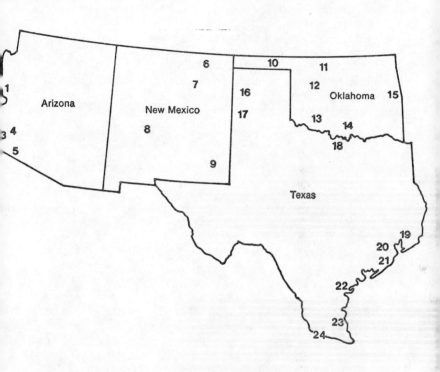

1 Havasu
2 Cibola
3 Imperial
4 Kofa
5 Cabeza Prieta
6 Maxwell
7 Las Vegas
8 Bosque del Apache
9 Bitter Lake
10 Optima
11 Salt Plains
12 Washita

13 Wichita Mountains
14 Tishomingo
15 Sequoyah
16 Buffalo Lake
17 Muleshoe
18 Hagerman
19 Anahuac
20 Attwater Prairie Chicken
21 San Bernard-Brazoria
22 Aransas
23 Laguna Atascosa
24 Santa Ana

ANAHUAC (Houston ● / ANAHUAC ★)

ANAHUAC (Texas)

Anahuac Refuge is one of the few places in the world where, until recently at least, the red wolf could be heard howling at night. Dogs in the area answer back, and sometimes the fur rises on their necks. It is a spine-tingling sound. How much longer it will be heard is problematical. The red wolf, once numerous over its range in the southeastern United States, has been so reduced in numbers scientists fear it may not be able to recover, at least as a pure strain, for as its population diminished it has bred with dogs and coyotes. Some have been captured and taken to Tacoma, Washington, as part of a plan to raise animals in captivity which then could be re-released in the wild. A pair has been freed on Bull's Island, South Carolina, in the Cape Romain Refuge.

But none of these efforts has been entirely encouraging; and meanwhile, this impressive animal which has survived so long now seems close to extinction. A recent count showed only thirty or fewer still in the wild, and the wolf seems to be making its last stand here. It is unlikely that most visitors will see one—they are extremely wary— but they are here. They can be told from the more numerous coyotes by their sturdier physiques and larger size. Tail position is not diagnostic and color varies—some coyotes are redder than "red wolves." Their flat mournful calls can be heard on many evenings.

To dwell too long and sadly on the red wolf would be to deny attention to the many wondrous sights and experiences for the visitor to this 9,837 acres of fresh- and salt-water ponds and marshland along the Texas Gulf Coast.

Anahuac is famous among birders for its rails—five and perhaps six species can be seen in spring migration (kings and clappers are common all year) and the refuge schedules marsh buggy trips in April when they all but guarantee to point out rails (sometimes tour leaders drag gravel-filled plastic bottles at the end of ropes to flush them). But reserve early—places are usually gone far in advance.

In any case there is much to see all the time. Large waterfowl concentrations are here from November to January—sometimes fifty thousand snow and blue geese and that many or more blue- and green-winged teal, pintail, wigeon, and others, twenty-five to thirty species in all. Mottled ducks are common all year and nest. Strikingly marked masked ducks are here from time to time—their first authenticated U.S. nesting record was on Shoveler Pond, where purple and common gallinules and pied-billed grebes also nest among the spike rushes and lily pads.

The list of shore birds seen commonly and abundantly in migration, and beautiful wading birds most of the year, is staggering—marbled godwits, golden plovers, long-billed curlews, pectoral, stilt, and upland sandpipers. Among wading birds are Wilson's phalaropes. Roseate spoonbills, wood storks, white-faced and white ibises, black-crowned and yellow-crowned night herons—some of these in sizable numbers—to mention a few.

Small bird migrations can be impressive too, in salt cedar brush—warblers, along with Swainson's thrushes, rose-breasted and blue grosbeaks, indigo buntings, scissor-tailed flycatchers, chuck-will's-widows, and occasional vermilion flycatchers and Le Conte's sparrows.

It is hard to imagine going out on the refuge trails without seeing numbers of interesting natural inhabitants, including some of the mammals as well—otter, raccoon, skunk, nutria which swim along with their young on their backs. Alligators also have been observed doing the same, giving a young one a ride on the adult's big flat scaly forehead.

How to get there: From Houston, take Route 10 east to Route 61, then south to Route 562, south to Route 1985 and southeast to refuge entrance.

Open: Twenty-four hours daily, all year.

Best times to visit: April for spring migrations; November to January for waterfowl in large numbers.

What to see: Six species of rails; large numbers of wading and shore-birds; wintering short-eared owls at dusk; otters; red wolves possible (though rare).

What to do: Miles of auto and walking trails; photography (blind available); guided tours to see rails in marsh by reservation in April; fishing from bayshore, excellent for flounder, redfish, trout, croaker, black drum, also crabbing.

Where to stay: MOTELS—In Baytown, Winnie, High Island and Anahuac. CAMPGROUNDS—Fort Anahuac and White County Parks, northwest of refuge; also permitted along bayshore on refuge, 3 nights only.

Weather notes: Summer can be hot, humid; January cool and blustery.

What to take and wear: Waterproof footgear if hiking around marsh.

Points of interest nearby: Big Thicket National Preserve, about 70 miles northeast—possible habitat of the ivory-billed woodpecker, if it still exists; Sea Rim State Park, 45 miles southeast; Vingt-et-Un Islands Audubon Sanctuary (permission required); and for general nature-watching in the area, contact the helpful Houston Audubon Society, 440 Wilchester, Houston 77079, phone: (713) 932-1392; or the Outdoor Nature Club, 10602 Cedarhurst, Houston 77096.

For more information: Anahuac National Wildlife Refuge, P.O. Box 278, Anahuac, Texas 77514. Phone: (713) 267-3337 and 267-3131.

ARANSAS
★
●Corpus Christi

ARANSAS (Texas)

The whooping crane, once seen, can never be forgotten. Strong and graceful, it is our tallest North American bird, standing up to five feet with a 7.5-foot wingspread. It is partly the cranes' regal presence that has inspired worldwide desire for their survival, and partly their lifestyle, dramatically exemplifying beauty in confrontation with great hazard at every turn. When a pair of the long white birds with scarlet crowns and black wingtips bow and dance with great aerial leaps in courtship, their "bugling" calls can be heard for miles. The call is sounded all along their 2,600-mile migration route from nesting grounds in remote Northwest Canada (only discovered in 1954 after a forest fire) to winter quarters at Aransas National Wildlife Refuge on the Texas Gulf Coast. It is a perilous journey undertaken mostly in threes—two adults with their usually lone chick between them. As the naturalist Aldo Leopold expressed it, "When we hear his call we hear no mere bird. He is the symbol of our untamable past."

Once reported to be extinct, in 1923, the whooping crane has come back from the brink of extinction and is not safe now. But the species has shown a gradual increase since there were only a total of twenty-one known to exist in the wild in 1944. A recent count showed almost one hundred, and there are a few others in small captive groups and in an experimental project using sandhill cranes as foster parents in the hope of establishing a separate migration flock (see Bosque del Apache Refuge in New Mexico). All this is watched carefully and uneasily, for a single disastrous occurrence—a wipeout on the nesting grounds, an oil spill on their winter feeding marshes—could cause losses beyond recovery.

Here on Aransas' ninety thousand acres is one of the few places where whooping cranes may be seen, and there is a very good chance of seeing them for any visitor who comes to Aransas from mid-October to late March (especially in the midpart of this period)—either from the observation tower or, for almost a certainty, from one of the tour boats.

The cranes have helped make Aransas probably the nation's best-known wildlife refuge—but its fame would be justified without them, for it is truly an outstanding place to see a great variety of flora and fauna, which can only be outlined here. It has the longest bird list of any refuge—350 species. Common at various times of the year are such stunning and interesting varieties as roseate spoonbills, wood storks, sandhill cranes, long-billed curlews, white pelicans, Rio Grande wild turkeys, Inca doves, pauraques, scissor-tailed flycatchers, buntings, tanagers, hummingbirds, various waterfowl, and fourteen species of warblers. Caracaras and Attwater's prairie chickens can be seen without difficulty, the latter on their booming grounds in spring. Broad-winged hawks migrate through in great kettles of five thousand or so in the fall.

Many rolls of film can be used on the beautiful white-tailed deer posing beside the trails with fine racks of antlers in winter and spotted fawns in the spring. Collared peccary, alligator, armadillo, and coyote are fairly common, and although rarely seen, bobcat, wild boar, and mountain lion are present on the refuge.

Aransas is admirably prepared to help enhance the visitor's stay with fine trail leaflets, including one for birding that gives seasonal highlights and locations, and with advice from refuge staff as to where, when, and how best to see everything. There is also an excellent set of bilingual "outdoor classroom" guides which may be requested in advance by teachers.

How to get there: From Rockport, go north on Route 35, turn right on Route 774 and follow refuge signs.

Open: Daylight hours all year.

Best times to visit: October to May (most wildlife here then, and weather generally best).

What to see: Whooping cranes, deer, and a great variety of others.

What to do: Many miles of walking and driving trails (including closed areas by permission); boat trips to see cranes; observation tower with wheelchair ramp and telescopes for viewing marsh and good chance of whooping cranes; photography (excellent, especially for deer, from car); limited hunting for deer and wild hogs; film showings on request for groups; educational packets for schoolchildren; fishing in bays for redfish, trout, flounder, also oystering and crabbing.

Where to stay: MOTELS—In Rockport and Port Lavaca. CAMP-GROUNDS—In Rockport, also Goose Island and Port Lavaca State Parks, and on refuge for youth groups with special permission.

Weather notes: Summer can be humid, and usually some cold rains January–February.

What to take and wear: Boots if walking off-trail, to protect against ticks and snakes.

Points of interest nearby: The whole Rockport area is wonderful birding, and refuge personnel are happy to direct visitors to spots where special things can be seen, eagles, caracaras, others; and several guided tours out of Rockport are well recommended. Also, Welder Wildlife Refuge; Padre Island National Seashore; and Second Chain of Islands, Audubon sanctuary open by permit only.

For more information: Aransas National Wildlife Refuge, P.O. Box 100, Austwell, Texas 77950. Phone: (512) 286-3559.

ATTWATER PRAIRIE CHICKEN ★ ● Houston

ATTWATER PRAIRIE CHICKEN (Texas)

Attwater prairie chickens are gallinaceous birds so inconspicuous most of the time you might not notice one if he were right beside you in the prairie grassland that is his required habitat. But when spring comes and courtship begins, all that changes. The males congregate on short grass areas ("booming grounds") and stake out territories. They proceed to advertise their presence and readiness to mate by stamping the ground, vibrating their erected feathers, and inflating bright orange sacs on each side of their necks. Under pressure, these orange sacs deflate to make loud booming sounds (a little like a foghorn). The stamping itself makes resounding echoes that can be heard for fifty feet or more; and under favorable weather conditions, the booming is audible for two miles. Often these strutting displays are interrupted by leaps into the air.

Once Attwater prairie chickens were so numerous in the coastal tall grass prairie of Texas that, old-timers said, the booming caused pain to sensitive eardrums. As if to lessen this threat, gunners practicing marksmanship used them as clay pigeons and held competitions in which teams of twenty or so would go out for a given period and kill as many of these inoffensive little fowl as possible; the party that killed the smallest number then would pay all the expenses of the outing. The tallies made, piles of sometimes thousands of birds were left to rot or be eaten by vultures.

Irresponsible hunting caused the loss of large numbers of birds, but the major cause of the population decline was habitat destruction. By 1937 the range of the Attwater prairie chicken (a race of the greater prairie chicken) had been reduced by 93 per cent, their population reduced by an estimated 99 per cent, and they were believed close to following their near relative, the heath hen of the Atlantic Coast, into extinction.

It has not happened. Awareness of their plight caused the close of the hunting season beginning in 1937; and despite a report in 1941 that predicted no possible measures could save these attractive little birds from extinction, they are still here. The Attwater Prairie Chicken National Wildlife Refuge, established in 1972, is dedicated to preserving habitat to ensure their survival. The Nature Conservancy originally purchased 3,500 acres and the Fish and Wildlife Service bought an additional 2,100 acres, bringing the total acreage to 5,600. Plans are to enlarge the refuge to 8,300 acres. Prairie chickens are not on the refuge in large numbers—a little over 150 in most years, out of perhaps 2,000 over the State of Texas—but they have been gradually increasing, so there is hope.

The refuge is closed to the general public, but one can observe the birds on booming grounds. Naturalists may obtain permission from the Refuge Manager for a conducted tour. All observations are made from towers which are placed at considerable distance from the booming grounds. With some advance notice (allow a month at least, since verbal permission has to be granted from Washington), permission may be granted to photograph the birds from blinds near one of the "leks."

In the future, a visitor's contact station is planned, along with interpretive walking and auto trails. School children will be hosted in environmental education programs. All public use activity will be conducted on remote areas at a distance from all known booming grounds.

A number of other interesting birds and mammals enjoy this same habitat—Sprague's pipits, Le Conte's and vesper sparrows, and yellow rails may be observed in winter. Dickcissels and painted buntings are common in the spring.

All disturbance cannot be eliminated. Refuge staff discovered recently that marsh hawks like to harass the male chickens at the height of their displays, swooping down as if to strike—terrorizing them briefly—but never actually striking. The hawks are apparently only taking a sporting interest in upsetting them. The male prairie chickens, after a few minutes, usually resume their strutting and booming as before. Observers of this odd behavior concluded it was aberrational on the part of the hawks, until an old account revealed that marsh hawks have been following this precise behavior pattern for generations. There seems to be no particular gain to the marsh hawks and no more than temporary agitation to the chickens.

How to get there: From Houston, take Route 10 west to Sealy, south on Route 36 for 1 mile to Route 3013 and about 10 miles southwest on 3013 to refuge sign.

Open: From 8 A.M. to 4:30 P.M. weekdays, otherwise by appointment.

Best times to visit: February through April.

What to see: Attwater prairie chickens.

What to do: Observe; photograph (blinds available by reservation only).

Where to stay: MOTELS—In Eagle Lake. Also, the Farris 1912, a South Texas landmark, is a restored Victorian hotel (prior reservations required). CAMPGROUNDS—Stephen F. Austin State Park, 12 miles northeast.

Weather notes: January and February can be blustery, summers hot and humid; otherwise, generally pleasant.

Points of interest nearby: The Eagle Lake area has some of the largest concentrations of wintering geese in Texas; thousands can generally be seen feeding in fallow rice fields along public roads. Information on recent nature sights may be learned by contacting the Houston Audubon Society, 440 Wilchester, Houston, Texas 77079, phone: (713) 932-1392; or the Outdoor Nature Club, 10602 Cedarhurst, Houston, Texas 77096.

For more information: Attwater Prairie Chicken National Wildlife Refuge. P.O. Box 518, Eagle Lake, Texas 77434. Phone: (713) 234-3021.

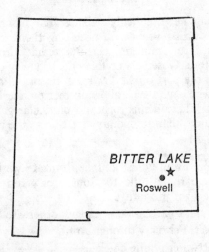

Roswell

BITTER LAKE (New Mexico)

The air is sometimes filled with snow geese and a large proportion of the world population of lesser sandhill cranes at this 23,350-acre refuge in southeast New Mexico. There is something of interest in the natural world during every season at Bitter Lake, whose name goes back before the earliest maps were drawn and refers to the alkaline water that feeds into it somewhat mysteriously from Lost River and subterranean springs. It tastes, some think, more sweet than bitter.

The snow geese may number sixty-six thousand at peak times and are here from October through February along with a hundred thousand ducks of twenty species, and up to seventy thousand cranes, at roughly the same times (though they may move off temporarily in midwinter if lakes and impoundments freeze over). They are a wonderful sight, flying off the lakes in the early morning to feed on farm fields and returning to roost at night, often silhouetted against one of the most spectacular sunsets to be seen anywhere. When they are here in force, local airports and nearby Cannon Air Force Base issue advisories on their numbers and location to avoid airspace conflicts.

Birding can be excellent. Because of its location near the 100th meridian in a plain rimmed by mountains, Bitter Lake gets representatives from both east and west and high and low elevations—eastern, western, and mountain bluebirds, for example, and red-winged and yellow-headed blackbirds. Cliff swallows colonize the bluffs.

Broad-tailed hummingbirds come when flowers are abundant. Snowy plovers nest on the salt flats. Roadrunners, the New Mexico state bird, are common all year, as are Say's phoebes, rock wrens, scaled quails, and introduced white-winged pheasants. White-necked ravens and ladder-backed woodpeckers nest.

Interesting sparrows common seasonally are the Cassin's, sage, lark, clay-colored, and Brewer's. Wilson's warblers are common in spring, and sometimes warblers migrate through in fair numbers. Birding is best along the foot trail (where a black-crowned heron rookery can be seen in summer) and around the headquarters area.

Bitter Lake has dozens of ponds and impoundments, and many can be viewed from the drive. There are also gypsum sinks, some ninety feet deep, of a striking blue (contrasting with the deep pink of a number of shallow ponds caused by an algae which blooms in August).

The Lake St. Francis Natural Area provides habitat for a marine algae found only here and along the Gulf of Mexico, as well as for the endangered mosquito fish *Pecos gambusia*, and the rare Pecos pupfish.

Arizona black-tailed prairie dogs, a threatened species, have a hundred or so burrow homes just outside the refuge entrance, some of which allow burrowing owls as near neighbors (and predatory marsh hawks for hovering observers). Mule deer are present, along with more secretive badgers and bobcats. The desert cottontail and black-tailed jackrabbit are to be seen nearly everywhere.

For a good introduction to some of Bitter Lake's striking bird species, visit the enclosure where birds which have been injured or temporarily incapacitated are kept until they are in good health and can be returned to the wild—the cranes, snow geese, various ducks and others are interestingly represented here from time to time.

How to get there: From downtown Roswell, take U.S. 70/285 north about a quarter mile to small refuge sign on right (opposite State Route 48 turnoff). Turn right and following winding road about 10 miles to refuge.

Open: One hour before sunrise to one hour after sunset.

Best times to visit: October through February but interesting all year.

What to see: Large concentrations of sandhill cranes, waterfowl; interesting small birding; such relative rarities as prairie falcons, eastern barking frogs, western spiny softshell turtles, Pecos ribbon snakes.

What to do: Eight miles of roads with self-guiding leaflet; observation platforms; seven overlooks with fine views of lakes; hiking trail, especially good spring and fall for small birds; fishing can be good for channel catfish, white bass; limited hunt for waterfowl, cranes; picnicking.

Where to stay: MOTELS—In Roswell. CAMPGROUNDS—Roswell; also Bottomless Lakes State Park, 15 miles east, and on refuge for youth groups by special permit.

Weather notes: Spring windy with blowing dust; fall weather usually mild and best for beautiful sunsets.

Points of interest nearby: Carlsbad Caverns National Park, 80 miles south; Lincoln National Forest, 70 miles west; Dexter National Fish Hatchery, 25 miles south, endangered fish research station; also good upland birding.

For more information: Bitter Lake National Wildlife Refuge, P.O. Box 7, Roswell, New Mexico 88201. Phone: (505) 622-6755.

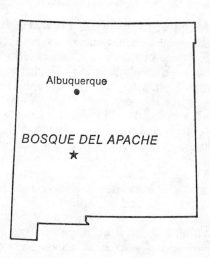

Albuquerque

BOSQUE DEL APACHE

★

BOSQUE DEL APACHE (New Mexico)

Young whooping cranes, already stately with their five-foot height and seven-foot wingspread and plumage blending from mottled rust to pure white, spend the winters at Bosque del Apache Refuge in central New Mexico with their sandhill crane foster parents. They are part of an experiment which may start a new migration flock and help save this majestic species, tallest bird in North America and often called the most beautiful, from extinction.

Like most of the interesting wildlife at this 57,191-acre refuge of marsh and grasslands in the shelter of the Magdalena Mountains, they can be seen readily by the visitor on the miles of roads and trails open to nature exploration. This is one of the nation's outstanding refuges, partly because of its widely varying wild inhabitants but also because of their high degree of visibility. Species which ordinarily are shy and wary often seem to show little fear here.

Mule deer, their long ears showing the reason for their name, are everywhere. Porcupines sleep in the forks of cottonwood trees when they are not chewing off bark and twigs. One pair of visitors started down an observation tower and found a mountain lion waiting at the bottom; they all exchanged stares until, curiosity satisfied, the lion ambled off.

But the dramatic time of the year is when the waterfowl are here between October and February—up to twenty-three thousand snow geese and two thousand Canadas and thirty-five thousand ducks of seventeen species (some of which also nest here in summer) along with fourteen thousand sandhill cranes. Go to the refuge at first light and watch while they stir and awaken and fly out to feed; or, just before sunset when they return to the roost again, filling the sky from horizon to horizon with calling birds, against a red sunset and a backdrop of silhouetted mountains. It is unforgettable.

In the late afternoon, a coyote may stalk a white goose flock—seldom getting close to these observant birds. But an eagle may feed on one which, weak or injured, lagged behind his fellows. A desert tortoise may plod across an arid stretch. Bats of fourteen species pour out of crevices in the spring and fall twilight to feed on insects.

Shorebird migrations can be interesting (avocets, stilts, phalaropes) and small birding excellent. Some of those common seasonally include cactus wrens, western bluebirds, black phoebes, blackheaded and blue grosbeaks, scrub jays, western and ash-throated flycatchers. Here all year round are cañon and rock wrens, Say's phoebes, roadrunners, Gambel's quails, and introduced white-winged pheasants. White-necked ravens nest, as do Cooper's hawks and ladder-backed woodpeckers.

Indian ruins dating back to 1300 are here (the refuge name refers to their camps in the "woods of the Apache").

Also administered by Bosque del Apache:

San Andres—57,215 acres in the San Andres Mountains, thirty miles northeast of Las Cruces, established for protection of desert bighorn sheep, of which some two hundred and fifty are there. Located entirely within the White Sands Missile Range, it is closed to public access except for a limited hunting season.

Sevilleta is a recent acquisition through The Nature Conservancy of 222,000 acres of varied habitat about twenty miles north of Socorro, supporting antelopes, mule deer, bobcats, mountain lions and various raptor, songbird, and upland species. Until recently at least, access has been limited to specific approved scientific studies.

How to get there: From Socorro, take I-25 to San Antonio exit ✕139, then Route 380 east to Route 1 (at Owl Cafe) and right (south) 8 miles to refuge.

Open: Half hour before sunrise to half hour after sunset.

Best times to visit: October to February (but all year interesting).

What to see: Sandhill cranes; whooping cranes; snow geese; mule deer; great variety of others.

What to do: Fifteen miles of roads for nature observation; interpretive trails; observation towers; photography (blinds on reservation basis); fishing; limited hunt for deer, geese, upland game; annual state retriever trials.

Where to stay: MOTELS—In Socorro. CAMPGROUNDS—In Socorro; also Cibola National Forest, 25 miles west of Socorro; primitive on refuge for organized youth groups.

Weather notes: Spring can be windy with dust storms, summer hot.

Points of interest nearby: Old Miguel Mission in Socorro; Gran Quivera National Monument, 70 miles northeast; VLA Laboratory (world's largest radio telescope), 70 miles west; Elephant Butte Reservoir, 60 miles south.

For more information: Bosque del Apache National Wildlife Refuge, Box 1246, Socorro, New Mexico 87801. Phone: (505) 835-1828.

Amarillo

★ BUFFALO LAKE

BUFFALO LAKE (Texas)

When Buffalo Lake has water, which is not every year, the birds at this 7,664-acre refuge in the central Texas panhandle can be outstanding—up to eighty thousand geese and a million ducks in fall and winter, and thousands of shorebirds in spring and fall migration.

When it is dry, there are still things to see—an excellent raptor population, a resident herd of mule deer, bobcat occasionally, a few small kit or "swift" fox, a sizable prairie dog town which the appealing rodents share with burrowing owls, and at times good birding along the canyons and draws.

Swainson's and red-tailed hawks nest commonly, and good numbers of Cooper's, rough-legged, sharp-shinned, marsh, and ferruginous hawks in fall and/or winter, with occasional peregrine and prairie falcons and ospreys.

Horned larks, mourning doves, and meadowlarks are everywhere; also rock wrens and quail, both the bobwhite and scaled. Ring-necked pheasant have increased in recent years. Vesper, lark, and Cassin's sparrows are common in summer, and grasshopper, chipping, and song sparrows in fair numbers over several seasons along with pine siskins and juncos of both the dark-eyed and gray-headed variety. Brewer's and Baird's sparrows can be found; lark buntings and green-tailed, brown, and rufous-sided towhees all are occasional through the year. Both orchard and northern orioles nest commonly. McCown's and chestnut-collared longspurs are sometimes around in large numbers—a recent Christmas Count showed 1,285 of the latter and 250 McCown's, along with ten Lapland longspurs, a few curve-billed thrashers, and both red-headed and ladder-backed woodpeckers.

Most visitors will enjoy the refuge's prairie dog town with three thousand or more of these alert little animals scurrying about, along with their young in spring—especially when burrowing owls take over some of their holes and start a neighborhood quarrel.

But Buffalo Lake is at its best in times of good rainfall when the shallow lake is full and moist flats line its banks. Then by the thousands come dowitchers, avocets, sanderlings, dunlins, yellowlegs, and others. Snowy plovers and black-necked stilts nest. Snowy egrets are common with more than a dozen species of ducks and both snow and Canada geese. There are always a few wintering eagles, both bald and golden, and when the ducks are here there may be a dozen or more.

Buffalo Lake's water situation is problematical; it is fed largely by rainfall and little Tierra Blanca Creek. Formerly there were springs as well, but irrigation use has lowered the water table and dried these up. So the future in dry years is uncertain.

It is also a beautiful refuge with its rose-colored caliche limestone outcrops, in places almost like a small grand canyon, and spring flowers over the rolling hills can be a lovely sight.

How to get there: From Amarillo, take I-40 west to Canyon Expressway, south to Canyon, then Route 60 west to Umbarger and Route 168 south 2 miles to refuge.

Open: Twenty-four hours all year.

Best times to visit: November through spring.

What to see: Wintering waterfowl, migrating shorebirds, numerous when water conditions permit; eagles; mule deer; prairie dogs; excellent small birding in canyons and draws.

What to do: Twenty miles of roads open to foot and vehicular travel; fishing, when water is up; bird dog training; horseback riding; bird-watching.

Where to stay: MOTELS—In Canyon, 10 miles east. CAMPGROUNDS— On refuge; also at Palo Duro Canyon State Park, 22 miles east.

Weather notes: Summer hot, dry, windy. Dust storms with 50 mph winds can come up suddenly in spring.

Points of interest nearby: Palo Duro State Park—scenically beautiful, good birding (see CAMPGROUNDS); Lake Meredith, 75 miles northeast—rated with Palo Duro and Buffalo Lake as best birding in area; Panhandle-Plains Historical Museum, Canyon.

For more information: Buffalo Lake National Wildlife Refuge, P.O. Box 228, Umbarger, Texas 79091. Phone: (806) 499-3382.

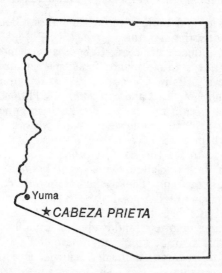

Yuma

★*CABEZA PRIETA*

CABEZA PRIETA (Arizona)

Cabeza Prieta is a mountain and desert refuge of more than a thousand square miles, set aside in 1939 largely at the instigation of the Boy Scouts of America to save the desert bighorn sheep from extinction. It has helped serve that function not only for the sheep but for the extremely rare Sonoran pronghorn antelope (one of the fastest animals on earth, clocked at seventy miles an hour) and for a number of rare-to-unique plants found here. These include the massive scaly-barked elephant tree, on which bighorns like to practice their charges; the Kearney sumac; organ pipe and senita cacti (the latter means old man's whiskers in Spanish); and the limberbush, whose slender branches can be tied in a knot.

Visitors can also see from time to time the rare to uncommon ferruginous hawk, prairie falcons, and sometimes tropical kingbirds, white-winged doves, and coatimundis over from Mexico.

Cabeza and Kofa both are administered from the Yuma office, and they are similar. Kofa's mountains are more jagged and dramatic-looking, and it has more bighorns and desert mule deer. It does not have Cabeza's pronghorns or its collared peccary (also called javelina), which are descended from gigantic wild pigs that lived here twenty-five million years ago. Cabeza is more arid. Each has its unique vegetation, and both have dazzling desert floral displays at times of sufficient spring moisture.

But if Kofa is difficult of access, Cabeza is even more so. Part of the road through it is an old pioneer track aptly named the Camino del Diablo—Devil's Highway—because it is so rough and rocky, and so many died there of thirst and exposure. In addition, the refuge is used as a military gunnery range, and refuge personnel must check on the gunnery practice schedule (normally weekdays) before anyone, including themselves, can enter.

The best place to see the herd of pronghorns—a small Sonoran race and one of the world's most endangered animals—is near a watering hole at the east end. The javelina are mostly on the flatlands or along old stream gullies. A good place to look for some of the brilliant flowers of the barrel and hedgehog cacti, as well as dune primroses, desert sunflowers, and verbenas, catchfly gentians, and pink pentstemons, is on the Pinta Sands, beyond Tule Well.

Remarkably, thirty-three mammal species manage to survive and even thrive here—ringtail cats, kit fox, badger, coyote, bobcat, and kangaroo rats as well as such relatively common (for the desert) birds as elf owls, white-winged and mourning doves, Gambel's quail, Cooper's hawks, kestrels, Costa's hummingbirds, Gila woodpeckers, verdins, cactus wrens, Scott's and Bullock's orioles, and sage and black-throated sparrows.

Beautiful sixteen-inch Gila monsters, their scales like ornate orange and black beading (sluggish, but watch out—they're poisonous) are here in small numbers, as is the relatively rare desert tortoise.

How to get there: Since a permit is required, go first to refuge headquarters in Yuma or subheadquarters in Ajo, next to the refuge. Offices are open weekdays only.

What to see: Bighorn sheep. Endangered Sonoran pronghorn antelopes. Javelinas, white-winged doves, unique desert wilderness.

What to do: Driving and walking trails (poorly marked and often nearly impassable). Photography at refuge blinds by permit.

Where to stay: MOTELS—In Ajo, or larger selection in Gila Bend or Yuma. CAMPGROUNDS—Primitive (no facilities) on refuge by permit. Also at Organ Pipe Cactus National Monument, adjoining refuge, and Painted Rock State Park, to the north.

Weather notes: Same as Kofa.

What to take and wear: Same as Kofa, only almost none of refuge should be attempted except by four-wheel drive vehicle (rentals available by reservation).

Points of interest nearby: Organ Pipe Cactus National Monument—spectacular cacti. Painted Rock State Park. Also, Kofa National Wildlife Refuge.

For more information: Cabeza Prieta National Wildlife Refuge, P.O. Box 1032, Yuma, Arizona 85364. Phone: (602) 726-2619.

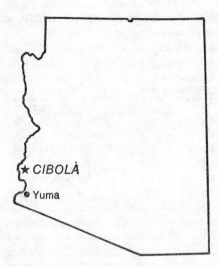

CIBOLA (Arizona-California)

Cibola is one of three national wildlife refuges on the lower Colorado River, and borders it for 9,463 acres of alluvial river bottom in Arizona and California, with dense growth of salt cedar, mesquite, and arrowwood surrounded by areas farmed largely for wildlife food. It differs from the others primarily in the latter respect—it is, in effect, a breadbasket, offering more sustenance for migrating waterfowl.

One of the best ways to see it is to put a canoe in the water and paddle or simply float down through the old river channel—about twelve miles, a leisurely one-day trip. Or, one can put in at Blythe to the north, float down through Cibola and on through Imperial Refuge on the south to Martinez Lake—a journey of about sixty miles, with campgrounds along the way (though not on the refuges). It can be an unforgettable experience.

Wildlife is similar at both refuges, though not identical because of their slightly different terrain. Imperial has more natural river channel winding through gorges with little backwater lakes. Cibola's natural old river channel, with its oxbows, parallels (in a sense) the new channelized portion, and has more wide flood-plain land.

Cibola has in addition some thirty miles of auto and walking trails. Arizona State University has done experimental work here in plantings for wildlife, and there are fine birding areas. Gambel's quail are common all year as are great blue herons and snowy egrets, pied-billed grebes, roadrunners, screech and great horned owls, Gila and ladder-backed woodpeckers, verdins, Abert's towhees, crissal thrashers, burrowing owls, and back-tailed gnatcatchers; and seasonally, the handsome phainopeplas, MacGillivray's warblers, black and Say's phoebes, Wilson's phalaropes, black-necked stilts, and white-winged and mourning doves (sometimes up to twenty thousand whitewings). The endangered Yuma clapper rail nests here, and a recent population count showed about a hundred birds.

Mammal populations are similar to Imperial's. Rare sightings of bighorn sheep are slightly more likely at Imperial; others like coyote, burros, and deer might be more likely to be seen while driving or walking along the dike roads early and late at Cibola.

Thousands of ducks and geese flock here in the winter from October through February—mostly Canada geese but some snows and whitefronts, and mallard, gadwall, pintail, cinnamon teal, wigeon, and shoveler ducks. Several hundred sandhill cranes may be here then, too, and in the summer interesting birds come up from the Gulf—a few brown pelicans, roseate spoonbills, and sometimes a hundred or so wood storks.

Wild flowers can be beautiful if triggered with sufficient rainfall— the green paloverde covered with masses of white blooms, the creosote bush with yellow, contrasting with the gnarled ironwood trees.

How to get there: From Blythe, California, take Route 78 south to Palo Verde, then three miles south to Colorado River Access Road, left on it around lake onto levee road south to refuge sign. (For Arizona side, take levee road *north* to bridge, cross and turn south on opposite side to refuge entrance.)

Open: Twenty-four hours daily all year.

Best times to visit: December through June.

What to see: Waterfowl; cranes; coyote; roadrunners; good variety of small birds; interesting old pioneer cottonwood log cabin on bluff overlooking area.

Where to stay: MOTELS—In Blythe. CAMPGROUNDS—A number of private, county and state facilities within 25 miles—3 adjacent to refuge boundaries.

Weather notes: Summer characteristically hot and dry until August, then hot and humid until mid-September.

What to take and wear: Hiking boots if doing much walking; high clearance vehicle and plenty of gas with food and water for emergencies (not much traffic on refuge roads in case of breakdown).

Points of interest nearby: Glamis Sand Dunes, 40 miles south. Desert bighorn sheep in Trigo Mountains, 5 miles east. Giant desert intaglios—huge figures of men and animals scoured out by Indians in desert north of Blythe. Also Imperial, Havasu, and Kofa National Wildlife Refuges.

For more information: Cibola National Wildlife Refuge, P.O. Box AP, Blythe, California 92225. Phone: (714) 922-4433.

HAGERMAN (Texas)

Those who visit Hagerman Refuge regularly all year say they always find something interesting—white pelicans, deer, coyote, bobcat, scissor-tailed flycatchers, migratory waterfowl, wading and shore-birds, depending on the season—all coexisting with some two hundred operating oil wells.

The wells, which pump some 5,400 barrels of oil a day, are spotted throughout the 11,319 acres of combined marsh, water, and upland habitat. This land was established as a refuge in 1946 on the Big Mineral Arm of Lake Texoma, formed by construction of the Denison Dam on the Red River which borders Texas and Oklahoma.

To some visitors, the wells are ugly; the wild inhabitants seem unconcerned. Most of the waterfowl species common to the Central Flyway settle down here for at least part of the year—more than a dozen kinds of ducks and up to fifteen thousand geese, mostly Canadas but also snows and white-fronts with a few brant and Ross'; most move farther south for the winter but a few stay through.

Flocks of thousands of white pelicans also drop by in spring and fall, and when mudflats offer feeding habitat (depending on rain-fall), notable shorebird groups stop: sometimes hundreds of Baird's sandpipers as well as the western, least, upland, pectoral, stilt, and solitary, with Wilson's phalaropes, dowitchers, and occasional golden plovers and long-billed curlews.

Small bird migrations can be impressive, too, with great numbers of swallows—bank, rough-winged, cliff, and tree—Swainson's thrushes, ruby-crowned kinglets, clay-colored, vesper, and Lincoln's sparrows, and Wilson's and yellow-throated warblers.

Wintering populations include good numbers of red-tailed hawks, horned larks, water pipits, cedar waxwings, purple finches, goldfinches, and white-crowned, white-throated, Harris', fox, and field sparrows, with a few Le Conte's (sometimes a dozen or more at a time) and sharptails and now and then a chestnut-collared longspur.

Painted and indigo buntings, blue grosbeaks, dickcissels, Bell's vireos, and the lovely scissor-tailed flycatchers, visible from every power line, nest regularly, and so, occasionally, do roadrunners and Swainson's hawks. Bluebirds, mockingbirds, great blue herons, bob-white quail, killdeer, and meadowlarks are here all year. All these are best sought before midsummer, when dense vegetation makes them hard to see—though the scissor-tailed, preparing for southern travel in the fall, sometimes masses in flocks of hundreds, an unfor-gettable sight of those streamered beauties.

The visitor who is willing to get out at daybreak has a better chance to get a look at the mammals. There are white-tailed deer, bobcat (sometimes with young in summer), mink (sometimes chased by the great blue herons when they compete for the same shoreline), armadillo, beaver, raccoon, skunk, and coyote (their calls heard nearly every evening).

Black and turkey vultures often preen themselves on the oil pipe-lines; geese browse beside the pumps and eagles perch on cotton-wood trees alongside the pumps, unconscious of any unnatural in-trusion—and to many Texans, this is indeed not only an appropriate part of the native scene along with the spring-flowering dogwoods and redbuds—they are ready to assert the whole thing is downright beautiful.

How to get there: From Sherman, take Route 82 west to Route 1417, then north about 5.5 miles to refuge sign; left there and continue to refuge headquarters.

Open: Twenty-four hours all year.

Best times to visit: October through spring.

What to see: Migratory and wintering waterfowl; deer; shorebirds; good assortment of small birds; unusual Cedar of Lebanon tree. (Excellent lists of refuge inhabitants are available.)

What to do: About 5 miles of roads for driving or hiking, 4 miles for foot travel; photography (portable blinds permitted); limited dove hunt; fishing for bass, crappie, bream, channel catfish.

Where to stay: MOTELS—In Denison and Sherman. CAMPGROUNDS— Flowing Wells (Army Corps of Engineers) Campground, 8 miles north; Eisenhower State Park, 9 miles northeast.

Weather notes: July–August hot, humid; January–February can be damp and cold.

Points of interest nearby: Denison Dam, recreation, museum, and tours, 9 miles north; Eisenhower State Park, various recreational facilities (see CAMPGROUNDS); Eisenhower birthplace in Denison; Rayburn home and library, 30 miles southeast; Tishomingo National Wildlife Refuge, 70 miles north.

For more information: Hagerman National Wildlife Refuge, Route 3, Box 123, Sherman, Texas 75090. Phone: (214) 786-2826.

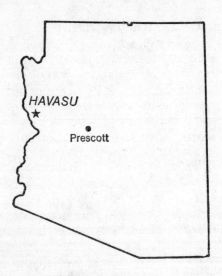

HAVASU (Arizona)

Havasu National Wildlife Refuge has some of the most spectacularly beautiful scenery and diverse and interesting wildlife of any place in the lower Colorado River Valley.

The many-colored cliffs in its eighteen-mile Topock Gorge rise sheer and rugged hundreds of feet from clear waters where great blue and black-crowned night herons visit.

Western grebes perform their courtship dances where the Colorado River and Lake Havasu meet, and endangered Yuma clapper rails breed in four-thousand-acre Topock Marsh, bordered on one side by the river and on the other by a narrow outwash plain.

But perhaps most remarkable is the unit named after a legendary mountain man named Bill Williams, which contains habitat that ranges from high rocky desert to mesa, desert floor and a creosote-ocotillo association, pockets of saguaro cactus and blue paloverde, and riverbottom delta land with marsh and open water and a dense forest of fifty-foot Frémont cottonwood trees. All this supports a tremendous range of plant and animal types, some highly rare and unusual.

Access to the best parts of these is not effortless. One can set out by vehicle and go into the Bill Williams unit, but to see most of it,

Turkeys, once declining, now have healthy populations at refuges such as White River in Arkansas, Erie, and Presquile. Woodcocks, grouse, partridges, quails, and pheasants are other upland fowl common on the refuges. *Laura Riley*

The magnificent frigatebird soars for hours on ninety-inch wings, never alighting on land or water because short legs and broad wings make takeoff difficult except from a height, such as a rock or tree limb. Males expand scarlet throat sacs during breeding. They are at Key Deer Refuge and others. *Laura Riley*

No other North American bird has this odd-shaped spoonbill—an efficient feeding instrument—or this superb coloration. The roseate spoonbill is seen at Gulf Coast refuges. *Laura Riley*

Gannets are noted for dramatic fifty-foot plunges when fishing and for "skypointing" behavior during courtship. They return to land only to breed. The rest of their lives are spent at sea, but they are commonly seen off Back Bay and Monomoy and occasionally seen off other coastal refuges along the Atlantic Coast. *Laura Riley*

The Louisiana state bird, the brown pelican, became extinct in that state and endangered over much of its range, harmed by pesticide pollution. But its status is improved since the banning of DDT, and it can be seen readily in Florida and occasionally at San Francisco Bay. *Laura and William Riley*

The green jay is a stunner, with brilliant green, blue, and golden plumage, locally common in woods at the southern tip of Texas and especially at Santa Ana Refuge. *Laura Riley*

The little burrowing owl, which hunts in the daytime and digs long tunnels for its home, is endangered over much of the West but can be seen at Cibola, Buffalo Lake, Muleshoe, and elsewhere. It catches frogs, lizards, and insects for food. *Laura Riley*

Mountain goats are not really goats but related to European and Asian antelopes, believed to have entered North America across the Bering Sea land bridge more than a half million years ago. They are in Alaska and at National Bison Range. *U. S. Fish and Wildlife*

Sometimes twelve thousand elk may gather in winter at National Elk Refuge in Wyoming. This large refuge was set aside after severe winter weather and shrinking habitat caused thousands to starve to death. *U. S. Fish and Wildlife*

Red-tailed hawks are one of our handsomest and best-known buteos, and prominent residents at most refuges across the country for at least part of the year. They perch on poles or treetops, rarely hovering. *Laura Riley*

The feet of bighorn sheep are especially constructed with spreading toes and hoofpads to deal with the habitat they like best—high mountain peaks. They can leap sixteen feet on level ground, thirty feet off a ledge. They are at most mountainous western refuges, their desert subspecies at Kofa and Cabeza Prieta. *U. S. Fish and Wildlife*

The attractive bobcat was once considered a destructive predator, with a bounty on its head. Now it is seen as a means of rodent control and is protected in many places (though high fur prices keep its numbers low). It is wary, for good reason, but present at refuges across the country. *U. S. Fish and Wildlife*

The beautiful pronghorn antelope can run faster than fifty miles an hour, leap twenty feet at a bound, see both backward and forward and pick out small objects four miles away. It exists only in North America; here, it is at Hart Mountain and Sheldon Antelope Range and elsewhere in the Northwest. *U. S. Fish and Wildlife*

The wood duck has been called the most beautiful waterfowl in the world. Since protection, its numbers have increased and it can be seen at many refuges, in particularly large numbers at Yazoo, Savannah, and Muscatatuck. *Laura Riley*

one must walk—and to experience Topock Gorge, it is necessary to go by boat. This can be managed by either canoe or houseboat without difficulty—the waters are not dangerous and boat rentals are readily available at concessions near the refuge—and whatever effort is involved is rewarded many times (particularly if a trip is scheduled for some time other than a crowded summer or holiday weekend).

Canada and snow geese winter here from early November through mid-March, occasionally with a few rare Ross's geese and Aleutian Canadas. A pair of southern bald eagles have found their way here in recent years and usually can be seen from a refuge observation tower overlooking the marsh. Common in fall and winter are Cooper's and marsh hawks, rock wrens, flickers, kingfishers, mallards, and gadwall ducks, and here all year are least bitterns, eared and western grebes, great and snowy egrets, red-tailed hawks, Gambel's quails, killdeers, roadrunners, verdins, crissal thrashers, Abert's towhees, black-throated sparrows, loggerhead shrikes, and black-tailed gnatcatchers. Common at some time during the year are white pelicans, snowy plovers, Inca doves, white-throated swifts, northern phalaropes, Hammond's flycatchers and seven other flycatcher species, to list but a few. Sometimes ten thousand or more doves abound in late August.

Beaver, muskrat, and coyote are common. Feral burros whose ancestors accompanied mining prospectors can be seen on the cliffsides, along with an occasional desert bighorn sheep. Porcupines feed on the cottonwoods and willows. Gray foxes, western pipistrel bats, antelope squirrels, and desert kangaroo rats (whose bodies manufacture their own water) thrive here, along with a few desert tortoises and Gila monsters.

Wild flowers in April (depending on moisture) are lovely masses of golds, yellows, and reds.

Havasu, with 42,655 acres, is one of three national wildlife refuges along the lower Colorado River which were set aside to attract and provide habitat for birds and mammals whose native areas had been altered by construction of dams and artificial river channels. The other two are Cibola and Imperial, which are contiguous with each other about a hundred river miles to the south. A visit to all three with their similar but distinctive attractions is a fine idea if schedule permits.

How to get there: Havasu has 3 distinct units. To get to Pintail Slough in the Topock Marsh unit, cross the river in Needles and take the Levee Road north toward Bullhead City. Turn right on Highway 95 and continue until you come to refuge signs.

Topock Gorge Unit is entered by water from either Lake Havasu to the south or at the Topock bridges from the north. For access to Bill Williams Unit, take Route 95 for 5 miles north from Parker Dam to large trailer court on righthand side; just before a new bridge over the Bill Williams River there is a dirt road immediately adjacent to the cliff, on the right heading southeast.

Open: Twenty-four hours, all year.

Best times to visit: Late fall to early spring.

What to see: Fantastically beautiful scenery. Wide variety of birds appropriate to desert and water habitat. (Sometimes tens of thousands of doves in late August.)

What to do: Boating (rentals available); photography (blind available); hiking, observation towers; hunting (limited for big and small game and waterfowl); fishing for catfish, bluegills, largemouth bass, crappie, striped bass, and in spring rainbow trout.

Where to stay: MOTELS—In Needles and Lake Havasu City. CAMPGROUNDS—Permitted on the refuge at Five-Mile Landing and Catfish Paradise, also at Lake Havasu (City) State Park.

Weather notes: Needles is often the hottest place in the nation. Summertime highs often *average* 115 degrees. (Dry, though, which helps.)

What to take and wear: A hat in the sun. Protective sun lotion. A water supply on any extended excursion (summer visitors should guard against overexertion or exposure).

Points of interest nearby: Mitchell Caverns, 40 miles west. Cibola, Imperial, and Kofa Refuges to the south.

For more information: Havasu National Wildlife Refuge, 1406 Bailey Avenue, P.O. Box A, Needles, California 92363. Phone: (714) 326-3853.

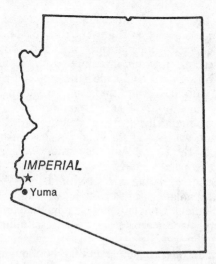

IMPERIAL

Yuma

IMPERIAL (Arizona)

Imperial National Wildlife Refuge has over 25,764 acres stretching for thirty miles along both sides of the Colorado River in California and Arizona. Exploring its waters by canoe, and its Sonoran desert uplands on foot along the five miles of Red Cloud Mine Road, is an exciting experience if only for its scenic beauty. For the naturalist willing to take a little time, it offers an entrancing range of plant and animal life as well.

Visitors can put in a canoe at the upper end and float or paddle down through the entire refuge, stopping to camp overnight at the Picacho State Recreation Area halfway down. It is even possible, if one's schedule permits, to start the trip at Cibola National Wildlife Refuge on the north and continue on down through both refuges to Imperial Dam, staying at campsites at intervals through, though not on, both refuges. It was Imperial Dam which led to establishment of these two refuges, to manage and protect wildlife at once displaced by its construction and attracted by backwaters formed thereby.

It is an easy trip—there is no raging whitewater here, only the wide river lined with canes, willows, and salt cedars. If the visitor is interested in observing wildlife, it is best to stop from time to time, tie up at a bank and look around, and take a walk through some of the brushy areas which small birds find hospitable. Most of the creatures of the refuge come down to the water at one time or other—great blue herons, snowy and great egrets, pied-billed grebes, killdeer, the endangered Yuma clapper rail, and some of the refuge mammals: raccoon, muskrat, antelope squirrel, feral burros (descendants of those that accompanied the gold miners), mule deer, a few gray fox, bobcat, coyote, and, in the summer, an occasional bighorn sheep, down from the desert mountains.

Beaver are common, living in riverbank burrows and feeding on cottonwoods and willows. There are also a few endangered Colorado River squawfish—the largest American minnow, sometimes reaching a length of five feet and a weight of eighty pounds.

Many species of wintering waterfowl find their way here—Canada geese, pintail, mallard, gadwall, redhead, cinnamon and green-winged teal. Shorebird migrations occur in the spring and fall, and include avocets, black-necked stilts, yellowlegs, killdeer, and western and least sandpipers.

The trip is pleasantest in spring and fall—but enjoyable all year.

Upland areas are rough; the best way to see these parts of the refuge is with a high clearance vehicle over Red Cloud Mine Road. Take a picnic lunch. Rough as it is, it is tremendously wild and beautiful and rewarding.

Gambel's quail are abundant all year, and common in their appropriate habitat are verdins, Gila and ladder-backed woodpeckers, black-tailed gnatcatchers, shrikes, Abert's towhees, roadrunners, crissal thrashers, song sparrows, and long-billed marsh wrens. Tremendous flights of tree, cliff, and barn swallows go through in spring and fall. Seasonally common or abundant are Costa's hummingbirds, white-winged doves, black and Say's phoebes, phainopeplas, yellow-breasted chats, MacGillivray's warblers, blue grosbeaks, warbling vireos, black and Forster's terns, Wilson's phalaropes, and black-necked stilts and an occasional golden eagle.

Both the rare desert tortoise and Gila monster are here.

Flowering plants can be stunning in a year with enough rain. The paloverde tree bursts forth in yellow blooms, as does the brittlebush. The smoketrees and ironwoods show lavender; pentstemons and chuparosas, red. The chollas are yellow, the beavertails pink, and the prickly pears varying shades of red. The saguaro cacti blossom in white. Bloom can occur almost any time with the proper combination of moisture and sunlight; sometimes, if conditions are right, some plants will seize the rare chance and bloom twice in a season.

How to get there: From Yuma, Arizona, take Route 95 north about 25 miles, then follow signs to Martinez Lake and refuge signs.

Open: Twenty-four hours a day, all year.

Best times to visit: Mid-October to late May.

What to see: A wide variety of desert and water wildlife.

What to do: Boating on Colorado River (rentals available); hiking and auto trails; photography (blinds available); observation tower; hunting, limited, for waterfowl, deer, upland game; fishing for bass, catfish, crappie, bluegill.

Where to stay: MOTELS—Many in Yuma. CAMPGROUNDS—In and near Yuma and at Picacho State Recreation Area on California side of river.

Weather notes: Summers very hot, often 110 degrees.

What to take and wear: High-clearance vehicle sometimes required for refuge roads. Water, spare tire, and jack for auto travel. Insect repellent and suntan lotion for canoeing.

Points of interest nearby: Picacho State Recreation Area (See CAMPGROUNDS); Mittry Lake State Area, on Arizona side, fine birding; and Cibola, Havasu, Kofa, and Salton Sea National Wildlife Refuges.

For more information: Imperial National Wildlife Refuge, P.O. Box 2217, Martinez Lake, Arizona 85364. Phone: (602) 783-3400.

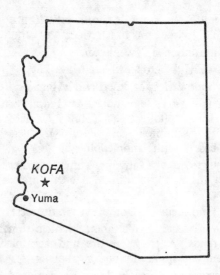

KOFA (Arizona)

The person seeing Kofa for the first time usually is awestruck by the scenic spectacle of jagged peaks rising abruptly for several thousand feet from the desert floor, altering in hue with every light change. It is particularly stunning during a spring burst of brilliant cacti and paloverde bloom, or if one is lucky enough to see one of the refuge's famed bighorn sheep marked out against the sky. Those who have seen this many times say this feeling never palls.

The outstanding sight at this thousand-square-mile Sonoran desert refuge near Yuma, Arizona, of which two thirds is mountains, canyons, and hills, is, of course, the desert bighorns, magnificent descendants of the wild sheep of Asia and residents of this continent only since they crossed the land bridge from Siberia a half million years ago. Once overhunted to the point of near extinction, their population here is now believed stable at about three hundred animals. But they are not easily seen—spotting them is an adventure, and even getting to the point where one is likely to see them can be a feat in itself which one should not undertake without preparation (see *What to take*).

Having made proper preparations, however, the best way to catch up with them is to get a refuge map and go to Kofa Queen Canyon. There, after entering this narrow pass, glance with binoculars over the horizon line—where the highest mountains meet the sky—and continue to do this as you proceed along. The sheep may be at lower elevations, but they are more readily visible outlined against the sky and this is where these remarkably adapted animals, with their hooves that are a combination of horny grippers and tough rubber-like pads, like to spend their time. The young are as adept soon after birth as their elders in leaping from crag to crag at breath-taking speed.

You need not worry about frightening them away with your appearance, either in or out of a vehicle. They have keen eyesight, comparable to a man's enhanced with eight-power binoculars, and will see you before you see them. Luckily they are supremely self-confident (rams have been known to challenge refuge personnel taking their census in a helicopter). They are also curious, and so will often come closer just to get a better look.

The other way to see them is to go in summer to one of the blinds set up near one of the waterholes (or "tanks" as they are called, from the Spanish "tanque" for spring). The original purpose of the blinds was to count wildlife populations, but they are available by permit for observation or photography. This should be undertaken only by those who can stand extreme heat, for the sheep, as well as other creatures, come to the tanks only to relieve their thirst in the hot, dry summers—and one should go prepared to stay in concealment all day.

If possible, get permission to camp overnight. There is much else to see here, and that is an excellent way to do it since denizens of the desert often prefer to repose out of sight during the hotter hours.

Golden eagles nest in the Kofa Mountains. Phainopeplas—handsome coal-black look-alikes of the cardinal—are commonly seen (or as common as anything in the desert) in the mesquite. One can also spot doves, swifts, thrashers, roadrunners, cactus and rock wrens, Gambel's quail, migrating warblers, and others—especially near water (a pair of bufflehead was once flushed from a small waterhole). Elf owls twitter at night.

Rare California fan palms have a fine stand here; the giant saguaro cactus, which can reach a height of 50 feet, an age of 250 years, and weigh 12 tons, provides food and shelter for numbers of creatures and is here in good numbers. The desert gold poppies, paloverdes, and all the various cacti burst into profuse and luxuriant bloom when conditions are right in April, carpeting the rocky desert floor.

And other desert animals are about—mule deer, coyote, bobcat, jackrabbit, feral burros, gray and kit fox, and kangaroo rats—both the latter adapted to live without free water, extracting; it from prey, forage, and their own life processes. Rattlesnakes are here, so don't plunge your hand quickly into a thicket or pack-rat nest.

("Kofa," incidentally, is a contraction of "King of Arizona," the name of a mine on the refuge whose expectations exceeded its accomplishments. The old workings can still be seen.)

How to get there: From Yuma take Route 95 north to milepost 77, or 12 miles farther. Turn right at either—these are the 2 refuge entrances (get map from refuge headquarters before venturing in).

Open: Twenty-four hours, all year.

Best times to visit: November to April.

What to see: Desert bighorn sheep, white-winged doves, and other desert wildlife. Rare California fan palms and Kofa mountain barberrys. Spectacular scenic views.

What to do: Explore—there are 300 miles of roads and trails. Photography—waterhole blinds available by permission best before August, which tends to be stormy. Limited approved hunting. No fishing on refuge.

Where to stay: MOTELS—In Yuma. CAMPGROUNDS—On refuge (no facilities); also at Quartzsite, north of refuge.

Weather notes: Winters pleasant but summers searingly hot and dangerous, with prolonged drought periods common.

What to take and wear: Sun lotion and hat; a spotting scope for distant sights; and if venturing any distance into the refuge a 4-wheel-drive vehicle (rentals available) with flashlight, food, *water*, compass, full gas tank, hiking boots, and notify someone of expected return time in case you get lost or stuck (as did the writers).

Points of interest nearby: Cabeza and Imperial National Wildlife Refuges.

For more information: Kofa National Wildlife Refuge, P.O. Box 1032, Yuma, Arizona 85364. Phone: (602) 726-2544.

Harlingen •

LAGUNA
ATASCOSA

LAGUNA ATASCOSA (Texas)

Laguna Atascosa, a 45,204-acre refuge on a former delta of the Rio Grande River at the southern tip of Texas, is a bridge between tropical and temperate biotic zones and home at various times of the year to a tremendous variety of wildlife from both. These include coyote, bobcat, and white-tailed deer which range over most of the United States. Also found is the javelina or collared peccary, wary descendant of a huge prehistoric wild pig, found in Mexico and just north of it, along with the rare but seldom seen jaguarundi and spotted ocelot.

Here are the familiar cardinals and meadowlarks, snow and Canada geese—and such border types seen in few other places in the United States as the chachalacas, pauraques, white-winged doves, least grebes, white-tailed and Harris' hawks, kiskadee flycatchers, and groove-billed anis.

Black-bellied whistling ducks, listed in most guides as only incidental stragglers from Mexico, are in abundance in spring and summer and nest in boxes put out by the refuge. These showy long-legged fowl have bright red, yellow, and blue bills, pink feet, and large white wingpatches visible when they fly. The houses they pass up for natural cavities often are taken by barn owls and their families.

This is a southernmost point in the long Central Flyway and 80 per cent of the continent's population of redhead ducks winters here, along with numbers of other waterfowl: pintails, wigeons, shovelers, sometimes more than a million birds in all, flying back and forth over Redhead Ridge—now a part of the refuge, but named when it was a famous hunting spot. In the 1700s, tens of thousands of redheads were killed in their traditional overflights there and used solely for their fat deposits, which were cut out and rendered for saddle ointment, the rest of the bird discarded.

Sometimes when these large concentrations take to the air from Laguna Madre they seem to stretch across the entire horizon, and one refuge staffer recalls seeing a great flight five miles long.

Spring migrations are spectacular for small birds as well, with stunning scissor-tailed and vermilion flycatchers, painted and indigo buntings, blue grosbeaks, northern orioles, dickcissels, and four kinds of swallows coming through in large flocks in April, along with yellowthroat, orange-crowned, black-and-white, and yellow-rumped warblers.

Shorebirds also appear in great numbers on mudflats and in fields along the roads—long-billed curlews, yellowlegs, dowitchers, and many others.

A large heron nesting island to the north is protected from public access but its birds feed on the refuge and are commonly seen most of the year—graceful tricolored (Louisiana) and great blue herons, reddish, snowy, and great egrets, sharing the marsh and tidewater shallows with an occasional roseate spoonbill.

This only suggests the wealth of bird and other life here, as does the annual Audubon Christmas Bird Count in which Laguna Atascosa almost always counts more than 150 species, along with top numbers for at least several of these. Its bird list, over 330 species in all, is second only to Aransas among the nation's refuges.

Photographic opportunities are splendid. Permission may be granted to put up a temporary blind but the birds are relatively unwary and with a telephoto lens and a little care, good pictures can be taken without one.

How to get there: From Harlingen, take Farm Road 106 east 25 miles to refuge sign.

Open: Daylight hours all year.

Best times to visit: Winter and spring, but interesting all year.

What to see: Great variety and numbers of birds of all kinds, as well as mammals.

What to do: About 25 miles of interpretive and on-your-own walking and driving trails; observation tower; photography; limited deer hunt; fishing, mainly for trout and redfish, on north end (night fishing permitted and limited camping).

Where to stay: MOTELS—In Harlingen (midway to Santa Ana Refuge). CAMPGROUNDS—Cameron County Park, on South Padre Island.

Weather notes: Generally pleasant—a sea breeze keeps humidity mostly bearable until August. Fall rains can make refuge roads impassable—check with office.

Points of interest nearby: Santa Ana Refuge, 60 miles west. Green Island, just north, a large wading bird sanctuary, access by permit only from National Audubon Society. The drive north from the refuge to Kingsville is good for spring wild flowers. The Brownsville dump, for Mexican crows and white-necked ravens, one of the few places these can be seen.

For more information: Laguna Atascosa National Wildlife Refuge, P.O. Box 2683, Harlingen, Texas 78550. Phone: (512) 423-8328 and 748-2426.

Santa Fe ● ★ *LAS VEGAS*

LAS VEGAS (New Mexico)

Las Vegas Refuge, 8,243 acres of prairie grasslands, piñon junipers, and steep canyons in north-central New Mexico, is known for its raptor populations. The rare prairie falcon is present all year and nesting. The endangered peregrine is usually here during migration, and red-tailed and Swainson's hawks are common in spring and fall. Golden and bald eagles are a common sight in winter in the cottonwood trees beside Lake McAllister. Kestrels are common all year, and almost always around seasonally are sharp-shinned, Cooper's, rough-legged, ferruginous, and marsh hawks and a few merlins.

The area has water problems—basically arid with 15.3 inches average precipitation and 90 inches evaporation, moisture depends largely on runoff from winter snowpack in the scenic Sangre de Cristo Mountains to the west. When there is plenty, the refuge may have seven hundred sandhill cranes and good numbers of waterfowl and shorebirds as well—sometimes peak populations of seventy-five hundred Canada geese with a few snows and white-fronts, and ten thousand ducks, mainly mallard, gadwall, pintail, and blue-winged teal. Eared and pied-billed grebes may be here, along with such nesting shorebirds as the long-billed curlews—well named with their eight-inch decurved beaks—Wilson's phalaropes, avocets, and spotted sandpipers, with western, Baird's, and least sandpipers common in migration.

But when there is little water, most migratory species pass up Las Vegas, and a trip of any distance to see them should not be taken without checking with refuge headquarters.

Las Vegas has one of the loveliest nature trails anywhere along the winding and verdant Gallinas Creek with sandstone and granite bluffs rising two hundred feet and more on each side, so steeply that the foot trail is its only access. Once there the visitor feels the remoteness of this wild spot where Indians carved petroglyph pictures in stone centuries ago, and cliff swallows build their tubular mud nests by the thousands—prey for the even swifter-flying falcons which nest on the ledges.

Small mammals abound—pocket gophers, mice, voles, ground squirrels—part of the attraction for the raptors. The large numbers of horned larks are another. Bobcat and badger are the most common larger mammals and are fairly readily seen by the quiet visitor out early or around dusk. Scaled quail are in the grasslands.

Small birding has not been outstanding but the careful searcher can find in the ponderosa pines and piñon junipers or other suitable habitat, both rock and canyon wrens, green-tailed towhees, mountain bluebirds, Stellar's jays, Lewis' woodpeckers, pine siskins, lark sparrows, and when moisture produces a display of desert flowers, black-chinned, rufous, and broad-tailed hummingbirds.

How to get there: From Las Vegas, take Route 104 east to Route 281, then south about 3.5 miles to refuge entrance.

Open: Daylight hours, but permit needed for some areas, check refuge office—open 8 A.M. to 4:30 P.M. weekdays. (Until recently the office was in Las Vegas. A new office is planned on the refuge.)

Best times to visit: Fall and winter.

What to see: Prairie falcons, eagles, sandhill cranes, waterfowl (depending on water conditions); relics of old Spanish ranches.

What to do: Seven miles of public road through refuge with interpretive leaflet; nature trail; fishing can be good in Lake McAllister for rainbow trout.

Where to stay: MOTELS—In Las Vegas. CAMPGROUNDS—Primitive, on refuge; also in Santa Fe National Forest and Storrie Lake State Park, northwest.

Weather notes: High winds, dust storms possible in spring; otherwise generally pleasant.

Points of interest nearby: Fort Union National Monument, 25 miles north; Pecos Pueblo National Monument, 40 miles southwest; Maxwell National Wildlife Refuge, 85 miles north.

For more information: Las Vegas National Wildlife Refuge, P.O. Box 1070, Las Vegas, New Mexico 87701. Phone: (505) 425-6819.

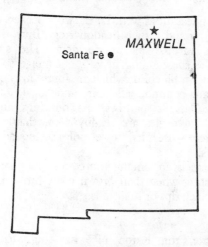

Santa Fe ●

★ MAXWELL

MAXWELL (New Mexico)

Maxwell Refuge is 3,584 acres of lakes, grass, and agricultural land in northeastern New Mexico. It is all but surrounded by a horseshoe of mountains which makes its weather almost impossible to predict. The wind can blow from four different directions in any two-hour period, sometimes bringing snow or rain that may deluge part or all of the area. None of this disturbs the sizable raptor and songbird populations which exist here in relative harmony—prairie falcons and golden eagles which are common all year; ferruginous hawks and bald eagles common in fall and winter; marsh and Swainson's hawks nesting and common in spring, summer, and fall; and songbirds in the clumps of deciduous and fruiting trees and shrubs which dot the terrain where a dozen former homesites existed before the refuge was established in 1966, as an important rest and feeding spot for waterfowl in the Central Flyway.

In dry periods Maxwell is not particularly hospitable, but when there is sufficient moisture the refuge may have five thousand Canada geese and up to fifteen thousand ducks of a dozen or more species in spring and fall. It can also have eared and pied-billed grebes, great blue herons, snowy egrets, white-faced ibises, and migrating flocks of white pelicans, and among the shorebirds avocets, Wilson's phalaropes, and yellowlegs.

Black-billed magpies are common everywhere, and scaled quail and ring-necked pheasant as well. Lewis' woodpeckers nest in wooded spots, including around refuge headquarters. Burrowing owls make homes in holes vacated by prairie dogs. The six-thousand-foot elevation plus the surrounding heights encourage such as the pine siskins and mountain bluebirds which are found in good numbers.

Rock wrens are common all year, and so seasonally are Say's phoebes, ravens, Cassin's sparrows, lark buntings, and rufous hummingbirds. Perching eagles are readily seen, thanks to man-made "trees" put up here—discarded power poles festooned with branches, ideal for lookouts.

Long-tailed weasels are among the commoner mammals, a handsome sight in winter when their brown coats turn entirely white except for the jet-black tips of their tails.

How to get there: From Raton, take I-25 south to Maxwell, then north on Route 85 and west on Route 505 to refuge entrance.

Open: Twenty-four hours, year-round.

Best times to visit: Spring, early summer, and fall.

What to see: Raptors, waterfowl, and many songbirds.

What to do: Twelve miles of roads through refuge, and most areas open to hiking by permit (check with headquarters). Guided tours given for groups by prior arrangement. Fishing—can be outstanding for rainbow trout.

Where to stay: MOTELS—In Raton. CAMPGROUNDS—Primitive, on refuge; also Cimarron Canyon Wildlife Area, 37 miles southwest.

Weather notes: Extremely erratic—can be 25 below in winter.

Points of interest nearby: Philmont Scout Ranch—field headquarters for Boy Scouts of America, with museum, trails, 29 miles southwest; Kit Carson's home, 35 miles southwest; Las Vegas National Wildlife Refuge, 85 miles south; many historic spots and outstanding trout fishing in area (refuge has information).

For more information: Maxwell National Wildlife Refuge, P.O. Box 276, Maxwell, New Mexico 87728. Phone: (505) 375-2331.

MULESHOE (Texas)

The spectacle of up to a hundred thousand stately sandhill cranes flying overhead and calling to one another on their way from their feeding grounds to their nightly roosts is almost incomparable in the natural world and unforgettable to anyone who has ever experienced it. It is an everyday occurrence at Muleshoe Refuge in the northwest Texas high plains during most years from September to March.

The number of cranes varies with moisture and temperature conditions; almost invariably they arrive the third week in September and their numbers build until December, when in years of severe weather some may move farther south. There are never fewer during the winter than ten thousand of these great majestic birds which can stand four feet tall with wingspreads up to seven feet. Muleshoe often has the nation's highest number of them in the annual Christmas Bird Count, more than a hundred thousand in some years.

The best place to see them is at Paul's Lake, for even in a drought year when the other runoff-fed lakes at this 5,809-acre refuge are dry, there is usually water here, and this is where they roost. You should arrive before daybreak as they awaken and take off, filling the air with their trumpeting k-r-r-r-oo and the sound of wings—or for a panoramic view against the sky, go to the pulloff on Highway 214. It is equally dramatic in the evening. They perform their extraordinary leaping dances in late afternoon and continue until sunset and dark —a sight that will etch itself indelibly on your mind.

This refuge of rolling, largely treeless sandhills is covered with short grasses, scattered yuccas, cacti, and mesquites, with reddish caliche limestone outcroppings, all of which can be suffused with springtime bloom.

In a good year, when the lakes fill up, waterfowl gather here in tremendous numbers—sometimes sixty thousand geese, both Canadas and snows, and up to seven hundred thousand ducks, mostly mallard but also pintail, wigeon, gadwall, and others. Birders at Muleshoe often record the highest number of many of these species on the Christmas Count.

Birding for songbirds can be excellent, too. An area of trees and shrubs behind refuge headquarters has the only vegetation over a foot tall for miles around and sometimes attracts large numbers of them, especially wood warblers in migration.

Ladder-backed woodpeckers and lark buntings are common all year, as are horned larks, mourning doves, Bullock's orioles, scissor-tailed flycatchers, lark sparrows, and curve-billed thrashers and western kingbirds nest, along with a few long-eared owls and white-necked ravens. Say's phoebes are usually here in winter and the watchful birder can almost always find McCown's and chestnut-collared longspurs in season and also seasonally clay-colored sparrows in the short grass and brushy draws.

Shorebird migrations can be fine in August and early fall when moisture is sufficient—sometimes a thousand or more Wilson's phalaropes and good numbers of Baird's western and least sandpipers, long-billed curlews, dowitchers, avocets, and others. Raptors are impressive always; red-tailed and Swainson's are common nesters and it is not unusual in midwinter to see eight or more species of raptors in one day—bald and golden eagles, kestrels, rough-legged, marsh, and ferruginous hawks, plus a Cooper's, sharp-shinned, or Harris' and perhaps a merlin or prairie falcon. Burrowing owls hole up at the prairie dog towns which they share with these engaging small rodents.

Grulla Refuge, thirty miles west in New Mexico, is also administered by Muleshoe. It has similar habitat but less water and no public access or visitor facilities.

How to get there: From Lubbock, take Route 84 northwest to Littlefield, then Route 54 west 19 miles to Route 214, then north 5 miles to refuge sign.

Open: Twenty-four hours all year.

Best times to visit: October–January.

What to see: Sandhill cranes; waterfowl; prairie dogs; good assortment of small birds.

What to do: Twenty-five miles of roads for driving and hiking; photography (blind available); picnicking.

Where to stay: MOTELS—In Muleshoe. CAMPING—On refuge.

Weather notes: Hot in summer; sudden sandstorms possible anytime spring and summer.

Points of interest nearby: National monument in Muleshoe to the beast which "without ancestral pride or hope for offspring . . . (has) helped all over the world to bear the burdens of mankind."

For more information: Muleshoe National Wildlife Refuge, P.O. Box 549, Muleshoe, Texas, 79347. Phone: (806) 946-3341.

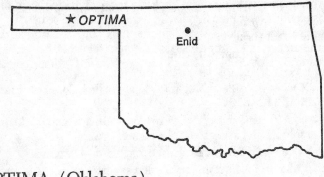

★ OPTIMA

Enid

OPTIMA (Oklahoma)

This 4,333-acre refuge of sand sage, grassland, and woods overlaid on a Corps of Engineers reservoir project supports impressive populations of raptors which are attracted by the small mammals living abundantly here. Red-tailed and Swainson's hawks are common nesters, as are kestrels; and ferruginous, Harlan's, Cooper's and rough-legged hawks and prairie falcons are here in fall and winter months.

Until recently public access was closed to Optima, one of the newest of the national wildlife refuges, while awaiting completion of the dam and reservoir on the North Canadian River near Guymon in the northwest Oklahoma panhandle. After facilities are developed, most of the waterfowl of the Central Flyway can be expected to stop here, along with wintering eagles, both bald and golden, which historically have frequented the area.

It is an important wildlife location: both white-tailed and mule deer and antelope are resident either on or just off refuge land. Badger are common as are coyote, bobcat, and various smaller mammals, including porcupines. Mississippi kites nest on the refuge, as do large numbers of streamered scissor-tailed flycatchers. Mourning doves nest abundantly in sand-plum thickets and small trees and on the ground as well. Both bobwhite and scaled quail are common, and Rio Grande turkey are present. Least terns, white-faced ibises, and long-billed curlews are among birds which appear in spring and fall migrations when water conditions offer suitable feeding and resting areas. Turkey vultures roost on the refuge in large numbers, seventy-five or so together, and nest in bluffs and cliffs nearby. Prairie chickens, rare through most of their range, are seen occasionally. Great blue herons are here most of the year.

Future plans include trails, photoblinds, and a headquarters site on the refuge, and campsites to become available on an adjacent Corps area. However, before planning to visit Optima, contact the refuge office: Optima National Wildlife Refuge, P.O. Box 628, Guymon, Oklahoma 73942. Phone: (405) 338-3479.

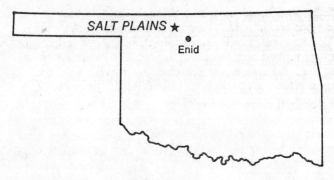

SALT PLAINS ★
Enid

SALT PLAINS (Oklahoma)

This 32,008-acre refuge in north-central Oklahoma has the largest salt flat in mid-America—Indians fought battles over it, wild creatures historically have been attracted to it, and such interesting birds as the avocet, snowy plover, and least tern nest on it in considerable numbers.

Its underground saline and gypsum solutions cause the constant formation—and breakdown—of selenite crystals found nowhere else in the world, containing a red-brown hourglass figure much sought by rock collectors.

And its combination with roughly one-third open water and the other third farm fields, grassland, river delta, and dense brush and woods gives it habitat for some of the best birding and general nature exploration anywhere around.

Stately whooping cranes, one of the world's most endangered birds, stop over on their long flight between the Far North and their Texas wintering grounds in greater numbers than at any other refuge along their 2,600-mile migration route. They cause anxiety when they coincide with goose-hunting season. The word goes out: "Shoot nothing white!"

Lovely scissor-tailed flycatchers with long streamered tails, the Oklahoma state bird, are here in large numbers from April to October. Wild turkey and quail are abundant, and ring-necked pheasant a common sight along the Eagle Roost Nature Trail, which goes through most of the habitat types.

Beaver are evident; so are white-tailed deer, sometimes wary but common badger, coyote, raccoon.

The Mississippi kites nest in numbers up to seventy-five or so, and waterfowl are here in impressive concentrations in fall and into the winter—sometimes thirty thousand ducks of more than a dozen species, and forty thousand geese including the Canada, white-fronted, and both blue and white forms of the snow.

Sometimes seventy-five to a hundred bald eagles are here in winter; sandhill cranes come through in flocks up to ten thousand with some staying through the cold months. Several thousand white pelicans are here in fall and spring; and a hundred or so turkey vultures often take up a summer roost behind refuge headquarters.

The raptor population year round is impressive. Swainson's are regular transients, as are rough-legged hawks in winter, marsh hawks, kestrels, and red-tailed hawks all the time, and Harlan's, red-shouldereds, and ospreys here from time to time seasonally. There are a few peregrine sightings most years.

Bank and cliff swallows colonize and gather with others of their swift-winged kind in post-breeding flocks of a hundred thousand or more. Bewick's wrens are common permanent residents; so are bluebirds, horned larks, loggerhead shrikes, meadowlarks, great blue herons, and screech and great horned owls; and, common seasonally, Bell's vireos, Harris' sparrows, painted buntings, blue grosbeaks, dickcissels, red-headed woodpeckers, and yellow and yellow-rumped warblers.

Migrations can bring hundreds of Baird's, stilt, and white-rumped sandpipers, and huge numbers of Franklin's gulls—a hundred thousand or in some years up to an estimated three million which fan out over the countryside to follow the plow and consume hordes of insects.

Three refuge plants have been given state endangered-species status: the eastern gamma grass, the sea purslane of the salt flats, and *Mirabilis exaltata,* a four-o'clock whose pink blooms are readily visible along the trailside ditches in June.

How to get there: From Enid, take Route 81-60-64 north and west to Jet, then right on Route 38 to refuge sign and west a mile to headquarters.

Open: Daylight hours all year.

Best times to visit: Something happening all the time, though activity dips in July–August heat.

What to see: Good assortment of birds from eagles and waterfowl to passerines and occasional migrant whooping cranes; white-tailed deer; coyote; selenite crystals; largest salt flat in midcontinent.

What to do: Two and a quarter miles of roads and trails, plus 6 miles of public roads through refuge; observation tower over salt flats (reachable via Fifth Street east from Cherokee); dig selenite crystals (limit 10 pounds and one crystal for personal use); limited deer hunt; fishing for catfish, sand bass.

Where to stay: MOTELS—In Cherokee and Jet, larger selection in Enid, 50 miles southeast. CAMPGROUNDS—On refuge in summer; year-round at Great Salt Plains State Park, adjacent.

Weather notes: Spring can be unsettled with sudden thunderstorms, tornadoes, and temporarily impassable roads. Summer humidity may bring high mosquito population.

What to take and wear: Protective lotion against brilliant sun reflection on white salt flats.

Points of interest nearby: Museum of Cherokee Strip, in Enid; Byron State Fish Hatchery, 4 miles north; original homesteader's sod house, 40 miles southwest; Great Salt Plains State Park, adjacent.

For more information: Salt Plains National Wildlife Refuge, Route 1, Box 76, Jet, Oklahoma 73749. Phone: (405) 626-4794.

Houston

SAN BERNARD ★

SAN BERNARD-BRAZORIA REFUGES (Texas)

These relatively new refuges along the Texas Gulf Coast offer wild and roadless habitat for large numbers of ducks, geese, and waders, along with rails and other marsh types, and interesting small birds. Public access is mostly by boat, except by special permission and for occasional tour groups conducted by refuge staff. Flat-bottomed johnboats are the only kind that can be recommended for water access since the waters are extremely shallow. The refuge office should be consulted on any plans for such a trip.

The wildlife potential in both refuges is enormous. Brazoria's 10,312 acres of coastal marsh edging a fertile farming area sometimes has a thousand or so wood storks, seven hundred mottled ducks (some of which stay all year and nest), up to four hundred roseate spoonbills, alligators, and on its upland areas bobwhite quail and sandhill cranes. San Bernard's 21,865 acres are about one-half marsh, ranging from fresh through brackish to salty, and Cow Trap Lake supports large numbers of diving ducks—merganser, scaup, redhead, canvasback, ruddy ducks—along with concentrations of up to 125,000 wintering snow geese. King and clapper rails are common all year; other rails, including black and yellow, are present in the marsh in winter.

Both refuges have sizable populations much of the year of herons and shorebirds. Warblers, sparrows, and other passerines, including scissor-tailed flycatchers, yellow-billed cuckoos, ruby-crowned kinglets, and yellowthroats, are found mostly in the wooded area at the northwest corner of San Bernard.

It is a wonderful birding area—Brazoria Refuge is part of the annual Audubon Christmas Bird Count which centers in nearby Freeport and which often is highest in the nation in the number of species seen at that time. Refuge staff members may be helpful in pointing out good places to go and observe, and a good contact as well would be two Houston groups, the Houston Audubon Society and the Outdoor Nature Club, both of whose members are extremely active and knowledgeable (see below, *Points of interest nearby*).

How to get there: Telephone refuge office for directions to headquarters in Angleton; there get maps and access information.

Open: Limited; daylight hours.

Best times to visit: October to March.

What to see: Waterfowl; wading birds; variety of others.

What to do: Nature observation (mostly by boat); waterfowl hunting by permit, oystering, crabbing, fishing for trout, flounder, redfish.

Where to stay: MOTELS—Lake Jackson. CAMPGROUNDS—Near Brazosport; also permitted on public beaches, and Bryan Beach State Park, Freeport.

Weather notes: Area subject to sudden downpours, high humidity.

What to take and wear: Raingear, powerful insect repellent (though refuge personnel say nothing protects against their mosquitoes and biting flies, especially in the summer).

Points of interest nearby: This is a wonderful birding area, especially in winter. For information on good birding spots contact Houston Audubon Society, 440 Wilchester, Houston 77079, phone: (713) 932-1392; or Outdoor Nature Club, 10602 Cedarhurst, Houston 77096. Visit the Brazosport Museum of Natural Science in Lake Jackson.

For more information: San Bernard-Brazoria National Wildlife Refuges, P.O. Drawer 1088, Angleton, Texas 77515. Phone: (713) 849-6062.

SANTA ANA ★ ● Harlingen

SANTA ANA (Texas)

Santa Ana is called the jewel of the national wildlife refuge system and the reason is immediately clear to one entering the winding tree-lined drive of this 3,913-acre sanctuary—one of the nation's smallest —and seeing, usually within minutes, some of its best-known and most colorful inhabitants in an exquisite natural setting.

Brilliant orange and black Lichtenstein's orioles and green jays appear in the mesquite. Hummingbirds, perhaps a buff-bellied one with bright orange bill, hover about the Turk's-cap blossoms. Chachalacas, resembling small hen turkeys, call loudly and sometimes look as if they might like a crumb from a sandwich (don't give it to them; they're flouting refuge rules).

Once much of the Texas-Mexico border along the Rio Grande River looked like this—a wildlife paradise, with rich bottomland and thick, jungle-like vegetation in which numbers of plant and animal species found nowhere else in the United States thrived at the northernmost limit of their range.

Agricultural and urban development have left only a remnant at

Santa Ana and a few other scattered tracts, several of which fortunately have been acquired and added as small satellite refuge areas managed by Santa Ana.

To mention only some of the rarest wildlife forms to be seen here, and for the most part readily seen, is a matter of difficult selection. Some of those present in this part of south Texas which naturalists come from around the world to observe include, among birds, the least grebe, black-bellied whistling duck, white-tailed hawk, tropical kingbird, kiskadee flycatcher, and long-billed thrasher. Unusual insects and plants are here also, and many are included in the refuge's excellent lists.

Mammals include coyote, bobcat, armadillo, commonly present and best seen early and late on the trails; they are hard to see in the dense vegetation which furnishes complete cover even a few feet away. The rare and secretive ocelot and jaguarundi are here, the latter called otter cat because it swims well. Both are extremely difficult to discern; look for the ocelot looking down at *you* from a forked tree branch, his spots blending perfectly with the dappled shade.

Five national champion trees grow here—including a 40-foot Texas ebony with a 131-inch girth which grows alongside the walking trails near cemetery, dating back over a hundred years.

The growing season averages 327 days; spring blooming starts in mid-February and a constant show of flowering plants continues (in years of normal rainfall) until late November. Rocks are rare on Santa Ana, so if you think you see a round gray rock about eight inches across, it might be a giant toad weighing a pound or more. A rustle of leaves could be the least shrew, at 2.2+ inches our shortest and hungriest mammal, often eating more than its weight daily.

Huge flights of white-winged doves roost in the refuge in mid to late September—eight thousand may pour over in a half hour at dusk. And great numbers of broad-winged hawks go through in late March—once seventy-three thousand in just a few days, stopping overnight and boiling up in kettles of hundreds to be on their way again early the next morning.

How to get there: From McAllen, take Expressway 83 east to Alamo, then south on F.M. 907 to end of road at U.S. Highway 281. Turn left to refuge sign, about .3 mile.

Open: Dawn to dusk all year. Scenic Drive hours are 8 A.M. to 6 P.M.

Best times to visit: Winter and spring (go early and try to avoid peak holidays and weekends).

What to see: Great variety and numbers of flora and fauna found seldom if at all elsewhere in United States—green jays, Lichtenstein's and black-headed orioles, buff-bellied hummingbirds, chachalacas; record-size trees; occasionally endangered ocelots and jaguarundis.

What to do: Scenic Drive auto tour (to be operated as a guided tram ride in peak visitor periods); 14 miles of foot trails; photography (blinds available). One trail to be adapted for use by handicapped, with wheelchair ramp and audio stations.

Where to stay: MOTELS—At McAllen, 16 miles northwest; or Harlingen, 35 miles east (midpoint between Santa Ana and Laguna Atascosa Refuge). CAMPGROUNDS—North of Pharr, 20 miles northwest; or Bentsen State Park, 25 miles west.

Weather notes: Summer can be humid, and early fall rainy.

What to take and wear: A field guide to birds of Texas and Mexico is useful—though the office has one for reference.

Points of interest nearby: Laguna Atascosa Refuge, 60 miles east; Bentsen State Park; also Falcon Dam State Park, 80 miles west, good birding for brown jays, green kingfishers, red-billed pigeons, others.

For more information: Santa Ana National Wildlife Refuge, Route 1, Box 202A, Alamo, Texas 78516. Phone: (512) 787-3079.

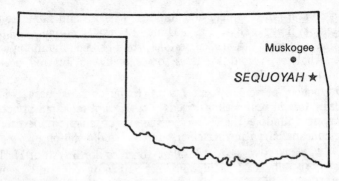

SEQUOYAH (Oklahoma)

Sometimes on a fall or winter day, sixty eagles can be seen in tall cottonwood trees on this 20,800-acre east-central Oklahoma refuge that nestles in the confluence of the Arkansas and Canadian rivers. These once formed the border between the Cherokee and Choctaw Indian nations.

The eagles follow the waterfowl which can be in the fall and again in spring (and sometimes through the winter) in great numbers—up to two hundred thousand ducks, mostly mallard (a main wintering area for them in the Central Flyway), but also gadwall, pintail, teal, wigeon, shoveler, and wood ducks; and up to thirty thousand geese—snows, Canadas, and white-fronted.

Sequoyah, named for the Indian who invented the Cherokee alphabet and whose home is preserved nearby, is half water, the rest rich river bottomland, scattered islands and sloughs and hilly or rocky upland featuring forest growth of cottonwood, hackberry, willow, pecan, hickory, oak, and elm. Overlaid on a Corps of Engineers project and established to replace loss of habitat resulting from that navigational work, it supports a wide variety of wildlife through the year.

The scissor-tailed flycatcher, the Oklahoma state bird and one of the loveliest in North America with its pearl and salmon plumage and long streamered tail, is common through the warmer months, seen on power lines and poles and sometimes nesting on the cross-bars. So are both yellow- and black-billed cuckoos, bank swallows, yellow-breasted chats, orioles, lark sparrows, dickcissels, little blue and green herons and great egrets. All year there are great blue herons, kingfishers, killdeer, red-tailed hawks, bobwhite quail, horned larks, shrikes, several kinds of woodpeckers, and cormorants, sometimes six thousand at one time and always around in good numbers.

Shorebird migrations can be notable, some of those appearing including golden plovers, snipes, and spotted, pectoral, white-rumped, and least sandpipers. Also there are Franklin's gulls, an occasional buff-breasted sandpiper and Hudsonian godwit, and several hundred white pelicans spring and fall.

Warbler migrations are irregular, but in a good year the tiny golden birds can seem to be everywhere in the woods and brush while may apples come up on the forest floor and redbuds and dogwoods display their bloom.

Bobcat are present in good numbers and perhaps more readily seen than at most refuges by the visitor willing to go out early and stay late and wend his way quietly. Occasionally they appear in spring with their kits. Coyote can be heard most evenings. Also fairly common are armadillo, raccoon, white-tailed deer, rabbit, squirrel, mink, opossum, and beaver, their working always evident. So are a variety of snakes, so watch where you put your hands and feet.

Armored gars can be dramatic when spawning, churing the waters and leaping from the surface like porpoises.

Both eagles and waterfowl are best seen off Tuff Landing and Stony Point and from the start of the Sandtown Woods trail, which is the best place for small birds.

On the opposite side are steep wooded hills and bluffs, reachable by canoe, beautiful and wild, so apparently untouched by civilization one can imagine the Choctaw and Cherokee are still there just beyond the next clump of trees.

How to get there: From Fort Smith, Arkansas, take Route 64 west to Roland, Oklahoma, then I-40 west to Vian exit; then left on Route 82 for 3 miles to refuge sign. Headquarters is in Sallisaw, 15 miles east of refuge.

Open: From 5 A.M. to 10 P.M. all year (wet weather can make some parts seasonally impassable).

Best times to visit: October through March.

What to see: Waterfowl, wading and shorebirds, eagles, good assortment of small birds.

What to do: Six miles of roads, 8 additional for walking only; photography; pecan-picking (1-gallon limit); limited hunt for water-fowl, small game; fishing can be excellent spring and fall, depending on water conditions, for crappie, white and black bass, channel catfish.

Where to stay: MOTELS—In Sallisaw. CAMPGROUNDS—In Sallisaw; also Sallisaw State Park, 5 miles west, and Corps of Engineers Recreational Area, 10 miles southeast.

Weather notes: Summer can be very hot with strong winds; March to May is tornado watch season.

Points of interest nearby: Sequoyah's birthplace, 20 miles northeast; Cookson Hills State Game Refuge, 18 miles northeast; Brushy Lake State Park, 12 miles northeast; Talimena Drive—scenic drive on Route 1 between Talihina, Oklahoma, and Mena, Arkansas.

For more information: Sequoyah National Wildlife Refuge, P.O. Box 398, Sallisaw, Oklahoma 74995. Phone: (918) 775-6223.

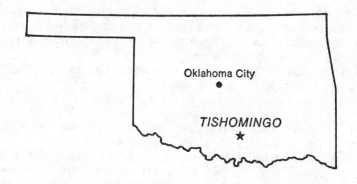

TISHOMINGO (Oklahoma)

Tishomingo, with 16,574 acres of woods, grass, and croplands and seasonally flooded mudflats can have large flocks of white pelicans, scissor-tailed flycatchers and ducks and geese. But it is best known as a locale where one can find a good assortment of widely varying wildlife, including deer and other mammals.

Sometimes up to seventy bald and golden eagles perch on trees about this southeast Oklahoma refuge when the migratory and wintering waterfowl are here. From those vantage points they watch for crippled or weakened birds on which they prey or swoop to a fish dinner from Lake Texoma, the Corps of Engineers project on which Tishomingo is overlaid.

Up to forty thousand geese—mostly Canadas but also whitefronteds and snows—and eighty thousand ducks of twenty or so species flock here at various times in fall and winter, along with numerous raptors—kestrels and marsh hawks and usually some Swainson's rough-legged, ferruginous, and Cooper's hawks as well (the Cooper's are nesters as are broadwings, red-shoulders, and redtaileds).

White pelicans may build to concentrations of five thousand or so in October, and again in smaller numbers in March, making spectacular flights over the refuge headquarters and gathering in large showy rafts offshore.

One of the stunning sights is the late afternoon flight of blackbirds in September and October, at times an estimated five million of seven species including red-winged, yellow-headed, rusty, and Brewer's, coming in to roost in large black funnel clouds across the western sky. Later in the fall a half million or more crows roost.

Beautiful wood ducks group when the pecans are ripening; some-times twenty thousand of these birds are in a single field feeding on the nuts, looking like a rolling wave as they leapfrog over each other while feeding on these delicacies.

Scissor-tailed flycatchers, one of America's loveliest small birds with their pearl and salmon plumage and long tail streamers, are abundant from spring through fall, as are painted and indigo bunt-ings, dickcissels, lark sparrows, and good numbers of blue grosbeaks, orchard orioles, barn swallows, chimney swifts, red-headed wood-peckers, summer tanagers, and blue-gray gnatcatchers.

Harris' and Lincoln's sparrows, purple finches, dark-eyed juncos, water pipits, and yellow-rumped warblers are here in sizable winter-ing populations; and great blue, little blue, and green herons and great egrets spend the summer. Doves and quail are always abun-dant. Shorebird migrations can be lively when moisture conditions encourage their stopovers, with Baird's and upland sandpipers, occa-sional long-billed curlews and golden plovers. Sometimes thirty thou-sand or more Franklin's and ring-billed gulls are present.

The quiet visitor at dawn and dusk may see a hundred or more white-tailed deer, along with a bobcat along the road edges, beaver on all the ponds, opossum, raccoon (which are adept at opening fishermen's baitboxes), armadillo, and perhaps a mink. There are also poisonous snakes; they are not aggressive, but one should watch where putting hands and feet, especially around rocks.

Indian paintbrush and devil's poker make a colorful spring bloom-ing along with redbud and dogwood trees through the woodlands.

Visitors wishing to see a particular kind of bird or animal should stop at the refuge office; the staff is glad to advise on what has been active lately.

How to get there: From Ardmore, take Route 70 east to Route 12, north on it to Route 22 east and through Tishomingo to refuge sign; turn right there onto blacktop 3 miles to headquarters.

Open: Twenty-four hours all year.

Best times to visit: Mid-October through early spring.

What to see: Deer; large numbers of water birds of all kinds—ducks, geese, white pelicans, shorebirds, herons; hawks and eagles; huge crow and blackbird roosts.

What to do: Fifteen miles of driving and hiking roads including in-terpretive Craven nature trail; spectacular Jemison's lookout; observation tower; picnicking; fishing can be excellent in March, October, for crappie, sand bass, catfish.

Where to stay: MOTELS—At Tishomingo and Ardmore. CAMPGROUNDS —On refuge; also Murray State Park, Ardmore.

Weather notes: Spring is tornado season (until about May).

Points of interest nearby: Platt National Park, 24 miles north; historic Chickasaw Council House in Tishomingo; Hagerman National Wildlife Refuge, 70 miles south; Tishomingo Wildlife Management Unit, adjoining refuge, jointly managed with state —various recreation facilities, including hunting for various game birds and mammals.

For more information: Tishomingo National Wildlife Refuge, P.O. Box 248, Tishomingo, Oklahoma 73460. Phone: (405) 371-2402.

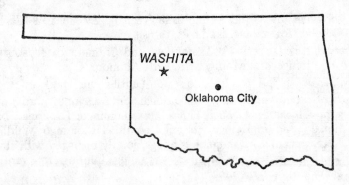

WASHITA (Oklahoma)

This 8,084-acre refuge of native grassland, farm fields, open water, and wooded creeks in west-central Oklahoma is an important link in the Central Flyway. For its relatively small size it accommodates a tremendous number of migratory and wintering waterfowl—as many as thirty-five thousand geese, mostly Canadas but with good numbers of snows and white-fronted and an occasional Ross'. In a good year there will be up to 140,000 ducks of more than a dozen species.

But with its varied habitat it supports a numerous and wide-ranging population of other wildlife, too.

Sometimes more than ten thousand stately sandhill cranes and a hundred or so white pelicans visit in their spring and fall migrations, and at rare intervals a pair of whooping cranes may touch down.

The prairies support a sizable rodent population as well which in turn attracts their predators—coyote, bobcat and hawks. Red-tailed and marsh hawks and kestrels are common to abundant all year; Swainson's common spring and fall, and others in fair to good numbers in all except summer—Cooper's, sharp-shinned, rough-legged, ferruginous, and from time to time the uncommon-to-rare falcons—merlin, prairie, and peregrine. (On one day, October 9, 1973, six hundred Swainson's hawks were counted on refuge fields.) Ospreys appear frequently, and both bald and golden eagles winter in small numbers.

Common all or part of the year are red-headed and red-bellied woodpeckers, great blue herons, bobwhite quails, killdeer, yellow-billed cuckoos, Bewick's wrens, Harris' and lark sparrows and—that loveliest of small birds—the streamered scissor-tailed flycatcher, here by the hundreds, nesting and posing on every high wire through the warm months.

Cliff and barn swallows nest abundantly under bridges along Highway 33; Mississippi kites, sometimes forty or so of them, nest in trees along the watercourses.

Shorebird migrations in a year of sufficient moisture can bring sizable groups of Baird's, least, and western sandpipers, Wilson's phalaropes, and sometimes upland sandpipers and long-billed curlews. Franklin's gulls can appear in large numbers spring and summer, consuming vast quantities of insects in newly tilled fields.

Birders are attracted by some of the less common varieties spotted from time to time—Sprague's pipits, ladder-backed woodpeckers, sage thrashers, lark buntings, and black-headed grosbeaks.

One can see almost everything, including the deer, prairie dogs, and horned toads, from the roads and trails, and the entire refuge is open part of the year to walking, which is easy and pleasant in the open grassland from eight access points. Washita is overlaid on a U. S. Bureau of Reclamation reservoir project and at no point is it more than a mile from the refuge boundary to the interior water. Some parts may be closed seasonally for waterfowl sanctuary but oftentimes permission may be obtained to enter these for quiet nature observation.

How to get there: From Clinton, take Route 183 north about 9 miles to Route 33, then west (left) to refuge sign, about 5 miles beyond Butler.

Open: Daylight hours all year (except during waterfowl season when parts closed to provide sanctuary).

Best times to visit: November through February.

What to see: Waterfowl concentrations; sandhill cranes; Mississippi kites; scissor-tailed flycatchers; occasional coyote, beaver, also fossils—partial remains of a woolly mammoth were found here in an eroded lakeshore cliff.

What to do: Five miles of roads, hiking trail; observation towers; photography (blinds available); boating October–April (limited rentals in adjacent state park); limited hunting for quail, rabbit; fishing, very good at times, for bass, crappie, walleye.

Where to stay: MOTELS—In Clinton, 28 miles southeast; Elk City, 28 miles southwest. CAMPGROUNDS—Foss State Park, adjacent.

Weather notes: Generally pleasant though sometimes quite windy spring–summer.

Points of interest nearby: Western Trails Museum, Clinton; Foss Lake State Park (see CAMPGROUNDS); Boiling Spring State Park, 50 miles north; Little Sahara State Park (with sand dunes, camels), 80 miles northeast.

For more information: Washita National Wildlife Refuge, Route 1, Box 68, Butler, Oklahoma 73625. Phone: (405) 473-2205.

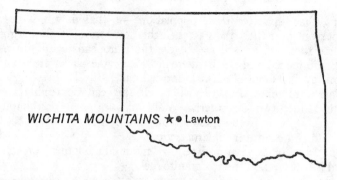

WICHITA MOUNTAINS ★ ● Lawton

WICHITA MOUNTAINS (Oklahoma)

Wichita Mountains is one of the showplaces of the national wildlife refuge system with stunning scenery, herds of buffalo, elk, Texas longhorn cattle, a prairie dog town, and a breath-taking variety of interesting birds, plants, reptiles, and rocks.

It is one of the places where it all began. Set aside by proclamation by President Theodore Roosevelt in 1905, it was the second, after tiny Pelican Island in Florida, of more than 386 U.S. refuges which now cover almost thirty-three million acres and protect wildlife of many thousands of species. And it was the first to be set aside for a mammal, the plains buffalo (or bison) of which only a few hundred remained at that time. Hunters had almost exterminated these monumental beasts which can stand six feet at the shoulder and weigh more than a ton, despite herds that had once darkened the plains for miles around, their numbers estimated at sixty to seventy millions.

A nucleus of fifteen was donated by the New York Zoological Society on condition Congress appropriate $15,000 to build a fence around them. They prospered, and later elk were reintroduced, and Texas longhorn cattle, great rangy animals whose horns commonly spread five feet or more, which developed in south Texas from ancestors brought over by early Spaniards.

Prairie dogs, once even more numerous than the bison—gregarious small rodents which once existed in the billions in the prairies, their burrow colonies spread over tens of thousands of square miles—were allowed to populate part of the refuge, away from farmers and cattlemen who nearly poisoned them out of existence.

Growing here are the tall native grasses, gone from much of the

Plains, that supported these populations—so that now it is possible to look out over the 59,019 acres in this southwest Oklahoma refuge and see the country as it was before the Europeans came, for much of it is unfenced and the herds roam free (some places are closed to permit management of animals and habitat).

There are miles of roads where all this can be readily viewed at any time; two interpretive trails, plus other varied habitat—canyons, streams, woods, mountains, more than twenty lakes and two wild and beautiful wilderness areas.

The handsome green and yellow "mountain boomer" or collared lizard is common on the red granite rocks.

Mississippi kites nest in the summer, along with streamered scissor-tailed flycatchers. Bald and golden eagles spend the winter. Large numbers of ducks of a dozen or more species come through in spring and fall migration. Wild turkey and bobwhite are common all year, as are bluebirds (eastern, with some mountain), red-tailed hawks, horned larks, red-bellied woodpeckers, Bewick's wrens (with some rock and cañon wrens), rufous-crowned sparrows, and, seasonally, painted buntings, pine siskins, purple finches, Harris' and Lincoln's sparrows, chestnut-collared longspurs, and chuck-will's-widows.

Campers almost certainly will hear coyote and great horned owls, and unless they put food away securely will probably meet a raccoon personally. Buffalo, too, have been known to wander through picnic or campsites, and these big creatures should be given a wide berth.

Young animals begin to appear in mid-March. Adult bison instinctively form a protective circle around the newborn calves. Indian blanket, Venus' looking-glass, false indigo, and other colorful wild flowers burst into bloom a few weeks later.

Elk tours are led through areas where they are starting their "bugling" during the mating season, beginning in mid-September. It is best to reserve ahead; tours are limited to twenty persons. Auction sales of surplus bison and longhorns, determined by carrying capacity of the land for healthy herds, are held in September and November and the public can attend.

There are many things to see here always, and an interested naturalist can spend an exciting time just beginning to explore the possibilities, with excellent lists and background material on all subjects available from refuge headquarters.

How to get there: From Lawton, take Route 62 west to Cache, then Route 115 north to refuge.

Open: Twenty-four hours all year.

Best times to visit: Spring and fall (but you can see wildlife anytime).

What to see: Buffalo; elk; longhorn cattle; white-tailed deer; prairie dogs; wonderful assortment of bird, plant, and small animal species.

What to do: Fifty miles of roads for driving or hiking; photography; fishing in designated areas; picnicking; scenic overlook from Mount Scott; guided tours and programs through the year on a wide range of natural history subjects, from elk and eagles to rocks and wild flowers. "Wildlife Under the Stars" programs on summer Friday nights.

Where to stay: MOTELS—In Lawton. CAMPGROUNDS—On refuge (limited, on first-come-first-served basis).

Weather notes: July–August hot; December–February can have ice storms.

What to take and wear: Hiking boots if going far on rocky terrain; compass if getting far off trail in wilderness areas.

Points of interest nearby: Quartz Mountain State Park, 50 miles northwest; Fort Sill Historical Museum; Museum of the Great Plains, in Lawton.

For more information: Wichita Mountains Wildlife Refuge, Box 448, Cache, Oklahoma 73527. Phone: (405) 429-3222.

VIII. THE MOUNTAIN STATES

The refuges of the mountain states are among the most beautiful, remote, and exciting of all. Many are located amid dramatic landscapes and some harbor numbers of the most exciting wild creatures left in the lower forty-eight states—bighorn sheep, antelope, elk, mountain lion, mule deer, and bison among the mammals; golden and bald eagles, goshawks, prairie falcons and gyrfalcons and peregrines among the raptors; trumpeter swans, whooping cranes, great colonies of nesting white pelicans, even rare fish such as the grayling at Red Rock Lakes.

IDAHO

Beginning in the north, in Idaho, there is *Camas*, named for the blue lily whose root bulb was a staple Indian food. This is a beautiful and remote refuge in southeast Idaho with habitat ranging from desert to irrigated meadows, marshes, and lakes and some native prairie as well.

Deer Flat is in southwest Idaho not far from Boise and is composed of two distinct units: Lowell Lake has large concentrations of waterfowl—up to seven hundred thousand ducks along with fifty or so bald eagles; the Snake River section extends 112 miles along the river from Walter's Ferry, Idaho, to Farewell Bend, Oregon, and includes eighty-six islands favored by nesting Canada Geese and great blue herons.

Grays Lake has been the site of an extraordinarily interesting experiment aimed at increasing the survival of the endangered whooping cranes. Eggs are taken from whooper nests in Canada (they lay two but hatch only one) and placed in sandhill crane nests here. The sandhills adopt the young whoopers which fly with them to their wintering grounds in New Mexico (see *Bosque del Apache*). The aim is to establish another whooper breeding population in addition to the one which winters along the Texas coast (see *Aransas*).

Kootenai near the Canadian border in northern Idaho, is a small refuge (less than three thousand acres) but with considerable diversity of habitat and wildlife including mule and white-tailed deer and

215 avian species, among them three kinds of hummingbirds (calliope, rufous, and black-chinned).

Minidoka lies on the Oregon Trail in southern Idaho and is an important migratory waterfowl stop. It has readily visible (with binoculars) nesting colonies of water birds including white-faced ibises, great blue herons, snowy egrets and double-crested cormorants.

MONTANA

Benton Lake may be at its best in May, when its dikes and ponds are filled with birds—gulls, terns, phalaropes, eared grebes, and a dozen species of ducks. Located only a short drive from Great Falls, it is one of Montana's more accessible refuges.

Bowdoin lies in Montana's "Big Sky" region where the subdued rolling landscape and great clarity of atmosphere make the sky stretch like a great bowl around the entire horizon, the airy expanse taking up vastly more space in one's vista than the earth beneath.

Charles M. Russell is one of the nation's great refuges, with almost one million acres (including forty-five hundred acres of prairie dog towns) stretching along the Missouri River in northeast Montana. The whole area is little changed since the days when Lewis and Clark explored its forested coulees, prairie grasslands, and rugged terrain in 1805. Its size and unexplored character make it a tremendously exciting place—one may see pronghorn antelope, mule and white-tailed deer, bighorn sheep, golden eagles, prairie falcons, merlins, peregrines, and gyrfalcons, to mention a few. It may be seen from horseback, four-wheeled drive vehicle, or, best of all, from a boat, floating down the great river and camping en route.

Medicine Lake is home to thousands of nesting white pelicans which produce up to three thousand young birds in a summer; it is a prodigious nesting area for other water and wading birds as well, including eared and horned grebes, with colonies of cormorants and herons and large colonies of California and ring-billed gulls.

Metcalf is a small (2,700 acres) refuge in the famous Bitterroot Valley of western Montana, with a varied raptor population including osprey, Cooper's, red-tailed, rough-legged, and goshawks as well as prairie falcons, bald and golden eagles.

National Bison Range is on the west slope of the Rockies, a range called "land of the Shining Mountains" by the Indians. President Theodore Roosevelt set this refuge aside in 1908 and visitors who travel the well-maintained auto tour route are likely to see elk, deer, pronghorn antelope, and quite possibly bighorn sheep.

Red Rock Lakes high in the Centennial Valley of Montana

against the Continental Divide is one of the most beautiful of all the nation's refuges. It harbors one of the most beautiful and stately of the world's birds, the rare and elegant trumpeter swan.

WYOMING

From December 26 to April 1 visitors to the *National Elk Range* can ride a sleigh which goes out among the herd of up to twelve thousand elk at this refuge adjacent to the town of Jackson. When needed, the sleigh takes supplemental feed to the elk which winter here returning from their summer breeding grounds high in Yellowstone National Park. There also are smaller populations of bison, mule deer, moose, antelope, bighorn sheep and coyote, as well as trumpeter swans.

Seedskadee means "River of the Prairie Hen" in Shoshone Indian, and sage grouse, the "prairie hen" of the Shoshones, is here in large numbers. So are golden eagles, those raptors of remote places, soaring with six-foot wingspreads over the sagebrush-covered fields and salt-grass bottomlands.

UTAH

Perhaps nowhere else in the nation do as many of the nation's beautiful and interesting birds gather in such numbers as at *Bear River*, a refuge of almost sixty-five thousand acres where this river empties into the Great Salt Lake of northern Utah. In spring and fall migrations, millions of birds may be here, their low, babbling "conversations" never stopping, even at night. Among them, in fall, are twenty thousand or so whistling swans, with peaks of up to a million ducks including hundreds of thousands of pintail and green-winged teal.

Fish Springs west of Salt Lake City is a remote jewel in the desert, a region of strong geothermal springs that well up in some of the least hospitable land to be found anywhere. Because of this it serves as a magnet for any wildlife in the area or migrating through, and for those willing to make the effort to get there, it offers a vista unchanged from that the Pony Express riders saw—an unpeopled oasis in the desert.

Ouray lies along the west bank of the Green River in the northeast corner of Utah where dinosaur bones have been found and Kit Carson used to hunt. It is an excellent place for raptors, mule deer, and, in migration, for cranes, including adopted whooping cranes, traveling with their sandhill-crane foster parents.

COLORADO

Alamosa is a 10,356-acre refuge located at 7,500 feet elevation in south-central Colorado. Despite its mountainous location it has breeding populations of waterfowl comparable to the pothole region of the Dakotas.

Arapaho, at 8,300 feet elevation next to the Continental Divide, is the highest U.S. refuge outside Alaska and offers a good example of the phenomenon of vertical migration in which some birds move seasonally not north and south but up and down the mountains. This is one of the least known refuges in the system, yet its location, in a beautiful and well-watered high meadow in north-central Colorado, makes it one of the most attractive.

Browns Park lies along the famed Green River in the northwest corner of Colorado. Once a haven for outlaws, this "park" or meadow still is one of the most remote of the country's refuges. Antelope, and mule deer are present here as are eagles, hawks, sage grouse, and numerous wading and water birds, including that curious small bird, the dipper, that walks under the water of mountain streams. All of this is in a region that seems almost untouched by the hand of man.

Monte Vista, not far from Alamosa in south-central Colorado, is the main stopover for young whooping cranes and their sandhill-crane foster parents between their nesting area at Grays Lake in Idaho and their wintering ground around Bosque del Apache in New Mexico. It also is a major nesting ground for waterfowl, 75 per cent of which spend most of their lives in this refuge and in the surrounding San Luis Valley.

NEVADA

Within sight of glittering Las Vegas is *Desert Wildlife Range*, the largest national wildlife refuge outside Alaska with more than one and a half million acres of habitat ranging from the burning Nevada desert floor to snowy mountains nearly ten thousand feet high. It was established in 1936 to preserve desert bighorn sheep and also harbors bobcat, badger, kit fox, mule deer, and pronghorn antelope as well as the rare and secretive mountain lion. Bird species include such specialties as the sage sparrow, hepatic tanager, and Le Conte's thrasher.

Ruby Lake is a verdant valley of about 38,000 acres of fresh-water marsh, salt-grass meadows, and open water fed by more than 130 gushing springs as well as snowmelt from the white-crowned Ruby Mountains which rim it and are home for one of the largest remaining populations of mountain lions in the nation.

Sheldon Antelope Range is administered from Hart Mountain Refuge across the border in Oregon (see West Coast section) and like that refuge has as its primary mission preserving habitat for the pronghorn antelope.

Stillwater in northwestern Nevada is a remnant of Pleistocene Lake Lahontan which once covered a closed mountain basin of almost nine thousand square miles in northwestern Nevada. Like some other western refuges, it has been put under increasing pressure in recent years as more and more scarce water is diverted from refuge use to irrigation of croplands and use in booming cities such as Reno.

The following is a list of some birds of special interest found in common or abundant status at the refuges of this region:

Birds Common or Abundant at Seasons Indicated:

S: Spring   s: Summer   F: Fall   W: Winter

White-faced Ibis: Bear River, SsF; Benton Lake, Ss;
    Browns Park, SsF; Camas, Ss; Ouray, Ss; Ruby Lake, SsF;
    Stillwater, s.
Trumpeter Swan: National Elk, SsFW; Red Rock Lakes, SsFW;
    Ruby Lake, SsFW.
Barrow's Goldeneye: National Elk, W; Red Rock Lakes, FW.
Cooper's Hawk: Bowdoin, SF.
Ferruginous Hawk: Arapaho, FW; Benton Lake, F; Bowdoin, SF.
Golden Eagle: Alamosa, W; Arapaho, FW; Bear River, W;
    Browns Park, SsFW; Charles M. Russell, SsFW; Desert, S;
    Minidoka, SW; Monte Vista, FW; National Bison, SsFW;
    National Elk, SFW; Ouray, SW; Red Rock Lakes, F;
    Seedskadee, SsFW.
Bald Eagle: Alamosa, W; River, W; Browns Park, W;
    Charles M. Russell, SW; Deer Flat, W; Minidoka, SW;
    Monte Vista, FW; National Elk, SFW; Ouray, W.
Osprey: Charles M. Russell, Ss; Kootenai, Ss.
Prairie Falcon: Arapaho, F; Benton Lake, S; Ruby Lake, SsFW.
Merlin: Charles M. Russell, SF.
Sharp-tailed Grouse: Bowdoin, SFW; Charles M. Russell, SsFW;
    Medicine Lake, SsFW.

Sage Grouse: Browns Park, SsF; Camas, F;
    Charles M. Russell, SsFW; Ruby Lake, SsFW;
    Seedskadee, SsFW.
California Quail: Deer Flat, SsFW; Stillwater, sF.
Gambel's Quail: Desert, SsFW.
Gray Partridge: Benton Lake, SsFW; Bowdoin, W;
    Charles M. Russell, SsFW; Minidoka, sF;
    National Bison, SsFW.
Long-billed Curlew: Bear River, Ss; Benton Lake, Ss; Bowdoin, F;
    Camas, Ss; Grays Lake, S; Minidoka, s; Red Rock Lakes, Ss;
    Ruby Lake, SsF.
Upland Sandpiper: Benton Lake, SsF; Medicine Lake, SsF.
Baird's Sandpiper: Bear River, sF; Bowdoin, Ss;
    Charles M. Russell, SF.
Marbled Godwit: Bear River, SsF; Benton Lake, SsF; Bowdoin, SsF;
    Medicine Lake, SsF; Ouray, Ss.
Northern Phalarope: Benton Lake, S; Ouray S; Stillwater, SsF.
Band-tailed Pigeon: Monte Vista, Ss.
Flammulated Owl: Desert, S.
Burrowing Owl: Benton Lake, Ss; Deer Flat, sF.
Saw-whet Owl: Charles M. Russell, SsFW.
Lesser Nighthawk: Desert, s.
Black Swift: National Bison, s.
White-throated Swift: Browns Park, SsF; Desert, s; Ouray, s.
Black-chinned Hummingbird: Browns Park, SsF; Ouray, s.
Broad-tailed Hummingbird: Desert s; Ouray, s.
Rufous Hummingbird: Desert, s; Kootenai, s.
Ladder-backed Woodpecker: Desert, SFW.
Lewis' Woodpecker: Kootenai, s; National Bison, Ss.
Ash-throated Flycatcher: Desert, s.
Dusky Flycatcher: Desert, s.
Gray Flycatcher: Desert, s.
Steller's Jay: Kootenai, FW.
Scrub Jay: Desert, SsFW.
Piñon Jay: Browns Park, SFW; Charles M. Russell, SsF;
    Ruby Lake, W.
Common Raven: Red Rock Lakes, W; Ruby Lake, SsFW;
    Stillwater, sF.
Clark's Nutcracker: Desert, SsFW; Kootenai, F; National Elk, SsFW;
    National Bison, SsFW; Red Rock Lakes, SsFW.
Mountain Chickadee: Desert, SsFW; National Bison, SFW;
    National Elk, W; Red Rock Lakes, SsFW.
Common Bushtit: Desert, SsFW; Ruby Lake, SsFW.

Pygmy Nuthatch: Desert, SsFW; National Bison, SFW.
Dipper: Browns Park, SsF; Kootenai, sF.
Rock Wren: Charles M. Russell, SF; Desert, SsFW;
    National Bison, SsF.
Sage Thrasher: Alamosa, Ss; Browns Park, SsF; Camas, s;
    Charles M. Russell, SsF; Ruby Lake, SsF.
Varied Thrush: Kootenai, S.
Western Bluebird: Charles M. Russell, SF; Desert, s.
Mountain Bluebird: Alamosa, S; Arapaho, Ss; Bowdoin, S;
    Charles M. Russell, SsF; Kootenai, S; Monte Vista, S;
    National Elk, SsF; National Bison, SF; National Elk, S;
    Red Rock Lakes, Ss; Ruby Lake, SF; Seedskadee, SsF.
Townsend's Solitaire: Desert, W; National Bison, FW.
Sprague's Pipit: Bowdoin, Ss; Charles M. Russell, Ss;
    Medicine Lake, Ss.
Bohemian Waxwing: Bowdoin, SFW; Charles M. Russell, SFW;
    National Bison, SFW.
Phainopepla: Desert, SsFW.
Northern Shrike: Charles M. Russell, SF.
Virginia's Warbler: Desert, s.
Grace's Warbler: Desert, Ss.
Western Tanager: Camas, S; Charles M. Russell, SF; Minidoka, S;
    National Bison, Ss; Red Rock Lakes, Ss.
Black-headed Grosbeak: Desert, s; Ouray, sF.
Lazuli Bunting: Deer Flat, s; Ruby Lake, S.
Cassin's Finch: Desert, SsFW; Red Rock Lakes, Ss.
Gray-crowned Rosy Finch: Arapaho, SW; National Elk, SW;
    Red Rock Lakes, SF; Seedskadee, W.
Black Rosy Finch: Arapaho, SW; Seedskadee, W.
Brown-capped Rosy Finch: Arapaho, S.
Green-tailed Towhee: Desert, SsF.
Baird's Sparrow: Benton Lake, SsF.
Black-throated Sparrow: Desert, SsF.
Sage Sparrow: Browns Park, SsF; Desert, SFW; Ruby Lake, SsF;
    Seedskadee, s.
Brewer's Sparrow: Arapaho, F; Desert, SF; National Elk, SsF;
    Red Rock Lakes, Ss; Ruby Lake, SsF.
Harris' Sparrow: Bowdoin, SF; Charles M. Russell, SF;
    Medicine Lake, SF.
McCown's Longspur: Medicine Lake, Ss.
Chestnut-collared Longspur: Benton Lake, SsF; Bowdoin, SsF;
    Charles M. Russell, s; Medicine Lake, SsF.
Lapland Longspur: Camas, W; Charles M. Russell, SFW.

THE MOUNTAIN STATES

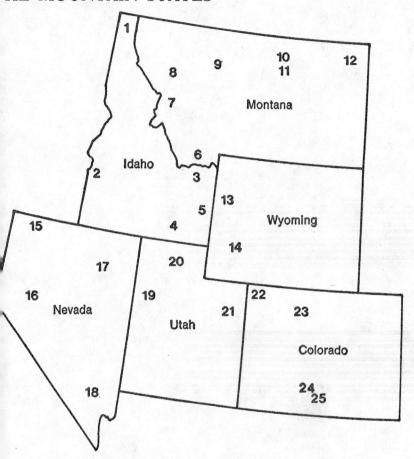

1 Kootenai
2 Deer Flat
3 Camas
4 Minidoka
5 Grays Lake
6 Red Rock Lakes
7 Metcalf
8 National Bison
9 Benton Lake
10 Bowdoin
11 Charles M. Russell
12 Medicine Lake
13 National Elk

14 Seedskadee
15 Sheldon Antelope
16 Stillwater
17 Ruby Lake
18 Desert
19 Fish Springs
20 Bear River
21 Ouray
22 Browns Park
23 Arapaho
24 Monte Vista
25 Alamosa

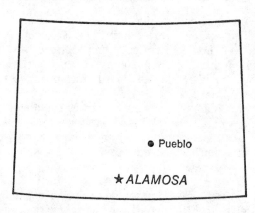

Pueblo

★ *ALAMOSA*

ALAMOSA (Colorado)

One can see almost all the wild creatures at this 10,356-acre south-central Colorado refuge at one time or another from the bluff alongside the refuge road overlooking the high mountain meadow (which has never seen a plow) with pond and riparian habitat along the meandering Rio Grande River.

Thousands of ducks and geese are here—mallard, gadwall, pintail, shoveler, cinnamon and blue- and green-winged teal, along with Canada geese, many with broods of young in early summer. For Alamosa, with its moist habitat and 7,500-foot elevation, has breeding waterfowl populations comparable to refuges hundreds of miles north in the prolific Dakota pothole country.

In fact, there is always something to see at Alamosa. Eagles, both bald and golden, winter here in large numbers; it is not uncommon to see fifty from one location on the bluff. Hundreds of sandhill cranes may come through in spring and fall migration, occasionally with a young whooping-crane foster offspring (part of the experimental program to produce a second migratory flock of this endangered species). There are also shorebirds such as snipes, black terns, avocets, and Wilson's phalaropes, all of which nest here as well (the female phalaropes are the colorful ones, not the male as is more usual among birds). Snowy egrets and black-crowned night herons nest here too.

Other raptors appear here seasonally and do much of their hunting in this meadow, where the visitor can sometimes get a bird's-eye view of *them*—rough-legged, red-tailed, Swainson's, and marsh all common, at least seasonally. The last two nest.

For some birds, of course, one must look more closely. One can spot black-billed magpies (great horned owls sometimes take over their huge nests), horned larks and song sparrows, and in summer sage thrashers and sizable populations of barn swallows and cliff-swallows which build mud-daub tube houses on almost every convenient vertical surface.

Until recently Alamosa has been relatively undeveloped; so until present facilities have been expanded one should check with the refuge office (a good idea anyway to learn what's around—particularly if wishing permission to visit on weekends).

How to get there: From Alamosa, Colorado, go east on Route 160 about 4 miles to El Rancho Lane and refuge sign, then right 2.5 miles to headquarters.

Open: Weekdays 8 A.M. to 4:30 P.M. (other times by arrangement).

Best times to visit: All year has interesting sights.

What to see: Cranes; eagles; hawks; waterfowl; shorebirds.

What to do: Five miles of roads and trails for riding, hiking; bluff overlook; limited hunt for waterfowl, small game.

Motels, weather: Special equipment and other information are similar to that at Monte Vista Refuge, 20 miles west.

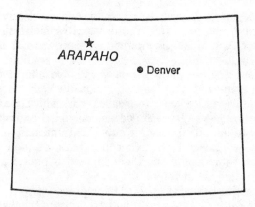

ARAPAHO
● Denver

ARAPAHO (Colorado)

The visitor to 12,814-acre Arapaho Refuge in north central Colorado can be almost certain to see pronghorn antelope, those decorative and keen-visioned beasts that can look in all directions at once, can pick out a small object four miles away, and have been clocked at speeds of seventy miles an hour.

Arapaho is also, at 8,300 feet elevation and lying alongside the Continental Divide, the highest of any U.S. refuge outside Alaska, and a good example of the phenomenon of vertical migration in which some birds move seasonally not north and south but up and down the mountains. This is the pattern followed here by the hardy mountain and black-capped chickadees, mountain bluebirds (which are sometimes seen in late summer at elevations up to twelve thousand feet) and the rosy finches, which spend the winter here, along with gray and Steller's jays and red crossbills, and breed above the timberline.

Three species of rosy finches occur at Arapaho—the gray-crowned, black and brown-capped, of which the last is found only in a relatively small range in this part of the United States.

Sage grouse are common in summer and fall and one can observe their colorful courtship displays, with the male strutting and inflating orange throat sacs. But no strutting grounds are located on the refuge proper. Consult refuge personnel for a good place to find them.

Waterfowl arrive as soon as the ice melts in late March or early April—some Canada geese but mostly ducks, predominantly mallard, but also gadwall, wigeon, teal, and shoveler peaking at about six thousand, many of which stay and nest in summer around small ponds and marshes fed by the Illinois River in this area known as North Park—the historical meaning of "park" in this sense being a mountain meadow.

During the relatively warm season, great blue and black-crowned night herons come and raise families, and so do Wilson's phalaropes, sora rails, willets, and a few avocets. Dippers, which manage somehow to walk underwater, are here occasionally, and Swainson's hawks are common to abundant spring through fall and nest. Ferruginous hawks, golden eagles, and prairie falcons all are common in fall, and the latter two sometimes nest. The white-tailed prairie dogs, whose holes are scattered about the refuge, along with Richardson's ground squirrels, sometimes serve as prey for the raptors.

Mule deer winter here as well, and elk are sometimes seen then, along with white-tailed jackrabbit. The latter turn white in the cold months, all except for their black eartips which sometimes can be seen bobbing like hundreds of black dots against the snowy background as they congregate around refuge field headquarters.

Arapaho also administers the following refuges:

Pathfinder is a 16,807-acre refuge southwest of Casper, Wyoming. It is used by numbers of waterfowl and shorebirds. Antelope and mule deer make their home here as do many rattlesnakes. There are no visitor facilities.

Bamforth covers 1,160 acres of largely salt flat. It is periodically flooded, and is visited by waterfowl, shorebirds, pronghorn antelopes. It is surrounded by private land with no public access.

Hutton Lake is a 1,969-acre refuge of five small lakes surrounded by marsh and upland. It is at a 7,150-foot elevation twelve miles southwest of Laramie, Wyoming. Although it is not staffed it can be an extremely interesting place to visit. Migrating ducks sometimes peak at 20,000 in April, including 7,500 redheads. A dozen species commonly nest, including canvasback, cinnamon teal, and ruddy ducks; also nesting are eared grebes, avocets, phalaropes, Forster's and black terns, Virginia rails, and various wading birds. Black-crowned night herons have a rookery. Golden eagles are common all year. Common in warmer months are mountain bluebirds, colonial cliff swallows, Say's phoebes, and ash-throated flycatchers, and in winter three kinds of rosy finches. Pronghorn antelope and mule deer visit.

How to get there: From Denver, take I-70 west to Route 40, through Granby, then north on Route 125 to refuge sign 8 miles south of Walden.

Open: From 4 A.M. to 9 P.M.

Best times to visit: Late spring and early fall.

What to see: Pronghorn antelope; sage grouse; rosy finches; waterfowl and shorebirds; prairie dogs; raptors.

What to do: Fourteen miles of roads open to driving, hiking—and entire refuge open to walking over pleasant terrain; limited antelope hunt; fishing can be excellent for brown trout; guided tours by prior arrangement.

Where to stay: MOTELS—In Walden. CAMPGROUNDS—North of Walden; also various national and state forests in area.

Weather notes: Winters severe, to minus 40° F. sometimes.

What to take and wear: Always a jacket (only 30 frost-free days a year here).

Points of interest nearby: Rocky Mountain National Park, 60 miles southeast; Mount Zirkel Wilderness Area, 20 miles west.

For more information: Arapaho National Wildlife Refuge, P.O. Box 457, Walden, Colorado 80480. Phone: (303) 723-4717.

★ *BEAR RIVER*

● Salt Lake City

BEAR RIVER (Utah)

The explorer Captain Howard Stansbury in 1849 said of Bear River, "I have seen large flocks of birds before . . . but never did I behold anything like the immense numbers here congregated together . . . as far as the eye can see." It can still seem that way at this 64,895-acre refuge of large shallow ponds and salt marsh where the Bear River empties into the Great Salt Lake in northern Utah.

Nowhere else do so many of the nation's beautiful and interesting birds gather in such large numbers, and so visibly that a visit here is invariably a treat for novice and seasoned birder alike.

Sometimes in spring and fall migration, millions of birds of all kinds may be here, their low babbling "conversations" never stopping, even at night. Some of the spectacles seen occasionally then can only be called amazing: a half million eared grebes covering the Bear River, a half million swallows like a tremendous windborne cloud, a half million marbled godwits and long-billed dowitchers.

The largest concentrations of whistling swans anywhere—around twenty thousand of these most graceful of snowy waterfowl—may come through in fall, with peaks of up to a million ducks, including a half million pintail, almost as many green-winged teal, as well as canvasback shoveler, cinnamon teal, and others. All are seen against a stunning scenic backdrop of the blue Promontory Mountains on the west and the snowy crests of the Wasatch Range on the east. Stay until dusk if possible—local folks claim "the West's most gorgeous sunsets" and this is hard to dispute.

In May, one cannot drive the twelve-mile auto tour route without seeing in the water, on the edges of the dikes; or in the roads, hundreds of young bird families. Killdeer do their "broken-wing" act to distract attention. There are willets, coot, lovely pink-legged black-necked stilts, and downy Canada goslings. Some of the goslings' parents volunteer for extra duties so that diligent pairs are sometimes seen herding along twenty or more young, theirs and their neighbors'. Of the 222 birds which have been identified as visiting Bear River at one time or another, 60 are known to nest.

Delicate, graceful avocets, their heads and necks russet with breeding color, are present in five thousand breeding pairs, by conservative estimates, on the dikes.

Ruddy ducks bob their heads toward their mates in frantic excitement, showing off their bright blue bills, freshly colored for the occasion.

Western grebes, sometimes called the "swan grebe" for their graceful curving white necks, perform remarkable courtship "water ballets" and later build floating nests and carry their young about on their backs, their offspring hanging on even when the parents dive for food around the spillways. Huge rolling carp weighing twenty to thirty-five pounds are a sight in themselves in May and June.

Great blue and black-crowned night herons have sizable nesting colonies as well. So do white-faced ibises, snowy egrets, California and Franklin's gulls, double-crested cormorants, Caspian terns, and many others, including cliff swallows which attach hundreds of tubular mud-daub nests to buildings and bridges in the headquarters area.

White pelicans with nine-foot wingspreads are here through the warmer months; so are long-billed curlews and willets, Wilson's phalaropes, spotted sandpipers, and Forster's terns. Marsh hawks are common all year, as are ring-necked pheasant, black-billed magpies, and ravens which often raise young under the observation tower steps. Bald and golden eagles abound in late fall, winter, and early spring, sometimes a hundred or more.

The airboat was first developed here so refuge personnel could oversee the almost sixty square miles of shallow water and marsh, much of which cannot be visited by any other means. Botulism, a serious illness that has killed millions of birds in the West, is studied at a research station here, one of the foremost units of its kind in the world.

Refuge personnel are extremely knowledgeable and helpful in suggesting how best to see everything—although excellent leaflets, both about the refuge and on numbers of related nature subjects, anticipate most questions.

How to get there: From Brigham City, turn west on Forrest Street which becomes Bird Refuge Road, 15 miles to headquarters.

Open: From 8 A.M. to 4:30 P.M., except Christmas, New Year's, and weekends January–March 15.

Best times to visit: Mid-April through December (but all year interesting).

What to see: Eagles most common in late fall and early spring when visitation is very low. Whole spectrum of birds, especially water-oriented, many in tremendous numbers.

What to do: Twelve-mile self-guided auto tour route; observation towers; photography—outstanding opportunities, many from car window but permits granted for temporary blinds; fishing; limited waterfowl, pheasant hunting; guided tours for groups and film available for off-refuge showing by prior arrangement.

Where to stay: MOTELS—In Brigham City. CAMPGROUNDS—On refuge; also Cache National Forest, 3 miles east of Brigham City.

Weather notes: Can have snow into May: summer hot, humid.

Points of interest nearby: Golden Spike National Monument, 25 miles northwest; Cache and Wasatch National Forests, east and southeast; interesting old buildings in Brigham City.

For more information: Bear River Migratory Bird Refuge, P.O. Box 459, Brigham City, Utah 84302. Phone: (801) 744-2488.

BENTON LAKE (Montana)

Great Falls

BENTON LAKE (Montana)

A drive down the dike road at Benton Lake Refuge can be almost a bewildering experience on a fine day in May. One may be surrounded by birds, on land, flying by, flushed from the roadside—gulls, terns, phalaropes in stunning array, while eared grebes and some of the dozen species of waterfowl that nest here, including Canada geese, plow the waters alongside.

The grebes in beautiful gold-festooned spring plumage and ruddy ducks with bright blue bills are common. So are avocets, killdeer, Wilson's phalaropes, black terns, willets, yellowlegs and spotted sandpipers, and a few horned grebes (which are just passing through to more northerly nesting spots), and a few black-necked stilts which have started to nest here in recent years. White-faced ibises often are here and stay through the summer, as do white pelicans and a few double-crested cormorants.

Benton Lake is largely a waterbird refuge—12,383 acres of marsh and wetlands in north-central Montana surrounded by native grasslands. These are perfect surroundings for the marbled godwits and long-billed curlews. The uncommon upland sandpiper, western burrowing owl, gray partridge, and ring-necked pheasant all abound here. Breeding ducks include mallard, gadwall, pintail, scaup, redhead, and canvasback and ruddy ducks, shoveler, and three species of teal; ten thousand to twenty thousand young are produced in an average year—nearly forty thousand in an outstanding one. Benton Lake also produces many thousands of eared grebes and Franklin gulls, both colonial nesting species.

Marsh hawks and short-eared owls are abundant, and nest, and so are other raptors in various seasons—rough-legged hawks in fall and winter, along with a few golden eagles, prairie falcons in spring and fall, and sometimes spectacular numbers of Swainson's hawks in late summer and fall, when as many as 150 of these splendid birds may be counted in a single day. Ferruginous hawks and peregrine falcons are occasionally seen during migrations.

The mudflats around the lake can attract impressive shore birds in migration—sometimes thousands of dowitchers, Wilson's phalaropes, and a variety of smaller sandpipers, lesser numbers of black-bellied plovers plus such occasional rarities as a whimbrel or Hudsonian godwit.

Cliff swallows nest in colonies under water control structures. Chestnut-collared longspurs are common to abundant, as are horned larks, water pipits, lark buntings, and a number of sparrows, including the Savannah grasshopper, vesper, and an occasional Baird's.

Winter usually brings snowy owls and snow buntings, and the mammal population—small numbers of coyote, jackrabbit, and an occasional pronghorn antelope—is more visible then. But the weather is bitter, and most creatures that can, move out.

Benton Lake also administers Waterfowl Production Areas and wetland easements in ten counties, maintained principally for their wildlife habitat, with few visitor facilities. To arrange a visit to any of these, consult refuge headquarters.

How to get there: From Great Falls take 15th Street (Route 87) north across Missouri River to Bootlegger Trail; follow it north 10 miles to refuge office.

Open: Dawn to dusk.

Best times to visit: Spring and fall.

What to see: Waterfowl, shore and marsh birds in nesting and migration; raptors, especially Swainson's hawks in the fall; historic Mullan Trail (can see remains of old wagon ruts).

What to do: Wildlife observation and photography (good from car window); limited waterfowl hunting in October and November.

Where to stay: MOTELS—In Great Falls. CAMPGROUNDS—Giant Springs State Park, 13 miles south; Thane Creek Forest Service, 50 miles east; Lewis and Clark National Forest, 60 miles southeast.

Weather notes: Can be frozen from mid-November to April.

Points of interest nearby: Giant Springs, largest fresh-water spring in the world—see this and other CAMPGROUNDS, above; Freezeout

State Wildlife Area, 40 miles west—fine birding area; C. M. Russell studio and gallery, in Great Falls.

For more information: Benton Lake National Wildlife Refuge, P.O. Box 450, Black Eagle, Montana 59414. Phone: (406) 727-7400.

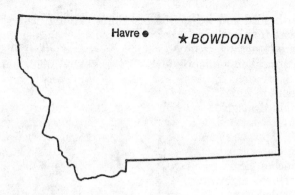

Havre ● ★ *BOWDOIN*

BOWDOIN (Montana)

Thousands of water birds of many kinds gather in spring to nest and bring up families at this 15,437-acre refuge of marsh, water, and grassland in northeast Montana. "Land of the Big Sky," it is called, because with the subdued rolling landscape and great clarity of sun-filled atmosphere stretching like a great bowl around the entire horizon, the airy expanse can often seem to take up far more space in one's vista than the earth beneath. The result is that sometimes the whole world except for a token foothold seems to be composed of a huge blue sky filled with avocets, marbled godwits, black and common terns, gulls, Wilson's phalaropes, and a great many others, calling, demonstrating breeding plumage, and later herding along young ones to flight stage before starting the southward trek in the fall.

Majestic white pelicans with nine-foot wingspreads reproduce in large numbers on islands in Lake Bowdoin. So do colonies of double-crested cormorants, California and ring-billed gulls and Franklin's gulls (favorites of the farmers for their insect-eating habit). Building floating nests in the marshes, thousands of eared grebes, lovely in their gold-accented head plumage, can seem to be everywhere about the marsh areas during the breeding season.

White-tailed deer and pronghorn antelope also are here, with their young appearing in June, often along the tour route that passes through most of the habitat types and affords views (though from a distance—bring a spotting scope) of many of the breeding bird colonies. Coyote, too—the "little prairie wolf"—prowl about. The engaging "flickertails" or Richardson's ground squirrels look like small prairie dogs at their holes.

Yellow-headed and red-winged blackbirds call and flare their brilliant colors from every patch of bullrush. Lark buntings and chestnut-collared longspurs are noticeable in the prairie growth. Cliff swallows construct substantial colonies of tubular mud nests under every bridge. Short-eared owls nest (so do a few long-eared) and can be conspicuous in late afternoon hunting forays.

Black-billed magpies and horned larks are abundant all year, and common at least seasonally are long-billed marsh wrens, mountain bluebirds, Sprague's pipits, cedar and Bohemian waxwings, yellow warblers, clay-colored, Brewer's, Lincoln's, and Harris' sparrows and Say's phoebes. Birding is good in any shrubby section and especially around refuge headquarters.

Sharp-tailed grouse and occasional sage grouse show off dramatic breeding effects on courtship dancing grounds, and ring-necked pheasants puff out their scarlet cheeks.

A dozen species of waterfowl breed—giant Canada geese, mallards, pintails, teals, goldeneyes, wigeons, shovelers, buffleheads, and ruddy ducks—and with others can build up to migratory concentrations of seventy thousand in fall. Raptors both spring and fall can be impressive—common almost every year are sharp-skinned, Cooper's, red-tailed, rough-legged, marsh and a few ferruginous, along with transient bald and golden eagles.

Bowdoin also administers four smaller refuges, *Black Coulee, Creedman, Hewitt Lake,* and *Lake Thibadeau,* with similar habitat and wildlife but no visitor facilities. To plan a visit to these, consult with the Bowdoin office.

How to get there: From Malta take Route 2 a mile east to refuge sign on right (*old* U.S. 2) and follow 6 miles to headquarters.

Open: Daylight hours.

Best times to visit: Spring and fall.

What to see: Nesting waterfowl, marsh birds, sharp-tailed grouse, and others in large numbers; deer; antelope.

What to do: Fifteen-mile self-guided auto tour; photography (blinds available, also can be good from car); limited hunt for waterfowl, upland birds.

Where to stay: MOTELS—In Malta, 7 miles west. CAMPGROUNDS—In Malta, also Nelson Reservoir State Recreation Area, 15 miles northeast.

Weather notes: Winters bitterly cold, snow and rain can make roads hazardous.

Points of interest nearby: Nelson Reservoir (see CAMPGROUNDS); Charles M. Russell National Wildlife Range, 70 miles south.

For more information: Bowdoin National Wildlife Refuge, P.O. Box J, Malta, Montana 59538. Phone: (406) 654-2863.

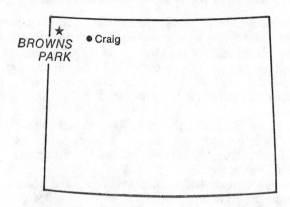

BROWNS PARK (Colorado)

Browns Park could be said to have been a haven for wildlife continually since before the dawn of history, when dinosaurs roamed here. Later came Indians, and fur trappers, and in the 1890s outlaws who took advantage of its relatively mild climate and advantageous location in a remote fastness where three states meet—to rustle cattle from one state, fatten them awhile on Browns Park, and sell them in another, then reverse the process and hide out successfully when difficulties arose.

Antelope and mule deer have always found it hospitable here, as have eagles, hawks, sage grouse, and various kinds of water birds on this 13,374-acre refuge along the Green River in the northwest corner of Colorado. More than half of it is "parkland," a word in this instance meaning mountain meadow, surrounded by rocky slopes.

The refuge was established in 1965 to restore habitat lost through construction of the Flaming Gorge Dam upstream (its canyons do seem almost to flame in the morning sun) and its roads, in the past sometimes barely passable, are being improved, which should result in one of the most striking wildlife drives anywhere. The remotely beautiful scene seems untouched by the hand of man, with marshes and old oxbows of the Green (really green) River paralleled by bluffs of fifty to several hundred feet. From them most of the wildlife at this refuge can be observed.

Deer swim across the river. Canada geese nest on river islands and on platforms in adjacent marshes but occasionally break tradition and raise broods in an old red-tailed hawk's nest high in the cotton-woods alongside. Great horned owls can sometimes be spotted in these trees, where they nest as well.

A half dozen or more golden eagles live here all year and nest in cliffs, as do cliff swallows, which sometimes gather with others of their fleet-winged family in huge migration groups. Bald eagles are here all winter.

Several dozen pairs of white-faced ibises usually summer in the bottoms. Black-crowned night herons take up residence on Hog Lake. And great blue herons and their nest activities can be seen from refuge headquarters.

Beaver are abundant, badger, fairly common, and bobcat also, al-though these are wary and hard to spot. White-tailed prairie dogs have loose colonies of several hundred along the roads, and scuttle among their burrows.

And there are numbers of others—a dozen nesting species of ducks, and common in all the warm months rufous and black-chinned hummingbirds, poor-wills, white-throated swifts, sage thrashers, sage sparrows, and, less common, that curious small bird that walks under the water of mountain streams, the dipper.

Occasionally visitors can see elk along this waterway where, it is said, Jim Bridger and Kit Carson came to sell their pelts. Just west of the refuge is the cabin where the outlaw Butch Cassidy could look out and call much of this—for a while at least—his own, sometimes with a female associate, Jodie Bassett. Jodie's sister was the famous "Queen Ann" Bassett, never convicted of rustling herself but only, according to local belief, because she was tried by a jury of her peers.

How to get there: From Craig take Route 40 west about 31 miles through Maybell, then right or north on Route 318, 51 miles to refuge entrance.

Open: Twenty-four hours all year.

Best times to visit: Fall and spring.

What to see: waterfowl, shore and wading birds; eagles; mule deer; antelopes; sage grouse; old rustlers' and outlaws' cabins.

What to do: Thirty miles of roads and trails for driving, hik-ing; fishing good June–February for rainbow and cutthroat trout; limited hunting for waterfowl, deer, rabbits; float trip through refuge on rafts or canoes on Green River (rentals near-by)—through refuge takes a day, or for beautiful 3-day 85-mile trip go from Flaming Gorge to Split Mountain.

Where to stay: MOTELS—Craig, 85 miles southeast. CAMPGROUNDS—
On refuge in specified areas; or in Flaming Gorge. Recreational
Area, 50 miles northwest.

Weather notes: Winters fairly mild but with sudden blizzards;
mosquitoes can be fierce in summer.

Points of interest nearby: Flaming Gorge Dam, Reservoir and Recreation Area (SEE CAMPGROUNDS); Dinosaur National Monument,
adjoining on south (quarry where dinosaur bones excavated);
Jones Hole National Fish Hatchery, 45 miles south—interesting,
with hiking, fishing, striking canyon scenery; Ouray National
Wildlife Refuge, 90 miles southwest.

For more information: Browns Park National Wildlife Refuge,
Greystone Route, Maybell, Colorado 81640. Phone: (303)
365-3695.

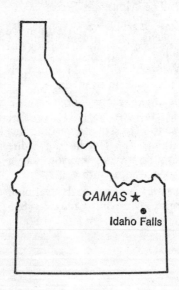

CAMAS ★
Idaho Falls

CAMAS (Idaho)

Camas, named for the blue lily whose rootbulb was a staple Indian food, is a beautiful 10,656-acre refuge in southeastern Idaho. Its habitat ranges from desert to irrigated meadows, marshes and open lakes with some native prairie. Up to two hundred thousand ducks may fly against a mountain backdrop of the snowy Lemhi Range to the west or the Grand Tetons to the east.

Visitors can watch mule deer usually in early morning and evening, as well as beaver and muskrat, often antelope, occasionally moose and, though they are wary, bobcat. Coyote are common in winter.

Greater sandhill cranes nest (sometimes on muskrat houses). So, often, do trumpeter swans. White-faced ibises share an impressive colony of several hundred nests with great blue and black-crowned night herons, snowy and great egrets and double-crested cormorants on Rays Lake. Long-billed curlews like the grassy meadows, avocets the marsh edges.

One can always see raptors—kestrels and ferruginous hawks nesting, sometimes in trees just east of headquarters. Swainson's, red-tailed, and marsh hawks are common, as are bald eagles in late fall and winter. The refuge has a raptor rehabilitation program for injured birds. Great horned and short-eared owls are always on the area, and great gray owls occasionally show up in winter. (The great horned can almost always be seen by inspecting the groves of trees near the canal.) Peregrines are sighted in small numbers every spring and fall.

Broods of ducklings, primarily redheads but also mallard, gadwall, shoveler and cinnamon teal with some Canada geese are on the waterways from early June on; but the prime waterfowl sights are in early April when the breeders and migrants combine in numbers that sometimes seem to cover every bit of surface water, and fill the air when they take flight. Sometimes there are thirty thousand gold-accented eared grebes at one time.

Migrating whistling swans can be impressive also; and white pelicans, which stay through most of the warm months.

Birders like to come out in spring for the small migrants that come through from mid-March through early June in the shrubbed and wooded area around headquarters. It is an attractive green oasis in this arid country that brings in large numbers and a wide variety of birds—warblers, mountain chickadees, kingbirds, juncos, rufous hummingbirds, thrushes, orioles—sometimes twenty or thirty species can be counted in a few hours.

Nighthawks are a common sight, wheeling and kiting about for insects all day, and then in the evening over the marshes. Pheasant and sage grouse are in the uplands.

More than anything else it is the solitude and intimacy of this remote and undisturbed setting that strike visitors here. Driving or walking quietly along and through the marshes, or paddling a canoe, you can almost always see something interesting—and then it is just you and the birds and the other sounds and sights of nature.

How to get there: From Idaho Falls take I-15 north to Hamer exit; from there follow signs 4 miles northwest to headquarters.

Open: Dawn to dark.

Best times to visit: Spring through fall.

What to see: Large concentrations of migratory waterfowl (especially spring); mule deer, sometimes antelope; moose; nesting shore and wading birds; trumpeter swans; sage grouse.

What to do: Twenty miles of improved roads for driving, hiking (plus 15 unimproved); canoeing around marsh units; limited waterfowl and upland game hunting. (Look, if you wish, but don't dig for gold taken in a stagecoach robbery, reportedly hidden along Camas Creek and never recovered.)

Where to stay: MOTELS—Idaho Falls and Rexburg, 36 miles south and southeast. CAMPGROUNDS—At Roberts, 20 miles south; also in Targhee National Forest, 30 miles north.

Weather notes: Snow often prevents access to refuge mid-December to mid-March.

Points of interest nearby: Mud Lake Wildlife Management Area, 5 miles southwest; Market Lake Wildlife Management Area, 20 miles south (can have huge pintail concentrations); wind-sculptured sand dunes, 20 miles east.

For more information: Camas National Wildlife Refuge, Hamer, Idaho 83425. Phone: (208) 662-5423.

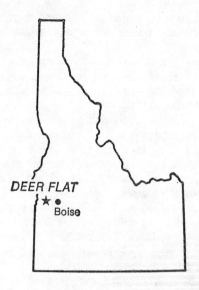

DEER FLAT (Idaho)

Deer Flat Refuge in southwest Idaho is 11,410 acres, composed of two different and interesting units: Lowell Lake, where the refuge headquarters is located and large concentrations of waterfowl winter —sometimes seven hundred thousand ducks including six hundred thousand mallard alone, along with fifty or so bald eagles; and the Snake River section, extending one hundred and twelve miles along the Snake River from Walter's Ferry, Idaho, to Farewell Bend, Oregon, which includes eighty-six islands in the river where Canada geese and great blue herons nest and a variety of wildlife make their homes.

Wintering geese gather in large numbers as well—up to nine thousand Great Basin Canadas with some whitefronts as well, both in Lake Lowell (one of the largest man-made lakes in the world, a Bureau of Reclamation project on which the refuge is superimposed) and in fields along roads around the lake. There are six access points where the visitor may park and walk in and look around, and the whole refuge is open to hiking, except during hunting season.

Photographers often find their best opportunities are from car windows, both for these and for shorebirds which congregate on sand and mudflats around the New York Canal at the southeast end in spring and fall—snipes, western sandpipers, long-billed dowitchers, and long-billed curlews, which have a nesting group of several hundred pairs on Bureau of Land Management land just west of the refuge in most years.

White pelicans are around in most warm months. Eared and western grebes are common nesters, as are great blue herons and several duck species, especially mallard but also pintail and cinnamon, blue- and green-winged teal.

Best time to see the waterfowl as well as the eagles that follow them here is from mid-September to March, although in years with a hard December freeze many may move to the river area. But a visitor can go out on almost any winter day and with diligence see at least a dozen eagles in the cottonwoods around headquarters, and another dozen or so along the lower embankment at the northwest end.

Small birding is best in these two places also and, while not spectacular, can be interesting with ruby-crowned kinglets, cedar waxwings, yellow warblers, Brewer's and yellow-headed blackbirds, lazuli buntings, magpies, Oregon juncos, and violet-green swallows common at various seasons. Red-tailed and Swainson's hawks are the common raptors, and nest, and rough-legged hawks and prairie falcons are present in winter.

Mule deer are the most common mammal, most often seen on the south side. Red fox sometimes make a den next to the observation tower.

Visitors can see the Snake River unit by driving along adjacent roads and entering at various access points to the shore where the islands, which range from a half to twenty-five acres and accommodate nesting geese as well as herons, gulls, terns, avocets, stilts, beavers, minks, and sometimes large numbers of goldeneyes, may be visible.

Closer access varies with the season—nesting islands are restricted (and patrolled) to reduce disturbance, and water conditions change. Boating and canoeing are possible during high water, and also an interesting method of locomotion employed by local fishermen, who attach waders to an inner tube and alternately paddle and walk the watery terrain (but weight your waders or risk being upended in the river current).

How to get there: From Nampa go south on 12th Avenue to Lake Lowell Avenue, then west to refuge sign 4 miles to Visitor Center, turning right at upper dam. To see refuge turn left at dam onto lake road, follow roads to left past various access points. For Snake River sector take Route 45 from Nampa south about

12 miles to Walter's Ferry, then follow river past various access points.

Open: Daylight hours.

Best times to visit: March–April and October–December.

What to see: Large waterfowl concentrations; bald eagles all winter.

What to do: Twenty-six miles of roads for driving, hiking; boating (rentals nearby); limited hunting for waterfowl, upland game; fishing good in spring for bullhead, crappie, largemouth bass; photography (blinds planned); recreation area for picnicking, general water-oriented activities.

Where to stay: MOTELS—In Nampa. CAMPGROUNDS—Several in Nampa; also municipal camping area in Holmdale and Marsing, and Boise National Forest, 30 miles north.

Points of interest nearby: Birds of Prey Natural Area, set aside for raptors especially nesting peregrine and prairie falcons, 55 miles southeast; Bruno Sand Dunes, 40 miles southeast; Bogus Mountain, 40 miles north; Indian pictographs, just north of Snake River Unit.

For more information: Deer Flat National Wildlife Refuge, P.O. Box 448, Nampa, Idaho 83651. Phone: (208) 467-9278.

DESERT

★

Las Vegas ●

DESERT (Nevada)

This is the largest national wildlife refuge outside Alaska, with more than one and a half million acres of habitat ranging from the burning Nevada desert floor to snowy mountains close to ten thousand feet. The scenery is spectacular and so are the natural inhabitants. Best known are the desert bighorn sheep for which the refuge was established in 1936—the largest population in existence of these majestic animals whose numbers were once close to extinction. But there is a fascinating variety of other flora and fauna which find ecological niches appropriate to their kind in six different elevational life zones. Here are the bristlecone pine, one of the oldest and certainly the hardiest plants on earth; a forest of joshua trees, and another of ponderosa pines.

Golden eagles soar above the mountains, a common sight in spring. Rare and secretive mountain lions roam the area. Some of the small birds which migrate do so not by flying to some distant place but by migrating up to a more comfortable zone to nest in summer, and return to a lower elevation in winter.

The annual Christmas Bird Count taken by the National Audubon Society usually shows some species in greater numbers here than any place else in the nation—most frequently the sage sparrow, hepatic tanager, and Le Conte's thrasher. These and a good number of other small birds are often visible at the Corn Creek subheadquarters, where there is a spring, a small pond (where the endangered Pahrump killifish lives) and a good amount of brushy habitat. Yellow-rumped (Audubon's) warblers, western bluebirds, Say's phoebes, ruby-crowned kinglets, and others can be spotted here in good numbers seasonally. If you go early and find a man in a tuxedo, he is one of the pit bosses at a Las Vegas casino, an avid birdwatcher who often checks in here on his way home.

The road out from Corn Creek forks right to the Mormon Well picnic area, and to the left through the passes to higher elevations where the sheep are most often found. This road also continues through the refuge, coming out at Route 93 toward the Pahranagat Refuge. A sign at the fork gives mileages to the various possible destinations. The Mormon Well way is regarded hereabouts as a nice Sunday drive, though it requires a pickup truck or, preferably, a four-wheel-drive truck to be sure of getting through. It traverses desert floor and comes at the Well to an attractive picnic area in the Ponderosa pines where small birds and some of the other refuge inhabitants, including some of the small mammals, congregate.

The Alamo Road passes side roads to the various springs in the mountain where the sheep are—but to see these, it is necessary to walk or go on horseback; and, while it can be done in a day (a very *full* day), it is better if at all possible to camp out (by permit only). This is truly a marvelous experience, whether one sees sheep or not. The stars seem to blaze at night. Coyote howl, owls twitter, and phainopepla flit among the mesquite. The ornate Gambel's quail with their improbable-looking topknots scurry along the paths.

Here one is believed to have about an 80 per cent chance of seeing the sheep by hiking up higher than they are, usually at least six thousand feet (three thousand feet above the road), finding a comfortable spot and sitting quietly for a few hours, binoculars at hand. If you don't see a bighorn, you might catch sight of the other interesting refuge residents at some point—a cliff chipmunk, bobcat, badger, black-tailed jackrabbit, mule deer, pronghorn antelope, spotted skunk, desert tortoise, kit fox (they often show up at campsites to see what's up), or one of the twelve species of bats.

Also administered from Desert headquarters is *Pahranagat* Refuge, covering 5,380 acres of water and marsh in this arid area, which attracts a wonderful range of wildlife. Drive or walk in from Route 93 on the eastern side of Desert Refuge. Common here at least part of the time are—to note but a few—green-tailed towhees, Brewer's, white-crowned, and black-throated sparrows, violet-green swallows, pine siskins, Bullock's orioles, MacGillivray's warblers, robins, water pipits, horned larks, kingfishers, marsh hawks, double-crested cormorants, great blue herons, and eight kinds of ducks, along with Canada geese and sandhill cranes from time to time.

Desert Refuge also maintains a refugium in Death Valley for preservation of the endangered killifish and devil's hole pupfish.

How to get there: From Las Vegas take Route 95 north about 23 miles to refuge sign and then 4 miles to the Corn Creek subheadquarters.

Open: Visitor hours are 5 A.M. to 9 P.M. Overnight camping by permit.

Best times to visit: September–October and early spring.

What to see: Desert bighorn sheep, mule deer, flora and fauna appropriate to 6 separate elevational life zones from 2,600 to nearly 10,000 feet.

What to do: About 150 miles of auto, hiking, and backpacking trails; primitive camping by permit; photography (no blinds, but may obtain permit to put one up temporarily); horseback riding; limited hunting for sheep; picnicking (about two thirds of refuge is an Air Force gunnery range and off limits).

Weather notes: Mean temperature is 60 degrees F., but this reflects range with elevation from around 120 on valley floor to below zero at 10,000 feet.

What to take and wear: Outer clothing for cold elevations; high-clearance or four-wheel drive vehicle (depending on destination); flashlight, compass, plenty of food and water, including water for your horse if riding; hiking boots—this is a rocky desert; spotting scope for distant sights.

Points of interest nearby: The Las Vegas wash, southeast of town, excellent birding. Death Valley National Monument, 50 miles west. Charleston Range in Toiyabe National Forest, opposite refuge on Route 95.

For more information: Desert National Wildlife Refuge, 1500 North Decatur Boulevard, Las Vegas, Nevada 89108. Phone: (702) 878-9617.

Salt Lake City

★ *FISH SPRINGS*

FISH SPRINGS (Utah)

Fish Springs is an oasis in the desert. This is the word that comes most often to those who have seen it, 17,992 acres of sparkling marshes reflecting a clear blue sky, fed by springs that come flowing out of the earth amid the southern fringes of the Great Salt Lake desert, against mountains that rise to eight thousand feet. This watery paradise acts as a magnet for wildlife in an arid, inhospitable environment—a peak of thirty-five thousand ducks in fall and spring migration, shorebirds, raptors, and a good many small birds.

Many stay and nest in the summer. There are snowy plovers, long-billed curlews, avocets, black-nested stilts, rails, eared grebes, Canada geese, at least ten species of ducks including pintail, canvasback, cinnamon teal, bufflehead, redhead, and ruddy ducks, and a colony of some six hundred nests of white-faced ibises, snowy egrets, and black-crowned night herons.

Others find the winters pleasant compared with alternatives elsewhere—especially the raptors, both kinds of eagles (the goldens often nest in the nearby mountains), marsh, rough-legged, red-tailed, and occasionally Swainson's and ferruginous hawks and prairie falcons. Whistling and some trumpeter swans are usually here in winter, and some of the other waterfowl remain.

Small birds can be numerous, especially in migration, around headquarters and in the other shrubbed, wooded section, the picnic area, where trees were planted for shade when it was a station on the Pony Express route. Yellow-rumped (Audubon's) warblers can be common, also flickers, nighthawks, western kingbirds, shrikes, Say's phoebes, marsh wrens, and Savannah sparrows.

Coyote are always around, most visible in winter, also muskrat (sometimes fifteen thousand of them), jackrabbit, antelope, ground squirrels, kangaroo rats, and a few bobcat, antelope, mule deer, and wild mustangs.

Visitors can see most of the refuge from thirty-eight miles of roads and trails. There is also canoeing (with your own canoe). A warning when driving anywhere in this area: watch closely for flash floods occurring with no warning after even a half inch of rain. These can leave a foot of water and boulders in a dip in the road.

But even more than the wildlife is the starkly beautiful isolation of this place. It is 150 miles southwest of Salt Lake City and there are 65 miles of gravel road between it and any other habitation. Climb up the mountainside on a clear day and you can see over a hundred miles, usually with no other human being in all that view. You can even, looking closely, discern the curvature of the earth.

For further information contact: Fish Springs National Wildlife Refuge, Dugway, Utah 84022. Phone: (801) 522-5353.

GRAYS LAKE
★
● Pocatello

GRAYS LAKE (Idaho)

Grays Lake in southeast Idaho has always been an outstanding wildlife area. It is on a remote high plateau of about fifteen thousand
acres covered almost entirely with marsh and water and surrounded
by national forest and the lofty Caribou Mountains. Wildlife here
includes moose, eagles, curlews, and many other creatures. These
days, however, its primary focus is on the beautiful white bird that
has made "endangered species" a household term: the majestic
whooping crane.

An ingenious, imaginative program started here will, it is hoped
cause the great white whooper—one of the world's largest birds,
standing four to five feet tall with wingspread up to seven feet—to
form a new flock with a shorter, safer migration route from Idaho to
New Mexico. This route covers about 850 miles as compared with
the long and hazardous traditional path of some 2,600 miles from
the whooper breeding grounds in the far north of Canada to wintering places in south Texas.

The plan is this: greater sandhill cranes, which nest densely at
Grays Lake (usually at least 250 pairs on the refuge) and take
the shorter route to New Mexico, are remarkably like whoopers in
almost every way. Why not take eggs from whooper nests (they

lay two, but raise only one), put them under sandhills to raise, and see if the whoopers thus hatched will follow the sandhills' route? Whooping crane populations have been so low, their survival possibilities so precarious for so many years, that the risk seemed minimal compared with possible reward.

This experiment began in 1975, but the final outcome will not be known for a while. Whoopers will not mate until they reach age four to six. Much can happen; and they are, and have been, subject to the same mortality and hazards of any wild creature. But there are encouraging signs. Sandhills have raised the foster chicks and they have flown together to Bosque del Apache Refuge and back (some young ones have loitered along the way as is characteristic of these birds). And, the older whooper offspring have seemed fairly independent, only occasionally associating with sandhills while feeding. (One fear has been hybridization.)

Meanwhile, both sandhills and young whoopers (which are rusty before they turn white) can be seen at Grays Lake, though not easily since they are protected from disturbance as much as possible during their time here, usually early April to mid-October. Even refuge staff closely connected with the sensitive project normally do not enter the area except to transplant the eggs in May and to band the chicks in August. The best ways to see them, and the whole refuge, are, first, along the county roads that border it on all sides, with several observation pulloffs, and, second, from the platform on a hill behind field headquarters. Drive or walk up; it is 150 feet above the valley floor and, especially with a spotting scope, much of the wildlife of various kinds can be seen from these vantage points. Refuge staff are helpful in suggesting where to look.

A third way, sometimes available by special permission in fall, is to accompany refuge staff on their occasional trips to Bear Island in the marsh.

Besides the cranes there are moose and mule deer which calve on Bear Island, red fox, coyote, and an occasional elk. Birds of special interest include prairie falcons, bald and golden eagles, Swainson's and marsh hawks, bitterns, eared and western grebes, nesting herons and egrets, and an impressive breeding waterfowl population. There are more than ten thousand ducklings in a good year, including ruddy ducks, redheads, Barrow's and common goldeneyes, plus Canada geese—and a large nesting colony of Franklin's and California gulls. There are also nesting long-billed curlews, white-faced ibises, migrating whistling swans, small birds such as mountain bluebirds, calliope hummingbirds, and sometimes black-headed grosbeaks, and beautiful wild flowers: lupines, flaxes, camas lilies, and scarlet gilas.

Impressive wildlife including mule deer, white-faced ibises, several colonies of western grebes, and sometimes moose can be seen on the 16,978 acres of marsh and water that comprise *Bear Lake Refuge.* The site is ten miles south of Montpelier and three miles east of Route 89 and was, until recently, administered by Grays Lake Refuge. Greater sandhill cranes also nest along with many waterfowl species —Canada geese, mallard, redhead, ruddy ducks, goldeneyes, and others, plus great blue and black-crowned night herons, avocets, and Wilson's phalaropes. There are five miles of refuge roads and miles of county roads from which to view most of the area. Winters are snowy but county roads are kept open, and eagles and rough-legged hawks are present then, along with many others similar to the mammal and bird species at Grays Lake.

How to get there: From Soda Springs go north on Route 34 about 34 miles to refuge sign (just before Wayan), turn left 3 miles to field headquarters.

Open: Viewing areas open 24 hours; Soda Springs office 8 A.M. to 4:30 P.M. weekdays.

Best times to visit: Late April through October 15.

What to see: Whooping and sandhill cranes; waterfowl and shorebirds, duck and goose broods; moose, occasional mule deer, red fox.

What to do: Observation platform; 25 miles of roads (mostly county roads) for driving, looking; limited waterfowl hunting; photography (waterfowl, shorebirds).

Where to stay: MOTELS—Soda Springs, 37 miles south. CAMPGROUNDS —Forest Service; Gravel Creek, 5 miles south, also Tin Cup and Pine Bar, 10 and 15 miles east.

Weather notes: Frost recorded in every month, 6 feet of snow cover most of winter.

Points of interest nearby: Ruts left by Oregon Trail, some on refuge, others in Caribou National Forest adjacent, and on Soda Springs golf course; Teton National Park, 75 miles northeast.

For more information: Grays Lake National Wildlife Refuge, Box 837, Soda Springs, Idaho 83276. Phone: (208) 547-4996.

★*KOOTENAI*

● Coeur D'Alene

KOOTENAI (Idaho)

Kootenai is a fine small refuge of woods, marsh, and upland in the
Kootenai Valley next to the Selkirk Range of the Rocky Mountains
just eighteen miles south of the Canadian border. Although it contains less than three thousand acres, it has as diverse and interesting
wildlife as any in the system.

Both mule and white-tailed deer live here, as well as coyote,
beaver, occasional moose and elk. There is always a chance of seeing
a black bear and rarely a mountain lion; in addition, this northern
tip of Idaho has been designated as critical grizzly bear habitat, so
there is always a remote possibility of seeing one of these in the vicinity. Watch for long-tailed weasel along the road.

As with the mammals and the other natural life including the
interesting amphibians, reptiles, and plants, bird life here is notable
more for diversity than for large concentrations (though some may
appear by the hundreds or even thousands during migration, as
sometimes a fall peak of forty thousand ducks).

More than 215 avian species have been identified. Nesters include
red-tailed and marsh hawks, Lewis' and pileated woodpeckers, western tanagers, both kinglets, six kinds of swallows, lazuli buntings, hermit, varied, and Swainson's thrushes, calliope, rufous, and black-

chinned hummingbirds, and ruffed and blue grouse. Five kinds of chickadees have been recorded. Dippers nest under bridges and rocks along streams, flying through the spray of waterfalls. Steller's jays and Clark's nutcrackers nest at higher elevations and return in cooler weather. Among the shorebirds are snipes, spotted sandpipers, and black terns.

Among water birds, common nesters include common goldeneye, blue-winged and cinnamon teal, pintail and beautiful wood ducks (Boy Scouts built and installed houses for them) and Canada geese; also some red-necked and pied-billed grebes.

Raptors are always on the refuge—bald and golden eagles in winter, along with rough-legged hawks and rarely a great gray or snowy owl. Great horned owls are around all the time, as are a few screech, pygmy, and saw-whets; ospreys are here spring and fall.

Small birds are common various places—around headquarters and along the county road which borders the refuge west side at the base of the mountains. This is the route taken for part of the National Breeding Bird Census each June, and sixty-eight nesting species are sometimes noted (not all on the refuge section).

Wild flowers can be lovely—wild clematis, mountain hollyhock, columbine, paintbrush, mariposa lilies—and there are many fruiting plants that attract bears and all kinds of creatures—Oregon grapes, elderberries, huckleberries, thimbleberries, and others that grow in abundance.

Be sure to take the short nature trail up through tamaracks and cedars, ferns, mosses, Indian pipes, and shining mica-filled rocks to Myrtle Falls. It is cool and pleasant on the hottest day, and beautiful all the time.

How to get there: From Bonners Ferry on Routes 2 and 95 on the south side of the Kootenai River, take road along south shore of river heading west, continue 5 miles through refuge to refuge headquarters.

Open: Daylight hours.

Best times to visit: Spring and fall.

What to see: Waterfowl, pileated woodpeckers, raptors, mule and white-tailed deer, coyote, chance of bear, broad wildlife spectrum.

What to do: County roads through and bordering refuge; 3-mile auto tour route; short foot trail and walking permitted over whole refuge except during nesting; trout fishing permitted; limited hunting for waterfowl, upland and big game.

Where to stay: MOTELS—Bonners Ferry, 5 miles east. CAMPGROUNDS —Forest Service, 25 miles north along Route 95.

Weather notes: Refuge roads can be blocked by winter snow, slippery in spring rains.

Points of interest nearby: Creston Valley Wildlife Area, 40 miles north—nature walks and talks, canoe trails; MacArthur Lake State Wildlife Area, 15 miles south.

For more information: Kootenai National Wildlife Refuge, Star Route 1, Box 160, Bonners Ferry, Idaho 83805. Phone: (208) 267-3888.

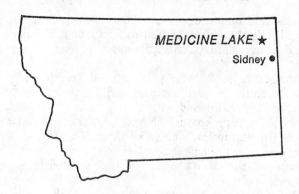

MEDICINE LAKE (Montana)

The white pelican, one of the world's most impressive and handsome birds with a length of almost six feet and wings that spread to almost nine in soaring flight, nests at Medicine Lake Refuge by the thousands, sometimes producing as many as three thousand young birds in a summer.

But there is much more besides at this 31,457 acres of meadows, pastureland, lakes and ponds in the northeast corner of Montana.

Eared and horned grebes, magnificent in gold head feathering in the breeding season, also come together to build colonies of floating nests. Although quiet and secretive, these birds are visible to one looking carefully in the bullrushes. More visible are the western grebes whose courtship is a breath-taking water ballet. Altogether they bring off hundreds and sometimes thousands of young grebes.

Double-crested cormorants and great blue herons also have breeding colonies, and nests of gulls—both California and ring-billed—whiten the islands seen from the shore.

It is a prodigious waterfowl nesting area as well with hundreds of Canada geese and sometimes more than thirty thousand ducklings hatched out—shoveler, gadwall, blue-winged teal, mallard, pintail, and others.

For this reason spring is an excellent time to visit Medicine Lake. Many of the breeding ducks can be seen in striking plumage from the eighteen-mile auto tour route. Visitors can also observe such nesting shorebirds as the marbled godwits, Wilson's phalaropes, upland sandpipers, avocets, and black terns, and numbers of small birds, many uncommon elsewhere. These include chestnut-collared longspurs by the hundreds, as well as McCown's, Sprague's pipits, and lark buntings, and Le Conte's, Baird's, lark, song and clay-colored sparrows.

But summer is fine too for pheasant and gray partridge Swainson's and marsh hawks, prairie falcons, and short-eared owls. Some of the waterfowl are young and with their parents (the Canada geese sometimes with "gang broods" of forty or more, accumulated by a pair whose parental instincts exceeded those of a neighbor). White-tailed deer, here in the largest numbers in this section of the country, become less shy about showing off their spotted fawns, and occasional antelope appear.

In fall some of those birds that stopped briefly in spring en route to breeding grounds farther north come through again, sometimes in larger numbers and, without such an urgent purpose, staying longer —whistling swans and up to 50,000 sandhill cranes, occasional ferruginous hawks and buildups of up to 200,000 Franklin's gulls and a quarter million waterfowl (sometimes 140,000 shoveler alone!).

Sharp-tailed grouse are numerous all year and have fourteen dancing grounds where more than seventy males may gather on one ground during early morning hours to stomp about and inflate lavender gular sacs to attract females (who sometimes, studies show, choose males not so preoccupied with display and mate with *them*).

Coyote are more visible as the weather turns cooler and they hunt more assiduously for prey. Both bald and golden eagles might be seen at any time of year.

Four research areas have been set aside for preservation of Indian archeological sites, important nesting areas, and unique botanical associations, and there is an 11,366-acre wilderness area.

Medicine Lake also administers *Lamesteer* Refuge, an 800-acre wetland easement, and a number of Waterfowl Production Areas, open to the public but with few visitor facilities. To arrange a visit to one of these, consult the refuge office.

How to get there: From Culbertson go north 24 miles on Route 16 across Medicine Lake bridge to refuge sign, then right 2 miles to headquarters.

Open: Sunrise to sunset.

Best times to visit: May through October.

What to see: Concentrations of nesting and migrating white pelicans, cormorants, waterfowl, shorebirds, sharp-tailed grouse,

Sprague's pipits, longspurs, raptors, white-tailed deer.

What to do: Sixteen-mile auto tour route; photo blinds; observation tower; canoeing; limited hunting for deer, waterfowl, upland game; fishing; picnicking; cross-country skiing and snowshoeing.

Where to stay: MOTELS—In Culbertson, 24 miles south, Plentywood, 25 miles north. CAMPGROUNDS—In Plentywood, also Lewis and Clark State Park, 90 miles southeast.

Weather notes: Winter temperatures can fall to 57 below.

Points of interest nearby: Theodore Roosevelt National Monument, 90 miles south; Fort Union Trading Post Historical Site, 35 miles south.

For more information: Medicine Lake National Wildlife Refuge, Medicine Lake, Montana 59247. Phone: (406) 789-2305.

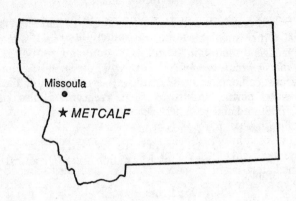

Missoula
★ *METCALF*

METCALF (Montana)

Ospreys share tree nests with majestic Canada geese (though not at the same time) at this fine small refuge of woods, fields, marsh, and open water along the Bitterroot River in western Montana.

For its 2,700 acres Metcalf (formerly called Ravalli) offers a tremendous wildlife diversity. White-tailed deer are at home all year, and coyote are here in the winter. Red fox sometimes build dens near the road, and the vixens and pups hunt in the fields in early summer, although popularity and high prices of long-haired furs in recent years have increased trapping on adjacent lands and reduced their numbers. Muskrat stack up mounds of vegetation for underwater dwellings which waterfowl use for resting and sometimes for nests above the waterline.

Raptors are present all year, especially the handsome little kestrels. Also apparent are several families of great horned owls and red-tailed hawks. Some Cooper's are always here and usually nesting. Goshawks breed in nearby mountains but hunt on the refuge all year, sometimes several together. Rough-legged hawks and prairie falcons can be counted on in winter, along with several bald eagles (sometimes nine can be seen at one time) and a few goldens.

Flame-crested foot-long pileated woodpeckers are a spectacular permanent resident but not the only woods bird of note; rosy-breasted Lewis' woodpeckers can always be found in warm months, and nest, along with downies and hairies, yellow-bellied and occasionally Williamson's sapsuckers. Steller's jays are common, and Clark's nutcrackers are here in all but summer, joined in the cool months by red crossbills and sometimes flocks of pine and evening grosbeaks. Other small birds especially in spring and summer are western tanagers, mountain bluebirds, pygmy and red-breasted nut-hatches, marsh wrens, veeries, yellowthroats, three nesting humming-birds—rufous, calliope, and black-chinned—six kinds of swallows, the western wood pewee, and likely the dusky and Hammond's fly-catchers. (Be prepared to hunt around for small birds, and ask the refuge office where to look. If possible, visit in the north end, sometimes closed but open by permit to careful, serious observers.)

Ospreys are highly visible starting in early April, when they arrive and immediately begin to harass, dive at, and dispossess the geese which have already taken up family duties in the bulky nests left by the big "fish hawks" from last year, these usually in dead cottonwood snags. Sometimes a half dozen geese will defend a nest. Luckily the geese are about finished at that point and the downy young climb on their mothers' backs and drop sometimes a hundred feet to the ground, where they head unhurt for the water. The ospreys then take over and are a delight to visitors who can easily watch the older birds hunt, catch fish, and "change the guard" as one takes over in-cubating and brooding chores from another.

Visitors can sight migrating birds from March to May and Sep-tember to November—up to twenty thousand ducks, including some of the nesting mallards, cinnamon teals, wood ducks, and hooded mergansers. One of the year's highlights is sometimes six hundred or so whistling swans. Raptor migrations can be good and are best seen by lying on one's back on a clear fall day and just looking.

Painted turtles are abundant and so enjoyed by local visitors that when a flood displaced their basking logs, numerous complaints were registered by citizens until the logs were replaced.

How to get there: From Stevensville take East Side Road to Water-fowl Lane and refuge sign, then north 1.5 miles to south refuge boundary.

Open: Daylight hours, year-round.

Best times to visit: All year can be interesting.

What to see: Nesting ospreys; resident and migratory waterfowl; white-tailed deer; raptors; pheasants.

What to do: County roads through refuge and along south boundary for driving, hiking; also short walking trail; picnic area; photog-raphy from hunting blinds in January; limited deer and water-fowl hunting; fishing, access to Bitterroot River for trout, also whitefish in winter. Tours can be arranged for organized groups.

Where to stay: MOTELS—Stevensville; also Missoula, 25 miles north. CAMPGROUNDS—Forest Service, just west; also various national forests (see below).

Points of interest nearby: Bitterroot National Forest surrounds refuge; Sapphire Mountains National Forest, 4 miles east; National Bison Range, 90 miles north; Fort Owen State Monument, 2 miles south, Montana's first white settlement; float trips along river from Hamilton to Missoula, beautiful in small boat or canoe.

For more information: Metcalf National Wildlife Refuge, P.O. Box 257, Stevensville, Montana 59870. Phone: (406) 777-5552.

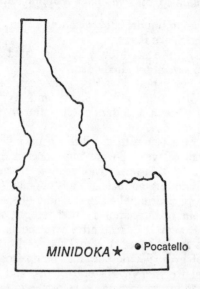

MINIDOKA ★ ● Pocatello

MINIDOKA (Idaho)

A visitor to Minidoka can stand in the ruts left by wagons on the Oregon Trail and watch the present-day north-south migration trails of up to a quarter of a million ducks and geese that stop by this 25,630-acre refuge in southern Idaho in spring and fall.

Many of these also nest, especially mallard, redhead, and ruddy ducks and Canada geese. Visitors can watch their broods and those of other water birds such as western, eared, and pied-billed grebes with their sizable floating nest colonies (the handsome westerns carrying their downy gray young about on their backs) on Lake Walcott from May through early summer.

Great blue herons raise their young on an island rookery which they share with snowy egrets and double-crested cormorants. These reuse the same nests year after year, adding material until they become like small chimneys. California gulls occupy the bare ground in the entire center space. Access is not permitted during nesting but it is only about four hundred feet from the south side dike and the young in the nests can be clearly observed with binoculars in mid-June.

Nighthawks wheel about for insects at all hours. White pelicans and others including hundreds of whistling swans in spring and fall congregate in the Snake River.

In recent years white-faced ibises have appeared in good numbers, sometimes up to several hundred or so.

Long-billed curlews nest. Avocets, yellowlegs, black-necked stilts, spotted and other sandpipers, willets, and Wilson's phalaropes (some nesting, some just loitering) like the marsh areas in late spring and early summer.

An osprey pair has begun to spend the warm months here. Golden eagles are present all year. So are mule deer and a few antelope, though these are not always readily seen. Beaver are here, too, though these interesting animals are not popular with local farmers and trapping keeps their numbers low. Bald eagles are here in winter.

Minidoka is one of the nation's oldest refuges, set aside by President Theodore Roosevelt in 1909 after construction of the Minidoka Dam across the Snake River created Lake Walcott. As the pioneer project in use of hydroelectric power to pump irrigation water, it is on the National Register of Historic Places, and a side effect has been its attraction for waterfowl in this formerly desert-like area.

Birding can be good for songbirds, too (but allow a little time for looking). A fine section to explore is the picnic area and the shrubby-grassy-wooded section behind refuge headquarters down to the lake, as well as the sandy-sagebrush tracts, for sage thrashers, larks, and sage and some Brewer's sparrows, northern (Bullock's) orioles, western tanagers, eastern and western kingbirds, marsh and rock wrens, sometimes lazuli buntings, black-headed grosbeaks, and a variety of warblers.

Areas judged sensitive to disturbance for nesting or other reasons are sometimes closed (as on the dike and marsh units) but ask at the office how best to see things. Permission is often granted to serious, careful observers even in these places.

How to get there: From Burley take I-80 east to Burley-Rupert exit, right onto Route 24 through Rupert to refuge sign, then 6 miles right to Minidoka Dam and another refuge sign.

Open: Dawn to dark.

Best times to visit: Spring and fall.

What to see: Migratory waterfowl concentrations; nesting water birds of various kinds; songbirds; mule deer; interesting lava formations; historic Oregon trail; active sand dunes.

What to do: Ten miles of improved roads for driving, hiking (others suitable for four-wheel drive, and hiking anywhere on refuge); boating, canoeing; photography (portable blind helpful); picnicking (at headquarters); trout fishing can be good.

Where to stay: MOTELS—Burley, 7 miles west; limited accommodations in Rupert. CAMPGROUNDS—At Declo I-80 interchange, 9 miles south; also primitive on Bureau of Reclamation land just below dam, and Massacre Rocks State Park, 30 miles east.

Weather notes: Wet, snowy winter weather can make roads impassable.

Points of interest: Massacre Rocks (see CAMPGROUNDS), and City of Rocks, 50 miles south, historic, good birding; pioneer hydroelectric irrigation project, tours; Minidoka State Bird Sanctuary, 30 miles west of Burley.

For more information: Minidoka National Wildlife Refuge, Route 4, Rupert, Idaho 83350. Phone: (208) 436-4545.

Durango
★ *MONTE VISTA*

MONTE VISTA (Colorado)

Monte Vista Refuge in south-central Colorado, almost fourteen thousand acres surrounded by magnificent high mountains and national forests, is the main stopover for young whooping cranes and their sandhill-crane foster parents between their nesting area at Grays Lake in Idaho and their wintering ground around Bosque del Apache Refuge in New Mexico. It is an important component in the experimental effort to establish a second flock of the endangered whoopers, America's largest and certainly one of its most majestic and beautiful birds. The eggs, taken from whooping cranes which nest in the Canadian Far North and migrate 2,600 miles to Texas, are hatched and raised by sandhills which have a shorter, less hazardous flight pattern. First results have been encouraging, and the young whoopers and their tall gray foster families can usually be seen at Monte Vista in October and November, and in March to mid-April.

Monte Vista, with a hundred or so small ponds, is also a major nesting ground for waterfowl. Seventy-five per cent of the ducks seen here do not go elsewhere but spend most of their lives on this refuge, and in the surrounding San Luis Valley, departing only during prolonged severe winter weather. These include mallard, redhead, shoveler, pintail, wigeon, gadwall, and green-winged, blue-winged and cinnamon teal, their populations sometimes peaking up to forty thousand when joined by migrants in spring and fall. Canada geese, re-established from a captive flock when the refuge was established, are now common nesters here also; and, in fact, have fanned out to nest wherever there is suitable habitat throughout the San Luis Valley.

With the waterfowl are those which often prey on them—both golden and bald eagles, common in fall and winter, sometimes several dozen perching in willows and cottonwoods and sometimes on fence posts. Because of the 7,500-foot elevation, few trees volunteer. Rough-legged and marsh hawks are also common in winter, and ferruginous occasional, Swainson's here in the fall, and prairie falcons, while not common, can be seen all year by anyone who seeks them out.

Avocets in russet-headed breeding feathers appear by the graceful hundreds in spring and summer, as do Wilson's phalaropes, whirling in mad circles as they feed in shallow waters (it is sometimes hard to see why they do not drop from dizziness).

The rare flammulated owl has been seen here, and great horned and short-eared owls, which hunt over the fields in the late afternoons, are common. Band-tailed pigeons, listed as common, are more often seen just off the refuge and are present in good numbers through the valley. Raucous, beautiful black-billed magpies are common all year, as are pheasants and horned larks.

Badger, coyote, bobcat, and rarely mule deer and elk are here, but are wary and seldom seen.

Water for the refuge comes from the Rio Grande and artesian wells, some of which continue to flow through the winter. Increased water use for irrigation has lowered the water table in recent years, however, so the flow is not as strong as formerly, and some wells have stopped entirely. Further loss could seriously hurt waterfowl in this area. But for now, waterfowl and snipe, which ordinarily might move south for the winter, stay all year around these hospitable springs.

How to get there: From Monte Vista take Route 15 south 6 miles to refuge.

Open: Daylight hours (tour route closed during waterfowl hunting).

Best times to visit: Spring and fall.

What to see: Whooping and sandhill cranes; bald and golden eagles; waterfowl; shorebirds.

What to do: Six-mile auto tour plus 12 miles county roads through refuge; photography (temporary blind available by arrangement); limited hunting for waterfowl, small game; guided tours for groups by prior arrangement.

Where to stay: MOTELS—At Monte Vista, Colorado. CAMPGROUNDS —In Monte Vista; also two forest service campgrounds in nearby mountains.

Weather notes: Can be dusty, windy in warm months (dust devils sometimes a half mile tall!) and winter temperatures can drop to 50 below.

What to take and wear: Warm clothing in winter and a jacket even in summer; spotting scope can help you view cranes.

Points of interest nearby: Great Sand Dunes National Monument, 25 miles northeast; Rio Grande State Wildlife Area, 10 miles northeast; Alamosa National Wildlife Refuge, 15 miles east. Good trout fishing in area.

For more information: Monte Vista National Wildlife Refuge, P.O. Box 511, Monte Vista, Colorado 81144. Phone: (303) 852-2435.

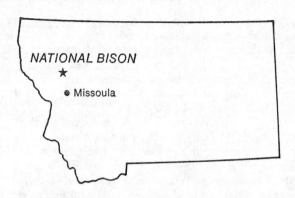

NATIONAL BISON
★
● Missoula

NATIONAL BISON RANGE (Montana)

National Bison Range sits on the west slope of the Rockies in a range called "land of the Shining Mountains" by the Indians. Once an island in a prehistoric lake, the refuge remains a treasure island for naturalists with its varied and abundant natural life of all kinds, including mammals, birds, botanical specimens, and great scenic beauty.

Many of the creatures that roamed this part of northwest Montana before people were here, are present now. Bison, once one of the most numerous mammals in the world, with perhaps seventy million in great herds on the western plains, were established here when their numbers were reduced by overhunting to fewer than three hundred in the wild. President Theodore Roosevelt set this refuge aside in 1908 and the newly formed National Bison Society found a nucleus herd (which had been saved by an Indian named Walking Coyote), and financed their transfer here by popular subscription. Now their descendants thrive.

Elk, with the most impressive antlers in America—often five feet across—live here along with swift and beautiful pronghorn antelope, Rocky Mountain goats and bighorn sheep, white-tailed and mule deer, coyote (the "little prairie wolf"), badger, mink, and great numbers of smaller interesting mammals—yellow-bellied marmots, Columbian ground squirrels, and yellow pine chipmunks.

And, while most visitors come for the impressive large animals, the bird population alone would make this a great refuge: golden eagles common all year and nesting; and common to abundant at one season or another are lazuli buntings, Lewis' woodpeckers, Clark's nutcrackers, Townsend's solitaires, red-breasted and pygmy nuthatches, mountain chickadees and bluebirds, Bohemian waxwings, red crossbills, black swifts, common goldeneyes, and short-eared owls. This is to mention only a few of the avian riches. Less common but still readily seen from time to time are ospreys, prairie falcons, blue and ruffed grouse, pygmy and long-eared owls, calliope and rufous hummingbirds, black-headed and pine grosbeaks.

The refuge, whose elevation rises more than two thousand feet from headquarters to the spectacular lookout point, is also a botanist's (as well as photographer's) delight with the varied habitat. Its 18,542 acres range through streambeds, prairie grasslands, deep woods of Douglas fir and ponderosa pine and heavily shrubbed areas of prairie roses, currants, chokecherries, and serviceberries. Here small birds are abundant and the wild flowers nothing short of awesome. Visitors seeing fields of lupines in the distance sometimes take out binoculars to be sure the shimmering blue is not a sparkling lake.

Visitors can see a great deal around headquarters, including some of the large mammals. Marmots are common and there is a short walking trail. But the best way to see it all is to take the nineteen-mile auto tour. Everything can be seen there, at one time or another. Drive slowly and plan to spend at least two hours, more if possible— most interested naturalists find that days could be consumed looking at everything here. For small birds stop by a thicket, especially along Pauline Creek, listen, and wait. The wait will not be long—the area can be alive with buntings, warblers, and orioles.

Stay in or near the car—a one-ton buffalo can be unpredictable and dangerous. It is best to go early or just before the tour route closes in the evenings to see the most. Scan the tops of slopes for bighorns, remembering that camouflage colors can make them look like a large rock (in late evening they often appear in large numbers on the roads). Young calves and fawns begin to appear in May; mating behavior starts in late July.

The route closes at night; but nightfall comes late in summer, and refuge staff do not hurry visitors who find something interesting to watch. It may also stay open later in the fall than the official Labor Day closing, if weather permits.

National Bison Range also administers *Ninepipe* Refuge, twelve miles north, and *Pablo* Refuge, thirty miles north—largely waterfowl refuges, sometimes with up to a quarter million birds in migration, and good fishing—a state record bass was taken at Ninepipe. It also manages a number of smaller refuges and Waterfowl Production

Areas. These are mostly open to the public but with few visitor facilities; to arrange a visit consult refuge headquarters.

How to get there: From Missoula take State Highway 93 north to Ravalli; then Route 200 west and north about 40 miles to Dixon, then Route 212 north 7.5 miles to refuge, following signs.

Open: Daylight hours weather permitting.

Best times to visit: Early summer and fall.

What to see: Bison; elk; deer; bighorn sheep; pronghorn antelope, golden eagles; great variety of other interesting animals, birds, plants, magnificent scenery.

What to do: Self-guided auto tour route; short nature walking trail; photography (good from car); picnicking; fishing can be good for cutthroat trout (up to 4 pounds). Group guided tours can be arranged.

Where to stay: MOTELS—Allentown, Polson, Ronan, or large selection in Missoula. CAMPGROUNDS—Allentown, also Lolo National Forest, 70 miles south; several state parks at Flathead Lake, 50 miles north.

Weather notes: Winters can be brisk—the nation's all-time cold spot in the lower 48 was 70 below at Rogers Pass, 90 miles southeast; world record for temperature variation, 100 degrees, from 44 above to 56 below one day at Browning, 100 miles northeast.

Points of interest nearby: Lolo National Forest; Creston National Fish Hatchery, 75 miles north; Lolo Hot Springs, 100 miles south; Glacier National Park, 100 miles north.

For more information: National Bison Range, Moiese, Montana 59824. Phone: (406) 644-2354.

★ NATIONAL ELK
● Jackson

NATIONAL ELK REFUGE (Wyoming)

Elk are the spectacular wildlife residents of this western Wyoming refuge. They are an awesome sight. The bulls can weigh up to a half ton with antlers up to six feet across, gathering against the snow and the stunning Rocky Mountain scenery in herds that have reached close to twelve thousand in midwinter. These are the largest congregations in North America of this majestic animal that, like the bison, once existed in many millions over much of the United States.

Come between December 26 and April 1 and ride along on sleighs which go out to the herds, taking alfalfa pellets as needed for supplemental feeding in severe winters (though much of the elk's forage is from natural grazing). Visitors can observe them at close range then, and also see some of the other wildlife—coyote and perhaps mule deer, moose, antelope, bighorn sheep, and trumpeter swans in patches of open water.

Supplemental feeding of the elk in winter and establishment of the 37-square-mile refuge itself started after homesteaders fenced elk winter range for cattle, causing loss of natural feeding areas. One year ten thousand elk died of starvation, and local people appealed for emergency help in providing enough to tide them over. There also was an extraordinary amount of persecution. Thousands were killed for their tusklike canine teeth alone, which were then sold for good luck charms, key chain and neck ornaments. Others were killed and their antlers ground up as aphrodisiacs. Finally the slaughter led to demands that it stop, and, with wide national support from individuals, including thousands of school children as well as conservation groups, this refuge was set up for the elk.

This was done in 1912. Since then elk have become the focus of life in this scenic little town where thousands of shed antlers (these great branched structures grow anew each year) have been piled up in high arches around the Jackson town square and are decorated with colored lights every Christmas. The elk are so close to town that they can be seen by school children from their classrooms, by patients from beds in the hospital, by housewives through their kitchen windows.

The elk are not, however, all there is to see on this refuge. Rare trumpeter swans, transplanted from a nucleus flock at Red Rock Lakes Refuge, nest, as do numbers of waterfowl—mallard, merganser, goldeneye, green-winged and cinnamon teal, and Canada geese. Barrow's and common goldeneye are present in winter, as are bald and golden eagles and rough-legged hawks. Golden eagles, prairie falcons, and red-tailed hawks nest. So do blue, sage, and ruffed grouse, long-billed curlews and sandhill cranes.

Small birds that can be common at various seasons include calliope hummingbirds, Clark's nutcrackers, dippers (walking through and under the water of valley streams), mountain chickadees, mountain bluebirds, yellow-rumped warblers, Townsend's solitaires, Steller's and gray jays, western tanagers, Lewis' woodpeckers, Williamson's sapsuckers, and the uncommon gray-crowned and black rosy finches, which often gather in winter flocks at feeders in town.

The elk can mistakenly be perceived as living inside a fence because of the high wire barrier between them and the road around the west refuge boundary. But this is not true; the fence only separates them from populated places. Behind and beyond are millions of acres of national park and forest land and wilderness areas where they are free to roam, leaving the refuge to spend the summers at higher elevations sometimes sixty miles away in South Yellowstone National Park. The summer visitor therefore is unlikely to see them without some special effort, such as exploring around the Timbered Island area of Grand Teton Park about twenty miles north beyond Moose, Wyoming. There they can be heard in September in the rutting season. Then the males bugle challenges to each other, audible for miles, one of the most wild and thrilling calls in the world of nature.

How to get there: Located next to Jackson. Go east on Broadway a mile to headquarters. Refuge entrance is ¼ mile east at base of mountain.

Open: Daylight hours, year-round.

Best times to visit: January through March.

What to see: Elk in large wintering concentrations, also coyote, possibly bighorn sheep, moose, mule deer, antelope, trumpeter swans.

What to do: Sleigh rides into elk herds December 26–April 1. Nine miles of roads for driving, observing (parts can be closed in winter), also pullouts on Route 187 overlooking marshes. Photography (blind available). Picnic area. Trout fishing can be good. Limited elk hunt.

Where to stay: MOTELS—Many in Jackson area. CAMPGROUNDS—Many around Jackson, including adjacent national forest and national park.

Weather notes: At 6,200 feet elevation, night cool even in summer and sometimes —50° F. in winter.

Points of interest nearby: Grand Teton National Park, adjacent north and west—walks and talks given from headquarters; Bridger-Teton National Forest to the east; Yellowstone National Park, 55 miles north; National Fish Hatchery, on refuge. Stop at Jackson Hole-Wyoming Highway Department Visitor Center just north of town for more information on scenic and natural areas.

For more information: National Elk Refuge, Box C, Jackson, Wyoming 83001. Phone: (307) 733-2627.

Salt Lake City
★
OURAY

OURAY (Utah)

Mule deer scramble agilely up shale and clay bluffs which turn light green, gold, and red with the changing light and humidity at this 11,363-acre refuge. Ouray encompasses both desert and marshland as well along the Green River in northeast Utah, where dinosaur bones have been found and Kit Carson used to hunt.

Bald and golden eagles are common in winter and spring and golden eagles nest, as do marsh and red-tailed hawks. Various other raptor species, including Swainson's and Cooper's, may be seen in good numbers in spring and fall migration.

Sandhill cranes also come through and in recent years have brought with them some of their famous adopted offspring—the endangered whooping cranes, part of a flock in which Idaho sandhills which winter in New Mexico have incubated and reared young from whooper eggs taken from nests in the Far North. It is an effort to establish a second whooping crane flock with a shorter and less hazardous migration route. Several times recently one of the young whoopers has stayed through the breeding season here and the hope is that eventually it might nest. To that end the refuge has created some secluded areas of the emergent marshes and open vistas which whooping cranes prefer (others like it as well).

Endangered fish species also live here—the Colorado squawfish and humpbacked chub. Fishermen are asked to return gently to the water anything not a catfish or carp, especially if it has a hump on its back. The fish are being propagated in ponds in national fish hatcheries with the hope of restocking them elsewhere in the world.

Nine species of ducks nest here—cinnamon, green-winged and blue-winged teal, mallard, gadwall, pintail, shoveler, redhead, and ruddy ducks; and Canada geese are here all year. So are ring-necked pheasant and colorful, raucous black-billed magpies, which build huge nests and are seen almost everywhere. Marbled godwits, avocets, and black-necked stilts are common in most warm months, and great blue herons have a rookery of a hundred or so nests in some years. Lewis' woodpeckers are common nesters.

Prairie dogs have burrows scattered throughout the refuge, some of which are appropriated by burrowing owls. Porcupines like to spend their time in forks of the cottonwood trees. Antelope occasionally show up on the east side of the refuge. Beaver are common around the waterways. Bear and mountain lion are seen at rare intervals. Dinosaurs used to be common here, and the Smithsonian Institution has been investigating a site where their remains have been found.

There are two ways to see the refuge to advantage. One is along the miles of roads and trails; the other is by canoe or raft in the Green River where one may see beaver at work, ducks loafing on sandbars, swallows along the steep banks, and an entirely different perspective. Try both if possible.

How to get there: From Vernal take Route 40 west 14 miles to refuge sign; then south on Route 88 for 15 miles to entrance. Office is in Vernal, open weekdays.

Open: Twenty-four hours all year.

Best times to visit: Spring and fall.

What to see: Waterfowl, eagles, hawks, migrating and sandhill and sometimes whooping cranes, mule deer, striking scenery.

What to do: Forty miles of roads open to driving, hiking; canoeing in Green River; fishing for channel catfish; limited hunting for ducks, pheasant, deer.

Where to stay: MOTELS—In Vernal. CAMPGROUNDS—In Vernal; also primitive on refuge; in Dinosaur National Monument, 45 miles northeast; on BLM land at Pelican Lake, adjoining; at Flaming Gorge Recreational Area, 60 miles north.

Weather notes: Summer can be desert-hot, with sudden strong winds in spring.

Points of interest nearby: Pelican Lake, access by BLM land (see

CAMPGROUNDS) can be marvelous birding and, some say, the best bluegill fishing on the North American continent; Browns Park National Wildlife Refuge, 90 miles northeast; Flaming Gorge and Dinosaur Monument (see CAMPGROUNDS) plus river trips, walking tours in Vernal—the area has many points of interest.

For more information: Ouray National Wildlife Refuge, 447 East Main Street, Vernal, Utah 84078. Phone: (801) 789-0351.

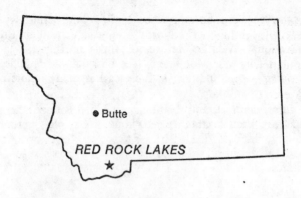

Butte

RED ROCK LAKES

RED ROCK LAKES (Montana)

One of the most beautiful and stately birds in the world was brought back from the edge of extinction in one of the most beautiful places in the world. The bird: the trumpeter swan. The place: Red Rock Lakes Refuge, in the remote, wild Centennial valley at the foot of the snowy Continental Divide in extreme southwestern Montana.

The trumpeter is distinguished from all other swans, including its near relative the whistling swan, by an extra loop in the windpipe making possible a deep, clear, resonant call that can be heard for miles. It is the largest waterfowl in the world. Over five feet long, it can weigh thirty pounds or more with a wingspread up to eight feet. It mates for life. Once it ranged over much of the United States. Archeologists have found its remains in Indian middens in Florida, Oregon, and Illinois.

But stern hunting pressure, both for meat and for feathers—thousands of feather robes were shipped to Europe—reduced its numbers. It also, in ways not fully understood, apparently altered its ancestral habits so as to limit its survival ability. Never highly gregarious, the majestic bird under pressure increased rather than reduced its territorial requirements (perhaps in a quest for sanctuary) so that now it needs a minimum of 15 and sometimes as much as 640 acres for each mated pair. Less than that and the bird apparently reduces its reproduction so that fewer young survive.

In 1912 the noted ornithologist Edward Howe Forbush wrote that "its trumpeting call will soon be locked in the silence of the past . . . total extinction is only a matter of years." Some believed it gone already. Then a small group was discovered in the Centennial Valley, and, with only 68 known still in the wild, steps were taken in 1935 to establish this refuge where the swan now survives in a stable population of 250 to 300. This is not very many, but it is saturation level here for this solitary swan that will tolerate no other large bird, even of a different species, to enter its home ground, driving away geese, cranes, all others. From the population here transplant pairs have been taken to other parks and refuges around the country; a large flock also has been discovered in Alaska and western Canada—so the beautiful trumpeter, while still rare in the lower United States (numbers total almost 1,500) is no longer endangered.

The visitor to Red Rock Lakes cannot be sure of seeing trumpeters—they often nest in remote marshes. But usually he can catch a glimpse of them, perhaps with gray cygnets in summer. Ask at the refuge office where they have been lately (and investigate Shambo Pond).

In any case, a trip to Red Rock Lakes is a superb experience. Some 13,000 acres of its 62 square miles are covered with shallow lakes, marshes, and meadows fed by snowmelt from mountains that rise from 6,660 to nearly 10,000 feet around it. Sandhill cranes nest, a common sight in the grasslands. Moose and antelopes are here, and in the streams are rare Arctic graylings. Fields, foothills, and mountains offer a profusion of flowers—lupines, shooting stars, paintbrushes, mallows, columbines, many others. There are also red fox, porcupine, badger, marmot, mule deer, coyote, and rarely black bear and mountain lion. Among the birdlife, at least seasonally, are white pelicans, whistling swans, seventeen nesting ducks including Barrow's goldeneye great horned and short-eared owls, long-billed curlews, great blue and black-crowned night herons, ruffed, sage, and blue grouse; among the smaller birds Clark's nutcrackers, mountain chickadees, mountain bluebirds, Cassin's finches, Lewis' woodpeckers, Townsend's solitaires, dippers, Steller's jays, and in winter gray-crowned rosy finches.

Winter is forbidding. Roads are closed most of the time. But if one can get through, the wildlife is more visible then; several hundred Canadian trumpeters join the local birds at warm springs, and the scenery, always stunning, is absolutely breath-taking.

How to get there: From Lima take I-15 south 14 miles to Monida exit and refuge sign, then 28 miles east on gravel road to headquarters at Lakeview.

Open: Twenty-four hours.

Best times to visit: Mid-May through October.

What to see: Trumpeter swans, sandhill cranes, eagles, waterfowl, wading birds, moose, variety of others plus wild flowers, spectacular scenery.

What to do: About 40 miles of roads for driving, hiking (walking permitted everywhere); canoe trail, restricted during nesting; photography; fishing for rainbow, brook, and cutthroat trout, grayling; limited hunting for waterfowl, big game; cross-country skiing and snowshoeing.

Where to stay: MOTELS—Guest ranch adjacent to refuge; also in Lima, 50 miles northwest. CAMPGROUNDS—Limited facilities on refuge; commercial camping 45 miles east near West Yellowstone, Montana; Bureau of Land Management land, adjacent on southwest, open to primitive or backpacking campers.

Weather notes: Summer rains through June may make roads impassable, and snows November–April may block roads to all but over-snow vehicles (average 151 inches snow yearly). Warm clothing may be needed spring and fall, frost possible even in midsummer.

Points of interest nearby: Yellowstone National Park, 50 miles east; Beaverhead National Forest, adjacent on north.

For more information: Red Rock Lakes National Wildlife Refuge, Monida Star Route, Box 15, Lima, Montana 59739. Phone: (406) 276-3347 or 276-3390.

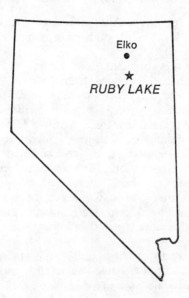

Elko

★
RUBY LAKE

RUBY LAKE (Nevada)

Ruby Lake is 37,630 acres of fresh-water marsh, salt-grass meadows, and open water. These are fed by more than 130 springs—some cool, some so hot they can burn the hand—and by snowmelt from the white-crowned Ruby Mountains that rise eleven thousand feet around it in a scenic rim that harbors one of the largest mountain lion populations left. Mountains and refuge both were named for the red stones that settlers found here and misidentified. They were garnets and some still can be picked up. The mountain lions are wary and seldom seen but they venture onto the refuge occasionally to prey on the abundant wintering deer herds.

Greater sandhill cranes court and nest here. So do trumpeter swans, largest and rarest of American waterfowl. There are also Canada geese and more than a dozen duck species, including the relatively uncommon canvasback and redhead which alone in a good year account for some four thousand ducklings.

There are also significant nesting colonies of white-faced ibises—up to three hundred pairs—great blue herons, snowy egrets, and black-crowned night herons.

Other nesters include avocets, stilts, phalaropes, bitterns, long-billed curlews, sage grouse (ten or more cocks gather on their courtship dancing grounds in April and May), Chukar and gray partridge, long-eared, short-eared, and great horned owls with a few burrowing and saw-whets.

Small birds can be abundant here. Lewis' woodpeckers can be seen most of the time in wooded Harrison Pass. In brushy places around springs, there are others such as bushtits, plain titmice, dippers (along hatchery raceways and Harrison Pass streams), mountain bluebirds, lazuli buntings, Cassin's finches, black-headed grosbeaks, sage thrashers, marsh wrens, Townsend's solitaire, dusky and other interesting flycatchers, and an assortment of swallows and sparrows, especially the sage, lark, Brewer's, and black-throated.

Rare prairie falcons are almost always here. Red-tailed, marsh, and rough-legged hawks are common. Golden eagles nest nearby and bald eagles are here in winter. Up to one hundred turkey vultures often roost behind field headquarters. Whistling swans and white pelicans visit seasonally.

Photographers can focus on sandhill crane families in the meadows in spring—fairly approachable—on wading birds and waterfowl broods in May and June near the dike roads, and on the ruggedly lovely scenery. Portable blinds can be used by permit.

Interesting mammals flourish as well, and while not as readily observable can usually be seen early and late in the day, most easily in winter—mule deer, coyote, muskrat (sometimes twenty thousand are here), also bobcat, porcupine, Townsend's ground squirrel, and a few badger.

The water is a cold forty-two degrees as it comes rushing out of Cave Creek spring in the mountain just behind headquarters at a maximum of twenty-seven cubic feet per second, so clear in the waterways that the abundant and large rainbow, brown, and brook trout can be seen distinctly ten feet down (and they rise and leap from the surface after flies at dusk like small sleek dolphins).

How to get there: From Elko take Lamoille Road south about 7 miles to Route 46, then south 27 miles to Jiggs; 4 miles south of Jiggs turn left at fork, go about 15 miles through Harrison Pass onto Ruby Valley Road and refuge sign, then 7 miles south.

Open: Daylight hours, year-round.

Best times to visit: May through October.

What to see: Nesting and migrating water birds; trumpeter swans; sandhill cranes; sage grouse; mule deer; variety of others—also historic sites (old homesteader cabin, Fort Ruby, pony express station).

What to do: Ten miles of roads for driving, hiking, also 18 miles of adjacent county roads (most of refuge open to overland hiking); photography; limited waterfowl hunting; small boating and canoeing (except in nesting season); fishing, outstanding for trout and largemouth bass. Slide shows and guided tours can be arranged for organized groups.

Where to stay: MOTELS—In Elko. CAMPGROUNDS—On Bureau of Land Management and Forest Service land in Humboldt National Forest, adjacent to refuge.

Weather notes: Harrison Pass roads en route to refuge can be closed by snow in winter; consult refuge on possible alternate route.

Points of interest nearby: State fish hatchery on refuge. Also fine hiking in national forest and mountains adjacent, excellent birding, alpine lakes, and rocky mountain goats can sometimes be seen.

For more information: Ruby Lake National Wildlife Refuge, P.O. Box 649, Elko, Nevada 89801. Phone: (702) 738-4320.

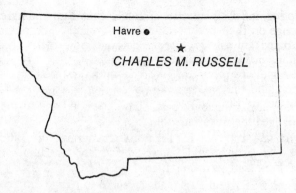

CHARLES M. RUSSELL (Montana)

Much of this vast wildlife refuge of almost a million acres in northeast Montana is unchanged from the time when Lewis and Clark traveled up the Missouri River here and explored the forested coulees, prairie grasslands, and rugged terrain around it in 1805. The grizzly bear are gone, but pronghorn antelope, mule and white-tailed deer, and bighorn sheep are here, along with more than forty other mammals. There is a tremendous variety of interesting birds, reptiles, plants, fossil remnants of some of its residents of pre-historic times—duck-billed dinosaurs and the great carnivore, *Ty-rannosaurus rex*. Paleontologists are still actively working the area and new discoveries of prehistoric activity continue to be made.

Much of this wild area is not fully explored. This is part of what makes it an extremely interesting place to visit, whether by the wind-ing twenty-mile auto tour route, hiking out over the badland "breaks," following some of the less well-traveled trails by horseback or four-wheel drive (take a compass) or going as Lewis and Clark did, following the waterways through unaltered wilderness, camping along the way. One can spend days, weeks, or longer here, and still not know on any given day what he may see—and always with the possibility of finding something no one even knew was here.

The black-footed ferret, one of the world's rarest animals, is still, it is hoped, making a last stand somewhere among the 4,500 acres of prairie dog towns here. In any case, these engaging little "dogs" share their colonial residences with such others as mountain plovers, burrowing owls, desert cottontails, and sometimes rattlesnakes.

Both sharp-tailed and sage grouse put on colorful courtship displays in spring, inflating lavender and gold gular sacs and extending their plumage on their traditional dancing grounds. Elk, one of the largest antlered animals in North America, grow racks of record size, spreading five feet and more in late summer.

Golden eagles are common in the summer, and nest, and many other raptors find this wild area to their liking. Rare prairie falcons are present spring through fall, as are, at various seasons, merlins, sharp-shinned, red-tailed, Swainson's rough-legged, and marsh hawks, bald eagles and ospreys, with occasional ferruginous, goshawks, peregrines, and gyrfalcons, and five common species of owl—the great horned, long- and short-eared and saw-whet, and the snowy in winter.

Wild turkey are here, white pelicans, common loons in spring, nesting great blue herons and Canada geese, large numbers of migratory waterfowl, shorebirds, and sandhill cranes, and such common to abundant small birds as piñon jays, red-breasted nuthatches, rock wrens, sage thrashers, mountain and western bluebirds, Bohemian waxwings, green-tailed towhees, lark buntings and Lapland and chestnut-collared longspurs.

Spring is prettiest and greenest with the most wild flowers—sometimes carpets of lupines, pentstemons, prairie roses—but there is bloom until freeze-up.

Strange paddlefish, ancient specimens with no true bones, grow up to 140 pounds and are sometimes snagged by fisherman.

The refuge was named after the cowboy artist who, with no instruction in painting, depicted in many great works the life he saw and knew here in the last century. His backgrounds show the land as much of it still can be seen here today. To describe it briefly is as difficult as trying to see it all in a brief time—but to make a start, consult the excellent maps and leaflets available at the refuge office, and the knowledgeable staff there.

UL Bend Refuge (named after the river's shape there) adjoins and complements C. M. Russell, and is administered by the Russell refuge. Its habitat and wildlife are similar except that it does not have bighorn sheep. If anything, it is more remote and difficult of access. Russell also administers four satellite waterfowl production refuges, *Halfbreed* National Wildlife Refuge, *Hailstone* National Wildlife Refuge, and *War Horse* National Wildlife Refuge, which have generally similar wildlife but no visitor facilities. Consult the refuge office about a visit to any of these.

How to get there: Enter the auto tour route by all-weather road from Route 191, 55 miles south of Malta. By four-wheel drive, various entrances, get map and consult refuge office. By boat (including raft or canoe) from Hell Creek or Rock Creek State Parks, also Pines and Fort Peck Recreation Areas on the east, or, from the west, James Kipp State Park on Route 191.

Open: Twenty-four hours year-round; Lewistown office 8 A.M. to 4:30 P.M. weekdays.

Best times to visit: Late spring and fall.

What to see: Mule and white-tailed deer, antelope, elk, prairie dogs, wild turkey, grouse, eagles, hawks, many others; excellent birding, interesting botanicals.

What to do: Twenty-one-mile auto tour route; 400 miles of roads open to four-wheel drive and hiking; boating, fishing, limited hunting for upland and big game, waterfowl; photography; horseback riding permitted, also cross-country skiing and snowshoeing, depending on snow conditions.

Where to stay: MOTELS—Fort Peck, Glasgow, Malta, Lewistown, Jordan. CAMPGROUNDS—At state parks and recreation areas (see *How to get there*).

Weather notes: Winters are harsh, roads frequently impassable.

What to take and wear: Jack, chains, shovel, food, water, hiking boots, and compass when driving or hiking off main roads.

Points of interest nearby: Montana State Fish Hatchery, Lewistown.

For more information: Charles M. Russell Refuge, P.O. Box 110, Lewistown, Montana 59457. Phone: (406) 538-8707.

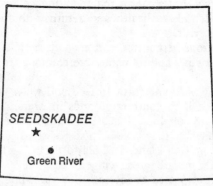

SEEDSKADEE

★

Green River

SEEDSKADEE (Wyoming)

The Oregon, Mormon, and California trails all went through the Green River Valley and so undisturbed has the land been by civilization that the visitor to 14,455-acre Seedskadee Refuge in southwest Wyoming can stand on the bluffs and see the wagon ruts left by those pioneers.

Wildlife have left their own trails. Sage grouse, for which the refuge is named—the word means "River of the Prairie Hen" in Shoshone Indian—are more numerous in this area than anywhere else. So are golden eagles, those raptors of remote places soaring with six-foot wingspreads over the sagebrush-covered fields and salt-grass bottomlands. They are common all year and nest here, and their wintering population on Seedskadee may be forty or so, sometimes highest in the nation on the annual Audubon Christmas Bird Count.

Gray-crowned and black rosy finches, whose rosy wings and rumps are visible both in flight and at rest, are here in good numbers in all but summer, when these hardy small birds retire to nest in the mountains above the timberline.

Pronghorn antelope and mule deer are here and fairly readily seen, as are wild horses and bobcat and occasional elk and moose. The numerous beaver keep the willows chewed down to low shrubs. The refuge is being fenced to keep out most open-range cattle with a special fence that allows passage of antelope, which prefer to go under an opening of sixteen inches, and deer which will leap thirty inches or more.

Birds of prey can be remarkable. Red-tailed and marsh hawks and prairie falcons nest on the bluffs overlooking the river. Rough-legged hawks, and sometimes a dozen or so bald eagles as well, are here in winter. The refuge has a raptor rehabilitation center where injured birds are nursed back to health and returned to the wild—an interesting place to visit.

Great blue herons nest in the cottonwoods, visible from the bluff road across the river. Sandhill cranes are common in spring and fall migration.

Sage grouse fly back and forth to feed and water, and can always be found—though their courting grounds in March may be located on the edge or just off the refuge. The refuge office can direct the careful visitor to where they have been seen recently.

Canada geese nest on islands and platforms in the river, and ducks nearby. Mallard, pintail, green-winged teal, shoveler, and wigeon are here and are expected to increase their breeding populations as water from the Green River is used to increase marsh habitat to compensate for similar areas lost when the Fontanelle Dam was built to the north in 1965. Common and Barrow's goldeneye sometimes spend the winter.

How to get there: From Green River take Route I-80 west 7 miles to LaBarge Road cutoff, then Route 374 north 30 miles to refuge sign, then east 2 miles to refuge headquarters.

Open: Twenty-four hours year-round (office 8 A.M. to 5 P.M. weekdays).

Best times to visit: Spring and fall.

What to see: Eagles; hawks; sage grouse; mule deer; antelope.

What to do: About 9 miles of desert roads and trails—whole refuge open to horseback riding and hiking except during nesting season; canoeing; limited hunting for deer, waterfowl, small game; fishing (fall best) for rainbow and brown trout.

Where to stay: MOTELS—In Green River, 39 miles southeast. CAMPGROUNDS—On refuge, primitive, by permit.

Weather notes: Winters at this 6,100-foot elevation can be cold, snowy, with roads impassable.

Points of interest nearby: Names Hill, 43 miles north (Jim Bridger scratched his name here); Fossil Butte National Monument, 40 miles west; Flaming Gorge Recreation Area, 60 miles south.

For more information: Seedskadee National Wildlife Refuge, P.O. Box 67, Green River, Wyoming 82935. Phone: (307) 877-6334.

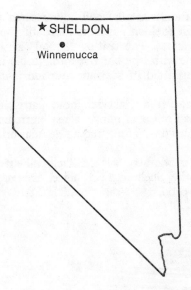

Winnemucca

SHELDON ANTELOPE REFUGE (Nevada)

On the (34,000-acre) Sheldon Antelope Range up to eight thousand
pronghorn antelope may spend the winter, usually on Big Springs
Table (which has a generally milder climate and less snow than
much of the surrounding area) although they may go farther east
to Jackass Flat during extremely severe conditions. They are not
easily seen by a visitor in these remote cliffbound places, however,
and winter weather can be harsh. The best times to visit and the
best things to see are similar here to those at Hart Mountain in
neighboring Oregon: antelope with their young appearing in May,
beginning to herd in groups of a hundred or so in summer, along
with such other mammals as mule deer, a few California bighorn
sheep, and burros. Like Hart Mountain these tracts are exceedingly
wild and remote. Sheldon may be somewhat easier for the average
visitor to observe since Route 140 goes through it for forty miles,
and there are also two graveled county roads which are passable
at least seasonally. However, for the hiker, backpacker, and horseback rider the whole refuge is open, with three primitive camping
areas available.

Bird populations also are similar to Hart Mountain (small birding habitat better on the mountain) and both refuges are popular with rockhounds, though Sheldon has more interesting specimens, including opals and sunstones. The visiting "hound" is permitted to take seven pounds home with him but not to dig or blast for them. Limited hunting is permitted in the range section, none in the refuge unit.

To get to Sheldon from Lakeview headquarters, take Route 140 southeast about 120 miles to refuge signs. Nearest standard motels are in Lakeview, Oregon, Winnemucca, Nevada, or Alturas, California, equidistant.

For further information contact the Sheldon-Hart Mountain office in Lakeview, or the Sheldon field office, Denio, Nevada 89404. Phone: (702) 941-0200.

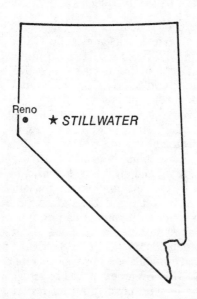

Reno ● ★ *STILLWATER*

STILLWATER (Nevada)

Stillwater Marsh, at 24,000 acres, and Pyramid Lake, site of its companion refuge, 248-acre *Anaho Island,* are remnants of Lake Lahontan, which once covered a closed mountain basin of almost nine thousand square miles in northwestern Nevada during the Pleistocene epoch. When first discovered by Europeans the basin still contained hundreds of thousands of acres of lakes and marsh, in spectacular contrast to the surrounding desert, a desert so dry that even sagebush cannot survive there.

The marsh, the lake, and nearby Carson Lake (not a refuge) depend entirely for their water on snowmelt from the eastern slope of the Sierra Nevada mountains which flows down through the Truckee and Carson rivers; no water leaves the basin except by transpiration and evaporation.

In early days Stillwater and Carson were prolific nesting areas for shore and water birds and prime stopovers for migrating waterfowl. Avocets and stilts nested by the thousands at Stillwater and white-faced ibises made Carson Lake one of their prime United States nesting sites. Migrating canvasback and redhead ducks were present in large numbers, as were long-billed curlews, geese, and whistling swans. Bald and golden eagles were common in fall and winter, here as elsewhere moving south with the waterfowl.

Little of this is left. Since the first irrigation ditches were completed about 1913 there has been steadily greater diversion of the basin's water from wildlife to cropland irrigation. In drought years more than 90 per cent of the former productive wetlands in Stillwater Marsh become arid salt flats; in such years Carson Lake is dry land, used only for grazing, its ibis rookeries destroyed.

While present water flows are sufficient to maintain Anaho Island as an island, its nesting colony of white pelicans, one of the largest in the country, is affected by the loss of feeding habitat at Stillwater. In addition to the pelican colony, Anaho has large numbers of nesting cormorants, gulls, terns, and great blue herons, all of which would be adversely affected by mammal and human predation should a potential land bridge, forty feet below the surface, be exposed by falling water. While this is not an imminent danger, it is of long range concern, since the lake's surface has dropped about eighty feet since water diversion began. To protect nesting activity and because of the abundant rattlesnake population on Anaho, public access is prohibited except when a visitor is accompanied by refuge personnel.

There are a few hopeful possibilities for restoring Stillwater. The refuge is drilling deep test wells in the hope of providing a little more water (but pumping costs are high and the water may be too salty). The area is active geothermally and there may be a possibility of using spent geothermal water, but if so it will be well in the future. Until then only several years of above-average snow pack offer much hope for Stillwater, so any person who is considering a visit to this refuge should first write or telephone the manager to determine its status.

In addition to Stillwater and Anaho Island this refuge administers *Fallon* National Wildlife Refuge which in high-water years provides about 2,500 acres of marsh and wetland. In most years, however, it is dry.

How to get there: From Reno take Interstate 80 east to Fernley, then Alternate U.S. 95 to Fallon. From Fallon take 50 east to Stillwater Road, then follow signs to refuge.

Open: Twenty-four hours a day, year-round.

Best times to visit: Spring and fall, but see *Weather notes.*

What to see: Summer, white pelicans, cormorants; fall and spring migrating waterfowl including canvasback, historically in large numbers; whistling swans, bald eagles, but see *Weather notes.*

What to do: Fishing, photography, wildlife observation; camping permitted. Limited duck hunting.

Where to stay: MOTELS—In Fallon, about 15 miles from refuge. CAMPGROUNDS—In Fallon. Primitive camping permitted on the refuge.

Weather notes: Annual precipitation averages only 5 inches, and refuge depends on snowpack runoff for water. Diversion of historic river flows to crop use have drastically reduced the size and quality of the refuge. Inquire as to present status before visiting.

Points of interest nearby: Lahontan Reservoir, water-oriented recreation is about 50 miles. Pyramid Lake (see text) is about 50 miles northwest, fishing and water-oriented recreation on Paiute Reservation; site of Anaho Island National Wildlife Refuge. The fault line from a 1954 earthquake with scarfs 15 to 20 feet high is about 80 miles southeast. Historic Pony Express trail is just south of Fallon.

For more information: Stillwater National Wildlife Refuge, P.O. Box 592, Fallon, Nevada 89406. Phone: (702) 423-5128.

IX. THE WEST COAST AND HAWAII

The refuges of the West Coast states embrace a wide variety of habitat from the wet and lush coastlands of Oregon, Washington, and northern California to *Salton Sea* in the southern California desert near the Mexican border. They include river deltas, mountains, volcanic remnants, and great marshes. Some of them are critically important as links in the Pacific Flyway; others provide sanctuary for endangered and threatened species. The Hawaiian refuges, which are for the most part not open to the public, are particularly important in this latter respect.

WASHINGTON

Columbia in southeastern Washington state is a curious and interesting place geologically. It rests on a great lava field—the Columbia Plateau—formed by an ancient earthquake which opened cracks thirty to fifty miles deep and sent lava pouring over the surface in layers up to 4,500 feet thick. Melting glaciers only twelve thousand years ago scoured the land into a spectacular complex of buttes, basins and rock mesas known as the Drumheller Channels.

The small subspecies of the white-tailed deer which gave its name to *Columbian White-tailed Deer* in southwest Washington has such a limited range that it may spend its entire life without leaving one large field. As settlers cleared and fenced the land for agricultural use its numbers diminished and by the 1930s it was thought to be extinct. A remnant herd of two hundred was discovered and this refuge of about 4,800 acres set aside for its protection. While the population has grown somewhat and is stable, the subspecies still is considered endangered. It can be seen readily here, along woods edges at morning and evening.

McNary is a small (3,629 acres) wildlife oasis in a rapidly developing section of southeast Washington. It was established to replace lands submerged by McNary dam and functions as both a stopover and a wintering area for waterfowl.

Nisqually is an astonishingly pure and unpolluted river delta located on Puget Sound in Olympia within a few miles of populations of around two million persons in the Seattle-Tacoma-Olympia area. It is one of the refuges that owes its existence to the efforts of local citizens who worked to save the area from proposals to turn it into either a sanitary landfill or a deep-water port. It attracts a variety of interesting sea birds such as three species of scoters, auks, murres, murrelets, and loons, four species of grebes, and nineteen of dabbling and diving ducks.

Ridgefield is a small (three-thousand-acre) refuge on the Columbia River floodplain in southwest Washington. It winters up to forty thousand ducks and fifteen thousand geese including the uncommon dusky Canada goose. During the cool months there are several hundred whistling swans.

Turnbull occupies a beautiful part of the "channeled scablands" of east-central Washington with a wide variety of interesting scenery and wildlife. Coyote are common; porcupine and beaver are readily visible. Rare trumpeter swans often nest not far from headquarters. Among interesting small birds here are pygmy nuthatches, mountain chickadees, and western and mountain bluebirds.

Willapa in the extreme southwest corner of the state on Willapa Bay is a secret national treasure with marvelous habitat for wildlife including ocean bay and tidelands, sand dunes, grasslands, and rain forest uplands. Its Leadbetter Point unit offers some of the best seabird viewing of any point on the Pacific Coast. Long Island, in the bay, has more than three thousand acres of marsh, meadow, and forest, some of it hundreds of years old. This island supports the densest black bear population in this part of the country along with elk, black-tailed deer, coyote, beaver, and river otter.

OREGON

Hart Mountain National Antelope Range is a primary refuge for the beautiful and graceful pronghorn—once almost as abundant as the buffalo with numbers in the central and western states estimated at forty million in the early 1800s. Within a hundred years overhunting and waste (thousands were killed to serve as bait for poisoning wolves and coyote) almost extinguished the species. This refuge was set aside in 1936—241,000 acres in eastern Oregon for summer range—and works in tandem with 570,000-acre Sheldon Antelope Range across the Nevada border about thirty miles southeast where the animals winter. Up to eight thousand antelope use the two ranges.

Malheur in southeastern Oregon not far from Hart Mountain is known for its wide variety of wildlife. Its 282 square miles of marsh, high desert, ponds, river bottom, and lakes harbor 57 species of mammals and over 260 of birds, including a hundred nesting bird species. Sandhill cranes perform spectacular and easily seen courtship dances here. Golden eagles nest in the rim rocks. Up to four hundred thousand avocets come through in migration, along with hundreds of thousands of geese and ducks. There are large breeding populations of ducks and long-legged wading birds, as many as twenty thousand whistling swans in spring migration, and a wide variety of interesting small birds.

Umatilla stretches for twenty miles along both sides of the Columbia River in Oregon and Washington with headquarters in northeastern Oregon. It was set aside to replace water-bird habitat lost when the John Day Dam was built, and it offers breeding, migration and wintering habitat for up to three hundred thousand waterfowl. It also provides, according to a study by Oregon State University, the densest wintering small bird population in the Northwest.

The *Willamette Valley Complex* is made up of three refuges— *Ankenny, Baskett Slough,* and *William Finley*—which provide wildlife habitat in this otherwise intensely farmed and developed valley, the western terminus of the Oregon Trail. A primary function of these refuges is to provide wintering grounds for the dusky Canada goose, but they provide interesting birding as well for such as band-tailed pigeons, varied thrushes, black-headed grosbeaks, and lazuli buntings.

CALIFORNIA

Humboldt Bay on the northern California redwood coast near Arcata was established to protect eelgrass beds and thereby provide protection for the West Coast subspecies of brant which dines almost exclusively on eelgrass during its migration. Almost the entire population stops here on its flight between its nests on the subarctic tundra and its wintering grounds in Mexico.

Kern and *Pixley* nestle in the lower San Joaquin Valley where Tulare Lake once spread over eight hundred square miles, supporting an abundance of wildlife—millions of waterfowl, trout weighing up to forty pounds, and great herds of elk and deer. It was drained in the late nineteenth century and now only scattered remnants of wetlands remain. These refuges are among them and when water is available they support hundreds of thousands of wintering water birds, along with good populations of raptors. Kern also harbors two endangered species—the San Joaquin kit fox and the blunt-nosed leopard lizard on which it often preys.

In the fall the refuges of the *Klamath Basin* of California and Oregon have some of the largest concentrations of migrating ducks and geese found anywhere in the world—sometimes several million passing through. Following them are up to five hundred bald eagles which winter here. Both bald and golden eagles also nest here along with eight species of hawks.

Modoc in the northeastern corner of the state is a lovely small refuge which harbors good populations of courting and nesting sandhill cranes, eleven species of breeding ducks, and a variety of other marsh and water birds. Antelope regularly cross the refuge in their spring and fall migrations between winter and summer range.

Sacramento with its three nearby satellite refuges provides one of the most important wintering areas for waterfowl in the Pacific Flyway. From October through January 300,000 or more geese and a million or more ducks are here along with tens of thousands of shorebirds.

Salton Sea in the southern California desert is the largest inland body of water west of the Rockies, 375 square miles with a 115-mile shoreline formed when the mighty Colorado burst its man-made channels in 1905 and rampaged for two years, spilling its waters and silt into this arid basin. From January through March there are large concentrations of wintering water birds. In spring and summer the refuge gets interesting visitors from Mexico, which lies only twenty miles south, including wood storks, blue-footed and brown boobies, roseate spoonbills, and fulvous tree ducks.

The 15,400-acre refuge at the south end of *San Francisco Bay* is one of the nation's newest and like Nisqually owes its existence to efforts of various citizens' groups—Sierra Club, Audubon, Nature Conservancy, and others. At one time or another during the year 70 per cent of the shorebirds in the Pacific Flyway stop here. The refuge also is home to two endangered species—the California clapper rail and the salt marsh harvest mouse.

San Luis lies in the San Joaquin Valley in the south-central interior lowlands. In addition to serving as an important station on the Pacific Flyway it has an impressive herd of scarce Tule elk and a varied and interesting bird population. The area including and around the refuge winters about half the world population of Ross' geese, up to 15,000 sandhill cranes, and in a good year 250,000 long-billed dowitchers, 100,000 phalaropes, and 20,000 snipes.

The Hawaiian and *Pacific Islands* group of refuges are critically important to a number of endangered species and subspecies driven to the edge of extinction by the pattern of rapid habitat destruction and promiscuous introduction of exotic species that has characterized development of these beautiful islands. The western Hawaiian Islands (generally known as the Leewards) are remote and unpeopled and serve as nesting habitat for such sea birds as sooty and fairy terns, the black-footed and Laysan albatrosses, and wedge-tailed and Christmas shearwaters. Because of the function these refuges serve most permit no public access. Exceptions are existing refuges and headquarters on Kauai and a refuge in the process of acquisition on Maui.

The following is a list of some birds of special interest found in common or abundant status at the refuges of this region.

Birds Common or Abundant at Seasons Indicated:

S: Spring   s: Summer   F: Fall   W: Winter

Arctic Loon: Dungeness, W; Willapa, SW.
Sooty Shearwater: Willapa, sF.
Brant's Cormorant: Dungeness, SsFW; Willapa, SFW.
Pelagic Cormorant: Willapa, SFW.
Wood Stork: Salton Sea, s.
White-faced Ibis: Malheur, sF; San Luis, W.
Black Brant: Willapa, SW.
Ross' Goose: Klamath Basin, S; Merced, SFW; Sacramento, FW; San Luis, W.
Fulvous Whistling Duck: Salton Sea, s.
Barrow's Goldeneye: Dungeness, FW; McNary, W.
Harlequin Duck: Dungeness, SFW.
White-tailed Kite: Sacramento, SsFW; San Francisco Bay, SsFW; San Luis, FW.
Goshawk: Willapa, SsFW.
Cooper's Hawk: Willapa, SsFW.
Golden Eagle: Hart Mountain, SsFW; Kern, W; Klamath Basin, W.
Bald Eagle: Dungeness, W; Klamath Basin, SW; Willapa, SsFW.
Blue Grouse: Willapa, SsFW.
Ruffed Grouse: Willamette Valley, SsFW; Willapa, SsFW.
Sage Grouse: Hart Mountain, SsFW.
California Quail: Columbia, SsFW; Dungeness, SsFW; Klamath Basin, SsFW; Malheur, SsFW; McNary, SsFW; Merced, SsFW; Modoc, SsFW; Turnbull, SsFW; Umatilla, SsFW; Willamette Valley, SsFW.

Chukar: Columbia, SsFW; Malheur, SsFW.
Snowy Plover: San Francisco Bay, sW; Willapa, Ss.
Mountain Plover: Kern, FW; Salton Sea, FW.
Baird's Sandpiper: Turnbull, F.
Surfbird: Dungeness, W.
Black Turnstone: Dungeness, SFW; Willapa, SFW.
Band-tailed Pigeon: Willamette Valley, s; Willapa, sF.
Northern Phalarope: Columbia, sW; Hart Mountain, F;
    Salton Sea, SF; San Francisco Bay, SsF; Willapa, SF.
Glaucous-winged Gull: Dungeness, SsFW; San Francisco Bay, SFW;
    Willapa, SFW.
Western Gull: Dungeness, SsFW; Willapa, SFW.
Thayer's Gull: Dungeness, W.
Mew Gull: Dungeness, SW; Willapa, SFW.
Heermann's Gull: Dungeness, F; Willapa, F.
Black-legged Kittiwake: Dungeness, W; Willapa, F.
Common Murre: Willapa, SsF.
Pigeon Guillemot: Dungeness, W; Willapa, SF.
Rhinoceros Auklet: Dungeness, sW.
Tufted Puffin: Dungeness, SW.
Roadrunner: Kern, SsFW; Salton Sea, SsFW.
Burrowing Owl: Kern, SsFW; McNary, SsFW; Merced, SW;
    Sacramento, SsFW; Salton Sea, SsFW; San Francisco Bay,
    SsFW; San Luis, SsFW; Umatilla, Ss.
Lesser Nighthawk: Kern, S; Salton Sea, Ss.
Rufous Hummingbird: Dungeness, Ss; Malheur, sF;
    Willamette Valley, Ss; Willapa, SsF.
Lewis' Woodpecker: San Luis, F.
Nuttall's Woodpecker: Sacramento, SsFW; San Luis, S.
Ash-throated Flycatcher: Hart Mountain, sF; McNary, Ss;
    Sacramento, Ss; San Luis, Ss.
Black Phoebe: Sacramento, SsFW; Salton Sea, SFW;
    San Francisco Bay, W; San Luis, SsFW.
Hammond's Flycatcher: Dungeness, Ss; Hart Mountain, sF.
Dusky Flycatcher: Hart Mountain, sF.
Western Flycatcher: Dungeness, Ss; Klamath Basin, s; Willapa, sF.
Olive-sided Flycatcher: Dungeness, s; Hart Mountain, sF; Willapa, Ss.
Common Raven: Hart Mountain, SsFW; Kern, SFW;
    Malheur, SsFW; San Luis, SFW; Umatilla, SsFW.
Scrub Jay: Ridgefield, W; Willamette Valley, SsFW.
Steller's Jay: Dungeness, SsFW; Klamath Basin, sF;
    Willamette Valley, SFW; Willapa, SsFW.
Northwestern Crow: Dungeness, SsFW; Willapa, SsFW.

Verdin: Salton Sea, SsFW.
Mountain Chickadee: Hart Mountain, sF; Modoc, SsFW:
    Turnbull, SsFW.
Chestnut-backed Chickadee: Dungeness, SsFW;
    Willapa, SsFW.
Pygmy Nuthatch: Turnbull, SsFW.
Common Bushtit: Willamette Valley, SsFW.
Bewick's Wren: Dungeness, SsFW; Ridgefield, SsFW;
    San Francisco Bay, W; San Luis, s; Willamette Valley, SsFW.
Cañon Wren: Hart Mountain, sF.
Rock Wren: Columbia, Ss; Malheur, SsF.
Sage Thrasher: Malheur, SsF; Modoc, sF.
Varied Thrush: Columbia, S; Dungeness, SFW; Ridgefield, SW;
    Sacramento, W; Willamette Valley, W; Willapa, SFW.
Western Bluebird: Turnbull, F.
Mountain Bluebird: Columbia, S; Hart Mountain, sF; Salton Sea, W;
    Turnbull, SF.
Townsend's Solitaire: Hart Mountain, sF; Willapa, Ss.
Bohemian Waxwing: McNary, FW.
Northern Shrike: Klamath Basin, W; Turnbull, W; Willapa, W.
Black-throated Gray Warbler: Willapa, SF.
Wilson's Warbler: Kern, S; McNary, s; Modoc, SF; Salton Sea, SF;
    Willapa, SsF.
Western Tanager: Dungeness, Ss; Hart Mountain, sF; Kern, SF;
    Klamath Basin, s; Malheur, SF; Salton Sea, S; San Luis, S.
Black-headed Grosbeak: Dungeness, Ss; San Francisco Bay, Ss;
    Willamette Valley, Ss.
Lazuli Bunting: Willamette Valley, s.
Lesser Goldfinch: San Francisco Bay, SsF.
Brown Towhee: San Luis, Ss.
Sage Sparrow: Columbia, Ss; Kern, F; Klamath Basin, SsF;
    Malheur, SsF; Modoc, SsF.
Brewer's Sparrow: Hart Mountain, sF; Klamath Basin, Ss;
    Malheur, SsF.
Golden-crowned Sparrow: Columbia, SF; San Luis, S;
    Willapa, SsW.

THE WEST COAST and HAWAII

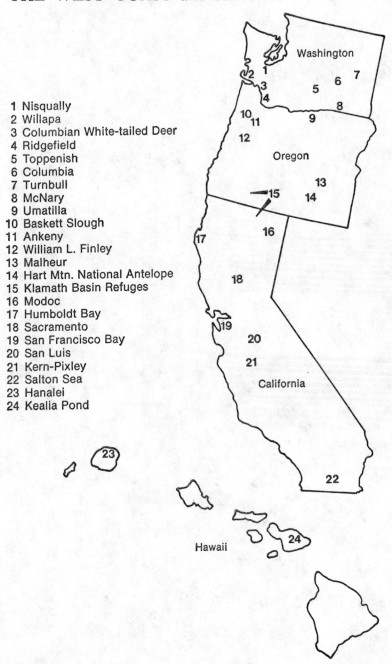

1 Nisqually
2 Willapa
3 Columbian White-tailed Deer
4 Ridgefield
5 Toppenish
6 Columbia
7 Turnbull
8 McNary
9 Umatilla
10 Baskett Slough
11 Ankeny
12 William L. Finley
13 Malheur
14 Hart Mtn. National Antelope
15 Klamath Basin Refuges
16 Modoc
17 Humboldt Bay
18 Sacramento
19 San Francisco Bay
20 San Luis
21 Kern-Pixley
22 Salton Sea
23 Hanalei
24 Kealia Pond

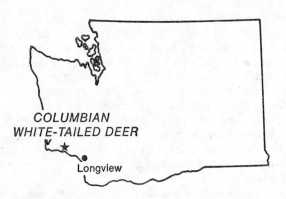

COLUMBIAN
WHITE-TAILED DEER

Longview

COLUMBIAN WHITE-TAILED DEER
(Washington and Oregon)

The explorers Lewis and Clark were the first white men to see the Columbian white-tailed deer, and it was abundant when they first set foot on this part of southeastern Washington in 1806. That situation did not last long, for this small subspecies has such a limited range it may live its entire life without leaving one large field—a lifestyle that ill suited it for adaptation and survival when settlers cleared much of the land for agriculture.

By the 1930s this lovely animal with the flashing snowy tail was believed to be extinct. Then a remnant herd of two hundred was discovered, and this refuge of 4,800 acres was set aside for them in 1972. The population has grown somewhat and is considered precariously stable, though still classed as endangered. Today the graceful Columbian can readily be seen, with spotted fawns in summer. It is even more visible when vegetation dies back in fall and winter; then it can be seen against the woods edges most mornings and evenings from the road which circles the refuge mainland section.

This relatively small refuge of mixed grassland interspersed with stands of sitka spruces, red alders, and willows and Columbia River bottomland has other interesting sights to offer as well.

Band-tailed pigeons appear, sometimes in large flocks on the Tenasillahe Island unit in the fall, and mink, beaver, river otter, and nutria may be seen there as well, either with binoculars or spotting scope from the mainland or by taking a boat across and hiking the nine-mile dike trail around it.

Elk usually come down from the uplands in mid-September to spend the winter, and long-tailed weasel and coyote are common.

Flocks of hundreds of goldfinches are a common sight in spring, as are golden-crowned sparrows, varied thrushes, Steller's jays, Bewick's wrens, Wilson's warblers, and a bird released from captivity which has thrived in its freedom here. This is the Japanese green pheasant, similar to its gorgeous ring-necked relative but with a greenish breast.

Loons are common in the sloughs in winter. Rufous humming-birds sun themselves in summer on wires and bare branches.

Great blue herons are around all year, as are red-tailed hawks with at least four nests on the refuge most years which usually can be seen with binoculars.

And an early springtime spectacular is the smelt run, when these silvery foot-long fish swim up the Columbia River in tremendous numbers to spawn from January to March. They attract tens of thousands of gulls—herring and ring-billed, western, glaucous-winged, California and a few Bonaparte's—for miles along the river between Longview and the refuge. Along with them are ten or twelve bald eagles which sit on dead snags and steal from the gulls or, if they have to (it's not very difficult with these huge numbers), catch their own.

Migrant waterfowl may build to a peak of 110,000 in fall, of which almost half may be wigeon, and a thousand geese, mostly dusky and lesser Canadas. Hundreds of snipe go through, and sometimes up to five hundred whistling swans stay the winter.

Also administered from the Columbian White-tailed Deer office is 8,300-acre *Lewis and Clark* Refuge (Oregon), made up largely of islands, sandbars, and open water in the estuary of the Columbia River. It provides wintering and resting areas for swans, waterfowl, and shorebirds, and is accessible only by boat, which in these tidal waters with sudden winds and changing river bottoms often requires an expert boatman. In any case, consult with refuge headquarters before planning such a trip.

How to get there: From Longview take Route 4 west 22 miles; 2 miles beyond Cathlamet is refuge sign.

Open: Daylight hours, year-round.

Best times to visit: Spring, fall, winter.

What to see: Columbian white-tailed deer; also elk, waterfowl, spectacular smelt runs.

What to do: Twelve miles of roads for driving, hiking, bicycling; photography (can be good from car window); limited waterfowl hunting; blackberry picking in August and September.

Where to stay: MOTELS—Longview, 22 miles east. CAMPGROUNDS—Fort Canby State Park, 45 miles west.

Weather notes: Rainy and overcast much of the time, especially in winter (annual precipitation 106 inches). Boots can be handy.

Points of interest nearby: Fort Columbia State Park, 35 miles west; Willapa National Wildlife Refuge, 30 miles west.

For more information: Columbian White-tailed Deer National Wildlife Refuge, Rt. 1, Box 376-C, Cathlamet, Washington 98612. Phone: (206) 795-4915.

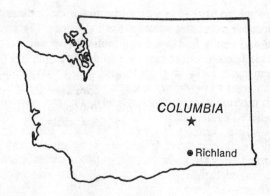

COLUMBIA (Washington)

Columbia Refuge in southeastern Washington is a 29,000-acre wintering area for more than a hundred thousand ducks and other waterfowl, including Canada geese and whistling swans. It is a fascinating and beautiful place geologically. Some of its rocks are sixty million years old, dating from a time well before violent earthquakes here opened cracks thirty to fifty miles deep from which volcanic eruptions sent molten lava pouring over the surface in layers which now form the Columbia Plateau, 4,500 feet thick in some places, one of the great lava fields of the world.

About a million years ago, the Cascade Mountain Range to the west was upthrust; then just twelve thousand years ago, during the Pleistocene Ice Age, melting glacial dams sent enormous walls of water into the area, scouring it into a spectacular complex of buttes, basins, rock mesas, and abandoned cataracts known as the Drumheller Channels, which can be seen along the auto tour route and are stunningly scenic and dramatic.

Since the creation of the nearby Columbia Basin irrigation project in 1952, seepage water has formed more than a hundred lakes, ponds, sloughs, streams, and wet meadows.

Wildlife abounds in the area. Coyote are common, and yellow-bellied marmots, "mini-bears" that look halfway between a squirrel and a woodchuck, are a frequent sight especially in spring and early summer. Beaver and muskrat also live here, with Townsend's ground squirrels, a few mule deer, and an occasional bobcat.

Nine species of ducks breed here, including cinnamon teal, mallard, and ruddy ducks, their broods conspicuous during the summer months. The refuge also is one of the most important resting and wintering areas for migratory waterfowl in the Pacific Flyway.

Red-tailed and marsh hawks are common all year and nest, as do a few rare prairie falcons. Great blue herons and ring-necked pheasants are a common sight. California quails and chukar partridges are usually around in good numbers but are less visible. Short-eared owls are often out on afternoon hunting forays, and the rare western burrowing owl is believed to nest here.

Interesting birds which are present at least seasonally include raucous and spectacular black-billed magpies, nighthawks (out all day in summer), Say's phoebes, rock and long-billed marsh wrens, horned larks, varied thrushes, mountain bluebirds, and a good assortment of sparrows—the vesper, sage, lark, white-crowned and golden-crowned. In winter there are sometimes flocks of gray-crowned rosy finches.

Among the shorebirds, Wilson's and northern phalaropes are usually present sometime during the warm months, along with long-billed curlews (some of which nest), long-billed dowitchers, yellow-legs, and spotted and western sandpipers. Bald and golden eagles usually spend the winter.

Columbia also administers *Saddle Mountain*, a 30,810-acre refuge of sagebrush-grasslands and sand dunes about thirty miles west of Columbia along the last free-flowing stretch of the Columbia River. It serves as a wintering waterfowl area where ducks and geese nest as well. Located within a nuclear reactor control zone, it is closed to all public use.

How to get there: From Othello take Broadway which becomes McManaman Road northwest 6 miles to Morgan Lake Road and refuge signs, then northeast ½ mile to field office. Tour route is a continuation on county roads past office.

Open: Twenty-four hours, year-round.

Best times to visit: November and March for migratory waterfowl, April and May for breeding birds.

What to see: Migrating and wintering waterfowl; whistling swans; coyote; spectacular scenery.

What to do: Twenty-five miles of roads for driving and hiking, including an auto tour route, nature trail, dikes in the marsh unit, and some public roads. Fishing can be very good for rainbow and brown trout, also bass, but season opening usually crowded. Limited hunting for waterfowl, upland game.

Where to stay: MOTELS—In Othello. CAMPGROUNDS—On refuge in designated areas; also Potholes Reservoir State Park, 2 miles northwest.

Weather notes: Temperature 100+ in summer, below zero in January–February.

Points of interest nearby: Dry Falls State Park (waterfalls), 50 miles north.

For more information: Columbia National Wildlife Refuge, P.O. Drawer F, Othello, Washington 99344. Phone: (509) 488-3831.

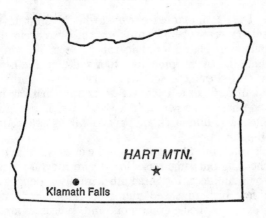

HART MTN.
★
Klamath Falls

HART MOUNTAIN (Oregon)

The pronghorn antelope, beautiful and graceful and swiftest of North American mammals, exists on no other continent. That it lives at all is due in part to two national wildlife refuges—Hart Mountain in Oregon and the Sheldon Antelope Range in Nevada.

This sturdy small-hoofed animal has as well perhaps the keenest vision of any mammal on the continent. Its protruding eyes can see both forward and backward and discern small moving objects four miles away. It once was almost as a abundant as the buffalo, its numbers in the central and western states estimated at forty million in the early 1800s. Within seventy-five years it was brought low by persecution and overhunting; thousands were killed for use as poison bait for wolves and coyote. Some felt it was already extinct. But a few remained, and the animals' supporters, including many private citizens and civic groups in this area who now belong to a local conservation group proudly called the Order of the Antelope to mark their achievement, worked for establishment of a sanctuary area for them.

The refuge was set aside in 1936—241,000 acres comprising Hart Mountain, a massive fault-block ridge where the antelope spend the summer and have their young; and 570,420-acre Sheldon Range and refuge, thirty miles southeast as the crow flies, where herds of eight thousand or more sometimes spend the winter (and many stay the summer as well). So successful have these efforts been that nucleus herds have been transplanted elsewhere in the west to re-establish this handsome species where its numbers had been decimated.

The antelope at Hart Mountain can be seen in spring, summer, and fall along the twenty-mile auto tour route on the high, flat desert plateau that rises 4,000 feet from lake-strewn Warner Valley to an elevation of 8,065 feet. There are other trails that can be followed as well if one has a four-wheel drive "and steel nerves," advises one refuge staffer; and horseback riding and hiking are permitted anywhere on the refuge.

But look carefully. Stop and scan the area with binoculars frequently, checking out large rocks to be sure they are rocks and not antelope, or mule deer, for these are here also, along with coyote, bobcat, a few bighorn sheep and wild horses and such smaller mammals as yellow-bellied marmots and kangaroo rats. Rarely a mountain lion passes through. There can be nighthawks, too, basking on the road at midday, looking exactly like rocks themselves.

Birding can be good for small birds, especially around the field headquarters and in a large grove of ponderosa pines at the tour route end. One can spot white-breasted and sometimes red-breasted and pygmy nuthatches, Steller's jays, Townsend's solitaires, mountain bluebirds and chickadees, cañon and rock wrens, evening grosbeaks, and sometimes calliope hummingbirds. Chukar partridge and sage grouse are common (the latter a marvelous sight on their courtship dancing grounds). So are short-eared owls, red-tailed hawks and seasonally Swainson's and rough-leggeds. Golden eagles nest. Prairie falcons and flammulated owls probably do likewise.

The whole Warner Valley from which Hart Mountain ascends is historically an outstanding ornithological area where great numbers of water birds stop in migration and some also nest—grebes, white pelicans, sandhill cranes, snowy and great egrets, white-fronted and Ross' geese, and nineteen species of ducks. One visitor looked back over the valley on a recent spring day to see ten thousand whistling swans covering one small lake. So keep an eye out—but at least one eye on that narrow twisting road!

How to get there: From Lakeview (where headquarters are located) take Route 395 north 5 miles to Route 140, east 25 miles to Plush cutoff and refuge sign, north on Route 313 to Plush; just after Plush follow pavement east and then north along base of Hart Mountain to field office at the end of Poker Jim Ridge.

Open: Twenty-four hours.

Best times to visit: Late April–late October.

What to see: Pronghorn antelope, mule deer, California bighorn sheep; Indian petroglyphs; birding can be good too.

What to do: Twenty-mile auto tour route (other roads for 4-wheel drive); picnicking; hiking and horseback riding anywhere; rockhounding; limited hunting for sheep, antelope; mule deer; fishing for crappie, cutthroat trout.

Where to stay: MOTELS—In Lakeview. CAMPGROUNDS—Primitive at Hot Springs on refuge; overnight permits for horseback, backpackers; various national forest sites in area.

Weather notes: Freezing weather likely any month of the year; snow closes many roads in winter; many roads may be closed throughout spring and early summer due to muddy road conditions and washouts.

What to take and wear: Four-wheel drive for secondary roads; emergency food, water, first-aid supplies.

Points of interest nearby: Sheldon National Wildlife Refuge, 90 miles southeast (by road); Malheur National Wildlife Refuge, 70 miles northeast (42 miles if the shorter road is open); Fremont National Forest, 40 miles southwest.

For more information: Hart Mountain National Antelope Refuge, P.O. Box 111, Lakeview, Oregon 97630. Phone: (503) 947-3315.

HUMBOLDT BAY (California)

On the map the range of the black brant appears as the slenderest of corridors barely skirting the West Coast of the United States and extending up the Pacific edge through to Alaska and even beyond the Arctic Circle. There this small, dark western subspecies of the brant nests on the subarctic tundra bordering the Bering Sea—the most beautiful nest, some believe, of any waterfowl, deep and downy and with no extraneous matter, only the soft pluckings from the breast of the female bird.

It is for the brant, which dines almost exclusively on eelgrass during migration from wintering areas, that this refuge has been established—for Humboldt Bay has eelgrass in abundance, one of only a half dozen such places on the West Coast. Almost the entire population of nearly two hundred thousand stops over here en route to and from its Mexican wintering grounds, peaking as high as forty thousand in early April. Duck hunting pressure in fall keeps the birds offshore. But as sanctuary areas become established in this relatively new refuge they should be seen more often then, too.

They are only one of the interesting wild inhabitants of this northern California refuge which is still in a state of development and land acquisition, its projected 8,600 acres of salt marsh, tidal mudflats, sandspit, uplands, and open water approved largely at the behest of local citizens.

The second largest colony of herons and egrets in California is in a stand of Monterey cypress and eucalyptus—mostly great egrets but some black-crowned and great blue herons, too.

A midwinter count of some sixty thousand ducks and one hundred and fifty thousand shorebirds is not uncommon—wigeon, pintail, green-winged teal, dunlins, willets, least sandpipers, black turnstones, long-billed dowitchers, among others. Whistling swans are here in fall and winter.

In fact, the whole bird list is formidable. Sightings include white-tailed kites, red-shouldered and red-tailed hawks, peregrine and prairie falcons, western and pied-billed grebes, double-crested and pelagic cormorants, brown pelicans, white-winged and surf scoters, Virginia rails, California quails. Among the small birds are Anna's hummingbirds, black phoebes, common bushtits, and for at least three seasons Swainson's thrushes, Lincoln's sparrows, pine siskins, water pipits, black-headed grosbeaks, violet-green swallows, orange-crowned and Wilson's warblers, and many others.

Several hundred harbor seals are here and have their pups in January and February. Pacific harbor porpoises and northern sea lions are occasionally seen, as are river otters.

December is the height of the gray whale southern migration, sometimes visible within a mile of the shore by their spouting and "rolling." One of the best vantage points for this is Table Bluff County Park overlooking the refuge and ocean with a 180-degree panoramic view from the ocean to the snow-capped peaks of the Siskiyou range to the Trinity National Forest.

Many of the walks and tour routes are still in planning and development so access to the various areas should be determined by a call to the refuge office (open weekdays).

How to get there: From Eureka take Route 101 south to Hookton Road which parallels the south end of the refuge and leads to the south spit. All refuge units can be reached from Route 101. (Refuge has office in Eureka.)

Open: Daylight hours all year (office weekdays only).

Best times to visit: All year.

What to see: Black brant, egrets, and excellent range of bird types; whales in migration.

What to do: Trails; observation tower; photography (blinds planned); fishing—so-so on refuge but outstanding in area for salmon, steelhead, and trout; clamming; limited duck hunting; pelagic research trips from Humboldt State University to view sea birds, migrating whales. Or rent a boat nearby for seal and sea-bird viewing (reserve ahead during salmon season).

Where to stay: MOTELS—Several in and near Eureka. CAMPGROUNDS —Patrick's Point, Trinidad Beach, Little River Beach, state parks, all within 30 miles north; Grizzly Creek, 35 miles southeast.

Weather notes: Temperatures generally pleasant but rains often during winter and periods of fog May through September (Arcata airport 10 miles north is renowned as the foggiest in the world).

What to take and wear: Waterproof clothing and footgear. Spotting scope for offshore viewing of sea birds, seals, and whales.

Points of interest nearby: Prairie Creek Redwoods State Park with herd of local coastal elk; many parks containing magnificent stands of redwoods in the area. If driving south on Route 101 take the parallel Avenue of the Giants through 25 miles of forest from Pepperwood.

For more information: Humboldt Bay National Wildlife Refuge, P.O. Box 1386, Eureka, California 95501. Phone: (707) 445-1352.

KERN-PIXLEY (California)

Tulare Lake, just west of Kern Refuge, once covered eight hundred square miles of California's lower San Joaquin Valley. It was the largest fresh-water lake west of the Mississippi River, with an abundance of wildlife—millions of waterfowl, trout weighing up to forty pounds, and great herds of elk and deer. In the late 1800s land was "claimed" from the lake bed by levees, and in a few years the lake bed was completely dried up. Rainfall is scarce—the valley lies in the rain shadow of the coast ranges—so the only surface water remaining in the valley came from river flooding. These floods now are contained by a series of dams and reservoirs in the Sierra Nevada foothills, and much of the former Tulare Lake area today is a semidesert.

It was to restore at least a part of this once vast waterfowl and wildlife habitat destroyed by reclamation that the Kern and Pixley refuges were established in the early 1960s. Together they amount to about fifteen thousand acres.

They have had partial success. When the refuges have water, they can support an impressive and abundant waterfowl population, with hundreds of thousands of wintering birds. But they have had no committed surface water and are dependent on deep wells or the purchase of surface water from the California aqueduct, which, during drought periods and with agricultural demands, becomes prohibitively costly. As a result, dry periods find the refuges able to offer little to attract and hold waterfowl.

During good years, however, the visitor may see large concentrations of ducks—mallard, gadwall, pintail, green-winged and cinnamon teal and ruddy ducks; great and snowy egrets; eared and pied-billed grebes; and impressive groupings of shorebirds as well—yellowlegs, long-billed curlews, dowitchers, avocets, stilts, and least and western sandpipers. Burrowing owls find good sites for their long underground tunnels (they lose when the others gain, since flooding destroys their homes).

Two endangered species, the San Joaquin kit fox and the blunt-nosed leopard lizard, on which it often preys, exist in uneasy juxtaposition in desert areas.

Swainson's hawks are common in fall and winter, and marsh, red-tailed, and sparrow hawks and golden eagles are easily seen most of the year. Ring-necked pheasant are common in brushy areas along with the introduced white-winged variety and a hybridized version of the two. Seasonally common small birds are horned larks, flickers, kingbirds, wood pewees, long-billed marsh wrens, yellow-rumped (Audubon's) and Wilson's warblers, western tanagers, goldfinches, and cliff, barn, and rough-winged swallows.

Striped and spotted skunk, raccoon, opossum, desert cottontail, black-tailed jackrabbit and coyote are resident, and muskrat are here when there is water.

The refuges support interesting and rare plants—the slough thistle, considered for endangered status, and brilliant blue phacelias in such numbers when there is sufficient moisture that they sometimes appear at a distance as sparkling bodies of water.

Pixley Refuge is located twenty miles northeast of Kern, and is open to visitors obtaining a permit from the Kern office. The two refuges are similar. Other areas administered from Kern are:

Hopper Mountain National Wildlife Refuge—1,871 acres of rugged mountains adjoining and acting as a buffer for the 53,000-acre Sespe Condor Sanctuary in the Los Padres National Forest. Visits by special arrangement only.

Seal Beach National Wildlife Refuge—977 acres superimposed on a United States Naval Weapons Station, established to preserve one of the largest remaining salt-marsh communities in southern California. No public use except by special permit.

How to get there: From Bakersfield take Route 99 north. Take first Delano exit, then left (west) about 20 miles on Garces Avenue which dead-ends at refuge headquarters.

Open: Daylight hours all year.

Best times to visit: September through March and April.

What to see: Waterfowl; shorebirds; pheasant (hybridized ringnecks and Afghan white-winged); coyote.

What to do: Short auto tour; hiking; limited hunting for waterfowl.

Where to stay: MOTELS—In Delano. CAMPGROUNDS—Buena Vista County Park, 24 miles south.

Weather notes: Summer hot, dry; often dense "Tule" fog in winter months.

Points of interest nearby: Sequoia National Forest, 65 miles northeast.

For more information: Kern-Pixley National Wildlife Refuges, P.O. Box 219, Delano, California 93215. Phone: (805) 725-2767.

KLAMATH
BASIN
REFUGES

★

● Klamath Falls

★

KLAMATH BASIN (California and Oregon)

The refuges of the Klamath Basin of California and Oregon are among the most exciting in the world, containing stunning concentrations of wildlife, sometimes several million ducks and geese in fall migration, the largest on the North American continent. There are also intimate glimpses of natural life of all kinds set against a background of spectacular scenic beauty in refuges covering almost a hundred thousand acres.

Some five hundred bald eagles winter here in the largest numbers outside Alaska. Sometimes more than a hundred can be counted from a single vantage point. Both bald and golden eagles nest, along with eight species of hawks and eight kinds of owls. In early summer, downy gray western grebe hatchlings are everywhere, riding about on the backs of their handsome ruby-eyed parents, sharing the marshes with young offspring of dozens of other water birds including more than sixty thousand ducklings and goslings that are produced here in a good year. Altogether more than 275 bird species have been counted, of which at least 180 have nested.

But it is the tremendous fall waterfowl concentrations on the Lower Klamath and Tule Lake units of this refuge complex that have attracted world renown. They can darken the sky when they come through in October and November, funneling southward from breeding grounds as far away as Siberia. Sometimes 250,000 snow geese can be seen in a single glance. The migration includes perhaps 80 per cent of the world population of their smaller cousins, the Ross' geese; plus Canadas, white-fronted, even an occasional emperor goose, and more than twenty duck species. It is an awesome and unforgettable sight and a particular delight to photographers, especially when the waterfowl fly up en masse in the late-day sun against a backdrop of snowy Mount Shasta.

Spring concentrations, usually in early March, are only a little less overwhelming—but whistling swans may be even more impressive in spring with up to ten thousand of these majestic white birds.

Significant nesting colonies are present on the complex as well, including white pelicans, double-crested cormorants, great blue herons, California and ring-billed gulls, Caspian terns, and sometimes hundreds of floating nests of the abundant eared grebes. Breeding avocets, coots, and black-necked stilts can be seen by the hundreds—as, in fact, can almost all the wildlife except some which congregate in inaccessible nesting groups where they are protected from disturbance. Even these can be viewed readily as they feed on the marsh and water areas in the early morning and late afternoon.

Mule deer are common year-round, and coyote in fall and winter; also yellow-bellied marmots and occasional antelope.

The best places to see the greatest numbers and variety are the tour roads on the Tule Lake and Lower Klamath units. The Clear Lake unit, while providing habitat for pronghorn antelope, is unimproved. Upper Klamath is almost entirely marsh and water, with a fine canoe trail where water birds, including red-necked grebes, can be seen. Boats are available for rental, and camping also, at a nearby Forest Service concession.

A new visitor center is evolving on an impressive overlook where Tule Lake Refuge adjoins the Lava Beds National Monument, bringing together the history of the land with the wildlife that inhabits it. There are extensive lava beds, with caves that can be explored in the Monument.

Large as the concentrations of birds are here, they were even higher a generation ago—up to seven million or more in the 1950s. Why? No one is quite sure. But the change points up the critical significance of refuges such as these, without which such populations would have nowhere to go for their continued existence.

How to get there: From Tule Lake, go west 5 miles on East-West Road, then ⅛ mile south via Hill Road to Klamath Basin headquarters. There get maps for all 5 refuge units.

Open: Daylight hours (office weekdays).

Best times to visit: March through May and mid-September through mid-November (but much to see all year).

What to see: Tremendous concentrations of migrating and nesting waterfowl as well as grebes, pelicans, waders, shorebirds, prairie falcons, coyote, mule deer, bald eagles in winter, many others.

What to do: Auto tour routes on Lower Klamath and Tule Lake, other roads of varying quality for driving, hiking (some may be closed in wet weather). Public roads also afford viewing. Photography (blinds available). Canoe trail on Upper Klamath. Fishing in Upper Klamath and Klamath Forest. Limited hunting for waterfowl, upland and big game. Guided tours for organized groups can be arranged.

Where to stay: MOTELS—In Tule Lake, also Klamath Falls, 25 miles north. CAMPGROUNDS—In Tule Lake, also Lava Beds National Monument, adjacent on south.

Weather notes: Winter travel can be difficult.

Points of interest nearby: Lava Beds National Monument (see CAMPGROUNDS); Miller Island State Wildlife Management Area, 25 miles northwest; Medicine Lake Highlands of Modoc National Forest, 25 miles south (one of the world's largest shield volcanoes); Crater Lake National Park, 75 miles northwest; Lower Klamath Refuge unit, 12 miles west; Upper Klamath unit, 50 miles north; Klamath Forest unit, 75 miles north; Clear Lake unit, 25 miles east (all located from Tule Lake unit refuge headquarters).

For more information: Klamath Basin National Wildlife Refuges, Route 1, Box 74, Tule Lake, California 96134. Phone: (916) 667-2231.

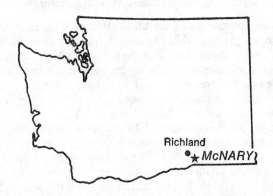

Richland
★ *McNARY*

McNARY (Washington)

This 3,631 acres of fields, marsh, and open water along with several islands in the Columbia and Snake rivers is a wildlife oasis amid increasing land development in this part of southeast Washington. Some thirty thousand ducks and forty thousand geese come here in spring and fall migration. Many, except in the most severe weather, stay through the winter.

Established in 1955 partly to replace wildlife lands submerged by construction of McNary Dam, it has not been highly developed for visitor use. There is a one-mile interpretive walking trail around one of the lakes and several miles of public roads where most of the refuge lands can be seen—chiefly along South Lake Road and the Humorist Road which borders on the south side, and the Hansen Loop Road on the west. A spotting scope would be helpful for identifying smaller species.

Nesting birds include Canada geese, mallard, gadwall, pintail, green and cinnamon teal, wigeon, shoveler, and some redheads and canvasback. Many of these are here in winter. Also wintering are scaup, ring-necked, bufflehead, and both common and Barrow's goldeneye. Among the raptors are marsh and red-tailed hawks, short-eared and burrowing owls. There are ring-necked pheasants; also great blue and black-crowned night herons (some of these nesting on adjoining state land but visiting the refuge), small numbers of avocets, long-billed curlews, and Wilson's phalaropes. A large colony of ring-billed and California gulls—some years ten thousand of them—nest on one of the islands, along with some Caspian and Forster's terns.

Black-billed magpies and long-billed marsh wrens are common, as, seasonally among the small birds, are ash-throated flycatchers, violet-green swallows, red-breasted nuthatches, Wilson's and yellow warblers in the willows and pond edges, vesper, white-crowned, and lark sparrows in the grasslands, and sometimes Bohemian waxwings in winter. White pelicans and whistling swans usually appear in small numbers in spring and fall.

Coyote are fairly common, hunting rodents. Mule deer and beaver sometimes also can be seen.

McNary also administers *Conboy Lake,* a beautiful refuge of forest and mountain meadow at the foot of snow-covered Mount Adams near Glenwood. It has marvelous wildlife—many kinds of birds, especially those of the higher elevations, along with black-tailed deer, beaver, coyote, and (though not easily seen) elk and black bear and sometimes river otter.

Waterfowl concentrations in fall and spring occasionally approach ten thousand and bald and golden eagles are around most of the year.

Until recently at least facilities have been minimal, though there is a self-guided walking trail—but for the most part the visitor must make his way on his own while land for this refuge still is being acquired. It can be well worth the effort.

Sandhill cranes stop over and in recent years there have been nest attempts. Ruffed grouse are common, blue and spruce grouse here also, along with occasional wild turkey, and usually several nests of red-tailed hawks and screech and great horned owls.

Among small birds, common at least seasonally are rufous and calliope hummingbirds, hairy woodpeckers (and occasionally pileated and Lewis'), mountain chickadees, mountain and western bluebirds, red-breasted nuthatches, varied thrushes, red crossbills, and sometimes dippers. There is also a wide variety of reptiles, amphibians, and plants, their inventory still being taken.

Fishing is permitted on Outlet Creek for rainbow and brook trout.

For further information contact McNary headquarters or Conboy Lake National Wildlife Refuge, Box 5, Glenwood, Washington 98948. Phone: (509) 364-3410.

Like Conboy Lake, *Toppenish* has been in a state of acquisition and development, but there is fine wildlife in this refuge of fields, marsh, and wetlands along Toppenish Creek in the Lower Yakima Valley of south-central Washington. Established largely to provide for the needs of nesting waterfowl, including up to a quarter of a million ducks that may appear in the area seasonally, it has much else as well.

Beaver maintain several colonies. Bobcat and coyote are here, along with badger and small numbers of river otter.

Pheasant and quail are abundant. Bald and golden eagles are around most of the time. Great horned owls nest, sometimes in a tree beside the field headquarters. Hawks common much of the year include red-tailed and Swainson's, rough-legged, marsh, kestrels, with prairie falcons and merlins occasional.

Wood ducks nest and can be seen commonly. There is a nesting colony of black-crowned night herons.

Birding can be excellent to outstanding, in the marshes, along the roads, and around the headquarters area, for a variety of flycatchers, finches, orioles, thrushes, warblers, sparrows, and others.

There is a self-guided walking trail and a pulloff on Route 97 which affords good viewing of the whole refuge. Otherwise at least until recently the visitor has been largely on his own here.

For further information contact McNary headquarters or Toppenish National Wildlife Refuge, Route 1, Box 210BB, Toppenish, Washington 98948. Phone: (509) 865-2405.

How to get there: From Pasco take Route 395 southeast 6 miles to refuge sign; turn left ¼ mile to headquarters.

Open: Twenty-four hours.

Best times to visit: Fall and early spring.

What to see: Migrating and wintering waterfowl, sometimes coyote.

What to do: Three miles of public roads for looking at refuge, also interpretive walking trail; photography blind available; limited hunting for waterfowl, upland game; fishing for bass, catfish, bluegill; tours for organized groups.

Where to stay: MOTELS—Pasco. CAMPGROUNDS—Pasco; also Sacajawea State Park, 5 miles northwest and Hood State Park, adjoining refuge.

Points of interest nearby: Whitman Mission National Historic Site, 20 miles southeast.

For more information: McNary National Wildlife Refuge, P.O. Box 308, Burbank, Washington 99323. Phone: (509) 547-4942.

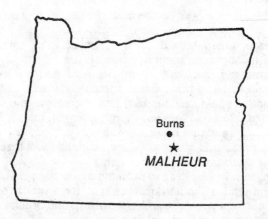

MALHEUR (Oregon)

Malheur Refuge with its 282 square miles of marsh, high desert, ponds, riverbottom, and three lakes in southeastern Oregon offers as diverse and interesting wildlife as any in the refuge system. It is home to 57 species of mammals and over 260 kinds of birds, of which more than a hundred nest and almost as many are listed as common or abundant at various times of the year.

Greater sandhill cranes perform their courtship dances in easy view of the springtime visitor, throwing sticks over their heads and leaping high into the air. Sometimes, they are activated by stress of any kind, not only courtship. Later in the year almost the entire Central Valley population of this majestic bird stage on Malheur in preparation for fall migration.

Up to 40,000 delicately beautiful avocets come through along with thousands of dowitchers, long-billed curlews, and concentrations of waterfowl—sometimes 100,000 snow geese and 250,000 ducks.

But Malheur is notable not so much for tremendous numbers as for a remarkable variety of wildlife of all kinds with something interesting to see in all but midwinter.

More than a dozen pairs of golden eagles nest in the rimrocks. Broods of ducklings, in a good year more than thirty thousand cinnamon teal, gadwall, redhead, and others, appear in July. Colonies of herons, egrets, cormorants, and terns are located in the middle of Malheur Lake (their then-threatened status caused establishment of the refuge in 1908) and can be seen over most of the watered areas.

Birding is excellent; in spring migration the careful observer may spot eighty or more species during a weekend excursion around the P-Ranch area and in trees around headquarters including common western tanagers, sage and Brewer's sparrows, mountain bluebirds, rock wrens, Wilson's warblers, and Say's phoebes.

Trumpeter swans, transplanted in a nucleus flock from Red Rock Lakes Refuge, live here year-round. As many as twenty thousand whistling swans are here in the spring. White pelicans are around in warm months. Chukar partridges, California quails, sage grouse, and ring-necked pheasants are common. Six species of hawks and five of owls, most noticeably the great horned, nest on the refuge.

Mule deer are common; so are coyotes. These and most of the other wildlife can be seen from the tour route, starting either at refuge headquarters, in Frenchglen (where an old hotel has been designated a state historic spot) or at either of two midway points. One can continue on from Frenchglen in summer over Steens Mountain through an alpine-like terrain with dramatic views and beautiful spring flowers.

In any case, do not hurry through; go slowly and stop frequently to examine the surroundings; listen, and let the feeling and beauty of one of the nation's largest inland marshes seep in. Otherwise much will be missed.

Excellent background brochures and lists are available as a guide in what to look for—other mammals such as beaver, porcupine, and yellow-bellied marmots; historic ranch buildings; old lava beds. Keep an eye out also on the road between the refuge and Burns; much of the area is managed in a way to attract wildlife, and some of the most spectacular sights may be along here.

The refuge is happy to be contacted ahead to consult on what the visitor most wishes to see and do, and to help plan a trip that will most likely accomplish these.

How to get there: From Burns, take Route 78 east, then Route 205 south 25 miles to refuge sign, then left 5 miles to headquarters.

Open: Dawn to dark.

Best times to visit: April through mid-October.

What to see: Large concentrations of waterfowl, shorebirds; sandhill cranes; trumpeter and whistling swans; songbirds; mule deer; others.

What to do: Forty-two-mile interpretive tour drive; self-guided canoe route on Blitzen River; photography (blind on display pond);

natural history museum; limited hunting for deer, waterfowl, upland game; trout fishing (fair); guided tours, films and slide shows can be arranged for organized groups.

Where to stay: MOTELS—At Burns, 32 miles north; also historic Frenchglen Hotel, by reservation. CAMPGROUNDS—Page Springs BLM campground and Camper Corral on south refuge boundary; also at Steens Mountain and national forests.

Weather notes: Summer nights usually cool; heavy rain and snow can close tour route.

Points of interest nearby: Steens Mountain loop drive, up to 10,000-foot elevation, remarkable scenic and wildlife view; Hart Mountain National Wildlife Refuge, 42 miles southwest (but road sometimes impassable); Ochoco National Forest, 45 miles northwest; Malheur National Forest, 50 miles northeast; Environmental Field Station, 4 miles west.

For more information: Malheur National Wildlife Refuge, P.O. Box 113, Burns, Oregon 97720. Phone: (503) 493-2323.

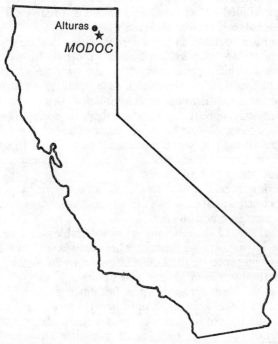

Alturas

MODOC

MODOC (California)

Modoc in the northeast corner of California is a lovely small refuge of about 6,283 acres with hospitable waterfowl habitat—almost two hundred small islands scattered over more than two dozen lakes and ponds. Around them is typical Great Basin sagebrush upland where pronghorn antelope sometimes appear by the hundreds in migration treks.

Late spring to early fall are the best times to see Modoc. Sandhill cranes perform courtship dances and nest. White pelicans are on hand in good numbers; and sometimes several dozen snowy and great egrets appear. Ducks and geese migrate through, peaking in the fall at up to sixty thousand ducks and fifteen thousand geese— mostly Canadas with some snows and white-fronted—and are seen again in smaller groups in spring. Many of the Canadas and eleven species of ducks stay through the summer to nest. They can be seen in breeding plumage in May and later with downy broods in ponds along the entrance road to headquarters. Here they accompany dusky coots and their startlingly bright-hued offspring, eared, western, and pied-billed grebes, and killdeer doing their "broken-wing" act to distract attention from their nests and young.

Mule deer are common in the summer; so are coyote, badger and mink, but these are wary and not readily spotted. Not so the Belding's ground squirrels, however—they are everywhere, especially along the dike road, scurrying at high speed only to brake to a sudden stop and assume their upright "picket-fence" pose.

Shorebirds may appear in large numbers in spring. Sometimes hundreds of snipes, Wilson's phalaropes, avocets, and black-necked stilts are around the ponds and meadows, and many of these remain to nest. There is usually a breeding colony of black-crowned night herons in the center of Teal Pond.

Small birding is best around refuge headquarters or by permission in certain closed areas (ask the office). Short-eared owls and red-tailed hawks are common all year.

The appearance of the antelope is unpredictable. Most often they are seen in November and March; when they come, five hundred may cross over a corner of the refuge in two or three days, apparently oblivious to their surroundings and easy to view.

Winter is the least agreeable time (although snow and freezing weather can be recorded in any month here), but a half dozen or so bald eagles often make Modoc their winter headquarters, and sometimes several can be seen in a single cottonwood tree near the office.

Modoc is located three miles south of Alturas, California. To get there go south from Alturas on Route 395, east on County Road 56, and south on County Road 115, following refuge signs. For further information contact the Refuge Manager: Modoc Refuge, P.O. Box 1610, Alturas, California 96101. Phone: (916) 233-3572.

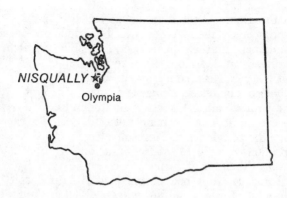

NISQUALLY

Olympia

NISQUALLY (Washington)

Nisqually is a wonderfully pure and unpolluted (1,796-acre Pacific Coast river delta on Puget Sound within a few miles of metropolitan populations of two million persons. Thousands of sea birds, shore-birds, and waterfowl live and rest here during migration. Both ter-restrial and marine mammals visit, including river otter, harbor and hair seal, Steller sea lions, porpoises, humpback and killer whales. On land there are coyote, fox, mountain beaver, and black-tailed deer.

That Nisqually is a refuge at all is due largely to the efforts of citi-zens who worked to save the area from proposals to turn it into ei-ther a sanitary landfill or a deep-water port. Their efforts continue as the Nisqually Delta Association. Meanwhile this developing refuge, where inventories still are being made on the rich variety of plant and animal life, is popular with naturalists who hike the five-mile dike trail to observe white-winged, surf, and common scoters, auks, murres, murrelets, arctic and red-throated loons, double-crested and pelagic cormorants, black brant, Canada geese, four species of grebes and nineteen species of dabbling and diving ducks including common and Barrow's goldeneye.

There is also a wooded and open upland trail, where California quail and ring-necked pheasant are common, and birders may ob-serve at various seasons Bewick's wrens, red-breasted nuthatches, bushtits, Bullock's orioles, varied, Swainson's, and hermit thrushes, chestnut-backed chickadees, and black-headed grosbeaks.

A pair of bald eagles nest on Anderson Island just north of the ref-uge, and can be seen soaring overhead. Rough-legged, Cooper's, and red-tailed hawks, and short-eared and great horned owls are common visitors to the Delta. Great blue herons are also common. Shorebirds in spring and fall migration usually include red-backed and western sandpipers, northern phalaropes, long-billed dowitchers, and yellowlegs. Band-tailed pigeons are here in summer, and glaucous-winged, Bonaparte's, Heermann's, and mew gulls all year.

Nisqually also administers *Dungeness*, one of the best birding locales in the United States. Visitors come from all over the world to observe species on its long list, many not easily seen elsewhere, especially among the pelagic types. This is due largely to its unique habitat and location—a 756-acre sandspit extending approximately five miles out into the Strait of Juan de Fuca from Washington State's Olympic Peninsula. It is one of the longest natural spits in the world, with a bit of woods and upland as well, all at the foot of the beautiful Olympic Mountains.

Winter is the best time for birding here. Common birds include arctic and red-throated loons, Brandt's cormorants, red-necked and three other species of grebes, black turnstones, mew gulls, black-legged kittiwakes, surfbirds, pigeon guillemots, bald eagles, Canada geese including both cackling and dusky types, more than a dozen species of ducks including harlequins, surf and white-winged scoters, common and Barrow's goldeneye, and up to fifteen thousand black brant feeding on the eelgrass.

Other seasons can be fine as well. Summer sometimes is crowded by vacationers on the refuge periphery, but rhinoceros auklets and tufted puffins are around, as are many small birds, commonly red-breasted sapsuckers, chestnut-backed chickadees, and many warblers. Refuge mammals include black-tailed deer, harbor and elephant seals, river and sea otters, killer whales in the outer bay—and an occasional red fox family.

Dungeness also provides habitat for the rosy day moth and golden sulphur butterfly (collecting forbidden) as well as ten species of salmon and four of trout (steelhead, rainbow, cutthroat, Dolly Varden) plus the justly famed Dungeness crab.

The refuge must be seen on foot. To reach the parking area, take Route 101 west from Sequim to Kitchen Road, then right to and through the Dungeness Recreation Area. Sequim has motels, and camping is permitted at Clallam County Park.

Fishing and clamming are permitted on the refuge. Various sight-seeing trips, both land and water, can be taken from Sequim.

San Juan Islands are a group of eighty-four islands in Puget Sound believed to be extensions of the beautiful nearby Olympic Mountains. Some islands are so small they are only a few rocks but even these are useful to large numbers of sea birds. Most are not accessible; several of those that are—Matia, Turn, and Jones—are managed cooperatively as state marine parks. The rest must be viewed by boat. This can be done from ferry and sightseeing boats that run in the area, or by small boat (nineteen-foot minimum suggested) which can be rented with or without guide nearby. Small boats should be handled by experts, severe riptides can be dangerous. But birding is most impressive, with Brandt's and pelagic cormorants, tufted puffins, pigeon guillemots, Cassin's, and rhinoceros auklets, black oystercatchers, and up to ten thousand glaucous-winged gulls, their largest nesting colony in the Northwest. There are often more than forty bald eagle nests as well, and seals, otters, and sometimes killer whales.

Winter days may be cool and foggy; otherwise there can be much to see at any time of year.

To get there, one can take a ferry from Anacortes to Friday Harbor and there charter or rent a boat. Motels are available there also, and camping is permitted on Matia Island.

How to get there: From Olympia take I-5 to Nisqually exit, turn left at end of exit ramp, go under highway then right on narrow paved road to refuge entrance.

Open: Daylight hours, year-round.

Best times to visit: Fall and winter.

What to see: Large numbers of wintering ducks, also wading and shorebirds, occasional bald eagles.

What to do: Six miles of dike road trails for hiking only, also a trail through wooded area in southeast section; boating and floating on McAllister Creek, where fishing can be good for steelhead and sea-run cutthroat trout; limited waterfowl hunting; clamming.

Where to stay: MOTELS—In Olympia. CAMPGROUNDS—On I-5 near Nisqually exit; also Millersylvania State Park, 18 miles south.

Weather notes: Cool and rainy much of the year.

Points of interest nearby: Mount Rainier National Park, 80 (driving miles) southeast; Olympic National Park, 70 miles northwest (don't miss the rain forest); Olympic Peninsula Scenic Drive, circling the peninsula along Puget Sound.

For more information: Nisqually National Wildlife Refuge, 2625 Parkmont Lane, Building A-2, Olympia, Washington 98502. Phone: (206) 753-9467.

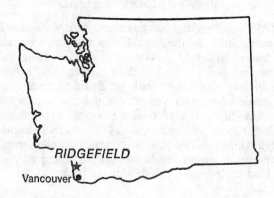

RIDGEFIELD (Washington)

This three-thousand-acre refuge on the Columbia River flood plain in southwest Washington winters up to forty thousand ducks and fifteen thousand geese, including many of the dusky Canada subspecies which has been in need of special protection because of its limited range. There may also be several hundred beautiful whistling swans through the cool months. Black-tailed deer are here; also numerous beaver and nutria.

At least ten species of duck stay and nest—principally wigeon and mallard but also some gadwall, pintail, shoveler, and cinnamon and blue- and green-winged teal.

Great blue herons have a large nesting colony of several hundred pairs just off the refuge, and these large wading birds are always about. So are red-tailed hawks, which have several nesting pairs on the refuge. Great horned owls are less readily seen but they are common also, and usually can be flushed along Bower Slough in the River S unit.

Snipe are abundant much of the year, and sometimes seem to adorn every fence post, posing for photographers.

Common small birds of interest include Bewick's wrens, scrub jays, varied thrushes, golden-crowned kinglets, Savannah sparrows, and violet-green swallows, with occasional bushtits, Steller's jays, red-breasted nuthatches, and golden-crowned sparrows. Up to five hundred sandhill cranes may stop over in spring and summer, and fair-sized flocks of band-tailed pigeons sometimes move through in the fall.

One of the most enjoyable ways to see this refuge is by canoe, drifting among flooded willows on the north unit, especially in winter when water conditions are good and the waterfowl have settled in. But there are also nine miles of roads and trails for driving and hiking, including the Oak Grove interpretive trail which winds through groves of massive Oregon white oak, some with trunks twelve feet around and a canopy spread of sixty feet or more.

Some of the roads and trails may not be in top condition during wet weather. In fact, it is well to remember that this is a recently established refuge, in the process of developing many of its visitor-use facilities.

How to get there: From Vancouver take I-5 north 10 miles to Ridgefield exit; then Route 501 into Ridgefield and refuge office, open weekdays, also signs to north and south units.

Open: Daylight hours, year-round.

Best times to visit: Spring, fall, and winter.

What to see: Nesting and wintering waterfowl; great blue herons; black-tailed deer.

What to do: Nine miles of roads and trails for driving, hiking, including interpretive walking trail. Limited waterfowl hunting. Canoeing. Blackberry picking.

Where to stay: MOTELS—Vancouver. CAMPGROUNDS—Paradise Point State Park, 5 miles north.

Points of interest nearby: Fort Vancouver National Historic Site.

For more information: Ridgefield National Wildlife Refuge, P.O. Box 457, Ridgefield, Washington 98642. Phone: (206) 887-8276.

SACRAMENTO (California)

Sacramento Refuge, with its three nearby subrefuges, is one of the most important wintering areas for waterfowl in the Pacific Flyway.

From October through January its eleven thousand acres of fields and ponds in the northern Central Valley of California, bordered by the Sierra Nevada mountains on the east and the South Coastal Range on the west and drained by the Sacramento River, may hold three hundred thousand or more geese and a million or more ducks, and tens of thousands of shorebirds as well.

Notable among these are the endangered Aleutian Canada geese, the rare Tule white-fronted geese (about fifteen hundred), Pacific white-fronted geese, cackling Canada geese, and Ross' geese, distinguished from their cousins the more numerous snow geese by absence of the "grinning patch" alongside the bill.

Every year, the annual Christmas Bird Count conducted by the National Audubon Society places Sacramento Valley highest in the nation in the numbers for various species (not always the same ones every year). These have included the Cooper's hawk, kestrel, barn owl, flicker, yellow-billed magpie, goldfinch, red-tailed hawk, white-tailed kite, pintail duck, white-crowned and golden-crowned sparrows, and numbers of others.

Sacramento is also listed by the Department of the Interior as affording some of the outstanding photographic opportunities among the national wildlife refuges—and for good reason. The sight of hundreds of thousands of waterfowl feeding in the shallow mirrorlike waters or rising and swirling in the air like leaves in the wind, taking flight against the background of the coastal range or red sunset, is never to be forgotten. While blinds are available, they are not necessary for such stunning panoramas as these.

Dowitchers are the most common shorebird and are here all year, as are Virginia rails, gallinules, great blue and black-crowned night herons and snowy and great egrets, which nest. Most common ducks are mallard, green-winged teal, shoveler, wigeon, pintail, and ruddy ducks.

Sacramento often has oddities show up as well. European wigeon are spotted almost every year, as are white-faced ibises; and the endangered peregrine falcon is usually seen in spring.

Mammals are present in fair numbers; most readily visible are black-tailed deer, but red fox, skunk, muskrat, jackrabbit, cottontails, ground squirrels, raccoons, a few ringtail cats (which sometimes use wood duck boxes for dens), and twelve species of bats—including some ten thousand Mexican freetails—are here as well.

Nuttall's woodpeckers nest along wooded areas, and cliff swallows construct their mud houses in colonies around bridges. Most of the other small birds migrate during breeding—some only six miles, however, to the westward coastal range. White-tailed kites prefer the large willows and cottonwoods for perching, and a few nest in these places. A visitor in winter or spring is almost certain to see one of these lovely white-plumaged predators hovering over an upland field, or to be treated at any time of year to a thrilling close-up view (through binoculars) of a marsh hawk or kestrel swooping down and carrying off a meal.

Brilliant ring-necked pheasants are a common sight along brushy areas, and burrowing owls find homes in more sparsely vegetated spots. California poppies and a variety of other wild flowers are a dazzling sight in spring.

Three subrefuges administered by Sacramento are located south and southeast, and are generally similar. They are:

Sutter National Wildlife Refuge—2,591 acres, has probably the highest per-acre waterfowl use of any United States refuge. At times, 10 per cent of the birds in the Pacific Flyway will be found here. There are no special visitor facilities, and the refuge usually floods at least part of every winter; but the area can be seen from a county road that bisects it.

Colusa National Wildlife Refuge—The endangered Aleutians have been seen on its 4,040 acres of ponds and uplands, and feral pigs are sometimes seen. There is an auto tour route.

Delevan National Wildlife Refuge—5,633 acres managed largely for waterfowl resting and feeding. No special visitor facilities but a small section on the east is open to fishing and bird-watching. Burrowing owls are a common sight.

How to get there: From Willows take Old Highway 99 (also called Tehama Street) south about 6 miles to refuge signs.

Open: Daylight hours all year.

Best times to visit: September through January (early December best).

What to see: Tremendous concentrations of waterfowl and shorebirds.

What to do: Self-guided auto and walking tours; photography (listed as one of best camera subjects in refuge system, photoblinds available); hunting, limited, for pheasant and waterfowl; fishing—so-so on refuge but good in Sacramento River and other streams nearby for salmon, striper, sturgeon up to 12 feet long; guided tours for groups on advance request.

Where to stay: MOTELS—Several in Willows. CAMPGROUNDS—Woodson Bridge State Recreation Area, west of Vina, all year; Colusa-Sacramento River State Area, near Colusa, except in winter.

Weather notes: Summer intensely hot and humid. Rains November–February *can* close tour route to cars.

Points of interest nearby: Mendocino National Forest, 20 miles west; Gray Lodge State Area, 40 miles east; Tehama-Colusa National Fish Facility (tagging and milking salmon), 50 miles north.

For more information: Sacramento National Wildlife Refuge, Route 1, Box 311, Willows, California 95988. Phone: (916) 934-2801.

Indio
SALTON SEA ★

SALTON SEA (California)

All but a few of the 35,484 acres of Salton Sea Refuge are under the sea itself, but what isn't affords a vantage point for some of the best birding anywhere.

Great concentrations of waterfowl, shore- and wading birds are here in season—probably the most significant numbers of those that migrate along the Colorado River and the inner Coastal Flyway. But there is also an abundance of others. During the Audubon Christmas Bird Count, Salton Sea often reports high counts in the nation for such species as rough-winged and bank swallows, Scott's orioles, orange-crowned and yellow-rumped (Audubon's) warblers (3,747 in one year), redstarts, burrowing owls, mountain plovers, long-billed dowitchers, long-billed curlews, long-billed marsh wrens, eared grebes (33,872), and ruddy ducks (17,050).

Part of the attraction is the sea itself—375 square miles with a 115-mile shoreline, the largest inland body of water west of the

Rockies. It was formed when the mighty Colorado burst its man-made channels in 1905, and rampaged for two years spilling its waters (and its silt) in this desert basin, which at 228 feet below sea level is one of the lowest spots in the United States. The area has some of the hottest and driest weather anywhere (rainfall sometimes is less than an inch a year).

The lake is supported now mostly by runoff from irrigated agricultural lands, and in fact has continued a gradual rise which has overtaken so much refuge area that additional acreage has been leased from the Imperial Irrigation District (a different problem from most southern California refuges where too little water is often the rule). Constant diking is required to keep some lands available for crops and feeding areas, and fresh-water ponds. Nor is the water of good quality, having a high saline content—with an interesting side effect. Barnacles introduced unintentionally by seaplanes during World War II have thrived and are relished as food by pintail ducks and others.

The best time to come for large concentrations are January through March, for wintering Canada and snow geese along with a few Ross' and white-fronted; ducks—as many as 190,000 pintail, along with green-winged teal, wigeon, and shoveler; white-faced ibises; and among the shorebirds, least and western sandpipers, marbled godwits and black-bellied plovers (many of these are present in fall also, but a hunting program keeps part of the refuge off limits then to afford quiet sanctuary).

White pelicans come through spring and fall, and migrating small birds can be seen—western tanagers, lazuli buntings, black-headed and blue grosbeaks, Bullock's orioles, warbling vireos and yellow and Wilson's warblers—the brushy areas around headquarters being as good a locale for these as any on the refuge.

In late spring and summer, the refuge often gets interesting visitors from Mexico just twenty miles south—wood storks, blue-footed and brown boobies, roseate spoonbills, fulvous whistling ducks. Gull-billed terns and laughing gulls, rare nesters in the western United States, are here in summer, and here commonly all year are snowy and cattle egrets, turkey vultures, coot, killdeer, avocets, and mourning doves. The Salton Sea area supports the largest population of doves in the west, including white-winged and Mexican ground doves. There also are verdins, long-billed marsh wrens, mockingbirds, roadrunners, loggerhead shrikes, yellow-throated warblers, and meadowlarks.

Coyote, raccoon, and jackrabbit are the most common mammals. Kit fox, kangaroo rats, bobcat, muskrat, striped skunk, and badger are also here though not in large numbers.

Trails are limited due to lack of land area. The best way to see the refuge is to drive to Rock Hill and walk around from there, climbing the hill for a good overview to the Superstition Mountains on the southwest and the Chocolate Mountains on the northeast, and by walking the dikes.

How to get there: From San Diego, take Route 8 east to El Centro, Route 86 north to Brawley, Route 111 north to Sinclair Road, then left about 6 miles to refuge.

Open: Daylight hours all year.

Best times to visit: September and January through March (but there's something interesting all year).

What to see: Good numbers and variety of waterfowl, shorebirds, songbirds, plus occasional odd visitors from Mexico. Occasional endangered Yuma clapper rails and Aleutian Canada geese.

What to do: Bird-watching; limited special-permit waterfowl hunting; fishing—not on refuge but in Salton Sea and canals, for corvina up to 27 pounds. Guided tours can be arranged for groups with advance notice.

Where to stay: MOTELS—In Brawley. CAMPGROUNDS—At Salton Sea State Recreation Area, 25 miles north; Red Hill County Boat Landing, 2 miles northwest; Finney-Ramer State Waterfowl Area, 16 miles southeast.

Weather notes: Winter days typically sunny, temperature 75–80. April to October hot, regarded locally as humid but not by midwest standards: 59 per cent.

What to take and wear: Boots can be useful in wet areas.

Points of interest nearby: All places mentioned under CAMPGROUNDS (above) are excellent for small birding. So is Spooney Bay (to get there go east from the refuge on Sinclair Road, turn north on Garst Road and follow it around). Joshua Tree National Monument is about 80 miles north.

For more information: Salton Sea National Wildlife Refuge, P.O. Box 247, Calipatria, California 92233. Phone: (714) 348-2323.

San Francisco ● ★ SAN FRANCISCO BAY

SAN FRANCISCO BAY (California)

It is sometimes possible at San Francisco Bay Refuge to see two endangered species in one marsh—the California clapper rail, of which
at least half the remaining population is here; and the salt-marsh
harvest mouse, one of the few mammals in the world able to drink
salt water. They coexist precariously in the salt marsh—readily visible at high tide when they are forced to the top of the vegetation.
Their small numbers contrast with the tremendous concentrations of
many of the wildlife species at this 15,400-acre refuge, one of the
country's newest, which is still being acquired and developed.

It is estimated that some 70 per cent of all the shorebirds in the
Pacific Flyway winter or stop here. Delicate and beautiful avocets
and black-necked stilts are here by the thousands all year, nesting and
delighting photographers as they probe for food on and close by the
shore. Marbled godwits, willets, western and least sandpipers, short-
and long-billed dowitchers do not usually nest but are gone and back

so quickly from their family chores that their presence on the fertile mudflats is noted at all seasons.

Snowy and common egrets and great blue and black-crowned night herons are common to abundant all the year (one small island has a large nesting colony of wading birds), along with pintail ducks, mallard, and seasonally gadwall, scaup, shoveler, cinnamon teal, and canvasback.

White-tailed kites, those consummate beauties of the raptor clan, hover in hunting flights and nest in the drought-resistant coyote bush, seldom more than ten feet off the ground. Forster's terns have their broods, sometimes seventeen hundred in a colony, in isolated, and protected, shore locations, along with Caspian terns—five hundred or so—snowy plovers and the rare California least terns. Both brown and white pelicans are here seasonally in good numbers.

Harbor seals historically have hunted and produced families along the edges of the tidal sloughs, hauling out to rest on the mudflats at low tide, and a blind and boardwalk for observing and photographing them is planned (young pups can sometimes be seen as early as April).

More than twenty miles of trails, mostly for hiking but with short stretches for cars and cyclists, are in existence or planned through the narrow twenty-five-mile shoreline of this refuge, which has more land below water than above it. It is a large part of what bay wetland remains and is here mostly as the result of efforts by various citizens' groups—Sierra Club, Audubon, Nature Conservancy and others, particularly the South San Francisco Baylands Refuge Committee—when rapid development threatened to overtake it all. Now, though surrounded by fairly dense development, with San Francisco but forty-five minutes' drive away, it retains a feeling of remoteness (often the result of a haze which obscures distances) and the approachable birds seem to feel it.

Several subrefuges are administered by San Francisco Bay headquarters:

San Pablo Bay National Wildlife Refuge—Marsh and open water north of Oakland established primarily to offer rest and feeding area for canvasback ducks; rafts of five thousand or so are a common sight, and more than half of all the Pacific Coast population is estimated to winter here. It also has good shorebird populations as well as clapper rails and the harvest mouse.

Ellicott Slough National Wildlife Refuge—A 119-acre tract with no visitor facilities, set aside to preserve habitat for the endangered Santa Cruz long-toed salamander.

Salinas Lagoon National Wildlife Refuge—A 518-acre coastal wetland eleven miles northeast of Monterey, managed jointly with the California Fish and Game Department. It has the brown pelican and the endangered Smith's blue butterfly. Hunting is permitted.

Elkhorn Slough National Wildlife Refuge—A tidal salt marsh, habitat for water birds of all kinds. Limited access with no visitor facilities: still under acquisition.

Farallon Islands National Wildlife Refuge and Wilderness Area— A group of small islands thirty miles west comprising the largest continental sea-bird colony south of Alaska. More than two hundred thousand birds summer here including breeding Cassin's auklets, murres, oystercatchers, puffins, and others, along with seals and sea lions. It is closely protected and patrolled with no public access. Bay Area Audubon groups sponsor annual boat trips around the islands.

How to get there: From San Francisco take Route 101 south to Route 84 which is the Dumbarton Bridge. Refuge headquarters is on the approach at the east end of the bridge. Visitor center will be found going farther south on 101 to 237 and refuge signs.

Open: Daylight hours all year.

Best times to visit: Weather generally pleasant and wildlife present all seasons.

What to see: Large numbers of shore- and wading birds; white-tailed kites; seals.

What to do: Driving and walking routes; observation platforms; photography (blind available but light often hazy); limited waterfowl hunting, including scullboating; fishing from causeways and piers for striper, sturgeon, others.

Where to stay: MOTELS—Numerous in San Francisco and surrounding area. CAMPGROUNDS—Numerous in San Francisco area; primitive camping in Mount Tamalpais State Park.

Points of interest nearby: Golden Gate National Recreation Area, including Mount Tamalpais State Park and Muir Woods National Monument, 14 miles north of San Francisco; Coyote Hills Regional Park, just north of refuge; Leslie Salt Company, solar salt production, adjacent to refuge.

For more information: San Francisco Bay National Wildlife Refuge, 3849 Peralta Boulevard, Fremont, California 94536. Phone: (415) 792-0222.

SAN LUIS (California)

San Luis and nearby Merced refuges offer sanctuary to some of the most spectacular concentrations of waterfowl and shorebirds on the Pacific Flyway, and in addition afford protection to an impressive herd of Tule elk, one of the few places where these rare animals can be seen at any time.

The Tule elk is the smallest of the North American elk but still imposing—an adult male weighs seven hundred pounds with antlers sometimes thirty inches across. This subspecies once "darkened the plains" according to old accounts, but overhunting brought them close to extinction around the turn of the century. They were saved partly through the efforts of an early cattle baron, Henry Miller, an immigrant German butcher who took the name when it accidentally appeared on his ticket west, and followed signs in a dream to become the owner of much of the land between here and Oregon. Miller paid hunters to bring him elk and release them alive on his property.

The animals still number less than a thousand, of which only about forty exist here; the rest are on a state preserve near Taft, California, and in the Owens Valley. Those that are at San Luis (in a five-mile fenced area) are an impressive sight, browsing and resting on the uplands, and in the late summer rutting (mating) season bellowing and "bugling" at all hours, occasionally charging at the enclosure when a visitor gets too close (their antlers have been known to go through the door of a refuge vehicle).

Huge numbers of migrant and wintering ducks, geese and shorebirds are sometimes here as well on this 7,430 acres of marsh and grassland. They include up to a million ducks (mostly mallard, pintail, green-winged teal, wigeon, and shoveler) and perhaps 50,000 geese—Canadas, often including up to 1,200 of the endangered Aleutian variety, plus white-fronted, snow, and a few Ross'. Most of the Ross' geese, sometimes half the world population of this rare species, appear at nearby Merced, along with as many as 15,000 sandhill cranes during the winter months.

Equally impressive are some of the others—in a good year the area will have up to 250,000 long-billed dowitchers, 100,000 phalaropes, 20,000 snipes, 12,000 each of black-necked stilts and long-billed curlews—and 20,000 Bewick's wrens, 1,000 burrowing owls, 5,000 kestrels, and 12,000 blackbirds, including the yellow-headed, red-winged, and tricolor. Whether it is a good year for water and shorebirds depends, of course, on the availability of water. California often has been subject to severe drought; and most of the river and runoff water in the lower Central Valley once drained by the San Joaquin River has been diverted to agricultural use, to the loss of the refuges.

Nevertheless, there is much to be seen here in any year. White-tailed kites, those stunning snowy raptors, are here in numbers, sometimes 150 in a single clump of trees, and birds of prey generally, especially marsh and red-tailed hawks, are a common sight soaring and hunting about the fields.

The endangered San Joaquin kit fox and giant garter snake also are here in reduced but, it is believed, stable numbers.

Merced Refuge, 2,562 acres of wild millet and other cultivated crops, is located fourteen miles south and west of the town of Merced. In addition to large winter populations of Ross' geese and cranes, it affords protection to the endangered Aleutian goose, and like San Luis, sometimes huge shore and waterfowl concentrations (as, 100,000 geese in a single day).

Kesterson Refuge, also administered by San Luis, is as yet largely undeveloped as a waterfowl habitat.

How to get there: From Merced take Route 140 west to Lander Avenue, then left to Wolfson Road, and left on Wolfson to refuge
signs.

Open: Sunrise until 2 hours after sunset, all year.

Best times to visit: Early spring, fall, and winter.

What to see: Large concentrations of waterfowl and shorebirds;
Tule elk; old adobe house—oldest house in Merced County,
maintains constant winter-summer temperature.

What to do: Auto and walking tour routes; photography; limited
hunting for geese, ducks, and snipe; fishing for catfish, black
bass, striper, crappie; mushroom picking 30 days after a good
rain.

Where to stay: MOTELS—In Los Banos. CAMPGROUNDS—Near Los
Banos and in San Luis State Recreation Area, 20 miles southwest.

Weather notes: Summers hot, dry; winters cool, mild, sometimes
rainy with periods of "Tule fog" so dense that state police close
roads and lead auto caravans through the areas.

What to take and wear: Boots for marshy areas.

Points of interest nearby: San Luis Reservoir, 15 miles west of Los
Banos (huge waterfowl concentrations); the Santa Fe Grade
Road, south of refuge, surrounded by brush, excellent birding;
and the refuge is 2½–3 hours from the Pacific Ocean, Kings
Canyon and Yosemite National Parks, Monterey and San Fran-
cisco.

For more information: San Luis-Merced National Wildlife Refuge,
P.O. Box 2176, Los Banos, California 93635. Phone: (209)
826-3508.

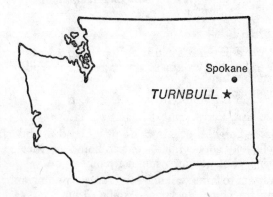

TURNBULL (Washington)

Turnbull is a scenically beautiful refuge with abundant and varied wildlife attracted by its fine habitat. There are more than a hundred lakes and marshes with interspersed woodlands of Ponderosa pine and quaking aspen. The 15,565-acre refuge is located in the "channeled scablands" created by a monstrous wall of water that overwhelmed this part of east-central Washington ten thousand years ago and left odd rock and earth formations.

White-tailed deer and coyote are common. Porcupine look down from tree notches. Beaver construct lodges. Rare trumpeter swans nest, often at Winslow pond near refuge headquarters where they and others that like this watery spot can be observed from the hill across the road. These often include Canada geese and some of the sixteen species of ducks that may breed here, including especially redhead, mallard, cinnamon teal, scaup, and ruddy ducks—for Turnbull is one of the best waterfowl nesting grounds in eastern Washington.

In fact, birding enthusiasts will find something of interest over a wide variety of species and in almost every season, except for a month or two when pond waters may be frozen over in midwinter.

Among the small birds, pygmy nuthatches are abundant all the time, and common at least seasonally are mountain chickadees, western and mountain bluebirds, hairy woodpeckers, western wood pewees—and some that are not listed as common can still show up in large numbers occasionally, as the thousands of Clark's nutcrackers that sometimes go through in the fall.

Black-billed magpies are always around; so are great horned owls which can often be flushed from the tops of thickets where pygmy owls occasionally occupy the understory. Screech owls take over some of the wood duck houses and peer out in the late afternoons as short-eared owls start to hunt over open areas.

California quail, ring-necked pheasant, and ruffed grouse are common all year. Black terns nest in good numbers, as do eared and pied-billed grebes, great blue herons, American bitterns, common snipes, and usually avocets.

Red-tailed hawks nest, goshawks occasionally, peregrine and prairie falcons and rough-legged hawks appear, and a dozen bald and golden eagles usually arrive with the waterfowl. These peak at up to twenty-five thousand in October and many, including Barrow's and common goldeneyes, stay the winter except when ice closes the waters. Whistling swans are here in spring.

There is a fine children's nature checklist, and a five-mile auto tour route where a visitor can spend hours, especially by stopping to walk some of the trails marked off it and noting the wild flowers—bitter-roots, lupines, wild delphiniums, sticky geraniums, and others—which bloom from early spring through much of summer.

Local people like the refuge, are proud of it, and use it heavily (though the trails are seldom crowded)—and justly so, since they are responsible for it. The lakes and marshes had been mostly drained for abortive land development projects when they decided it should be restored for wildlife, and worked and petitioned the government until this was done in 1937, and over the years it became the fine place it is today.

How to get there: From Spokane take I-90 to Cheney Four Lakes exit; in Cheney turn left at K Street and refuge sign onto Cheney Plaza highway and go 4 miles south and 2 miles east on Smith Road to headquarters.

Open: Daylight hours, year-round.

Best times to visit: April through November.

What to see: Trumpeter swans, other nesting and migrating water birds; also white-tailed deer, coyotes.

What to do: Seven miles of roads, including self-guided auto tour, with nine short marked hiking trails off (but visitors can walk anywhere in the public use area); photography (blind available); slide show for organized groups by arrangement; skiing, cross-country skiing when enough snow (one regular user takes his dog sled out).

Where to stay: MOTELS—In Cheney, and large selection in Spokane area. CAMPGROUNDS—One mile west of Cheney; also in Newman Lake State Park 75 miles northeast.

Weather notes: Seldom prolonged extremes.

Points of interest nearby: Mount Spokane State Park, 55 miles northeast; Finch Arboretum, Coeur d'Alene Park, many others in Spokane area; Little Pend Oreille State Game Refuge near Colville, 100 miles north.

For more information: Turnbull National Wildlife Refuge, Route 3, Box 385, Cheney, Washington 99004. Phone: (509) 235-4723.

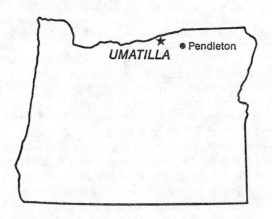

UMATILLA (Oregon and Washington)

Umatilla, stretching for twenty miles along both sides of the Columbia River in Washington and Oregon, is a place of contrasts among arid desert forms of life. It includes grasslands where one of the largest populations of long-billed curlews in the Pacific Northwest make their homes, and sparkling lakes and marshes that offer wintering, breeding and migration habitat for up to three hundred thousand waterfowl, including Canada geese and more than a dozen duck species. There are also noteworthy populations of raptors and small birds, as well as mule deer, coyote, beaver, badger, and small numbers of river otter.

This refuge of 23,000 acres was set aside to replace waterfowl habitat inundated when the John Day Dam was built, a loss at least partly compensated by formation of two backwater areas known as McCormack and Patterson sloughs. Dense thickets of Russian olive have grown up in moist sections, and one covering more than sixty acres shelters, according to a study by Oregon State University, the densest wintering small bird population in the Northwest, as well as numbers of larger species such as great horned owls.

Rare western burrowing owls nest. So do long-eared, short-eared, barn, and screech owls, and marsh, red-tailed, and Swainson's hawks. Prairie falcons are seen regularly, and bald and golden eagles, usually a dozen or so of each, spend the winter. Great blue herons and double-crested cormorants share nest colonies on some of the river islands (the herons housekeeping sometimes on Coast Guard channel markers) and ring-billed gulls and Caspian terns occupy others in one of their few known breeding sites in this part of the country.

Horned larks are sometimes around in scattered groupings of thousands in the winter. Ring-necked pheasant are as numerous as anywhere in Oregon. Hundreds of whistling swans visit in spring and fall.

But the stars of Umatilla refuge are the long-billed curlews. Those medium-sized marbled brown shorebirds with the improbable eight-inch curved bills and loud plaintive call arrive every year on March 16 and signal for everyone around here the first day of spring. On March 16 no one can call in by telephone because the locals are all calling each other to report the first sighting. There has been a strong move to declare an official Curlew Day every year; in any case studies have been started to see if more nesting habitat can be provided on the refuge for this interesting bird which is conspicuous here from the time of its arrival through its nesting in June. There are usually at least five hundred of them nesting now, and if local people can arrange it, there will be more.

There is also a desert area of moving sand dunes with dryland reptiles, plants, insects, and birds. These can be fascinating to study by observing tracks where, for example, a black-billed magpie has swooped down and carried off a wriggling snake. Not far away the river cuts a sparkling blue slash through the arid land and in the distance one can see the Blue Mountains and on a clear day, snow-covered Mount Hood in the Cascade Range.

Also administered by Umatilla: *Cold Springs*—Large concentrations of waterfowl, including most of the species common to the Pacific Flyway, stay here the winter. A few breed at this 3,117-acre refuge which was superimposed on an irrigation reservoir six miles east of Hermiston, Oregon. It is a scenically lovely place with a large and varied raptor population as well. Swans and pelicans visit during the winter, and deer may be seen. There are several miles of primitive roads and trails that can be followed to view wildlife. Take along a refuge map and compass. Visitors get lost sometimes.

McKay Creek. Also superimposed on an irrigation reservoir project, 1,837-acre McKay Creek Refuge, located five miles south of Pendleton, Oregon, provides wintering habitat for some twenty-five thousand ducks and ten thousand geese. Visitor facilities are not highly developed. Fishing is permitted, and there is a picnic area.

How to get there: From Umatilla take Route 730 west to Irrigon; 3 miles farther turn right on Patterson Ferry Road and proceed about 2 miles to refuge entrance.

Open: Twenty-four hours, year-round.

Best times to visit: Spring, fall, and winter.

What to see: Long-billed curlews; large concentrations of migrating and wintering waterfowl; good numbers of raptors, shorebirds, and songbirds; mule deer; coyote; Indian petroglyphs (visible from a boat).

What to do: Ten miles of roads for driving, hiking; photography (blind available); boating on Columbia River; limited hunting for waterfowl, upland game birds; fishing for bass, sturgeon. Environmental study areas for school and other groups, with tours by arrangement.

Where to stay: MOTELS—In Umatilla, Hermiston, also Boardman adjacent to refuge. CAMPGROUNDS—In Boardman; also Crow Butte State Park and Plymouth Corps of Engineers Park on Washington side.

Weather notes: Frequent dust storms in spring; summer 100+, dry.

Points of interest nearby: McNary Dam, especially the windows for viewing salmon and steelhead trout on the fish ladders on the Washington side.

For more information: Umatilla National Wildlife Refuge, P.O. Box 239, Umatilla, Oregon 97882. Phone: (503) 922-3232.

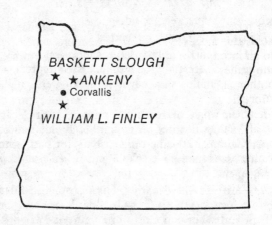

BASKETT SLOUGH
★ ★ANKENY
● Corvallis
★
WILLIAM L. FINLEY

WILLAMETTE VALLEY COMPLEX
(Oregon)

It is easy to see why settlers on the Oregon Trail ended their long trek in the green and fertile Willamette Valley—from Independence, Missouri, to Independence, Oregon—and why numbers of waterfowl have always found it so hospitable as well. Historically one of these has been the smaller and more uncommon subspecies known as the dusky Canada goose, distinguished by its smaller size and charcoal breast. Hunting and land development in this century have gradually diminished the population and areas open to the attractive little dusky whose whole population winters in the Willamette and along the lower Columbia River (it nests in an equally restricted area of the Alaskan coast, primarily on the Copper River delta).

To safeguard its decreasing numbers, three refuges were set aside in 1964 and 1965, and the dusky has responded well, its population apparently stable and even slightly increased. It can be seen on its wintering grounds, its numbers close to forty thousand, divided roughly between the 2,800-acre Ankeny Refuge, 2,500-acre Baskett Slough Refuge, and 5,325-acre William Finley Refuge which administers all three. Certain areas are set aside for quiet sanctuary for these sometimes nervous birds (especially in hunting season) but they can almost always be seen, and sometimes from fairly close by, when they venture into the fields to feed.

The three refuges, located not far apart, are similar but Finley probably holds the most for a visitor, with more varied habitat and wildlife and an interpretive walking trail. Most of the animals indigenous to the valley and the coast range have been seen at one time or another, including pileated woodpeckers and the first nesting record for the white-tailed kite in Oregon. Gray fox sometimes build dens near the workshop and bobcat are occasionally around.

Common all year at all three refuges are red-tailed hawks, kestrels, ruffed grouse, California quails, ring-necked pheasant, great horned owls, great blue herons, and a variety of small birds, especially bush-tits, Bewick's wrens, scrub and usually Steller's jays, white-breasted and often red-breasted nuthatches, killdeer, flickers, and handsome wood ducks.

Common seasonally are whistling swans, band-tailed pigeons, Swainson's and varied thrushes, black-headed grosbeaks, lazuli buntings, yellow-breasted chats, golden-crowned sparrows and orange-crowned and Wilson's warblers, which also nest. Warbler migrations can be interesting. Best times for small birding are April through June 15.

Black-tailed deer are fairly common; red fox cyclically common; coyote are seen occasionally. All three refuges have trails that can be hiked (sometimes closed in wet weather). There are excellent lists, particularly of the plants.

Information on all, and maps and directions for getting there are available from the Finley Refuge office, open weekdays. To get there from Corvallis, take Route 99 W, 8.5 miles south to the refuge sign, then west on a gravel road two miles. For further information contact: Willamette Valley Refuge Complex, Route 2, Box 208, Corvallis, Oregon 97330. Phone: (503) 753-7236.

Hundreds of thousands of sea birds come ashore in spring and summer to nest on these wild uninhabited rocky coastal refuges administered from the Willamette Valley Complex. *Cape Meares* Refuge, the main land-based one of the three, is located on a coastal headland just south of Tillamook Bay about eight miles west of the town of Tillamook and two miles north of Oceanside; *Three Arch Rocks* Refuge is a group of arched rocky islands about two miles south of Cape Meares; and *Oregon Islands* Refuge consists of a string of islands, some only a few rocks themselves, scattered for 290 miles from the north Oregon coast to the California border.

Huge concentrations of common murres, tufted puffins, guillemots, petrels, Brandt's and pelagic cormorants use these, as well as several species of sea lions and harbor seals. Except for the land portion of Cape Meares, all are inaccessible (and off limits in any case for all but scientific study by special permission) but some can easily be seen and a fantastic sight they are with these birds packed shoulder to shoulder on every available space of rock, sometimes a hundred thousand or more at a time, occasionally diving to the water or flying low overhead.

The best view of Three Arch Rocks is from a pleasant motel on a hill just beside Oceanside, where the proprietors seem to enjoy having bird-watching visitors. For a closer look at the murre congregations, go to the lighthouse two miles north adjoining the Cape Meares tract. You can either drive to the lighthouse parking lot and walk around, or take the trail through Cape Meares Refuge which is in itself worth the trip: a small section of the Oregon coastal walking trail system and probably one of the most beautiful short hikes in America, through tall old hemlocks and fir trees, every step offering a new woodland garden of ferns, trilliums, hepaticas, star mosses.

The various holdings in the Oregon Islands Refuge range in size from rocks that are awash in rough weather to the fairly substantial Goat Island, and can be viewed from the many state parks and waysides that line the Oregon coast (camping is often available at these, too). Consult the refuge office for advice on which present the best sights when, and how to see them. A spotting scope would be helpful but binoculars are often satisfactory.

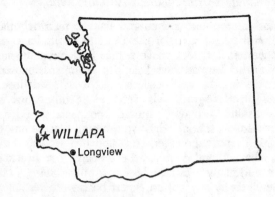

WILLAPA (Washington)

Willapa Refuge on the extreme southwest corner of Washington state is a secret national treasure of almost 10,000 acres with marvelous habitat ranging through ocean bay and tidelands, sand dunes, grasslands and rain forest uplands and wildlife such as is seldom seen—and until recently at least, few visitors, so that it has remained remote-seeming even while located not far from busy vacation areas.

Among the natural inhabitants that find their way here either to make permanent homes or just to pass through in migration are gray whales, black bear, blue and ruffed grouse, elk, bald eagles, black brant, rare Aleutian Canada geese, great rafts of sea ducks—to note but a few.

It is composed of three separate units in and around Willapa Bay, all open to foot travel only in order to preserve the wilderness quality of the place. Leadbetter Point is the northern end of the peninsula of Long Beach which separates the bay from the Pacific Ocean, and has long been known among birders for its outstanding sightings of shore- and sea birds some of which are rarely seen elsewhere. These include masses of sooty shearwaters, for example, that go through every August en route from summering territories off Alaska to nesting islands off the coast of New Zealand.

The mainland unit at the south end of the bay offers miles of dikes around and through the sloughs and fresh-water marshes where large numbers of surf and white-winged scoter, goldeneye, bufflehead, old-squaw, and now and then harlequin ducks may gather, and brant feed of the eelgrass.

Long Island, more than six thousand acres of meadow, marshland, and virgin forest where some of the Douglas firs, Sitka spruces, red cedars, and western hemlocks have trunks twelve feet through, supports not only the densest black bear population in this part of the country but the impressive Roosevelt elk, black-tailed deer, coyote, beaver, river otter, pygmy owls (and eight other owl species), Cooper's hawks and goshawks, pileated woodpeckers, and numerous songbirds. It also has several primitive camping areas. Long Island is accessible only by boat, however, and though it is only a short trip across it can be perilous. Winds arise quickly with swells of eight feet or more, and many lives have been lost in this place, so it should not be undertaken by any but an expert boatman after consultation with the refuge office. In any case much of the island wildlife also can often be seen from the mainland headquarters.

There are also great blue heron colonies, and, common at least seasonally on one or another of the refuge tracts, Brandt's and pelagic cormorants, whistling and trumpeter swans, black turnstones, whimbrels, band-tailed pigeons, western and mew gulls, black-legged kittiwakes, common murres, pigeon guillemots, chestnut-backed chickadees, red crossbills and black-throated gray warblers, to mention but a sampling, along with occasional wandering tattlers, commonly wintering rough-legged hawks and snowy owls, and migrating whales in spring, when as many as three hundred thousand shorebirds and that many ducks may stop by on their journey north, and again a few months later southward bound.

Willapa also administers *Washington Islands* Refuge. This unusual refuge of 870 rugged islands stretching more than a hundred miles along the coast of Washington state from Cape Flattery to Copalis Beach supports enormous numbers of nesting and resting sea birds—sometimes more than a million birds are estimated to occupy these islands and nearby waters during the various seasons. These include tufted puffins, Leach's petrels, rhinoceros auklets, fork-tailed petrels, black oystercatchers, pigeon guillemots, Brandt's and pelagic cormorants, sooty shearwaters, common murres, peregrine falcons, and others, along with harbor seals and sea lions, sea and river otters, gray, piked, and killer whales. Some of the islands are only a few rocks barely above the water. Access to all is forbidden except by special permit, and to many any approach is so difficult it is likely they have never been visited by humans. But many are visible from various shore points—a spotting scope is helpful but not always necessary—one of the best viewpoints being at La Push, fifteen miles west of Forks, where one might observe a half million or so shearwaters and scoters in spring or fall, along with the migrating whales.

There are also boat services which undertake pelagic observation trips from time to time; contact the refuge office to learn about these.

How to get there: From Long Beach take Route 103 south to 101, then north 8 miles beyond Astoria junction to refuge headquarters. There get maps, directions for various refuge units.

Open: Daylight hours (office weekdays only), year-round.

Best times to visit: Spring, fall, and winter.

What to see: Tremendous variety and numbers of water-oriented birds, many seldom seen elsewhere, also mammals—black-tailed deer, possibly bear, elk, otter, whales.

What to do: Twenty-six miles of roads and trails for hiking, as well as open wilderness areas; photography (blinds available, one with removable one-way glass); observation pond at headquarters where sampling of wildlife often seen; shellfishing for steamer clams; archeological sites; limited waterfowl and big game hunting; beachcombing for agates, glass balls, driftwood, other sea finds. Mushrooming—30 edible species in fall—at Long Beach and throughout peninsula.

Where to stay: MOTELS—At Long Beach and throughout peninsula. CAMPGROUNDS—Throughout peninsula; also Fort Canby and Fort Columbia State Parks, 15 miles south, and primitive on Long Island.

Weather notes: Snow is rare but winter months average 15″ rain each. Sudden windstorms can cause 8-foot swells on the bay.

What to take and wear: Raingear and rubberized hiking boots.

Points of interest nearby: Historic village of Oysterville; Nahcotta State Shellfish Laboratory; Leadbetter Point State Park, adjoining refuge on the south; Lewis and Clark Interpretive Center at Fort Canby.

For more information: Willapa National Wildlife Refuge, Ilwaco, Washington 98624. Phone: (206) 484-3482.

HAWAIIAN AND PACIFIC ISLANDS

The Hawaiian Islands in the mid-Pacific Ocean are nearly twenty-four hundred miles from the nearest continental land mass and they are among the most beautiful and idyllic on the face of the earth. High volcanic mountains and lush green valleys are surrounded by green crystalline waters, and there is fine weather all year, ranging from an average seventy-four degrees in February to eighty in September, and varying but little from day to night.

Eleven units of the national wildlife refuge system are located in Hawaii and on other Pacific islands. All of those on the populated Hawaiian islands protect endangered birds; the Central and South Pacific refuges support both endangered species and large nesting sea-bird colonies.

On the remote and mostly unpopulated "out" islands are some of the largest sea-bird colonies in the world—sometimes up to ten million albatrosses, frigatebirds, shearwaters, boobies, sooty and fairy terns and petrels. These refuges also harbor four endemic species of land birds—the Nihoa finch and millerbird and the Laysan finch and duck—and provide vital habitat for the endangered monk seal, the world's only tropical seal.

When Captain James Cook first visited Hawaii in 1778, there were seventy kinds of birds here that were found nowhere else in the world. Of these, twenty-five have become extinct and twenty-eight are threatened, and so many exotics—both plant and animal—have been introduced to compete with them that on the populated islands one generally must go to places over fifteen hundred feet elevation, preferably in forested land, to see native plants and birds. Most of those visible at lower elevations have been introduced. Also, the limited amount of available land is at such a premium that refuges sometimes must make do with what is left in the more populous centers—as, on Oahu, the Pearl City unit is twenty-four and a half acres adjacent to a landfill. The unit contains a small but precious bit of wetland, where the endangered Hawaiian stilt finds sanctuary.

The Kilauea Point lighthouse headquarters for the Hanalei and

Huleia refuges on the island of Kauai is probably the most interesting refuge area open to the public. Red-footed boobies nest and the young try their wings from the office weathervane; wedge-tailed shearwaters wheel and soar, and there are red-billed and white-tailed tropicbirds and green sea turtles.

The naturalist visitor to the populated Hawaiian islands also may enjoy the beautiful state parks where there are trails and camping; national parks where volcanic activity is evident; and dozens of hiking trails throughout the islands. There is excellent material available on these at bookstores and park and refuge offices, including an information-packed *Atlas of Hawaii* by the University of Hawaii, which also produces a booklet on Hawaiian National Parks; a bird booklet by the Hawaiian Audubon Society; a booklet which describes the hiking trails; and other information available from the State Department of Land and Natural Resources, 1151 Punchbowl Street, Honolulu, Hawaii 96813. Several good booklets have been published by the state and U. S. Interior Departments on Hawaii's endangered wildlife, endangered water birds, and endangered forest birds.

There are camping areas, lovely drives, and pleasant natural areas within a short distance of almost any place on these islands, especially as one gets away from the large airports and population centers. Air shuttles commute regularly among the various islands and some have stops away from the main jetports.

The refuges on the main islands, other than those on Kauai, are not generally intended for public access; they harbor endangered species, are not very large, and public access would disturb the creatures the refuges are there to protect. Refuge lands are gradually being added, however, and existing refuges developed so the traveler who finds himself here should by all means check with the refuge complex office for recent information at Hawaiian and Pacific Islands National Wildlife Refuge Complex, 300 Ala Moana Boulevard, Room 5302, P.O. Box 50167, Honolulu, Hawaii 96850. Phone: (808) 546-5608.

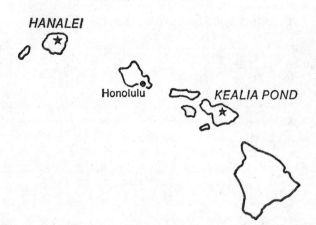

HANALEI

Honolulu

KEALIA POND

KILAUEA POINT, HANALEI, AND HULEIA
(Kauai)

Wedge-tailed shearwaters and red-footed boobies are abundant in burrows alongside the refuge office located at Kilauea lighthouse station and there is a dramatic view of steep cliffs rising from the Kauai coastline. These drop off sharply into the clear water where green sea turtles and spinner dolphins often can be seen.

Hundreds of birds can be seen wheeling around this dramatic spot —red-billed and white-tailed tropicbirds, both brown and red-footed boobies, frigatebirds, and, from December through March the great Laysan albatross, sailing along on seven-foot wingspread, one of the few places in the United States where this impressive bird is readily observable from land. There can be good chances to photograph some of these beautiful sea birds in flight as they hover, often at eye level, facing into the wind.

Young boobies can be perched almost anyplace during the time they are learning to fly—often they are on the office weathervane. Shearwaters are best seen at dusk between March and November; short-eared owls are possible anytime, here and elsewhere on Kauai. Some of the small introduced species are common here also—common mynahs, Japanese white-eyes, the shama and melodious laughing thrush, and several native plants such as 'akoko.

To get to Lighthouse Point from Lihue take the Kuhio Highway north about twenty miles to Kilauea, then the Kilauea Road to the office. The gate is open from noon to 4 P.M. except Saturdays.

The other two refuge tracts on Kauai are 917-acre Hanalei and 238-acre Huleia. They consist of taro fields (Hanalei) and seasonally flooded riverbottom (Huleia) where the endangered stilt, coot, gallinule, and Hawaiian duck can be found (Kauai is the only place where a self-sustaining population of this duck remains). There are a number of other species, primarily introduced, but also some migratory golden plovers and wandering tattlers.

To view the Hanalei tract, continue on the Kuhio Highway from the lighthouse five miles to Princeville, and past it a mile, staying on the main road. There is an overlook above Hanalei's lush green valley on the left-hand side of this road. A spotting scope is helpful here.

There is also a good chance to see the golden plovers and tattlers at Hanalei from September to March by continuing on the main road past a covered bridge and turning left on a county road which dead-ends shortly afterward (the turn-around can be muddy).

For Huleia, follow road signs from Lihue toward Nawiliwili Harbor and then to Menahune Fish Pond.

Some persons say Kauai, "the garden isle," is the loveliest place in the islands. The movie *South Pacific* was photographed here and there is much lush, rolling greenery as well as high mountains, the topmost peak of which, Mount Waialeale, is the wettest place on earth (rain falls here an average 335 days a year and totals an average 486 inches). There are particularly striking scenic views in Kokee and Alakai State Parks and nearby Waimea Canyon and native forest birds can often be seen in these places.

Information on trails and camping and permission to enter restricted areas can be obtained from the State Department of Land and Natural Resources in Lihue, and there are numerous motels on the island. For further information, contact: Hanalei and Huleia National Wildlife Refuges, P.O. Box 87, Kilauea, Kauai, Hawaii 96754. Phone: (808) 828-1431.

KEALIA POND (Maui)

This valuable wetland has been in the process of acquisition as a refuge for water birds on the island of Maui. Eventually public use facilities are planned—interpretive centers and walks around the five hundred acres of pond and surrounding rim of upland—though until recently no timetable has been set for this. But the site is readily visible and so are many of the birds for which it is to be set aside—the endangered subspecies of Hawaiian coots and stilts. There also are black-crowned night herons, cattle egrets, and some migrant shorebirds along with various of the introduced small species, the omnipresent mynah as well as munias, Japanese white-eyes, shama thrushes and others. Ospreys and ring-billed and herring gulls also are occasionally seen here.

To get to the refuge, take Route 38 from the Maui airport to Route 36, then south to Route 32, west to Route 30, south to 31, and east to the point from which the pond may be seen.

Haleakala National Park is on Maui, preserving 28,660 acres that was a Hawaiian spiritual and cultural center in a beautiful wilderness area for centuries before others came. It encompasses stunning overlooks, rare botanical species, hiking trails in a volcanic crater, cabins, and campgrounds. Maui also has botanical gardens and state and county parks—in fact, much of the island is interlaced with lovely walks and drives, with lush vegetation, waterfalls, and an altogether enchanting and other-worldly tropical beauty. Charles Lindbergh, having seen most of the world, chose Maui as his final home.

PEARL HARBOR AND JAMES CAMPBELL (Oahu)

The 61-acre Pearl Harbor and 142-acre James Campbell refuges as well as the headquarters office for all the Hawaiian and Pacific Islands complex are located on Oahu. These small refuge tracts were established specifically for protection of the endangered Hawaiian coot, gallinule, and stilt. A number of other species use the refuge as well, including the American golden plover, cattle egret, ruddy turnstones, and such introduced species as the spotted and barred dove and spotted munia.

The two Pearl Harbor units are on the south shore inside the Pearl Harbor naval base, and protect dense nesting concentrations of the stilt. Neither has public facilities, but one, containing a ten-acre wetland basin adjacent to a landfill, can be viewed from behind a chain link fence constructed to protect the birds.

The James Campbell units on the northeastern shore contain ponds and impoundments and are used mainly by the coots and stilts, although gallinules and koloas are sometimes present. Some interpretive development is planned but until recently none had been completed.

Related places of interest for the visitor on Oahu include excellent snorkeling and viewing on the island's south side in Hanauma Bay, a state marine sanctuary with dazzling tropical fish and several possible birding locales described in the booklet on "Hawaii's Endangered Waterbirds."

KAKAHAIA (Molokai)

This forty-two-acre refuge adjacent to the south shore of beautiful Molokai is a small pond fed by artesian wells and bordered by dense roundstem bullrush marsh, a tiny but rare and valuable bit of remnant wetland, primarily habitat for the endangered coot which lives and nests here. Migrant ducks and cattle egrets also use it. The immediate area is not open to public entry but the ocean beachfront has been developed by the county for public access and general viewing as well as picnicking, swimming, and snorkeling, and is open daily. Kakahaia is located on Kamehameha Highway, just east of Kaunakakai. For the visitor to Molokai, Halawa Valley at the eastern end has several state areas with waterfalls and hiking trails.

CENTRAL AND SOUTH PACIFIC OCEAN

Some of the largest concentrations of sea birds in the world inhabit these tiny, remote island refuges—over ten million frigatebirds, sooty terns, shearwaters, petrels, albatrosses, tropicbirds, and others, as well as the endangered Hawaiian monk seal; hawksbill and green sea turtles and hundreds of marine species. Altogether these are six separate refuges in this complex, one of which has eight individual units. These island refuges extend more than four thousand miles across the Pacific.

Among them is an island chain a thousand miles long encompassing only 1,769 acres of land but over 300,000 acres of reefs and water known as the Leewards or the Northwest Hawaiian Islands—plus the separate island refuges of *Baker, Howland,* and *Jarvis* and *Johnston* and *Rose* atolls. Howland was the destination of Amelia Earhart when she disappeared in 1937; Rose Atoll in American Samoa (eight degrees below the Equator) was named "for a lady especially dear" to its discoverer, and is one of the smallest atolls in the world. It is the southernmost of U.S. refuges.

The largest of these island refuges, *Laysan,* is but two square miles. Access to many of them is difficult, often dangerous, and in any case public use would be hazardous to the bird colonies. Therefore, except for rare calls by special permit (granted by the Oahu refuge office) and by refuge staff itself, the islands are visited by none except their avian inhabitants.

There are several geologic forms visible in the Hawaiian Islands Refuge chain. Tremendous underwater volcanic peaks rise in sheer cliffs without beaches; there are coral-encrusted collapsed cones, as in the atolls, and low sandy islands surrounded by submerged coral. Four bird species found nowhere else in the world are found in this group—the Nihoa millerbird and finch, and the Laysan teal and finch, as well as unique plants such as the Nihoa palm.

One of the most abundant birds is the sooty tern. Sometimes up to two million can be present on Laysan. This bird is said to be able to fly for months at a time without ever touching down on either land or water. One of the loveliest inhabitants is the white tern (often called the most beautiful of all sea birds) which lays a single egg on a bare branch or rock with no nest construction whatever. Somehow both egg and young manage to stay in place and survive.

The black-footed albatross is abundant on some of the islands, as is the Laysan albatross; and present at various times are noddy terns, wedge-tailed and Christmas shearwaters, red-billed tropicbirds, several species of boobies, petrels, and many others.

As notable as the tremendous size of these congregations is the life pattern of many of the species. The albatross relies on its great wingspread to balance so delicately on air currents that it can glide for miles at sea without seeming to move more than a few feathers, and uses its remarkable homing ability to return three thousand miles over unmarked seas in ten days. Shearwaters have tubular nostrils and the ability to drink sea water safely, excreting the salt through its nostrils. Tiny swift petrels nest deep in the ground and ride the air cushions inches above the ocean swells. Then there are graybacked terns, whose eggs have pink yolks; streamer-tailed tropicbirds, said to be able to fly backward; and frigate- or man-o'-war birds, earning their nickname from a piratical habit of stealing other birds' fish. Birds which nest in Alaska's Far North stop here for the winter—golden plovers, bristle-thighed curlews, wandering tattlers, and ruddy turnstones.

The Hawaiian Islands National Wildlife Refuge was established in 1909. Before then visitors had slaughtered birds for their decorative feathers, and introduced competitive or predatory creatures such as rabbits and rats that laid waste with devastating effect. Between 1902 and 1911 the bird population on Laysan was reduced from an estimated seven to ten million to a little over one million. Recovery has been slow.

But during breeding season some of these now-undisturbed tiny islets can be so covered with birds—nest, eggs, young—that it is hard to see how the parents recognize their own offspring. The activity is bewildering, the din deafening. But the neighbors on these tiny islands (which truly are national treasures) don't seem to mind.

X. ALASKA

Alaska comes from the Aleut Eskimo word meaning "great land," a name given it when few if any persons could more than imagine its greatness. But they imagined correctly. To see a small part of it even today—a glimpse of a herd of caribou crowding one another with spreading yard-wide antlers; a cliffside literally covered with tens of thousands of sea-bird nests overhanging the sea; the scream of a bald eagle high in the air over a streambed where tens of thousands of salmon are struggling upstream; the vastness of miles and miles of Arctic tundra awash with multihued wild flowers in the spring, blanketed with scarlet and gold moss and lichen in the fall; mountains and rivers, some of the highest and longest in the world, that have been wild and undisturbed since their cataclysmic creation by natural forces—is to sense something of the greatness of the whole.

Moose, reindeer, Arctic fox, and polar bear make their home here; also great Kodiak bear and at least representative numbers of some of the wild populations that have largely disappeared from the southern United States—lynx, wolverines, and timber wolves. There also are mountain goats and sheep, and many others. Whales, seals, and walruses swim offshore, and upstream, five species of North Pacific salmon spawn.

Some of the great sea-bird colonies of the world are here—millions of puffins, murres, fulmars, cormorants—as well as shorebirds and passerines and waterfowl which come here to nest in the short northern summer and then return to spend the fall and winter over the entire United States, and in fact the whole hemisphere. This ecologically fragile land is the nursery for the waterfowl and other bird populations of much of this part of the world.

Alaska is by far our largest state—more than twice the size of Texas. From its eastern end to the western tip of the Aleutian archipelago, it stretches almost over a map of the contiguous United States. It has a glacier the size of Rhode Island. It encompasses four time zones. Its weather can be warm and sunny in summer—Anchorage and the Kenai Peninsula often have conditions not unlike the midwestern United States—but near the sea it can be shrouded much of the time in fog, and above the Arctic Coast, there are always ice floes. Winters there are long and cold with deeply sub-zero temperatures, and the daylight, which lasts around the clock in midsummer, disappears entirely, leaving only the aurora borealis to light up the darkness.

Refuges are represented in almost every significant natural section of Alaska, from sixty-five-acre *St. Lazaria,* a vital home for oceanic birds to the 8,900,000-acre *Arctic Wildlife Range* with its Porcupine River caribou herds, one of the largest in the world. The *Aleutian Islands Refuge* with its sea otters and other marine mammals stretches over a thousand miles along that southwestern archipelago; *Izembek* is at the head of that chain, where the entire world population of black brant can be seen during fall migration; the beautiful *Kenai Moose Range* is located on the Kenai Peninsula, where moose and many other wild creatures make their homes in a huge de facto wilderness just two hours' drive from Anchorage; *Kodiak* encompasses most of Kodiak Island off the Alaskan Peninsula, home of the great Kodiak brown bear; *Clarence Rhode Refuge* faces the Bering Sea and is one of the world's great nesting colonies of waterfowl, shorebirds and songbirds; finally there is 3,330,632-acre *Nunivak Island,* where the musk-ox lives.

The large refuges need to be large. While Alaskan wildlife populations of some species are abundant, the state could not be described as teeming with wildlife in the usual sense. The climate, short growing season, and general ecological conditions are too harsh for that. An animal in this northern area requires a larger territory to survive than the same species needs in a more hospitable clime. So while wildlife occur in good numbers, they are spread over a wide area. Therefore, one does not simply set foot on one of these refuges and automatically find great herds and flocks of wild creatures presenting themselves before him. As at any refuge, observation of wild birds and animals requires time and patience—perhaps even a bit more here.

The refuges also may not be easy to see because of their weather conditions and relative inaccessibility. Only Kenai, on the Alaska highway system and with numerous hiking trails, canoe routes, and campsites, is fairly easy to visit and look around.

For the others it can be quite a different story. Best plan on seeing them, between May and October—the rest of the year can be too harsh for all but the hardiest. Even then it is not always simple. On most there are few if any roads, few if any places to stay close by. Access to some is not possible at all—as in the case of some of the rocky nesting islands surrounded by treacherous waters. To others, access to interior sections is by hiking or charter airplane only. This can be costly and "bush" pilots are not invariably reliable—sometimes because the conditions in which they are flying are not reliable. Fog and rain especially near the sea can stop flying for weeks at a time. All this should be said so that one will not go to an Alaskan refuge unprepared. The visitor who is willing and able to take nature on its own terms, as actual, true wilderness, expecting no more special conveniences for his comfort than are offered the wild inhabitants, will make out best. With these caveats, it can be one of the most glorious places on earth, especially in the summer, and when the sun shines.

Nature observations and hiking are among the most rewarding things to do. Backpacking can be one of the best (though not only) ways of doing this. Camping is permitted in most places, also hunting, with limitations, and fishing—some of the best salmon and trout fishing in the world. Photographic opportunities can be marvelous with the long hours of summer daylight, especially for scenery—the grandeur of Alaskan scenery is unsurpassed (though coastal areas can be misty much of the time); success in photographing wildlife, here as any place, goes to the person who is patient. Cross-country skiing and snowshoeing are possible for those not frozen out by Thanksgiving. From then until February it is pretty grim going but according to Dave Spencer, a longtime Alaska refuge manager now at the University of Alaska, "March and April can't be beat. Ski touring is unsurpassed as long days give a foretaste of spring."

There are many places of related interest for one planning a trip to Alaska, prime among them being McKinley National Park, with hiking, camping, backpacking, breath-taking scenery, wildlife populations—everything, and excellent guidebooks for seeing it all. Two magnificent national forests, the Chugach and Tongass, occupy large parts of southeast and south-central Alaska. There are brochures on scenic drives, hiking and canoe routes, and campgrounds around the state by the Bureau of Land Management, available from the BLM state director, U. S. Department of the Interior, 555 Cordova Street, Anchorage, Alaska 99501, and the state parks are among the best in the nation.

There are ferry trips to various places, including spectacular Glacier Bay and the Inside Passage up from Seattle. There are raft trips, side trips to the Pribilof Islands, and many, many others.

About all of this there is abundant informational material available (though it should be spelled out more clearly that Alaskan tourist costs generally are quite high). The Alaska Geographic Society has a series of beautiful booklets on various sections of the state—

Cook Inlet, Admiralty Island, and others. Probably the best and most comprehensive is the fact-filled "Milepost," printed annually by the same publishers, and available at most bookstores. It covers almost every possible subject related to Alaska.

Finally, the visitor should contact in advance either the Alaskan regional refuge office in Anchorage, or any of the refuges included therein. Refuge staff members can be extremely helpful in suggesting how to plan a trip best suited to individual wishes and capabilities. The regional refuge office is: U. S. Fish and Wildlife Service, 1011 East Tudor, Anchorage, Alaska 99503. Phone: (907) 276-3800.

The following is a list of some birds of special interest found in common or abundant status at the refuges of this region.

Birds Common or Abundant at Seasons Indicated:

S: Spring   s: Summer   F: Fall   W: Winter

Yellow-billed Loon: Aleutian Islands, W; Arctic, s.
Arctic Loon: Arctic, s; Kenai, Ss; Kodiak, W; Rhode, s.
Northern Fulmar: Aleutian Islands, s.
Pink-footed Shearwater: Kodiak, s.
Sooty Shearwater: Aleutian Islands, Ss; Kodiak, s.
Short-tailed Shearwater: Aleutian Islands, s.
Fork-tailed Storm-petrel: Aleutian Islands, s.
Pelagic Cormorant: Aleutian Islands, SsFW; Kodiak, SsFW.
Red-faced Cormorant: Aleutian Islands, s; Kodiak, s.
Trumpeter Swan: Kenai, SsF.
Emperor Goose: Aleutian Islands, W; Izembek SFW; Rhode, SsF.
White-fronted Goose: Rhode, SsF.
Barrow's Goldeneye: Kenai, SsF; Kodiak, W.
Harlequin Duck: Aleutian Islands, SsFW; Arctic, s; Izembek, SsFW; Kodiak, SsFW.
Steller's Eider: Aleutian Islands, W; Izembek, W; Kodiak, W.
King Eider: Arctic SsF; Rhode, SF.
Spectacled Eider: Rhode, SsF.
Goshawk: Kenai, SsFW; Kodiak, SF.
Bald Eagle: Aleutian Islands, SsFW; Kenai, SsFW; Kodiak, SsFW.
Merlin: Arctic, s.
Gyrfalcon: Arctic, s; Izembek, W.
Peregrine Falcon: Aleutian Islands, SsFW.
Willow Ptarmigan: Arctic, SsFW; Izembek, SsFW; Kenai, SsFW; Kodiak, SsFW; Rhode, SsFW.

Rock Ptarmigan: Aleutian Islands, SsFW; Arctic, SsFW; Izembek, SsFW; Kodiak, SsFW.

White-tailed Ptarmigan: Kenai, SsFW.

Black Oystercatcher: Aleutian Islands, SsFW; Kodiak, SsFW.

American Golden Plover: Arctic, s; Rhode, SsF.

Bar-tailed Godwit: Izembek, F; Rhode, s.

Wandering Tattler: Aleutian Islands, SF; Arctic, s; Kodiak, SF.

Black Turnstone: Kodiak, SsFW; Rhode, SsF.

Rock Sandpiper: Aleutian Islands, SsFW; Izembek, SsFW; Kodiak, SsFW.

Baird's Sandpiper: Arctic, s.

Red Phalarope: Aleutian Islands, SF; Arctic, s; Izembek, SF; Rhode, SsF; Kodiak, SF.

Northern Phalarope: Aleutian Islands, SsF; Arctic, s; Izembek, SsF; Kenai, Ss; Kodiak, SsF; Rhode, SsF.

Parasitic Jaeger: Aleutian Islands, SsF; Arctic, s; Kodiak, s; Rhode, SsF.

Pomarine Jaeger: Aleutian Islands, SsF; Arctic, s.

Long-tailed Jaeger: Arctic, s; Rhode, SsF.

Glaucous Gull: Arctic, s; Rhode, SsF.

Glaucous-winged Gull: Aleutian Islands, SsFW; Izembek, SsFW; Kenai, SsF; Kodiak, SsFW.

Mew Gull: Arctic, s; Kenai, SsF; Kodiak, SsFW; Rhode, SsF.

Black-legged Kittiwake: Aleutian Islands, SsF; Izembek, SsF; Kodiak, s.

Red-legged Kittiwake: Aleutian Islands, s.

Sabine's Gull: Arctic, s; Rhode, SsF.

Arctic Tern: Aleutian Island, Ss; Arctic, s; Izembek, s; Kenai, Ss; Kodiak, s; Rhode, s.

Aleutian Tern: Aleutian Islands, Ss; Izembek, s; Kodiak, Ss.

Common Murre: Aleutian Islands, SsFW; Kodiak, SsFW.

Thick-billed Murre: Aleutian Islands, SsFW; Arctic, s.

Black Guillemot: Arctic, s.

Pigeon Guillemot: Aleutian Islands, SsFW; Kodiak, SsFW.

Ancient Murrelet: Aleutian Islands, s; Kodiak, W.

Parakeet Auklet: Aleutian Islands, s.

Crested Auklet: Aleutian Islands s.

Least Auklet: Aleutian Islands, s.

Whiskered Auklet: Aleutian Islands, s.

Horned Puffin: Aleutian Islands, s; Kodiak, s.

Tufted Puffin: Aleutian Islands, s; Kodiak, s.

Snowy Owl: Arctic, SsFW.

Gray Jay: Arctic, SsFW; Kenai, SsFW.

Northwestern Crow: Kodiak, SsFW.
Boreal Chickadee: Arctic, SsFW; Kenai, SsFW.
Dipper: Arctic, s; Kodiak, SsFW.
Varied Thrush: Kenai, SsF; Kodiak, SsFW.
Wheatear: Arctic, s.
Arctic Warbler: Arctic, s.
Yellow Wagtail: Arctic, s; Rhode, SsF.
Bohemian Waxwing: Arctic, s; Kenai, SsF.
Gray-crowned Rosy Finch: Aleutian Islands, SsFW; Izembek, SsFW.
Hoary Redpoll: Arctic, SsFW.
Lapland Longspur: Aleutian Islands, Ss; Arctic, s; Izembek, s;
    Kenai, S; Kodiak, Ss; Rhode, s.
McKay's Bunting: Izembek, W; Rhode, SsF.

ALASKA

Alaska

1 Arctic
2 Clarence Rhode
3 Aleutian Islands
4 Izembek
5 Kodiak
6 Kenai National Moose Range

Anchorage

ALEUTIAN
ISLANDS

ALEUTIAN ISLANDS (Alaska)

The Aleutian Islands Refuge is a chain of volcanic islands more than a thousand miles long stretching from Alaska almost to Siberia. Originally set aside chiefly to bring back the persecuted sea otter from near-extinction, it not only has accomplished this but provided sanctuary for many other creatures as well. Some of the largest sea-bird colonies in the world are here—their nests crowd the cliffsides by the millions—along with bald eagles, sea lions, caribou, brown bear, reindeer, and others.

The two-hundred-odd islands in the archipelago cover 2.7 million acres, most of which is included in the refuge. They were discovered in the early 1700s by Russian explorers who quickly noticed the rich, luxuriant fur of the sea otter, then present in the thousands. The Russians had a hunting quota, but after the United States acquired Alaska unrestricted hunting greatly reduced both the otters and the native Aleuts, who were impressed into the traders' service. By 1911, when hunting was halted, and 1913, when the refuge was established, the survival of the sea otter seemed all but impossible.

But they have come back, and population figures now are estimated at well over sixty thousand for this beautiful, intelligent marine mammal which has the world's most valuable fur and the interesting habits of floating on its back in the ocean while nuzzling its young and cracking open its shellfish food with rocks, occasionally anchoring itself and young with a ribbon of kelp while taking a nap, shading its eyes with a paw. (The Aleuts fared less well, their final viable communities largely gone by the end of World War II.)

Birds scarce almost everywhere else are here in numbers to stagger the imagination: fulmars, petrels, cormorants, kittiwakes, murres, auklets, and puffins in vast colonies along the steep ledges, on beaches, and in caves and burrows. The largest known fulmar colony in the world, some 450,000 birds, is on Chagulak Island, and there are hundreds of nesting bald eagles and peregrine falcons, a few gyrfalcons and snowy owls, along with the tiny Aleutian Canada goose, almost wiped out by introduced Arctic foxes in the Western Aleutians, now gradually being restored. There are great numbers of songbirds—multitudes of Lapland longspurs, gray-crowned rosy finches, snow buntings—and the rock ptarmigans which nest in summer and change into white plumage to plunge into the snowbanks for winter cover.

Bird life is active throughout the year. Harlequin ducks, Steller's and king eider, old-squaw and most of the world's emperor geese spend the winter, and thousands of shorebirds touch down during migration; and with the proximity of Siberia there are Asiatic species seldom if ever seen elsewhere in the United States—whooper swans, Mongolian plover, Steller's sea eagles, long-toed stints, falcated teals, spotted redshanks, smews, and among the small birds the bramblings, oriental cukoos, Siberian rubythroats, Asiatic rose finches, and reed buntings.

Ancient murrelets stage mass migrations of young, tumbling down from burrow nests to the sea when only a few days old. Parakeet, crested, least, and whiskered auklets all raise numbers of offspring, as do red-faced cormorants and many others.

Sea lion colonies are common, also harbor seals, and walruses occasionally haul out on Amak Island in winter. Fur seals migrate through and so do several species of whales and porpoises.

Reindeer live on Atka. Three native species of salmon spawn. Orchids and lady's slippers, pink Siberian spring beauties and Kamchatkan rhododendrons bloom.

Much of this wildlife abundance as well as the spectacular scenery against which it exists—some still active volcanoes spew smoke and steam about the landscape—are seen by few but the wild inhabitants (perhaps one reason why they thrive). This is because most of the islands are difficult to get to, hard to get around when one is there, and sometimes difficult to get out of. In recent years Reeve Airline has scheduled flights to Cold Bay, Adak, Attu, Umnak, and Shemya but most airfields are in military zones and military clearance is required to go there. The weather, while mostly in a tolerable temperature range—usually sixty degrees in summer and down to ten in winter—is subject to violent storms and periods of dense fog that can last for weeks. Further, beyond Cold Bay most places have no place to stay whatever. Attu has a Coast Guard Station; Adak has a Bachelor Officers Quarters sometimes available to persons who can get Navy clearance. Permission is sometimes granted to camp out. Occasionally the Navy has boat trips and may agree to take along a visitor on an infrequent charter trip. But all these arrangements must be cleared well in advance. For anyone prepared to be entirely self-sufficient in a wild situation, these can be fascinating places, and further information can be obtained from: Aleutian Islands National Wildlife Refuge, Box 5251, FPO Seattle, Washington 98791. Phone: (907) 579-8418.

The Aleutian Islands office also administers *Bogoslov* Refuge, two rocky islands totaling 160 acres about thirty miles north of Umnak Island with sea-bird colonies and a sea lion herd of about eight hundred. Interesting geologically, this volcanic outcrop rose from the sea about two hundred years ago and has changed form several times since then. Access requires an oceangoing vessel and is, if anything, more difficult than for the other islands.

Fairbanks

ARCTIC

The Arctic National Wildlife Range is the largest wildlife refuge in the United States and one of the largest in the world—8,900,000 acres bounded by the Arctic Ocean on the north and Canada on the east and supporting caribou, grizzly bear, mountain sheep, eagles, wolves, and great flocks of birds that come from the southern forty-eight states and at least three other continents to breed in the isolation of the tundra.

There are ice floes along its northern shores even in the summer, some of the most imposing mountains on the continent and blankets of wild flowers in spring and summer—Arctic poppies, lupines, and rhododendrons together with scarlet bunchberries and orange and gold lichens and mosses that explode in color in the fall.

It has lynx, Arctic fox, polar bear, seals, marten, black bear, wolverines, musk-oxen, and nesting ptarmigans, peregrine and gyrfalcons, snowy owls, merlins, rough-legged hawks, Arctic and red-throated loons, golden and black-bellied plovers, harlequin ducks, phalaropes, jaegers, dippers, snow buntings, and many others—and most of the species on its bird list are nesters.

Its winters have no daylight and temperatures can fall to fifty below; its summers, in the 35–75-degree range, have no darkness—the sun does not set between May 10 and August 2 and the refuge leaflet suggests the best way to see wildlife is to hike around "from evening until about noon the next day."

It is so close to the North Pole that compass readings must be adjusted thirty-six degrees to compensate for the magnetic declination.

It is so quiet, most of the time, that a tiny shrew can be heard scampering across the sphagnum moss.

From its south boundary to the foothills of the spectacular Brooks Range which divides it into north- and south-draining slopes it is open spruce forests and muskeg and winding rivers as far as the eye can see. From the towering snowclad peaks and glacier-mantled valleys the slope drops north into rounded hills covered with deep cushiony moss and finally into the treeless Arctic plain dotted with lakes and interlaced with streams, underlaid two thousand feet deep with permafrost that helps prevent moisture loss—even though the four- to eight-inch yearly precipitation is about like the southwest U.S. desert, the low vegetation is thick and lush. Ten major rivers drain into the Arctic Ocean through a vast lacework of streams, deltas, lagoons, and marshes, a tremendous undisturbed and vital feeding ground for millions of waterfowl before they go south for the winter.

It is one of the most scenically beautiful and magnificent wildlife and wilderness areas in North America, as well as one of the most fragile and ecologically sensitive, and the sight of it alone, stretching for miles and miles over spectacular vistas of lands and waters that have made their own way forever unaltered except by the natural cataclysms that created them is a stunning and memorable experience.

It is not a trip to be taken lightly—one of the largest uninhabited wilderness areas of the continent—no help—you are on your own—hazardous streams, mountains, weather, animals. You have to be equipped and know what you face. There are no auto tour routes or hiking trails. It is, on the other hand, available to any person willing to go a bit more than halfway. Camping is permitted anywhere. So is hiking. Some visitors hike across the range for several weeks at a time, supported by what they can carry in a backpack, but that is not necessary. It is possible, after flying from Fairbanks to Fort Yukon, Arctic Village, or Barter Island, to charter a plane which will put one down alongside a river where he can canoe or put up a tent and stay several days or a week exploring that place or walking out around the area. Charter planes cost, recently, about a dollar a mile but the cost of the time actually in the wilderness is figured to be only about seven dollars a day. It is appropriate for persons of all ages in average health and the refuge staff makes every effort to assist visitors in planning, well in advance if possible, a trip likely to suit their individual wishes and capabilities. For general information the refuge has prepared an excellent and detailed refuge leaflet called "Experiencing the Arctic Wildlife Range."

The possible sights and experiences can only be suggested.

Almost anyone who hikes around at the right time can see caribou —the herd is estimated at 120,000—small groups of calves or huge crowds in migration presenting a sight that can seem to be a rolling sea of antlers, along with the strange and clearly audible sounds of clicking hoofs and anklebones (one visitor who had laboriously negotiated the steep, rocky inclines that are covered with ease by these impressive animals said he could understand why their bones click). Both males and females grow large antlers and swim well, with airfilled hair giving buoyance and splayed hoofs paddling. They usually will swim across a lake rather than walk around it. The caribou calve on the coastal plain of the refuge and then migrate in the fall across the border to Canada where they winter.

Fossils are in the streambeds, for most of the refuge was once under the sea. Moose are not numerous but range throughout the refuge. Dall sheep are in the mountain ranges. Wolves and bear might be anyplace, but a prime area to spot them is the lovely Sheenjek Valley. The smaller mammals are relatively unwary. Weasels, Arctic ground squirrels, and others sometimes can be observed with great intimacy.

Birds can be everywhere, depending on species and appropriate habitat—longspurs, wheatears, and gray-crowned rosy finches in the alpine tundra; wagtails, hoary redpolls, and Arctic warblers in riparian thickets. But probably the most important bird habitat in the entire range is the strip of marshy land and coastal lagoons along the northern Arctic coastal plain. A half-million old-squaw may migrate along here, with a million common and king eider that nest on offshore islands, whistling swans, and hundreds of thousands of snow geese. There also are pintail, wigeon, teal, bufflehead, and shorebirds that require these quiet places to rest and feed, both adults and young, in order safely to make the long migration south to wintering grounds over much of the lower forty-eight states.

Finally it should be said that the Arctic, while presenting a wide variety of living things, is not teeming with wildlife in the usual sense. The Arctic environment is too harsh for that. They are all here but each one requires a large territory in order to survive; therefore they exist in scattered numbers. Nowhere is the Arctic effect better seen than in the vegetation, most of which hugs the ground in a lovely mosaic. This is one reason the geologic forms appear so spectacular: no tall trees soften their spare outlines. Even willow trees, the same species that grow to twenty feet elsewhere, are here but a few inches high.

For further information contact: Arctic National Wildlife Refuge, Room 266 Federal Building, 101-12th Avenue, Box 20, Fairbanks, Alaska 99701. Phone: (907) 452-1951, ext. 250.

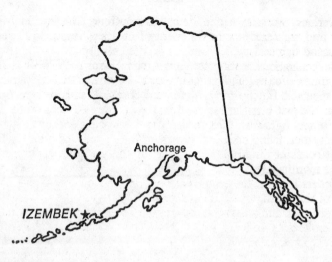

Anchorage

IZEMBEK ★

IZEMBEK (Alaska)

The entire world population of the black brant subspecies is at Izembek lagoon in the fall, feeding on the eelgrass, an aquatic plant named for its resemblance to the eel and the main food of this small dark goose which breeds above the Arctic Circle and winters as far south as Baja California. The world's largest eelgrass beds are on this 321,000-acre refuge of marshes, lagoons, low heath vegetation, and soaringly beautiful and rugged volcanic peaks at the lower end of the Alaska Peninsula between the Bering Sea and the Pacific Ocean, and the dependence on them of this bird, the western equivalent of the brant of the Atlantic Coast, was the reason this refuge was established. But many other species have been attracted as well.

A good part of the world's emperor goose population comes through, along with sixty thousand or so lesser Canada geese; sometimes a hundred thousand dabbling ducks—pintail, teal, mallard, —bound for the lower forty-eight states; flocks of rock sandpipers, along with ruddy turnstones, semipalmated plovers, least and western sandpipers; and sometimes huge numbers of others that stay the winter—great waves of colorful old-squaw, Steller's, common, and king eider, harlequin ducks, and white-winged scoter, along with smaller numbers of common and yellow-billed loons.

There are also substantial populations of Alaskan brown bear, called the world's largest land carnivore, caribou, wolves, along with wolverines, weasels, Arctic hares, river otters, and, cyclically, red fox, and in nearby waters sea otters and sea lions, with several thousand hair seals which bask on exposed sandspits.

Concentrations of waterfowl are present in spring but not as many at a time or for as long—usually from mid-April to mid-May. But the fall spectacle can be truly awesome, starting as early as late August when the first brant arrive, customarily on the first cool north wind, and others follow on each succeeding north wind and until they are all together, flying back and forth and calling and gabbling in an almost constant din, finally departing, often all in one night, perhaps three months later.

Others feed on the eelgrass as well but also on the abundant berries of the heath, especially the crowberries.

Both rock and willow ptarmigans are here, and nest, the former in the mountains and the willow sometimes in great numbers in the alder thickets.

Gyrfalcons, peregrines, bald eagles, and very rarely golden eagles all breed here. So do many rock sandpipers, gray-crowned rosy finches, golden-crowned and Savannah sparrows, Lapland longspurs, wandering tattlers and snow buntings, and on the shore islands, Arctic and Aleutian terns and glaucous-winged gulls.

Four native species of salmon spawn, the red, silver, pink, and chum, crowding the streams and attracting sometimes a hundred or more eagles as well as the huge brown bears and—following warily after—the wolverines, minks, otters, and glaucous-winged gulls.

Izembek's jagged Aghileen Pinnacles, Mount Dutton and Frosty Peak and its broad treeless valleys which can be covered with beautiful wild flowers are a scenic splendor as well (though marred in places by damage and debris left from World War II military activity).

Like many Alaskan refuges, Izembek is not easy to see—not only because of access—but simply visibility. Temperatures are equable—seldom below zero in winter or over sixty-five degrees in summer—but fog and clouds dominate much of the time, and the winds can seem incessant. Izembek occupies a low pass in the Alaska-Aleutian range and serves as a venturi where wind velocities increase and weather is constantly in change from the Pacific to the Bering regions. Residents are fond of saying there is relief only when the wind is changing direction. There are frequent cyclonic storms.

To get there, one can fly by commercial airline to Cold Bay, where there are limited hotel-boardinghouse accommodations. From there one can hike and camp out; or be flown out by charter aircraft; or drive over parts of the refuge if a car can be rented, as is only sometimes possible—rentals cars are few and high-priced. Try to arrange ahead, if possible, for a four-wheel drive. The refuge has thirty miles of roads, of which a two-wheel drive can manage something more than half. Another good way to travel is by boat through Izembek Bay, but only if one can be chartered with a knowledgeable boatman.

With these caveats, Izembek can be a stirring natural experience —especially for the lucky visitor who is there when the sun breaks through.

For further information contact refuge operations headquarters in Anchorage or: Izembek National Wildlife Range, Pouch 2, Cold Bay, Alaska 99571. Phone: (907) 532-2445. The Cold Bay staff also administers three other refuge units. They are:

Semidi—Encompasses a dozen or so treeless, rocky, remote, inaccessible islands and islets 110 miles southwest of Kodiak Island, totaling about 8,400 acres of land and a quarter million of water with large nesting colonies of common and thick-billed murres, black-legged kittiwakes, Pacific fulmars and horned puffins, as well as peregrine falcons and bald eagles, harbor seals and sea lions. Access is by permit only, requiring extended travel by oceangoing vessel and is not to be attempted under most circumstances because of dangerous rough waters and, much of the time, dense fog.

Simeonof—A remote 26,000-acre island in the Pacific Ocean south of the Alaskan Peninsula, established as a sanctuary for sea otters and visited also by bald eagles, oystercatchers, seals, and sea lions. Access is by permit only and should be attempted only by accomplished boathandlers.

Unimak—The first and largest island in the windswept and fog-bound Aleutian chain, almost one million acres of snow-topped peaks, active volcanoes, moving glaciers, and vast tundra covered with lakes and streams and supporting a variety of wildlife, including caribou, brown bear, wolves, fox, bald eagles, peregrine falcons, whistling swans, sea lions, and harbor seals. Large waterfowl concentrations may appear in migrations, resting and feeding on the lagoons and eelgrass—brant, lesser Canada geese, emperor geese, eider, scoter, and others. Pelagic cormorants, kittiwakes, and murres rest on the cliffs, and several million slender-billed shearwaters have sometimes been sighted in Unimak Pass. There are no visitor facilities and no roads, but a determined individual can fly to the small native village of False Pass via commercial airline, hike from there and camp out, or be flown out by small charter aircraft. Aircraft landings are allowed only on the lakes and below mean high tide on the beaches.

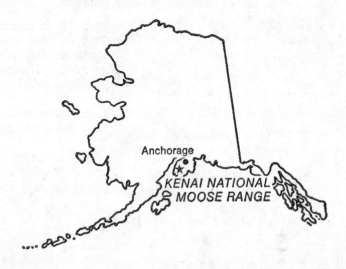

Anchorage

KENAI NATIONAL
MOOSE RANGE

KENAI (Alaska)

The Kenai Moose Range has in microcosm almost every kind of geologic feature and wildlife habitat that can be found over the whole of Alaska and most of its wild creatures as well.

Several thousand moose roam over the range. Dall sheep and mountain goats are on the high peaks. Wolves, lynx, fox, black and brown bear, and over 160 species of birds find homes on this almost-3,000-square-mile refuge in south-central Alaska, which has heathland muskeg, rolling hills, meadows, and spruce-birch-aspen forests. There are more than 1,200 lakes ranging in size from small potholes to 73,000-acre Tustumena, all drained by more than a thousand miles of rivers and streams in which four kinds of salmon spawn.

Loons call from almost every pond. Willow, rock, and white-tailed ptarmigans change their brown plumage to white when winter comes, the better to seek concealment by plunging into snowbanks. Spruce grouse are in the forest. Goshawks are common residents. Bald eagles nest as do trumpeter swans.

There are thousands of acres of de facto wilderness where one may go and see no other human being for days. There are also more than a hundred miles of paved and graveled roads, another hundred miles of hiking trails, 140 miles of canoe routes, thirteen campgrounds, and hundreds of fishing lakes and streams which have been mapped and charted for visitors. The trails are mapped for length, elevation, and difficulty; the lakes and streams for size, depth, and fish species available (fifteen species, including salmon, Dolly Varden, Arctic char, grayling, and rainbow trout); camping spots for their various facilities; and canoe trails covering much of the north part of the range. Information on the trails includes what may be seen, terrain that may be encountered, and length of time each trip probably will require. Canoes can be rented in the area.

In winter there are cross-country skiing and snowshoeing—some roads are kept open all year, and though cold, winters are often no worse than in the upper midwestern states of the lower forty-eight.

A principal landscape feature is the Kenai Mountain area covering about a third of the Moose Range and reaching from near sea level to over six thousand feet. Here are mountains interespersed with large lakes and capped by the extensive Harding ice field—a plateau of ice that heads extensive glaciers leading down the valleys of the range.

All this is within two hours' drive, 120 miles south, of Anchorage on State Route 1 which bisects the refuge. There are places to stay in Kenai, Soldotna, and several other towns nearby, and other campgrounds in adjacent Chugach National Forest and nearby state parks.

Kenai became a refuge largely at the urging of local people and conservation groups to ensure preservation here of sufficient habitat for the wide-ranging moose and several thousand of these great antlered animals, largest deer in the world, are here now. Standing up to seven and a half feet at the shoulder, and weighing up to fourteen hundred pounds (with antlers as much as four feet across) they may be seen along any of the graveled roads or even along the state highway. The bulls sometimes appear clumsy with their high muscled shoulders and lower hindquarters (which enable them to negotiate snowdrifts handily) but they are the picture of light-footed grace when in motion, trotting along at the speed of a fast horse.

Coyote are an occasional sight along the roadways and trails, especially early and late in the day (which in the northern summer can mean almost until midnight). Kenai has a dense black bear population. While they are wary, they might be spotted anywhere, as may wolves, lynx, porcupines, wolverine, otter, weasel, and snowshoe hare. A small herd of caribou is present, and hoary marmots colonize high valleys. Beaver are in many streams and ponds, and mink hunt along the water's edges.

Alaskan brown bears stay warily out of view but sometimes are lured to streams where salmon are spawning in summer. These great

fish challenge rapids and waterfalls, attempting and sometimes succeeding in negotiating a rise of perhaps thirty feet in elevation over
two-hundred-feet distance against swift-running waters. Some fall
back to rest in a quiet eddy only to try again and perhaps succeed,
or, spent, to die. It is one of the most dramatic and moving sights in
nature.

Mountain goats and sheep are on high mountain outcrops and
sometimes may be seen from a point where the Russian and Kenai
rivers join along Route 1 just off the refuge. Telescopes are set up
there but binoculars are usually sufficient. Stop and scan the moun-
tainsides carefully for what may appear at first to be small white
moving dots resembling patches of snow. Once spotted they can be
observed easily as they leap about the steep inclines, after early June
often with their lambs.

A dozen kinds of waterfowl nest, including harlequin ducks, Barrow's goldeneye, pintail, green-winged teal; also horned and red-
necked grebes, northern phalaropes, Arctic terns, glaucous-winged
and mew gulls, greater and lesser yellowlegs, and some wandering
tattlers. Ravens, magpies, redpolls, boreal and black-capped chickadees, and gray jays are always about, the last a common visitor at
campgrounds; and less so but present and often of special interest to
visitors are gray-crowned rosy finches, black-backed and northern
three-toed woodpeckers. The great horned owl is frequently seen or
heard; less so are great gray, boreal and hawk owls. Pine grosbeaks,
golden-crowned sparrows, varied thrushes, and Bohemian waxwings
all are common nesters.

Wild flowers can be beautiful—poppies, lupines, shooting stars,
and acres of fireweed in the summer at low elevations, with miniature varieties on the alpine terrain.

Visitors are urged to plan trips at times other than summer holiday weekends or the first week of moose season. Even at such times
in this most accessible of all Alaskan refuges, it is possible to be in
places that seem like utter wilderness, particularly backpacking in
the southern part of the refuge. This is a designated natural area,
where snowy six-thousand-foot peaks are reflected in mirrorlike lakes
rippled only by the passage of beaver or a moose. The only
sounds are the calling of birds and rustling of leaves, and each vista
seems more splendid than the last.

Also administered by Kenai Refuge is *Tuxedni*, consisting of
6,439-acre Chisik Island and tiny neighboring Duck Island, where
thousands of black-legged kittiwakes, and also horned puffins, common murres, pigeon guillemots, and glaucous-winged gulls nest on
the cliffs about 120 air miles southwest of Anchorage in Cook Inlet.

It is a wilderness area critical for nesting sea birds; access is by chartered aircraft or boat. Tides can be extremely hazardous, and visitors are asked to check with the Kenai office before planning any visit.

For more information: Refuge Manager, Kenai National Moose Range, Box 500, Kenai, Alaska 99611. Phone: (907) 283-4877.

Anchorage

KODIAK

KODIAK (Alaska)

Kodiak belongs to the bears, the eagles, and the salmon, and the first two flourish largely because of the abundance of the last. When one of the five species of Pacific salmon are spawning there may be hundreds of eagles and huge brown Kodiak bears, largest land carnivore on earth, congregated about the streams to gather up some of the great fish as they fight their way up the fast streams and rivers.

Spawning salmon are one of the awesome sights of nature on this large, rugged, beautiful island off the coast of southwest Alaska. Tens of thousands return in waves from June to September and in lesser numbers through the fall. They engage what seem and often are insuperable odds, swimming against rapids so strong it seems unlikely that even their great exertions could get past them to spawn and lay their eggs in the places upstream where they themselves began life. Many die before achieving this; others as soon as they have spawned. And waiting for them are the eagles—some two hundred pairs nest here—and the great bears for which this almost 3,000-square-mile refuge, more than two thirds of Kodiak Island, was set aside in 1941.

Sometimes several dozen bears of the two thousand on the refuge may be gathered along a few miles of streambed, and it is a daunting sight. One who has never seen a Kodiak brown bear can hardly imagine the size, presence, and power of these great mammals. The skull of a male may be eighteen inches long and he may stand nine feet tall and weigh fourteen hundred pounds. A visitor should carefully observe *all* the rules laid down to avoid unintentional confrontation and provocation of these powerful animals. Make plenty of noise as you move along; don't cook in the same place where you're camping; don't camp on a stream.

Kodiak brown bears are ordinarily mild-mannered and even playful with one another and individually, sliding down hillsides for enjoyment or turning somersaults in high spirits when thinking themselves unobserved. But the danger of confrontation cannot be overstated, and while the bears are not aggressive, once one is met the cause of the meeting becomes academic (and the bears can and do climb trees!).

Kodiak was made a refuge by Executive Order to protect the bears against overhunting and provide the large territories they require with buffer zones against human activity (cattlemen had urged their extermination). Before the refuge was established other mammals were transplanted here—Sitka black-tailed deer, reindeer, snowshoe hare, and beaver, and all have established viable populations. Mountains goats were introduced later. Deer are especially abundant here. Red fox, otter, and weasel are common—the latter two often den under refuge cabins. There are occasional silver and cross foxes. Whales, porpoises, sea otters, seals, and Steller's sea lions are in the estuaries.

Kodiak's location, bordered by Shelikof Strait, the Gulf of Alaska and the Pacific Ocean and only thirty miles from the Alaska Peninsula, gives it a blend of land and oceanic birds with occasional Asiatic species. Spring migration from early April through May brings yellowlegs, black-bellied and golden plovers, and thousands of sea birds which nest on nearby islands and cliffs—sooty and short-tailed shearwaters, double-crested, pelagic, and red-faced cormorants, and kittiwakes along with the common murres, pigeon guillemots, and horned and tufted puffins. Fall migration, July through October, ends with the return of waterfowl from farther north to spend the winter—sometimes two hundred thousand old-squaws, Steller's eiders, white-winged and surf scoters, emperor geese, and others.

Common nesters—some of them year-round residents—include willow and rock ptarmigans, rock sandpipers, common loons, with some boreal owls, dippers, redpolls, gray-crowned rosy finches, white-winged crossbills, Lapland longspurs, a few peregrine falcons, and commonly a dozen species of waterfowl including pintail, common and Barrow's goldeneye, harlequin ducks, common eider, black scoter, and scaup.

Eagles are always in view and reach a total population of well over a thousand in fall.

Wild flowers can be beautiful, with orchids, irises, fields of fireweed, shooting stars, Indian paintbrushes, and thousands of fruiting plants—salmonberries, blueberries, and elderberries—all nourished by the mild, moist climate. It is seldom down to zero in winter and sometimes up to eighty degrees in summer, with sixty inches annual precipitation, the reason this is called Alaska's Emerald Isle and said to be as green as any place on earth.

Scenery is magnificent—four-thousand-foot mountains, blanketed with low Arctic tundra vegetation ranging to dense stands of alders and willows in foothills and valleys and finally to Sitka spruce climax forest. There are hundreds of lakes and eight hundred miles of convoluted shoreline indented by dramatic fjordlike inlets. (Unfortunately all this can often be obscured by rain and fog.)

To get there, fly from Seattle or Anchorage or take a ferry from Seward or Homer. Refuge headquarters is located in the town of Kodiak where there are motels, rental cars, charter planes, and *sometimes* boats for hire to look at sea-bird colonies in the bay, all best reserved ahead. There is camping in nearby Fort Abercrombie State Park as well as on the refuge, by permit. Contact the refuge office to plan how to see the refuge, for Kodiak is a true wilderness. There are no roads leading to the refuge. There are seven cabins available on a limited basis, with no facilities other than shelter, and these must be reserved well ahead. To get to a cabin one must be flown out by charter aircraft, or taken to a nearby coastal point by boat, then hike some distance.

Take good-quality raingear and hip boots! Hiking can be difficult, which little level ground, much of it covered with shoulder-high, damp vegetation. Be prepared to be self-sufficient in a wet, wild, wonderful place—for Kodiak is that, most of it probably unchanged since the Russion explorer Vitus Bering discovered Alaska in 1741 (and sailed right by Kodiak, not seeing it in the fog).

For further information contact: Kodiak National Wildlife Refuge, Box 825, Kodiak, Alaska 99615. Phone: (907) 486-3325.

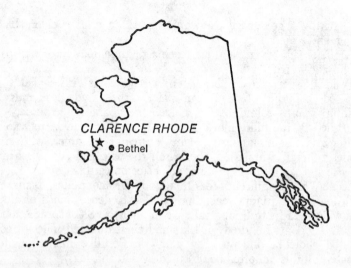

CLARENCE RHODE
● Bethel

CLARENCE RHODE (Alaska)˙

The road ends at Anchorage; beyond that it is necessary to fly—but that is what most of the residents of this remote and windswept refuge of tidal marsh and tundra do best. Clarence Rhode Refuge, five hundred miles west of Anchorage facing the Bering Sea, is the largest water-bird refuge in North America—2,887,000 acres—and the wildest and most isolated. Birds nest here in almost incredible numbers—tens of millions of waterfowl, shorebirds, and passerines (estimates sometimes exceed a hundred million). They fly here every year from six continents in almost every part of the western hemisphere and beyond—southeast Asia, New Zealand, and Antarctica, as well as over most of the lower United States. Here they raise their young, hurrying to complete the task in the short northern summertime, and then return again in some of the longest and most arduous migration journeys known.

Golden plovers, bar-tailed godwits, bristle-thighed curlews, and ruddy turnstones fly to islands throughout the South Pacific and some to Australia, sometimes two thousand miles nonstop over open sea.

Whimbrels, Hudsonian godwits, black-bellied plovers, sanderlings, dowitchers, and spotted, solitary, least, pectoral, western, and semi-palmated sandpipers move along the Pacific Coast and inland to winter in Central and South America as far south as Cape Horn or Tierra del Fuego.

Mew gulls migrate to the lower West Coast; Bonaparte's to both West and East coasts and Sabines to Cape Horn and as far as Antarctica. Arctic terns may travel 22,000 miles round-trip between breeding and wintering grounds, the longest migration trip of any living thing. White-fronted geese fly 2,500 miles to the interior California valleys. Old-squaw move to the Bering Sea, where they mingle with sea ducks from the Soviet Union. Greater scaup ducks divide and about half move down the Pacific Flyway, the other half southeasterly across Canada to the Great Lakes and eventually to the Atlantic Coast. Probably no other area of similar size is so critical to so many species of water birds.

The refuge together with adjoining habitat in the twenty-million-acre Yukon-Kuskokwin Delta provides nesting habitat for 80 per cent of the population of emperor geese and whistling swans of the Pacific Flyway and for a good part of the whistling swans of the Atlantic Flyway as well.

It is the major nesting area for the spectacled eider in North America. More than half the continental population of black brant nest here, as do all the continental population of cackling geese. It is the most important breeding area in the range of the lesser sandhill crane. The entire world population of bristle-thighed curlews, known to nest only in the mountainous areas north of the refuge, are on the Yukon Delta region during the fall.

It can be an almost unbelievable sight, this vast coastal tundra covered with literally uncounted tens of thousands of lakes, ponds, and streams. It appears as much water as land. That part which is not under water is in most places less than ten feet above sea level. All of it is filled with calling and flying birds from the time of ice breakup in June until the end of the short northern summer (and some birds are already starting to flock for a three-thousand-mile southern migration in late July).

Small birds can be everywhere, too—yellow wagtails, redpolls, snow buntings, Lapland longspurs, Savannah, tree, and fox sparrows, gray-cheeked thrushes, and still others: long-tailed and parasitic jaegers, red phalaropes, black turnstones, Arctic and red-throated loons, short-eared and some snowy owls. All these varied species can breed because even in this limited elevation there is diversity of habitat: heath tundra with mosses, lichens and dwarf prostrate shrubs; grasslands; both fresh and salt marshes and bogs; and small thickets of willows and alders where willow ptarmigans obtain food and cover in winter.

Pacific salmon are here in season, especially chum, and four kinds of seals (the harbor, bearded, ringed, and ribbon), mostly in early spring and late fall. There are occasional walruses, Beluga whales in the rivers in the early spring, and a few land mammals—tundra hare, large and numerous mink, many muskrat and fewer otter, red and Arctic fox.

But the birds own this refuge—though visiting them is no easy matter, nor necessarily always desirable. Disturbance to this fragile area and to any nesting area, even one so large, is never beneficial. One must check first with refuge headquarters in Bethel. Fly to Bethel by commercial airline from Anchorage. From there, the refuge is 125 miles by air, and there are no roads. It may be possible to charter a flight over the refuge, or arrange to ride with a regularly scheduled mail plane to a nearby village. One can sometimes find a boatman who will take visitors out. There are motel accommodations in Bethel, and restricted tent camping is permitted. Another warning: weather can be rainy and overcast much of the time with high winds, so one can never be sure when it will be possible to leave.

In any case, don't come bird-watching in winter (October to April) since few species stay to brave the northern blasts on a frozen wasteland: the indomitable ravens, ptarmigans, snowy owls, gyrfalcons, McKay's and snow buntings on land and some sea ducks in open leads offshore.

For further information contact: Clarence Rhode National Wildlife Refuge, P.O. Box 346, Bethel, Alaska 99559. Phone: (907) 543-3151.

Nunivak Refuge, which covers 1,109,000 acres of Nunivak Island in the Bering Sea twenty miles west of the Alaskan coast, administered by the refuge staff in Bethel, is the main home today of the musk-oxen in Alaska. Once they ranged over much of Asia and North America. At one time, they moved south with the glaciers as far as Iowa and New York, but by 1920, when the species became protected, most populations had been slaughtered indiscriminately. A nucleus group of thirty-one was brought to Alaska from Greenland in the mid-thirties. They have done so well on Nunivak that small groups have been taken to reinstate them elsewhere in their former range in Arctic Alaska.

Musk-oxen are odd, bulky animals, standing almost four feet high at the shoulder and covered with long, shaggy black fur almost to their feet. Their name derives from glands under their eyes which emit a musky odor when excited by predators. Eskimos called them "Oomingmak," the bearded ones. They are known for their stolid herd defense against an enemy in which the entire group will stand its ground with backs against a wall or cliff or in a circle with massive horns facing outward while one male dashes out briefly to threaten the aggressor from time to time. This worked well against wolves but not against the rifle, and musk-oxen were killed off in Alaska by hunting around 1865.

Nunivak is one of the few places where a sizable herd of musk-oxen can be seen in the wild—and they cannot be seen easily even here, for five hundred animals, which is about the maximum that can be supported on Nunivak, can space themselves fairly widely when grazing over an island of this size. Also, Nunivak is a *de facto* wilderness, inhabited almost solely by Eskimos and wild animals for the past two thousand years, so there are no roads or other easy means of getting about. The best way would be to fly to Mekoryuk, Nunivak's only village, by scheduled airline, and there hike out or arrange to be taken out by a local boatman. The refuge has planned to start a field office in Mekoryuk, which could be helpful. Restricted tent camping is permitted. Otherwise there is no place to stay although local families sometimes take in visitors. The weather can be worse, if anything, than at most coastal Alaskan areas—windy, foggy, rainy, cold in winter, subject to sudden severe storms. But it is a fascinating island, with a large herd of reindeer and on its precipitous western cliffs some of the largest nesting sea-bird colonies in the world for kittiwakes, murres, pelagic cormorants, horned and tufted puffins, parakeet and crested auklets, and pigeon guillemots. There are also many songbirds, including occasional Asian drop-ins and the rare McKay's bunting, a winter visitor which nests only on Bering Sea islands.

Also administered from the Bethel office are four smaller refuges: *Bering Sea* Refuge, *Cape Newenham*, *Chamisso*, and *Hazen Bay*.

All are interesting and important nesting areas and all have limited access, partly because of their sensitive nesting situation but also because they can be extremely difficult and hazardous to approach, being rocky, located in or facing the open sea, with most of the colonies on steep cliff faces. Refuge offices in Bethel or Anchorage must be contacted by anyone proposing such a visit.

The Bering Sea Refuge comprises three islands 250 miles west of the Alaskan coast. This is the only known nesting place of the rare McKay's bunting. It also has one of the largest fulmar colonies anywhere, with parakeet auklets, horned puffins, pelagic cormorants, and thick-billed murres.

Cape Newenham occupies a peninsula between Bristol and Kuskokwim bays. On its steep cliffs are huge nesting colonies of murres, kittiwakes, puffins, and other marine birds. Two large coastal lagoons support heavy eelgrass growth and are an important feeding ground for waterfowl.

Chamisso is a highly important nesting area for horned puffins, thick-billed murres, and others on Chamisso and Puffin islands in Kotzebue Sound.

Hazen Bay, an extension of Clarence Rhode, is a 6,800-acre island which provides dense nesting area for black brants and cackling Canada geese as well as for emperor geese, old-squaws, greater scaups, and other waterfowl.

Three additional refuges, administered from the Alaska refuge complex office in Anchorage, are *Forrester Island, Hazy Islands,* and St. Lazaria refuges. Forrester and St. Lazaria are timbered islands important to burrow-nesting birds such as the storm-petrels and auklets. St. Lazaria, an unusually scenic small island, is accessible by small boat from Sitka. Hazy Island provides habitat for glaucous-winged gulls, murres, and sea lions and is essentially not accessible; Forrester may be reached only by large vessels. For further information contact the Anchorage office.

Acknowledgments by Regions

II. THE NORTHEAST AND MID-ATLANTIC STATES

For contributing to this section special thanks are due to: Richard Antonette; J. C. Appel; Herbert Bell; Walter Benning; Glen W. Bond; Edwin Chandler; Bruce Fellman; John Fillio; George W. Gavutis; Linda Gintoli; Lisa Gordon; Ron Harrell; Grady Hocutt; Allen Hundley; Gaylord L. Inman; Marion Ireland; William H. Julian, Jr.; Ralph Keel; Stanley McConvey; John Miller; John Morse; Mickey Novak; Richard Nugent; Harold C. Olson; George O'Shay; Don R. Perkuchin; Mary Ellen Rainey; Rogert N. Steelman, Jr.

III. THE SOUTHEAST

Thanks to: Jim Baker; Tom Barnes; Bruce Blihovde; George Campbell; Edward Collinsworth; John P. Davis; John R. Eadie; John C. Fields; George R. Garris; John Hoffman; Jerry L. Holloman; Marvin T. Hurdle; Harold Johnson; Donald J. Kosin; Clyde Lee; Thomas W. Martin; John Matthews; Delano A. Pierce; Ernest Rauber; James H. Roberts; John Schorer; Ron L. Shell; Henry Stevenson; Harry T. Stone; Stephen R. Vehrs; George Weymouth; Joe D. White; John Williamson; Patricia Young.

IV. THE GREAT LAKES STATES

Thanks to: Wayne Adams; James Carroll; Stanley S. Cornelius; John R. Frye; Charles W. Gibbons; David Heffernan; Leland Herzberger; Robert Johnson; Joseph Kotok; Howard Lipke; Will Nidecker; Carl E. Pospichal; Charles E. Scheffe; Omer N. Swenson; John Toll; Laurel Van Camp; Edward Wagner; Norrel Wallace.

V. THE MID-SOUTH

Thanks to: Edward Alexander; Thomas Z. Atkeson; Samuel W. Barton; Herbert Bell; Bobby W. Brown; J. C. Bryant; Jerome Carroll; Vandiver L. Childs; Ben Coffey; Wendell E. Crews; James M. Dale; Paul D. Daly; Daniel Doshier; William A. Grabill; Edith Halberg; Larry M. Ivy; Stephen K. Joyner; Raymond R. McMaster; Cecil McMullan; Marvin L. Nichols; Charles Strickland; Don Temple; John R. Walther.

VI. THE NORTH-CENTRAL STATES

Thanks to: Harold H. Burgess; Forrest W. Cameron; Gerald L. Clawson; Charles R. Darling; Robert M. Ellis; John R. Foster; George E. Gage; Ann Gammell; Robert Gammell; John Guthrie; Linda Hagen; Keith S. Hansen; Robert R. Johnson; James Kline; Rolland Krieger; Michael J. Long; Jon M. Malcolm; Alfred O. Manke; David C. McGlachlin; R. G. Rollings; Jean Schulenberg; Erik Sipko; Ted Stans; Lyle A. Stemmerman; Sam Waldstein; Maurice B. Wright; Gary R. Zahm; Fred C. Zeillemaker.

VII. THE SOUTHWEST

Thanks to: John R. Aiken; John Beall; Stephen S. Berlinger; Tyrus W. Berry; Ronald Bisbee, Bert E. Blair, Jr.; Ken Butts; Russel W. Clapper; George Constantino; Jodi Corrie; Monte M. Dodson; Gerald E. Duncan; Steve Gniadek; Delbert Griego; Karl Haller; Kelly Himmel; Ernest S. Jemison; E. Frank Johnson; Allen C. Jones; Robert A. Karges; Evan V. Klett; LeMoyne B. Marlatt; Bill Mobley; Jim Neaville; James Norman; Arthur R. Rauch; Richard W. Rigby; Joe Rodriguez; Kenneth E. Schwindt; Wayne A. Shifflett; Ron Shupe; Robert A. Stratton, Jr.; Ronald S. Sullivan; Milton Suthers; George Unland; Ken Voget; Ray Washtak; Larry Wynn.

VIII. THE MOUNTAIN STATES

Thanks to: Mark Barber; Jay R. Bellinger; Steve Breeser; James Brown; Robert C. Brown; Larry L. Calvert; James A. Creasey; Robert Darnell; Roger di Rosa; Milt Haderlie; John D. Hill; Russell R. Hoffman; Lynn C. Howard; Huyson J. Johnson; Larry Kline; Rolf H. Kraft; Rod Krey; Edward Loth; Melvin T. Nail; Larry Napier; Lois Parker; Ned I. Peabody; Robert L. Pearson; Joe Quiroz; Jack Richardson; Gene Sipe; Eugene D. Stroops; Herbert L. Troester; Robert C. Twist; John E. Wilbrecht; William J. Wilson; Robert Yoder.

IX. THE WEST COAST AND HAWAII

Thanks to: Clark Bloom; Vernon Byrd; Thomas J. Charmley; Elizabeth Cummings; Ada Davis; Jack Davis; Robert C. Fields; Judy Fisher; Duane Gahimer; Marion Gebhart; Brent Giezentanner; Henry A. Hansen; Stanley Harris; Jack Helvie; Willard B. Hesselbart; Marvin R. Kaschke; John E. Kurtz; Leon A. Littlefield; Joseph P. Mazzoni; Hugh Null; Robert Personius; Jim Rees; Palmer Sekora; Darwin Sisson; John Taylor; Owen H. Vivion; Joseph M. Welch; Donald M. White.

X. ALASKA

Thanks to: Robert L. Delaney; James E. Frates; Donald N. Frickie; Richard L. Hensel; John Martin; Michael Rearden; Don E. Redfearn; John E. Sarvis; David L. Spencer; Michael Spindler, Averill S. Thayer; Michael T. Vivion.

INDEX

Species are indexed in the singular. When the principal entry is in the plural followed by page numbers it indicates either groups of related species (e.g. Bitterns, Herons, Rails) or notable numbers of a single species.